FOODS OF PLANT ORIGIN
Production, Technology, and Human Nutrition

FOODS OF PLANT ORIGIN

Production, Technology, and Human Nutrition

Edited by

D. K. Salunkhe, Ph.D.

Department of Nutrition and Food Science
Utah State University, Logan, Utah

S. S. Deshpande, Ph.D.

Morden Research Station, Agriculture Canada
Morden, Manitoba

An AVI Book
Published by Van Nostrand Reinhold
New York

An AVI Book
(AVI is an imprint of Van Nostrand Reinhold)
Copyright © 1991 by Van Nostrand Reinhold

Library of Congress Catalog Card Number 91-11853

ISBN 0-442-23917-3

Manufactured in the United States of America

Published by Van Nostrand Reinhold
115 Fifth Avenue
New York, New York 10003

Chapman and Hall
2-6 Boundary Row
London, SE 1 8HN, England

Thomas Nelson Australia
102 Dodds Street
South Melbourne 3205
Victoria, Australia

Nelson Canada
1120 Birchmont Road
Scarborough, Ontario M1K 5G4, Canada

16 15 14 13 12 11 10 9 8 7 6 5 4 3 2 1

Library of Congress Cataloging-in-Publication Data

Foods of plant origin : production, technology, and human nutrition /
    edited by D. K. Salunkhe and S. S. Deshpande.
        p.   cm.
    Includes bibliographical references and index.
    ISBN 0-442-23917-3
    1. Food crops. 2. Food. 3. Food crops—Processing. 4. Food industry and trade.
    5. Nutrition. I. Salunkhe, D. K. II. Deshpande, S. S.
    SB175.F66   1991
    664—dc20   91–11853
                                                                      CIP

To the rivers and soils of this planet,
and to the environment
for sustaining global agriculture

Contributors

B. B. Desai
Department of Biochemistry
Mahatma Phule Agricultural University
Rahuri, Maharashtra State, India

S. S. Deshpande
Food Science and Technology Laboratory
Morden Research Station
Agriculture Canada
Morden, Manitoba, Canada

Usha S. Deshpande
Department of Plant Sciences
University of Manitoba
Winnipeg, Manitoba, Canada

D. K. Salunkhe
Department of Nutrition and Food Science
Utah State University
Logan, Utah, USA

B. Singh
Department of Food Science and Technology
Alabama A&M University
Normal, Alabama, USA

U. Singh
ICRISAT
Patancheru, Andhra Pradesh, India

Contents

Preface

The present world population of about five billion and its projected growth create enormous pressures and demands for food and industrial raw materials. It is to crop plants, one of our precious few renewable resources, that we must look to meet most of these needs. Globally, about 88% of our caloric requirements and 90% of our protein ultimately derive from plant sources—ample evidence of their importance to humankind. Our survival will therefore continue to depend on the world's largest and certainly most important industry: agriculture. Yet in spite of our long history of domestication and civilization, the number of crop species involved in sustaining human life is strictly limited: Essentially, some twenty-four crops protect us from starvation.

To know these basic food crop plants—to study how they function and how their productivity may be improved—is the first step in solving the world food problem. The primary objectives in writing this book were to address this challenge and to review comprehensively the wealth of available yet scattered information on food crop productivity and processing. Unlike several other texts and monographs in this field, the present work was intended to give, in a single volume, a quick, informative view of the various problems from field to table concerning the major food crops worldwide. It covers all aspects, from crop production to processing and utilization, with special emphasis on biological nitrogen fixation, photosynthesis, breeding for yield-limiting environments, and loss-reduction technology—areas rarely covered elsewhere but that will require priority research in years to come.

Over 80% of the edible dry weight of world food prodution is derived from only eleven crop species, and two-thirds of those are cereals. A few cereal species predominate, but several others play important roles in our sustenance. Even in highly developed Western countries—where much of the diet is of animal origin and only about a third of protein intake comes directly from plant sources—cereal grain crops are still essential for the maintenance of comestible herbivorous animals. Food legumes, meanwhile, provide nearly a quarter of the world's dietary protein requirements—over 50% in the developing countries. Although legumes have traditionally been described as "poor man's meat," ever-increasing costs and the unfavorable energy balance of animal food production may well force a greater reliance on them in the foreseeable future.

In view of their major protein and caloric contributions to human nutrition, cereal and legume food crops involve the two biggest sections of this book, Chapters 1 and 2, respectively. Chapter 3 deals with several fruits and vegetables, including potato, that enrich and improve our diet both aesthetically and nutritionally. Chapter 4 covers sugar crops, which, although not serving as food directly, still find their way into our diet after processing and are the mainstay ingredients of food and beverage manufacturing industry worldwide.

We hope that this book, with its state-of-the-art information on food crop production, nutritional quality, processing, and loss-reduction technology, will serve as a useful reference for students, scientists, and professionals involved in research and processing areas related to agriculture, food technology, and human nutrition. Although some aspects, especially processing, are considered primarily from the viewpoint of a developed country, every effort was made to include information on the local production and technology practices of various countries. This was especially true for third world countries, where professionals would find these two contrasting viewpoints extremely useful in their research work.

ACKNOWLEDGMENTS

The editors would like to thank the Department of Nutrition and Food Science, Utah State University, for providing the secretarial assistance. Most of SSD's contributions to this book were written during his sojourn with Idetek, Inc., San Bruno, California. He gratefully acknowledges the excellent encouragement and cooperation of Mr. Mark C. Platshon, President and CEO, and others at Idetek during this period. Sincere gratitude is also extended to Dr. Jim Bole, Director, and Dr. G. Mazza of Agriculture Canada Research Station, Morden, for ensuring the conditions to complete this book. One of the most pleasing experiences in writing this book has been the splendid spirit of cooperation on the part of various publishers and scientific institutions for graciously allowing us to reproduce material from their publications. Finally, it was a delightful experience to have worked with Dr. Eleanor Riemer, Constance Carmody, Michael Beck, Michael Gnat, and their staff at VNR, without whose cooperation and assistance this book would never have been written. They exhibited tremendous patience and perseverance, particularly when deadlines arrived but manuscript did not.

Introduction

D. K. Salunkhe and S. S. Deshpande

Never in the history of humankind did we face such monumental challenges and daunting prospects as we do approaching the dawn of the twenty-first century. The present world population of about 5 billion and its projected growth create enormous pressures and demands for food and industrial raw materials. It is to crop plants, one of our precious few renewable resources, that we must look to meet most of these needs. However, just to keep up with current population growth, modern agricultural technology must double crop productivity by the year 2000.

Residents of highly developed Western countries may not always be aware of our dependence on plants: Much of their diet is of animal origin, and only about a third of their protein intake comes directly from plant sources. However, since both grain crops and forage plants are essential for the maintenance of the herbivorous animals processed by the meat industry, we are in the long run concerned with plant production just the same. In any case, on the global level, about 88% of the caloric requirements and 90% of the protein ultimately comes from plant sources.

To meet the demand for food, humankind has developed a range of crop plants; but, considering the long history of domestication, the number of crop species involved is strictly limited. Over 80% of the edible dry weight is derived from only eleven crop species, two-thirds of which are cereals. We must, therefore, get to know these plants thoroughly in order to safeguard and preferably to improve their productivity. Even though only a few species of cereals predominate, several others play an important role in sustaining human life. Legumes provide nearly a quarter of the world's dietary protein requirements and over 50% in the developing countries. Although they have traditionally been described as "poor man's meat," the ever-increasing costs and unfavorable energy balance of animal food production may well force us to place a greater reliance on these plants in years to come. Potatoes do not occupy a large proportion of

1

the total cultivated area of the world, yet their productivity per unit area is very high. Fruits and vegetables enrich and improve our diet both aesthetically and nutritionally. Several other crops do not serve as food directly but find their way into our diet after processing. For example, sugarcane and sugar beet provide sweeteners; peanut, soybean, and sunflower yield oils and fats; and barleys, potatoes, and other crops are used for the production of alcoholic beverages.

PLANT PRODUCTION AND CONSUMPTION TRENDS

The use of plants to meet the world's food needs is vital to our survival. On a global basis, over 65% of food protein and more than 80% of food energy is supplied by plants. In terms of gross tonnage, approximately 98% of the total world food production is harvested from land sources and only 2% from the ocean and inland waters (Table 0-1). Of the total world food harvest, plant products directly contribute about 82% of the gross tonnage, whereas animal and marine products together contribute only 17% (FAO 1988a). The average production of plant protein potentially edible by humans was estimated to be 196.8 million metric tons (MT), compared to 49.1 MT of animal protein (Deshpande and Damodaran 1990).

There are approximately 350,000 species of plants that have been documented in the annals of botany and plant sciences. Historically, over 3,000 species of plants have been used to feed humans (Borlaug 1981). At least 150 different species of these plants have been grown in sufficient quantities to have entered world trade. People currently depend primarily upon these twenty-four (in approximate order of importance): rice, wheat, corn,[1] potato, barley, sweet potato, cassava, soybean, oats, sorghum, millet, sugarcane, sugar beet, rye, peanut, field bean, chick-pea, pigeon pea, mung bean, cowpea, broad bean, yam, banana, and coconut. Cereal grains constitute the largest and the most important single group of foods (Table 0-1). Because of the high-yielding ability of their genotypes, cereals are expected to play an even more dominant role in the total world food supply in years to come.

Food production is partially offset by severe problems of wastage (Table 0-2). Food losses occur throughout production, harvesting, threshing, drying, storage, processing, marketing, and distribution. Under the best of circumstances, global crop losses are estimated to be over 2 million metric tons, representing over U.S.$140 billion. The potential for such losses is even greater. Insect pests, diseases, and weeds together account for about 70% of total losses.

---

[1]Throughout this volume, the word "corn" is used in the American sense, referring to *Zea mays*, which the British call "maize." (The British use the word "corn" to refer either to wheat [in England] or to oats [in Scotland and Ireland].)

Table 0-1. World Food Production, 1988.

Source	Production (1,000 MT)	Proportion (% Grand Total)
Land		
Total cereals	1,742,985	42.3
Wheat	509,952	
Rice	483,466	
Corn	405,460	
Barley	168,423	
Other	175,684	
Total root crops	571,182	13.8
Potatoes	269,702	
Other	301,480	
Total pulses	54,652	1.3
Vegetables and melons	426,187	10.3
Total fruits	329,506	8.0
Total nuts	4,098	0.1
Oil crops (oil equiv.)	66,275	1.6
Sugar	102,779	2.5
Coffee, tea, cocoa	10,244	0.2
Meat	163,540	4.0
Milk	525,223	12.7
Eggs	34,880	0.8
Total food from land	4,031,551	97.8
Water		
Total catch from ocean and inland waters	92,693	2.2
Total land and water	4,124,244	100.0

Adapted from: FAO (1988a,b). Courtesy Food and Agriculture Organization of the United Nations.

The magnitude of the data presented in Table 0-2 would be even greater if we were to consider all other losses presently occurring in agriculture and the food system that will have long-term ramifications on our global food supply. Substantial losses of the topsoil due to erosion result in lower crop productivity, and will ultimately be reflected in lower total food production. The application of fertilizers is imperfect, and a substantial amount does not reach the plant in the proper quantity or at the appropriate time. Similar losses occur in the use of water, and production may decline because of water mismanagement, lack of irrigation, or bad weather. Even proper storage, including refrigeration and

Table 0-2. Annual World Crop Losses.

Commodity	Tonnage (Value)[a]		Crop Loss Cause			
	Actual	Potential	Insects	Disease	Weeds	All
Cereals	961.1	1,467.5	203.7	135.3	167.4	506.4
	(63.9)	(98.0)	(14.4)	(8.7)	(11.0)	(34.1)
Potatoes	270.8	400.0	23.8	88.9	16.5	129.2
	(10.6)	(15.6)	(1.0)	(3.4)	(0.6)	(5.0)
Sugar beet/cane	694.6	1,330.4	228.4	232.3	175.1	635.8
	(7.6)	(13.9)	(2.3)	(2.3)	(1.7)	(6.3)
Vegetables	201.7	279.9	23.4	31.3	23.7	78.2
	(16.7)	(23.1)	(2.0)	(2.3)	(2.0)	(6.3)
Fruits	141.7	197.2	11.3	32.6	11.6	55.5
	(14.3)	(20.1)	(1.2)	(3.3)	(1.2)	(5.7)
Stimulants	10.2	16.5	1.9	1.6	1.8	6.3
	(7.2)	(11.4)	(1.3)	(1.7)	(1.2)	(4.2)
Oils	94.7	137.0	14.5	13.5	14.3	42.3
	(10.6)	(15.7)	(1.8)	(1.6)	(1.7)	(5.1)
Fibers & rubber	18.3	26.2	3.1	3.1	1.7	7.9
	(8.6)	(12.7)	(1.8)	(1.5)	(0.8)	(4.1)
All crops	2,393.1	3,854.7	510.1	539.6	412.1	1461.6
	(139.7)	(210.5)	(25.8)	(24.8)	(20.2)	(70.8)

Adapted from: Cramer (1967).
[a]Tonnage in millions of metric tons, value in U.S.$10^9 (in parentheses).

freezing, cannot completely stop the process of biological degradation. In the processing of a crop into a food product, or in the preparation of food for eating, there is yet another set of chemical and physical losses—usually involving a decrease in energy, protein, and vitamin content of the food. The physical loss in food processing alone is estimated to be 10% of the input. Processing is necessary to make some crops edible; however, in many instances, such as those of wheat and rice (removing the protein and vitamin-rich bran), the processing is primarily motivated by tradition and taste preference. In the home, food may be wasted at the dinner table, in improper distribution among the family members, and within the human body. For example, certain infectious diseases can reduce the efficiency of food absorption by as much as 30%. Finally, too much food may be consumed, giving rise to obesity and other health problems. Losses in energy therefore occur at every stage of the food system, though accurate measurements of such losses are difficult to obtain.

Improvements in pre- and postharvest technologies can increase the global food supply by at least 30–40% without bringing any additional area under cultivation or incurring expensive inputs (e.g., various intensive crop-management practices). Thus loss-prevention technology should receive at least as much attention as increased planting.

The following chapters cover the four plant food groups—cereals, legumes, fruits and vegetables, and sugar crops—that make sizable contributions to caloric and protein intake of the humankind, and describe some of the major problems in the global food production system. For each major food group, a brief reference is made to world production and major producer countries. Discussions on evolutionary and botanical background of each class are followed by current information on crop production technology. The postharvest discussions include various options and methods for processing of individual food groups, their modes of utilization, and their contributions to the human diet. Finally, where applicable, future research needs are identified and strategies to ensure a safe and adequate food supply to all of humankind are outlined.

REFERENCES

Borlaug, N. E. 1981. Using plants to meet world food needs. In *Future Dimensions of World Food and Population*, ed. R. G. Woods, pp. 101–82. Boulder: Westview Press.

Cramer, H. H. 1967. *Plant Protection and World Crop Production*. Leverkusen (W. Germany):Bayer Pflanzenschutz.

Deshpande, S. S., and Damodaran, S. 1990. Food legumes: Chemistry and technology. *Adv. Cereal Sci. Technol.* 10:147–241.

FAO. 1988a. *Production Yearbook*. Rome: Food and Agriculture Organization.

FAO. 1988b. *Yearbook of Fishery Statistics*. Rome: Food and Agriculture Organization.

1

Cereals

S. S. Deshpande, B. Singh, and U. Singh[1]

INTRODUCTION

Cereal grains are the major food of humankind. In many of the less developed countries of the world, cereals provide two-thirds or more of the dietary calories (Deshpande and Damodaran 1990). Rice in Asia, corn (maize) in South America, sorghum in Africa, and wheat in the Middle East are recognized as the staple foods on whose yields famine or feast depends. Among the developed countries there are many, such as Russia and Japan, in which cereals still provide more than half the dietary calories. Although cereals make a smaller direct contribution to the diet of such developed countries as the United States and Canada, total cereal use per person is extremely high; however, most of the grain is fed to livestock and becomes an indirect component of human diets.

Rising standards of living in several parts of the world, especially traditional third world developing countries, are generally associated with higher consumption of meat and hence, indirectly, more grain. It takes an average cow 17 kg of vegetable protein to gain 1 kg of edible animal protein (Holmes 1971; Borlaug 1974). Thus, whereas in India the average per capita consumption of cereal grains is 158–170 kg per annum, in the United States it is 675 kg (Salunkhe, Chavan, and Kadam 1985; Pomeranz 1987). Japan is a classic example of the switch to a meat diet as prosperity increases. Between 1960 and 1972, annual meat consumption increased from 6.4 kg per person to 23.3 kg, an increase of 264% during a period when incomes increased by 204% (Allaby et al. 1975). It has been estimated that of every 30 metric tons (MT) average annual growth of world grain output, approximately 22 are absorbed by population growth and 8 by rises in per capita incomes (FAO 1988).

---

[1] Sincere appreciation is extended to Usha Deshpande for her assistance in the literature survey and the compilation of references.

World production of cereals over the past thirty years has increased more rapidly than the world population, but with much more variation from year to year; for the world as a whole, increase in yield per unit area has contributed much more than the increase in the area under cereal crops (FAO 1988). This is particularly so in the developed countries; but in the less developed countries, the rather smaller increases in grain production have been due about equally to increases in yield and in area.

The world average yield of cereal grains is approximately 2.5 metric tons per hectare (MT/ha), two to three times greater than that of legume crops and oilseeds. Partly because of their higher yielding ability and greater economic returns, especially under subsistence farming, cereals are displacing pulses and legumes in many less developed countries, even though they complement one another both agronomically and nutritionally. Also, the rate of increase in yield, on a world scale, is much greater in the major cereals than in the legumes; consequently, cereals are becoming a progressively more predominant component of the total world food supply.

Given the restrictions on further increase in the area of land under cultivation, greater cereal yields are the key to increased food supplies. Improved agronomy, such as better weed control and more timely and effective fertilizer applications, has contributed greatly to the recent increases in cereal yields, as has better control of diseases and pests, whether by genetic or chemical means. Plant breeding has played a major role in three ways:

1. the selection of disease- and pest-resistant cultivars,
2. the development of shorter-statured varieties that do not lodge at high levels of fertilizer application, and
3. the selection of cultivars with greater yield potential that can respond to higher inputs.

All three plant-breeding approaches are essential and must be linked, so it is difficult to partition actual progress among them. At the lower yield levels, improved agronomy may be the major requirement for progress, as with corn in Africa (Evans and Wardlaw 1976). As fertilizer inputs increase, lodging resistance becomes more important, while in high-input systems increase in yield potential may be rate limiting.

Compared to developments in crop physiology, genetics, and agronomy, much less attention has been paid worldwide on reducing the tremendous losses that occur during the storage and handling of cereals. As much as 50% losses occur alone during the postharvest handling and processing of cereals, especially in the developing countries, where development infrastructure was too marginal or nonexistent to handle the tremendous yield increases achieved in cereal production during the recent decade.

Given the vast literature available on various aspects of cereal production and technology and the constraints of summarizing such information in one chapter, the present review is intended to be only a bird's-eye view of the recent developments in these areas. Although most aspects of cereal production and technology are briefly dealt with here, attention has been primarily focused on areas that need our attention in the coming years if we are to meet the increasing demands on our food supplies that would be made in the twenty-first century.

PRODUCTION AND DISTRIBUTION

According to Frey (1984), total world cereal production can be roughly divided into four groups: The first three are wheat, rice, and corn; the fourth includes barley, oats, rye, sorghum, various millets, and buckwheat. World cereal production in the recent past has shown variable trends (Table 1-1). Total production increased up to 1986 and then decreased slightly during 1987–8. In 1988, although rice production in the tropics increased, that of wheat, barley, and other coarse grains declined. This could be attributed to a decrease in cereal production in the United States and Canada, two of the largest cereal producers in the world, both of which recently experienced drought conditions (Table 1-2). The decrease of 31.5% in total U.S. cereal production in 1988 alone as compared to 1979–81 could also be attributed, in part, to land being taken out of cultivation as a part of government subsidy programs (FAO 1988).

Comparison of the 1960 and 1980 figures shows a large increase in the production of corn, wheat, rice, and barley, varying from a 75% increase in rice production to 92% for barley (Frey 1984). Sorghum and millet production in Africa and Asia increased nearly 66% and 100%, respectively, whereas Latin America has seen a spectacular sixfold increase in millet production. Total cereal grain output was about 1,800 million MT for 1986–8. The increase over 1969–71 was 22.6%, or a 22.3% increase per year (USDA 1989). Not only the production of cereal grains has increased during the past two decades; the cereal grain productivity (i.e., the yield per hectare) has also increased signifi-

Table 1-1. Worldwide Production[a] Trends of Cereal Grains, 1983–8.

	1983	1984	1985	1986	1987	1988
Total cereals	1642.7	1805.3	1844.5	1863.9	1803.1	1743.0
Wheat	494.0	517.3	505.9	536.7	517.2	509.9
Rice	451.2	470.4	472.6	472.5	464.5	483.5
Coarse grains	697.4	817.7	865.2	854.7	821.5	749.6
Corn	347.8	452.7	487.7	485.1	458.0	405.5
Barley	161.9	172.5	176.6	182.4	181.7	168.4
Other	197.7	192.5	200.9	187.2	181.8	175.7

Source: FAO (1988), courtesy Food and Agriculture Organization of the United Nations.
[a]In thousands of metric tons.

Table 1-2. Production of Total Cereals in Different Regions of the World.

Region	Production (10^6 MT)		
	1979–81[a]	1988	% change
World	1590.3	1743.0	+ 9.6
Africa	72.6	89.2	+ 22.9
N. America	369.5	269.3	− 27.1
USA	301.3	206.5	− 31.5
S. America	66.8	80.2	+ 20.0
Asia	640.0	797.2	+ 24.6
China	286.6	352.3	+ 22.9
India	138.2	175.6	+ 27.1
Europe	248.9	296.9	+ 19.3
Oceania	219.6	230.4	+ 4.9

Source: FAO (1988), courtesy Food and Agriculture Organization of the United Nations.
[a]Mean of three years.

Table 1-3. Grain Yield of Some Barley Cultivars Released during 1960–80 and Grown at the Plant Breeding Institute, Cambridge, England.

Cultivar	Year of Introduction	Grain Yield (kg/ha)
Vada	1960	5,700
Zephyr	1966	5,960
Golden Promise	1966	5,510
Julia	1968	6,200
Maris Mink	1973	5,930
Sundance	1976	6,320
Georgie	1976	6,300
Ark Royal	1976	6,350
Egmont	1980	6,930
Koru	1980	6,740
Triumph	1980	6,680

Source: Riggs et al. (1981).

cantly. The average yield for 1961–79 was highest for corn, followed by rice, barley, wheat, rye, oats, sorghum, and millet. It is, however, difficult to make valid comparison of yields of different cereals because of environmental conditions: The yield trend would vary depending on the cultivars and the year of introduction of the crop. For example, barley cultivars showed a large variation in grain yield (Table 1-3).

Total world production of the eight major cereals in recent years is sufficient to provide approximately 370–390 kg of cereal grains per person per annum, or slightly more than 1 kg/person/day, if shared equally among the entire world population. However, the average human consumption of cereals is only about one-third of this figure. This is largely due to a major proportion of cereal production being used for purposes other than human food—mainly as animal feed, industrial processing, and seed. In addition, there is considerable wastage of grains during storage and postharvest handling and processing of cereals.

The United States, Canada, Argentina, Australia, New Zealand, South Africa, and Thailand have been the net exporters of cereal grains (USDA 1989). Eighty percent of the total export came from the United States and Canada alone, despite the fact that their share of total world cereal grain production is only about 25%. It is quite apparent that world cereal production is not related geographically to food needs. Total per capita grain consumption varies from less than 200 kg per year in Pakistan, Philippines, Indonesia, India, and Nigeria to over 700 kg in the United States. Of the 700 kg consumed per person in the United States, about 100 kg is consumed directly as bread, pastries, and breakfast foods; the remaining 600 kg is fed to livestock (USDA 1989).

World agricultural production and population grew at an annual rate of 2.2% and 1.85%, respectively, from 1971 to 1980 (FAO 1981). If such production and population trends continue for the next twenty years, demand growth in the ninety developing countries (2.9%) will exceed projected agricultural production growth, according to projections by the FAO (1981, *Agriculture Towards 2000*). The imbalance will be greatest in Africa and West Asia. Self-sufficiency in cereals in developing countries would decline from 91% in 1979 to 83% in the year 2000, again with the situation being much worse in Africa and West Asia than in other regions. The ninety developing countries (including China) are projected to have a cereal deficit of 165 million MT by the year 2000. Most experts believe that the world is now probably producing enough to feed its people. However, because population distribution is not uniform worldwide, most experts predict that, by the year 2000, there will be an insufficient supply as well as inequitable distribution of food grains, primarily that of cereals.

ORIGIN AND BOTANICAL CLASSIFICATION

The term "cereal" is derived from *Cerealia munera,* the gifts of the goddess Ceres. It is commonly used to refer not only to the grain itself, and to the many foods manufactured from it (including flour, meals, bread, and flaked, shredded, or puffed breakfast cereals), but also to the cultivated grass plants (wheat, rice, corn, barley, oats, sorghum, rye, and millet) that yield the grain. All these grasses belong to the large monocotyledonous family Gramineae (Fig. 1-1).

At least two other species belonging to this family are economically important sources of food: sugarcane (*Saccharum* spp., Tribe Andropogoneae), the

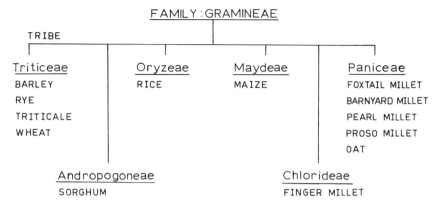

Fig. 1-1. Botanical classification of cereals.

principal source of sugar worldwide, and bamboo (*Arundinaria* spp., Tribe Bambuseae), whose young tender shoots are commonly consumed as vegetables in several East and Southeast Asian countries.

The cultivated grasses are cereals in the strictly botanical sense; but several other botanically different plants, often called "pseudocereals" (Brouk 1975), must be grouped with cereals because of the similarity of their use. Since most pseudocereals did not require cultivation but were simply gathered, it appears that many of these were used for human food long before grasses were successfully cultivated. Some pseudocereals, such as buckwheat, were cultivated in China and by Native Americans.

At present, the pseudocereals are a relatively insignificant group of crops. In contrast, the true cereals represent the world's most important source of food. In fact, if any one of the other commodity groups were to become unavailable, humankind could still survive and remain tolerably healthy; but a failure of the cereal crops would bring starvation and malnutrition to most parts of the world.

The cultivation of cereal crops, together with the domestication of animals and the invention of pottery, marked the beginning of the Neolithic period (Brouk 1975; Langer and Hill 1982). Except for corn, which originated in America, all the cereals are native to the Old World. The important characteristics of the cereals and pseudocereals are briefly described below.

Cereals

Wheat (Triticum *spp.*)

Wheat has been known since prehistoric times. The oldest grains, found in excavations of the Jarmo site in the upland of eastern Iraq, date from 6750 B.C. (Brouk 1975). It rapidly became the most important cereal, a position it still occupies in today's world.

The wild diploid progenitor of wheat occurs throughout the Fertile Crescent of the Middle East, where it was first domesticated about 10,000 years ago along with barley and several pulses (Harlan and Zohary 1966) by the selection of nonshattering, larger-seeded forms. Tetraploid wheats also developed in this area at about the same time. The final step in the evolution of wheat was the hybridization of the tetraploids with *Aegilops squarrosa* to give the hexaploid bread wheat *T. aestivum. A. squarrosa* occupies a wider range of environments than do the other wheat progenitors. As such it may have conferred on wheat not only the protein characteristics required for bread making but also a greatly increased adaptive range (Evans and Wardlaw 1976). Thus wheat became a crop of both subhumid and semiarid steppes, and adapted to more acidic soils (Zohary, Harlan, and Vardi 1969; Slootmaker 1974). This has led to its subsequent spread through central Europe to higher altitudes and more humid environments. In its original environment, wheat germinated with the onset of autumn rains, grew through the winter to flower in early spring and mature its grains before the summer drought, and was a vernalizable, long-day plant (Evans and Wardlaw 1976).

The members of the tribe Triticeae, wheat species can be grouped according to the *genomes* or sets of chromosomes their somatic cells contain (Table 1-4). "Einkorn" wheat has been known since the Stone Age and was developed from the wild wheat, *T. boeoticum,* that still grows wild in Asia Minor and southeastern Europe. It carries two A-genomes. The tetraploid wheats were derived from wild "emmer" wheat, *T. dicoccum,* still found in Syria and Palestine. They contain the two A-genomes of the einkorn parent plus the two B-genomes derived from a wild grass, *Aegilops speltoides,* and thus have the genotype AABB. Hexaploid wheats were then developed from a further crossing that occurred when the cultivated tetraploid wheat came into contact with the weed *A. squarrosa,* probably growing on the borders of the fields of the mid-European lake-dwellers of the Neolithic period (Brouk 1975). The hexaploid wheat contains two genomes contributed by the weed, so its genotype is AABBDD.

The einkorn wheats are no longer of any importance and are grown only rarely, primarily as a fodder plant in the mountain regions of Spain. The cultivation of emmer wheat also is limited, being now mainly restricted to the Soviet Union and parts of Germany. In contrast, the tetraploid wheat *T. durum* grows best in warmer regions and is an important source of semolina flour used for the manufacture of pasta products. However, the type of wheat most widespread throughout the world is hexaploid wheat, mainly *T. aestivum vulgare.* It is the choice wheat for bread making.

From the practical standpoint, wheat is differentiated into two main classes: hard and soft. Respectively, these yield the strong and weak flours known to bakers (Pomeranz 1987). The strong flour from hard wheat is of a coarse texture and is required for bread making. The weak flour from soft wheat, howev-

Table 1-4. Genomic Classification of Cultivated Wheat Species.

Einkorn group: 7 pairs of chromosomes, diploid wheats
    Wild form, fragile rachis, kernel in hull
        Triticum boeoticum
    Cultivated form, fragile rachis, kernel in hull
        T. monococcum Einkorn

Emmer group: 14 pairs of chromosomes, tetraploid wheats
    Wild form, fragile rachis, kernel in hull`
        T. dicoccoides
    Cultivated form, partly fragile rachis, kernel in hull
        T. dicoccum Emmer (emmer wheat)
        T. timopheevi (Timopheevi wheat)
    Cultivated form, tough rachis, free kernel
        T. durum (durum wheat)
        T. turgidum (poulard or rivet wheat)
        T. polonicum (Polish wheat)
        T. carthlicum (= *persicum*) (Persian wheat)
        T. turanicum (= *orientale*)

Vulgare group: 21 pairs of chromosomes, hexaploid wheats
    Wild form, none; synthetic type only
    Cultivated form, partly fragile rachis, kernel in hull
        T. aestivum subsp. *spelta* (spelt wheat)
        T. aestivum subsp. *vavilovi* (Vavilov wheat)
        T. aestivum subsp. *macha* (Macha wheat)
    Cultivated form, tough rachis, free kernel
        T. aestivum subsp. *vulgare* (common or bread wheat)
        T. aestivum subsp. *compactum* (club wheat)
        T. aestivum subsp. *sphaerococcum* (short wheat)

Source: Briggle and Reitz (1963).

er, is a fine powdery flour that, although of little use for bread making, is very good for biscuit manufacture. As will be described later (under "Processing Technology"), various grades of flours can be obtained from different kinds of wheats, or sometimes by blending strong and weak flours together.

Hard wheat is commonly grown in the United States and Canada as well as in the warmer parts of Europe; soft wheat is primarily grown in the United Kingdom and in northern and central Europe. Varieties described as "red" have a reddish-colored grain due to the presence of an anthocyanin pigment in the bran.

Bulgur, primarily used as a substitute for rice, is prepared from varieties of both common and durum wheat by parboiling, drying, cracking, and removing some of the bran.

Rice (Oryza spp.)

The rice species and their varieties (Tribe Oryzeae, Fig. 1-1) are certainly the main and often the only cereal used by several nations of the Far East and by Southeast Asian countries. According to ancient records, rice has been cultivated in China for 5,000 years, and Theophrastus mentions its cultivation in India (Langer and Hill 1982). It was first brought to Europe by Alexander the Great, but its cultivation started no earlier than the eighth century A.D. In A.D. 711, the Moors began to grow rice in Spain. The only European country producing rice in large quantities today, however, is Italy, where the plantations are situated in the north along the River Po.

Rice has two parallel series of species ranging from wild perennial to cultivated annual. One species, *Oryza glaberrima,* was domesticated in West Africa; the other, *O. sativa,* in Asia (Evans and Wardlaw 1976). It is predominantly a rain-fed crop, its most characteristic environment being the flooded fields of the tropics. As in other cereals of tropical origin, the response of rice to daylength has been considerably modified as the crop spread to higher latitudes. However, most wild forms and tropical cultivars are short-day plants and exhibit strong photoperiodism, although a few of the traditional upland rice varieties are relatively insensitive to daylength (Evans and Wardlaw 1976).

The commonest species of rice is *Oryza sativa.* Its varieties are subdivided into three subspecies: *japonica, javanica,* and *indica.* The *japonica* types are short-grained, the *javanica* of intermediate types, and the *indica* rices are long-grained. In general, *japonica* rices adapt to cooler temperatures and longer days better than the *indica* rices long ago selected in China, Japan, and elsewhere (Chang and Oka 1976). At higher latitudes, the cultivars become even less sensitive. There are over 2,400 varieties of cultivated rice; in India alone, about 1,100 of them are cultivated (Langer and Hill 1982; Brouk 1975; Pomeranz 1987).

Rice is the only cereal cultivated in flooded fields that remain flooded for the major part of the growing season and are normally drained a few weeks before harvest. Drainage of the fields creates favorable conditions for the grain to complete its development. There are, however, also varieties of rice that grow like other cereals in soils that are not flooded: These so-called dry, upland, or hill rices, although the oldest cultivated rice form, are today of no economic importance. The bulk of the rice consumed is produced from flooded fields and is called wet, aquatic, or lowland rice. The seedlings planted in the flooded fields are produced in nurseries that are also either wet or dry. In some countries, rice is sown directly in the flooded fields, but this method of cultivation is wasteful.

The so-called wild rice growing in Africa, Southeast Asia, and North America is in fact a plant of another genus, *Zizania,* but belongs to the same tribe,

Oryzeae (Brouk 1975). *Z. aquatica* was an important cereal for Native Americans, although it is not a cultivated grass. Wild rice is also used in China, but more as a vegetable than as a cereal, the green parts and not the grain being eaten.

Corn (Zea mays)

Corn (maize) is the only cultivated cereal to originate from the American continent. The "discoverers" of America found the plant already in a state of cultivation, and there is ample evidence of its having been cultivated for at least 4,000 years, since the time of Mayas and Aztecs.

Corn is native to tropical Central America, the wild plant nearest to it being teosinte or *Zea (=Euchlaena) mexicana;* however, teosinte is not the true ancestor of cultivated corn. According to Brouk (1975), both plants had a common ancestor, now extinct, which by hybridization with another grass, *Tripsacum,* produced both corn and teosinte. Corn is intolerant to both shade and drought, and presumably originated in an area with alternately wet and dry seasons, where control of life cycle timing by daylength was very important (Evans and Wardlaw 1976). Many tropical races of corn are short-day plants, whereas modern temperate-zone cultivars appear to be almost wholly indifferent to daylength (Stevenson and Goodman 1972).

Corn also differs from other cereals in that its spikelets are unisexual, forming separate male and female inflorescences on the same individual. The staminate flowers form the terminal panicle, or so-called tassel, and the pistillate flowers in spikelets form the spadix, or cob, from which the grain develops. The cob arises laterally in the axil of the foliage leaf in which it is ensheathed.

There are many varieties of corn. *Zea mays* var. *saccharata* is the common sweet corn, mostly used as "corn on the cob" in the United States. *Z. m.* var. *everta* is a special variety from which popcorn is produced: Its small, hard seeds have a hard and glossy outer endosperm; the kernels burst when exposed to high temperatures, everting the soft palatable inner endosperm. Other varieties of corn normally cultivated include dent corn, *Z. m.* var *americana,* which is characterized by an indentation or depression on the top of the grain, caused by shrinkage of the soft endosperm. This is the typical corn of the American corn belt. Flint corn, *Z. m.* var. *praecox (=indurata),* with a hard endosperm and no indentation, is normally cultivated in Europe. Flour or soft corn, *Z. m.* var *amylacea,* is without the horny endosperm and is cultivated almost exclusively by Native Americans for their own use. Finally, waxy corn, although not regarded as a distinct variety, is valuable because its starch consists entirely of amylopectin. Other cornstarches normally have a 25 : 75 ratio of amylose to amylopectin.

Barley (Hordeum *spp.*)

The origin of barley has been dated as far back as 8000 B.C. (Brouk 1975; Langer and Hill 1982). Neolithic excavations at Fayum in Egypt have revealed that barley was grown by the ancient Egyptians. It was also known to the Greeks and Romans, and was cultivated in ancient China, whence it was introduced to Japan about 100 B.C. Barley thus appears to have been domesticated at the same time and place as wheat, and may have been even more important than wheat in the early stages of domestication. A wholly diploid crop, its history of change is similar to that of wheat, though it is not so well adapted to extreme cold. Today, as a cereal, barley plays only a minor role, the bulk of its production being used for brewing.

The commonest species, *H. distichum,* is a two-rowed barley type in which only the central spikelet is fertile and awned. In *H. vulgare* (=*hexastichum*), a six-rowed barley, all three spikelets are fertile and awned. Four-rowed barley in which all three spikelets are fertile but are asymmetrically arranged is also grown.

The cultivated varieties of barley were thought to be derived from the wild two-rowed barley, *H. spontaneum* of Southwest Asia. However, the more recent discovery of a wild six-rowed barley, *H. agriocrithon,* growing in Tibet has led to a reexamination of the theories of the origin of cultivated barley (Langer and Hill 1982; Brouk 1975). It appears likely that either *H. agriocrithon* gave rise to the cultivated species *H. vulgare,* and that *H. spontaneum* was the parent of *H. distichum,* or that a cross between *H. agriocrithon* and *H. spontaneum* produced the ancestors of both cultivated varieties.

Oats (Avena *spp.*)

Oats are of uncertain origin, although believed to be native to Asia. Oats may have appeared as weeds in wheat and barley fields in the Middle East. They became a secondary crop of increasing importance as the temperate cereals spread to higher latitudes and cooler, wetter climates (Evans and Wardlaw 1976). Oats derive from a polyploid series like wheat. The commonest cultivated species, the hexaploid *Avena sativa,* was derived from wild oats, *A. fatua,* whereas the cultivated red oat, *A. byzantina,* was believed to be descended from the wild red oat *A. sterilis.* However, recent genetic, physiological, and pathological studies have indicated that *A. sativa* is more likely to have been derived directly from *A. byzantina;* hence, *A. sterilis* is most probably the progenitor of all the other species of oats, including *A. byzantina, A. sativa, A. orientalis, A. fatua,* and *A. nuda* (Brouk 1975).

Although oats are a highly nutritive cereal, they are widely cultivated as an animal food plant, especially as fodder for horses in the colder parts of the temperate zone. In recent years, oat bran and fiber have become increasingly popular as breakfast cereal because of their alleged cholesterol-lowering effects in human nutrition.

Rye (Secale cereale)

Rye is one of the most recently domesticated cereals, being known to the ancient Greeks and Romans, but not to the ancient Egyptians. It is believed to have originated in Afghanistan and Turkey, where its wild ancestor, *S. montanum,* is still found (Lorenz 1982). Another wild form of rye, *S. anatolicum,* is also found in Syria and Iraq. Similar to oats, rye may have appeared as a weed crop in the ancient wheat and barley fields of the Middle East. Like barley, rye is a diploid with a notable winter hardiness and a capacity to grow on light and acid soils (Evans and Wardlaw 1976). There are only a few cultivated varieties of rye, and over 90% of the world production comes from Europe, where rye bread is preferred in countries such as Germany, Austria, Czechoslovakia, Poland, and the USSR. The Soviet Union is the largest producer of rye, since the crop is well adapted to colder climates with short summers.

Triticale

Triticale is the first man-made cereal and is a product of a cross between the genera *Triticum* and *Secale*. It was first described in the scientific literature in 1876 when A. S. Wilson reported the production of two sterile plants by crossing hexaploid wheat (*T. aestivum*) and diploid rye (*S. cereale*) (Skovmand, Fox, and Villareat 1984). The F_1 hybrids were very vigorous but sterile. Many years later in prerevolutionary Russia, spontaneous chromosome doubling apparently occurred in some wheat × rye F_1 hybrids, resulting in the first true-breeding diploid triticale.

Triticale is currently produced primarily in developed countries that are noted for their already high levels of small grain production. Spring triticale is commonly grown in Australia, Argentina, and Canada; the USSR, United States, France, and China are the largest producers of winter triticale.

Sorghum (Sorghum vulgare, S. bicolor)

A member of the tribe Andropogoneae (Fig. 1-1), sorghum was known as a cereal in ancient Egypt by 2200 B.C. It was probably domesticated in Africa, possibly 5,000 years ago (de Wet and Harlan 1971), in the savanna belt stretching from Lake Chad to the Sudan (Harlan 1971). From there it spread through Africa and India to China. Many tropical sorghums are strict short-day plants in which local adaptation of daylength response is very important (Evans and

Wardlaw 1976). The requirement for short days initially confined sorghum to the southern United States, but the selection of earlier maturing varieties and hybrids led to its cultivation at higher latitudes (Ross and Eastin 1972). Sorghum is not yet as well adapted to cool temperatures as is corn, but it is more drought resistant. The commonest species (which is often erroneously called millet) is *Sorghum vulgare*. The major cultivated varieties developed include *S. vulgare* var. *durra* (durra sorghum), *S. v.* var. *caffrorum* (kaffir sorghum of Africa), *S. v.* var. *rexburgii* (Indian sorghum, also known as *shallu*), and *S. v.* var. *nervosum* (Chinese sorghum, *kaoliang*). Sorghum is a tropical plant and grows only in warmer countries including those of the Mediterranean region and the U.S. South. It is an important human food in China, India, and Africa; elsewhere, the plant and grain are mainly used for fodder.

Millets

Finger Millet (*Eleusine coracana*)

This is the only millet that belongs to the tribe Chlorideae; all others belong to the tribe Paniceae. In various parts of the world, finger millet is also known as *ragi, nagli, telabun, marua, korakan,* bird's-foot millet, or African millet. The plant probably originated in India, and is now widely cultivated in India, Malaya, China, and the wetter parts of Central Africa.

Foxtail Millet (*Setaria italica*)

Depending on its country of origin, this millet is also known as Italian, German, Hungarian, or Siberian millet. In ancient times, foxtail millet was commonly used for human food in Europe; but today, because of higher economic standards, it is cultivated only for fodder. This plant is probably of Asiatic origin, and was being cultivated in China in the year 2700 B.C. (Brouk 1975). In Europe, it is known to have been grown by the lake-dwellers.

Japanese Barnyard Millet (*Echinochloa crusgalli* var. *frumentqacea*)

Japanese barnyard millet, also called *sanwa* millet, is used in Japan and Korea as human food, mostly prepared as a form of porridge. It is cultivated as a forage plant in the United States.

Pearl Millet (*Pennisetum typhoideum, P. glaucum*)

Pearl or bulrush millet was known in Asia and Europe in prehistoric times, but seems to have originated in tropical Africa. It is cultivated mainly in India and Africa, where it is ground into flour and made into bread or cooked as a porridge.

Proso Millet (*Panicum miliaceum*)

Proso millet (also known as hog or broom millet) is the true millet of the ancient Romans who called it *milium*. *Proso* is a Russian word for millet. The plant is generally believed to have originated in Egypt or Arabia and to have spread to the Soviet Union, India, China, and Japan, where it is mainly cultivated today. Some is also grown in the Mediterranean region.

Pseudocereals

All plants outside the Gramineae having fruits and seeds that can be ground into flour for making bread and similar products might be called *pseudocereals*. Although this group includes acorns, beechmast, sweet chestnuts, seeds of leguminous plants, and so on, these plants have today lost their importance as pseudocereals and have mainly acquired another function for human consumption (e.g., as nuts or pulses). Thus the true pseudocereals are nowadays mainly plants with small seeds used in the same way as cereals and also cultivated like cereals in fields. These include buckwheat, still sown in Asia and some parts of Europe and America; amaranth species, mainly of Central and South America, which were cultivated by the Aztecs; quinoa, the "cereal" of ancient Incas, still grown in Ecuador, Bolivia, and Peru; and the Mexican chia, another pseudocereal of the Aztecs (Brouk 1975). The only pseudocereal greatly dissimilar to cereals is the water chestnut, an annual aquatic plant bearing submerged large nuts. This was cultivated in Neolithic times in Europe but today it is grown only in China and the Far East.

In chemical composition, the seeds of pseudocereals are similar to those of the true cereals; unfortunately, figures are available only for buckwheat (described later under "Chemical Composition and Nutritional Quality"). Also, of all the pseudocereals, only buckwheat is mentioned in the world statistics of agricultural production of the Food and Agriculture Organization. Some of the economically important pseudocereals are briefly described below.

Amaranth (**Amaranthus** *spp.*)

The genus *Amaranthus* belongs to the family Amaranthaceae, which is very closely related to the family Chenopodiaceae. *Amaranthus leucocarpus* grows in the New World and is native to Central America. It is primarily cultivated in Mexico and Guatemala. In Mexico, it has been an important crop since 5000–3000 B.C., and the Aztec Emperor Montezuma received annual tribute from his subjects in amaranth grain (Brouk 1975). *A. cruentus* is cultivated in Guatemala and other parts of Central America, whereas *A. caudatus* is grown in the Andean region of Bolivia, Peru, and northern Argentina. *A. paniculatus* is a grain crop of Southeast Asia. Leaves from plants of this genus are also widely used as a vegetable on the Indian subcontinent.

Buckwheat (Fagopyrum *spp.*)

Buckwheat is a member of the dicotyledonous family Polygonaceae. As the name implies, it is cultivated much the same way as wheat, and its seeds are separated from the pericarp and ground into flour to be used in making porridge (i.e., Russian kasha) or pancakes. Sometimes the whole unmilled seed is consumed.

Buckwheat is a native of Central Asia, where it still grows wild. For several centuries, it has been cultivated in China, whence it was introduced into Europe at the end of the Middle Ages. It is still an important crop for human consumption in the USSR. In other European countries, however, it is grown mainly as a fodder plant.

There are three distinct species in the genus *Fagopyrum*: *F. esculentum* Moench (*F. sagittatum* Gilib, common buckwheat), *F. tartaricum* (tartary buckwheat), and *F. cymosum* (wild perennial buckwheat). Both diploid ($2n = 16$) and tetraploid ($2n = 32$) species are known to occur in common and perennial buckwheats, whereas tetraploids have not been reported in tartary buckwheat. Most species of the genus *Fagopyrum* are variable in plant habit and are markedly affected by habitat conditions, thus making them extremely difficult to differentiate from one another. The most consistent method of identifying these plants is on the basis of their fruit (achene) characteristics. The species of buckwheat most commonly grown in the North American continent is *F. esculentum*, whereas tartary buckwheat is cultivated for food purposes in the Himalayan regions of India and China (Pomeranz 1983).

Chia (Salvia columbarie)

Widely cultivated by the ancient Aztec civilization, chia and its related species belong to the same genus as sage (*S. officinalis*) and to the family Labiatae. Chia species are native to Mexico, whereas sage is of Mediterranean origin. Chia was a staple food of the Aztecs, along with corn, amaranth, and beans.

Quinoa (Chenopodium quinoa)

This is a member of the family Chenopodiaceae and a native of Peru, where it was used in large quantities by the ancient Incas. The seeds may be ground into flour from which bread and cakes are prepared, or the entire grain may be eaten in soups. Quinoa is still grown to a large extent in mountainous regions of Ecuador, Bolivia, and Peru, where corn cannot be cultivated. Excavation records of several settlements show that another species, *C. nuttalliae,* was grown in Mexico in pre-Columbian times, whereas in Iron Age Europe the species *C. album* was cultivated (Brouk 1975). Leaves of some species of quinoa are also used like spinach.

Table 1-5. Chromosome Numbers and Centers of Diversity of Commonly Grown Cereal Crops.

Cereal	Chromosome No. (2n)	Centers of Diversity[a]
Wheat		
Einkorn	14	NE
Emmer	28	NE, ES
Bread wheat	42	CJ, HI, CE
Club wheat	42	ES, NE, CE
Rice	24	CJ, II, HI
Wild rice	30	NA
Corn	20	MA, SA, CJ
Barley	14, 28	NE, ME, CJ
Oats	42, 48, 63	ME, NE, CJ
Sorghum	20	CJ, HI, ME
Rye	14–29	CE, NE, CJ
Millets		
Finger millet	36	HI, AF
Italian millet	18	CJ
Pearl millet	14	AF
Proso millet	36, 54, 72	CJ
Triticale	42, 56	NA, ES
Buckwheat	16, 32	NE

Adapted from: Jung (1978) and Hanson (1990).
[a]The possible center of origin is listed first. Abbreviations: AF, Africa; CE, Central Asia; CJ, China, Japan; ES, Euro-Siberian; HI, Hindustani (India); II, Indochina, Indonesia; MA, Middle America; ME, Mediterranean; NA, North America; NE, Near East; SA, South America.

Water Chestnut (Trapa *spp.*)

Water chestnut (*Trapa natans*) belongs to the family Onagraceae, and is an annual aquatic plant native to the territory marked by Persia, Egypt, and southern Europe. In Neolithic times it was a common food of most of the European peoples, and grew at that time in central and even northern Europe. Nowadays water chestnut is a rare plant found in Europe only in the warmer countries (e.g., in Italy). The water chestnut still consumed as grain in China, Korea, and Japan belongs to another species of *Trapa, T. bicornuta*. It is mainly used in the form of flour, and in pre-Communist China was one of the five most important "grains" (Brouk 1975). The third edible species, *T. bispinosa,* is a native of tropical Asia and is known as the *singhara* (horny) nut. It is mainly the food of people living by lakes in the northern Indian state of Kashmir, and is usually consumed in the form of a porridge.

Table 1-5 summarizes the chromosome numbers and primary and secondary centers of diversity of the commonly cultivated cereal crops.

ANATOMICAL STRUCTURES OF SEEDS

The grain or kernel of a cereal is a nutlike fruit, or *caryopsis*. The fruit contains only one seed and, as it ripens, the ovary wall (or *pericarp*) becomes rather firmly attached to the wall of the seed proper and forms the outer tissue of the bran. The monocotyledonous embryo that develops into a new plant upon germination occupies only a small part of the seed. The bulk of the seed is composed of the flour portion (the *endosperm*), which constitutes a food reservoir.

In the grass family, the floral envelopes (modified leaves), or chaffy parts, within which the caryopsis develops, persist to maturity. In some cereals such as rice and most varieties of oats and barley, some of the chaffy structures constitute the hull of such grains (which are said to be "covered"). In the common wheats, rye, hull-less barleys, and the common varieties of corn, the caryopsis readily separates from the floral envelopes on threshing; these grains are said to be "naked."

The anatomical structure of various cereal grains are quite similar and have been extensively studied. Although numerous reports are available on the topic, studies on kernel structure of wheat (MacMasters, Hinton, and Bradbury 1972), rice (Bechtel and Pomeranz 1980), corn (Wolf et al. 1952), and sorghum (Rooney and Miller 1982) are the most commonly referred to. Generally, in most cereals, the endosperm constitutes nearly 80% of the total seed weight and consists of highly packed starch granules embedded in a matrix of protein. The germ, bran, pericarp, and seed coat are the other important components of cereal grains. The germ is usually distinctly separated from other components, whereas the bran, pericarp, and seed coat are described in association with one another. Sometimes the pericarp, the testa, and the aleurone layers are collectively called the bran. Endosperm hardness, which is generally determined by the relative proportion of corneous to floury type within the grain, plays a very important role in determining the processing quality and industrial uses of cereal grains.

Wheat

The structure of the wheat kernel is shown in Fig. 1-2. The dorsal side of the grain is round; the ventral has a deep groove along the entire length of the kernel. At the apex end (small end), a brush of small hairs is present. Except for durum wheats, the grains are either red or white.

Wheat kernel consists of germ and endosperm enclosed in a seed coat. The seed coat or pericarp consists of four outer layers: epidermis, hypodermis, cross cells, and tube cells (Salunkhe, Chavan, and Kadam 1985). The pericarp with aleurone constitutes the bran, which is rich in protein, cellulose, hemicellulose, and minerals. The germ consists of plumule, radicle, and scutellum, while the

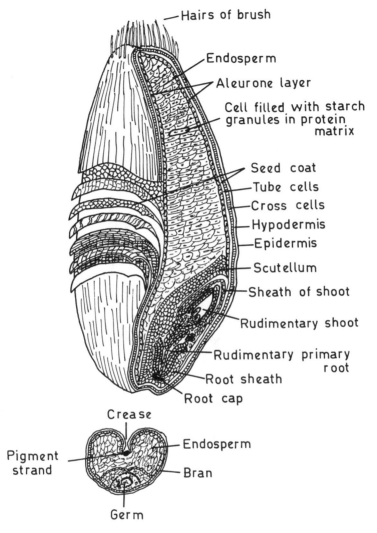

Fig. 1-2. Longitudinal and cross-section through a wheat kernel. *Source:* Wheat Flour Institute, Washington, D.C.

endosperm is highly packed starch grains in a matrix of protein. The outer portion of the endosperm is vitreous; the inner portion is floury. The durum wheats have a greater proportion of vitreous endosperm, whereas the soft red wheats have more floury endosperm. The relative proportions of the various constituents are as follows: 83% endosperm, 2.5% germ, and 14% bran.

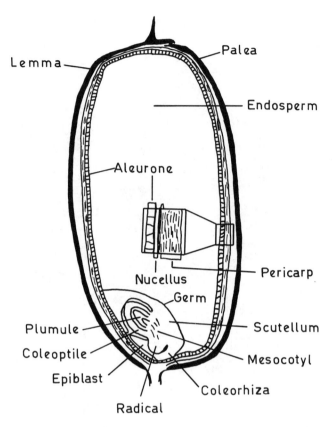

Fig. 1-3. Schematic diagram of a midlongitudinal section of rice caryopsis. *Source:* Pomeranz, Y., and Ory, R. L. 1982. In *Handbook of Processing and Utilization in Agriculture, vol. II, pt. 1, Plant Products,* ed. I. A. Wolff. CRC Press, Boca Raton, Fla., p. 139. Reprinted with permission.

Rice

Bechtel and Pomeranz (1980) described the fine structure of rice kernel in relation to its postharvest technology, storage, and nutritional and processing quality. Hull or husk, pericarp, seed coat (integument or testa), aleurone, endosperm, and germ are the principal components of rice seed (Fig. 1-3). In rice, the pericarp consists of outer pericarp, hypoderm, mesocarp, and cross cells; it constitutes about 4–5% of the kernel weight. The pericarp, along with the seed coat or testa, nucellus, and aleurone layer, forms the bran, which constitutes about 5–7% of the weight of the brown rice. The endosperm is predominantly made up of starch.

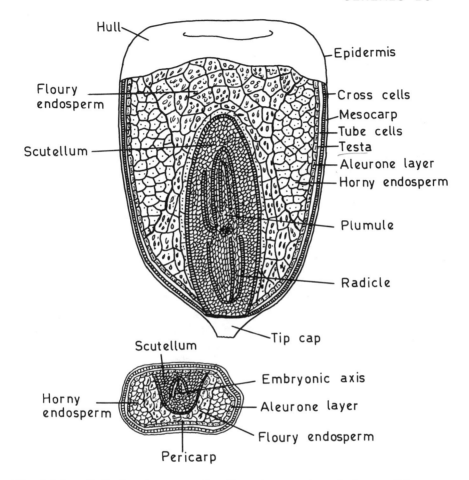

Fig. 1-4. Longitudinal and cross section through a corn kernel. *Source:* Wheat Flour Institute, Washington, D.C.

Corn

Studies on the structure of corn kernel have been recently reviewed (Salunkhe, Chavan, and Kadam 1985; Pomeranz 1987). Corn kernel is the largest of all the cereals. It is flattened, wedge-shaped, and broader at the apex end than at the point of attachment to the cob (Fig. 1-4). The size and weight (150–600 mg/ kernel) of the kernel differs significantly from different types of plants and often even within the same ear. The color of the grain may be white, orange, yellow, cherry red, red, dark red, or brown. The pericarp and testa, endosperm, and the germ are the principal anatomical parts of the corn kernel. Their relative proportions vary considerably with grain type.

Corn pericarp consists of epidermis, mesocarp, and cross and tube cells, and constitutes 4–6% of the whole kernel. It mainly consists of insoluble non-starchy carbohydrates.

The endosperm consists of aleurone (2.2%), an outer two- or three-cell region (3.9%), and outer corneous (58.1%) and central floury (17.6%) portions (Salunkhe, Chavan, and Kadam 1985). The endosperm contributes about 80–85% of the kernel weight.

Corn kernel also has a relatively larger germ than other cereals. It is placed in the lower portion of the endosperm and contributes 10–14% of the kernel weight. Most of the oil (81–86%) and minerals (80%) are present in the germ. The higher proportion of protein and minerals also makes it susceptible to insect attacks, while the oil causes rancidity upon prolonged storage.

Barley

In barley grain, the husk, pericarp and testa, aleurone, endosperm, and germ are the important structures (Fig. 1-5). The husk accounts for about 10% of the dry weight of the grain. The pericarp, which is fused with the testa, is a mass of compressed cellulosic cells separated from the husk by a thin waxy layer; the testa is made up of two distinct bands containing fat and waxy material (Palmer and Bathgate 1976; Salunkhe, Chavan, and Kadam 1985). The aleurone is a distinct layer of cells between the testa and the endosperm. It secretes α-amylase, protease, and β-glucanase during malting (Palmer and Bathgate 1976; Pomeranz 1987). Similar to other cereal grains, barley endosperm is the major

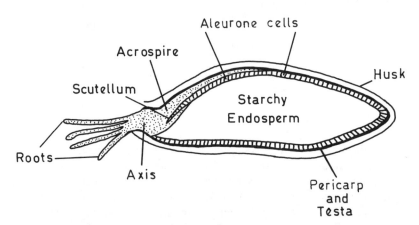

Fig. 1-5. Longitudinal section of a germinated barley kernel. *Source:* Burger, W. C. 1982. In *Handbook of Processing and Utilization in Agriculture, vol. II, pt. 1, Plant Products,* ed. I. A. Wolff. CRC Press, Boca Raton, Fla., p. 187. Reprinted with permission.

storage organ for protein bodies and starch granules. The embryo is partly embedded in the endosperm at the base of the kernel and is held at an oblique angle to the axis of the kernel. The literature on the structural and biochemical changes in embryo and endosperm of barley kernels during germination has been extensively reviewed (Palmer and Bathgate 1976; Pomeranz 1987).

Oats

With the exception of being covered with a fuzzy layer of trichomes or short hairs, the kernels (groats) of oats are similar in structure to the caryopsis of other cereal grains. In the common varieties of oats, the caryopsis is enveloped in a hull comprising certain of the floral envelopes; naked or hull-less varieties exist but are not extensively grown.

The hull content in oats varies with the test weight. In light, thin oats of low test weight, the hulls may comprise as much as 45% of the grain, but in very heavy or plump oats, they may represent only 20%. The dehulled kernels are called groats and contain 28–40% bran, 3% germ, and 55–68% endosperm.

Sorghum

Rooney and Miller (1982) have described the kernel structure of sorghum using light, fluorescence, and electron microscopy. The seed coat in sorghum is composed of pericarp and testa (Fig. 1-6). The pericarp comprises three to four layers: epicarp, mesocarp, cross-cell layer, and tuber-cell layer. The epicarp may be further subdivided into epidermis and hypodermis. The endosperm consists of the aleurone layer and peripheral corneous, intermediate, and floury portions. The aleurone is a single layer of blocklike rectangular cells beneath the testa. Sorghum germ contributes about 8–12% of the dry weight of the kernel and is made up of scutellum and the embryonic axis.

Rye

The mature rye kernels are more slender than those of wheat, and grayish-yellow, brown, or somewhat greenish in color. The crease or furrow extends the full length of the grain on the ventral side; the embryo is located at the base on the dorsal side. As in other cereal grains, the major components are pericarp, testa and aleurone, embryo and scutellum, and the endosperm. The mature kernels have a wrinkled pericarp, which gives them a rough appearance. The starchy endosperm represents the bulk of the kernel, and is composed of peripheral, prismatic, and central portions that differ in shape, size, and location within the kernels (Salunkhe, Chavan, and Kadam 1985; Pomeranz 1987). The embryo closely resembles that of wheat and is rich in oil and protein, whereas the aleurone layer is a major storage reserve of lipids.

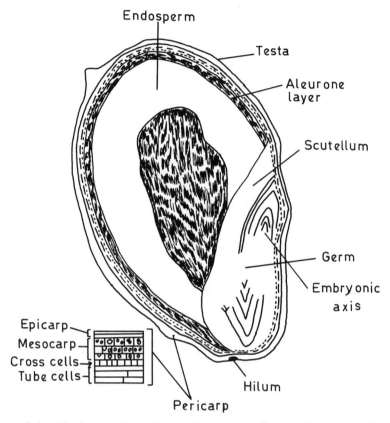

Fig. 1-6. Longitudinal section of a sorghum kernel. *Source:* Rooney, L. W., and Miller, F. R. 1982. *Proc. Int. Symp. Sorghum Grain Quality,* 28–31 October 1981. ICRISAT, Patancheru, India, p. 143.

Millets

Compared to other cereal grains, millets generally have smaller seeds. They also exhibit a wider range of size, shape, and color. For example, the pearl millet grain may be near white, pale yellow, brown, gray, slate blue, or purple in color, whereas finger millet grains may be white, orange-red, deep brown, purple, or almost black. In millets the pericarp, endosperm, and germ are the principal grain components. The aleurone is a single layer of blocklike cells extending around the periphery of the entire kernel. The starchy endosperm may be divided into peripheral, corneous, and floury regions. The grains of most minor millets also tend to be smaller than those of pearl millet, and have lemma and palea adhering to their pericarp. As a general rule, the seeds of common millets are flattened, oval, or smooth.

Table 1-6. Approximate Grain Size and Proportions of the Principal Parts Comprising the Mature Kernel of Different Cereals.

Cereal	Grain Wt. (mg)	Embryo (%)	Scutellum (%)	Pericarp (%)	Aleurone (%)	Endosperm (%)
Wheat						
Bread wheat	30–45	1.2	1.54	7.9	6.7–7.0	81–84
Durum wheat	34–46	1.6[a]		12.0		86.4[b]
Rice	23–27	2–3	1.5	1.5	4–6	89–94
Corn	150–600	1.15	7.25	5.5[b]		82
Barley	36–45	1.85	1.53	18.3		79.0[b]
Oats	15–23	1.6	2.13	28.7–41.4[b]		55.8–68.3
Sorghum	8–50	7.8–12.1[a]		7.3–9.3[b]		80–85
Rye	15–40	1.8	1.73	12.0		85.1[b]
Millets	7–14	2.3[a]		8.4–12.1		88–91[b]
Triticale	38–53	3.7[a]		14.4		81.9[b]

[a]Includes scutellum.
[b]Includes aleurone layer.
Adapted from: Simmonds (1978), which includes the original references.

Buckwheat

Buckwheat is not a true cereal. The fruit of a dicotyledonous plant, it is, however, classed in agriculture and commerce with the cereals. With the exception of the floral envelopes being absent, like the cereals, the grain of buckwheat is a dry fruit (achene). The kernels or achenes are triangular, either glossy, dull gray, dark brown, or black in color, and have a thick fibrous pericarp, which is not fused or cemented to the seed as in the true cereals.

The fruit in most varieties is 4–6 mm long, but 6–9 mm in Japanese types. It consists of hulls, spermoderm, endosperm, and embryo (Javornik and Kreft 1980). The kernels are easily dehulled. The hulls represent 17–26% (up to 33% in tartary buckwheat) of the kernel weight. The diploid varieties tend to have fewer hulls than the tetraploid. In common with the cereal grains, buckwheat has an aleurone layer of large, starch-free cells that surrounds the starchy endosperm (Marshall 1969; Pomeranz 1983). The embryo is dicotyledonous and is embedded in the white endosperm that forms the bulk of the seed. The embryo, however, is removed during the milling process.

Table 1-6 summarizes data on grain size and the proportions of the principal parts comprising the mature seed of different cereals.

NITROGEN FIXATION

The largest single industrial input into agricultural food production is nitrogen fertilizer. It accounts for 30–40% of total crop productivity (Wittwer 1980), but is energy intensive and demanding of nonrenewable energy resources. Natural gas equivalent to 300×10^6 barrels of oil is consumed annually for the synthesis of anhydrous ammonia by the Haber–Bosche process of nitrogen fertilizer production (Wittwer 1980). Nitrogen fertilizer now accounts for about one-third of all the energy going into agricultural production.

The alternative is biological nitrogen fixation, which constitutes approximately 70% of the total nitrogen fixed worldwide (Power and Papendick 1985). Next to photosynthesis, it is the second most important biochemical process on earth (Wittwer 1979). In fact, symbiotic nitrogen is the most efficient way of providing fixed nitrogen for plant growth (Deshpande and Damodaran 1990).

While legumes have the capacity of being at least partially self-sufficient through symbiotic N_2 fixation, the grain crops have relied mostly on commercial nitrogen sources of manures and fertilizers. In fact, increased use of nitrogen fertilizer is probably the most important single factor that has enabled cereal grain production to increase significantly in the past two decades. It is not surprising that increasing cereal grain production at the world level would require the use of increasing amounts of nitrogen fertilizer. However, in the less developed countries, the availability and the high prices of nitrogen fertilizer are limiting factors for its use on a large scale. In addition, in tropical regions considerable amounts of nitrogen, mostly in the form of NO_3, are lost from the soil by leaching (Neyra and Dobereiner 1977).

Although improved technologies of nitrogen fertilizer production and increased efficiency of fertilizer use by plants could make more nitrogen available for the plants, alternative technologies should be found to lessen the dependence of plants on nitrogen fertilizer. Developing nitrogen self-sufficiency in grain crops may constitute a major breakthrough in the years ahead. Efforts along these lines may include the incorporation of *nif* (nitrogen-fixing) genes into cells that normally do not fix N_2 (Brill 1975) or the development of already present plant-bacteria associations.

Some cereals, such as corn and sorghum, that are able to support significant nitrogenase activity possess the photosynthetic C-4 pathway. The amount of light required to saturate photosynthesis and the maximum photosynthetic rate attainable are much greater in C-4 than in C-3 plants (Chollet and Ogren 1975). At high light intensities and low temperatures, the rate of photosynthesis is essentially the same in C-3 and C-4 species, but at higher temperatures C-4 plants show higher photosynthetic rates. Furthermore, losses of carbon due to photorespiration are minimal in C-4 plants. This suggests that some cereals may be very efficient in harvesting light energy for nitrogen fixation. Maximization of N_2 fixation in cereal–bacteria associations and the elaboration of agronomic practices to enhance or promote N_2 fixation will depend on the identification of the various limiting factors controlling this process under field conditions.

High nitrogenase activities (up to 9,000 nmol C_2H_4/g roots per hour) have been reported on excised, preincubated corn and sorghum roots in lowland soil in Rio de Janeiro, Brazil (von Bulow and Dobereiner 1975). Other estimates by this method range between 100 and 2,000 nmol C_2H_4/g roots per hour. *Spirillum lipoferum* was found to be abundant in all N_2-fixing corn and sorghum roots examined. Field-grown corn plants in Wisconsin inoculated with strains of *S. lipoferum* isolated from *Digitaria* roots in Brazil showed establishment of the bacteria inside the roots (Dobereiner, Marriel, and Nery 1976). Inoculated plants showed higher nitrogenase activity than uninoculated ones, whereas nitrogen-fertilized plants had no activity.

There is little doubt as to the substantial contribution of biological N_2 fixation to the nitrogen economy of rice crop. For instance, a total of twenty-three rice crops, in an eleven-year experiment at the International Rice Research Institute in the Philippines, were obtained from a nonfertilized field with no apparent decline in the nitrogen fertility of the soil. About 45–60 kg N/ha per crop were removed through straw and grain (Watanabe and Kuk-Ki-Lee 1975). This represents a substantial amount of nitrogen that had to be replaced to maintain the fertility level of the soil. Blue-green algae and photosynthetic bacteria account for a large part of the N_2 in rice fields (Stewart 1975).

Bacterial counts indicate that *Beijerinckia* sp. and *Enterobacter cloacae* are the most common N_2-fixing bacteria in the rhizosphere of rice (Yoshida 1971; Neyra and Dobereiner 1977). However, most of the nitrogen fixation in the rice system has been attributed to rhizosphere soil rather than to the roots themselves. Higher numbers of aerobic than of anaerobic N_2-fixing bacteria in the rhizosphere of rice were also found by Watanabe and Kuk-Ki-Lee (1975). Methane-oxidizing bacteria, which are able to fix N_2, are also found in rice fields. The large amount of methane that can accumulate in these soils should not be overlooked as a potential carbon source for N_2 fixation (De Bont and Mulder 1976). However, oxygen diffusion seems to be a limiting factor for this system. De Bont and Mulder (1976) also reported very high numbers (up to 3.6×10^7) of N_2-fixing, methane-oxidizing organisms in the rice rhizosphere.

Nitrogen fixation in wheat fields has also been reported in the literature. A nitrogen balance study in the famous Broadbalk continuous wheat experiment carried out from 1843 to 1967 in England showed an average annual gain of 34 kg N/ha, of which 24 kg N/ha were removed with straw and grain (Jenkinson 1973). However, values extrapolated from the acetylene reduction assays on soil cores were much lower (2–3 kg N/ha per year). It was also shown that nitrogenase activity of soil cores containing wheat was significantly higher than in bare soils. Wheat cores assayed in Oregon have been calculated to fix 2 g N/ha/day (Barber, Tjepkema, and Evans 1976), whereas much higher nitrogenase activities have been observed in wheat cores assayed in Rio de Janeiro, Brazil (Neyra and Dobereiner 1977).

In the Broadbalk experiment, a large part of N_2 fixation was attributed to blue-green algae, whereas the root nitrogenase activity was attributed to anaerobic or facultative bacteria (Day, Neves, and Dobereiner 1975). Barber, Tjepkema, and Evans (1976) isolated N_2-fixing strains of *Enterobacter cloacae, Bacillus macerans,* and *B. polymyxa* from wheat roots in Oregon soils.

Larson and Neal (1976) described a highly specific association of a facultative *Bacillus* sp. with a disomic chromosome substitution line of wheat. The *Bacillus* was isolated from a soil where wheat had been growing for thirty years without nitrogen fertilizer. The rhizosphere of this wheat line contained also more nitrate-reducing bacteria and a lower total number of microorganisms. In monoxenic culture, the bacterium closely associated itself with the root surface. Abundant numbers of bacterial cells were found on the root surface as well as in the intercellular spaces between the cortical root cells.

The identification of the factors that limit nitrogenase activity and hence N_2 fixation under field conditions and in vivo is essential for any attempt to find agriculturally viable practice that may increase biological N_2 fixation in cereals. Some of the important factors in this regard, as described by Neyra and Dobereiner (1977), are briefly discussed below.

Seasonal and Diurnal Fluctuations

Nitrogenase activity fluctuates throughout the growth cycle of the plants. In general, maximal activities are found during reproductive growth of the plant. In field-grown corn, two peaks of nitrogenase activity, the first associated with silk emergence and the second with the onset of grain filling, are observed. Conversely, very little nitrogenase activity is observed before tasseling and after midgrain filling. Similarly, in sorghum maximal enzyme activities occur at flowering, and then decline linearly with the onset of grain filling. It is quite likely that competition for available photosynthate by the grain causes the observed decline of nitrogenase activity during the seed-filling stages.

Diurnal fluctuations also affect N_2 fixation in cereals. Peak enzyme activity is usually observed around midday, but in C-4 plants such as corn, sorghum, and millets, a second peak is observed at night. The latter peak is attributed to hydrolysis of carbon storage products accumulated during the day and their subsequent translocation and exudation in the rhizosphere. In general, most of the nitrogenase activity computed over a 24-h period occurs during the light period; this may reflect the dependence of nitrogenase activity in cereals upon the available photosynthate, as in the case of symbiotic systems of legume plants.

Plant Genotype

Nitrogenase activities vary widely with different genotypes of a given cereal species. Such effects have been shown for corn, millets, and wheat (Day,

Neaves, and Dobereiner 1975; Larson and Neal 1976; Neyra and Dobereiner 1977). Crosses between higher-fixing versus lower-fixing cultivars show significant heterosis effects. This suggests the importance of plant genotype for optimal associations and the possibility of improvement of N_2-fixing associations by plant breeding.

Temperature

Soil temperatures below 22–25 °C are a major limiting factor in N_2 fixation in cereals. However, differences among plant species are expected to occur in relation to tolerance to relatively low temperatures.

Oxygen

Optimal nitrogenase activities are found at pO_2 far below that of air. The activity is almost completely inhibited in air. Most N_2-fixing organisms associated with cereals have very poor oxygen protection mechanisms for their nitrogenases (Abrantes, Day, and Dobereiner 1975).

Combined Nitrogen

High levels of combined nitrogen (NO_3, NO_2, and NH_4) in the soil, or the application of heavy nitrogen fertilization, reduce the potential for nitrogen fixation in cereals. It is quite likely that, at low levels of combined nitrogen in the soil, the simultaneous utilization of biological N_2 fixation and mineral nitrogen fertilizer may be possible. On the other hand, in areas receiving continuously high doses of N fertilizer, the potential for N_2 fixation may not be realized.

It is quite evident from the foregoing brief discussion that biological nitrogen fixation is possible in cereal crops, although not quite to the same extent as in legume–rhizobia symbiotic systems. Various nitrogen-fixing organisms associated with cereal crop systems are listed in Table 1-7. Although the cereal–bacteria associations contribute significantly to the overall nitrogen economy of the plants, the actual contribution of N_2 fixation in cereal crops is not known. The seasonal pattern of nitrogenase activity associated with plant life cycle and the genotypic differences observed with several species show that the physiology of the host can control the level of nitrogenase activity of the bacteria associated with their roots. While biological nitrogen fixation could be sufficient for the maintenance of cereals growing in their natural habitat, it is unlikely that it alone could satisfy all the nitrogen requirements of high-yielding agricultural cereal crops; therefore, studies on the interaction between combined nitrogen and biological N_2 assimilation should be ranked as a high research priority. Similarly, although good progress has been made in understanding the impor-

Table 1-7. Nitrogen-fixing Organisms Associated with Cereal Crops.

Organism	Reference
Azotobacter spp.	
A. paspali	Dobereiner (1970)
A. chroococcum	Watanabe (1975); Alexander (1985)
A. vinelandii	Neyra & Dobereiner (1977)
Beijerinckia spp.	Yoshida (1971)
B. indica	Dobereiner (1973)
B. fluminensis	Quispel (1974)
B. derxii	Alexander (1985)
Azospirillium spp.	Barber, Russel, & Evans (1979)
Spirillum lipoferum	Dobereiner, Marriel, & Nery (1976)
Rhodospirillum rubrum	Quispel (1974); Neyra & Dobereiner (1977)
Enterobacter cloacae	Yoshida (1971); Barber, Tjepkema, & Evans (1976); Neyra & Dobereiner (1977)
Pseudomonas spp.	Mendez-Castro & Alexander (1983)
Bacillus spp.	
B. macerans	Barber, Tjepkema, & Evans (1976)
B. polymyxa	Barber, Tjepkema, & Evans (1976); Larson & Neal (1976)
Clostridium pasteurianum	Neyra & Dobereiner (1977)
Klebsiella aerobacter	Neyra & Dobereiner (1977)
Blue-green algae	Stewart (1975); Alexander (1985)

tance of environmental and plant factors, the exact nature of cereal–bacteria association is still unclear. Until such information is made available, we may not be able to apply the modern biotechnological approaches for improving biological nitrogen fixation in cereals.

BREEDING APPROACHES

In a review dealing with the capacity of conventional plant breeding for crop yield improvement, Frey (1984) summarized data showing that, during this century, the yield potential of wheat and corn in the United States has increased by approximately 50% as a result of genetic improvement. It was estimated that 60% of the observed yield improvement in wheat could be attributed to genetic improvement, whereas for barley and oats the proportions attributable were 42% and 29%, respectively.

Cereal crop cultivars are homozygous and hence are genetically stable; that is, they can be grown year after year without losing their genetic identity. The most commonly used breeding approaches for cereal yield improvement are the pedigree method, the bulk method, backcrossing, and haploid breeding. These methods have been reviewed by Stoskopf (1985). There are several excellent examples of improving yield and quality of cereals by following suitable breeding methods: Hexaploid semidwarf wheat was utilized to transfer genes to durum wheat with continued backcrossing (Frey 1984), and hexaploid triticale was developed via crosses between *Triticum* and *Secale* for several years.

The gene pool concept for plant breeding of cereals was conceived by Harlan and de Wet (1971), who divided the genetic materials into primary, secondary, and tertiary genes. In case of primary genes, the progenitors of a crop species are used for increasing crop productivity. This approach has already been successful in improving the yields of oats and barley (Frey 1984). In a barley introgression study, matings among three barley cultivars and nine collections were backcrossed four times to the cultivated plants; the resulting lines had improved plant height, heading date, and harvest index (Frey 1984). Considerable gains in corn yield have been achieved using intrapopulation recurrent selection breeding techniques (Sprague and Eberthart 1977).

Breeding for specific traits, such as disease resistance and desirable quality characteristics in cereals, has made considerable progress over the past three decades. Several simultaneous backcrossing programs are required to recombine the various resistances with the background of the recurrent parent. An alternative method for achieving a combination of resistances in a crop, without the backcrossing requirement of multilines, is to blend existing varieties that differ in their resistance genes. The effectiveness of this approach in reducing yield losses from yellow rust and powdery mildew in barley has been demonstrated in field studies in the United Kingdom and Denmark (Walsh 1984).

Interspecific Gene Transfer

Deficiencies in crop cultivars for desirable characteristics (resistance to pests, diseases, drought, etc.) and their availability in wild relatives are now well documented in the agricultural literature. Although significant progress in conventional cereal breeding has been made in this regard in recent decades, such approaches are time consuming, and the natural barriers of cross incompatibility between species limit the possibilities of combining genomes and transferring desired traits from one species to another. Recent advances in gene manipulation and transfer have opened new vistas in agricultural research, generating considerable interest in interspecific breeding for effecting transfer of desirable genes from wild species into related cultivars (Stalker 1980; Stalker and Moss 1987; Singh, Moss, and Smartt 1990). When the donor and the recipient species are closely related, there is generally no genetic barrier in the production of a hybrid with a satisfactory level of chromosome pairing. In such cases, gene transfer can be and has been accomplished by conventional methods such as hybridization and backcrossing. Unfortunately, a majority of wild relatives of crop species have developed reproductive isolating mechanisms that may limit interspecific hybridization or inhibit genetic introgression through inadequate chromosomal meiotic pairing (Fehar and Hadley 1980; Sastry 1984; Gupta and Bahl 1985). Even where pairing occurs, linkage may restrict recombination between desirable and undesirable genes, thus preventing production of lines with desired agronomic characteristics.

Barriers to interspecific hybridization occur as a result of either sexual incompatibility or hybrid breakdown. Sexual incompatibility is caused by disharmonious pollen–pistil interaction resulting in a failure of the egg to form a viable zygote. In contrast, hybrid breakdown, hybrid weakness, and hybrid sterility are the main crossability barriers to interspecific hybridization. These may be caused by arrested embryo development, endosperm disintegration, abnormal development of ovular tissue, or chromosomal or genetic instability (Singh, Moss, and Smartt 1990). The two main requirements of interspecific hybridization to incorporate alien genetic variation therefore are

1. the initial production and establishment of viable hybrids, and
2. the subsequent integration of desirable genomic segment(s) from the donor species into the genome of the cultivated species.

In this regard, polyploidy has been particularly helpful in the production and propagation of many interspecific hybrid combinations with subsequent genome duplication. The most successful examples of using ploidy level and chromosome manipulations for introducing alien genetic variation are from *Triticum aestivum,* bread wheat. Sears (1956) was first to demonstrate the role of an integrated set of manipulations in the transfer of genes conferring resistance to leaf rust (*Puccinia recondita*) from *Aegilops umbellulata* to *T. aestivum.* Some of the other studies in this regard are summarized in Table 1-8. Some of the studies using more recent genetic engineering techniques, such as DNA transfer to protoplasts of barley, rice, wheat, and corn, are summarized in Table 1-9.

Direct gene transfer offers new possibilities for combining genomes and genes that so far could not be brought together by conventional means. Such approaches as microinjection of DNA into cells, injection of genetic material directly into plants, the use of pollen or embryos for DNA uptake, and the use of vector systems based on *Agrobacterium* or viruses have been suggested as alternative gene transfer methods applicable to cereals (Gobel and Lorz 1988). Excellent progress has been made toward cloning the genes of major storage proteins of wheat , corn, and barley (Table 1-10). Several genetic engineering approaches and their potential in cloning seed proteins have been reviewed by Croy and Gatehouse (1985).

Recently, there has been growing interest in crop improvement by exploiting exotic germ plasm. The most important characteristics of interest are resistances unavailable in crop species to diseases and pests that are major constraints in

Table 1-8. Ploidy Manipulations for Interspecific Hybridization and Gene Transfer in Wheat and Oats.

Species	Nature of Manipulation	Objectives Achieved	Reference
Wheat (*Triticum aestivum*)			
Triticum × Triticum, *Triticum × Aegilops*	Interploid hybrid, backcrossing	Genetic introgression	Vardi (1974)
		Herbicide resistance	Gill, Multani, & Dhaliwal (1986)
		Resistance to stem rust to 6x via 4x	Kerber & Dyck (1969)
		Direct gene transfer 2x to 6x	Gill & Raupp (1987)
	Amphiploidy	Resistance to leaf rust	Dyck & Kerber (1970)
	Amphiploidy	Addition line	Sears (1956)
	Amphiploidy, aneuploidy	Homologous pairing, resistance to yellow rust	Riley, Chapman, & Johnson (1968)
	Aneuploidy	Homologous pairing	Sears (1973)
Triticum × Agropyron	Interploid hybrid, backcrossing, amphiploidy	Hybrid establishment, genetic introgression	Cauderon (1978)
	Amphiploidy, aneuploidy	Resistance to wheat rust	Cauderon (1978)
	Aneuploidy	Resistance to stem rust	Knott (1961)
Agropyron × Agropyron	Autoploidy	Overcoming incompatibility	Dewey (1977)
Oats (*Avena sativa*)	Interploid hybrid	Addition line, genetic introgression	Thomas, Haki, & Arangzeb (1980)
	Amphiploidy	Resistance to powdery mildew	Kummer (1984)
	Amphiploidy, aneuploidy	Homologous pairing, resistance to powdery mildew	Thomas, Powell, & Aung (1980)

crop production. However, interspecific gene transfer has been devised in only a few cereal crops, such as wheat, rice, and oats, for which there has been a large research effort and for which genome structure and cytogenetic affinities between related species are very well understood and documented. Such studies for other important cereal crops, such as the millets, are lacking. Although existing cytogenetic methods of genetic manipulation will continue to be the principal means of effecting interspecific gene transfer for the foreseeable future, novel techniques for transformation at the cellular and/or molecular levels provide enormous opportunities for extending the range of gene introductions.

Table 1-9. Direct Gene Transfer and Vector-Dependent DNA Transfer to Cereals.

Transfer Type and Crop	Reference
Direct gene transfer	
(a) DNA transfer to protoplasts	
Wheat	Lorz, Baker, & Schell (1985)
Rice	Ou-Lee, Turgeon, & Wu (1986)
Corn	Rhodes et al. (1988); Junker et al. (1987); Gordonkamm et al. (1990)
Barley	Junker et al. (1987)
Sorghum	Ou-Lee, Turgeon, & Wu (1986)
(b) Injection of DNA into floral tillers	
Rye	De La Pena, Lorz, & Schell (1987)
(c) Pollen-mediated transformation	
Corn	de Wet et al. (1985)
Vector-dependent DNA transfer	
Agrobacterium as a vector	
Corn	Grimsley et al. (1987)

Table 1-10. Examples of Cloning and Isolation of cDNAs Encoding Cereal Proteins.

mRNA source	Vector	Seed Protein Encoded	Reference
Wheat endosperm poly(A) RNA	pBR 322/Pst-I	Gliadins	Bartles & Thompson (1983)
Corn endosperm poly(A) polysomal RNA	pBR 322/Pst-I	Zeins	Weinand, Bruschke, & Feix (1979)
Corn endosperm protein bodies poly(A) RNA	pMB 9/Eco-RI	Zeins	Burr et al. (1982)
Barley endosperm poly(A) RNA from membrane-bound polysomes	pBR 322/Hind-III	Hordeins	Brandt (1979)
Barley endosperm poly(A) RNA from membrane-bound polysomes	pBR 322/Pst-I	Hordeins	Forde et al. (1981)

Nevertheless, much work is still required to perfect the techniques of chromosome engineering in many cereal crops, which could reduce the size of the alien chromosome segment that can be transferred. Since wheat has provided such scope for improvement using these techniques, it is quite likely that, given serious research efforts, other cereal crops would respond to these approaches in the near future.

Breeding for Drought Resistance

The ability of a crop to grow satisfactorily in areas subjected to water deficits has been termed its "drought resistance"; its structural and functional modification to increase its probability of survival and reproduction in a particular environment is termed an "adaptation" (Turner and Kramer 1980; Turner 1986). Adaptations can be heritable or nonheritable, constitutive or facultative. Plants, for example, adapt their photosynthetic rate to moisture and temperature depending on habitat, and additionally acclimate photosynthetically to the seasonal changes in these two factors in their habitat.

In the past two decades there has been considerable effort devoted to breeding for improved drought resistance in cereals. While the benefit of this research by the development of new cultivars has yet to be realized on a large scale, it does point the way to future crop breeding methodologies for water-limited environments.

Four basic approaches to breeding for drought resistance have emerged (Turner 1986; Ludlow and Muchow 1990). The first is to breed for high yields under optimal conditions—that is, to breed for yield potential—and then to assume that this will provide a yield advantage under suboptimal conditions. Fischer and Maurer (1978), working with a wide range (up to 53) of bread wheats, durum wheats, triticales, and barleys, found that a high yield potential gave improved yields when the crops were stressed with drought. However, even in the severely stressed crops, grain yields were 2,000 kg/ha compared to 5000 kg/ha in the well-irrigated crops. Clearly yields were high compared with those in severely water-limited environments, where grain yields can be an order of magnitude lower.

The second approach to breeding for drought resistance is to breed for maximum yield in the target environment. However, water-limited environments are notably variable from year to year, so the environmental selection indices and pressures on the breeders' populations change drastically from generation to generation. Compounded with the low heritabilities for yield and yield components (Roy and Murty 1970; Turner 1986), this makes for slow breeding progress and a costly breeding program, and accounts for the low yield increases observed from breeding programs in water-limited environments compared to environments with optimal rainfall (Turner and Begg 1981).

Hence, some breeders developing cultivars for water-limited environments have suggested the selection and incorporation of physiological and morphological mechanisms of drought resistance into traditional breeding programs. This third approach requires the identification of the characters in each generation. To this end, considerable progress in rapid screening methods has been made (Mussell and Staples 1979; IRRI 1982; Ludlow and Muchow 1990). Having identified a range of characters with putatively useful qualities in conferring some measure of drought resistance, Ludlow and Muchow (1990) recommended selection for these characters at the F_5 and F_6 generations in an established program for selection for agronomic types, yield, and yield components under optimal environmental conditions.

Rather than utilizing multiple physiological selection criteria, an alternative, fourth approach to breeding under water-limited conditions aims to prove beyond doubt that a single drought-resistance character will benefit yield under water-limited conditions, and then to incorporate that character into an existing yield breeding program. A ten-year breeding program to incorporate a high hydraulic root resistance into wheat has provided results suggesting that lines with narrow xylem vessels in the seminal roots outyield lines with large vessels by 5–10% in water-limited environments (Passioura 1986). Likewise, selection for lines of wheat with high endogenous levels of abscisic acid have increased yields by 16% and 10% at two sites, the higher improvement being at the drier site (Quarrie 1985).

It thus appears, because of the variability in amount and temporal distribution of available moisture from year to year, breeding improved genotypes for the arid and semiarid tropics by selecting solely for grain yield is difficult. The genotypic variance in yield is low under these conditions. It is therefore essential to understand how plants survive drought and how traits influence yield by enhancing the determinants of survival. To survive periods of water deficit, higher plants may use one of two main strategies: drought escape and drought resistance (Table 1-11). Desert ephemerals and short-season annuals have such a short life cycle that they germinate (after rain), grow rapidly, flower, and set seed before the soil water is exhausted in arid environments with low and variable rainfall. These plants are said to "escape" drought or water deficits in their tissues. The cost of such a strategy, however, is lost opportunity and low yield in better-than-average seasons (Ludlow and Muchow 1990).

Longer-season annuals and perennials survive water stress by one of two drought-resistance strategies (Table 1-11). The first involves the avoidance of water deficits in tissues—despite the absence of rainfall and the presence of hot, dry atmospheres—by maintaining cell turgor and cell volume. This is achieved by maintaining water uptake, reducing water loss, and changing tissue characteristics (e.g., osmotic adjustment or increased tissue elasticity). The second strategy relies on tissues that are able to tolerate dehydration, usually because of superior protoplasmic tolerance of desiccation. Putative traits that improve yield per unit of precipitation by enhancing plant survival must act through one or more of the determinants given in Table 1-11.

Not all the mechanisms listed in the table are without metabolic cost to productive processes. Turner (1982, 1986) considered the influence of the adaptive mechanisms on crop productivity and concluded that only those mechanisms that aided in drought escape, maintenance of water uptake, and maintenance of turgor pressure did not reduce photosynthesis, crop growth, and yield (Table

Table 1-11. Mechanisms of Adaptation to Water Deficits and Their Influence on Productive Processes.

Mechanism	Productive Processes Reduced?
Drought escape	
Rapid phenological development	No
Developmental plasticity	No
Drought resistance	
Dehydration avoidance/postponement	
Maintenance of turgor	
Increased root density and depth	No
Increased liquid-phase conductance	No
Maintenance of volume	
Increase in elasticity	No
Reduction of water loss	
Reduction of leaf area	Yes
Increase in stomatal and cuticular resistance	Yes
Reduction in radiation absorbed	Yes
Osmotic adjustment	No
Changes in tissue characteristics	Yes
Dehydration tolerance	
Protoplasmic tolerance	Yes

Compiled from: Levitt (1980), Turner (1986), and Ludlow and Muchow (1990).

1-11). While it is relatively easy to decide whether a particular adaptive mechanism affects a short-term process such as the instantaneous rate of photosynthesis, it is much more difficult to determine whether it has long-term consequences. For example, maintenance of water uptake by the development of deep roots into a wet profile will maintain the assimilation rate of leaves, but the diversion of carbon from new leaves to new roots and the maintenance of a deep root system will ultimately reduce the aboveground productive capacity of the plant relative to one with an adequate supply of water (Turner 1986).

Many traits have been proposed for improving the performance of drought-affected crops; these are summarized in Table 1-12. (For details on the role of these traits in breeding drought-resistant cereal crops, see Begg and Turner [1976], IRRI [1983], Turner [1986], and Ludlow and Muchow [1990].) These traits may differ in priority when breeding drought-resistant varieties of different cereal crops. The recommendations of Ludlow and Muchow (1990) for breeding for drought-resistant sorghum in intermittent and terminal stress environments in both modern and subsistence agriculture systems are summarized in Table 1-13 as an example. It is quite likely that similar approaches may be successful in breeding other drought-resistant cereal crops.

Table 1-12. Traits That Control Drought Resistance of Cereal Cultivars.

1. Matching phenology to the water supply
2. Photoperiod sensitivity
3. Developmental plasticity
4. Mobilization of preanthesis assimilate to grain
5. Rooting depth and density
6. Root hydraulic conductance
7. Early vigor
8. Leaf area maintenance
9. Osmotic adjustment
10. Low lethal water status
11. Reduced stomatal conductance
12. Leaf movements
13. Leaf reflectance
14. Epidermal conductance
15. Transpiration efficiency
16. High-temperature tolerance

Compiled from: Begg and Turner (1976), IRRI (1983), Turner (1986), and Ludlow and Muchow (1990).

PHYSIOLOGICAL CONSIDERATIONS

Carbon Metabolism

The cultivated cereal crop species exhibit significant differences in their carbon metabolism pathway. Some of these aspects and their influence on certain parameters associated with their yield potential are briefly described below.

Two basic pathways of carbon metabolism operate in cereal crops: the Calvin cycle (Benson–Calvin–Bassham cycle) and the Hatch–Slack pathway (Hatch, Osmond, and Slatyer 1971; Evans and Wardlaw 1976; Tootill 1984). These are shown in Figs. 1-7(a) and 1-7(b), respectively, and are differentiated based on whether the first product generated during the photosynthesis process is a three- or four-carbon compound.

Any plant that produces the three-carbon compound phosphoglyceric acid as the first step in photosynthesis is termed a C-3 plant. Most plants of temperate regions are C-3 plants; among cereals, wheat, oats, rye, and rice are examples. Generally, C-3 plants exhibit photorespiration and are relatively inefficient photosynthetically as compared to C-4 plants. They also have lower CO_2-fixation rates and higher compensation points than C-4 plants.

C-4 plants produce, as the first step in photosynthesis, either oxaloacetic acid, maleic acid, or aspartic acid, which all contain four carbon atoms (Moss and Musgrave 1971). Over 100 species of C-4 plant have been identified, most

Table 1-13. Recommended Traits, in Order of Priority, for Grain Sorghum Grown in Intermittent and Terminal Stress Environments in Both Modern (Opportunistic) and Subsistence (Conservative) Agriculture.

Modern Agriculture[a]		Subsistence Agriculture[a]	
Intermittent Stress	Terminal Stress[b]	Intermittent Stress	Terminal Stress[b]
1. Matching phenology to water supply	1. Matching phenology to water supply	1. Matching phenology to water supply	1. Matching phenology to water supply
2. Osmotic adjustment of shoots and roots	2. Osmotic adjustment of shoots and roots	2. Osmotic adjustment of shoots and roots	2. Mobilization of preanthesis dry matter
3. Rooting depth and density	3. Rooting depth and density	3. Rooting depth and density	3. Increased leaf reflectance[c]
4. Early vigor	4. Increased leaf reflectance	4. Increased leaf reflectance	4. Photoperiod sensitivity[c]
5. Leaf area maintenance	5. Early vigor	5. Low lethal water stress	
6. Increased leaf reflectance[d]	6. Mobilization of preanthesis dry matter[c]	6. Leaf movements	
7. Low lethal water stress		7. Low epidermal conductance	
		8. Early vigor	
		9. Leaf area maintenance	
		10. Photoperiod sensitivity	

Source: Ludlow and Muchow (1990).

[a]Seedling tolerance of high temperature is an important trait in environments where soil surface temperature at emergence exceeds 50 °C.
[b]When lodging of grain sorghum is a problem in a particular environment, any trait that is shown to reduce lodging is desirable. It remains to be shown whether stay-green is such a trait without a yield penalty.
[c]Could be disadvantageous for grain sorghum in some environments if it promotes lodging.
[d]The scope for improvement may be small if current varieties are glaucous or bloomed.

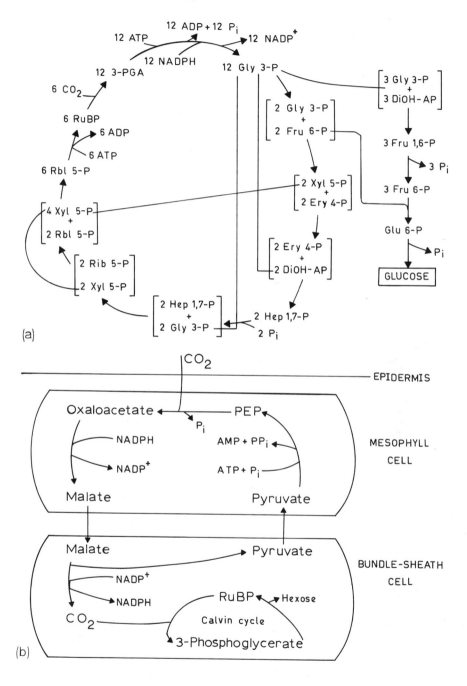

(a)

(b)

of which are tropical. Examples include corn, sorghum, millets, sugarcane, Bermuda grass, and many desert plants. C-4 plants require thirty molecules of ATP and twenty-four molecules of water to synthesize a molecule of glucose, whereas C-3 plants need only eighteen molecules of ATP and twelve molecules of water (Tootill 1984). However, C-4 plants produce more glucose for a given leaf area than do C-3 plants, and consequently grow more quickly. They can also continue to photosynthesize at high light intensities and low CO_2 concentrations, and, most significantly, do not exhibit photorespiration.

Photorespiration occurs in plants in light. It differs from dark respiration in that it does not occur in the mitochondria and is not coupled to oxidative phosphorylation. The rate of CO_2 release by photorespiration in C-3 plants can be three to five times greater than that of dark respiration (Tootill 1984). Since the process does not generate ATP, it appears to be extremely wasteful. It has been estimated that the photosynthetic efficiency could be improved by 50% if photorespiration were inhibited (Evans and Wardlaw 1976). In C-4 plants photorespiration is hardly detectable, possibly because the synthesis of glycolic acid,

Fig. 1-7 (facing). (**A**) Calvin cycle (Benson–Calvin–Bassham cycle), which produces a three-carbon compound, phosphoglyceric acid, as the first step in photosynthesis in C-3 type plants. The sequence of reactions constitutes the dark or light-independent reactions of photosynthesis in which CO_2 is reduced to glucose using ATP and NADPH derived from the light-dependent reactions. The overall series of reactions is as follows:

$$6 \text{ Ribulose 1,5-biphosphate} + 6\,CO_2 + 18 \text{ ATP} + 12 \text{ NADPH} + 12\,H^+ + 12\,H_2O$$
$$\rightarrow 6 \text{ Ribulose 1,5-biphosphate} + \text{glucose} + 18\,P_i + 18 \text{ ADP} + 12 \text{ NADP}^+$$

The glucose is subsequently converted to starch, cellulose, and other polysaccharides. *Abbreviations:* Gly 3-P, glyceraldehyde 3-phosphate; DiOH-AP, dihydroxyacetone phosphate; Fru 6-P, fructose 6-phosphate; Fru 1,6-P, fructose 1,6-biphosphate; Glu 6-P, glucose 6-phosphate; Xyl 5-P, xylulose 5-phosphate; Ery 4-P, erythrose 4-phosphate; Hep 1,7-P, sedoheptulose 1,7-biphosphate; Rib 5-P, ribose 5-phosphate; Rbl 5-P, ribulose 5-phosphate; RuBP, ribulose 1,5-biphosphate; 3-PGA, 3-phosphoglyceric acid. (**B**) Hatch–Slack pathway of alternative form of CO_2 fixation in C-4 plants. The first product of photosynthesis is a four-carbon compound, oxaloacetate, which is formed by the carboxylation of phosphoenolpyruvate (PEP) by PEP carboxylase. Oxaloacetate is then either reduced to malate or transaminated to yield aspartate. All these reactions take place in the cells of the mesophyll. The malate or aspartate is then transported to bundle-sheath cells and decarboxylated to form CO_2 and pyruvate. The CO_2 released reacts with ribulose 1,5-biphosphate to yield two molecules of phosphoglyceric acid. The normal Calvin cycle then commences to yield glucose. The pyruvate is then returned to the mesophyll cells, where it is converted back to PEP. Because of this last reaction, which uses two high-energy phosphate bonds (ATP to AMP), C-4 plants require thirty molecules of ATP for each molecule of glucose synthesized, compared to eighteen molecules in C-3 plants. *Source:* E. Tootill (ed.), *The Penguin Dictionary of Botany.* London: Penguin, pp. 54–5, 170. © Market House Books Ltd., 1984. Reproduced by permission of Penguin Books Ltd.

the substrate for photorespiration, is much lower in C-4 plants (about 10% of that of C-3 plants). This may be due to the high concentration of CO_2 in the bundle sheath cells that prevents the oxidation (instead of carboxylation) of ribulose biphosphate.

Another major difference between C-3 and C-4 plants is related to their *compensation points,* defined as the lowest steady-state CO_2 concentrations achievable in a closed system containing a photosynthesizing plant. These points are higher for the C-3 than for the C-4 plants (Tootill 1984). When the minimum level is reached, the photosynthetic uptake of CO_2 is exactly balanced by its respiratory release, indicating that the rate of synthesis of organic material equals the rate of breakdown by respiration. Low compensation points are indicative of photosynthetic efficiency, as the plant is then using the maximum amount of available CO_2.

Yet another form of photosynthesis, first observed in the family Crassulaceae and since found in many other succulent plants, is the crassulacean acid metabolism (CAM) pathway (Tootill 1984). CAM plants keep their stomata closed during the day to reduce water loss by transpiration. Carbon dioxide can therefore only enter at night, when, instead of combining with ribulose biphosphate (as in conventional C-3 plants) it combines with the three-carbon compound phosphoenol pyruvate to give the four-carbon oxaloacetate. This is then converted to malic acid, which can be stored in the cell vacuoles until daylight, when it is transferred to the cytoplasm. Here it is broken down to release CO_2, which is then fixed in the normal manner. This adaptation allows such plants to flourish in arid habitats, but their growth rate is slow. CAM can be induced in certain C-3 plants by water shortage.

The differences between C-3 and C-4 plants are reflected in their photosynthetic rates. McCree (1974) found the action spectrum for photosynthesis by leaves to be closely similar in wheat, oats, barley, triticale, rice, corn, and sorghum. As mentioned above, rice and the temperate small-grain cereals, such as wheat, barley, oats, and rye, depend entirely on the Calvin cycle; in corn, sorghum, and millets, however, the Calvin cycle is preceded by CO_2 fixation in the C-4 dicarboxylic acids. The Michaelis–Menten constant for the carboxylating enzyme in C-3 plants (RuBP carboxylase) is not much greater than that of PEP carboxylase, which mediates the primary carboxylation in C-4 plants (Evans and Wardlaw 1976). More important, refixation of CO_2 by RuDP carboxylase in the bundle-sheath cells of C-4 cereals, after transfer and decarboxylation of malate or aspartate from the mesophyll, probably takes place at a much higher CO_2 concentration, and is therefore less susceptible to photorespiratory decarboxylation. Consequently, the minimum values for mesophyll (or residual) resistance (r_m) to CO_2 uptake by leaves appear to be substantially lower in the C-4 cereals than in the Calvin cycle species. For example, r_m values of $0.7–0.9$ s cm^{-1} (Gifford and Musgrave 1973) and 1.0 s cm^{-1} (El Sharkawy and Hesketh 1965) for corn are to be compared with minimum values of 4.1 $s\,cm^{-1}$ for oats (El Sharkawy and Hesketh 1965) and 2.7–3.1 $s\,cm^{-1}$ for a range of wheat species (Dunstone, Gifford, and Evans 1973).

The smaller r_m of the leaves of C-4 compared with C-3 cereals tends to be associated with a greater stomatal resistance r_s; hence the greater efficiency of the C-4 cereals in dry-matter production per unit of water transpired (discussed later in this section). Stomatal opening in the C-4 cereals increases up to very high flux densities of light, as in corn (Hatch, Osmond, and Slatyer 1971). Consequently, whereas photosynthesis by single leaves of the C-3 cereals tends to reach light saturation at 33–50% of full sunlight, that of the C-4 cereals increases with increasing intensity up to full sunlight (Hesketh and Musgrave 1962; Hesketh 1963). Even so, the minimum recorded gas phase resistances to CO_2 uptake tend to be rather lower in the C-3 cereals (e.g., 0.7–0.8 $s\,cm^{-1}$ in wheat [Dunstone, Gifford, and Evans 1973] compared with 1.5 $s\,cm^{-1}$ in corn [El Sharkawy and Hesketh 1965]).

The maximum photosynthetic rates achieved by the C-4 cereals are distinctly greater than those of the C-3 cereals. Rates up to 240–280 $ng\,CO_2\,cm^{-2}\,s^{-1}$ have been recorded in corn, sorghum (Downes 1971), and pearl millet (McPherson and Slatyer 1973), compared with up to 120 $ng\,cm^{-2}\,s^{-1}$ in wheat cultivars at atmospheric CO_2 levels. However, rates up to 200 $ng\,cm^{-2}\,s^{-1}$ have been measured in the wild diploid wheats (Evans and Dunstone 1970).

The greater rates of photosynthesis in C-4 plants, associated with their reduced photorespiratory losses and other characteristics mentioned above, have led to them being called "efficient" plants, and to a search for nonphotorespiring forms among the temperate cereals such as oats and wheat (Moss and Musgrave 1971), but without success. Other characteristics of the C-4 pathway in cereals should be considered, however. Although their greater photosynthetic rate may be of advantage at high light intensities, especially in view of their more efficient use of water, at low light intensities (such as overcast weather or for leaves deep in the canopy) their photosynthetic rate may be lower than that of C-3 plants (Evans and Wardlaw 1976). This is particularly true when cooler temperatures are associated with low light, the conditions under which the temperate cereals usually make their early growth. For example, the tropical C-4 grasses show poor photosynthetic performance at cool temperatures (around 10 °C) relative to temperate C-3 grasses and cereals such as barley and wheat (Evans 1975). At high temperatures, in contrast, photosynthesis by the C-3 cereals falls off rapidly at temperatures above 30 °C, as in wheat (Milthorpe and Ivins 1966), whereas photosynthesis by the C-4 cereals may reach its peak at temperatures of 30–40 °C as in corn, sorghum, and pearl millet (El Sharkawy and Hesketh 1964; Hofstra and Hesketh 1969; McPherson and Slatyer 1973). Although rice is a crop of tropical origin, its photosynthetic response to temperature resembles that of the other C-3 cereals in having a broad optimum (Murata

1961) with a rapid fall in the rate at high temperatures. Cool temperatures, however, have a more adverse effect on photosynthesis in rice than in the temperate cereals, particularly on the *indica* varieties (Evans and Wardlaw 1976).

The differences among C-3, C-4, and CAM plants are also reflected in their water-use efficiency, perhaps the most critical component of crop production. The transpiration ratio R_T, which is the loss of water by evaporation from a plant surface, is generally much lower for the C-4 metabolism plants (<400 with a mean of 320 ± 43) compared to that for C-3 metabolism plants (640 ± 165) (Stanhill 1986). These values are even lower for CAM plants, such as pineapple, with mean values ranging from 103 ± 41 (Ting 1976). The lower transpiration ratio found in C-4 plants can be attributed to their ability to continue photosynthesis at CO_2 concentrations that are one-third to one-fifteenth of those needed to sustain the process in C-3 plants (Stanhill 1986). This leads to an increased CO_2 gradient and hence flux, and is associated with a specialized leaf anatomy that enhances CO_2 but not H_2O gas exchange.

The marked yield improvements achieved in modern crop production are largely ascribable to the greater proportion of the crop's total dry-matter production harvested as yield, rather than to increases in dry matter production per se: Where total dry matter production has been increased, this has nearly always been achieved via larger and longer-lasting photosynthetic apparatuses (i.e., leaf canopies) rather than by a greater photosynthetic efficiency per unit leaf area (Gifford and Evans 1981).

Larger crop canopies and longer cropping seasons imply an increase in transpiration, which suggests that significant decreases in R_T are not to be expected when expressed on a dry matter rather than yield basis. However, the adoption of new varieties and improved fertilizer, irrigation, and plant protection practices continues to increase yields. Similarly, the larger and longer-lasting crop canopies resulting from these changes can be expected to reduce evaporation losses from bare soil, shaded to a greater degree by larger crop canopies.

An important exception to the strong coupling between dry-matter production and transpiration is the previously noted difference in the R_T values of plants with C-4, C-3, and CAM metabolisms. If the carbon metabolism responsible for the high net dry-matter production rates of C-4 plants could be transferred to C-3 crop species, a major increase in yields could be achieved without necessitating any increase in transpiration. In arid regions, the transfer of CAM metabolism to C-3 or C-4 plants would allow crop production at transpiration rates below those currently capable of supporting economic crop production.

The feasibility of transferring the different photosynthetic pathways from one species to another has been demonstrated, although not, to date, in crop plants. One major problem is that many of the first-generation hybrids between species of different metabolisms are not fertile. However, fertile hybrids have been produced between C-3 and C-4 *Atriplex* species from the same subgenus (Nobs 1976), and from a number of other genera, some between C-3 and intermediate

C-3 : C-4 species (Powell 1978; Brown et al. 1985; Holaday, Talkmitt, and Doohan 1985).

The prospects for achieving metabolism transfer selectively through genetic engineering rather than by plant breeding are distant. This is because each system of carbon metabolism involves a major complex of enzymatic, organelle, and cellular specializations, each of which in turn involves many groups of gene sequences. Even after the sites of all of the controlling genes have been identified, there are formidable difficulties involved in their transfer. One major problem is that of handling the large number of genes concerned. Another is the fact that one of the relevant genes for the large subunit of the central rubisco enzyme (ribulose-biphosphate carboxylase) is coded by DNA in the chloroplast genome (Stanhill 1986); as yet there is no transfer system available for gene manipulation within the chloroplast.

The possibility of incorporating the even lower values of R_T common to plants with CAM metabolism into other crop species is even more problematic. The fact that a number of C-3 plants utilize the CAM carbon pathway only under conditions of water stress shows that there is no fundamental incompatibility between these two metabolisms. However, the very energy-demanding nature of this metabolism reduces the absolute levels of dry-matter production by CAM plants to levels that are too low for economic crop production. An exception could be for high-value seed crops produced at the end of a wetter growing season. This same water-conserving strategy achieved by shifting from C-3 to CAM metabolism during the final reproductive growth phase has been reported for a plant growing in an arid Mediterranean habitat (Turner and Kramer 1980).

To incorporate the CAM metabolism into crop species by genetic engineering requires the same progress needed for the transfer of C-4 metabolism to C-3 plants: the identification of the controlling gene sequences and the development within the chloroplast genome of a transfer system capable of dealing with the large number of genes involved. Nevertheless, the practical benefits to be derived from progress in this field suggest that such research is worthy of our greater attention in years to come.

Vernalization

Vernalization may be defined as the promotion of flowering by exposure of young plants to a cold treatment. For example, the winter varieties of wheat, barley, oats, and rye will normally flower in early summer if they were sown before the onset of winter. However, in areas experiencing very harsh winters, this may not be possible; therefore, the plants are given an artificial cold treatment and are planted in the spring.

Russian researcher T. D. Lysenko was the first deliberately to chill seeds of winter wheats and demonstrate that this treatment hastened development when they were planted in spring (Salisbury 1963; Flood and Halloran 1986). Hence, winter wheats were made to act like spring wheats, for which Lysenko coined the term "jarovization" (Russian: *jarovizacija*). Vernalization (from the Latin *vernalis,* pertaining to spring) has now come to embrace other physiological processes unrelated to its original meaning—for example, the breaking of dormancy in bulb crops. This section focuses on vernalization in wheat.

Vernalization in wheat is generally considered to be affected by temperatures ≤10 °C, although the upper limit has not been critically established, and temperatures as high as 11–15 °C have been reported as being vernalizing (Vavilov 1951; Salisbury 1963; Flood and Halloran 1986). It is an unusual biological process in that it generally appears to have a negative Q_{10} value; that is, the lower the temperature, the faster it proceeds (Bidwell 1979). Ahrens and Loomis (1963) found that 1 °C had a vernalizing effect in winter wheat although there was no vernalization at –2 °C. The possibility of an optimum vernalization temperature was supported by Trione and Metzger (1970), who found that rate of vernalization was maximal at 7 °C but much lower at both 9° and 3 °C.

Since low temperatures influence the rates of both growth and development, the most effective vernalizing temperature for early induction of flowering cereal is not yet resolved. It is generally considered, however, that the weaker the vernalization response, the higher the vernalizing temperature needed for maximum rate of vernalization. As a corollary, the higher the optimum temperature for vernalization, the shorter the vernalization period. Citing the pioneering work of a Russian researcher by the name of Dolgusin, Flood and Halloran (1986) summarized the optimal temperature–time treatments for vernalization in a range of wheats as shown in Table 1-14.

As constant temperatures are not experienced in the field, vernalization in these situations must be considered in the context of the vernalizing component of diurnal temperature fluctuation and the possible influence of higher (nonvernalizing) day temperatures on this process. Gregory and Purvis (1948) were the first to demonstrate reversal of vernalization with the rye variety Petkus by imposing a temperature of 35 °C for three days on vernalized seed. They also found that the longer the period of cold treatment, the less reversible was the

Table 1-14. Optimal Temperature–Time Treatments for Vernalization in Wheat.

Varieties	Temperature–Time Treatment	
Early spring varieties	8–15 °C	for 5–8 days
Late spring varieties	3–6 °C	for 10–15 days
Intermediate varieties	2–5 °C	for 20–25 days
Winter wheats	1–4 °C	for 30–35 days
Extreme winter wheats	0–3 °C	for 30–45 days

Source: Flood and Halloran (1986).

vernalized condition. This was the trend up to a certain period of cold, beyond which the vernalized condition was irreversible.

Summarizing the available literature, Flood and Halloran (1986) suggest that vernalization could be satisfied at three stages in the life cycle of the wheat plant: (1) during germination, (2) during plant growth, and (3) during seed formation and ripening. These researchers also found that the vernalization response in wheat is controlled by one to four genes, and that some varieties may display polygenic control of this process.

Vernalization has the adaptive value of delaying the initiation of floral development. Under the moderately long photoperiods and warm temperatures subsequent to sowing in many autumn-sown wheat areas of the world, it ensures against precocious photoperiod induction of reproductive development before the onset of winter cold. In prolonging vegetative development, it minimizes or prevents the damaging effects of winter freezing temperatures on the differential head during the period from apex initiation to flowering. By delaying the initiation of reproductive development, it can ensure closer-to-optimum fitness, as higher reproductive potential, of the species in particular environments.

Physiology of Grain Yield

Crop yield is an agroindustrial concept; thus it does not necessarily relate to natural selection or to crop evolution, but rather is expressed by the nonbiological criterion of weight of product per unit area. In some crops a vegetative part is harvested; in others, a reproductive organ. Yet whatever plant part is used, natural crop evolution on the one hand and trends in crop yields on the other must be recognized as separate, if interrelated, phenomena. Increased understanding of the factors governing crop photosynthesis and respiration, distribution of assimilates, and seed growth permits us to compare and contrast the performance of annual seed crops such as cereals and legumes in terms of their branching, leafiness, light profile, photosynthesis, biomass, flowering, seed setting, grain filling, harvest index, and yield, and/or in terms of agronomic factors such as soil fertility, plant density, and plant arrangement. The prime need for farmers has always been the quantity of seed in the bag or basket—the crop yield per unit area of land—rather than the size of the individual seed or the seed yield per plant. A cereal breeder may therefore gain leverage in producing higher-yielding plants by selecting types capable of producing a higher proportion of grain to straw. Since over 90% of the dry weight of a plant is the product of photosynthesis, and since a plant is limited by time in the amount of assimilate it can produce, a better distribution of assimilates (i.e., the photosynthates) into grain and less into straw should produce a more efficient plant. Here literature pertaining to grain-yield physiology in major cereal crops is reviewed.

Partitioning of photosynthate—the differential distribution and deposition of assimilate among the organs, tissues, and cells plants—is an important component of economic yield. *Partitioning efficiency* is then defined as the amount of product produced per unit of resource used (Snyder and Carlson 1984). In modern cropping systems, it is the ratio of the amount of food, feed, or fiber energy produced per unit or radiant energy absorbed. Synthesis, translocation, partitioning, and accumulation of the photosynthetic products within the plants are controlled genetically, influenced by the environmental factors, and involve a number of complex physiological processes (Donald and Hamblin 1976, 1983; Evans and Wardlaw 1976; Snyder and Carlson 1984).

"Source" and "sink" are the two terms often used in conjunction with partitioning. Leaves and other green tissues and organs of plants that produce photosynthate are called *sources,* as are organs or tissues that receive products, temporarily store them, and later release them to other sites. All sites within the plant that utilize the photosynthetically derived products, either in situ or after receiving the products, are called *sinks* (Cooper 1975; Donald and Hamblin 1983). There is a close relationship between net photosynthesis and crop yield as well as the need for improved translocation and larger sink capacity.

Environmental factors significantly influence the partitioning of photosynthates and the subsequent dry-matter accumulation. For example, the optimum temperature for growth of roots and shoots differs in many species. Although shading and other practices may modify temperature within the crop canopy and the soil, for crops grown in the field, it is generally not possible to control temperature. Therefore, the greatest opportunity for manipulating temperature effects on partitioning lies in changing the plant genotype itself.

Light also affects dry-matter production and partitioning in a number of ways. More light (by either increased duration or intensity) increases the biomass and, therefore, the proportion of root weight and economic yield of many crops (Donald and Hamblin 1983). As irradiance levels increase, the capacity of sources to produce assimilates also increases.

Deficiencies in water and mineral nutrients result in a smaller source, lower photosynthetic rates, and altered partitioning. Water and nitrogen deficits tend to increase the proportion of root to total biomass as well as of root to shoot (Caloin, Khodre, and Atry 1980). The effect of water stress on dry-matter accumulation by the cereal grains depends upon the time and intensity of stress during grain development (Donald and Hamblin 1976, 1983).

Snyder and Carlson (1984), reviewing the literature on the effects of CO_2 and O_2 concentrations on growth and distribution in a number of crop plants, reported that high CO_2 promoted some increases in height and leaf area. C-4 plants are generally less responsive than C-3 plants. High CO_2 promotes tillering in barley and rice, and rice partitions relatively more dry matter to roots than to leaves when exposed to relatively higher CO_2 (Donald and Hamblin 1983; Snyder and Carlson 1984). In contrast, the growth of corn, a C-4 plant, is promoted less by high CO_2 and suppressed less by low CO_2.

Plant stand densities can also be selected to complement environmental factors that will produce the greatest economic yield per hectare (Donald and Hamblin 1976, 1983; Snyder and Carlson 1984). Generally, the yield of above-ground biomass is greater for high-density than for low-density stands. Cereal crops such as wheat, oats, and rice tiller less at high density than at low density; thus the partitioning response to stand density in the vegetative state compensates to quite a degree, and tends to lessen differences in economic yields caused by differences in stand density (Donald and Hamblin 1976, 1983). However, when water or nutrient stress occurs, the economic yield may be greater at somewhat lower stand densities than at higher densities. In general, the optimum stand density for cereals tends to be more variable because of their capacity to tiller as compared to that for root crops (Snyder and Carlson 1984).

The efficiency of partitioning of photosynthates is further reflected in the biological yield (BY), harvest index (HI), and grain yield (GY) of cereal crops. Donald and Hamblin (1976) defined the BY of a cereal crop as the total yield of plant material, and HI as the ratio GY : BY. The relationships between BY and GY in cereal crops display some important differences.

The BY of cereals increases with density until it reaches a plateau (Donald 1963; Donald and Hamblin 1983). This is maintained up to very high densities unless crop failure occurs from lodging or the advent of disease or pests among the attenuated plants. The GY increases to a maximum at a density approximating the minimum density giving the full BY. To the extent that, when maximum seed yield is attained, there is a maximum exploitation of the environment in terms of BY, cereals are efficient in ensuring this prolificacy. Donald and Hamblin (1983) further speculated (Fig. 1-8) on future trends in the relationship be-

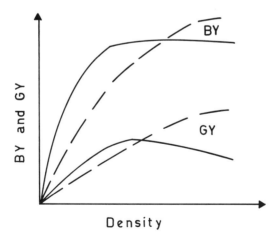

Fig. 1-8. Present relationship (solid lines) and possible future relationship (broken lines) between biological yield (BY) and grain yield (GY) as related to stand density under field conditions of cereal genotypes. *Source:* Donald and Hamblin (1983).

tween BY and GY of cereal crops. If nonbranched plants are used, the density (plants/ha) required to give the full BY will be greater. The main contribution to potential yield will then be an improved HI, perhaps 0.35–0.40 or 0.50 in cereals, representing an increase of about 25% in GY of modern cultivars. Donald and Hamblin (1983) also suggested that an increase of 10% in BY and 25% in HI would increase the GY by 37%.

The HI is correlated positively with GY and negatively with BY in barley (Singh and Stoskopf 1971), oats (Takeda, Frey, and Bailey 1980), rye (Singh and Stoskopf 1971), and wheat (Singh and Stoskopf 1971; Luthra and Dawari 1979). Based on these and several other studies, Snyder and Carlson (1984) suggested that selecting for higher HI should increase the GY in most cereals, particularly where BY is relatively stable.

Donald and Hamblin (1976) studied various models and actual relationships between BY and GY within a series of genotypes or agronomic treatments; these are summarized in Fig. 1-9. Model 1A depicts a situation in which a number of varieties all have precisely the same BY but different GY; in model 1B, these genotypes are ranked in order of increasing GY. In both these cases, the GY is proportional to HI and their correlation is 1.0 (Table 1-15), whereas the BY and HI are unrelated.

In some situations, the GY shows dependence on the BY. As shown in model 2, the GY is strictly proportional to the BY with a correlation of 1.0. Similar relationships may be observed in relation to responses to water and nitrogen fertilizers (models 3 and 4, respectively). However, in a complex case where water is deficient, the BY shows a negative correlation with HI and GY with increasing application of nitrogen. This relationship is shown in model 5. In fact, models 3–5 are in effect variations of model 2, where GY is proportional to BY. Each of these relationships has been reported frequently in agronomic studies, and each is also feasible in comparisons of genotypes. With an increase in BY, the GY may rise more than proportionately (model 3), rise less than proportionately (model 4), or decline (model 5).

Cereal crops suffering from water stress not only have lower BY and GY, but also lower HI (Donald and Hamblin 1976). Citing the results of Poostchi, Rovhani, and Razmi (1972) of supplementary spring irrigation of wheat under semiarid conditions in southern Iran, they found a characteristic response pattern that was remarkably consistent for each of the three years of the experiment (Fig. 1-10). As the water supply was increased, the BY rose from 9.5 to 15.8 MT, the GY from 1.6 to 3.6 MT, and the HI from 0.172 to 0.229.

The application of nitrogen to cereals also tends to influence the BY with a concurrent decrease in HI. This relationship was demonstrated at the Rothamsted Experimental Station in England as early as last century by the application of nitrogen to wheat for the period 1852–63 (Fig. 1-11). The increase in BY (3.4–8.5 MT) greatly exceeded the decline in HI (0.36–0.30) such that the GY rose from 1.2 to 2.6 MT with 192 kg N/ha.

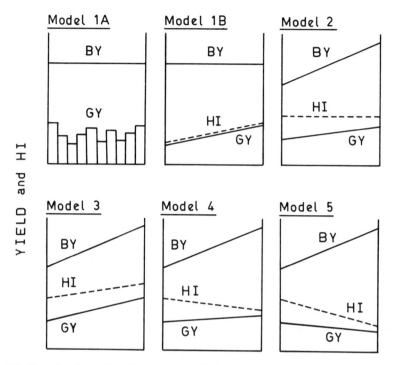

Fig. 1-9. Models of relationships between biological yield (BY), grain yield (GY), and harvest index (HI). BY is shown as constant or as increasing from left to right; however, the graphs can also be considered in mirror image. In model IA the varieties are unranked; in 1B they are ranked. In both cases, GY is directly proportional to HI. Model 2 represents tendency of genotypes in mixtures where, as BY increases, GY increases proportionately. Model 3 is typical of responses to water where, as BY increases, GY increases more than proportionately. Responses to nitrogen are shown in Model 4 where, as BY increases, GY increases less than proportionately. Model 5 depicts an inverse relationship between BY and GY and is characteristic of responses to nitrogen when water is deficient. *Source:* Donald and Hamblin (1976).

Table 1-15. Correlation Coefficients Showing Interrelationships among the Biological Yield (BY), Grain Yield (GY), and Harvest Index (HI), as Shown in Fig. 1-9.

Model	GY vs. BY	GY vs. HI	BY vs. HI
1A, 1B	0	1	0
2	1	0	0
3	1	1	1
4	1	–1	–1
5	–1	1	–1

Adapted from: Donald and Hamblin (1976).

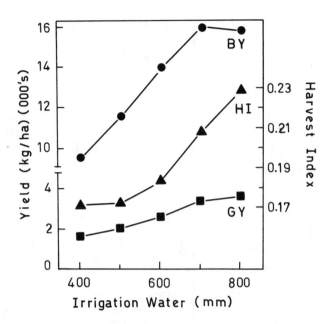

Fig. 1-10. The responses of wheat to irrigation in southern Iran. The data shown are means of three seasons. *Abbreviations:* BY, biological yield; HI, harvest index; GY, grain yield. *Source:* Adapted from the data of Poostchi, Rovhani, and Razmi (1972).

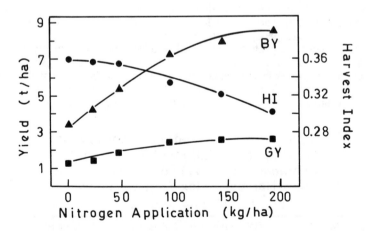

Fig. 1-11. The influence of nitrogen on biological yield (BY), grain yield (GY), and harvest index (HI). The experiments were conducted at the Rothamsted Experimental Station in England and represent means of twelve years (1852–63). The data were taken from Russell and Watson (1940) as reported by Donald and Hamblin (1976). This was the first classic experiment on the influence of nitrogen fertilizers on yields of field crops. Subsequently, similar relationships were shown by several researchers worldwide for different cereal crops.

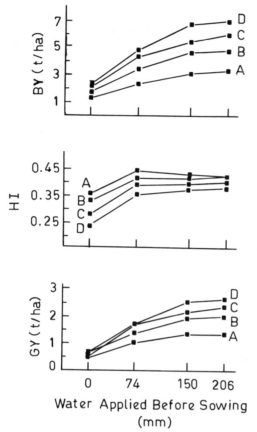

Fig. 1-12. The interaction of nitrogen and water on the biological (BY) and grain (GY) yields and harvest index (HI) of wheat at North Platte, Nebraska. Nitrogen application rates: (A) 0, (B) 20, (C) 40, and (D) 80 lbs/acre. *Source:* Ramig and Rhoades (1963); redrawn from Donald and Hamblin (1976).

When water is in limited supply, as generally is the case for a considerable part of the world's cereal growing regions, the fall in HI associated with applied nitrogen may be more marked than the increase in BY and the decline in GY. Ramig and Rhoades (1963) made a factorial study of the interaction of nitrogen and water on wheat at North Platte, Nebraska. The natural rainfall (mean 328 mm, October 1–June 30) was supplemented with several levels of water supply prior to sowing during the three years of study. Nitrogen and water each gave increased BY (grain + straw) with a strong positive correlation (Fig. 1-12). However, nitrogen severely lowered the HI at low water (0.36 at N_0 to 0.24 at N_{80}), and to an appreciable though lesser extent at high water (from 0.41 to 0.38). The outcome was a modest absolute increase in GY with a small nitro-

Table 1-16. Harvest Indices (HI) of Some Commonly Cultivated Cereal Crops.

Crop	HI	Reference
Wheat		
3 semidwarf winter vars.		Vogel, Allan, & Peterson (1963)
Medium fertility level	0.385	
High fertility level	0.385	
5 standard height vars.		Vogel, Allan, & Peterson (1963)
Medium fertility level	0.305	
High fertility level	0.276	
Standard wheat	0.40	Spiertz & van der Haar (1978)
Semidwarf wheat	0.47	
Tall wheats (86 cm)	0.38	Singh & Stoskopf (1971)
Medium wheats (78 cm)	0.40	
Dwarf wheats (58 cm)	0.42	
6 Australian and 1 German vars. (all normal height) and 2 Mexican semidwarf vars.	0.243–0.396	Syme (1970)
Plant density (000/ha)		Puckridge & Donald (1967)
14	0.364	
70	0.358	
350	0.304	
1540	0.262	
4470	0.251	
Nitrogen application (kg/ha)		Barley & Naidu (1964)
0	0.36	
67	0.28	
134	0.27	
Rice		
Soil saturation level		Enyi (1968)
Upland variety		
60%	0.17	
80%	0.19	
100%	0.21	
Flooded	0.16	
Swamp rice		
60%	0.13	
80%	0.13	
100%	0.21	
Flooded	0.26	
Growth type		Jeanings & de Jesus (1968)
Short, erect, compact	0.53–0.56	
Intermediate	0.48	
Tall, leafy, spreading	0.39–0.42	
Corn		
11 hybrid maize vars.		Hanway & Russell (1969)
Low-density planting	0.44	
High-density planting	0.40	

Table 1-16. (*Continued*)

Crop	HI	Reference
Plant density (000/ha)		
20	0.475	Scarsbrook & Doss (1973)
40	0.420	
80	0.389	
21	0.494	Fairbourn, Kemper, & Gardner
32	0.494	(1970)
37	0.474	
42	0.373	
Water stress		Downey (1971)
No stress	0.28	
Early stress	0.42	
Late stress	0.21	
Barley		
Plant height		Hayes (1968)
Very tall variety	0.401	
Tall variety	0.487	
3 medium vars.	0.535–0.571	
Nitrogen application (kg/ha)		Luebs & Laag (1969)
0	0.45	
45	0.37	
90	0.13	
Sorghum		
Plant density (000/ha)		Gerakis & Tsangarakis (1969)
80	0.169	
120	0.141	
160	0.141	
200	0.125	
Percent daylight		Fischer & Wilson (1975)
100	0.49	
72	0.46	
48	0.42	
35	0.39	
N and P (kg/ha) application		Roy & Wright (1973)
0/0	0.37	
60/0	0.42	
120/0	0.43	
0/26	0.43	
60/26	0.50	
120/26	0.49	

gen dressing at low water (470 kg/ha at N_0 and 538 kg/ha at N_{20}) and a GY strongly related to BY at high water.

The HI thus has been used extensively both for measuring the partitioning of photosynthates in cereal crops and in selecting for increased economic yields. The HI values for major cereals are shown in Table 1-16.

Table 1-17. Principal Characteristics of an Ideal Cereal Ideotype.

1. Strictly annual habit
2. Erect growth form
3. Dwarf structure
4. Strong stems
5. Unbranched or nontillered habit
6. Reduced foliage (smaller, shorter, narrower or fewer leaves)
7. Erect leaf disposition
8. Determinate habit
9. High harvest index
10. Nonphotoperiodic for most but not all situations
11. Early flowering for most but not all situations
12. High population density
13. Narrow rows or square planted

Source: Donald and Hamblin (1983).

Based on the various interactions among plant genotypes and characteristics, water, nitrogen application, and their interrelationships with HI, BY, and GY, Donald and Hamblin (1976, 1983) have proposed several characteristics for an ideal cereal "ideotype" (i.e., a biological model that is expected to perform and behave in a predictable manner within a defined environment). They further suggest that these characteristics be considered in breeding future cereal cultivars. The principal characteristics of the ideotype proposed for all cereal and other annual seed crops and their cultures are summarized in Table 1-17. Based on these, they have further postulated other useful features and practices for annual seed crops (Table 1-18).

The various studies described above suggest the need for considerable additional information of the physiological mechanisms that control growth and ultimate size of the individual plant and its potential for economic yield, if more rapid progress in increasing crop yields is to be achieved. In addition, information is needed on the role of specific genes and the heritability of morphological and physiological traits to help breeders operate more efficiently. Interdisciplinary research teams are needed to understand the complex interrelationships among the mechanisms controlling growth, development, and partitioning, and to develop techniques and guidelines for improving management practices and for selecting for increased economic yield of cereal crops.

Table 1-18. The Features of a Common Ideotype for All Cereal Crops, Together with Associated Cultural Practices.

Feature of Crop	Features of Ideotype
Pure culture sown at high density	Good plant performance among like neighbors sown at high density, hence communal plants needed; plant yield in isolation or in competition with other genotypes of no relevance
Strictly annual habit	Determinate growth; plant death at seed ripeness; loss of residual features of perenniality (i.e., of vegetative branching, tillering or vegetative storage organs)
Crop must not lodge or collapse	Plants of sound physical structure; short stature, strong or flexible stems, nonbranching, nontillering, nonleafy
Effective form and disposition of foliage for light utilization	Deep light penetration within the leafy canopy; small, narrow or divided, erect leaves
High seed yield sought	High biological yield, attainable through high sowing rate, rapid emergence, rapid attainment of optimum leaf area index, high net assimilation rate High harvest index, involving annual habit, no excessive use of resources on plant framework, short stature, light stems, nonbranching, nonleafy Large sink for photosynthates, many seeds per unit of biological yield, long interval flowering to maturity, no sterility at high plant density
Minimal competition between plants	Absence of those features associated with strong competitive ability (i.e., absence of tallness, large or horizontally disposed leaves, branching or widely ramifying root system)
Plant density and plant arrangement to be appropriate to the communal plant form	High plant density to compensate for lack of branching and lack of leafiness; close approach to uniform spacing through use of narrow rows
Effective response to high nutrient levels	Limited increase in competition between plants as fertility is raised; absence of plant responses giving increased competitive ability, especially minimal increase in height, leafiness, or branching
Wide climatic adaptation	As appropriate to the climatic region but commonly including nonphotoperiodicity; earliness of flowering to avoid early or late frosts, cold soil or cold irrigation water early in the season, drought, or wet or wintery conditions at harvest; wide temperature tolerance

Source: Donald and Hamblin (1983).

AGRONOMY

Agronomic practices for the cultivation of different cereal crops vary not only from one geographical location to another, but often also from one location to another within the same geographical area. They are a function of several variables, differing significantly with variety, cultivar, and genotype. More intensive cultivation practices are required for high-yielding genotypes than for cultivars grown under traditional subsistence farming, where any grain and fodder yield is preferable and desired. The high-yielding genotypes require significant inputs of irrigation, fertilizers, and pesticides at timely intervals if their full potential is to be realized. Cereal cultivation in the developing countries is still labor intensive where land preparation, seeding, cultural operations, harvesting, and threshing are done manually; fortunately, these countries also enjoy the benefits of cheap and abundant farm labor throughout the year.

The effects of the green revolution, as well as the increasing awareness among farmers of the potential benefits and economic rewards of resorting to high-yielding modern cereal genotypes, are quite evident throughout the developing countries. The characteristics of these genotypes (especially of rice and wheat) and of their use include the following:

higher, often doubled yield of grain per unit land area, combined with a similar protein content (thus giving the possibility of doubled yield of protein);

larger return of grain per unit of fertilizer applied and per person-hour of labor expended;

higher yield of protein per unit of irrigation water;

early maturation;

less sensitivity to daylength, thus allowing greater flexibility in planting time and the possibility of two or even three crops per year; and

shortness of height, making them resistant to lodging under the windy conditions prevalent in the tropics and subtropics, which include most of the world's developing countries.

It is neither intended nor feasible to cover here in detail the various agronomic practices employed in cereal cultivation worldwide. Moreover, production systems are not fixed packages to be used year after year. For example, the correct seeding rate depends on the area of production, the cultivar, the intended end use of the crop, and soil fertility. For any given genotype, where moisture is plentiful throughout the growing season, a higher seeding rate may be used than in areas of limited rainfall. The planting date may be varied if a particular disease or pest is known to invade a given locality or geographical area during a certain time of year. Similarly, the crop may be harvested early if bad weather conditions that may ruin the entire crop are forecasted. Fixed guidelines are therefore practically impossible when dealing with a system so dependent upon the vagaries of the surrounding environment and of nature itself.

Some of the textbooks and monographs available on various topics covering the broad area of cereal agronomy, including individual cereal crops, include the following: Inglett (1970, 1979), Pomeranz (1971), Chandler (1979), Esmay, Soemangat, and Phillips (1979), Yamazaki and Greenwood (1981), Gallagher (1982), Lorenz (1982), Kent (1983), Stoskopf (1985), DuPont and Osman (1987), ICAR (1988), and Palmer (1989). Readers are also referred to *Advances in Agronomy,* an excellent series of continually updated reviews on various production aspects of cereals. Information on newly developed genotypes and cultivars of various cereals and their cultural requirements is also published annually by the various national agricultural agencies of different countries, as well as by such international research institutions as CIMMYT in Mexico, IRRI in Philippines, and ICRISAT in India. Therefore, only the salient features of cultivation of some of the important cereal crops, mostly taken from the above references, are described below.

Wheat

The cultural practices for wheat depend on the type of wheat grown. The hard red spring (HRS) wheat is grown in the northcentral United States, mostly where the winters are too severe for the production of winter wheat. HRS wheats are also grown in Canada, Poland, and the USSR. Durum wheat is also commonly grown in these countries. The hard red winter (HRW) wheats are adapted to the central and southern Great Plains, where the annual rainfall is <35 in.; they are also grown extensively in Europe, Argentina, and the southern USSR. The soft red winter (SRW) wheats are grown principally in the eastern United States, where the average annual rainfall is <30 in., but also in Western Europe. White wheats are grown in the far western U.S. states and the rest of Europe, as well as in Australia, South Africa, western South America, and Asia.

Wheat, a cold-weather crop, prefers soils with pH in the range 4.5–8.6 for bread wheat and 5.3–8.3 for durum wheat types, and an average temperature of 5–27 °C and 7–20 °C during the growing season for bread and durum wheats, respectively. The crop is generally sown in drills at a depth of 1.5–3 in. in well-prepared seedbeds. Seed rates for bread wheat are in the range 30–120 lb/acre, and for durum types, 60–90 lb/acre. The time of seeding varies with geographical location. In the semiarid Great Plains of the United States and Canada, the optimum date for winter wheat seeding is generally at the beginning of September, becoming progressively later to the south. Spring wheats are also grown from fall or winter sowing in China, India, southern Europe, Africa, and parts of Latin America. Early seeding of the spring wheats usually results in the highest yields, since the crop is most likely to escape injury from drought, heat, and diseases that become more prevalent as the season advances.

The crop is harvested with combines in developed countries, whereas both harvesting and subsequent threshing are still largely manual operations in developing countries.

Rice

Rice is unique among the cereals in being able to germinate and thrive in water. Without oxygen, a condition associated with wet or flooded soil conditions, most cereal crop plants turn yellow, wilt, and eventually die. Oxygen-deprived cereal plants show restricted shoot and root growth. Under normal, aerobic soil conditions, water and air fill the porous structure from which roots obtain the oxygen necessary to function. Lowland rice does not rely on soilborne oxygen for its survival and is thus able to grow under submerged conditions. There are three main adaptive mechanisms that enable rice to grow under these conditions (Martin and Leonard 1967; Gallagher 1982):

1. A highly developed system of anaerobic respiration, especially during early growth stages, allows the plant to tolerate oxygen-deprived conditions.
2. An ability to transport oxygen from leaves to roots through tubelike structures ("aerenchyma" cells in leaves, stems, and roots) permits air to move from the leaves to root surfaces. This supplies the submerged roots with sufficient oxygen for normal respiration, subsequent growth, and nutrient absorption.
3. A special system of very fine, abundantly branched, negatively geotropic roots on the soil surface (developed at the time of panicle initiation) supplies oxygen to the roots when stem elongation temporarily disrupts the downward internal flow of oxygen.

Rice is grown in the tropics and subtropics where both rain and sunshine are abundant. It is also grown in the temperate regions of the world. *Indica* rices predominate in the tropical rice-growing areas, whereas *japonica* types are suited to the temperate regions. Although typically a swamp cereal, rice can be grown either on dry land (upland rices) or underwater (lowland cultivation). Yields under dry upland conditions, however, are much lower than those for submersion.

The best soils for rice are slightly acidic to neutral, but the crop can be grown on soils in the pH range 4.3–8.3. Heavy soils with an impervious underlying subsoil 1.5–5 ft from the surface are required to minimize water drainage. The common practice of flooding the paddies has been adopted both as a means of irrigation and also to control weeds.

The crop is sown either broadcast or with grain drills. Seed rates may vary from 67 to 160 lb/acre depending upon the variety. In many oriental countries, the seeds are first grown in rice nurseries and transplanted after four to eight weeks to the main fields. Transplanting offers the advantages of better land use (growing two different crops per year), savings on irrigation water, and better weed control. In hand transplanting, the rows are spaced for convenient weeding, harvesting, and fertilizer application, all of which are done manually. The seed is generally sown in beds while the fields are still occupied by other crops.

Rice is a highly mechanized crop in the United States, where planting, fertilizer treatment, and weeding are all carried out on a large scale by means of aircraft, and the crop is harvested by combine harvesters. In contrast, over 90% of the world crop is managed entirely without mechanization.

In order to produce maximum yields of high milling quality, rice should be harvested when the moisture content of the grain of standing rice has dropped to 23–28%. At this stage, the kernels in the lower portion of the heads are in the hard-dough stage while those in the upper portion are fully ripe. Increased shattering occurs in some varieties if the harvest is delayed beyond this stage. When grown as a lowland crop, the fields are drained about two to three weeks before harvest. The harvest is then dried to about 14% moisture content prior to threshing.

Rice yields become stabilized at low yield levels when grown continuously on the same land. In the southern and western United States, rice is usually grown on the same land for two or three years, which is then seeded to pasture crops. Crops frequently grown in rotation with rice on well-drained soils include safflower, sorghum, wheat, and barley.

Corn

Corn has a remarkable diversity of vegetative types and is grown in a wide range of environmental conditions. From latitude 58° N in Canada, corn cultivation passes without interruption through the tropical regions and on to the frontiers of agriculture in the Southern Hemisphere (35°–45° S latitude). Corn is cultivated in regions that experience periods of at least ninety days of frost-free conditions. The annual rainfall where it is grown ranges from 10 in. in the semiarid plains of the USSR to >200 in. in tropical India. Suitable types are available for these varying conditions.

Corn requires an abundance of readily available plant nutrients and soils with pH ranging from 5.5 to 8.0 for the best production. Fertile, well-drained loam soils found in the North American prairie region are best suited for corn cultivation.

The crop is usually planted 2–3 in. deep in rows 36–44 in. apart. Seed rates vary depending upon the end use of the crop, rates of 6–18 lb/acre commonly being used for grain production, 8–18 lb/acre for silage, 3–6 lb/acre for popcorn, and 12–18 lb/acre for sweet corn types. It is harvested for grain with a corn picker, picker-sheller, or corn combine. In the developing countries, the cobs are manually picked, dehusked, and shelled.

Almost the entire U.S. corn crop is planted to hybrid corn varieties, which normally outyield by 15–20%, and sometimes up to 50%, those of inbred lines.

Barley

Barley is grown throughout the more temperate regions of the world, mainly as a spring crop, and has a geographic distribution generally similar to that of wheat. It withstands more heat under semiarid than under humid conditions. In the warmer climates, barley is sown in the fall or winter.

The best barley soils appear to be well-drained loams, which need not be as fertile as those required by wheat. It produces a poor crop of low grain quality on heavy, poorly drained soils in regions of frequent rains. Light sandy soils are unsuitable since crop growth is often erratic and ripening may be premature. In spite of the stringent requirements to produce a crop of high grain quality, especially for the brewing industry, barley is one of the most dependable cereal crops under extreme conditions of salinity, frost, or drought (Martin and Leonard 1967).

Where moisture is plentiful throughout the growing season, a higher seeding rate may be used than in areas of limited rainfall. Large-seeded, two-row barley cultivars should be seeded at a slightly higher rate than average-sized, six-row cultivars. Seeding rates for barley in western Canada vary 35 to 90 lb/acre (40–100 kg/ha) (Gallagher 1982). The crop is usually planted in drills. In general, most cultural operations, including harvesting and threshing of barley, are similar to those used in wheat production.

Oats

Common oats are best adapted to cooler, more temperate regions, where the annual rainfall is ≥30 in., or where the land is irrigated. Thus they are more successful than wheat or barley in wet climates. Oats are a major crop in the Pacific Northwest and in valleys of the Rocky Mountain regions of the United States, as well as in northern Europe and Canada. Because of drought and heat, the crop often fails in the Great Plains.

Oats produce a satisfactory crop on a wide range of soil types, provided the soil is well drained and reasonably fertile. In general, loam soils, especially silt and clay loams, are best suited for oat cultivation. Heavy, poorly drained clays are likely to cause the crop to lodge. Oats generally follow corn or some other row crop; consequently, the seedbed often is prepared by disking and harrowing without plowing. The crop is seeded at 50–130 lb/acre as early in the spring as a seedbed can be prepared, but after the prolonged cold weather is past.

In the United States and Canada, over 95% of the crop for grain is threshed with a combine. Sometimes the crop is harvested with a binder in order to save more of the straw. Nearly 40% of the crop is windrowed before combining, in order to avoid losses from lodging and shattering of the grain.

Sorghum

Sorghum crop is grown in latitudes below 45° on all continents, in warm or hot regions that have summer rainfall as well as in hot, irrigated areas. The most favorable mean temperature for the crop is 27 °C (80°F). Sorghum withstands extensive heat better than other crops, but extremely high temperatures during the fruiting period reduce the seed yield.

Sorghums are well adapted to summer rainfall regions where the average annual rainfall is only 17–25 in. The plants remain practically dormant during periods of drought but resume growth as soon as there is sufficient rain to wet the soil. Sorghum is grown successfully on all types of soil. In rainy seasons, the highest yields are obtained on heavy soils, but in dry seasons, it does best on sandy soils. Sorghum also tolerates considerable salinity. The crop is not troubled by serious pests and diseases, and has the added advantage that it can be sown late, if other crops fail.

A warm, mellow seedbed is essential to good seed germination for sorghum. High temperatures of 23 °C at planting depth favor rapid germination; therefore, the crop must be planted after the soil is sufficiently warm. In general, sorghum planting may extend from midspring or early March to about the beginning of July in areas with an extended growing season. The seed is best planted in rows 30–42 in. apart and about 1 in. deep in moist soil, or at 2 in. depth in dry warm soil. Shallow seeding depths are generally recommended in the cooler regions. Seed rates for grain crop vary from 2 to 5 lb/acre. The crop is harvested with a combine, or manually in the developing countries of the world.

Rye

Winter rye is the hardiest of all cereals (Martin and Leonard 1967). On good soils, it is a less profitable crop than wheat. The highest yields are usually obtained on rich, well-drained loam soils. It is more productive than other grains on infertile, sandy, or acidic soils, and is the only small grain crop that succeeds on coarse, sandy soils.

Winter rye can be seeded at almost any time during the late summer or early fall, but early seeding produces the most fall pasture. In contrast, spring rye, like other spring small grains, should be sown as early as is feasible. The seed is generally planted in drills at a rate of about 30–110 lb/acre. Most other cultural operations are similar to those used in wheat and barley production.

Millets

Millets are grown throughout the drier parts of tropics and in drier areas of Africa, India, and China. In recent years, they are being increasingly cultivated in the United States, Australia, and South Africa. As a general rule, they are well adapted to drought conditions, well suited to arid tropics with high temperatures, and have good yields under low rainfall. In areas receiving <45 cm annual rainfall, they are not usually grown as a dryland crop, and often require irrigation. Millets are susceptible to frost during the growing period, and plants may be killed if the temperatures are sufficiently low. Optimum temperatures for millet cultivation are in the range 16–40 °C. Early frosts also cause premature ripening of grain; the seeds may mature badly frostbitten and shriveled.

Millets are adapted to a wide range of soil types varying from light loams to heavy clays, but light soils are generally preferred. They thrive best on free-working soils of high fertility. Millets are often the most productive grain crops in extremely dry and infertile soils of India and Africa.

Generally, millets require firmly prepared seedbeds due to their small seed size. It is essential to control weeds thoroughly up to the time of sowing because millet seedlings are small and compete poorly with weeds until they have attained some size. The crop is planted when the soil is warm and after the danger of frost is passed. They are seeded, with an ordinary grain drill, 2–5 cm deep and 5–10 cm apart; closer spacings help the crop suppress weeds. Seed rates vary with soil type, species, variety, and the availability of irrigation water during the growing season.

Millets respond well to nitrogen and phosphorus fertilizers. Under dry conditions, weekly irrigations are usually necessary for good yields. In tropics, two to four cultivations are usually necessary to control weeds. For seed, the crop is usually harvested with a binder and allowed to stand in the field until the seed can be rubbed from the head. The crop may be windrowed to be threshed later with a combine with pickup attachment. Direct combining is less successful because part of the seeds shatter before the later seeds are ripe. In tropical countries the heads are cut by hand and dried in heaps on the ground or on the threshing floor. For proper storage, millet seeds should be dried down to 12–13% moisture.

Buckwheat

Although cultivated primarily to produce seed for human consumption, buckwheat is often used as a green manure crop, as a smother crop to suppress weeds, and as a source of buckwheat honey. Buckwheat grows best in a cool, moist climate. It is extremely susceptible to frost and can be severely damaged by late spring or early fall frost. Seeding, therefore, is generally delayed until the danger of spring frost is past. The crop is also sensitive to high temperatures and hot, dry winds, especially when moisture is scarce. These conditions during flowering can cause flower blasting, which reduces seed set and yield.

Buckwheat is adapted to a wide range of soil types and has high tolerance to soil acidity. It grows best on well-drained sand or silt loam soils. Although it grows well on hastily prepared land, careful plowing and seedbed preparation give higher yields. Seeds are either broadcast or drilled 2.5–5 cm apart in rows 15–40 cm wide. Seed rates generally vary between 25 and 40 kg/ha.

On poor soils, buckwheat responds well to fertilizers. Phosphorus application is generally beneficial. In contrast, excess nitrogen encourages vegetative growth and increased tendency to lodge, thereby reducing seed yields. Serious losses due to diseases and pests are rare in buckwheat.

Because of its indeterminate growth habit, ripening in buckwheat is rarely uniform. The crop is normally harvested after ten weeks, when seeds at the base of the plants are fully ripe. Buckwheat is usually swathed and then harvested with a combine after the plants and seeds have dried. To reduce losses due to shattering, the crop is usually cut early in the morning or in dull weather when the plants are moist; it is then combined when the seed in the swath contains <16% moisture. Average seed yields range from 800 to 1,000 kg/ha, although yields of up to 2,000 kg/ha are produced under favorable conditions in the Prairie Provinces of Canada.

Some of the relevant agronomic data on various cereals are summarized in Tables 1-19, 1-20, and 1-21. Although the values for soil pH, annual precipitation, and temperature shown in Table 1-19 are extreme ranges, best yields are generally obtained in the middle of the ranges given. The cold weather crops— spring wheat, barley, and oats—show the highest resistance to frost, whereas rice and corn are quite susceptible to these conditions, especially during the fruiting season (Table 1-20). Data on the nutrient uptake from soils by the high-yielding genotypes of various cereals (Table 1-21) could be used as a rough index for the application of fertilizers; actual levels will, of course, be determined by the nutrient analyses of the soil and the previous crop grown on the same piece of land. In general, C-4 crops such as corn and sorghum are nutrient demanding as compared to C-3 crops, and thus should not be grown continuously on the same land.

The advantages of cereal–legume intercropping systems, especially under the subsistence farming systems, as well as the technology of drying and storage of grains, are described at great length in Chapter 2, and hence will not be discussed here.

Table 1-19. Some Agronomic Requirements of Various Cereal Crops.

Cereal	Growth Type[a]	Soil pH	Rainfall (dm/yr)	Annual Temp. (°C)[b]	Seed Rate (lb/acre) Drills	Seed Rate (lb/acre) Rows	Germination Time (days)	Temp. Type[c]
Wheat								
Bread	A,G	4.5–8.6	3–25	5–27	30–120		7	C
Club	A,G	5.8–8.3	3–16	6–16	60–90		7	C
Durum	A,G	5.3–8.3	3–16	7–19	60–90		10	C
Rice	A,G	4.3–8.3	5–42	9–29	67–100		14	W
Wild	A,G	5.8–7.8	4–13	7–19				
Corn	A,G	4.3–8.3	3–40		5–29	6–18	7	W
Barley	A,G	4.5–8.3	5–25	5–24	72–96		7	C
Oats	A,G	4.5–8.6	2–21	5–26	48–128		10	C
Sorghum	A,G	4.3–8.7	4–41	8–27		2–5	10	W
Rye	A,G	4.5–8.3	3–17	5–21	28–112		7	C
Millets								
Finger millet	A,G	4.3–8.4	3–42	12–27	12–20	5–10	7	W
Italian millet	A,G	5.0–8.3	3–42	6–27	20–30		10	W
Pearl millet	A,G	4.5–8.3	2–26	12–27	16–20	4–6	7	W
Proso millet	A,G	4.8–8.5	3–42	6–27	15–35		7	W
Triticale	A,G	5.3–7.5	4–25	6–26	30–90		8	C
Buckwheat	A,H	4.8–8.2	4–13	6–25	36–60		6	W

Compiled from: Jung (1978), Gallagher (1982), Kent (1983), Stoskopf (1985), and Hanson (1990).
[a]Growth type: A, annual; H, herb; G, grass.
[b]Average of monthly means with values below 0 °C treated as 0.
[c]Temperature type: C, cold weather crop; W, warm weather crop.

Table 1-20. Resistance of Cereals to Frost in Different Developmental Phases.

Frost Resistance	Temperature (°C) Harmful to Plant in the Phases of: Germination	Flowering	Fruiting
High			
Spring wheat	−9 , −10	−1 , −2	−2 , −4
Oats	−8 , −9	−1 , −2	−2 , −4
Barley	−7 , −8	−1 , −2	−2 , −4
Medium			
Italian millet	−3 , −4	−1 , −2	−2 , −3
Low			
Corn	−2 , −3	−1 , −2	−2 , −3
Millet	−2 , −3	−1 , −2	−2 , −3
Sorghum	−2 , −3	−1 , −2	−2 , −3
None			
Buckwheat	−1 , −2	−1 , −2	−0.5, −2
Rice	−0.5, −1	−0.5, −1	−0.5, −1

Adapted from: Chang (1968).

Table 1-21. Uptake of Nutrients (kg/ha) by the High-Yielding Varieties of Cereals.

Cereal	Yield/ha, Plant Part	N	P_2O_5	K_2O	Mg	S
Wheat	5,376 kg grain	106	49	30	13	6
	Straw	47	11	151	13	17
	Total	153	60	181	26	23
Rice	7,840 kg grain	86	52	31	9	6
	Straw	39	16	134	7	8
	Total	125	68	165	16	14
Corn	12,544 kg grain	168	97	64	20	17
	Stover	130	30	234	53	20
	Total	298	127	298	73	37
Barley	5,376 kg grain	123	45	39	9	11
	Straw	45	17	129	10	11
	Total	168	62	168	19	22
Oats	3,584 kg grain	90	28	22	6	9
	Straw	39	17	140	17	12
	Total	129	45	162	23	21
Sorghum	8,960 kg grain	134	67	34	16	25
	Stover	146	34	190	34	18
	Total	280	101	224	50	43
Buckwheat	1,613 kg grain	34	17	11	—	6
	Straw	13	6	28	—	3
	Total	47	23	39	—	9

Source: Courtesy Potash and Phosphate Institute, Atlanta, Georgia.

DISEASES AND PESTS

The three most important constraints in the production of field crops are water, nitrogen fertilizers, and pests and diseases. World crop losses to the three major pest groups—insects, pathogens, and weeds—are currently estimated at about 35% (Pimentel 1981; Davidson and Lyon 1987). Mammal and bird losses appear to be more severe in the tropics and subtropics than in the temperate region, but still are low compared with losses to these three pest groups. Representative data on losses in world cereal crops from insects and pathogens are summarized in Table 1-22; data on losses due to various arthropod pests of selected cereals are shown in Table 1-23.

Losses to pests have been intensified by the use of the intensive crop production technology introduced with the green revolution. The new high-yielding cereal cultivars in use today are often more susceptible to pests than were their old counterparts. Before the green revolution, farmers usually selected seeds from individual plants that survived and yielded best under the native cultural conditions. These plants contained genes resistant to insects and pathogens, and competed successfully with weeds (Pimentel 1981).

Table 1-22. Estimated Losses (%) in World Cereal Crops from Insects and Diseases.

Cereal	Insects	Diseases	Total
Wheat	5	9	14
Rice	27	9	36
Corn	12	9	21
Barley	4	8	12
Oats	8	9	17
Sorghum and millets	10	11	21
Rye	2	3	5

Source: McEwen (1978).

Table 1-23. Losses of Various Cereal Crops Caused by Arthropod Pests.

Crop and Pest	Calculated Yield Loss (%)	
	Without Control	With Control
Wheat, oats, rye, & millets		
Banks grass mite	61	18
Brown wheat mite	100	21
Cutworms	54.7 ± 12.4	7.7 ± 3.2
Rice		
Leafhoppers	42	9
Rice water weevil	5.2 ± 4.6	1.5 ± 1.5
Corn (field)		
Corn field ant	20	3
Corn rootworms	15.7 ± 4.6	5.0 ± 1.3
Garden symphalid	14	7
Leafhoppers	74.7 ± 15.7	38.3 ± 14.8
Southwestern corn borer	34.4 ± 10.4	9.9 ± 2.7
White grubs	43	11
Wireworms[a]	48.3	18.4
Cutworms	22	7
European corn borer	4.3 ± 4.3	0.3 ± 0.3
Fall armyworm	67.5 ± 1.5	27.0 ± 1.0
Rootworms	45.5 ± 45.5	0.0 ± 0.0
Barley		
Greenbug	84	7
Sorghum		
Fall armyworm	19.4 ± 7.2	0.0 ± 0.0
Sorghum midge	5.0 ± 5.0	0.2 ± 0.2
Sorghum webworm	3	0
Southwestern corn borer	24	4
White grubs	39.0 ± 26.3	9.3 ±4.7

[a]For sweet corn: 29.0 ± 19.0 without control, 4.0 ± 2.0 with control.
Source: Schwartz and Klassen (1981).

Worldwide postharvest losses of food plants to pests are estimated to range from 10% to 20% (Salunkhe, Chavan, and Kadam 1985). The major pests of harvested foods are microorganisms, insects, and rodents. When these losses are added to preharvest losses, worldwide food losses due to pests amount to a staggering 45% of total crop production. This significant loss of valuable food occurs in spite of all of the methods used to control pests.

Pimentel (1981) estimated U.S. preharvest losses of food plants to pests to be about 37% even with the use of modern pest control technology. Insects account for 13% of these losses, plant pathogens 12%, and weeds 12%. U.S. postharvest food losses are estimated to be about 9%. Thus, total losses to pests in the United States alone are estimated to be more than 40%. It is quite possible that such losses would be even higher in the developing countries where the advanced pest control technology is neither available nor economically feasible.

Diseases

Major diseases of economic importance in cereal crops and their geographic distribution are summarized in Table 1-24. Fungi and bacteria are the major disease-causing agents, although in several places viruses, nematodes, and mycoplasmas are also important.

Bacteria

Bacteria are disseminated primarily by water, insects, seeds, plant parts, machinery, tools, or any method that can move soil from place to place. They are, however, infrequently disseminated by wind. Free water on the plant surface is necessary for motility of bacterial cells, which enter a plant through a natural opening or wounds. Once a cell enters a plant, it begins to multiply and establish an infection if environmental conditions are favorable. Survival, overwintering, or overseasoning is accomplished as survival spores directly in soil or in the dead tissue; in live infected perennial plants, insects, and on or in seed; and as saprophytes on plant residue (Jones and Clifford 1979; Nyvall 1989).

Symptoms of diseases caused by bacteria are varied. Infected below-ground plant parts may have galls on roots, discoloration only of xylem tissue or of other tissue, and decomposition typified by wet, slimy, and smelly rot. Above-ground plant parts may have wet-appearing or water-soaked spots as well as chlorotic or yellow spots, tan spots, or streaks with or without a chlorotic halo (Nyvall 1989). Stalks or stems may have a wet and smelly rot. The entire plant may wilt showing a grayish-green foliage and, often, a discoloration of seeds.

Fungi

Fungi are disseminated by wind, water, insects, seeds, plant parts, machinery, and tools. They enter plants by spores or propagules forming a germ tube that

Table 1-24. Major Diseases of Cereal Crops and Their Distribution.

Crop and Disease	Organism[a]	Distribution
Wheat		
Bacteria		
Bacterial leaf blight	*Pseudomonas syringae*	Northcentral USA
Bacterial mosaic	*Corynebacterium* spp.	Central USA
Basal glume rot	*Pseudomonas atrofaciens*	Worldwide
Black chaff	*Xanthomonas translucens*	Worldwide
Pink seed	*Erwinia rhapontici*	Canada, Europe
Spike blight	*Corynebacterium tritici*	Australia, Canada, China, Egypt, Ethiopia, India
Fungi		
Anthracnose	*Colletotrichum graminicola*	Worldwide
Ascochyta leaf spot	*Ascochyta tritici*	Europe, Japan, N. America
Cephalosporium stripe	*Cephalosporium gramineum*	England, Japan, N. America
Common bunt	*Tilletia caries*	Worldwide
Common root rot	*Helminthosporium sativum*	Worldwide
Downy mildew	*Sclerophthora macrospora*	Worldwide
Dwarf bunt	*Tilletia controversa*	Canada, Europe, USA
Ergot	*Claviceps purpurea*	Worldwide
Eyespot	*Pseudocercosporella herpotrichoides*	Worldwide
Flag smut	*Urocystis agropyri*	Australia, USA
Glume blotch	*Septoria nodorum*	Worldwide
Halo spot	*Selenophoma donacis*	England, northern Europe, USA
Leaf rust	*Puccinia recondita*	Worldwide
Leaf spot	*Ascochyta sorghi*	Eastern USA
Leaf spot	*Phaeoseptoria urvilleana*	England, USA
Leptosphaeria leaf spot	*Leptosphaeria herpotrichoides*	Canada, Europe, USA
Loose smut	*Ustilago tritici*	Worldwide
Phoma glume blotch	*Phoma insidiosa*	India
Pink snow mold	*Calonectria nivalis*	Canada, central and northern Europe, and USA
Platyspora leaf spot	*Platyspora pentamera*	Northcentral USA and Canada
Powdery mildew	*Erysiphe graminis*	Worldwide
Pythium root rot	*Pythium* spp.	Worldwide
Scab	*Gibberella zeae*	Worldwide
Sclerotinia snow mold	*Sclerotinia borealis*	Canada, Europe, Japan, Scandinavia, USSR
Septoria leaf blotch	*Septoria tritici*	Worldwide
Sharp eyespot	*Rhizoctonia solani*	Worldwide
Snow rot	*Pythium aristosporum*	Northwestern USA
Stem rust	*Puccinia graminis*	Worldwide
Stripe rust	*Puccinia striiformis*	N. and S. America, Asia, central Europe
Take all	*Gaeumannomyces graminis*	Worldwide
Twist	*Dilophospora alopecuri*	Canada, Europe, India, USA
Yellow leaf spot	*Pyrenophora trichostoma*	Worldwide
Mycoplasmas		
Aster yellows	Aster leafhoppers	Eastern Europe, Japan, N. America

Table 1-24. (*Continued*)

Crop and Disease	Organism[a]	Distribution
Nematodes		
Oat cyst	*Heterodera avenae*	Africa, Australia, southeastern Canada, Europe, Japan, USSR, USA
Root gall	*Subanguina radicicola*	Canada, Northern Europe
Root knot	*Meloidogyne* spp.	Worldwide
Root lesion	*Pratylenchus* spp.	Worldwide
Seed gall	*Anguina tritica*	E. Asia, Europe, India, southeastern USA
Stubby root	*Paratrichodorus* spp.	Worldwide
Stunt	*Merlineus brevidens*	Indigenous to most soils
Viruses		
American wheat striate mosaic	*Endria inimica, Elymana virescens*	Central USA, Canada
African cereal streak	*Toya catilina*	E. Africa
Barley stripe mosaic	Wind, hail, animals, and infected pollen	Australia, S. Asia, Europe, Japan, western N. America, USSR
Barley yellow dwarf	11 species of aphids	Worldwide
Eastern wheat striate	*Cicadulina mbila*	India
Soilborne wheat mosaic	*Polymyxa graminis*	Eastern and central USA
Tobacco mosaic	Soilborne	Central USA
Spindle streak mosaic	*Polymyxa graminis*	Northeastern USA, Canada
Wheat streak mosaic	*Aceria tulipae*	Eastern Europe, west-central USA

Rice

Bacteria		
Bacterial blight	*Xanthomonas oryzae*	Africa, Asia, Caribbean, Central and S. America
Glume blotch	*Pseudomonas oryzicola*	Asia, Australia
Leaf streak	*Xanthomonas translucens* sp. *orizicola*	Tropical Asia
Fungi		
Bakanae disease	*Fusarium moniliforme*	Worldwide
Blast	*Pyricularia oryzae*	Worldwide
Brown bordered leaf and sheath spot	*Rhizoctonia oryzae*	Japan, USA, Vietnam
Brown leaf spot	*Helminthosporium oryzae*	Africa, Asia
Crown sheath rot	*Ophiobolus oryzinus*	Africa, India, Japan, USA
Downy mildew	*Sclerophthora macrospora*	Australia, China, India, Italy, Japan, USA
False smut	*Ustilaginoidea virens*	Worldwide
Kernel smut	*Tilletia barcclayana*	Worldwide
Leaf scald	*Rhynchosporium oryzae*	W. Africa, Central America, Southeast Asia, USA
Leaf spot	*Helminthosporium rostratum*	India
Leaf smut	*Entyloma oryzae*	Worldwide
Narrow brown leaf spot	*Cercospora oryzae*	Worldwide except Europe
Phoma seedling blight	*Phoma glomerata*	Ghana

Table 1-24. (*Continued*)

Crop and Disease	Organism[a]	Distribution
Fungi (*continued*)		
Pithomyces glume blotch	*Pithomyces chartarum*	India
Rust	*Puccinia graminis*	Worldwide
Seed and seedling blight	Several fungi	Temperate rice-growing areas
Sheath blight	*Rhizoctonia solani*	Worldwide
Sheath rot	*Acrocylindrium oryzae*	Southeast Asia, USA
Stackburn disease	*Alternaria padwickii*	Worldwide
Stem rot	*Leptosphaeria salvinii*	Asia, USA
Nematodes		
Stem nematode	*Ditylenchus angustus*	Southeast Asia, India, Egypt
White tip	*Aphelenchoides besseyi*	Southeast Asia, Australia, Cuba, Japan, USA
Viruses		
African cereal streak	Leafhopper	E. Africa
Grassy stunt	Brown planthopper	India, Malaysia, Philippines, Sri Lanka, Thailand
Hoja blanca	Leafhoppers	Western Hemisphere
Orange leaf	Zigzag leafhoppper	Malaysia, Philippines, Sri Lanka, Thailand
Ragged stunt	Brown leafhopper	Philippines, India, Indonesia, Sri Lanka
Yellow mottle	Mechanical transmission	Africa
Tungro	Green rice leafhopper	India, Bangladesh, Indonesia, Malaysia, Philippines, Thailand
Waika disease	Green rice leafhopper	Japan
Yellow dwarf	Leafhoppers	Tropical Asia
Corn		
Bacteria		
Bacterial leaf blight	*Pseudomonas avenae*	Southeastern USA
Bacterial stalk rot	*Erwinia* spp., *Pseudomonas* spp.	Worldwide
Bacterial stripe	*Pseudomonas andropogoni*	Eastern USA
Bacterial top rot	Unknown bacteria	Central USA
Chocolate spot	*Pseudomonas coronafaciens*	Central USA
Goss's bacterial wilt and blight	*Corynebacterium nebraskense*	Central USA
Holcus spot	*Pseudomonas syringae*	Eastern and midwestern USA
Stewart's wilt	*Erwinia stewartii*	Central America, China, Eastern and Southern Europe, eastern USA, USSR
Yellow leaf blotch	*Pseudomonas* spp.	W. Africa
Fungi		
Anthracnose	*Colletotrichum graminicola*	France, Germany, India, Philippines, eastern USA
Ascochyta leaf and sheat spots	*Ascochyta zeae*	USA
Aspergillus ear rot	*Aspergillus* spp.	Worldwide
Brown stripe downy mildew	*Sclerophthora rayssiae*	India

Table 1-24. (*Continued*)

Crop and Disease	Organism[a]	Distribution
Charcoal rot	*Macrophomina phaseoli*	Europe, N. America, S. Africa
Cladosporium rot	*Cladosporium herbarium*	Worldwide
Common rust	*Puccinia sorghi*	Worldwide
Common smut	*Ustilago maydis*	Worldwide
Corticium ear rot	*Corticium saskii*	India
Crazy top	*Sclerophthora macrospora*	Africa, N. and Central America, Asia, Europe
Curvularia leaf spots	*Curvularia* spp.	Warmer and milder climates
Diplodia ear and stalk rot	*Diplodia maydis*	Africa, Australia, Philippines, Romania, USA
Diplodia leaf spot	*Diplodia macrospora*	Central America
Downy mildew	*Sclerospora graminicola*	Worldwide
Ear and stalk rot	*Nigrospsora oryzae*	Worldwide
Ergot	*Claviceps gigantea*	Central Mexico
Eyespot	*Kabatiella zeae*	Northcentral USA and Ontario
False smut	*Ustilaginoidea virens*	Worldwide
Fusarium kernel and stalk rot, leaf spot	*Fusarium moniliforme*	Worldwide
Gibberella ear and stalk rot	*Gibberella roseum*	Worldwide
Gray ear rot	*Physalospora zeae*	Eastern USA
Gray leaf spot	*Cercospora zeae-maydis*	Africa, Southeast Asia, China, Europe, India, eastern USA
Head smut	*Sphacelotheca reiliana*	Australia, India, western Mexico, New Zealand, S. Africa, USSR, Yugoslavia, western and southeastern USA
Leaf disease	*Helminthosporium rostratum*	Worldwide
Leaf spot	*Helminthosporium carbonum*	Eastern and midwestern USA
Northern corn leaf blight	*Helminthosporium turcicum*	Worldwide
Northern leaf spot	*Helminthosporium* spp.	Northcentral USA
Penicillium rot	*Penicillium oxalicum*	Worldwide
Phomopsis seed rot	*Phomopsis* spp.	USA
Physoderma brown spot	*Physoderma maydis*	Southeastern and midwestern USA
Pythium root rot	*Pythium graminicola*	Worldwide
Pythium stalk rot	*Pythium aphanidermatum*	Worldwide
Red kernel disease	*Epicoccum nigrum*	USA
Sclerotium ear rot	*Sclerotium rolfsii*	India
Seed and seedling blight	*Pythium* spp., *Diplodia maydis, Gibberella zeae, Fusarium moniliforme, Rhizoctonia solani*	Worldwide Worldwide
Sorghum downy mildew	*Sclerospora sorghi*	Africa, Asia, India, USA
Southern corn leaf blight	*Helminthosporium maydis*	Worldwide
Southern rust	*Puccinia polysora*	Africa, Southeast Asia, Central and S. America, USA
Sugarcane downy mildew	*Sclerospora sacchari*	Southeast Asia
Tropical rust	*Physopella zeae*	Central and S. America, Caribbean

Table 1-24. (*Continued*)

Crop and Disease	Organism[a]	Distribution
Fungi (*continued*)		
Yellow leaf blight	*Phyllosticta maydis*	Africa, Asia, Brazil, Canada, Romania, USA
Zonate leaf spot	*Gloeocercospora sorghi*	Africa, S. America, USA
Mycoplasmas/Spiroplasmas		
Corn stunt	Leafhoppers	Southern and southeastern USA
Nematodes		
Root lesion nematodes	*Pratylenchus* spp.	Probably worldwide
Lance nematode	*Hoploaimus* spp.	Probably worldwide
Viruses		
American wheat striate mosaic	*Endria inimica, Elymana virescens*	Canada, northcentral USA
Corn lethal necrosis	Plant-sucking bugs	Central USA
Maize chlorotic dwarf	*Graminella nigrifrons*	Eastern USA
Maize chlorotic mottle	6 species of beetles	Peru, USA
Maize dwarf mosaic	*Rhopalosiphun maidis, Schizaphis graminun, Myzus persicae*	Australia, USA
Maize mosaic	*Peregrinus maidis*	Africa, Australia, Caribbean, Hawaii, India, N.–S. USA
Maize streak disease	*Cicadulina mbila, C. zeae, C. nicholsi*	Africa, Asia
Rayadofino (fine stripping)	*Dalbulus maidis*	Central America
Wheat streak mosaic	*Aceria tulipae*	Northern Africa, N. America, Europe
White leaf of corn	*Peregrinus maydis*	Venezuela
Barley		
Bacteria		
Bacterial stripe blight	*Pseudomonas striafaciens*	Australia, N. and S. America, Europe
Basal glume rot	*Pseudomonas atrofaciens*	Worldwide
Black chaff	*Xanthomonas translucens*	Worldwide
Fungi		
Anthracnose	*Colletotrichum graminicola*	Worldwide
Ascochyta leaf spot	*Ascochyta graminea*	Eastern USA
Aster yellows	*Macrosteles fascifrons*	Eastern Europe, Japan, N. America
Cephalosporium stripe	*Cephalosporium gramineum*	N. America, England, Japan
Common root rot	*Helminthosporium sativum*	Worldwide
Covered smut	*Ustilago hordei*	Worldwide
Downy mildew	*Sclerophthora macrospora*	Worldwide
Dwarf bunt	*Tilletia controversa*	Western USA
Ergot	*Claviceps purpurea*	Worldwide
Eyespot	*Pseudocercosporella herpotrichoides*	Worldwide
Glume blotch	*Septoria nodorum*	Worldwide
Halo spot	*Selenophoma donacis*	England, N. Europe, USA
Leaf rust	*Puccinia hordei*	Worldwide

Table 1-24. (*Continued*)

Crop and Disease	Organism[a]	Distribution
Leaf spot	*Leptosphaeria herpotrichoides*	Canada, Europe, USA
Loose smut	*Ustilago tritici*	Worldwide
Net blotch	*Helminthosporium teres*	Worldwide
Powdery mildew	*Erysiphe graminis*	Worldwide
Pythium root rot	*Pythium* spp.	Worldwide
Scab	*Gibberella zeae*	Worldwide
Scald	*Rhynchosporium secalis*	Worldwide
Seedling blight	*Gibberella zeae*	Worldwide
Semiloose smut	*Ustilago nigra*	Worldwide
Septoria leaf blotch	*Septoria avenae*	Worldwide
Sharp eyespot	*Rhizoctonia solani*	Worldwide
Spot blotch, associated seedling and crown rots	*Helminthosporium sativum*	Worldwide
Stem rust	*Puccinia graminis tritici*	Worldwide
Stripe disease	*Helminthosporium gramineum*	Worldwide on winter barley
Stripe rust	*Puccinia striiformis*	N. and S. America, mountain areas of Europe and Asia
Take all	*Gaeumannomyces graminis*	Worldwide
Nematodes		
Root gall	*Subanguina radicicola*	Canada, N. Europe
Root knot	*Meloidogyne* spp.	Worldwide
Root lesion	*Pratylenchus* spp.	Worldwide
Viruses		
African cereal streak	*Toya catilina*	E. Africa
American wheat striate mosaic	*Endria inimica, Elymana virescens*	Central USA, Canada
Barley stripe mosaic	Infected pollen	S. Asia, Australia, Europe, Japan, western N. America, USSR
Barley yellow dwarf	11 species of aphids	Worldwide
Eastern wheat striate	Plant hopper	India
Moderate barley dwarf	Leafhoppers	Canada, Europe, northcentral USA
Wheat soilborne mosaic	*Polymyxa graminis*	Argentina, Brazil, Egypt, Italy, Japan, eastern and central USA
Wheat streak mosaic	*Aceria tulipae*	Eastern Europe, western and central N. America, USSR

Rye

Bacteria		
Blight	*Xanthomonas translucens*	Australia, N. America
Halo blight	*Pseudomonas coronafaciens*	Worldwide
Fungi		
Anthracnose	*Colletotrichum graminicola*	Worldwide
Cephalosporium stripe	*Cephalosporium gramineum*	England, Japan, N. America
Common bunt	*Tilletia caries*	Worldwide
Common root rot	*Helminthosporium sativum*	Worldwide
Downy mildew	*Sclerophthora macrospora*	Worldwide
Ergot	*Claviceps purpurea*	Worldwide

Table 1-24. (*Continued*)

Crop and Disease	Organism[a]	Distribution
Fungi (*continued*)		
Eyespot	*Pseudocercosporella herpotrichoides*	Worldwide
Glume blotch	*Septoria nodorum*	Worldwide
Leaf rust	*Puccinia rubigo-vera*	Worldwide
Leaf spot	*Leptosphaeria herpotrichoides*	Canada, Europe, USA
Loose smut	*Ustilago tritici*	Worldwide
Pink snow mold	*Calonectria nivalis*	Canada, USA, central and northern Europe
Platyspora leaf spot	*Platyspora pentamera*	Northcentral USA, Canada
Powdery mildew	*Erysiphe graminis* sp. *secalis*	Worldwide
Scald	*Rhynchosporium secalis*	Worldwide
Septoria leaf blotch	*Septoria secalis*	Worldwide
Sharp eyespot	*Rhizoctonia solani*	Worldwide
Speckled snow mold	*Typhula incarnata*	Canada, central and northern Europe, Japan, northwestern USA
Spot blotch, associated seedling/common rots	*Helminthosporium sativum*	Worldwide
Stalk smut	*Urocystis occulta*	Worldwide
Stem rust	*Puccinia graminis*	Worldwide
Stripe rust	*Puccinia striiformis*	N. and S. America, mountain areas of central Europe and Asia
Take all	*Gaeumannomyces graminis*	Worldwide
Yellow leaf spot	*Pyrenophora trichostoma*	Worldwide
Mycoplasmas		
Aster yellows	Aster leafhopper	Eastern Europe, Japan, USA
Nematodes		
Root gall	*Subanguina radicicola*	Canada, Northern Europe
Root lesion	*Pratylenchus* spp.	Worldwide
Seed gall	*Anguina tritici*	Eastern Asia, parts of Europe, India, southeastern USA
Stubby root	*Paratrichodorus* spp.	Worldwide
Viruses		
African cereal streak	Delphacid leafhopper	E. Africa
Wheat soilborne mosaic	Soilborne	Argentina, Brazil, Egypt, eastern and central Europe, Italy, Japan
Wheat streak mosaic	wheat curl mite	Eastern Europe, western and central N. America, USSR
Oats		
Bacteria		
Black chaff	*Xanthomonas translucens*	Worldwide
Halo/blade blight	*Pseudomonas coronafaciens*	Australia, Europe, N. and S. America
Stripe blight	*Pseudomonas striafaciens*	Australia, Europe, N. and S. America
Fungi		
Anthracnose	*Colletotrichum graminicola*	Worldwide
Cephalosporium stripe	*Cephalosporium gramineum*	England, Japan, N. America

Table 1-24. (*Continued*)

Crop and Disease	Organism[a]	Distribution
Covered smut	*Ustilago kolleri*	Worldwide
Crown rust	*Puccinia coronata*	Worldwide
Downy mildew	*Sclerospora macrospora*	Worldwide
Ergot	*Claviceps purpurea*	Worldwide
Eyespot	*Pseudocercosporella herpotrichoides*	Ireland
Foot rot	*Helminthosporium sativum*	Worldwide
Leaf blotch	*Scoleocotrichum graminis* var. *avenae*	Worldwide
Leaf blotch, seedling blight, crown and lower stem rot	*Helminthosporium avenae*	Worldwide
Loose smut	*Ustilago avenae*	Worldwide
Powdery mildew	*Erysiphe graminis* sp. *avenae*	Worldwide
Root rot	*Fusarium roseum*	Worldwide
Scab	*Gibberella zeae*	Worldwide
Seed and seedling rot	*Pythium debaryanum*	Worldwide
Septoria diseases	*Septoria avenae*	Africa, Australia, Europe, and N. America
Sharp eyespot	*Rhizoctonia solani*	Worldwide
Snow mold	*Fusarium nivale*	N. America, central and northern Europe
Stem rust	*Puccinia graminis* sp. *avenae*	Worldwide
White head	*Gaeumannomyces graminis*	Worldwide
Mycoplasmas		
Aster yellows	Leafhopper	Eastern Europe, Japan, N. America
Nematodes		
Cyst nematodes	*Heterodera latipons, H. avenae, Longidorus cohni*	Africa, Australia, Canada, Europe, Japan, USA, USSR
Root gall	*Subanguina radicicola*	Canada, Europe
Root lesions	*Pratylenchus* spp.	Worldwide
Stubby root	*Paratrichodorus* spp.	Worldwide
Viruses		
African cereal streak	Leafhoppers	E. Africa
Blue dwarf	Leafhoppers	Canada, Northcentral USA
Oat mosaic	Soilborne	Europe, N. America
Red leaf	Aphids	Worldwide
Streak mosaic	Wheat curl mite	Eastern Europe, western and central N. America, USSR
Wheat striate mosaic	Leafhoppers	Central USA, Canada

Sorghum

Bacteria		
Bacterial spot	*Pseudomonas syringae*	Worldwide
Bacterial streak	*Xanthomonas holcicola*	Argentina, Australia, S. Africa, USA
Bacterial stripe	*Pseudomonas andropogoni*	Argentina, Australia, China, Nigeria, Taiwan, USA
Yellow leaf blotch	*Pseudomonas* spp.	W. Africa

Table 1-24. (*Continued*)

Crop and Disease	Organism[a]	Distribution
Fungi		
Anthracnose	*Colletotrichum graminicola*	Worldwide
Charcoal rot	*Macrophomina phaseoli*	Worldwide
Covered kernel smut	*Sphacelotheca sorghi*	Worldwide
Crazy top	*Sclerophthora macrospora*	Worldwide
Curvularia kernel rot	*Curvularia lunata*	Mexico
Downy mildew	*Sclerospora sorghi*	Africa, India, Southeast Asia, USA
Fusarium leaf blight, root and stalk rot	*Fusarium moniliforme*	Worldwide
Gray leaf spot	*Cercospora sorghi*	Worldwide
Green ear	*Sclerospora graminicola*	Worldwide
Head smut	*Sphacelotheca reiliana*	Worldwide
Leaf spot	*Helminthosporium rostratum*	Africa, USA
Long smut	*Tolyposporium ehrenbergii*	Africa, Asia
Loose kernel smut	*Spacelotheca crucenta*	Worldwide
Northern leaf blight, seed and seedling blight	*Helminthosporium turcicum*	Worldwide
Periconia root rot	*Periconia circinata*	Southern USA
Phoma leaf spot	*Phoma insidiosa*	Worldwide
Pokkah boeng	*Fusarium moniliforme*	Tropics and semitropics
Red rot	*Colletotrichum graminicola*	Worldwide
Rhizoctonia stalk rot	*Rhizoctonia solani*	Worldwide
Rough leaf spot	*Ascochyta sorghina*	Africa, Asia, southern Europe, USA
Rust	*Puccinia purpurea*	Worldwide
Seed and seedling blight	*Pythium* spp.	Worldwide
Sooty stripe	*Ramulispora sorghi*	Africa, Asia, S. America, USA
Southern leaf blight	*Helminthosporium maydis*	Worldwide
Southern sclerotial rot	*Sclerotium rolfsii*	Warmer sorghum-growing areas
Target leaf spot	*Helminthosporium sorghicola*	Cyprus, India, Israel, Sudan, USA
Zonate leaf spot	*Gloeocercospora sorghi*	Africa, Asia, Central and S. America, USA, West Indies
Nematodes		
Root knot	*Meloidogyne* spp.	Warmer sorghum-growing areas
Root lesion	*Pratylenchus* spp.	Warmer sorghum-growing areas
Stubby root	*Trichodorus* spp.	Warmer sorghum-growing areas
Sting nematodes	*Belonolaimus* spp.	Warmer sorghum-growing areas
Viruses		
Maize dwarf mosaic	Aphids	USA
Maize dwarf head blight	*Graminella nigrifrons*	Southern USA
Red stripe	Johnson grass	New South Wales (Australia)
Yellow sorghum stunt	Insects	USA
Millets		
Bacteria		
Bacterial blight	*Xanthomonas coracanae*	Africa, India
Bacterial stripe	*Xanthomonas panici*	USA
Yellow leaf blotch	*Pseudomonas* spp.	W. Africa

Table 1-24. (*Continued*)

Crop and Disease	Organism[a]	Distribution
Fungi		
Blast	*Pyricularia setariae*	India
Cercospora leaf spot	*Cercospora penniseti*	USA
Downy mildew	*Sclerophthora macrospora, S. graminicola*	Africa, India
Ergot	*Claviceps microcephala*	India
Foot rot	*Sclerotium rolfsii*	Africa, India
Head mold	Several fungii	Africa, India, USA
Head smut	*Sphacelotheca destruens*	Worldwide
Helminthosporiosis	*Helminthosporium nodulosum*	Africa, India
Kernel smuts	*Ustilago crameri*	Africa, Asia, USA
Leaf mold	*Curvularia* spp.	India, USA
Leaf spot	*Helminthosporium frumentacei*	India
Leaf spot	*Helminthosporium stenospilum*	USA
Long smut	*Ustilago penniseti*	Africa, Asia
Rhizoctonia blight	*Rhizoctonia solani*	USA
Rust	*Puccinia substriata*	Africa, India, USA
Smut	*Melanopsichium elesinis*	India
Viruses		
Bajra streak	Leafhoppers	India
Panicum mosaic	Mechanical transmission	USA
Buckwheat		
Fungi		
Chlorotic leaf spot and stipple spot	*Bipolaris sorokinione, Alternaria alternata*	Manitoba Province (Canada)
Downy mildew	*Peronospora ducometi*	Canada, Europe, Japan

Compiled from: Jones and Clifford (1979), Lucas, Campbell, and Lucas (1985), and Nyvall (1989).
[a]Includes the vectors of mycoplasmas and viral agents.

penetrates the plant directly or grows through a natural opening or wound (Davidson and Lyon 1987; Nyvall 1989). They survive by saprophytic growth on plant residues, or through survival spores in soil or infected plants, reproductive structures on infected plants, and mycelia in perennial plants, insects, seeds, or plant residue.

Symptoms of plant diseases caused by fungi are also varied and may resemble those caused by bacteria (Nyvall 1989). Below-ground plant parts, including seeds, emerging seedlings, and roots, become discolored and rotted to various degrees. Aboveground plant parts display spots of various shapes and sizes that can occur on any part of the plant from the cotyledonary leaves to the grain or fruit. Some cause pustules to form in which spores are produced, giving the plant a rusty appearance. Galls that become dusty when mature may be produced on any aboveground plant part. In some diseases, the seeds may be replaced by either dusty-appearing groups of spores of the fungus or a hard, almost rocklike appearing object called a "sclerotium." Soft rots on stems and fruits may become overgrown with fungus mycelia during moist conditions. Many fungal diseases also occur inside a stem, showing little outward evidence that the plant is diseased until it topples over or is harvested; the rotted stalk interior or discoloration inside a stem is then evident. An overall wilting of the plant may occur with some vascular wilt fungi (Nyvall 1989).

Mycoplasmas

Mycoplasmas somewhat resemble bacteria, but are usually smaller in size, lack rigid cell walls, and are variable in shape. They disseminate from plant to plant mainly by insects. Entrance into the plant is accomplished during feeding activities of the insect vector. Mycoplasmas overwinter in infected perennial plants and possibly in certain insect vectors. Usual symptoms of mycoplasma infection are distortion, yellowing, and proliferation of aboveground plant parts.

Nematodes

Nematodes infect the plants using their stylet to probe a plant cell. Fluids are injected into the plant through the stylet to soften or predigest plant tissue. Survival is by eggs in the soil or in cysts (the resistant body of a dead female) and by larvae in the soil.

Nematode symptoms are mostly confined to below-ground plant parts, although some are capable of infecting aboveground parts. Galls on roots, numerous short or short and stubby roots, lesions, and a poorly developed root system are the characteristic symptoms of nematode infection. Often, wounds caused by nematodes provide an entry for root rot and wilt organisms into the plant. The most common aboveground symptom is a general unthriftiness of the entire plant. Other symptoms include leaf distortion, discoloration, and formation of galls in seed.

Viruses

Viruses disseminate by several means, such as insects, nematodes, soil fungi, and seed. They enter plants through the feeding activity of a vector, and survive

Table 1-25. Major Insect Pests of Cereal Crops.

Family	Common Name	Scientific Name
Aphididae	Corn root aphid	*Anuraphis maidiradicis*
	Green bug	*Schizaphis graminum*
	Apple grain aphid	*Rhopalosiphum fitchii*
	Corn leaf aphid	*Rhopalosiphum maidis*
	English grain aphid	*Macrosiphum avenae*
	Cherry oat aphid	*Rhopalosiphum padi*
Carabidae	Slender seedcorn beetle	*Clivina impressifrons*
Cecidomyiidae	Sorghum midge	*Contarinia sorghicola*
	Hessian fly	*Mayetiola destructor*
	Wheat midge	*Sitodiplosis mosellana*
Cephidae	Wheat stem sawfly	*Cephus cinctus norton*
	Black grain stem sawfly	*Trachelus tabidus*
Chrysomelidae	Cereal leaf beetle	*Oulema melanopus*
	Corn rootworms	*Diabrotica* spp.
	Southern corn rootworm	*Diabrotica undecimpunctata howardi*
	Northern corn rootworm	*D. longicornis barberi*
	Western corn rootworm	*D. virgifera virgifera*
	Mexican corn rootworm	*D. virgifera zeae*
	Banded cucumber beetle	*D. balteata*
	Western spotted cucumber beetle	*D. undecimpunctata*
	Corn flea beetle	*Chaetocnema pulicaria*
	Toothed flea beetle	*C. denticulata*
	Desert corn flea beetle	*C. ectypa*
	Pale-striped flea beetle	*Systena blanda*
	Red-headed flea beetle	*S. frontalis*
	Western black flea beetle	*Phyllotreta pusilla*
Curculionidae	Maize billbug	*Sphenophorus maidis*
	Clay-colored billbug	*S. aequalis*
	Bluegrass billbug	*S. parvulus*
	Southern corn billbug	*S. callosus*
	Corn or timothy billbug	*S. zeae*
	Hunting billbug	*S. venatus vestitus*
	Nutgrass billbug	*S. cariosus*
	Rice water weevil	*Lissorhoptrus oryzophilus kuschel*
Eurytomidae	Wheat jointworm	*Tetramesa tritici*
	Wheat strawworm	*Tetramesa grandis*
	Wheat sheath jointworm	*Tetramesa vaginicola*
	Rye jointworm	*Tetramesa secale*
	Rye strawworm	*Tetramesa websteri*
	Barley jointworm	*Tetramesa hordei*
Lygaeidae	Chinch bugs	*Blissus leucopterus*
Noctuidae	Corn earworm	*Heliothis zea*
	Sorghum webworm	*Celama sorghiella*
	Rice worm	*Apamea apamiformis*
Pentatomidae	Rice stink bug	*Oebalus pugnax*
Pyralidae	European corn borer	*Ostrinia nubilalis*
	Southwestern corn borer	*Diatraea grandiosella*
	Southern cornstalk borer	*Diatraea crambidoides*
	Lesser cornstalk borer	*Elasmopalpus lignosellus*
	Rice stalkborer	*Chiloplejadellus zincken*

Compiled from: Hill (1983) and Davidson and Lyon (1987).

in perennial plants, seeds, and (sometimes) insect vectors. Viral symptoms are visible most commonly on the aboveground parts. Leaves, pods, and fruits may be malformed or have varying patterns of discoloration. Leaves or other tissues may proliferate, causing the plant to appear bushy. Streaks and spots of various colors and patterns may also be present, and stems may be cracked, pitted, or cankered (Nyvall 1989).

The methods for the control of plant diseases are discussed at length in Chapter 2, and hence will not be described here.

Pests

Major insect pests attacking various cereal crops are listed in Table 1-25. The characteristics of various insect pests of field crops and methods for their control are discussed in Chapter 2 with regard to legumes; similar approaches may be used for the control of cereal pests.

CHEMICAL COMPOSITION AND NUTRITIONAL QUALITY

The proximate composition of important cereal grains is summarized in Table 1-26. A large variation appears to exist in various chemical constituents of cereals. These differences could be primarily attributed to differences in cultivars and analytical techniques used by different researchers. Starch is the major constituent of cereal endosperms, comprising 58–70% of the total kernel weight; total carbohydrates may account for as much as 68–90% of the seed weight (Table 1-27). The starchy carbohydrates are present in the endosperm, whereas the nonstarchy carbohydrates are primarily concentrated in the bran fractions. Processed cereal products, such as polished white rice and milled wheat flour of 72% or lower extraction rates, are generally lower in dietary fiber as compared to brown rice and whole wheat flour. The bran fractions of various cereals contain 9–12% of dietary fiber (Table 1-27).

In cereals, bran and germ are generally richer in proteins than is the endosperm, and protein content decreases toward the grain center. Protein content also shows great variation among cereal grains, ranging from 5.6% to 21% in wheat (Mattern, Schmidt, and Johnson 1970) and from 8% to 18.2% in corn kernel (Bressani and Mertz 1958); more recently developed corn cultivars have shown a larger variation in protein content (Salunkhe, Chavan, and Kadam 1985). Generally, selection for higher protein results in decreased yield in cereals (Gallagher 1982; Palmer 1989).

Even though the protein content of cereal grains is only half that of various food legumes, they still supply over 70% of the total dietary intake of proteins worldwide (Deshpande and Damodaran 1990). The amino acid composition of

Table 1-26. Proximate Composition of Cereal Grains (% Dry Weight).

Cereal	Nitrogen	Protein[a]	Fat	Fiber	Ash	NFE[b]
Wheat						
Bread	1.4 –2.6	12	1.9	2.5	1.4	71.7
Durum	2.1 –2.4	13			1.5	70.0
Rice						
Brown	1.4 –1.7	8	2.4	1.8	1.5	77.4
Milled			0.8	0.4	0.8	
Wild	2.3 –2.5	14	0.7	1.5	1.2	74.4
Corn	1.4 –1.9	10	4.7	2.4	1.5	72.2
Barley						
Grain	1.2 –2.2	11	2.1	6.0	3.1	—
Kernel	1.2 –2.5	9	2.1	2.1	2.3	78.8
Oats						
Grain	1.5 –2.5	14	5.5	11.8	3.7	—
Kernel	1.7 –3.9	16	7.7	1.6	2.0	68.2
Sorghum	1.5 –2.3	10	3.6	2.2	1.6	73.0
Rye	1.2 –2.4	10	1.8	2.6	2.1	73.4
Millets	1.7 –2.0	11	3.3	8.1	3.4	72.9
Triticale	2.0 –2.8	14	1.5	3.1	2.0	71.0

Adapted from: Simmonds (1978), which includes the original references.
[a]Typical or average figure.
[b]NFE = Nitrogen-free extract (an approximate measure of total carbohydrates other than fiber).

various cereal proteins indicates lysine as the first and tryptophan as the second limiting amino acids (Table 1-28). Cereal proteins are, however, rich in sulfur-amino acids (met + cys), and therefore complement very well the lysine-rich, sulfur-amino acid–deficient legume proteins. The major storage proteins of cereals are either prolamins or glutelins; oats are the only exception, with their major protein a globulin (Croy and Gatehouse 1985).

Being deficient in lysine, cereal proteins perform poorly in animal studies. Their protein efficiency ratio (PER) ranges from 0.8 to 2.0; that of milk casein is 2.5 (Table 1-29). Among various cereals, rice and oat proteins have better PER values; however, some of their good-quality protein is lost during processing. Sorghum and corn proteins have PER values comparatively low among those of the various cereals. Consumption of sorghum is also associated with poor absorption and retention of nitrogen, and with higher fecal losses of energy and nitrogen than is other cereals; it is also found to be inferior to wheat or corn in promoting growth of weaning rats (MacLean et al. 1982).

Representative data on the true digestibility of protein of various cereals and cereal products are shown in Table 1-30. The digestibility of wheat gluten is the highest, and is closely followed by that of wheat white flour. The protein

Table 1-27. Carbohydrate Contents of Cereal Grains and Their Products.

Cereal	Product	Total Carbohydrates (g/100 g)	Fiber (g/100 g)
Wheat	Durum	70.1	1.8
	Hard red spring	69.1	2.3
	Hard red winter	71.7	2.3
	Soft red winter	72.1	2.3
	White	75.4	1.9
	Bulgur		
	Club wheat	79.5	1.7
	Hard red winter	75.7	1.7
	White wheat	78.1	1.3
	Wheat flour		
	80% extraction	74.1	0.5
	Patent, all purpose	76.1	0.3
	Straight, hard wheat	74.5	0.4
	Straight, soft wheat	76.9	0.4
	Wheat bran	61.9	9.1
	Wheat germ	46.7	2.5
Rice	Brown	77.4	0.9
	Bran	50.8	11.5
	Polished	57.7	2.4
	White	80.4	0.3
Corn	Field corn	72.2	2.0
	Sweet corn, raw	22.1	0.7
	Popcorn		
	Unpopped	72.1	2.1
	Popped, plain	76.7	2.2
	Corn flour	76.8	0.7
Barley	Pearled	78.8	0.5
	Malt, dry	77.4	5.7
	Malt extract, dried	89.2	trace
Oats	Dry oatmeal	68.2	1.2
Sorghum	Grain	73.0	1.7
Rye		73.4	2.0
	Rye flour		
	Light	77.9	0.4
	Medium	74.8	1.0
	Dark	68.1	2.4
Millet	Proso	72.9	3.2
Buckwheat	Whole grain	72.9	9.9
	Buckwheat flour		
	Dark	72.0	1.6
	Light	79.5	0.5

Adapted from: Watt and Merrill (1963) and Lockhard and Nesheim (1978).

Table 1-28. Amino Acid Composition of Cereals (% by Weight).

Amino Acid	Wheat (HRS)	Rice (Brown)	Corn (Field)	Barley	Oats	Sorghum	Rye	Pearl Millet	Triticale
Ala	3.50	3.56	9.95	4.60	6.11	—[a]	5.13	—	3.53
Arg	4.79	5.76	3.52	5.15	6.58	3.79	4.88	4.60	4.99
Asp	5.46	4.72	12.42	5.56	4.13	—	7.16	—	5.00
Cys	2.19	1.36	1.30	2.01	2.18	1.66	1.99	1.33	1.55
Glu	31.25	13.69	17.65	22.35	20.14	21.92	21.26	—	31.80
Gly	6.11	6.84	3.39	4.55	4.55	—	4.79	—	4.05
His	2.04	1.68	2.06	1.87	1.84	1.92	2.28	2.11	2.48
Ile	4.34	4.69	4.62	4.26	5.16	5.44	4.26	5.57	3.71
Leu	6.71	8.61	12.96	6.95	7.50	16.06	6.72	15.32	6.87
Lys	2.82	3.95	2.88	3.38	3.67	2.72	4.08	3.36	2.77
Met	1.29	1.80	1.86	1.44	1.47	1.73	1.58	2.37	1.44
Phe	4.94	5.03	4.54	5.16	5.34	4.97	4.72	4.44	5.26
Pro	10.44	4.84	8.35	9.02	5.70	—	5.20	—	12.06
Ser	4.61	5.08	5.65	4.65	4.00	5.05	4.13	—	4.70
Thr	2.88	3.92	3.98	3.38	3.31	3.58	3.70	4.00	3.11
Trp	1.24	1.08	0.61	1.25	1.29	1.12	1.13	2.18	1.08
Tyr	3.74	4.57	6.11	3.64	3.69	2.75	3.22	—	2.14
Val	4.63	6.99	5.10	5.02	5.95	5.71	5.21	5.98	4.39

Adapted from: Simmonds (1978), which includes original references.
[a]Not estimated.

Table 1-29. Protein Quality of Cereal Grains (PER).

Cereal	Actual	Estimate[a]	Cereal	Actual	Estimate[a]
Wheat			Corn		
Whole	1.5	1.3	Normal	1.2	1.2
Germ	2.5	2.5	Opaque-2	2.3	1.9
Gluten	—	0.7	Barley	—	1.6
Flour			Oats	1.9	1.7
80–90% extraction	—	1.1	Sorghum	1.8	0.9
70–80% extraction	—	1.0	Rye	1.6	1.6
60–70% extraction	—	0.8	Millets		
Bulgur	—	1.2	Finger millet	0.8	—
Rice			Foxtail millet	—	1.0
Brown	1.9	1.8	Pearl millet	1.8	1.6
Polished	1.7	1.7	Proso millet	—	1.4
Buckwheat	—	1.8	Triticale	1.6	1.4

Adapted from: Simmonds (1978), which includes the original references.
[a]Estimated from the amino acid content assuming availability of amino acids the same as the amino acids in casein.

Table 1-30. True Digestibility by Adults of Protein in Some Cereal Protein Sources.

Protein Source	Processed Version	No. of Reports	Digestibility (%) Mean	Range
Wheat	Whole	6	87	90 – 93
	Flour (white)	2	96	96 – 97
	Bread (white)	5	97	95 –101
	Bread (coarse, brown, or whole wheat)	2	92	91 – 92
	Gluten	4	99	96 –104
	Ready-to-eat cereal	9	77	53 – 88
Rice	Polished	4	89	82 – 91
	Ready-to-eat cereal	3	75	77 – 85
Corn	Whole	4	87	84 – 92
	Ready-to-eat cereal	5	70	62 – 78
Oats	Ready-to-eat cereal	4	72	63 – 89
Animal protein		41	96	90 –106

Source: Hopkins (1981).

Table 1-31. Utilizable Protein and Growth of Weaning Rats on Cereals Fed Alone (100%) and from 90% Cereal + 10% Bean Mixtures.

Protein Source	Protein in Diet (%)	Utilizable Protein (%)	Average Weight Gain (g/4 weeks)	PER
Wheat	11.0	4.28	19	1.05
+ bean	12.0	5.94	41	1.73
Rice	6.9	4.01	43	2.15
+ bean	7.9	4.96	56	2.32
Corn	8.5	2.41	13	0.87
+ bean	10.3	4.10	32	1.40
Oats	13.8	8.22	34	1.60
+ bean	14.6	8.73	75	2.37
Sorghum	7.7	2.23	12	0.88
+ bean	8.6	3.93	30	1.39
Casein	10.7	8.02	75	2.37

Source: Bressani (1975). Reprinted with permission.

digestibility of whole corn, rice, and wheat flour is comparable, but considerably reduced as a result of processing—that of ready-to-eat wheat, corn, and rice was 77%, 70%, and 72%, respectively (Table 1-30). The availability of proteins primarily depends upon their digestibility; incomplete digestion adversely affects the absorption and utilization of protein by the body. Utilizable protein is lowest in sorghum and highest in oats (Table 1-31).

Table 1-32. Mineral Contents (mg/100 g Dry Weight) of Cereal Grains and Cereal Products.

Cereal	Ca	Fe	Mg	P	K	Na	Cu	Mn	Zn
Wheat									
Grain	50	10	160	360	520	3	0.72	4.88	3.40
Bran	140	70	550	1,170	1,240	9	1.23	11.57	9.80
Rice									
Brown	40	3	60	230	150	9	0.33	1.76	1.80
White	30	1	20	120	130	5	0.29	1.09	1.30
Corn									
Grain	30	2	120	270	280	1	0.21	0.51	1.69
Bran	30	—	260	190	730	—	—	1.61	—
Germ	90	90	280	560	130	—	1.10	0.90	—
Barley	80	10	120	420	560	3	0.76	1.63	1.53
Oats	100	10	170	350	370	2	0.59	3.82	3.40
Sorghum	40	4	170	310	340	—	0.96	1.45	1.37
Rye	60	10	120	340	460	1	0.78	6.69	3.05
Millet (proso)	50	10	160	280	430	—	2.16	2.91	1.39
Triticale	20	4	—	—	385	—	0.52	4.26	0.02
Buckwheat	110	4	390	330	450	—	0.95	3.37	0.87

Adapted from: Lockhart and Nesheim (1978), which includes the original references.

The mineral and vitamin contents of cereal grains and their products are summarized in Tables 1-32 and 1-33, respectively. Cereals are excellent sources of phosphorus and potassium and are fairly rich in calcium, iron, and magnesium. About 70–80% of the total phosphorus in cereals is present as phytic acid (Reddy, Sathe, and Salunkhe 1982). Cereals are also important sources of thiamin, niacin, and pyridoxin; they do not, however, contain significant amounts of fat-soluble vitamins. Over 80% of the total minerals and vitamins in cereal grains are present in aleurone layers that are usually removed during processing operations such as polishing, pearling, or milling. Whole-grain cereals are therefore generally more nutritious than their processed counterparts.

As compared to food legumes, cereals generally do not contain appreciable amounts of antinutrients, such as enzyme inhibitors and lectins. Phytic acid (*myo*-inositol 1,2,3,5/4,6-hexakis [dihydrogen phosphate]), which chelates important dietary minerals (such as iron, calcium, and zinc) and lowers their bioavailability, is the major antinutritional compound in cereals; it is generally regarded as the primary storage form of both phosphate and inositol in cereal grains (Reddy, Sathe, and Salunkhe 1982).

Phytate is located in aleurone particles or grains (as globoids) in the aleurone layer (Lasztity and Lasztity 1990). The globoid particles contain high levels of phytic acid (25–70%) and are rich in potassium (2–20%) and magnesium (1.5–12%). Thus, phytate probably occurs in cereals as a K–Mg salt.

Table 1-33. Vitamin Contents[a] of Cereal Grains and Cereal Products.

Cereal	Thiamin	Ribo-flavin	Niacin	Vitamin B_6	Folic Acid	Pantothenic Acid	Biotin	Vitamin E
Wheat								
Grain	0.57	0.12	7.4	0.35	78	1	6	1
Germ	2.01	0.68	4.2	0.92	328	2		
Bran	0.72	0.35	21.0	1.38	223	3	14	—
Patent flour	0.13	0.04	2.1	0.05	25	1	1	—
Rice								
Brown	0.34	0.05	4.7	0.62	20	2	12	2
Polished	0.07	0.03	1.6	0.04	16	1	5	1
Corn	0.37	0.12	2.2	0.47	26	1	21	2
Barley	0.23	0.13	4.52	0.26	67	0	6	1
Oats	0.67	0.11	0.8	0.21	104	1	13	3
Sorghum	0.38	0.15	3.9					
Rye	0.44	0.18	1.5	0.33	34	1	—	2
Millet	0.73	0.38	2.3					1
Buckwheat	0.60		4.4			1		

Adapted from: Lockhart and Nesheim (1978), which includes the original references.
[a]Vitamin contents are in mg/100 g except folic acid and biotin (μg) and vitamin E (IU/100 g).

Representative data on phytate content of various cereals are summarized in Table 1-34. According to Nelson, Ferrara, and Storer (1968), phytate accounts for over 81% of the total phosphorus in brown rice, 60–80% in wheat, 18–53% in triticale, 83–88% in corn, 66–70% in barley, 59–66% in oats, and 72% and 89% in low- and high-tannin sorghum, respectively. Morphological distribution of phytic acid in various cereals suggests that it is primarily concentrated in the aleurone layer and to a lesser extent in the germ (Table 1-35).

Since aleurone layers are removed during the milling of cereals, phytate becomes concentrated in the bran portion. Thus, products prepared from whole-grain flours or those fortified with cereal brans are generally the richest in phytic acid, whereas white breads prepared from low-extraction flours are the poorest. The chemistry, biochemistry, and nutritional and processing aspects of phytate in various cereals have been recently reviewed (Lasztity and Lasztity 1990).

Among other antinutrients, tannins are present in significant amounts in certain cereals, such as sorghum and millets (Deshpande, Sathe, and Salunkhe 1984). High-tannin sorghums thrive well under drought conditions and are resistant to bird attack. The red-pigmented, high-tannin sorghum varieties may contain as much as 7–8% tannins, although the normal levels range from 1% to 3% (Deshpande, Cheryan, and Salunkhe 1986).

The various deleterious effects of tannins in human nutrition have been reviewed (Deshpande, Sathe, and Salunkhe 1984). In animal studies, when fed

Table 1-34. Phytate Content (% Dry Weight) of Various Cereals.

Cereal	McCance & Widdowson (1935)	Averill & King (1926)	Oke (1965)	Lolas, Palamidis, & Markakis (1976)	Other Researchers
Wheat (whole grain)	0.596	1.230		0.62 –1.35	
Rice (unpolished)	0.851		0.284		
Corn			0.532		0.89[a]
Barley		1.130		0.97 –1.16	
Oats	0.770			0.79 –1.01	
Sorghum					0.57 –0.96[b]
Rye		1.340			0.97[c]
Millet		1.120	0.532		0.17 –0.47[d]
Triticale					0.50 –1.89[c]

Adapted from: Lasztity and Lasztity (1990).
[a]De Boland, Garner, and O'Dell (1975).
[b]Radhakrishnan and Sivaprasad (1980).
[c]Singh and Reddy (1977).
[d]Lorenz (1983).

Table 1-35. Phytic Acid Content (%) in Morphological Parts of Some Cereals.

Cereal	Type	Morphological Part	O'Dell, De Boland, & Koirtyohann (1972)	Lorenz (1983)	Lasztity (1988)
Wheat	Hard winter	Endosperm			0.001–0.01
		Germ			0.86 –1.35
		Aleurone			0.91 –1.42
	Soft	Endosperm	0.001		
		Germ	1.10		
		Aleurone	1.16		
Rice	Brown	Endosperm	0.004		
		Germ	0.98		
		Pericarp	0.95		
Corn	Yellow dent	Endosperm			0.01 –0.03
		Germ			0.72 –1.78
		Hull			0.05 –0.19
	High-lysine	Endosperm	0.01		
		Germ	1.61		
		Hull	0.07		
Millet	Proso	Hull		0.51 –1.60	
		Dehulled grain		0.18 –0.27	

Adapted from: Lasztity and Lasztity (1990).

at levels that commonly occur in cereals (approximately 1–2%), tannins have depressed the growth rate and resulted in poor feed efficiency ratio and an increase in the amount of feed required per unit weight gain. Other deleterious effects of tannins include damage to mucosal lining of the GI tract, alteration in the excretion of certain cations, and increased excretion of proteins and essential amino acids. The deleterious effects of tannins in the diet are generally related to their interactions with dietary proteins (Deshpande and Damodaran 1990).

PROCESSING AND PRODUCTS

Wheat

Processing

Wheat must be converted to flour before different products can be prepared. The miller thus desires a wheat that mills easily and gives a high flour yield. Wheat kernels should be plump and uniformly large for ready separation of foreign material without undue loss of millable wheat (Lawande and Adsule 1985; D'Appolonia 1987; Pomeranz 1987; Yamazaki 1987). The wheat should produce a high yield of flour with maximum and clean separation from the bran and germ. Since the endosperm is denser, high-density wheats produce more flour. Some environmental factors also influence the ease of milling; for example, the bran of weathered and frosted wheats tends to pulverize, and it is difficult to secure clean separation of flour from bran (Pomeranz 1987).

Wheat as harvested is not suitable for milling; therefore, processing overall includes preparation (wheat selection and blending, cleaning, tempering, and conditioning), followed by milling (breaking, sifting or sieving, purification, and reduction), and finally treatment (bleaching, enrichment, and supplementation). Roller milling operations for wheat processing have been comprehensively reviewed by Lawande and Adsule (1985) and Pomeranz (1987), upon whose excellent work much of this section is based.

The primary objective in the production of wheat flour is separation of the starchy endosperm of the wheat kernels from the bran and germ. The separated endosperm is then pulverized. A partial separation of the starchy endosperm is possible since its physical properties differ from those of the fibrous pericarp and oily germ. The bran is tough because of its high fiber content, whereas the starchy endosperm is friable; the oily germ flakes when passed between smooth rolls. In addition, particles from various parts of the wheat kernels differ in density, allowing their separation by the use of air currents. The differences in friability of the bran and the starchy endosperm are enhanced by wheat conditioning. The addition of water before milling toughens the bran and mellows the endosperm. The actual milling process comprises a gradual reduction in particle size, first between corrugated break rolls and later between smooth reduction rolls. This process results in the production of many streams of flour and offals that can be combined in different ways to produce different grades of flour.

Preparation

Selection and Blending. The selection of wheats and binning according to quality for proper blending are essential phases of modern milling. Flours of desired characteristics can be obtained by blending different varieties or types of wheat in different proportions.

Cleaning. Wheat received in the mill contains many impurities that affect the uniformity and appearance of flour, flour yield, and ultimately the flour quality. These impurities must be removed before the milling of wheat. The types of impurity present in wheat include vegetable matter (foreign seeds and plant residues), animal matter (rodent excreta, hairs, insects, mites, etc.), mineral matter (mud, dust, stones, nails, etc.), and such other impurities as binder twine, string, and miscellaneous rubbish. Wheat is initially conveyed through a water trough to the base of a centrifugal machine to remove adhering dirt. Wire screens are then used to remove impurities based on their size and shape. Magnetic separators remove metal impurities, and aspirators remove lighter materials such as chaff, straw, and small seeds. Dry scourers are used to remove by friction hair and dirt adherent to grain. In this process, wheat is forced against a perforated iron casting by beaters fixed to a rapidly revolving drum. Depending upon the nature and extent of impurities, the miller follows a suitable combination and sequence of the above operations.

Tempering. Wheat is tempered by the addition of water to raise its moisture content to 15–19% for hard wheat and 14.5–17% for soft wheat. During this process, wheat is allowed to lie in tempering bins for periods of 18–72 h with little or no temperature control. The moisture enters the bran and diffuses inward.

Conditioning. Conditioning involves the use of heat for quick diffusion of water into the kernels. It improves milling properties with the consequent saving of time. There are three conditioning methods: In *warm conditioning,* wheat is conditioned for 1–1.5 h at temperatures of up to 46 °C. The warm-conditioned wheat is then rested for 24 h prior to milling. *Hot conditioning* is similar except that temperatures are raised to 60 °C or higher. *Steam conditioning* is the most time saving of the three. It requires less power and gives higher yields of flour.

Milling

The cleaned and conditioned wheat is now ready for milling. The grinding of wheat evolved from primitive hand methods to air- and water-power sources turning heavy stones. Milling evolution continued with the introduction of screw conveyors, bucket elevators, steel rollers, and purifier machines. Subsequently, several patents were issued covering improvements and refinements for cleaners, dust collectors, grain washers, mechanical purifiers, and other milling operations. Advances in science and technology have led to the development of automatic modern flour mills. In most of these mills, wheat is milled by rollers, which are of two types: break and reduction. A flowchart of modern wheat flour milling is shown in Fig. 1-13.

Breaking. The first part of the grinding process is carried out on corrugated rolls (break rolls), usually 24–30 in. long and 9 in. in diameter. Each stand has two pairs of rolls revolving in opposite directions at a speed differential of about 2.5 : 1. In the first set of break rolls, there are usually ten or twelve corrugations per inch, which increases to twenty-six or twenty-eight corrugations on the fifth break roll. During the breaking process, the grains are cracked. After each break, the resulting mixture of bran, free endosperm, and bran that contains endosperm is sieved, the coarsest material is conveyed to the second break roll, and so on. The material that goes to each succeeding break contains less and less endosperm. After the last break, the longest fragments consist of flakes of the wheat pericarp. They are passed through a wheat bran duster that removes a small quantity of low-grade flour.

Sieving or Sifting. After each set of break rolls, the crushed material ("stock" or "chop") is subjected to a combination of sieving operations (plan sifters) and air aspirators (purifiers). The process results in separation of three classes of material:

1. coarse fragments that are fed to the next break until only the bran remains;
2. flour or fine particles that pass through the finest flour sieve; and
3. intermediate granular particles or "middlings."

Purification. Purifiers consist of long oscillating sieves inclined downward through which air current is passed upwardly. This causes the flour to stratify into bran and middlings of different sizes. The middlings are taken to appropriate reduction rolls. The "overtails," including bran and the bran + endosperm, are taken back to the break roll or to the mill feed stock. The number of purifiers may range up to twelve for a system with four break rolls.

Reduction. Reduction rolls differ from break rolls in two important aspects: The roll surfaces are quite smooth, and the speed differential between the two rolls is lower, usually 1.25 : 1 or 1.50 : 1. The purified and classified middlings are gradually pulverized to flour between the smooth reduction rolls. Endosperm fragments passing through the rolls are reduced to finer middlings and flour, and the bran is flaked or flattened. After each reduction step, the resulting

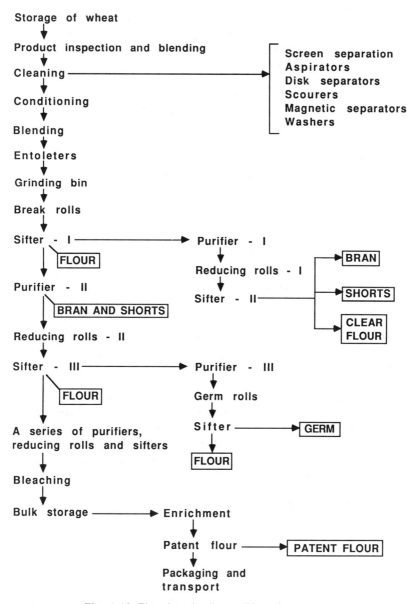

Fig. 1-13. Flowchart for flour milling of wheat.

stock is sifted. Most of the bran is removed on the top sieve, the flour passes through the finest bottom sieve, and the remaining middlings are separated according to size, moved to their respective purifiers, and passed to other reduction rolls. The entire process is repeated until most of the endosperm is converted to flour and the bran has been removed as offal by the reduction sifters. What remains is a mixture of fine middlings and bran with a little germ: This is called "feed middlings."

Scratching. In addition to the break and reduction system, a scratch system is sometimes employed as a standby to maintain proper release of endosperm from the bran. The system contains fluted rolls, similar to lower break rolls, which scratch off the adhering husk or bran from the endosperm.

Entoleter. The stock from the earliest reduction rolls is treated on a specially designed "entoleter" machine, which acts almost like a detacher and increases the yield of flour. The entoleter contains disks with concentric rings rotating at high speed: Any living matter present, such as insects, is killed due to the centrifugal force. This machine thus avoids the use of chemicals to control these organisms.

Air Classifiers. Some flour mills add yet another system to their millstream for further separation of particles. Wheat flour produced by conventional roller milling contains particles of different sizes (1–150 μm). These include large endosperm chunks, small particles of free protein, free starch granules, and small chunks of protein attached to starch granules. The flour can be ground—pin-milled to avoid excessive starch damage—to fine particles in which the protein is freed from the starch. The pin-milled flour is then passed through an air classifier (Fig. 1-14). A fine fraction of $\leq$40-μm particles is removed and passed through a second classifier, where particles of $\leq$20 μm are separated. This fraction comprises about 10% of the original flour and contains up to twice the protein of the unfractionated flour. Air classification has created considerable interest within the milling industry and is relatively inexpensive. It produces more uniform flours from different wheats, increases the protein content of the bread flour (and decreases that of cake and cookie flours), controls particle size and chemical composition, and produces special flours for specific end uses. The technology of the process is well known; however, its benefits and potential have not been fully explored, primarily because of the availability of low- and high-protein wheats and the high energy costs involved in air classification.

Milling Soft and Durum Wheats. Soft wheats are also milled by the method of gradual reduction with minor alterations, such as processing variables, grinding technique, and stream selection (Lawande and Adsule 1985; Pomeranz 1987). Patent flours milled from soft red winter wheats containing 7–9% protein are especially suitable for chemically leavened biscuits and hot breads. Special mixes of soft wheats containing $\leq$8% protein and milled to very short patents (about 30%) are used to make cake flours.

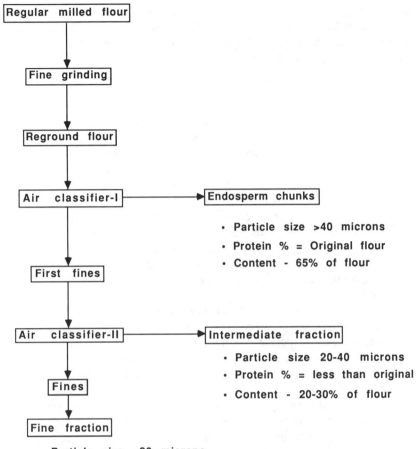

Fig. 1-14. Flowchart for air classification of wheat flour.

In durum wheat milling, the main objective is to produce a maximum yield of highly purified semolina. Although the sequence of operations involved in the production of semolina and flour is the same, the milling systems differ in their design. In semolina manufacture, impurities and mill offals must be removed by cleaning and purification systems. The breaking, sizing, and purification systems are much more elaborate and extensive than in flour mills, but the reduction systems are shorter since the primary product is removed in a granular condition. For maximum yield of large endosperm particles, break rolls with

U-cut corrugations are employed. A durum wheat of good milling quality normally yields 62% semolina, 16% clear flour, and 22% feeds. The particle size distribution and granulation of semolina are highly important in the production of macaroni (Pomeranz 1987).

Flour Grades and Improvements

Each milling operation in the roller flour mill results in a stream of flour of individual characteristics and properties. If all streams are combined, the resulting flour is a straight-run flour that represents about 72% of the wheat kernel. The remaining 28% is called "mill feed" and includes 16% bran and 12% shorts. Frequently, only highly refined streams are taken off and sold separately as "patent flours"; the remaining streams containing more bran and germ are known as "clear flours." The percent recovery of wheat kernel in patent flour is lower than that in straight-run flour and is still lower in case of extra short or fancy patent flour. The ordinary power-driven stone mills commonly used on the Indian subcontinent do not completely separate the bran from the endosperm, and thus yield a long extraction flour that represents 90–95% of the whole kernel.

The quality and nutritive value of wheat flour can be improved by certain chemical additives and physical means. Flour is bleached by chemicals such as chlorine, nitrogen trichloride, chlorine dioxide, benzoyl peroxide, and potassium bromate and iodate. During this process, xanthophyll, a yellow flour pigment, is oxidized to yield a white flour. Maturing agents—including potassium bromate, ascorbic acid, and azodicarbonamide—improve the baking properties of the flour by modifying gluten during fermentation. They oxidize the thiol group of cysteine to disulfide bonds, thereby tightening the dough, improving dough handling properties, loaf volume, and the fineness of crumb texture. Self-raising flour contains a mixture of sodium bicarbonate and one or more acid-reacting substances added to produce at least 0.5% carbon dioxide.

Wheat flours are also nutritionally enriched with vitamins such as thiamin, riboflavin, and niacin, and minerals such as calcium and iron. They can also be mixed with suitable legume flour to produce composite flours with improved nutritive value.

Products

Wheat flour is the basic ingredient for making bread, biscuits, pastry products, and semolina and farina for alimentary pasta. A small portion is also converted into breakfast foods. Unlike other cereals, wheat, due to its high price, has limited uses for industrial purposes; these include the manufacture of malt, potable spirits, starch, gluten, pastes, and core binders. *Wheat malt* is usually too costly to be used in the brewing industry. It is mainly used by the flour milling industry to increase the α-amylase activity of the high-grade flours (Pomeranz 1987). In the United States, small quantities of wheat flour (mainly low-grade clears) are used to manufacture *wheat starch* as a by-product of viable (functionally in bread making) gluten. *Wheat gluten* is used to supplement flour proteins in specialty baked goods, such as hamburger buns, hotdog buns, and hearth-type breads. It is also used as a raw material for the manufacture of monosodium glutamate. Some low-grade wheat flours are also used in the manufacture of pastes for bookbinding and paper hangings, in plywood adhesives, and in iron foundries as a core binder in the preparation of molds for castings.

Several monographs and texts have been written on the technology of bread, breakfast cereals, and other products prepared from wheats and other cereals (Pomeranz 1971; Pomeranz and Shellenberger 1971; Matz 1972; Williams 1975; Kent 1983; Pomeranz 1987). Only the salient features of these products are described below.

Bread

Bread is made by baking a dough whose principal ingredients are wheat flour, water, yeast, and salt. Other cereals, fat, malt flour, soy flour, emulsifiers, yeast foods, milk and milk products, fruits, and gluten may also be added for specialty breads.

There are three essential processes in bread making:

1. formation of a gluten network (mixing and dough development),
2. aeration of the mixture by incorporation of a gas, and
3. coagulation of the material to stabilize the structure (oven baking).

The dough generally used in commercial bakeries is of a standard consistency, usually requiring 55–61% water by flour weight. More water is added to flour with high protein (i.e., from strong wheats) or damaged starch content (i.e., from hard wheats) to attain this consistency. The starch in the dough is first hydrolyzed by amylases to maltose, which is then broken down to glucose by maltase. The resulting reducing sugars are fermented by the yeast to carbon dioxide and alcohol; the latter is evaporated during the baking process.

A dough undergoing fermentation with intermittent mechanical mixing is said to be "ripening." It becomes less sticky as ripening proceeds, and more rubbery when molded. A ripe dough has maximum elasticity after molding and gives maximum spring in the oven. There are two main processes by which dough is prepared. Both systems are examples of *bulk* or *long fermentation*.

In the *straight dough method,* the ingredients are mixed, allowed to ferment for about two hours of a three-hour fermentation process, then knocked back to mix the dough thoroughly and even out the temperature, and allowed to rest for another hour. It is then divided into loaf-sized portions that, after 10–15 min at about 27 °C ("first proof"), are molded into the final shape. During this stage, the dough is mechanically worked to tighten it, so that the gas is better distributed and retained, and is placed in pans. The final mold is very important in giving good texture in bulk-fermented bread. The dough rests again in the pans for the final proof of 45–60 min at 43 °C and is then baked in the oven at a temperature of about 235 °C for 25–40 min.

In the *sponge and dough system,* widely used in the United States, only a part of the flour is mixed at first with all the yeast and sufficient water to make a dough, which is allowed to ferment for a few hours. This so-called sponge is then broken down by mixing, and the remaining ingredients are added to make a dough of standard consistency. This is then given only a short fermentation time prior to proofing and baking. The sponge and dough system is believed to produce bread with a fuller flavor than that from the straight dough system.

In the *mechanical development* processes, the ingredients are mixed with a prefermentation brew containing the yeast. The dough is allowed no fermentation time, but instead subjected to intense mechanical mixing to achieve the correct degree of ripeness for proofing and baking.

Unleavened breads, called *chapatties,* are commonly used in the Indian subcontinent. For the preparation of *chapatti,* a strong gluten is not required, but the water absorption of the flour should be high. Chapatties are made by mixing whole wheat flour with water to form a dough that is rested for about an hour. It is then divided into small portions, flattened by hand or roller, and baked on an iron plate over an open fire. Sorghum and millet flours are also used for the making of *chapatties.*

Breakfast Cereals

The breakfast cereal foods can be classified based on the amount of domestic cooking required, the form of the product or dish, and the cereal used as raw material. In the case of hot cereals, cooking is carried out domestically, whereas ready-to-eat cereals are cooked during manufacture. Ready-cooked porridges can be made merely by stirring the material with hot or boiling water in the bowl. Generally, they are prepared from the cream of wheat or rolled oats. Other ready-to-eat cereals comprise flaked, puffed, shredded, or granular products, generally made from wheat, corn, or rice, although barley and oats are also used. The basic cereal may be enriched with sugar, syrup, honey, or malt extract. All types are prepared by processes that tend to cause dextrinization rather than gelatinization of the starch. For flaked products, the cereal (generally wheat, corn, or rice) is conditioned to a suitable moisture content and then lightly rolled between smooth rolls to fracture the outer layers. They are then cooked at elevated pressure and the flavorings are added. The cooked cereal is then dried to 15–20% moisture content and rested for 24–72 h while conditioning takes place. The conditioned grain is flaked on heavy flaking rolls, toasted in a tunnel or traveling oven, and then cooled and packaged.

For the manufacture of puffed cereals, whole-grain wheat (or rice, oats, or pearl barley) is prepared by cleaning, conditioning, and depericarping. It is cooked for 20 min at 20 psi pressure, dried to 14–16% moisture content, and pelleted by extrusion through a die. The pelleted dough is then fed into a pressure chamber, which is sealed and heated both externally and by the injection of steam so that the internal pressure rapidly builds up to about 200 psi. The pressure is then suddenly released by opening the chamber, called a "puffing gun." The expansion of water vapor on release of the pressure blows up the grains or pellets to several times their original size. The puffed product is then dried to 3% moisture content by toasting, and finally cooled and packaged.

Shredded wheat breakfast cereals are prepared by cleaning and cooking the whole grain by the application of external heat and the injection of steam. The conditions are such that the cooked grain is soft and rubbery, the moisture content is about 43%, and the starch is fully gelatinized. The cooked grain is then cooled and rested for about 18 h to condition. The conditioned grain is fed to shredders comprising a pair of metal rolls—one smooth and the other with circular grooves between which the material emerges as long parallel shreds. The shreds fall onto a slowly traveling band, and a thick mat is built up by superimposition of several layers. The mat is then cut into tablets and later baked for 20 min at 260 °C in a gas-heated oven. After baking, the product is dried to 1% moisture content, passed through a metal detector, and packaged.

Pasta

Various pasta products (e.g., macaroni, spaghetti, vermicelli, noodles) are made from semolina milled from hard wheat by a special process described earlier (see "Milling Soft and Durum Wheats"). The highest-quality pasta products are made from durum wheats alone; other wheats are not suitable for this purpose. The semolina is made into a stiff dough using 25–30% water at 32–38 °C and mixing for 10–15 min. After a rest period, the dough is kneaded at about 30 °C in a cylindrical machine equipped with beveled helical blades. Kneading is carried out under vacuum to avoid bubbles, which would affect the quality, and to yield a brighter and more transparent product. Mixing and kneading take about 15 min. The dough is then extruded through the die of a press to make tubular or strap-shaped products. Heavy pressure is employed to ensure that the product is translucent and to squeeze out any small air bubbles. The extruded product is cut to the required length by rotating knives, and dried to about 12.5% from about 30% moisture content at emergence from the die.

Cakes

As discussed earlier (see "Milling Soft and Durum Wheats"), cake flours are derived from special blends of soft wheats. Cake premixes sold commercially often contain all the necessary ingredients, requiring only the addition of water before baking. Sometimes, eggs and/or milk are omitted, since the addition of fresh eggs makes lighter cakes of larger volume.

Rice

Processing

The primary objective of rice milling is to remove the hull, bran, and germ with a minimum breakage of the endosperm (Webb 1987). In the threshed grain (rough rice or "paddy"), the kernel is enclosed in a tough, siliceous hull, rendering it unsuitable for human consumption. The paddy is cleaned and conveyed to shelling machines that loosen the hulls. Conventional shellers consist of two steel plates, mounted horizontally, whose inner surfaces are coated with a mixture of cement and carborundum. As the moving plate revolves around the stationary plate, the pressure on the ends of the upturned grains disengages the hulls, which are removed by aspiration. The mixture of (de)hulled and unhulled grains is separated on a large box shaker fitted with vertical, smooth steel plates set on a slight incline to form zigzag ducts. The plates and the shaking action cause the less dense paddy grains to move upward and the heavier hulled grains to move downward. Paddy may also be shelled with rubber rollers or with a rubber belt operating against a ribbed steel roll. The rubber shellers cause less mechanical damage and improve the stability against rancidity.

Hulled (brown) rice is then milled to remove the outer and inner bran layers, the aleurone layers, and the germ. The milling and polishing machines consist of grooved, tapering cylinders that revolve rapidly in stationary, uniformly perforated cylinders. The entire machine is filled with grain, and the packing force is regulated by a blade that protrudes between the upper and lower halves of the perforated cylinders. The bran, aleurone, and germ are removed by the scouring action of the rice grains against each other near the surface of the perforated cylinders. After passing through a succession of hullers, the rice is practically free from germ and outer bran. Scouring is usually completed by polishing in a brush machine. The polished (white) rice is then sorted according to size class: *whole kernel (head)* rice is at least three-quarters of the whole endosperm; *second-head* comprises large pieces of broken milled kernels; *screenings* are smaller pieces of broken milled kernels; and very small pieces of broken milled kernels are called *brewer's rice*. Fig. 1-15 is a flowchart of the rice milling process.

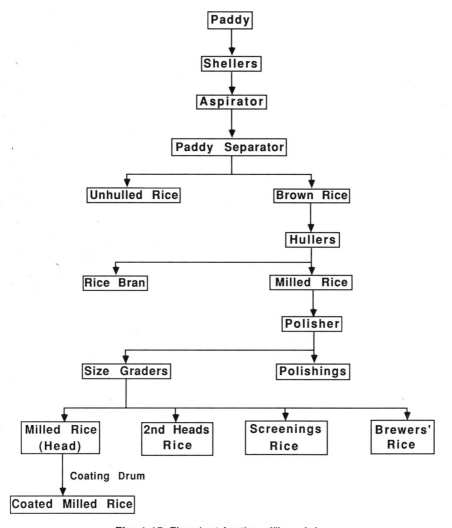

Fig. 1-15. Flowchart for the milling of rice.

Based on the weight of rough rice or paddy, the yield of white rice normally varies between 60% and 70%. The yield of head rice ultimately determines the milling quality of rough rice. The price obtained for the various classes of rice decreases with size (Pomeranz 1987). The yields of head rice vary widely depending upon the variety, grain type, cultural practices, and other environmental factors affecting the chalkiness and plumpness of the grains, and the conditions of handling, drying, storage, and milling (Webb 1987). The extent to which the bran layers and germ are removed from the endosperm during milling is referred to as the "degree of milling." The U.S. National Bureau of Standards recognizes four degrees of milling: well milled, reasonably well milled, lightly milled, and undermilled (Webb 1987).

A solvent extraction process is also developed to increase the yield of whole-grain rice (Pomeranz 1987). Hulled brown rice is softened with rice oil to improve bran removal. Fully milled rice is sometimes treated with a talc and glucose solution to improve its appearance. After the coating is evenly distributed on the kernels and dried with warm air, the rice emerges from the equipment with a smooth, glistening luster and is known as "coated rice."

Brown rice—though little in demand as food since it tends to become rancid and is prone to insect infestation—is more nutritious than polished, white rice. This is because protein, vitamins, and minerals are predominantly concentrated in the bran and aleurone layers of the kernel, their concentration decreasing progressively toward the center of the grain. Among the minerals, iron, potassium, phosphorus, and manganese are concentrated in the aleurone layers; these last three are particularly high in the subcellular particles of the aleurone layer, whereas calcium is abundant in the pericarp (Bhattacharya and Ali 1985). The conversion of brown rice to white or polished rice removes about 15% of the protein, 65% of the fat and fiber, and 55% of the minerals. Similarly, head rice contains only 20% as much thiamin, 45% as much riboflavin, and 35% as much niacin as brown rice (Pomeranz 1987). These losses have necessitated the development of several practical methods to retain more of the B-vitamins and minerals in the milled rice kernel. This is usually achieved by processing the paddy or rough rice before milling to diffuse the vitamins and other water-soluble nutrients from the outer portion of the grain into the endosperm. The processing of paddy to increase the retention of these nutrients involves parboiling or some modification thereof (Bhattacharya and Ali 1985). A flowchart of various steps involved in the preparation of different kinds of parboiled, expanded, and/or flaked rices is shown in Fig. 1-16. For parboiling, the paddy is soaked in water either at room or at elevated temperatures, then drained, steamed, and dried.

Parboiling improves both the nutrition of rice and its storage and cooking qualities. The major changes include the transfer of some vitamins and minerals from the aleurone and the germ into the starchy endosperm, dispersion of lipids into the endosperm, inactivation of lipolytic enzymes, and the destruction of molds and insects (Bhattacharya and Ali 1985; Gariboldi 1974). These changes are accompanied by reduced chalkiness and increased vitreousness and translucence of the milled parboiled rice. Compared to nonparboiled rices, parboiled rices disintegrate less during cooking and remain better separated and less sticky after cooking. This is mainly due to the reduction of solids leached into the cooking water and the extent to which the kernels solubilize during cooking (Pomeranz 1987).

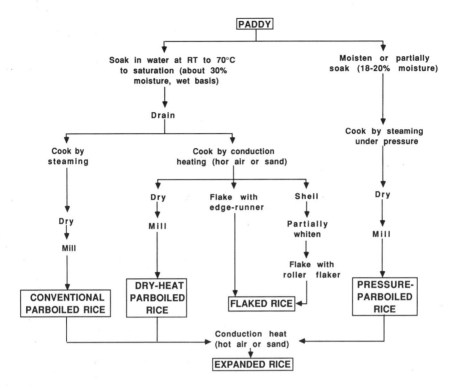

Fig. 1-16. Flowchart showing various processes for the parboiling of rice. *Source:* Bhattacharya and Ali (1985).

Products

The rice milling industry generates considerable amounts of by-products: There is an annual potential of 5 million metric tons of food protein and 6 million MT of edible oil (from rice bran), 256,000 billion kcal as fuel (from husks), and 30,000 billion kcal as metabolizable energy for cattle (from straw) (Pomeranz 1987).

In the United States, rice is classified for marketing purposes into long-, short-, and medium-grain types. Each type is associated with specific cooking and processing behavior. U.S. long-grain varieties cook dry and fluffy, and the cooked grains tend to remain separate. In contrast, the cooked kernels of high-quality medium- and short-grain varieties are more moist and chewy than those of the long-grain varieties, and the kernels tend to cling together. Different ethnic and cultural groups prefer specific and varied textures in home-cooked rice.

The modern trend in processed foods is toward convenience items. Quick-cooking rices may be prepared by precooking in water and then drying under controlled conditions, or by the application of dry heat (Pomeranz 1987). Other convenience items include canned and frozen cooked rice.

As mentioned above (under "Wheat Products"), some breakfast cereals are made from rice.

Corn

Processing

Corn processing is one of the largest food-processing industries in the United States. About three-fifths of the processed corn is used to produce cornstarch, sweeteners, corn oil, and various feed by-products. The remainder is used to prepare various food products and alcoholic beverages.

The milling of corn is centered on the transformation of a basic agricultural product into even more basic fractions for consumption by people and animals. There are two main types of process: dry milling and wet milling.

Dry Milling

Dry milling of corn is carried out both by old-process milling from non-degermed grain and by new-process milling from degermed grain (Pomeranz 1987). In old-process milling, corn is ground to a coarse meal between mill-stones run slowly at a low temperature, with the meal frequently not being sifted. In the larger mills, about 5% of the coarse particles of the hulls are sifted out. The meal is essentially a whole corn product and has a rich oily flavor; the lipids, however, lower its storage stability. In some large mills, the corn is dried to 10–12% moisture before grinding. Kiln drying facilitates rapid grinding and improves the keeping qualities of the meal (Pomeranz 1987).

In new-process milling, steel rolls are used to remove the bran and germ and to recover the endosperm in the form of hominy or corn grits, coarse meal, fine meal, and corn flour. (A flowchart is shown in Fig. 1-17.) The corn is cleaned and passed through a scourer to remove the tip cap from the germ end of the kernel. The hilar layer under the tip is frequently black and causes black specks in the meal. Depending on the variations of the processes, the corn is either un-tempered or tempered by the addition of water to a moisture content of 21–24%. Subsequently, it is passed through a corn degerminator, which frees the bran and germ and breaks the endosperm into two or more pieces. The stock from the degerminator is dried to 14–16% moisture and cooled in revolving or gravity type coolers.

The large endosperm pieces obtained from the first break are used for making corn flakes. The stocks are passed through a hominy separator first to separate the fine particles, and then to grade the larger fragments to various sizes

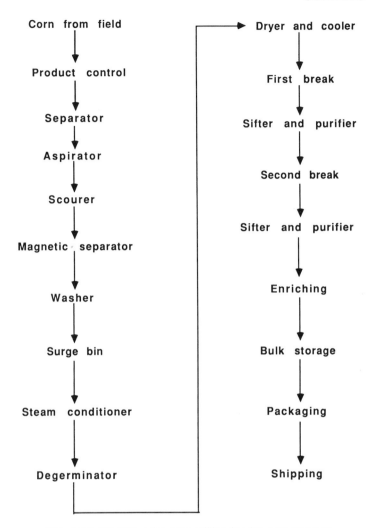

Fig. 1-17. Flowchart for corn milling by the new process.

and polish them. The various grades of broken corn are passed through aspirators to remove the loose bran from the endosperm fragments. These are reduced to coarse, medium, and fine grits by gradual reduction between corrugated rolls and subsequent sifting of the stock. The coarsest stock from the aspirator, which is highly contaminated with germ, goes to the first break rolls. The germ is flattened between the break rolls with minimum endosperm grinding and separated by sieving. The successive steps in the gradual reduction for corn are similar to those used in wheat milling (Pomeranz 1987).

Wet Milling

In the wet-milling process, the clean corn is first softened by steeping in a very dilute solution of SO_2 at 48–52 °C for 30–50 h. For optimum milling and separation of corn components, the corn should have absorbed about 45% water at the end of the steeping period, released about 6.0–6.5% of its dry solids as solubles into the steepwater, absorbed about 0.2–0.4 g SO_2/kg, and become quite soft (Pomeranz 1987). When corn has been optimally steeped, the germ can be removed easily and intact in the degerminating mills. After the removal of germ, the kernels are transported to the grinding mills, where they are broken down in a slurry mixture of starch, gluten protein, and hull. The hulls are removed by specially designed screens to produce a slurry of gluten and starch. This slurry is then sent through a hydrocyclone that separates out a purified cornstarch stream and a gluten feed stream. This entire process lends itself to a continuous operation in the wet-milling plants.

Corn Oil. In the manufacture of corn oil, the germ—the first major fraction isolated in the corn processing—is removed by centrifugation. It is then sent to a continuous screw press where its oil content is reduced from roughly 50% to 20%. In larger commercial processing plants, the remaining 20% residual oil is reduced further by solvent extraction, after which the germ meal contains 1–3% oil. The germ meal is used as an animal feed.

The crude corn oil from the extraction process must be refined further before it is acceptable for use in food products. The undesirable components of the corn oil (free fatty acids, phospholipids, waxes, carotenoids, odors, and flavors) lower the quality of the oil. They are removed during the oil refining process (Fig. 1-18). After refinement, the oil consists of approximately 99% triglycerides, phytosterols, and tocopherols.

Sweeteners. Corn-derived sweeteners are produced by hydrolyzing the starch that has been refined during wet-milling operations. The corn sweeteners produced by the wet-milling industry are very diverse and can range from little or no sweetness to very high levels of sweetness. The characteristics and functional properties of corn syrups vary according to their composition. The simplest means of identifying a syrup is by referring to its dextrose equivalent (DE) value. The DE represents a measurement of the total reducing sugars on a dry solids basis in the syrup, and indicates the level of starch hydrolysis used to produce the product. Based on DE value, corn syrups are classified into four types (Pomeranz 1987):

Type I,   20–38 DE   Type III, 58–73 DE
Type II, 38–58 DE   Type IV,   >73 DE

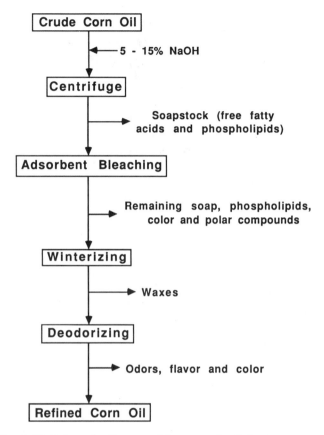

Fig. 1-18. Schematic diagram of the corn oil refining process.

The manufacture of corn sweeteners is a multistep process. There are three commonly used methods for syrup production, with the final type of syrup indicating which method is used (Pomeranz 1987):

1. acid catalyzed hydrolysis (acid conversion),
2. acid-enzyme conversion, and
3. enzyme conversion.

A flowchart of commercial corn syrup production using these three methods is outlined in Fig. 1-19. Each method produces a certain type of syrup with different saccharide distributions that give them their specific qualities.

In the *acid conversion process,* a starch slurry of about 35–40% dry matter is acidified with hydrochloric acid to pH of about 2 and pumped to a converter. Here, the steam pressure is adjusted to 30 psi, and the starch is gelatinized and

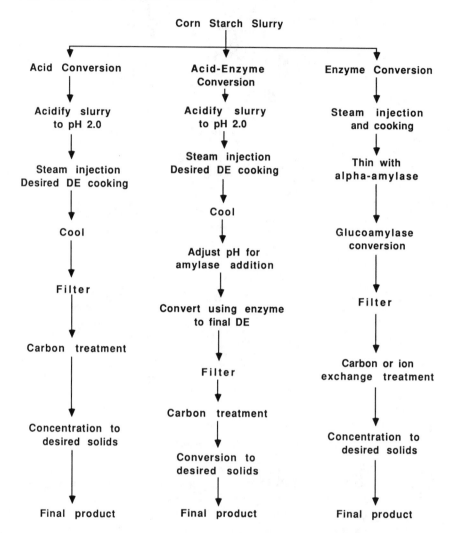

Fig. 1-19. Flowchart for the preparation of corn syrups by various methods.

depolymerized to a predetermined level. The process is ended by adjusting the pH to 4–5 with an alkali. The liquor is clarified by filtration and/or centrifugation, and concentrated by evaporation to ~60% dry matter. The syrup is further clarified and decolorized by activated carbon treatment, and refined by ion-exchange to remove soluble minerals and proteins and to deodorize and decolorize. It is further concentrated in large vacuum pans or continuous evaporators.

In the *acid-enzyme process,* the liquor, containing a partially converted product, is treated with an appropriate enzyme or combination of enzymes to complete the conversion. Thus, in the production of 42-DE high-maltose syrup, acid conversion is carried out until dextrose production is negligible; at this point, β-amylase (a maltose-producing enzyme) is added to complete the conversion. The enzyme is deactivated, and purification and concentration are continued as in the acid process (Fig. 1-19).

In the *enzyme conversion process,* the starch granules are cooked, preliminary starch depolymerization is done by starch-liquefying α-amylase, and the final depolymerization is effected by either a single enzyme or a combination of enzymes. Different enzyme combinations make possible the production of syrups with specific composition and/or properties (e.g., high maltose or high fermentable syrup).

Products

Corn is utilized in several ways as human food: parched to be eaten whole; ground to make hominy, corn meal, or corn flour; treated with alkali to remove the pericarp and germ to make lye hominy; and converted to a variety of breakfast foods (see "Breakfast Cereals" in the discussion of wheat).

Dry Milling

Modern corn mills can produce a variety of grits, meals, and flours. They are dried at 65 °C and cooled before packing. The flattened germs are used to produce corn oil. For such industrial uses as brewing and wallpaper paste manufacture, hominy or grits are flaked: The grits are steamed and passed between heavy-duty heated iron rolls, and the flakes are dried. The heating process gelatinizes the cornstarch.

The relative yields of various products from dry milling of corn depend on whether the main objective is to produce grits or meal and whether the corn was degermed before grinding. In milling corn for grits and meal by the degerminating process, the following average yields are obtained: grits 52%, meal and flour 8%, hominy feed 35%, and crude corn oil 1%. When the corn is not degermed before grinding, about 72% corn meal and 20% feed are produced (Pomeranz 1987). Of the total meal produced, about two-thirds contain 1.4% fat and the rest 4.6% fat. The grits and meal are largely produced from the horny or vitreous endosperm, and they contain less than 1.0% and 1.5% fat, respectively. The flour produced by grinding the starchy endosperm contains 2–3% fat from broken germ during process.

Wet Milling

The main products of corn wet milling are starch (unmodified and modified, including syrups and dextrose) and several coproducts. Cornstarch is a widely used stabilizer in food systems. The preparation, properties, and uses of both modified and unmodified cornstarches have been comprehensively reviewed (Pomeranz 1987). The coproducts of cornstarch wet milling amount to about one-third of the total output. Except for corn oil (which is very bland in flavor and odor and can be used in an assortment of food applications) and steep liquor (condensed corn fermentation extractives, used in industrial fermentations), the coproducts are mainly sold as feed ingredients. In decreasing commercial value, these include corn gluten meal, corn gluten feed, spent germ meal, cornstarch molasses or hydrol, steep liquor, corn bran, and hydrolyzed fatty acids.

In recent years, isomerized corn syrups have become a sizable part of the total production of syrups by the U.S. corn wet-milling industry (Pomeranz 1987). Commercial isomerized corn syrups are clear, bland, sweet, low-viscosity sweeteners high in dextrose (glucose) and fructose (levulose). High-fructose corn syrups (HFCS) are functionally equivalent to liquid invert sugar in most foods and beverages, and can be substituted with little or no change in formulation, processing, or final product. HFCS is prepared by the enzymatic action of glucose isomerase, which isomerizes glucose into fructose. The fructose content in the syrup may be 50% or more, depending on the substrate and the method of preparation; the principal HFCS marketed in the United States contains 42% fructose. HFCS and other corn sweeteners are widely used in bakery products, candy manufacture, and beverages.

Barley

Barley is often consumed as pot barley or pearl barley. They both are manufactured by gradually removing the hull and the outer portions of the barley kernels by abrasive action, although pearl barley is decorticated or pearled to a greater extent: Typically, 100 lb of barley yields 65 lb of pot barley or 35 lb of pearl barley (Pomeranz 1987). Barley flour is a secondary product, and the polishings are a by-product of the pearling process. This flour is milled from barley grain that has been pearled, steamed, and ground to produce a stable product. It is commonly used as a thickener, stabilizer, binder, or protein source for baby foods, malt beverages, prepared meats, and pet foods (Pomeranz 1974). Sometimes, quick-cooking barley is used as a major ingredient in dry soups and as a thickener. Barley flakes are a creamy white, pearled barley that has been steamed and rolled into thin flakes; these provide a less chewy texture than oat flakes and are used in granola products. The various uses of barley and barley products are summarized in Table 1-36.

Since barley produces many hydrolytic enzymes (including large amounts of α- and β-amylase) during malting, it occupies a unique position in the brewing industry. The combination of the two amylases result in a more complete and

Table 1-36. Present Uses of Barley and Barley Products.

Type	Use
Feed	Livestock, poultry
Pearling	Pot barley for soups and dressings; pearled barley for soups and dressings, flour, feed
Milling	Flour for baby foods and food specialties, grits, feed
Malting	Brewed beverages; brewer's grains for dairy feeds; brewer's yeast for animal feed, human food, and fine chemicals; distiller's alcohol or spirits; distiller's solubles or grains for livestock and poultry feeds
Specialty malts	High-dried, dextrin, caramel, or black for breakfast cereals, sugar colorings, dark beers, and coffee substitutes
Export	Malt flour for wheat flour supplements and human and animal food production; malted milk concentrates for malted milk, malted milk beverages, and infant foods; malted syrups for medicinal, textile, baking uses, and for breakfast cereals and candies; malted sprouts for dairy feeds, vinegar manufacture, and industrial fermentations

Source: Phillips and Boerner (1935).

rapid degradation of starch than in malts from most other cereal grains. Two general types of malt are produced commercially: brewer's and distiller's malts. *Brewer's malts* are made from barleys of plumper, heavier kernels with a mellow or friable starch mass. They are steeped and germinated at moisture contents ranging from 43% to 46%, and the final temperature used in drying them to about 4% moisture content is in the 71–82 °C range. The high final drying temperature reduces the enzymatic activities of the malt and the wort made from it and increases the flavor and aroma. *Distiller's* (or *high-diastatic*) *malts* are made from small-kerneled barley high in protein content and enzymatic potential (Pomeranz 1987). The barley is steeped and malted at higher moistures (45–49%) and dried at lower temperatures (49–60 °C) to higher finished moisture contents (5–7%) than is brewer's malt. *Malt sprouts* are the main by-products of barley malting. They are easily separated from the kilned malt by passing the malt through revolving reels of a wire screen, and are mainly used in feed formulation.

Pomeranz (1987) has reviewed the various brewing processes and the associated chemical changes. In a typical brewhouse process, the dried barley malt is milled and then extracted with water ("mashing") in one of two basic ways: In the traditional (and simpler) *infusion mashing process,* the mixed grist and liquor are allowed to stand in a mash tub, and the temperature is gradually raised but kept below the boiling point. In the *decoction method,* a part of the mash is withdrawn, boiled, and returned to the mash tub to raise the temperature of the whole mash. In both processes, the mash passes to a lauter tub with a false bottom. The grain husks deposit on this false bottom and form a filter bed for the subsequent straining of the sugar-rich wort. After the spent grains are separated from the wort, the clear extract (sweet wort) is then boiled with hops, strained, and cooked. Yeast is then added and the whole mixture pumped to settlers. After 10–12 h, it is transferred to fermentation tanks where it remains until the fermentation is completed. The fermented wort is allowed to age and is prefiltered, chill-proofed, filtered, carbonated, and bottled. The bottled or canned beer is either pasteurized or sterilized by ultrafiltration. The main by-products of the brewing process are spent grains, trub (break), spent hops, and yeast. They are mostly used as adjuncts in feed formulations.

Oats

Oat spikelets typically contain two or three kernels: the primary, which is the largest, the somewhat smaller secondary, and the occasional, quite small tertiary. Each kernel has a two-part hull (lemma and palea), which when removed exposes the groat. The groats are milled to provide oatmeal for porridge and oatcake, rolled oats for porridge, oat flour for baby foods, and ready-to-eat breakfast cereals (see "Breakfast Cereals" in the discussion of wheat). Rolled oats and oatmeal are essentially whole-grain products (Doggett 1970; Pomeranz 1987).

The schematics of oat processing are shown in Fig. 1-20. Only high-grade oats are employed in milling. The initial stages include cleaning and drying or slow-roasting of the kernels to reduce their moisture content to about 6%; this increases the brittleness of the hulls, thus facilitating their easy removal. The size-graded oats are then (de)hulled. Most of the oats destined for food are rolled. There are two major types of rolled oats (actually rolled groats): regular (old-fashioned) and quick. Regular rolled oats are made from primary groats. The entire groat is rolled to produce large flakes. These take longer to cook, but have a desirable texture. In contrast, quick-rolled oats are made from secondary or small broken groats. They are steel-cut into two or three pieces and rolled into thinner-than-regular flakes to produce a product that cooks rapidly. In either case, the groats are steamed prior to rolling to inactivate the lipases and precondition the groats for rolling. The medium-quality grade no. 2 white oats yield about 42% good-quality rolled oats, 30% hulls, and 28% other products (including oat shorts, oat middlings, cereal grains, weed seeds and other material removed in the cleaning process) (Pomeranz 1987).

Oat hulls are an important by-product of oat milling. The pentosans in the hulls are used for commercial production of furfural, which is used extensively in the manufacture of phenolic resins and as a solvent (Pomeranz 1987).

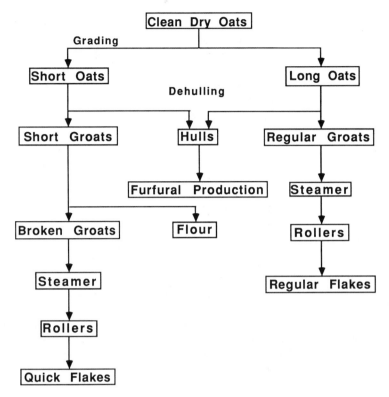

Fig. 1-20. Schematic diagram showing the various steps in oat processing.

Sorghum

Sorghum is often cultivated as a staple food crop in the semiarid agricultural regions, especially of the developing countries, where it serves two purposes: sorghum fodder and stover are used as feed for dairy and farm animals, and the grain is used as human food. In the developed countries, however, it is primarily used for industrial or animal feed purposes. In recent years, sorghum has attracted the attention of researchers because of its potential use in the form of composite flour with wheat (Jadhav and Joglekar 1984). The development of suitable technology to improve the acceptability of sorghum products is essential for popularizing its use and for meeting human nutritional requirements.

Sorghum processing is not fully developed on a commercial scale. Dehusking of the grain is followed only if it is utilized for special food products; however, modern concepts in cereal grain processing can also be used for sorghum.

Nevertheless, household and traditional techniques of sorghum processing that have been followed in African and Asian villages are of considerable importance. They generally involve the use of mortar and pestle and the stone mill. The husk (bran) is removed from the grain by pounding and discarded by winnowing, and the remaining grains are further pounded until the flour is suitable for sieving (Muller 1970; Joglekar and Jadhav 1984). The stone mill consists of two grooved circular stone slabs. The upper slab is manually rotated around a short axle at the center of the lower, stationary slab while grain is periodically fed through the hole on the top of the upper slab. The flour is released around the lower slab. Mechanical grinding of grain sorghum into whole flour is common in India, where it is done in a *chakki,* essentially based on the principle of the traditional stone mill. Grinding of sorghum by these traditional methods, however, results in high losses of important nutrients (Carr 1961).

The conventional dry, roller-milling process can be employed for the preparation of whole and refined sorghum products. Sorghum is harder to grind than wheat, barley, or oats, but slightly easier than corn (Pomeranz 1987). The preliminary operations in dry milling of sorghum involve the removal of impurities such as adhering glumes, broken kernels, chaff, dirt, foreign seeds, sticks, and stones. The addition of moisture to the grain (i.e., conditioning or tempering) prior to milling is a common practice. Preconditioning of the grains offers such advantages as swelling and separation of the germ from the cementing layer of endosperm, toughening of the bran, and mellowing of the endosperm (Larsen 1959). Also enabled are removal of pericarp in large pieces (due to the hydration of cellulose and hemicellulose) and efficient separation of the products with desirable properties. Conditioning also makes the endosperm soft and friable (Joglekar and Jadhav 1984).

In conventional roller milling, the grooved or corrugated rollers break open the grains. The exposed endosperm is then crushed between a series of smooth reduction rollers and freed from the toughened bran. The fine grains are separated by screening, and the coarse fraction is further fed to the next set of rollers after every pass. The bran is generally removed by screening and aspiration. The utility of dry milling largely depends upon the maximum yield of endosperm and the use of germ and bran as valuable by-products. The break flour (10–15% yield) obtained from the first set of rollers is mostly floury endosperm and contains little protein (4.0–4.5% as compared to 8–9% in whole grain) (Pomeranz 1987). The roller-milled flours are sieved to yield products varying in extraction and composition. A product obtained in 70% yield contains 0.5% ash and 0.8% fiber, and is reasonably free of objectionable specks. For the production of high-extraction flours (i.e., 90%), impact grinding is preferred as it requires less space and equipment than the roller-mill system.

Since the sorghum kernel is round, the bran can be removed mechanically by abrasion. Without tempering, a 75–80% yield of almost completely dehulled sorghum can be obtained (Pomeranz 1987). Proper tempering to assist in loosening the hull can increase the yield to 85%. Joglekar and Jadhav (1984) reported that a 15.5% moisture content in the peeled grain is essential for germ removal and further milling. Most polishers or decorticating machines are designed to remove the outer bran layers from the kernel. The sorghum is fed to a cylindrical millstone rotating continuously inside a cylindrical screen. Pearling is continued until adequate amount of bran is removed. The bran is separated from the grain by sifting while fine particles are aspirated.

Peeling of bran layers from sorghum kernels can also be achieved chemically (Pomeranz 1961). A caustic dip (0.25%) of sorghum grain after solvent extraction loosens the seed coat, which is then removed by rinsing and brushing (Thrasher 1950). Barta, Kilpatrick, and Morgan (1966) described another caustic method in which the grains are soaked in 25% sodium hydroxide at 82 °C for several minutes.

Attrition milling has also been used for the dehusking of sorghum grains. De Man et al. (1973) described a Palyi compact attrition mill fitted with sawtooth-blade plates that provide the dehulling action. The grains were further abraded by a drum rotating in a cylindrical screen. Finally, hulls were separated from kernels by an air separator. Most attrition-type dehullers are comprised of two stone or metal disks, either or both of which rotate around a vertical or horizontal axis (Joglekar and Jadhav 1984). The attrition is provided by introducing metal pins or blades into the surface of either or both rotors, or of the rotor and the stator.

Reichert and Young (1976) compared two commercial mills, an abrasive and an attrition type, with a laboratory-type barley pearler for the dehusking of pigmented Nigerian sorghum. They found the abrasive mill (Hill grain thresher) more suitable. The abrasive mill consists of thirteen carborundum stones (12-in. diameter) driven at a speed of up to 200 rpm. In a continuous operation, the grains are fed through a hopper at one end and released after stone action through an overflow outlet at the other end. The amount of kernels removed as fine is determined by the retention time in the mill, which in turn depends upon the grain-feeding rate. The grains are then passed through an air separator on the attrition mill to remove the fines.

Degermination of the dehusked sorghum is essential to obtain products with low lipids for better storage stability. The germ can be removed by passing the dehusked kernel through cracking rolls or impact machines (Pomeranz 1987). The germ separation is then achieved by flattening and sieving, air classification, or by gravity separation. The by-products of sorghum dry milling (bran, germ, and shorts) are used in the production of hominy feed.

Wet-milling processes similar to that of corn have also been used for sorghum processing. However, finer-mesh screens are necessary for efficient operation (Pomeranz 1987). Chemically and microscopically, sorghum starch is similar to cornstarch. Milo starch is blander in flavor and does not develop rancidity. Other products of sorghum wet-milling operations include oil and gluten feeds.

Some sweet sorghum varieties produce large quantities of sugar in the stalks. The pressed juice is boiled to produce a distinctively flavored syrup, which is then used for sugar and alcohol production. Sugar production from sweet sorghum is described in detail in Chapter 4.

Rye

Rye breads are quite popular in Europe and Russia. The quality characteristics of rye with regard to bread production have been comprehensively reviewed by Weipert and Zwingelberg (1980). It is impossible to wash out gluten from a dough made entirely of rye flour; thus rye flour is inferior to wheat flour in yeast-leavened bread. In the United States, most of the so-called rye bread is baked from mixtures of rye and wheat flour (Pomeranz 1987; Webb 1987). Most of the major mills market rye blends made from a mixture of strong spring or hard winter wheat and rye. They roughly follow the pattern of 80% clear and 20% dark rye, 70% clear and 30% medium rye, or 50% clear and 50% white rye.

Pomeranz (1987) has reviewed the technology of rye milling. Rye is milled into flour by a process similar to that of wheat milling. However, because the bran in rye adheres tenaciously to the endosperm, it is not practical to produce clear "middlings" from rye or to purify them by aspiration. Also, if ground between smooth rolls, rye middlings tend to flake or flatten rather than pulverize. The primary objective of rye milling is to produce flour during the breaking process. The break rolls are therefore set relatively close and have finer corrugations than those used for corresponding breaks in milling wheat. The highest grade of flour is produced by the first break rolls. As the purity of the flour decreases, it becomes increasingly dark: The light (white) rye flour represents 50–65% of the grain, the medium flour corresponds to straight-grade wheat flour, and the dark rye flour corresponds to the "clear." Sometimes, "cut" or "stuffed" straights are also produced. The former is a medium rye flour from which a small percentage of white rye flour has been removed; the latter has a small amount of dark rye flour added to it. The milling of rye normally yields 65% light or patent rye, 15–20% dark rye, and 15–20% offal (CIGI 1975; Bushuk 1976).

Millets

Millets are processed and utilized in ways quite similar to sorghum, which are elaborated above.

Buckwheat

Over two-thirds of the buckwheat grain production in the United States and Canada is used as a feed for livestock and poultry; the remainder is milled into buckwheat flour (Pomeranz 1983). Buckwheat flour is usually dark in color due to the presence of hull fragments not removed during the milling process. For this reason, millers prefer Japanese buckwheat, the hulls of which are easier to remove. Buckwheat may be milled either for flour or for groats (hulled grains). Tartary buckwheat is not used for milling because of its darker color and a bitter taste.

Buckwheat flour is primarily used for making buckwheat griddle cakes. It is more commonly marketed as pancake mixes than as pure buckwheat flour. These mixes may contain wheat, corn, rice, or oat flours and a leavening agent (Marshall and Pomeranz 1982). Buckwheat is also used in mixtures with wheat flour for bread, noodles, spaghetti, macaroni, and ready-to-eat breakfast cereals.

Two types of milling process are used for the manufacture of breakfast flour. In one process, the seeds are dehulled and then milled. In the other, the whole seeds are milled and the flour then screened to remove hulls. Rohrlich and Thomas (1967) have described a detailed commercial process for buckwheat milling. The freshly harvested seed is cleaned to remove sand, weeds, small and immature seeds, and other foreign material. The cleaned seeds are then steamed at 145 °C for 5 min and kilned. Steaming is essential to improve the swelling capacity and to reduce the cooking time of the final product. Kilning reduces the moisture content to about 7–8% and facilitates husk removal. After cooling and cold-conditioning, the seeds are separated by sieving into four fractions of various sizes and then dehulled. The dehulled groats are sized, and the hulls and flour are separated by screening. The whole groats are cut and sieved, and the hulls still adhering to them are removed. Buckwheat flour is produced by milling small groat pieces on smooth reduction rolls, similar to those used in wheat milling. As many as four types of flour are produced. These range in protein from 4.7% to 15.9%, in crude fiber from 0.4% to 1.2%, and in ash from 0.6% to 2.2%. High-quality buckwheat yields 60–65% groats and flour, 30% hulls, and 10–12% flour-containing bran. The hulls are an excellent packaging material and a good source of fuel, whereas the bran is used in swine feeding (Pomeranz 1983).

Sobagiri noodles prepared from buckwheat flour are quite popular in Japan. Since buckwheat flour itself is not glutinous, it is usually mixed with wheat flour. The mixture is kneaded into a tight dough, which is then rolled into a thin sheet. The sheet is cut into long, solid strips. The noodles are boiled in water, put into a bamboo basket, and dipped into cold water. The water is swished off the noodles before they are cooked. *Sobagiri* noodles are either used in soups (*kake-soba*) or eaten after being dipped into a thick soy sauce (*mori-soba*).

FUTURE RESEARCH NEEDS

The importance of cereals in nurturing our civilizations cannot be overemphasized. These earliest domesticated plant sources still play the most vital and pivotal role in sustaining our daily lives and our very existence on this planet. In fact, if any of the other food groups were to become unavailable, humankind still could survive and remain tolerably healthy; a failure of cereal crops, however, would bring starvation and malnutrition to most parts of the world.

Global cereal production has increased rapidly during the past three decades. The introduction of new high-yielding genotypes (especially of rice and wheat), the success in developing hybrid varieties of corn and sorghum, and new agronomic practices account for much of the success of the so-called green revolution in many parts of the world. The United States, Canada, the Soviet Union, China, and India together produce over 70% of the world's cereals. Yet, both global environmental and political trends during the past couple of years suggest that their production may decline in the coming few years. The Soviet Union, in the midst of a prolonged drought and a rapidly changing political scene, is expected to become a major importer of cereal grains for the next few years. Similarly, continuous drought conditions during the past five years in vast areas of both the United States and Canada will certainly add to the global shortfall of cereal supply. Agriculture in India still depends on the vagaries of nature. In fact, a failure of monsoon in the Indian subcontinent and the Eastern Hemisphere for two years in a row still has a large ripple effect on the world's food supply and economy. Increased production and loss-reduction technology rather than improved processing will thus continue to dominate research on the cereal front. Some of these research challenges are briefly highlighted below.

Commercial Fertilizers and Biological Nitrogen Fixation

Unlike legumes, which are partially self-sufficient through symbiotic N_2 fixation, cereals primarily rely on commercial nitrogen sources of manures and fertilizers for their growth. In fact, it is the single most important economic constraint in cereal production. Continuous increase in global cereal production no doubt will depend on a sustained economic supply of commercial nitrogen fertilizers. Nevertheless, several bacteria and blue-green algae are capable of fixing atmospheric nitrogen in cereal fields. Although cereal–bacteria associations contribute significantly to the overall nitrogen economy of the plants, the actual contribution of N_2 fixation in cereal crops is not known. However, at least in the foreseeable future, it is unlikely that biological nitrogen fixation alone would satisfy all the nitrogen requirements of the high-yielding cereal genotypes.

Fertilizers are the most important industrial inputs into modern agricultural production systems, accounting for about one-third of the total energy input.

They also account for about the same degree of increase in the total crop productivity achieved during the past three decades. Fertilizer management under field conditions will therefore be of increasing importance in the coming years. For example, nitrogen fertilizer inputs exceed over $1 billion annually in the United States for corn alone. Yet only 50% of the nitrogen and less than 35% of the phosphorus and potassium applied as fertilizers in the United States are recovered by crops (Wittwer 1980). In contrast, the recovery of fertilizer nitrogen in the rice paddies of the tropics is only 25–35%, the balance being lost to the environment. Worldwide, about 12–15 million metric tons of nitrogen fertilizers are lost to denitrification alone. Both natural and synthetic nitrification inhibitors, which could be applied with ammonia or urea to effectively deter leaching and atmospheric losses of nitrogen, must be expeditiously researched on a global scale to preserve our ever-depleting natural hydrocarbon resources. Since denitrification occurs only under anaerobic soil conditions, such research should go hand in hand with newer and better soil compaction methods, improved drainage, use of soil-improving crops, and careful attention to irrigation procedures.

Foliar application of fertilizer has long been declared the most efficient method of fertilizer placement (Wittwer and Bukovac 1969), yet technology of application on a large scale is still lacking. Future yield barriers may well be broken up, by utilizing the absorptive capacity of leaves and roots, for applying nutrients at crucial stages of development. Although research results in this area are not very encouraging, the rising costs of fertilizer and its nonrenewable resource requirement should be continuing stimuli for further developments of this technology.

Although improved technologies of fertilizer nitrogen production and increased efficiency of fertilizer use by plants could make more nitrogen available for the plants, alternative technologies must be developed to lessen the dependence of plants on fertilizer nitrogen. In fact, development of high-yielding cereal genotypes that are also self-sufficient in their nitrogen requirements may indeed prove to be the most crucial breakthrough in the years ahead. The possible transfer of nitrogen-fixing (*nif*) genes from free-living bacteria such as *Klebsiella* to higher plants has been proposed quite frequently in recent years. There have been rapid advances made in understanding the seventeen *nif* genes in nitrogen-fixing bacteria, particularly their order, gene products, and regulation of expression (Roberts and Brill 1981), but complications do arise in their transfer and expression in higher plants. Nitrogenases that catalyze the ATP-dependent six-electron reduction of dinitrogen (N_2) to ammonia are oxygen-labile. This fact is circumvented in *Azotobacter* by rapid respiration to reduce oxygen tension, and by the presence of leghemoglobin in *Rhizobium* nodules, which facilitates oxygen diffusion to bacteroids without inactivating the enzyme. Therefore, all efforts of transferring the genes to higher plants should include some methods for the protection of the nitrogenase enzyme system. In addition, extra host genes will be required to assimilate and transport the ammonia produced during this process. The bacterial gene control sequences may also have to be modified for the expression in higher plants. Newer biotechnological approaches of gene transfer will undoubtedly offer some solutions in this regard in the years to come.

Interspecific Gene Transfer

Genetic improvement by conventional plant breeding techniques accounts for at least half of the increased productivity of the high-yielding cereal genotypes. Breeding for specific traits, such as resistance to pests and diseases and other quality characteristics desirable in cereals, has also made considerable progress over the past few decades. In fact, one of the major reasons for the vast increase in global wheat production is due to the transfer of rust resistance to wheat genotypes from its wild relatives. Conventional plant breeding techniques, however, are time consuming, and their success is limited due to the natural barriers of cross incompatibility between species that restrict the possibility of combining genomes and the transfer of desired traits from one species to another. Recent advances in gene manipulation and interspecific gene transfer technology will prove quite useful in effecting transfer of desired genes from wild species into related cultivars, as also between different species. These techniques will also be useful in enhancing the nutritional quality of cereal proteins by breeding for high-lysine genotypes. Such approaches as microinjection of DNA into plant cells, injection of genetic material into plants, the use of pollen and embryos for DNA uptake, and *Agrobacterium-* and viral-based vector systems have been suggested and tried under laboratory conditions for gene transfer applicable to cereals. We may have, in the not too distant future, genetically improved species and genotypes for crop production.

Breeding for Drought and Salinity Tolerance

Two other areas will require our continuing attention and research efforts in plant breeding: development of drought- and salinity-tolerant cultivars. We need to expand our data base regarding underlying drought-tolerant mechanisms and their influence on crop productivity. Much of our agriculture still depends on annual rainfall. To maintain a sustained level of cereal production, we must identify traits that will allow crops to grow under water-stressed environments and yet maintain a high level of productivity. Genetic links, if any, need to be established in this regard.

The reckless use of irrigation water in several parts of the world has created hitherto unknown problems. Salt levels in irrigated soils have been continually rising, making vast areas of fertile lands unavailable for economic crop production. Improvements in irrigation systems and techniques are required to minimize this problem. For soils that already have high levels of salinity and alkalinity, genotypes must be developed that are tolerant to these conditions.

Photorespiration and Photosynthesis

Great challenges lie ahead in developing varieties of cereals having low photorespiration and in the formulation of chemicals that will modify plant architecture and increase photosynthesis. In no research area are the opportunities more attractive and the potentials greater for achieving results, reflected in increased crop productivity, than in maximization of the photosynthetic process. Photosynthesis still remains the most important biochemical energy-producing process on earth. The greatest challenge we face in food-producing systems today is how to manipulate plants under varying environmental conditions to maximize this energy conversion process. The importance of building a stock of plants for agricultural purposes with the C-4 pathway in photosynthesis has long been recognized. Thus far, this approach has been notably unsuccessful. Of the larger research investments allocated to a better understanding of the photosynthetic process, there has been little payoff with food crops under field conditions. Nevertheless, there are some specific examples of photosynthesis enhancement. The new, short, stiff-strawed rice varieties have a higher proportion of grain to plant. The short, erect leaves capture light more efficiently and have better light-receiving systems in the the densely planted, heavily fertilized, tropical rice paddies.

The feasibility of transferring the different photosynthetic pathways from one species to another has been demonstrated, although not to date in crop plants. The prospects for achieving this through genetic engineering are also distant due to the large number of genes that need to be transferred. Nevertheless, the practical benefits to be derived from progress in this field suggest that such research is worthy of our greater attention in the decade ahead.

Research on the physiological mechanisms that control growth and ultimate size of the individual plant and its potential for economic yield also needs to be expedited. Over 90% of the dry weight of a plant is the net product of photosynthesis. A plant is limited by time in the amount of assimilate it can produce. Both environmental factors and agronomic practices significantly influence the partitioning of photosynthates and the subsequent dry-matter accumulation. Continuing interdisciplinary research is needed to understand the complex interrelationships among the mechanisms that control plant growth, development, and partitioning of photosynthates, so as to develop techniques and guidelines for improved management practices and select for increased economic yield of cereal crops.

Pre- and Postharvest Losses

In spite of the best pest control and management practices, preharvest losses in cereals generally exceed 20% in the developed countries. World crop losses to pests and diseases amount to over 35%. High-yielding genotypes of cereals are generally more susceptible to pests and diseases than were their old counterparts. Reliance on pesticides as the single line of defense during the past two decades has now introduced several new problems of pesticide resistance, destruction of natural enemies, outbreaks of secondary pests, reductions in pollinators, potential environmental and groundwater contamination, and health hazards. To circumvent these problems, research on integrated pest management techniques should be expedited. Similarly the tremendous losses (up to 50% of total grain production) that occur during the storage and handling of cereals, particularly in the developing countries, need to be minimized. In this regard, particular attention must be paid to developing the necessary infrastructure to handle the yield increases achieved in cereal production in tropical developing countries. If such losses are eliminated through improved storage, postharvest handling, and prompt processing, the world food supply could be increased by at least 30–40% without bringing any additional land under cultivation or incurring any expensive inputs.

With regard to processing, a major improvement may be expected in the Western countries to expand the uses of cereal grains in traditional ethnic foods for local markets. A greater reliance would certainly be placed on making the various cereal processing operations more energy efficient. Computer-aided technologies will play a key role in both process management and quality control. In contrast, most efforts in this regard in the developing countries should be aimed at formulating technologies that suit given environments, are cost effective, use indigenous energy resources, and take into consideration local food habits and customs. Wherever possible, industries should be established to process food crops for export markets—not only to earn the valuable foreign exchange that most developing countries need, but also to utilize the vast, untapped labor pool that is frequently found in these regions.

REFERENCES

Abrantes, G. T. V., Day, J. M., and Dobereiner, J. 1975. *Bull. Int. Inf. Biol. Sol.,* Lyon no. 21 (cited by Neyra and Dobereiner [1977]).

Ahrens, J. F., and Loomis, W. E. 1963. Floral induction and development in winter wheat. *Crop Sci.* 3:463–6.

Alexander, M. 1985. Enhancing nitrogen fixation by use of pesticides: A review. *Adv. Agron.* 38:267–82.

Allaby, M., Blythe, C., Hines, C., and Wardle, C. 1975. *Losing Ground.* London: Earth Resources Research Ltd.

Averill, H. P., and King, C. G. 1926. The phytin content of food stuffs. *J. Am. Chem. Soc.* 48:724–8.

Barber, L. E., Russell, S. A., and Evans, H. J. 1979. Inoculation of millet with *Azospirillum. Plant Soil* 52:49–57.

Barber, L. E., Tjepkema, J. D., and Evans, H. J. 1976. *Environmental Role of Nitrogen-Fixing Blue-Green Algae and Asymbiotic Bacteria.* Int. Symp., Uppsala, Sweden.

Barley, K. P., and Naidu, N. A. 1964. The performance of three Australian wheat varieties at high levels of nitrogen supply. *Aust. J. Exp. Agric. Anim. Husb.* 4:39–48.

Barta, E. J., Kilpatrick, P. W., and Morgan, A. J. 1966. Methods of peeling wheat. U.S. Patent no. 3,264,113, August 2.

Bartles, D., and Thompson, R. 1983. The characterization of cDNA clones coding for wheat storage proteins. *Nucleic Acids Res.* 11:2961–77.

Bechtel, D. B., and Pomeranz, Y. 1980. The rice kernel. *Adv. Cereal Sci. Technol.* 3:73–93.

Begg, J. E., and Turner, N. C. 1976. Crop water deficits. *Adv. Agron.* 28:161–217.

Bhattacharya, K. R., and Ali, Z. A. 1985. Changes in rice during parboiling and properties of parboiled rice. *Adv. Cereal Sci. Technol.* 7:105–68.

Bidwell, R. G. S. 1979. *Plant Physiology.* New York: Macmillan.

Borlaug, N. E. 1974. The destiny of man and world civilization. *Second Lecture of the Gov. Winthrop Rockefeller Distinguished Lecture Series,* Univ. of Arkansas at Little Rock, January 29.

Brandt, A. 1979. Cloning of double stranded DNA coding for hordein polypeptides. *Carlsburg Res. Commun.* 44:255–67.

Bressani, R. 1975. Legumes in human diets and how they might be improved. In *Nutritional Improvement of Food Legumes by Breeding,* ed. M. Milner, pp. 15–42. New York: Wiley.

Bressani, R., and Mertz, E. T. 1958. Studies on corn proteins. Protein and amino acid content of different corn varieties. *Cereal Chem.* 35:227–34.

Briggle, L. W. and Reitz, L. P. 1963. *Classification of Triticum Species and of Wheat Varieties Grown in the United States.* USDA Tech. Bull. no. 1278. Washington, D.C.: USDA.

Brill, W. J. 1975. Regulation and genetics of bacterial nitrogen fixation. *Annu. Rev. Microbiol.* 29:109–29.

Brouk, B. 1975. *Plants Consumed by Man.* London: Academic Press.

Brown, R. H., Bouton, J. H., Evans, P. T., Malter, H. E., and Rigsby, L. L. 1985. Photosynthesis, morphology, leaf anatomy and cytogenetics of hybrids between C_3 and C_3/C_4 *Panicum* species. *Plant Physiol.* 77:653–8.

Burger, W. C. 1982. Barley. In *Handbook of Processing and Utilization in Agriculture, vol. II, pt. I. Plant Products,* ed. I. A. Wolff, pp. 187–222. Boca Raton: CRC Press.

Burr, B., Burr, F. A., St. John, T. P., Thomas, M., and Davis, R. W. 1982. Zein storage protein gene family of maize. *J. Mol. Biol.* 154:33–49.

Bushuk, W. 1976. *Rye: Production, Chemistry, Technology.* St. Paul: Am. Assoc. Cereal Chem.

Caloin, M., Khodre, E. A., and Atry, M. 1980. Effect of nitrate concentration on the root: shoot ratio in *Dactylis glomerata* L. and on the kinetics of growth in the vegetative phase. *Ann. Bot. (London) [n.s.]* 46:165–73.

Carr, W. R. 1961. Observations on the nutritive value of traditionally ground cereals in Southern Rhodesia. *Brit. J. Nutr.* 15:339–43.

Cauderon, Y. 1978. *Interspecific Hybridization and Plant Breeding.* Proc. 8th Congr. EUCARPIA, Madrid, Spain.

Chandler, R. F. 1979. *Rice in the Tropics. A Guide to the Development of National Programs.* Boulder: Westview Press.

Chang, J. H. 1968. *Climate and Agriculture.* Chicago: Aldine.

Chang, T. T., and Oka, H. I. 1976. *Climate and Rice.* Los Banos (Philippines): Int. Rice Res. Inst.

Chollet, R., and Ogren, W. 1975. Regulation of photorespiration in C_3 and C_4 species. *Bot. Rev.* 41:137–79.

CIGI. 1975. *Grains and Oilseeds: Handling, Marketing, Processing,* 2nd ed. Winnipeg: Canadian International Grains Institute.

Cooper, J. P. 1975. *Photosynthesis and Productivity in Different Environments.* Cambridge: Cambridge Univ. Press.

Croy, R. R. D., and Gatehouse, J. A. 1985. Genetic engineering of seed proteins: Current and potential applications. In *Plant Genetic Engineering,* ed. J. H. Dodds, pp. 143–268. Cambridge: Cambridge Univ. Press.

D'Appolonia, B. L. 1987. Factors involved in the quality of bread wheats. In *Cereals and Legumes in the Food Supply,* ed. J. DuPont and E. M. Osman, pp. 121–6. Ames: Iowa State Univ. Press.

Davidson, R. H., and Lyon, W. F. 1987. *Insect Pests of Farm, Garden and Orchard.* New York: Wiley.

Day, J. M., Neaves, M. C. P., and Dobereiner, J. 1975. Nitrogenase activity on the roots of tropical forage grasses. *Soil Biol. Biochem.* 7:107–12.

De Boland, A., Garner, G. B., and O'Dell, B. L. 1975. Identification and properties of phytate in cereal grains and oilseed products. *J. Agric. Food Chem.* 23:1186–9.

De Bont, J. A. M., and Mulder, E. G. 1976. Invalidity of the acetylene production assay in alkane-utilizing, nitrogen-fixing bacteria. *Appl. Environ. Microbiol.* 31:640–7.

De La Pena, A., Lorz, H., and Schell, J. 1987. Transgenic rye plants obtained by injecting DNA into young floral tillers. *Nature* 325:274–6.

de Man, J. M., Banigo, E. O. I., Rasper, V., Gade, H., and Slinger, S. J. 1973. Dehulling of sorghum and millet with the Palyi compact milling system. *Can. Inst. Food Sci. Technol. J.* 6:188–93.

de Wet, J. M. J., Begquist, R. R., Harlan, J. R., Brink, D. E., Cohen, C. C., NeWell, C. A., and de Wet, A. E. 1985. Exogenous gene transfer in maize (*Zea mays*) using DNA-treated polled. In *Experimental Manipulation of Ovule Tissues,* ed. G. P. Chapman, S. H. Mantell, and R. W. Daniels, pp. 197–209. London: Academic Press.

de Wet, J. M. J., and Harlan, J. R. 1971. The origin and domestication of *Sorghum bicolor. Econ. Bot.* 25:128–35.

Deshpande, S. S., Cheryan, M., and Salunkhe, D. K. 1986. Tannin analysis of food products. *CRC Crit. Rev. Food Sci. Nutr.* 24:401–49.

Deshpande, S. S., and Damodaran, S. 1990. Food legumes: Chemistry and technology. *Adv. Cereal Sci. Technol.* 10:147–241.

Deshpande, S. S., Sathe, S. K., and Salunkhe, D. K. 1984. Chemistry and safety of plant polyphenols. In *Nutritional and Metabolic Aspects of Food Safety,* ed. M. Friedman, pp. 457–95. New York: Plenum.

Dewey, D. R. 1977. A method of transferring genes from tetraploid to diploid crested wheatgrass. *Crop Sci.* 17:803–5.

Dobereiner, J. 1970. Zentralbl bakteriol parasitend infektionskr. *Hyg. Abt.* 2 124:224–30.

Dobereiner, J. 1973. *Fellow Report.* Sussex Univ., Sussex, England.

Dobereiner, J., Marriel, I. E., and Nery, M. 1976. Ecological distribution of *Spirillum lipoferum* Beijerinck. *Can. J. Microbiol.* 22:1464–73.

Doggett, H. 1970. *Sorghum.* London: Longmans, Green and Co.

Donald, C. M. 1963. Competition among crop and pasture plants. *Adv. Agron.* 15:1–118.

Donald, C. M., and Hamblin, J. 1976. The biological yield and harvest index of cereals as agronomic and plant breeding criteria. *Adv. Agron.* 28:361–405.

Donald, C. M., and Hamblin, J. 1983. The convergent evolution of annual seed crops in agriculture. *Adv. Agron.* 36:97–143.

Downes, R. W. 1971. Relationship between evolutionary adaptation and gas exchange characteristics of diverse *Sorghum* taxa. *Aust. J. Biol. Sci.* 24:843–52.

Downey, L. A. 1971. Effect of gypsum and drought stress on maize (*Zea mays* L.). I. Growth, light absorption and yield. *Agron. J.* 63:569–72.

Dunstone, R. L., Gifford, R. M., and Evans, L. T. 1973. Photosynthetic characteristics of modern and primitive wheat species in relation to aontogeny and adaptation to light. *Aust. J. Biol. Sci.* 26:295–307.

DuPont, J., and Osman, E. M. 1987. *Cereals and Legumes in the Food Supply.* Ames: Iowa State Univ. Press.

Dyck, P. L., and Kerber, E. R. 1970. Inheritance in hexaploid wheat of adult-plant leaf rust resistance derived from *Aegilops squarrosa. Can. J. Genet. Cytol.* 12:175–80.

El Sharkawy, M. A., and Hesketh, J. D. 1964. Effects of temperature and water deficit on leaf photosynthetic rates of different species. *Crop Sci.* 4:514–18.

El Sharkawy, M. A., and Hesketh, J. D. 1965. Photosynthesis among species in relation to characteristics of leaf anatomy and CO_2 diffusion resistances. *Crop Sci.* 5:517–21.

Enyi, B. A. L. 1968. Comparative studies of upland and swamp rice varieties (*Oryza sativa* L.). *J. Agric. Sci. (Camb.)* 71:1–13.

Esmay, M. L., Soemangat, E., and Phillips, A. 1979. *Rice: Postproduction Technology in the Tropics.* Honolulu: East–West Center Univ. Press.

Evans, L. T. 1975. *Crop Physiology.* Cambridge: Cambridge Univ. Press.

Evans, L. T., and Dunstone, R. L. 1970. Some physiological aspects of evolution in wheat. *Aust. J. Biol. Sci.* 23:725–41.

Evans, L. T., and Wardlaw, I. F. 1976. Aspects of the comparative physiology of grain yield in cereals. *Adv. Agron.* 28:301–58.

Fairbourn, M. L., Kemper, W. D., and Gardner, H. R. 1970. Effects of row spacing on evapotranspiration and yields of corn in a semi-arid environment. *Agron. J.* 62:795–7.

FAO. 1981. *Agriculture Towards 2000.* Rome: Food and Agriculture Organization.

FAO. 1988. *Production Yearbook.* Rome: Food and Agriculture Organization.

Fehar, W. R., and Hadley, H. H. 1980. *Hybridization of Crop Plants.* Madison: Am. Soc. Agron. and Crop Sci. Soc. Am.

Fischer, K. S., and Wilson, G. L. 1975. Studies of grain production in *Sorghum bicolor* L. Moench grain growth capacity and transport system. *Aust. J. Agric. Res.* 26:11–23.

Fischer, R. A., and Maurer, R. 1978. Drought resistance in spring wheat cultivars. I. Grain yield responses. *Aust. J. Agric. Res.* 29:277–317.

Flood, R. G., and Halloran, G. M. 1986. Genetics and physiology of vernalization response in wheat. *Adv. Agron.* 39:87–125.

Forde, B. G., Kreis, M., Bahramian, M. B., Matthews, J. A., and Miflin, B. J. 1981. Molecular cloning and analysis of cDNA sequences derived from poly A^+ RNA from barley endosperm: Identification of B-hordein related clones. *Nucleic Acids Res.* 9:6689–707.

Frey, K. J. 1984. Breeding approaches for increasing crop yields. In *Cereal Production,* ed. E. J. Gallagher, pp. 47–68. London: Butterworths.

Gallagher, E. J. 1982. *Cereal Production.* London: Butterworths.

Gariboldi, F. 1974. *Rice Parboiling.* FAO Agric. Dev. Paper no. 97. Rome: Food and Agriculture Organization.

Gerakis, P. A., and Tsangarakis, C. Z. 1969. Response of sorghum, sesame and groundnuts to plant population density in the Central Sudan. *Agron. J.* 61:872–5.

Gifford, R. M., and Evans, L. T. 1981. Photosynthesis, carbon partitioning and yield. *Annu. Rev. Plant Physiol.* 32:485–509.

Gifford, R. M., and Musgrave, R. B. 1973. Stomatal role in the variability of net CO_2 exchange rates by two maize inbreds. *Aust. J. Biol. Sci.* 26:35–44.

Gill, B. S., and Raupp, W. J. 1987. Direct genetic transfers from *Aegilops squarrosa* L. to hexaploid wheat. *Crop Sci.* 27:445–50.

Gill, R. S., Multani, D. S., and Dhaliwal, H. S. 1986. *Crop Improv.* 13:200–3 (cited by Singh, Moss, and Smartt [1990]).

Gobel, E., and Lorz, H. 1988. Genetic manipulation of cereals. *Oxford Surveys of Plant Molecular Biology* 5:1–22.

Gordonkamm, W. J., Spencer, T. M., Mangano, M. L., Adams, T. R., Daines, R. J., Start, W. G., O'Brien, J. V., Chambers, S. A., Adams, W. R., and Willetts, N. G. 1990. Transformation of maize cells and regeneration of fertile transgenic plants. *Plant Cell* 2:603–18.

Gregory, F. G., and Purvis, O. N. 1948. Reversal of vernalization by high temperature. *Nature* 161:859–60.

Grimsley, N., Nohn, T., Davies, J. W., and Hohn, B. 1987. Agrobacterium-mediated oblinery of infectious maize streak virus into maize plants. *Nature* 325:172–9.

Gupta, P. K., and Bahl, J. R. 1985. *Advances in Genetics and Crop Improvement.* Meerut (India): Rastogi.

Hanson, A. A. 1990. *Practical Handbook of Agricultural Science.* Boca Raton: CRC Press.

Hanway, J. J., and Russell, W. A. 1969. Dry matter accumulation in corn (*Zea mays* L.) plants: Comparisons among single-cross hybrids. *Agron. J.* 61:947–51.

Harlan, J. R. 1971. Agricultural origins: Centers and non-centers. *Science* 174:468–74.

Harlan, J. R., and de Wet, J. M. J. 1971. Toward a rational classification of cultivated plants. *Taxon.* 20:509–17.

Harlan, J. R., and Zohary, D. 1966. Distribution of wild wheats and barleys. *Science* 153:1074–80.

Hatch, M. D., Osmond, C. B., and Slatyer, R. O. 1971. *Photosynthesis and Photorespiration.* New York: Wiley.

Hayes, J. D. 1968. *Annual Report.* Welsh Plant Breeding Stn., Aberystwyth, Wales.

Hesketh, J. D. 1963. Limitations to photosynthesis responsible for differences among species. *Crop Sci.* 3:493–6.

Hesketh, J. D., and Musgrave, R. B. 1962. Photosynthesis under field conditions. IV. Light studies with individual corn leaves. *Crop Sci.* 2:311–15.

Hill, D. S. 1983. *Agricultural Insect Pests of the Tropics and Their Control.* Cambridge: Cambridge Univ. Press.

Hofstra, G., and Hesketh, J. D. 1969. Effects of temperature on the gas exchange of leaves in the light and dark. *Planta* 85:228–37.

Holaday, A. S., Talkmitt, S., and Doohan, M. E. 1985. Anatomical and enzymic studies of leaves of a $C_3 \times C_4$ Flaveria F_1 hybrid exhibiting reduced photorespiration. *Plant Sci.* 41:31–9.

Holmes, W. 1971. Efficiency of food production by the animal industries. In *Potential Crop Production*, ed. P. F. Waareing and J. P. Cooper, pp. 31–59. London: Heinemann Educational Books.

Hopkins, D. T. 1981. *Protein Quality in Humans: Assessment and Evaluation.* Westport: AVI Publ. Co.

ICAR. 1988. *Handbook of Agriculture.* New Delhi: Indian Council of Agriculture Research.

Inglett, G. E. 1970. *Corn Culture, Processing and Products.* Westport: AVI Publ. Co.

Inglett, G. E. 1979. *Tropical Foods*, vols. 1 and 2. New York: Academic Press.

IRRI. 1982. *Annual Report.* Los Banos (Philippines): Int. Rice Res. Inst.

IRRI. 1983. *Annual Report.* Los Banos (Philippines): Int. Rice Res. Inst.

Jadhav, S. J., and Joglekar, N. V. 1984. Traditional processing of sorghum in India. In *Nutritional and Processing of Grain Sorghum*, ed. D. K. Salunkhe, J. K. Chavan, and S. J. Jadhav, pp. 129–39. New Delhi: Oxford and IBH Publ. Co.

Javornik, B. and Kreft, I. 1980. Structure of buckwheat kernel. In *Buckwheat: Genetics, Plant Breeding and Utilization*, ed. I. Kreft, B. Javornik, and B. Dolinsek, pp. 105–13. Ljubljana (Yugoslavia): VTOZD za Agronomijo Biotehniske Fakultete.

Jeanings, P. R., and de Jesus, J. 1968. Studies on competition in rice. I. Competition in mixtures of varieties. *Evolution* 22:119–24.

Jenkinson, D. S. 1973. Organic matter and nitrogen in soils of the Rothamsted classical experiments. *J. Sci. Food Agric.* 24:1149–50.

Joglekar, N. V., and Jadhav, S. J. 1984. Dry milling of grain sorghum. In *Nutritional and Processing Quality of Sorghum*. D. K. Salunkhe, J. K. Chavan, and S. J. Jadhav (ed.), pp. 140–55. New Delhi: Oxford and IBH Publ. Co.

Jones, D. G., and Clifford, B. C. 1979. *Cereal Diseases: Their Pathology and Control*. England: BASF Perivan Press Ltd.

Jung, G. A. 1978. *Crop Tolerance to Suboptimal Land Conditions*. Madison: Am. Soc. Agron.

Junker, B., Zimmy, J., Luhrs, R., and Lorz, H. 1987. Transformation experiments of chimaeric genes in dividing and non-dividing cereal protoplasts after PEG-induced DNA uptake. *Plant Cell Reports* 6:329–32.

Kent, N. L. 1983. *Technology of Cereals*. Oxford: Pergamon Press.

Kerber, E. R., and Dyck, P. L. 1969. Inheritance in hexaploid wheat of leaf rust resistance and other characteristics derived from *Aegilops squarrosa*. *Can. J. Genet. Cytol.* 11:639–47.

Knott, D. R. 1961. The inheritance of rust resistance. VI. The transfer of stem rust resistance from *Agropyron elongatum* to common wheat. *Can. J. Plant Sci.* 41:109–23.

Kummer, M. 1984. *Tagungsber. Akad. Landwirtschaftswiss. Dtsch. Dem. Repub.* 225:191–9 (cited by Singh, Moss, and Smartt [1990]).

Langer, R. H. M., and Hill, G. D. 1982. *Agricultural Plants*. Cambridge: Cambridge Univ. Press.

Larsen, R. A. 1959. Milling. In *The Chemistry and Technology of Cereals as Food and Feed*, ed. S. A. Matz, pp. 69–112. Westport: AVI Publ. Co.

Larson, R. I., and Neal, J. L. 1976. *Environmental Role of Nitrogen-Fixing Blue-Green Algae and Asymbiotic Bacteria*, Int. Symp., Uppsala, Sweden.

Lasztity, L. 1988. Phytic acid in foods. D.Sc. thesis, Academy of Sciences, Budapest, Hungary.

Lasztity, R., and Lasztity, L. 1990. Phytic acid in cereal technology. *Adv. Cereal Sci. Technol.* 10:309–71.

Lawande, K. M., and Adsule, R. N. 1985. Wheat milling. In *Quality of Wheat and Wheat Products*, ed. D. K. Salunkhe, S. S. Kadam, and A. Austin, pp. 205–19. New Delhi: Metropolitan Book Co.

Levitt, J. 1980. *Responses of Plants to Environmental Stresses*, 2nd ed., vol. 2. New York: Academic Press.

Lockhart, H. B., and Nesheim, R. O. 1978. Nutritional quality of cereal grains. In *Cereals '78: Better Nutrition for the World's Millions*, ed. Y. Pomeranz, pp. 201–22. St. Paul: Am. Assoc. Cereal Chem.

Lolas, G. M., Palamidis, N., and Markakis, P. 1976. The phytic acid–total phosphorus relationship in barley, oats, soybeans and wheat. *Cereal Chem.* 53:867–71.

Lorenz, K. 1982. Rye: Utilization and processing. In *Handbook of Processing and Utilization in Agriculture, vol. II, pt.1. Plant Products*, ed. A. Wolff, pp. 243–58. Boca Raton: CRC Press.

Lorenz, K. 1983. Tannins and phytate content of proso millets (*Panicum miliaceum*). *Cereal Chem.* 53:867–71.

Lorz, H., Baker, J. B., and Schell, J. 1985. Gene transfer to cereal cells mediated by protoplasts transformation. *Mol. Gen. Genet.* 199:178–82.

Lucas, G. B., Campbell, C. L., and Lucas, L. T. 1985. *Introduction to Plant Diseases: Identification and Management.* Westport: AVI Publ. Co.

Ludlow, M. M., and Muchow, R. C. 1990. A critical evaluation of traits for improving crop yields in water-limited environments. *Adv. Agron.* 43:107–53.

Luebs, R. E., and Laag, A. E. 1969. Evapotranspiration and water stress of barley with increased nitrogen. *Agron. J.* 61:921–4.

Luthra, O. P., and Dawari, N. H. 1979. Relationship of harvest index with yield and its components in wheat (*Triticum aestivum* L.). *Haryana Agric. Univ. J. Res.* 9:36–42.

McCance, R. A., and Widdowson, E. M. 1935. Phytin in human nutrition. *Biochem. J.* 298:2694–9.

McCree, K. J. 1974. Equations for the rate of dark respiration of white clover and grain sorghum as functions of dry weight, photosynthetic rate and temperature. *Crop Sci.* 14:509–14.

McEwen, F. L. 1978. Food production: The challenge for pesticides. *BioScience* 28:773–7.

MacLean, W. C., Lopez, G. de Romana, Placko, R. P., and Graham, G. G. 1982. Nutritional value of sorghum in preschool children: Digestibility, utilization and plasma free amino acids. *Proc. Int. Symp. Sorghum Quality.* Patancheru (India): ICRISAT.

MacMasters, M. M., Hinton, J. J. C., and Bradbury, D. 1972. Microscopic structure and composition of the wheat kernel. In *Wheat: Chemistry and Technology,* 2nd ed., ed. Y. Pomeranz, pp. 51–113. St. Paul: Am. Assoc. Cereal Chem.

McPherson, H. G., and Slatyer, R. O. 1973. Mechanisms regulating photosynthesis in *Pennisetum typhoides*. *Aust. J. Biol. Sci.* 26:324–39.

Marshall, H. G. 1969. *Description and Culture of Buckwheat.* Penn. State Univ. Coll. Agric., Agr. Exp. Stn. Bull. no. 754, 26 pp.

Marshall, H. G., and Pomeranz, Y. 1982. Buckwheat: Description, breeding, production and utilization. *Adv. Cereal Sci. Technol.* 5:157–210.

Martin, J. H., and Leonard, W. H. 1967. *Principles of Field Crop Production,* 2nd ed. New York: Macmillan.

Mattern, P. J., Schmidt, J. W., and Johnson, V. A. 1970. Screening for high lysine content in wheat. *Cereal Sci. Today* 15:409–12.

Matz, S. A. 1972. *Baking Technology and Engineering.* Westport: AVI Publ. Co.

Mendez-Castro, F. A., and Alexander, M. 1983. *Appl. Environ. Microbiol.* 45:28–254.

Milthorpe, F. L., and Ivins, J. D. 1966. *The Growth of Cereals and Grasses.* London: Butterworths.

Moss, D. H., and Musgrave, R. B. 1971. Photosynthesis and crop production. *Adv. Agron.* 23:317–36.

Muller, H. G. 1970. Traditional cereal processing in Nigeria and Ghana. *Ghana J. Agric.* 3:187–95.

Murata, Y. 1961. *Bull. Natl. Inst. Agric. Sci. Series D-9.* Tokyo: Ministry of Agriculture.

Mussell, H., and Staples, R. C. 1979. *Stress Physiology in Crop Plants.* New York: Wiley.

Nelson, T. S., Ferrara, L. W., and Storer, N. L. 1968. Phytate phosphorus content of feed ingredients derived from plants. *Poultry Sci.* 47:1372–4.

Neyra, C. A., and Dobereiner, J. 1977. Nitrogen fixation in grasses. *Adv. Agron.* 29:1–38.

Nobs, M. A. 1976. *Annual Report. Director, Dep. Plant Biol. 1975–1976.* Washington, D.C.: Carnegie Inst.

Nyvall, R. F. 1989. *Field Crop Diseases Handbook.* New York: Van Nostrand Reinhold.

O'Dell, B. L., De Boland, A. R., and Koirtyohann, S. R. 1972. Distribution of phytate and nutritionally important elements among the morphological components of cereal grains. *J. Agric. Food Chem.* 20:718–21.

Oke, O. L. 1965. Phytic acid phosphorus content of Nigerian foodstuffs. *Indian J. Med. Res.* 53:417–21.

Ou-Lee, T. M., Turgeon, R., and Wu, R. 1986. Expression of a foreign gene linked to either a plant virus or a *Drosophila* promoter after electroporation of protoplasts of rice, wheat and sorghum. *Proc. Natl. Acad. Sci. (USA)* 83:6815–19.

Palmer, G. P. 1989. *Cereal Science and Technology.* Aberdeen: The University Press.

Palmer, G. H., and Bathgate, G. N. 1976. Malting and brewing. *Adv. Cereal Sci. Technol.* 1:237–324.

Passioura, J. B. 1986. Resistance to drought and salinity: Avenues for improvement. *Aust. J. Plant Physiol.* 13:191–201.

Phillips, C. L., and Boerner, E. G. 1935. Present use of barley and barley products. Washington, D.C.: USDA Bureau of Agric. Econ., 13 pp.

Pimentel, D. 1981. *Handbook of Pest Management in Agriculture,* vol. 1. Boca Raton: CRC Press.

Pomeranz, Y. 1961. The problems involved in the pearling of wheat kernels. *Cereal Sci. Today* 6:76–9.

Pomeranz, Y. 1971. *Wheat: Chemistry and Technology.* St. Paul: Am. Assoc. Cereal Chem.

Pomeranz, Y. 1974. Food uses of barley. *CRC Crit. Rev. Food Technol.* 4:377–94.

Pomeranz, Y. 1983. Buckwheat: Structure, composition and utilization. *CRC Crit. Rev. Food Sci. Nutr.* 19:213–58.

Pomeranz, Y. 1987. *Modern Cereal Science and Technology.* New York: VCH Publ.

Pomeranz, Y., and Ory, R. L. 1982. Rice. In *Handbook of Processing and Utilization in Agriculture, vol. II, pt. I, Plant Products,* ed. I. A. Wolff, pp. 139–55. Boca Raton: CRC Press.

Pomeranz, Y., and Shellenberger, J. A. 1971. *Bread Science and Technology.* Westport: AVI Publ. Co.

Poostchi, I., Rovhani, I., and Razmi, K. 1972. Influence of levels of spring irrigation and fertility on yield of winter wheat (*Triticum aestivum* L.) under semi-arid conditions. *Agron. J.* 64:438–40.

Powell, A. M. 1978. *Ann. Mo. Bot. Gard.* 65:590–636 (cited by Stanhill [1986]).

Power, J. F., and Papendick, R. I. 1985. Organic sources of nutrients. In *Fertilizer Technology and Use,* ed. O. P. Engelstad, pp. 503–30. Madison: Soil Sci. Soc. Am.

Puckridge, D. W., and Donald, C. M. 1967. Competition among wheat plants sown at a wide range of densities. *Aust. J. Agric. Res.* 18:193–211.

Quarrie, S. A. 1985. *Annual Report of the Plant Breeding Institute—1984.* Cambridge: Plant Breeding Inst.

Quispel, A. 1974. *The Biology of Nitrogen Fixation.* Amsterdam: North Holland Publ.

Radhakrishnan, M. R., and Sivaprasad, J. 1980. Tannin content of sorghum varieties and their role in iron bioavailability. *J. Agric. Food Chem.* 28:55–7.

Ramig, R. E., and Rhoades, H. F. 1963. Interrelationships of soil moisture level at planting time and nitrogen fertilization on winter wheat production. *Agron. J.* 55:123–7.

Reddy, N. R., Sathe, S. K., and Salunkhe, D. K. 1982. Phytates in legumes and cereals. *Adv. Food Res.* 28:1–92.

Reichert, R. D., and Young, C. G. 1976. Dehulling cereal grains and grain legumes for developing countries. I. Quantitative comparison between attrition and abrasive type mills. *Cereal Chem.* 53:829–39.

Rhodes, C. A., Pierce, D. A., Mettler, I. J., Mascarenhas, D., and Detner, J. J. 1988. Genetically transformed maize plants from protoplasts. *Science* 240:204–7.

Riggs, T. J., Hanson, P. R., Start, N. D., Miles, D. M., Morgan, C. L., and Ford, M. A. 1981. Comparison of spring barley varieties grown in England and Wales between 1880 and 1980. *J. Agric. Sci.* (Cambridge) 97:599–610.

Riley, R., Chapman, V., and Johnson, R. 1968. Introduction of yellow rust resistance of *Aegilops comosa* into wheat by genetically induced homoeologous recombination. *Nature* 217:383–4.

Roberts, P., and Brill, W. J. 1981. Genetics and regulation of nitrogen fixation. *Annu. Rev. Microbiol.* 35:207–35.

Rohrlich, A., and Thomas, B. 1967. *Getreide und Getreide Mahlprodukte.* Berlin: Springer–Verlag.

Rooney, L. W., and Miller, F. R. 1982. Variation in the structure and kernel characteristics of sorghum. *Proc. Symp. Sorghum Grain Quality.* Patancheru (India): ICRISAT.

Ross, W. M., and Eastin, J. D. 1972. Grain sorghum in the USA. *Field Crop Abstr.* 25: 169–74.

Roy, N. N., and Murty, B. R. 1970. A selection procedure in wheat for stress environment. *Euphytica* 19:509–21.

Roy, R. N., and Wright, B. C. 1973. Sorghum growth and nutrient uptake in relation to soil fertility. I. Dry matter accumulation patterns, yield and N content of grain. *Agron. J.* 65: 709–11.

Russell, E. J., and Watson, D. J. 1940. The Rothamsted field experiments on the growth of wheat. *Imp. Bur. Soil Sci. Tech. Commun. no. 40,* 163 pp.

Salisbury, F. B. 1963. *The Flowering Process.* Oxford: Pergamon.

Salunkhe, D. K., Chavan, J. K., and Kadam, S. S. 1985. *Postharvest Biotechnology of Cereals.* Boca Raton: CRC Press.

Sastry, D. C. 1984. Incompatibility in angiosperms: Significance in crop improvement. *Adv. Appl. Biol.* 10:71–111.

Scarsbrook, C. E., and Doss, B. D. 1973. Leaf area index and radiation as related to corn yields. *Agron. J.* 65:459–61.

Schwartz, P. H., and Klassen, W. 1981. Estimate of losses caused by insects and mites to agricultural crops. In *Handbook of Pest Management in Agriculture,* vol. 1, D. Pimentel (ed.), pp. 15–77. Boca Raton: CRC Press.

Sears, E. R. 1956. The transfer of leaf rust resistance from *Aegilops umbellulata* to wheat. In *Genetics in Plant Breeding,* Brookhaven Symp. Biol. no. 9, pp. 1–22. Upton (New York): Brookhaven Natl. Lab.

Sears, E. R. 1973. *Proc. 4th Int. Wheat Genet. Symp.* Mexico: CIMMYT.

Simmonds, D. H. 1978. Structure, composition and biochemistry of cereal grains. In *Cereals '78: Better Nutrition for the World's Millions,* ed. Y. Pomeranz, pp. 105–38. St. Paul: Am. Assoc. Cereal Chem.

Singh, A. K., Moss, J. P., and Smartt, J. 1990. Ploidy manipulations for interspecific gene transfer. *Adv. Agron.* 43:199–240.

Singh, B., and Reddy, N. R. 1977. Phytic acid and mineral compositions of triticales. *J. Food Sci.* 42:1077–83.

Singh, I. D., and Stoskopf, N. C. 1971. Harvest index in cereals. *Agron. J.* 63:224–6.

Skovmand, B., Fox, P. N., and Villareal, R. L. 1984. Triticale in commercial agriculture: Progress and promise. *Adv. Agron.* 37:1–45.

Slootmaker, L. A. J. 1974. Tolerance to high soil acid in wheat related species, rye and triticale. *Euphytica* 23:505–13.

Snyder, F. W., and Carlson, G. E. 1984. Selecting for partitioning of photosynthetic products in crops. *Adv. Agron.* 37:47–72.

Spiertz, J. H. J., and van de Haar 1978. Differences in grain growth, crop photosynthesis and distribution of assimilates between a semi-dwarf and a standard cultivar of wheat. *Neth. J. Agric. Sci.* 26:233–49.

Sprague, G. F., and Eberthart, S. A. 1977. *Corn Breeding.* Madison: Am. Soc. Agron.

Stalker, H. T. 1980. Utilization of wild species for crop improvement. *Adv. Agron.* 33:111–47.

Stalker, H. T., and Moss, J. P. 1987. Speciation, cytogenetics and utilization of *Arachis* species. *Adv. Agron.* 41:1–40.

Stanhill, G. 1986. Water use efficiency. *Adv. Agron.* 39:53–85.

Stevenson, J. C., and Goodman, M. M. 1972. Ecology of exotic races of maize. I. Leaf number and tillering of 16 races under four temperatures and two photoperiods. *Crop Sci.* 12: 864–8.

Stewart, W. D. P. 1975. *Nitrogen Fixation by Free-Living Microorganisms.* Cambridge: Cambridge Univ. Press.

Stoskopf, N. C. 1985. *Cereal Grain Crops.* Reston: Reston Publ. Co.

Syme, J. R. 1970. A high yielding Mexican semi-dwarf wheat and the relationship of yield to harvest index and other varietal characteristics. *Aust. J. Exp. Agric. Anim. Husb.* 10: 350–3.

Takeda, K., Frey, K. J., and Bailey, T. B. 1980. Contribution of growth rate and harvest index to grain yield in F_9–derived lines of oats (*Avena sativa* L.). *Can. J. Plant Sci.* 60:379–84.

Thomas, H., Haki, J. M., and Arangzeb, S. 1980. The introgression of characters of the wild oat *Avena magna* (2n = 4x = 28) into the cultivated oat *A. sativa* (2n = 6x = 42). *Euphytica* 29:391–9.

Thomas, H., Powell, W., and Aung, T. 1980. Interfering with regular meiotic behavior in *Avena sativa* as a method of incorporating the gene for mildew resistance from *A. barbata. Euphytica* 29:635–40.

Thrasher, W. B. 1950. Process for removing seed coat from grain. U.S. Patent no. 2,530,272, November 14.

Ting, I. P. 1976. Crassulacean acid metabolism in natural ecosystems in relation to annual CO_2 uptake patterns and water utilization. In *CO_2 Metabolism and Plant Productivity,* ed. R. H. Burris and C. C. Black, pp. 251–68. Baltimore: Univ. Park Press.

Tootill, E. 1984. *The Penguin Dictionary of Botany.* Middlesex: Penguin Books Ltd.

Trione, E. J., and Metzger, R. J. 1970. Wheat and barley vernalization in a precise temperature gradient. *Crop Sci.* 10:390–2.

Turner, N. C. 1982. *Drought Resistance in Crops with Emphasis on Rice.* Los Banos (Philippines): Int. Rice Res. Inst.

Turner, N. C. 1986. Crop water deficits: A decade of progress. *Adv. Agron.* 39:1–51.

Turner, N. C., and Begg, J. E. 1981. Plant water relations and adaptation to stress. *Plant Soil* 58:97–131.

Turner, N. C., and Kramer, P. J. 1980. *Adaptation of Plants to Water and High Temperature Stress.* New York: Wiley.

USDA. 1989. *Agricultural Statistics.* Washington, D.C.: USGPO.

Vardi, A. 1974. Introgression from tetraploid durum wheats to diploid *Aegilops longissima* and *Aegilops speltoides. Heredity* 32:171–81.

Vavilov, N. I. 1951. *The Origin, Variation, Immunity and Breeding of Cultivated Plants* (trans. from Russian by K. S. Chester). New York: Ronald Press.

Vogel, O. A., Allan, R. E., and Peterson, C. J. 1963. Plant and performance characteristics of semi-dwarf winter wheats producing most efficiently in Eastern Washington. *Agron. J.* 55:397–8.

von Bulow, J. F. W., and Dobereiner, J. 1975. Potential for N₂ fixation in maize genotypes in Brazil. *Proc. Natl. Acad. Sci. USA* 72:2389–93.

Walsh, E. J. 1984. Developing yield potentials of cereals. In *Cereal Production,* ed. E. J. Gallagher, pp. 69–93. London: Butterworths.

Watanabe, I. 1975. *Research Results Report, Soil Microbiology.* Los Banos (Philippines): Int. Rice Res. Inst.

Watanabe, I., and Kuk-Ki-Lee 1975. *Int. Symp. Biological Nitrogen Fixation Farming Systems in Humid Tropics.* Ibadan (Nigeria): Int. Inst. Trop. Agric.

Watt, B. K., and Merrill, A. L. 1963. *Composition of Foods: Raw, Processed and Prepared. Agric. Handbook no. 8,* Washington, D.C.: USDA.

Webb, B. D. 1987. Factors involved in the quality of rice. In *Cereals and Legumes in the Food Supply,* ed. J. DuPont and E. M. Osman, pp. 133–54. Ames: Iowa State University Press.

Weinand, U., Bruschke, C., and Feix, G. 1979. Cloning of double stranded DNA's derived from polysomal mRNA of maize endosperm: Isolation and characterization of zein clones. *Nucleic Acids Res.* 6:2707–15.

Weipert, D., and Zwingelberg, H. 1980. *Getreide Mehl. Brot.* 34:97–100 (cited by Pomeranz [1987, pp. 419–52]).

Williams, A. 1975. *Breadmaking: The Modern Revolution.* London: Hutchinsons Benham.

Wittwer, S. H. 1979. *Agriculture for the 21st Century.* Coromandel Lecture no. 9, September 4, Coromandel Fertilizers Ltd.: New Delhi.

Wittwer, S. H. 1980. The shape of things to come. In *The Biology of Crop Productivity,* ed. Carlson, P., pp. 413–59. New York: Academic Press.

Wittwer, S. H., and Bukovac, M. J. 1969. In *Handbuch der Pflanzenernahrung und Dungung,* ed. K. Scharrer and H. Linser, pp. 235–61. Berlin: Springer–Verlag (cited by Wittwer [1980]).

Wolf, M. J., Buznan, C. L., MacMasters, M. M., and Rist, C. E. 1952. Structure of the mature corn kernel. IV. Microscopic structure of dent corn. *Cereal Chem.* 29:362–98.

Yamazaki, W. T. 1987. Factors involved in the quality of soft wheat. In *Cereals and Legumes in the Food Supply,* ed. J. DuPont and E. M. Osman, pp. 127–32. Ames: Iowa State Univ. Press.

Yamazaki, W. T., and Greenwood, C. T. 1981. *Soft Wheat: Production, Breeding, Milling and Uses.* St. Paul: Am. Assoc. Cereal Chem.

Yoshida, T. 1971. *Research Results Report: Soil Microbiology.* Los Banos (Philippines): Int. Rice Res. Inst.

Zohary, D., Harlan, J. R., and Vardi, A. 1969. The wild diploid progenitors of wheat and their breeding value. *Euphytica* 18:58–65.

2

Legumes

Usha S. Deshpande and S. S. Deshpande

INTRODUCTION

Production and Consumption

Legumes (including soybeans and peanuts) are ranked fifth in terms of annual world grain production, at around 170 million metric tons, after wheat, rice, corn, and barley (Table 2-1; cf. Table 0-1). With the exception of soybeans, legume production has remained stationary and in some areas even fell during the past decade. The major reasons for this decline in legume production include the higher yields of cereal crops (and thus better returns under traditional farming systems), a failure to obtain significant breakthrough in the genetics of legumes, and the inherent low productivity of legume genotypes. Legumes are also usually grown under rain-fed conditions and in poor soils with very little if any chemical inputs, such as fertilizers and pesticides.

Legume production in different regions of the world indicates that over 50% of the total land area under legumes is used for soybeans and peanuts alone (FAO 1988a). The American subcontinent produces over 70% of the world's soybeans, with the United States alone contributing about 50%. Tropical Asian countries produce the bulk of the remaining legumes. With the exception of soybeans, over 60% of pulses and nearly all peanuts are produced by developing nations. However, the mean yields of legumes in the developing nations are approximately half those of the advanced farming systems in the developed countries, with mean yields ranging from 500 to 2,000 kg/ha (FAO 1988a). This indicates tremendous growth potential for legume production in the developing nations. Well-defined preferences for legumes are found in various regions of the world. Distinct differences also exist in both the types and amounts of legumes produced. India produces nearly a quarter of total dry beans grown

Table 2-1. World Acreage, Production, and Protein and Lysine Yields of the Major Food Legumes Compared with Cereals, 1988.

Crops	Protein		Area (10⁶ ha)	Production (1,000 metric tons)		
	% Amount	% Lysine		Crop	Protein	Lysine
Legumes						
Total pulses	25[a]	7.0[b]	68.5	54,652	13,663	956
Dry beans	22		27.3	15,533		
Peas	22		9.9	15,505		
Chick-peas	21		8.7	5,803		
Soybeans	40	7.0	54.7	92,333	36,933	2,585
Peanuts	27	4.1	19.5	22,752[c]	3,003	123
Total				169,737	53,599	3,664
Cereals						
Wheat	12	1.8	220	4,509,952	61,194	1,101
Rice	7	3.9	145	6,483,466	33,843	1,320
Corn	8	3.0	126	6,405,460	32,437	973
Total					127,474	3,394

Source: FAO (1988a).
[a]From Rockland and Hahn (1977) and Powell, Matthews, and Oliveira (1984).
[b]From Rockland and Hahn (1977).
[c]In-shell basis.

and nearly 80% of the chick-peas, and China is the leading producer of broad beans. India and Africa produce the greatest diversity of pulses, but Central America almost exclusively produces cultivars of dry beans.

The availability of legumes in different regions of the world shows distinct patterns and preferences. In South and Latin America, the availability of legumes ranges from very low in Argentina to very high in Mexico (Hellendoorn 1979). On the other hand, legume consumption in North America and most European countries is rather low. The Indian subcontinent seems to be the area of greatest dependence on pulses. Although the per capita availability of legumes is about 50 g/day, the daily intake of pulses in the different regions of India ranges from 14 to 140 g/day/person (Salunkhe 1983). The pulses grown in India are also predominantly those of the Old World; those grown extensively include green gram, black gram, chick-pea, pigeon pea, pea, lentil, and *kesari dhal*. Only peanuts and to some extent dry beans among the New World legumes have found acceptance in this region. The Far East (China and Japan) is also an area of high legume utilization, although most of it comes from soybeans. Japan is a rare example of a technologically advanced society with a high level of pulse utilization. The African continent is characterized by moderate to intensive use of pulses. In fact, in some African countries, the intake of beans is so large that 65% of caloric intake is in the form of legumes and only 35% from other food sources (Smartt 1976). The indigenous legume of Africa is the cowpea, which is widely grown and consumed throughout most of the continent. Dry beans and broad beans—and, to a lesser extent, chick-peas and lentils—have also found acceptance in African diets.

Nutritional Aspects

Legumes have a special place in the human diet because they contain nearly two to three times more protein than cereals. In fact, for vegetarians, legumes are the principal source of dietary protein. Although the total protein production from cereals in 1988 was about two and a half times that from legumes, the yield of lysine was in fact greater from legumes (Table 2-1). Since lysine is the principal amino acid deficient in most plant proteins, the importance of legumes in human nutrition may be vastly underestimated. Although cereals supply nearly 50% of the protein in the human diet worldwide (see Chapter 1), their unfavorable balance of amino acids requires that complementary protein be provided for optimal nutrition. In Western developed countries, animal proteins (meat, fish, poultry, eggs, and milk) comprise a substantial portion of the diet. This preference may be based on intuitive recognition of their higher intrinsic nutritional value or a more favorable balance of the amino acids (Rockland and Nishi 1979). In Western diets, therefore, the poor quality of cereal proteins is hardly of any importance. In developing countries, however, animal proteins are either too expensive (e.g., in Latin America and Africa) or are not readily accepted (e.g., in India). Legumes serve as main sources of both protein and calories in many of these tropical and subtropical areas. Dry legumes and legume products are in fact the richest source of food protein from plants (Deshpande and Damodaran 1990).

Although legumes also provide calories and are important sources of several B-complex vitamins, minerals, and fiber, their major importance lies in their actual and potential value as a source of plant protein for human nutrition. Legume proteins alone, however, are of poor quality; it is when consumed with cereals that their complementary effect is exemplified. The relative proportion of legumes in such combinations varies in different countries. In Latin America, legumes constitute about 10% of the diet; in different regions of India, the proportion is in the range 30–50%. The mutually supplementary effect is due to the fact that the sulfur-containing amino acids (methionine and cystine) are first limiting in legumes whereas lysine is limiting in cereals. The maximum complementary effect often occurs near a 50 : 50 ratio of the two proteins (Hellendoorn 1979). The maximum increase in nutritive value is obtained for cereals such as corn and sorghum, which are poor in protein quality, followed by wheat, rice, and oats.

Research

Research on tropical food legumes was comparatively neglected until about 1950, partly because many tropical countries' primary need seemed to be increased output and profitability of export crops, particularly fibers, rubber, beverages, and palm oils. Food crops were largely left to look after themselves. When the emphasis began to shift to them, the first priority, both nationally and internationally, was the principal cereal crop—whether rice (which feeds half of humankind), wheat, or corn. At the international level, the International Rice Research Institute (IRRI) was opened in the Philippines in 1960, and the International Center for the Improvement of Wheat and Maize (CIMMYT) in Mexico in 1966. But each of the next two international centers to be established—the International Center for Tropical Agriculture (CIAT) in Colombia (1967) and the International Institute of Tropical Agriculture (IITA) in Nigeria (1968)—included one or more legumes in its programs: *Phaseolus* beans at CIAT and cowpea and tropic-adapted soya at IITA. The International Crops Research Institute for the Semi-Arid Tropics (ICRISAT), set up in India in 1972, works on pigeon pea, chick-pea, and peanuts, and the program of the International Center for Agricultural Research in Dry Area (ICARDA) in Syria and other countries of the Middle East and North Africa (1976) includes lentils, chick-peas, and fava beans.

Recent renewed interest in legume research is thus quite evident. This could be at least partially attributed to their nutritional quality and potential for development of acceptable food products. The present critical situation in world food supplies demands that all our agricultural resources be utilized to the fullest. The green revolution demonstrated that much more effective use could be made of cereal crops in the tropics than had previously been thought feasible; a similar demonstration is long overdue for legume crops. Serious consideration will probably be given to oilseed meals as a direct source of dietary protein. Alternative sources, such as the production and use of fish protein concentrate, single-cell protein, and extractable leaf protein, will also be explored. Fortification of these sources with synthetic amino acids is another important aspect. However, genetic enhancement of productivity and protein quality in traditionally accepted crop plants deserves particular attention, since by following this approach people requiring better sources of protein need not be forced to adopt new foods, and no new economic infrastructure for processing, fortification, and distribution is essential.

In the past, major research interests were focused on soybeans and peanuts because of their important role in the food industry and in human nutrition. However, their mode of consumption is quite different than that of the high protein–low fat common food legumes. These two legumes, along with winged beans, are typically classified as oilseeds.

Chapter Overview

Because of the obvious limitations of space, and the fact that several excellent reviews and books on various aspects of individual food legume species are available, a complete review of the work in this field is impossible. The present review is thus intended to be a "bird's-eye view" in which certain preharvest biotechnological aspects of food legumes as a group are described. Most of the literature herein covered deals with the twelve food legume species commonly grown worldwide. A brief discussion on the origin, diversity, and phylogenicity of these legumes is followed by a look at their contribution to the biological nitrogen cycle. In this regard, the role of legume–rhizobial symbiotic association and the importance of legumes in agricultural systems, especially under subsistence farming, will be addressed. The general agronomic practices involved in monocropped legume culture are described, as are various cereal–legume intercropping systems and their advantages and disadvantages. Problems related to pests and diseases and their control in legume cultivation are then discussed, followed by the importance of proper storage and some problems related to stored legume seed quality. Finally, future research needs on preharvest biotechnology of food legumes are identified.

ORIGIN, DIVERSITY, AND PHYLOGENICITY

Origin

The chronology of origin and domestication of food legumes is probably impossible to reconstruct; however, radiocarbon dating has been successfully used to determine the approximate ages of materials found in archaeological sites. The Leguminosae are believed to have originated in the late Jurassic period, and to have expanded and diversified in the Cretaceous (Delwiche 1978). Renfrew (1966) reported seeds of *Pisum, Vicia,* and *Lens* from Neolithic sites in Greece. Although these sites have not as yet been dated, Renfrew pointed out that they showed a virtually simultaneous arrival of the full complement of cereals and legumes. Zohari and Hopf (1973) also confirmed the presence of lentils and chick-peas at sites dating back to 7000–6000 B.C. and 5450 B.C., respectively. In the New World also, grain legumes have been under cultivation for at least 4,000 years (Bressani and Elias 1974). Legume cultivation therefore seems to be quite ancient and dates back to prehistoric times.

Grain legumes have clearly originated in both the Old and New Worlds. Old World grain legumes can readily be referred to one or more of the following regions: the Mediterranean, Central Asia, Asia Minor, Africa, India, and the Sino–Japanese area. In the New World, Central and South America are the most important centers (Smartt and Hymowitz 1985). However, domestication of a single legume species could have occurred in more than one gene center. The Mediterranean and Asia Minor gene centers are considered of great importance in the evolution of the major Old World temperate grain legumes. The tropical grain legumes of the Old World probably originated in the Asian and African gene centers, whereas those of the New World were developed in Central and South America. The Indonesian, Australian, and North American regions are believed to be involved only as secondary centers of origin (Smartt and Hymowitz 1985). With the exception of the peanut, grain legumes are known to have been domesticated from the wild by prehistoric planters who both cultivated these species and made selections within them to suit their evolving environment.

Since these early origins, grain legumes have spread widely so that, in some cases, the region of major production is far removed from the region of origin, as exemplified by the soybean and peanut. Such migration to new areas, often associated with partial or complete failure of nodulation, tends to accentuate the changes that occur as a result of domestication. The most obvious effects of pulse domestication involve the modification of growth habit (Hutchinson 1969). Stems tend to be thicker, leaves larger, branches fewer, node number lower, and internode length shorter. This process culminates in the evolution of self-supporting plants well adapted to monocrop farming systems (Smartt 1976). Other consequences of domestication include a change from perennial to annual life form, earlier flowering, increasing self-pollination, loss of seed dormancy and pod dehiscence mechanisms, and increased seed size at the expense of seed numbers per pod. Such changes have led to an increase in yield potential. Following domestication, seed coats have become more readily permeable to water (almost certainly as a consequence of human selection), thus decreasing their dormancy and leading to uniform germination as well as ease and speed of cooking. Local consumer preference may have led to selection of a particular seed color and consequently remarkable diversity, especially in *Phaseolus vulgaris, P. lunatus,* and *Vigna unguiculata.*

Since legumes present such large diversity in so many aspects of their biology, it is certainly reasonable to ask whether there are any distinguishing characteristics or features of their origin and distribution shared by the majority of species. Are the legumes unique in any significant way from other plant groups with respect to their origin, ties to wild ancestors or near relatives, patterns of variability, or distribution? As reviewed by Adams and Pipoly (1980) and Isely (1982), the following inferences can be drawn.

1. Although the Asian Near East is cited as the region of primary diversity more frequently than any other part of the world, useful legume species have originated on every continent.

2. The concept of centers of diversity appears valid for legume species.
3. At some stage in their evolution, many legume species have experienced atypically rapid increases in variability.
4. Several mechanisms were responsible for this increase in variability, probably including introgression from close relatives, outcrossing, alternate outcrossing and selfing cycles, polyploidy, populational subdivision, and exploitation of noncompetitive environments, which allowed a greater range of survivors from recombinational events.
5. Landraces and local ecotypes still exist in several species.
6. At least some species (e.g., cowpeas and broad beans) are probably still actively evolving.
7. In several cases, wild ancestors have been identified and genetic bridges to domesticated forms are available.
8. The present patterns of genetic diversity are not closely correlated with geographical diversity.
9. Although unique in those morphological characteristics that distinguish the legumes taxonomically, and in some physiological and architectural traits, the legumes are not otherwise significantly different from many plant groups in the consequences of their breeding systems, in their manner of origin or distribution, or in their patterns of diversity.

Such studies on grain legume evolution and domestication have over the past three decades enabled us to arrive at a much better assessment of the value of the crops, the necessity for collecting wild germplasm, the potential for their improvement, and the nature and extent of the resources available for this task. However, one major question still remains to be answered. Why are so few legume genera or species of the literally hundreds and thousands known particularly dominant as food sources? The answer rests upon the hypothesis that if humans determine that a plant is useful, especially as a food source, they will find ways of cultivating that plant. Perhaps the food legumes were unusually rich in genetic potential for increases (from the wild types) in seed size and contained larger concentrations of protein than cereals. This concentration depends greatly upon the symbiotic system for nitrogen fixation, which is almost unique to the legumes. In essence, humanity itself, seeking to exploit species rich in genetic potential for meeting its needs, has played a vital role in influencing the present-day distribution and usage patterns of the economic legumes.

Ecological Diversity

One of the largest of flowering plant families of the world, legumes are also one of the very few groups that are almost cosmopolitan in their distribution.

Representatives of the family are found on all continents, from the hot, humid Asian lowland tropics to the cold, barren Siberian steppes; from sea level to mountain meadows; and from the semidesert savanna of Africa to the cool altiplanos of South America (Isely 1982). Important legumes may be found growing from the equator to the Arctic Circle, and at least two useful species (*Medicago falcata* and *Trifolium lupinaster*) survive winter temperatures as cold as −68 °C on the tundra in Siberia, where the subsoil is frozen permanently. Such adaptation is based upon fitting the plant's specific requirements and capabilities to the specific resources of an environment. Although no legume species seemed to have approached universal adaptation, the ecological diversity is often described in terms of physiological adaptations, anatomical variations, morphological pattern, and the structure and genetics of population. For a detailed description of the origin, genetics, and evolutionary and ecological diversity of legumes, the reader is referred to several excellent reviews (Adams and Pipoly 1980; Isely 1982; Smartt and Hymowitz 1985).

Phylogenicity

After Compositae and Orchidaceae, Leguminosae (or Fabaceae) is the third largest family of flowering plant; in economic importance, it is second only to the grasses (Gramineae). The family has a currently estimated 16,000–19,000 species in about 750 genera (Allen and Allen 1981). The traditional classification of the Leguminosae is that of Taubert (1891–4), largely derived from Bentham (1865). Taubert subdivided the family further into three subfamilies: Caesalpinioideae, Mimosoideae, and Papilionoideae (or Faboideae). However, there is still controversy regarding whether to subdivide the legumes into families or subfamilies. The connections between the three main groups seem fairly well demonstrated as a view expressed by a single family. The alternative of these treated as separate families is expressed as Caesalpiniaceae, Mimosaceae, and Papilionaceae (or Fabaceae).

The term "legume" (from the Latin *legere*, to gather), although botanically meaning the seed pod itself, is often applied both to the fruit or seed and to the plant or plant family. The caesalpinioid legumes are the basic, presumably most primitive, and in some ways most diversified subfamily, and primarily include tropical, woody plants (Isely 1982). Many are not nitrogen-fixers, lending support to the theory that the other two subfamilies probably evolved from it. The proportion of mimosoids (which seemingly are derived from the caesalpinioids) that fix nitrogen is much higher (Allen 1973). They are also mostly woody plants of the tropics and warm regions. The papilionoid legumes, which are characterized by papilionaceous (butterfly-like) flowers, show many characteristics of their immediate caesalpinioid ancestors. The most primitive species of

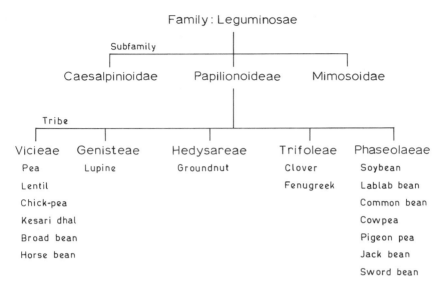

Fig. 2-1. Botanical classification of food legumes.

this group are mostly woody, tropical, and warm-weather plants, from which they proliferated in habit and in ecological adaptation. They are by far the dominant legumes of the temperate, developed countries, and constitute the most important agents of biological nitrogen fixation in the world. The human food they supply is of three kinds: edible tubers; leaves, green pods, and unripe seeds (vegetable legumes); and ripe dry seeds (grain legumes, pulses).

The domesticated legumes or pulses are all members of the Papilionoideae. This subfamily is classified in ten botanical tribes, three of which together contain the major vegetable and grain legumes (Fig. 2-1). The tribe Vicieae (or Fabeae) includes the lentils, peas, chick-peas, *kesari dhal,* and the broad and horse beans. Hedysareae includes the peanut, which is primarily grown as an oilseed and to a relatively minor extent as a pulse. Soybeans, lablab beans, common beans and grams, cowpeas, pigeon peas, and sword and jack beans all belong to the tribe Phaseolaeae. The various common and scientific names of the domesticated grain legume species ordinarily used for food purposes are summarized in Table 2-2. Of the species listed here, only twelve are so widely grown as to constitute the bulk of the legumes grown and consumed worldwide. These include common beans, green peas, chick-peas, cowpeas, pigeon peas, lentils, green and black grams, broad and lima beans, and the two oilseeds, soybeans and peanuts.

Table 2-2. Grain Legume Species Commonly Used for Food Purposes.

Botanical Name	Common Name[a]
Arachis hypogaea	Peanut, goober, groundnut,[b] earth pea,* earth nut,[c] monkey-nut
Cajanus cajan	Pigeon pea,* red gram, *arhar, tur*
Cajanus indicus	Pigeon pea,* Congo pea, yellow *dhal*
Canavalia ensiformis	Jack bean, horse bean,* *gotani* bean
Canavalia gladiata	Sword bean
Ceratonia siliqua	Carob, St. John's bread, locust bean
Cicer arietinum	Chick-pea, gram, bengal gram, garbanzo,* *ceci,* gram pea, Egyptian pea, *chana, deshi chana*
Cicer minotinum	Garbanzo,* *kabuli chana*
Cyamopsis tetragonoloba	Cluster bean, guar*
Cyamopsis psoralioides[d]	Guar*
Dolichos biflorus	Horse gram*
Dolichos lablab	Hyacinth bean, lablab,* *bonavist*
Ervum vulgaris	Lentil,* *masur dhal*
Faba vulgaris	Windsor bean
Glycine hispida	
Glycine max	} Soybean, soya bean, soja
Glycine soja	
Lablab niger	Lablab* bean
Lablab purpureus	Indian bean, lubia bean, kidney bean,* hyacinth bean*
Lathyrus sativus	Grass pea, *kesari dhal,* vetchling, chickling pea
Lathyrus niger	Flat pea
Lathyrus odoratus	Sweet pea
Lens esculenta	Lentil,* *masur dhal, red dhal*
Lens culinaris	Lentil*
Lupinus spp.	Lupine, *tarwi, tarin,* pearl lupin, sweet lupine
Macrotyloma uniflorum	Horse gram*
Mucuna pruriens	Velvet bean*
Phaseolus aconitifolius	Moth bean*
Phaseolus acutifolius	Tepary bean, *pavi, yorimuni*
Phaseolus angularis	*Adzuki* bean
Phaseolus aureus[e]	Mung bean,* green gram,* golden gram*
Phaseolus calcaratus[f]	Rice bean*
Phaseolus coccineus	Scarlet runner bean
Phaseolus limensis	Baby lima bean*
Phaseolus lunatus	Large lima bean,* sieva bean, Madagascar bean, sugar bean, *towe* bean
Phaseolus multiflorus	Indian runner bean
Phaseolus mungo[g]	Mung bean, mungo bean, *urd dhal,* black gram*
Phaseolus radiatus	Mung bean,* golden gram,* green gram*
Phaseolus vulgaris	*Ripe seed:* common bean, kidney bean,* navy bean; black, pink, or red bean; pinto bean, roman bean, great northern bean, dry bean, *feijao, frijol,* French kidney, *kintocki*

Table 2-2. (*Continued*)

Botanical Name	Common Name[a]
	Young pod: string bean, wax bean, green bean, snap bean, French bean, haricot
	Unripe seed: shell bean
Pisum angularis	
Pisum arvense }	Dried pea, green pea, garden pea, field pea
Pisum sativum	
Psophocarpus tetragonolobus	Winged bean* (humid tropics), goa bean
Sphenostylis stenocarpa	Yam bean
Stizolobium spp.	Velvet beans
Tetragonolobus purpureus	Winged bean* (Europe)
Trigonella foenumgraecum	Fenugreek, methi
Tylosema esculentum	Marama bean
Vicia faba	Broad bean, horse bean,[h]* fava (or faba) bean, common bean
Vicia sativa	Common vetch
Vigna aconitifolia	Moth bean,* matki, mouth bean, mat, math
Vigna aureus	Mung bean*
Vigna radiata	Green gram*
Vigna glabra	Cowpea*
Vigna mungo	Black gram*
Vigna sesquipedalis	Yardlong cowpea
Vigna sinensis	Cowpea,* black-eyed pea,* black-eyed bean, dried cowpea
Vigna umbellata	Rice bean,* red bean, mambi bean
Vigna unguiculata	Black-eyed cowpea, black-eyed pea,* cowpea*
Voandzeia subterranea	Bambara groundnut, Madagascar groundnut, earth pea*

[a]Asterisks indicate names that appear more than once.
[b]In U.K.; in U.S., refers to *Apios tuberosa*.
[c]In U.K., earth nut=peanut *or* tuber of *Conopodium flexuosum* (= arnut, pig-nut, earth-chestnut). In U.S., pignut = hickory nut (*Carya glabra, C. ovalis, C. cordiformis*).
[d]Wild ancestor.
[e]New classification is *Vigna radiata*.
[f]New classification is *Vigna umbellata*.
[g]New classification is *Vigna mungo*.
[h]Also U.S. name for Jerusalem thorn (*Parkinsonia aculeata*), used as emergency forage.
Compiled from: Smartt (1976), NAS (1978, 1979), Rockland and Nishi (1979), and Bhatia (1983).

BIOLOGICAL NITROGEN FIXATION BY LEGUMES

Importance of Nitrogen in Plant World

Nitrogen, in its elemental gaseous form N_2, constitutes four-fifths of the atmosphere. This is virtually an inexhaustible supply, and yet very few plants and no animals can assimilate nitrogen in its free form. Since nitrogen is the essential constituent of proteins, all organisms depend on having it available in a

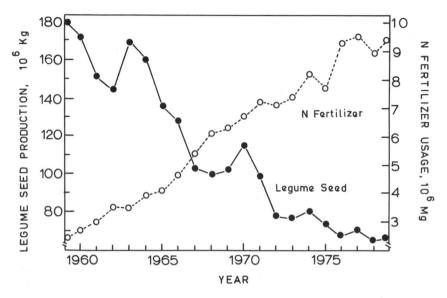

Fig. 2-2. Changes in the United States legume seed production and nitrogen fertilizer usage, 1959–79. *Source:* Power and Papendick (1985).

utilizable form. Most plants derive their nitrogen from the mineralization of soil organic matter and plant residues. To obtain high yields of crops used for human and animal food, the naturally occurring supply is augmented by the application of synthetic nitrogen fertilizers. Their widespread availability in many nations has resulted in a major decrease in the cultivation of legumes (Fig. 2-2). The energy crisis of the 1970s, however, with the concurrent increases in the cost and reduced availability of nitrogen fertilizers, caused many producers to evaluate the stability of continued dependence on synthetic nitrogen fertilizers as their only nitrogen input. Even though the initial energy crisis has abated somewhat in recent years, economic stress in agriculture, coupled with the fear that prices of such fertilizers will again increase greatly in the near future, has prompted current, worldwide interest in legume crops as a renewable source of nitrogen in farming systems.

Furthermore, the use of nitrogen fertilizers aggravates other already serious problems, such as nitrogen losses from the soil, nitrate movement into the subsoil, and disturbances in the water quality of lakes and streams. In addition, the nutritional demand that will be placed on our supplies of fixed nitrogen by an estimated doubling of the global population (to exceed 7 billion by the year 2000) carries grave implications. The need to conserve fixed nitrogen supplies extends beyond the basic need for food and fodder for all living things, whether they be economically important or purely ornamental and aesthetic: Modern ecology has recently shown this to be one of the primary focal points of vegetational adaptation. Indeed, living plants and ecosystems are organized specifically to obtain and preserve usable nitrogen.

Biological nitrogen fixation, especially of the symbiotic variety, plays a crucial ecological role in maintaining adequate nitrogen resources in the plant world. Stewart (1966) has described three kinds of biological nitrogen fixation:

1. symbiotic legume–*Rhizobium* relationships,
2. symbiotic relationships between miscellaneous woody species and *Actinomyces,* and
3. free-living blue-green algae and bacteria.

Most ecologists agree that the biological world predominantly depends on the Leguminosae–*Rhizobium* consortium. Legumes, having established a mutually beneficial association with bacteria of *Rhizobium* species, can thrive either with no fixed nitrogen or with a minimal supply from the soil. The bacteria invade the root hairs, where, inside the cortical root swellings or nodules, free air nitrogen is converted into fixed nitrogen for eventual plant protein assimilation and storage. The complexities of nodule tissues, and the high degree of specialization for gaseous and enzyme regulations and vascular transport, indicate a long-standing coevolution between these two groups. Recent intensification of studies of tropical grain legumes and their associated rhizobia stems from the pressing need of densely populated nations to maximize their productivity of high-protein food crops without depleting their fixed nitrogen resources.

The ecological uniqueness of legume nodular root systems was depicted in some of the earliest printed botanical illustrations, including the famous herbals of Fuchs (1542), Bock (1556), Dalechamps (1587), and Malpighi (1679) (all cited by Allen and Allen, 1981). So characteristic and so seemingly constant was their occurrence on leguminous plants that Wydler (1860) considered them of diagnostic value for taxonomic identification. However, the general opinion that legumes and nodules are always associated is not true: The ability to nodulate seems to be consistently absent within certain sections of the legume family (Allen and Allen, 1981). It must also be noted that even though a species is capable of symbiotic relationship, nodulation cannot occur unless the compatible rhizobia are present in the rhizosphere.

The Symbiotic Process

Although the soil-improving properties of legumes were known for several centuries, it was only in the mid nineteenth century that scientific research efforts were made to identify the sources of nitrogen available to green plants. Hellriegal and Wilfarth (1888) were the first to establish beyond doubt that root nodules bore a causal relationship to the assimilation of free nitrogen. Subsequently, Beijerinck (1888) isolated pure-culture nodule bacteria from several legume species and proved, using Koch's postulates, that they were the causative microsymbionts. The agronomic significance of this discovery was soon realized in the production of annual food crops such as peas and beans, and in the planting of pasture legumes. Since then, effective cultures of root-nodule bacteria appropriate for a given legume have been commercially developed for use as inocula for coating seeds to ensure that the proper types of root-nodule bacteria are present in the rhizosphere during seed germination.

Rhizobia in the free-living state are almost ubiquitous soil inhabitants. They occur more abundantly along and in the rhizosphere of legumes than of other plants. They are aerobic, non–spore-forming, Gram-positive short rods, and readily isolated by plating out surface-sterilized crushed nodules onto suitable nutrients, such as yeast-extract mannitol agar (Allen and Allen 1981). The various *Rhizobium* species could be distinguished by such physiological characteristics as fast or slow growth, acid or alkaline production, copious or scant gum formation, and serum zone production or absence thereof in litmus milk. The one characteristic that validates all of them as members of the genus *Rhizobium* is their ability to form root nodules on a leguminous host (Smartt 1976; Allen and Allen 1981).

At first all rhizobia were thought as a single species capable of nodulating all leguminous plants. However, as attention focused more critically on differences in the ineffectiveness of various strains, it was apparent that the ability of a given bacterial strain to produce nodules on certain plants and not on others tended to be specific (Smartt 1976; Allen and Allen 1981). Extensive cross testing of many different strains on multiple hosts led to the establishment of bacteria–plant cross-inoculation groups—groups of plants within which the root-nodule organisms are mutually interchangeable. Thus, with few exceptions, particular strains of rhizobia are able to nodulate only plants within a certain group of legumes. Species of *Rhizobium* are therefore designated by their host range (Table 2-3). The necessity for inoculating seed of a legume

Table 2-3. *Rhizobium* Species and Their Host Range.

Microsymbiont	Growth Rate	Cultural Reaction	Host Affinities	Plant Group
R. japonicum	Slow	Alkaline	*Glycine*	Soybean
R. leguminosorum	Fast	Acid	*Pisum, Lathyrus, Vicia, Lens, Cicer*	Pea
R. lupini	Slow	Alkaline	*Lupinus* spp.	Lupine
R. meliloti	Fast	Acid	*Melilotus, Medicago, Trigonella*	Alfalfa
R. phaseoli	Fast	Acid	*Phaseolus* (temperate zone spp.)	Bean
R. trifolii	Fast	Acid	*Trifolium*	Clover

Compiled from: Smartt (1976) and Allen and Allen (1981).

species newly introduced to a locality becomes quite evident where a strain of *Rhizobium* actually able to induce nodule formation is lacking. Even within the *Rhizobium* group capable of infecting a given legume species, there are apparently differing levels of efficiency in their fixation of nitrogen (Smartt 1976). Effective nodules can be readily distinguished from ineffective ones. The mature nodule consists of an outer protective layer of small cells with a connection to the main vascular system of the root. This surrounds the functional root-nodule tissue. This tissue in effective nodules is pink or reddish and becomes greenish with age, whereas ineffective nodules do not develop pigmentation.

Root Growth and Nodulation

The establishment of a good root system by sustained root growth is important to legumes not only because it provides anchorage and an absorption and translocation system for water and mineral nutrients as in other crop plants, but also because it is the site of action of the root-nodule bacteria. Nodule initiation, development, and function entail intricate biochemical and biophysical processes, many of which are still not fully understood. According to Allen and Allen (1981), nodule initiation involves at least six distinctive processes:

1. rhizobia-host recognition factors at loci on root hair surfaces;
2. rhizobial entry and progressive invasion via infection threads into the root cortex;
3. evocation of meristematic loci with active cell proliferation accompanied by hypertrophy and usually polyploidy of the invaded cells;
4. release of microorganisms from the infection threads;
5. rapid bacterial and plant cell division; and
6. differentiation of the tissue into nodule zones, with the central bacteroid zone as the site of hemoglobin, essential in the fixation process, and the peripheral vascular strands as the transport system linked with the parent root.

A diagrammatic representation of nodule formation in legumes and the life cycle of the root-nodule bacteria is shown in Fig. 2-3. Studies on soybeans indicate that nodulation may become effective in supplying nitrogen to the plant by about the fifteenth day (Howell 1963); recognizable nodules can, however, be detected by about the ninth day of seed germination. As Howell further comments, the speed of the process is impressive. The ability of the nodules actually present on the plant to fix nitrogen does not extend indefinitely: The active life of a nodule may not exceed four weeks, but they are produced continuously during the life of the plant and, in some cases, may be active at least until late stages of seed maturation (Smartt 1976).

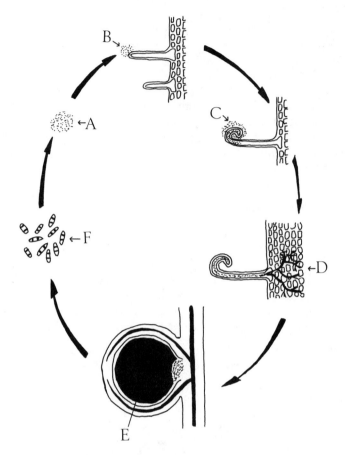

Fig. 2-3. Diagrammatic representation of nodule formation in legumes and the life cycle of the root-nodule bacteria (*Rhizobium* spp): (A) *Rhizobium* cocci free-living in soil; (B) *Rhizobium* colony develops around the tip of the root hair; (C) root hair twists around the colony and infection starts; (D) infection threads penetrate the cortex of the root; (E) large cell filled with bacteria; (F) banded rods (bacteroids) liberate in soil as the old nodules disintegrate. *Source:* Cobley (1976), *Introduction to the Botany of Tropical Crops,* courtesy of the Longman Group UK.

The shape and size of the nodules also appear to be characteristic of the species. In the early stages, all nodules are small and spherical. The shape of the nodule is thereafter governed by the extent and location of the meristem, which is the site of active cell division and tissue differentiation (Allen and Allen 1981). Hemispherical peripheral meristems produce spherical nodules, such as those of *Arachis, Glycine,* and *Vigna.* Elongated, cylindrical finger forms result from the distal growth of apical meristems. If portions of the meristem grow at unequal rates, or if cleavage occurs, then bifurcated, digitate, palmate,

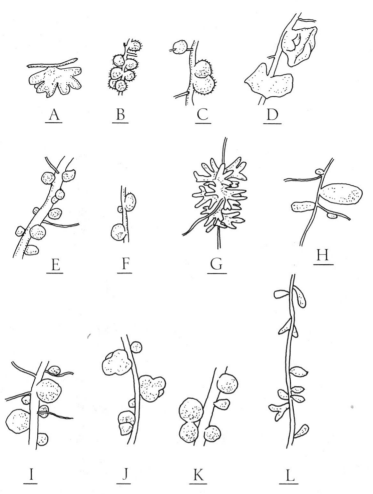

Fig. 2-4. Size and shapes of root nodules of some food legumes. (A) *Pisum sativum* (x1.14), (B) *Vicia faba* (x1.14), (C) *Glycine max* (x1.14), (D) *Cicer arietinum* (x1.14), (E) *Phaseolus mungo* (x0.57), (F) *Arachis hypogaea* (x1.14), (G) *Lathyrus sativus* (x1.14), (H) *Cajanus cajan* (x1.14), (I) *Phaseolus vulgaris* (x1.14), (J) *Lablab niger* (x0.57), (K) *Vigna unguiculata* (x1.14), (L) *Lens esculenta* (x1.14). *Source:* Cobley (1976), *Introduction to the Botany of Tropical Crops,* courtesy of the Longman Group UK.

or coralloid nodules result. In these nodule types, typical of *Trifolium* and *Vicia*, the vascular connecting tissue between the mother root cortex and the nodule outgrowth is constricted and rather narrow. Divided lateral meristems are responsible for the nodules found on *Lupinus* species. The diversity in shapes of root nodules found on some tropical legumes is shown in Fig. 2-4.

Factors Influencing Symbiosis

Effective symbiosis between the host plant and the bacteria is influenced by several factors. The mere absence of nodules does not necessarily indicate an inability on the host plant to enter into such a relationship, but may reflect an unfavorable temporary situation. According to Allen and Allen (1981), there are four common reasons for the absence of nodules concomitant with natural plant growth:

1. Shedding of nodules may be a consequence of drought, flooding, or clipping of the plant's foliage. However, if these occur at an early stage of plant growth, new nodules usually will form when plant growth is renewed.
2. Unfavorable soil type and soil pH (pH < 5 depresses nodulation), insufficient solar radiation, and temperature extremes all adversely affect rhizobial populations and nodule formation.
3. The absence of compatible rhizobia in the rhizosphere obviously precludes infection.
4. At the genetic level, a resistant or noninvasive line may result from plant breeding and selection.

Thus conditions that favor vigorous host growth generally also favor active or effective nodulation. High photosynthetic rates and adequate soil moisture and aeration, together with suitable pH and balance of mineral nutrients in soil, are highly critical for effective host–bacteria symbiosis. This relationship can be easily disturbed if the host's nutrition is disturbed: Under such conditions, the symbionts still get their energy requirements from the host plant, thus turning the relationship into one of parasitism. Effective nitrogen fixation thus depends on both the genetic constitution of the bacterium and the environment in which it operates (Smartt 1976). Certain basic phylogenetic factors of the host plant, including the following, may also depress effective nodulation:

the presence of physical and morphological barriers to bacterial invasion (Allen and Allen 1981);
the presence of cell constituents containing tannins, flavonoids, quinones, or other phenolic compounds, which exert an antibiotic or physicochemical restriction to rhizobial invasion and growth (Allen and Allen 1976); and
the absence of lectins and essential enzymes from the root hairs, leading to failure in recognition or binding between the rhizobia and the root surface (Lis and Sharon 1973).

Quantity of Nitrogen Fixed

Although there are many published tabulations of the amount of nitrogen fixed by legume crops, most are derived from only a very few sources. Burns and

Hardy (1975) averaged a great many published estimates to arrive at a figure of 140 kg of nitrogen fixed per year per hectare of arable land under legumes. Much of the work reported on estimating fixation, however, cannot be extrapolated to field conditions, since these studies are often carried out in experimental or demonstration plots, where yields are much higher than the areal average. Also, symbiotic fixation is probably lower on the farm. Nevertheless, many grain legumes are efficient at nitrogen fixation. Representative data on the quantity of nitrogen biologically fixed annually by some important legumes are summarized in Table 2-4. As discussed earlier, variables affecting the quantity of nitrogen fixed include not only the legume species and cultivars, but also such factors as soil type and texture, pH, soil nitrate nitrogen levels (high levels depress nodulation), temperature and water regimes, availability of other nutrients, and crop (especially harvest) management. This last factor is extremely important: Alfalfa (*Medicago sativa*), for instance, may add to the soil up to several hundred kilograms of nitrogen per hectare if a final cutting of the hay is not removed, as compared to <150 kg N/ha if only the roots and stubbles remain (Heichel 1987).

It is difficult to put an economic tag on the nitrogen fixed by legumes. Biological nitrogen fixation is energy expensive and represents a genuine symbiosis: In return for the energy-rich materials metabolized, the bacteria produce mineralized nitrogen. Unfortunately, this fact is often ignored when the yields of food legumes are compared with those of cereals, usually to the disadvantage of the farmer. The fact of the matter is that very substantial yields of legumes can be obtained on nodule-fixed nitrogen if other mineral nutrient levels are adequately maintained. Much too often, particularly in the farming systems of the developing countries, legumes have to shift for themselves—not only for nitrogen but for other mineral elements as well—even when conditions may be

Table 2-4. Reported Quantities of Nitrogen Fixed by Various Legume Species.

Species	N fixed (kg/ha/yr)
Alfalfa	114 – 223
Clover	21 – 36
Chick-pea	24 – 84
Common bean (*P. vulgaris*)	2 – 121
Fava bean	178 – 251
Field pea	174 – 196
Peanut (groundnut)	87 – 222
Hairy vetch	111 – 130
Lentil	167 – 189
Lupine	121 – 157
Soybean	22 – 310

Compiled from: LaRue and Patterson (1981) and Heichel (1987).

such that efficient nodulation and nitrogen fixation do not occur. The last factor is probably a direct result of legumes usually being grown under rain-fed conditions much too often on poor soils with very little, if any, in the way of such inputs as chemical fertilizers and pesticides. However, legume cultivation on some poor soils has several long-term benefits that are difficult to convert into monetary value. Both short- and long-term cropping rotations involving legumes result in enhanced soil organic matter content and mineralizable nitrogen. This provides not only better control of nitrogen availability, but also improved soil structure, less energy for cultivation, and reduced soil erosion (Hoyt and Hargrove 1986). Even a minor reduction in the soil erosion rate over a period of decades can have a major impact on the properties and productivity of some soils. The enhanced mineralizable nitrogen levels in soils with legume rotations, compared to those for continuously cereal-cropped soils, also aids greatly in the control of groundwater quality. With legumes, not only is less fertilizer nitrogen required, but the level of nitrate nitrogen in the soil at any given time is usually lower, so there are fewer nitrates to leach below the root zone. Today, the use of legumes in agriculture provides an annual input of fixed nitrogen approximately equal to that fixed industrially for fertilizers, and these two combined are approximately equal to the estimated input of fixed nitrogen from all sources prior to human intervention (Hardy and Havelka 1975; Delwiche 1978).

AGRONOMY

Monocropping

The ultimate goal of all crop production practices is to achieve maximum yield potential of a given cultivar or crop species. Yield is a product not only of a crop's genetic constitution but also of its interactions with the environment. Environmental factors influence the expression of the genotype, many by limiting crop growth and yield. Some of these (weeds, insects, rodents, birds, fungi, bacteria, nematodes, and viruses) directly reduce the yield irrespective of the potential yield level in a given environment; others (nutrients, stand density or plant population, spacing, leaf orientation) may add or subtract from the yielding ability of a crop in any environment. Most crop management practices are therefore aimed at balancing these variable factors to achieve optimum yields.

The agronomic practices described below for some of the important food legume species are intended only as general guidelines. For detailed information on various aspects of legume monocropping, as well as on various individual legumes, the reader is referred to following reviews and monographs: ICAR (1970), Doku (1976), Summerfield and Bunting (1980), Duke (1981), Smartt (1976), Bhatia (1983), Matthews (1989), and Power (1987). Agronomic practices vary not only from locality to locality but also by geographical region; however, judging from the literature, legume monocrops are given hardly any special attention (especially under subsistence farming) as compared to the high-yielding cereal crops, such as rice, wheat, and corn. Most legume crops are also cultivated on marginal lands—indicating that, even with minor attention, their yields should be greatly improved. Nitrogenous fertilizer input is generally not required for legumes, and in many cases may be detrimental to crop yields since it results in excessive vegetative growth at the expense of seed yields. Application of phosphate and potash, however, appears to have beneficial results in many instances. The importance of proper rhizobial inoculum for the seeds cannot be stressed any further. Although in many places legumes are grown under rain-fed conditions, the application of one or two irrigations, wherever facilities exist—especially at the flowering stage and under drought conditions—increases their yield potential. Certain legume species (i.e., peanut, soybean, pigeon pea, and cowpea) appear to be far more susceptible to pests and diseases than many others, and may require special attention in this regard. As a general rule, good agronomic and farm practices should help in maximizing the yield potential of various food legumes.

Peanut (Arachis hypogaea)

Native to South America, peanuts (groundnuts) are widely grown in tropics and subtropics throughout most of the world. They are drought resistant, but notably susceptible to frost. The crop requires hot, dry conditions for maturing. Peanuts are primarily grown as an oilseed and seldom as a pulse. They are annuals, with ascending- to decumbent- to prostrate-type, geocarpic, glabrate to hirsute herbs. Peanuts grow best on light, friable, well-drained sandy loams, but can also be grown in heavier soils.

All commercial varieties of peanut are propagated from seed: Virginia-type (alternately branched) seeds have a dormancy period; Spanish–Valencia types (sequentially branched) have little or no dormancy. Seedbed should be prepared either flat or widely ridged. Spacing and seed rate vary with growth habit and production methods. Seed rates of up to 45 kg/ha are used for runner types, and of ≤90 kg/ha for bunch varieties.Short-season cultivars in semiarid regions respond to early application of nitrogen, whereas phosphorus is added on tropical red earths. Calcium supply in the pegging zone is essential for high yield of good-quality seeds in large-podded Virginia types. Seeds produced on calcium-deficient soils often have poor germination and poor seedling growth.

Although flowering may commence in 30 days, 80–150 days or more are required for fruit maturation. In harvesting by hand, plants are pulled and turned over on the ground, or stacked or placed on racks to cure. The pods are picked and allowed to dry on trays at depths of ≤5 cm, or spread in the sun in the dry-season tropics. In fully mechanized harvesting, a single operation pulls, inverts, and windrows the plants, which remain a few days for preliminary drying. The pods are removed by combines and either elevated into attached baskets or blown directly into trailing "drying wagons"; these, when full, are towed to a drying station where warm or ambient air is forced through the load of peanuts. The crop is usually marketed as dried seeds instead of dried pods. Seed yields under subsistence farming range from 400 to 1,500 kg/ha; up to 6,000 kg/ha are possible under advanced farming systems.

Pigeon pea (Cajanus cajan)

Pigeon pea (red gram) is commonly grown in several tropical and subtropical countries of Asia and Africa. It is one of the most prized pulse crops of India. It is a short-lived, 2–12 ft high, perennial shrub, but is usually grown as an annual crop, often for green manure or for cover in plantations. Its deep and penetrating root system makes it specially valuable as a renovating and contour-hedge crop for checking soil erosion. The roots also aerate the soil and subsoil, and the vegetative parts add a lot of organic material to the soil by way of leaf and flower shedding. This property renders it an economic success in India, even though the return from the crop is not commensurate with the period for which it occupies the field.

In India, pigeon pea is normally sown in July with the onset of first monsoon rains; it ripens about March, thus occupying the land during one rainy and one cold-weather season. The plant is hardy and requires little attention in the field. However, being native to tropics and subtropics, it cannot withstand even light frost.

A deep-rooted crop, pigeon pea responds well to cultivation. The surface soil should be well tilled. Young seedlings, although not delicate, show only scanty growth for the first couple of months, but then start off vigorously. Once well established, the crop requires little attention; however, it pays to give it a reasonable amount of cultivation.

Row spacing and seed rate depend on the manner of cropping and the final intended use of the crop. In pure crops, especially the spreading types, sowings are usually made 2 ft apart in rows 4 ft wide. Such a planting requires about 10–12 kg seeds/ha. Usually a plant population of 30,000 plants/ha is required for optimal yields.

The crop usually responds to phosphate fertilizers at the time of sowing. Nitrogen and potassium are rarely beneficial, though lime application may be so on very acid soils. Even though pigeon pea is among the most drought resistant cultivated crops known in the tropics, it usually responds generously to a reasonable amount of irrigation during dry seasons. Watering in excess of actual needs, however, retards seed production and encourages vegetative growth.

One irrigation at the end of December or in the first week of January is effective in protecting the crop from the winter frost damage.

The crop is harvested according to the cultivar used, date of sowing, and location—optimally when a large percentage of the pods is mature. The pods are indehiscent even when they are roughly handled. Although pods are hand picked in harvesting the first crop, in the final harvest, the matured crop is harvested by cutting the whole plant. After allowing the leaves to dry and shed, the plants bearing the pods are collected at one place and the pods separated by beating with sticks. The seeds are then separated from the pods either by beating or by a thresher. The proportion of seeds to pods is generally 50–60%. The forage and pods, after the seeds have been winnowed, make an excellent roughage for livestock. Seed yields vary from 500 to 1,100 kg/ha.

Chick-pea (Cicer arietinum)

Chick-peas are commonly grown in subtropics or during the cool season in the tropics. They are widely cultivated in India and in several Near East and Mediterranean countries. They are moderately resistant to drought and high temperatures. Chick-peas are herbaceous annuals that branch close to the ground. Some varieties are semierect with a main stem and only a few branches; others are semispreading types with profuse branching. They are always grown as a cold-weather crop.

Chick-peas do not need a very fine seedbed: A deep plowing followed by a harrowing is generally sufficient. No fine tilth is attempted; the soil is not compacted, but is left loose on the surface. Planting is done in late October or early November in rows 12–18 in. apart. Depending on the cultivar, seed rates may vary from 30 to 45 kg/ha.

The crop is generally not supplied with nitrogen fertilizers, but often responds well to phosphate application. Although it may be irrigated once or twice during the early growth period, further irrigations may not be needed.

Depending on the variety, the crop matures within 95–150 days after sowing. Yields range from 400 to 1,800 kg/ha. Harvesting is done when most of the leaves and pods have turned brown. The plants are either uprooted or cut aboveground, then dried completely before threshing and winnowing.

Guar (Cyamopsis tetragonoloba)

Guar (cluster bean) has been grown in India since ancient times for vegetable and forage purposes. Up to the beginning of the twentieth century, guar was not much known outside India. Although first introduced to the United States from India in 1905 (Poats 1960), it is only recently that the industrial applications of guar gum were recognized. Guar gum is now widely used as thickener in food products and for sizing textiles and paper products.

Guar is a hardy, bushy annual, and is notably drought resistant. It grows well in deep alluvial and sandy loam soils, but does not withstand waterlogging conditions or excessive wetness. When raised for green manure or forage, sowing is done broadcast; for seed or vegetable crop, it is sown in rows 1.5–2 ft apart with 0.5–1 ft between the plants. Seed rates in the latter case vary from 10 to 25 kg/ha.

Guar pods begin to set about 45–55 days after sowing; the seeds ripen 110–160 days after sowing. Guar pods usually do not shatter. For the best-quality seed, the crop should be harvested soon after maturity, when pods are brown and dry, or when the moisture content is <14%. Pods are harvested by hand and manually threshed. Seed yields of up to 900 kg/ha have been reported under dryland conditions; yields twice that are possible with irrigation.

Horse Gram (Dolichos biflorus)

Horse gram is the most extensively grown legume in Southern India in areas of moderate (<75-cm) rainfall. It is drought resistant and hardy, and tolerates a wide range of soil types. Good, deep red loams, black cotton soils, clayey paddy soils, stony and gravelly upland soils, rough jungle cleared and being newly brought under cultivation—all can be sown with horse gram. It is therefore a kind of preparatory crop on new land. In Southern India, it is almost considered a "famine year" if even horse gram cannot be grown. When used for seed, horse gram is sown in October or November; for fodder, it is sown thrice on the same field—in June, August, and November.

No special land preparation is required for horse gram. It is sown in rows but is generally broadcast. The crop is always sown thick at a rate of about 40 kg/ha. By the time the pods mature and the crop is ready for harvest, a considerable part of the leaves dry and drop on the field. The whole plants are harvested, dried for about a week, and threshed and winnowed to separate the seeds. Yields range from 200 to 500 kg/ha.

Soybean (Glycine max)

Soybeans originated and have been extensively cultivated in China since prehistoric times. They are now widely grown in the United States, Brazil, Far East Asia, and, to a limited extent, in Africa and the Near East. They thrive well in subtropical climate with good rainfall and warm sun, but may require irrigation in semiarid regions. Although soybeans can be grown on a wide variety of soils, the crop performs best in alluvial soils. A well-pulverized seedbed up to 15–20 cm deep is required for optimal seed germination and plant growth. Inoculation with proper rhizobial strains is essential when the crop is newly introduced to a locality; otherwise, 80–100 kg N/ha is considered adequate. Soybeans also require more phosphorus and potash than most other food legume crops. Seed rates range from 40 to 50 kg/ha, and the seed should not be sown more than 5 cm deep to ensure good germination. The grain crop is sown in rows 1.5–2 ft apart; for fodder, it is sown broadcast.

Soybean is very sensitive to photoperiod; it is inherently a short-day plant. The crop usually matures within four or five months, and yields in excess of 2,000 kg/ha can be obtained. Ripening is usually very even. At maturity, the leaves shed easily and the stems dry. In varieties that tend to shatter, harvesting must be done when the pod color starts changing from yellow to brown and the leaves begin to shed: A delay of even two days results in pods bursting and the eventual shedding of seeds. Harvesting is done by combine, and special care is required to prevent mechanical damage to seeds. Pods can be threshed manually or mechanically.

Kesari Dhal (Lathyrus sativus)

Kesari dhal, or chickling pea, is mainly grown in India. It is a hardy, drought-resistant annual that thrives on poor soils. In the central plains of India, it is an important "famine crop," surviving or cultivated after cereals have failed from drought. (Under such circumstances, its excessive consumption often leads to the outbreak of neurolathyrism.) Outside India, this crop is rarely grown. Lathyrus is a winter crop and requires a cool climate. It is affected neither by excessive water in the field at the time of sowing, nor by water shortage during the growing season. It is generally grown on clayey soils, which remain wet long after the growing season is over.

There is hardly any tillage given when this legume is sown in rice fields before the rice is harvested. On lands submerged in water, until late October to November, it is sown broadcast on muddy soils, where it sprouts and grows in spite of the subsequent hardening of the soil almost to the consistency of stone. Its cultivation is most common in the late paddy areas. Seed is broadcast at a rate of 35–45 kg/ha. No interculture is necessary, and aftercare is almost nil.

The crop usually matures in four to six months, and seed yields range from 1,000 to 1,500 kg/ha. It is harvested as soon as the leaves begin to turn yellow, but when the pods are not fully ripe—pods, when fully ripe, easily dehisce and scatter the seeds. The harvested crop is allowed to dry in heaps in the fields for about a week, then threshed and winnowed to separate the seeds.

Lentil (Lens esculenta)

Lentil, a cool-season crop of the Mediterranean region and the Near East, is now cultivated worldwide. It prefers warm, dry climate and, although quite unsuited to cultivation in the wet tropics, can be raised in the cool, dry season at higher altitudes in the monsoon tropics under irrigation. It is quite susceptible to winter frost. Lentil is an herbaceous annual characterized by highly dehiscent pods, and can be grown on a wide range of soil types.

Seeds may be sown either broadcast or in drills at 50 kg/ha. The crop requires a very thoroughly prepared seedbed, but no attention by way of weeding or interculture, and irrigation is seldom required.

Lentil is a short-duration crop and is ready for harvest in three or four months. Usually, the plants are cut to ground level, dried for a week or so, and threshed; seeds are then separated by winnowing. Seed yields range from 500 to 700 kg/ha under rain-fed conditions, but 1500-1700 kg/ha are obtained with irrigation.

Lupine (**Lupinus** *spp.*)

Lupines have been used for human food purposes predominantly by ancient cultures surrounding the Mediterranean and by those living in the Andean highlands. Species commonly used for food purposes include *L. albus, L. luteus,* and *L. mutabilis.* The first two are native to Southern Europe; the third is common to the Andean regions. Although the significance of lupines as green fodder or for silage has been accepted without reservation, its use in human nutrition has consistently decreased due to the presence of bitter-tasting alkaloids. Modern varieties have been bred for low alkaloid content (i.e., low toxicity), and are commonly called "sweet lupines." The most interesting species are the blue-, yellow-, and white-flowering types. Blue lupine, widely grown in Western Australia, thrives on deep, fertile soils but is susceptible to *Fusarium* wilt and ripens very late. Yellow lupine is grown for seed in northeastern Europe, but is best used for green manuring when reclaiming very acidic, sandy soils. White lupine is the most promising for grain production. Its high-yielding potential (up to 5,000 kg/ha), disease resistance, early ripening (120–140-day growing period), and indehiscent pod characteristics are quite promising. It can be grown on acid, sandy soils, but does better on deep, well-limed, free-draining loams. It requires a thoroughly prepared seedbed, and seed rates of about 50–60 kg/ha.

Harvesting lupines is a big problem, since most varieties ripen very unevenly. Because the large, fleshy pods are slow to dry out and shatter far too easily, the crop must be combined quite carefully to reduce these losses. The threshed seeds should be dried to a moisture content of about 13–14%.

Moth Bean (**Phaseolus aconitifolius**)

The moth bean is grown as a crop only on the Indian subcontinent. It is an herbaceous annual with a spreading prostrate habit. Among the *kharif* pulses of

India (i.e., those sown before the monsoon to ripen in autumn), moth bean is considered to be the most drought resistant. It is mostly grown as a dry crop on light sandy soils, and requires minimal land preparation. It is usually sown broadcast with the onset of monsoon rains at rates of 3–4 kg/ha. The crop matures within three or four months of sowing, and yields range from 1,500 to 2,000 kg/ha. Harvesting, threshing, and drying practices are similar to those used for other dryland pulses of India.

Green Gram (Phaseolus aureus) and Black Gram (P. mungo)

These legumes are botanically very similar. Black gram can be distinguished from green gram, however, by much shorter, stout, very hairy pods and longer oblong seeds, which vary in color from blackish to olive. The current nomenclature for green gram is *Vigna radiata;* that for black gram, *V. mungo*. Both are now commonly grown in several tropical Asian countries. They thrive best under hot, dry climate. Green gram is slightly less tolerant to drought and humidity. Among all the pulses grown in India, black gram is the most highly prized for its nutritional value and food uses. These pulses can be cultivated on a variety of soils ranging from red laterite, black cotton, medium loamy, sandy, light, or shallow stony soils to clay soils. Black gram requires slightly rougher tilth for maximum seed production than green gram. The crops may be sown broadcast or in rows, the commonly used seed rates being 25–30 kg/ha. Desirable plant population densities for good growing conditions are about 150,000–200,000 plants/ha. Both pulses mature within three or four months, and harvesting and threshing practices are similar to those of other dryland-grown pulse crops. Seed yields vary between 500 and 2,000 kg/ha.

Rice Bean (Phaseolus calcaratus)

The cultivation of rice bean is largely limited to India. It is mostly grown in the hills up to an altitude of 2,000 m in the Western Himalayas as a *kharif* crop, and is usually sown broadcast at relatively high seed rates (60–80 kg/ha). It is very vigorous in growth, giving a thick, dense mass of foliage, and is therefore often used as a cover crop to check soil erosion. Its cultivation practices are otherwise similar to those used for green and black gram; however, its yield potential is quite low (250–300 kg/ha). Among the pulses, rice beans are the richest sources of calcium.

Lima Beans (Phaseolus lunatus)

Lima beans are native to tropical America but now widely grown throughout the humid and subhumid tropics and subtropics. The crop is fairly tolerant to high temperatures, poor soil conditions, and drought, but cannot withstand frost. It is a perennial, but is often cultivated as an annual or biennial.

Lima beans can be grown on all types of soil, but prefer moderately rich and well-drained soils. Very rich soils are conducive to greater vegetative growth and less pod formation, whereas heavy soils prone to waterlogging are detrimental for the proper growth of the crop. The land is prepared thoroughly and brought to a fine tilth by repeated plowing and harrowing. Seed rates depend on the seed size of the variety used, and vary from 50–150 kg/ha. Lower seed rates are also required for space-planted pole beans. The crop matures within seven to nine months, and dry-seed yields range from 1,000 to 3,000 kg/ha.

Dry Bean (Phaseolus vulgaris)

Dry beans (common beans), native to the American continent, are widely grown throughout the world in warm temperate or subtropic climate. They are also grown in the cool season or at high altitudes in tropics. The crop is susceptible to high temperatures, frost, and drought. Dry beans grow well on clays and heavy loams that have a good structure, are well-drained, and have a pH > 6.5 (so that nodule bacteria work better). Organic soils and too much nitrogen usually result in overabundant straw, lodging, and low grain yields.

Dry beans require a well-prepared seedbed. Seed rates used depend on seed size: As little as 25 kg/ha may be required for small-seeded varieties, whereas rates ≤70 kg/ha may be necessary for the largest-seeded cultivars. Plant populations should be about 150,000/ha under good conditions. Sowing methods can vary, the seed usually being sown deeper in light soils than in heavy soils. The crop responds well to both potash and phosphorus applications. Good crops can be produced with very little moisture applied during the season; but light irrigation just before blooming helps in setting pods, and another irrigation is given soon after these have set.

The dwarf varieties of dry bean mature in about three months; climbing varieties take longer and mature continuously. Seed yields range from 250 to 2,500 kg/ha. The beans are harvested when a sizable percentage of pods are fully ripe and most of the remainder have turned yellow. Harvesting should begin before the lower pods become dry enough to shatter: Nearly mature pods continue to ripen after plants are cut, and heavy shattering losses occur when plants are cut and too many pods are dry. Combines are used for mechanical harvesting of beans. The harvested beans are quickly removed to a factory, where they are processed for canning, quick-freezing, and freeze-drying.

When used as fresh, green beans, the young pods are hand-picked into shallow baskets and removed to a cool packing shed to retain quality. The harvested bean pods must be whole, undamaged, separated (i.e., not in clusters), and free of soil contamination.

Pea (Pisum sativum)

Peas are widely cultivated in the cool, moist temperate climate or in the cool season at high altitudes in the tropics and subtropics. The crop is highly susceptible to high temperatures and drought. It is a short-lived herbaceous annual, glaucous and climbing by means of leaflet tendrils. The taproot is well developed with many slender lateral branches.

Peas grow best on loams and lighter types of soils; seedbed preparation and harvesting can be difficult on heavy soils. All soils must be well drained and have a pH > 5.5. Peas require a fine seedbed such that the seeds can be sown about 5 cm deep in a fairly loose tilth. Depending on the purpose for which they are grown, seed rates vary between 60 and 300 kg/ha: Lower seed rates are used for green vegetable production, high rates for dry-seed production. In subsistence farming, seed rates are probably lower, and they may be broadcast or sown in rows. Plant populations of the order of 200,000/ha are necessary to obtain satisfactory yields.

Peas often respond to phosphorus and potassium applications, although nitrogen is not normally required. Except under very dry conditions, irrigation is not normally required.

There are three main types of pea used for human consumption: *Vining peas* are used for canning fresh ("garden peas"), quick-freezing, or artificial drying; *threshed dry peas* are sold dry or canned; and *pulling peas* are sold as fresh peas in pods. Vining peas are ready when the crop is just starting to lose its green color and the peas are still soft. The firmness of the peas is tested daily near harvest with a tenderometer, which indicates the best time to start cutting: The reading for freezing peas is about 100, though they can be a little firmer for canning, at 120. When ready, the crop must be cut as soon as possible. The pods are then separated either manually or mechanically, and the shelled peas rushed to the processing plant for freezing, canning, or drying. Threshed peas are not harvested until the vines and pods have turned a yellow or light brown color, and before the seed starts to shed. After partly drying on the ground, the pods are removed, threshed, and the shelled peas are then further dried slowly in a mechanical dryer at low temperatures (43 °C). Pulling peas are harvested manually by removing the pods when the peas are in a fresh, sweet condition. The yield of green pods varies with the variety, climatic conditions, soil, fertilizers, and irrigation. Dry-seed yields of about 2,000–4,000 kg/ha are possible under good farming conditions.

Winged Bean (Psophocarpus tetragonolobus)

Probably originated in India, winged bean (goa bean) is now grown to a limited extent in Southeast Asia, the Pacific region, Africa, and the Caribbean. It is primarily cultivated for its immature edible pods and cooked as a vegetable; young pods are even eaten raw. The leaves, young sprouts, flowers, and fruits are also used as vegetables. The dried seeds are excellent sources of oil and protein. Winged bean is a perennial vine, twining, and glabrous, but is usually grown as an annual. The main lateral roots run horizontally at a shallow depth, later becoming thick, tuberous, and nodulous. It can be grown in a range of soil types, but good drainage is essential. It is sensitive to drought, frost, salinity, and waterlogging.

Winged bean crop is usually space planted, and populations are of the order of 10,000–12,000 plants/ha. The seed is sown 1–3 in. deep at the beginning of the rains in drills spaced 2–4 ft apart. The crop requires stakes or trellises for support. The flowers are usually plucked to increase root yields. After fruiting the top dies, but the plant is perennial. The stored food in tubers allows resumption of growth the following year when rains begin.

The first green pods are ready for consumption six to ten weeks after sowing (or two weeks after pollination). After three weeks, the pods become tough; after three more weeks, the seeds mature. The plant may bear pods indefinitely but production declines; this is why, although perennial, it is often treated as an annual. When grown for seed, the harvesting, threshing, and drying practices are similar to those for other legume crops. Dry-seed yields range from 500 to 2,000 kg/ha; those of edible tubers from 2,000 to 10,000 kg/ha.

Broad Bean (Vicia faba)

Broad beans (fava beans, vetches) are widely grown in the temperate and subtropical countries with good rainfall in the Mediterranean region. They are also cultivated during the cool season at high altitudes in tropics. The crop is highly susceptible to drought and high temperatures. *Vicia* includes both annual and perennial species, although those commonly grown are either annual or biennial. They are more tolerant to acid soil conditions than are most legume crops.

Tillage requirements vary depending on the soil type. It is, however, desirable to have a reasonably firm seedbed to ensure better surface moisture conditions and, consequently, good seed germination. Seed rates are quite high (130–160 kg/ha), and plant populations of about 200,000 plants/ha are essential for optimal yields. The depth of planting should not exceed 4 in.

Fertilizers usually are not necessary for the successful growth of this crop. However, in planting vetch for the first time on land that has neither been used for legumes nor received application of nitrogen, nitrogen in some available form should be included. On acid soils, the crop responds well to liming. Soil phosphorus is essential for proper fruiting and seed production.

Vetches are ordinarily cut for hay when the first pods are well developed, and are cured in the stocks for several days. With most vetches, it is difficult to obtain a bright green-colored hay. When grown for seed purposes, the general practice is to cut common, hairy, smooth, woolly pods, and other shattering vetches as soon as the lower pods are fully ripe. At this time, the upper pods are fully formed and the plant carries a maximum quantity of seed. If harvesting is delayed until the upper pods are ripe, losses from shattering become enormous. After threshing, the seeds are cleaned with ordinary fanning mills. When beans are harvested by combine, the crop should be fully matured and as dry as possible. In most varieties, the attachment point of the bean seeds to the pod is black when the crop is ripe. The moisture contents of the combine-harvested beans are usually higher than those of cereal crops. Seed yields generally range from 3,000 to 6,000 kg/ha.

Cowpea (Vigna unguiculata)

Cowpeas (black-eyed peas) probably originated in India but are now widely cultivated throughout the world. They are grown in semiarid to subhumid tropics and are tolerant of drought and high temperatures, but have specific daylength requirements. Cowpea is a vigorously growing annual legume, with a strong taproot bearing numerous horizontally spreading lateral roots. It is adapted to a variety of soil types (red loam, black clayey loam, rice fields, black cotton soils, coarse gravel, sandy and light sandy loams). It is also more tolerant of heavy rainfall than are most other pulses. In India, it is usually raised as a dryland *kharif* crop or as a pre- and late-monsoon crop.

Land for cowpea is neither prepared in any special way nor heavily manured. Cowpeas are seldom supplied with any fertilizers, and in most countries are grown as a rain-fed crop. The usual pre- and postcultivations for any rain-fed crop also apply to cowpea fields. As a pure crop, cowpea is sown in rows 2–4 ft apart, depending upon the cultivar habit. The commonly used seed rates are in the range 25–35 kg/ha, giving plant populations of the order of 150,000/ha.

Cowpea crop ripens unevenly, and the proper stage of harvesting is difficult to determine. Flowers, green pods, and ripe pods usually occur on vines at the same time. In some varieties, if the mature pods are left too long on the vines, they are likely to shatter. Usually, the crop is harvested for seed when one-half to two-thirds of the pods are ripe. Either the pods are hand-picked or the entire plants are pulled out. The seeds are then separated after drying on a threshing floor, trod by cattle or beaten with sticks, then winnowed as for other dryland crops. Seed yields are 400–600 kg/ha in the tropics, but yields of 1,000–3,000 kg/ha are obtained in the subtropical countries.

As a ready reference, some of the important agronomic characteristics of these food legumes are summarized in Table 2-5. The variations in cultural practices, especially in the maturity period and yields, indicate that much extension work

Table 2-5. Field Characteristics of Some Important Food Legumes.

Legume and Botany	Ecology	Soil Type	Cultivation	Maturity, Seed Yield
Arachis hypogaea (peanut, groundnut)				
Annual ascending to decumbent to prostrate type; geocarpic, glabrate to hirsute herbs	Suitable for tropics, subtropics, and warm, temperate regions; frost sensitive, drought resistant; needs hot, dry conditions for maturing, 30–100 cm rainfall, 10–28 °C temp.	Best on light, friable, well-drained sandy loams, but will grow in heavier soils, pH 4.3–8.7	Spacing and seed rate vary with growth habit and production method; sown on flat or widely ridged seedbeds; 45 kg/ha for runner and 90 kg/ha for bunch types; responds well to Ca and S	3.5–5 mo; 400–1,500 kg/ha (2,000–6,000 kg/ha in advanced farming systems)
Cajanus cajan (pigeon pea, red gram)				
Perennial, woody shrub, mostly grown as an annual for seed	Drought resistant; tolerates <65 cm annual rainfall; 18–29 °C temp.; sensitive to frost and waterlogging	All types from sand to heavy clay loams, well-drained; medium heavy loams best	10–12 kg/ha in 2 × 4-ft rows or broadcast, sown 1–2 in. deep; little response to N; P application beneficial	5–6 mo (range 4–12); 500–1,100 kg/ha
Cicer arietinum (chick-pea)				
Annual herb, erect or spreading, much branched	Rain-fed, cool weather or as dry-climate crop; 60–100 cm rainfall; 18–26 °C temp.; moderately resistant to drought and high temperatures; sensitive to frost, hailstones, and excess rains	Prefers well-drained soils (clayey but not too heavy) of pH 5.5–8.6; generally sown on heavy black or red soils	30–45 kg/ha broadcast or in rows 1–2 ft apart at a depth of 1–4 in.; little response to N; P beneficial; 1–2 irrigations desirable 45 and 75 days after planting	3–6 mo; 400–1,800 kg/ha
Cyamopsis tetragonoloba (guar, cluster bean)				
Hardy, bushy branching annual	Drought-tolerant summer legume; thrives well on alluvial and sandy	Wide range of soils; 40–50 cm rainfall; 25–30 °C	10–25 kg/ha broadcast or in rows 1.5–2 ft apart at 1-in. depth;	4–6 mo; 900 kg/ha; double under

	temp.; sensitive to frost and shade	loams with well-drained subsoil; pH 7.5–8.0	requires P	irrigated conditions
Dolichos biflorus (horse gram)				
Hardy, annual herb, semierect, twining branches	Notably drought resistant; moderate rainfall of up to 75 cm; 25–30 °C temp.	Wide range of soil types	Generally broadcast at 40 kg/ha	3–4 mo; 200–500 kg/ha
Glycine max (soybean)				
Bushy, rather coarse annual herb	Subtropical plant; 50 cm annual rainfall; 15–28 °C temp.; susceptible to excessive heat or severe winters; short-day plant	Performs best in fertile, well-drained alluvial soils, but tolerates wide range of soil conditions; pH 6.0–6.5	40–50 kg/ha in rows 1.5–2 ft apart at a depth of 2 in.; P and K beneficial; inoculum essential when newly introduced to a locality	4–5 mo; up to 2,000 kg/ha
Lathyrus sativus (kesari dhal)				
Much-branched, climbing, suberect annual herb	Hardy crop suited to dry climates; drought resistant; 30–70 cm rainfall; 5–28 °C temp.; sensitive to acidity	All types of soils; black, deep, retentive soils best; pH 4.5–8.3; requires lime on acid soils	Generally broadcast at 35–45 kg/ha	4–6 mo; 1,000–1,500 kg/ha
Lens esculenta (L. culinaris) (lentil)				
Annual, bushy herb; erect or suberect; softly hairy; much branched	Cold-weather crop or winter crop in tropics; not suited to humid tropics; 30–80 cm rainfall; 18–21 °C temp.; long-day plant; sensitive to waterlogging	Thrives well on wide range of soils; best on clay soils; pH 4.5–8.2; slightly tolerant to salinity	Broadcast or in rows 1 ft apart at 50 kg/ha	3–4 mo; 500–700 kg/ha

Table 2-5. (Continued)

Legume and Botany	Ecology	Soil Type	Cultivation	Maturity, Seed Yield
Lupinus spp. (lupine)				
Short, hairy annual	Winter crop; long-day plant; intolerant to waterlogging; 40–100 cm rainfall; 6–26 °C temp.; good frost and cold resistance	Well-drained, fertile, neutral soils; native in acid soils; somewhat tolerant to salinity	Depending upon species, 60–180 kg/ha in rows 1–3 ft apart and 1–2 in. deep; needs P	3–5 mo; 1,000–2,000 kg/ha
Phaseolus aconitifolius (*Vigna aconitifolia*) (moth bean)				
Slender, trailing, hairy annual herb	Most drought resistant among "Kharif" pulses of India; dry rain-fed crop; 50–75 cm rainfall; 21–28 °C temp.; frost sensitive	Light sandy soils; pH 5.0–8.1	Usually broadcast at 3–4 kg/ha; not much care required	3–4 mo; 1,500–2,000 kg/ha
Phaseolus aureus (*Vigna radiata*) (green gram, mung bean)				
Erect or semierect; rather hairy annual shrubby herb	Drought resistant; sensitive to frost, waterlogging, and salinity; 70–90 cm well-distributed rainfall; 8–28 °C temp.	Good loamy or black cotton soils; also sufficiently deep-red light loams or alluvial soils; pH 4.3–8.1	Broadcast or drilled in rows 1–2 ft apart at 25–30 kg/ha; responds to P; irrigation beneficial under dry conditions	3–4 mo; 500–2,000 kg/ha
Phaseolus calcaratus (*Vigna umbellata*) (rice bean)				
Annual or short-lived perennial; suberect; vining branches	Tolerates high temperatures and drought but not frost; 100–150 cm rainfall; 18–30 °C temp.; short-day plant	Best on fertile loams; pH 6.8–7.5	Generally broadcast at 60–80 kg/ha or in rows 3 ft apart; responds to P	2–5 mo; 250–300 kg/ha

Phaseolus lunatus (P. limensis) (lima bean)			
Annual or perennial bushy herb	Tropical crop; can be grown in humid, subhumid, and subtropic regions; fairly tolerant of high temperatures, poor soil conditions, and drought; susceptible to frost and waterlogging; 30–150 cm rainfall; 9–28 °C temp.	Best on well-drained, well-aerated fertile soils; in general, on all types of soils; pH 4.5-8.4	50–150 kg/ha, depending on seed size, in rows 3 ft apart; responds to P and K	7–9 mo; 1,000–3,000 kg/ha

Phaseolus mungo (Vigna mungo) (black gram, mung bean)			
Decumbent or erect; diffusely branched annual herb	Moderately resistant to drought; intolerant to frost and prolonged cloudiness; up to 90 cm rainfall; 8–28 °C temp.	Clays, black cotton, or red light loams; pH 4.5–7.5	Broadcast or drilled in rows 1 ft apart at 13–22 kg/ha; responds to P and K	3–4 mo; 400–1,600 kg/ha

Phaseolus vulgaris (dry bean, common bean)			
Highly polymorphic species; annual herb; erect and bushy	Tolerates most environmental conditions in tropical and temperate zones, but does poorly in very wet tropics; sensitive to frost and waterlogging; 10–100 cm rainfall; 6–28 °C temp.	Best in well-drained sandy loam, silt loam, or clay loam soils rich in organic matter; sensitive to Al, B, Mn, and Na; pH 4.2–8.7	20–120 kg/ha, depending on seed size, in rows 2.5–3 ft apart and 2–3 in. deep; responds to P and K; irrigation beneficial in semiarid regions	*Green beans:* 4–6 wk; 4,500 kg/ha; *Dry beans:* 2–5 mo; 250–2,500 kg/ha

Pisum sativum (pea)			
Annual herb; climbing or bushy; glabrous, usually glaucous	Requires cool, relatively humid climate or high altitude in tropics; susceptible to high temperatures and drought; 80–100 cm well-distributed rainfall; 5–27 °C temp.	Variety of soils; prefer well-drained clay loams or silt loams; pH 4.2–8.3	*Green peas:* in rows 2–3 ft apart, 1–3 in. deep at 67–113 kg/ha; *Dry peas:* 200–300 kg/ha; responds to P and K	*Green peas:* 1.5–2.5 mo; *Dry peas:* 2–4 mo; 400–4,000 kg/ha

Table 2-5. (Continued)

Legume and Botany	Ecology	Soil Type	Cultivation	Maturity, Seed Yield
Psophocarpus tetragonolobus (winged bean)				
Perennial vine; twining, glabrous; usually grown as annual; tuberous and nodulous roots	Moist tropics; twining, glabrous; sensitive to drought, frost, salinity, and water-logging; 150–250 cm annual rainfall; 15–28 °C temp.; short-day plant	Variety of soils but should be well-drained; pH 4.3–7.5	Sown 1–3 in. deep in drills spaced 2–4 ft apart; seed rates vary with cultivar and seed size	*Green pods*: 6–10 wk *Dry seeds*: 4–6 mo; 500–2,000 kg/ha *Tubers*: 2,000–10,000 kg/ha
Vicia faba (broad bean, fava bean, vetch)				
Coarse, erect annual herb	Winter annual in warm-temperature and subtropic areas; highly susceptible to high temperatures and drought; 20–150 cm rainfall; 6–27 °C temp.	Tolerates nearly any soil type; grows best on rich loams; pH 4.5–8.3	Sown 2–4 in. deep in rows 2–3 ft apart at 130–160 kg/ha	3-7 mo.; 3,000–6,000 kg/ha
Vigna unguiculata (cowpea, black-eyed pea)				
Herbaceous annual; erect, semierect, or spreading type; glabrous except at nodes	Semiarid to subhumid tropics; requires reasonably warm growing season, fairly good distribution of 70–150 cm rainfall followed by bright weather during and after flowering; tolerates drought and high temperatures; photoperiod sensitive; 12–28 °C temp.	Does well on well-drained moderately light or medium loam soils; lime is essential on acid soils; soil of medium fertility best; pH 5.0–7.5	25–35 kg/ha in rows 2–4 ft apart; responds to P and K	3–8 mo.; 400–600 kg/ha (tropics); 1,000–3,000 kg/ha (subtropics)

needs to be done in educating farmers as to the benefits of proper monocropping of various legume species. It is also quite evident from the data presented in Table 2-5 that we should easily be able to double legume production worldwide merely by improving agronomic practices and using high-yielding, pest- and disease-tolerant legume cultivars.

Cereal–Legume Intercropping Systems

Growing crops in mixed stands is often regarded as more productive in terms of land use than growing them separately (Willey 1979). Mixed cropping is traditionally practiced in several nations of Asia, Africa and Latin America. In the Western world, interest in cereal–legume intercropping is developing in some temperate regions with warm climates, such as Australia and the United States (Chui and Shibles 1984; Ofori and Stern 1987). The main reasons for this appears to be some of the established and speculated advantages for intercropping systems, such as higher grain yields, greater land use efficiency per unit land area, and improvement of soil fertility through the addition of nitrogen fixation and excretion from the component legume. The intercropping of legumes with cereals also offers scope for developing energy-efficient and sustainable agriculture (IAEA 1980).

Intercropping may be broadly defined as the growing of two or more crop species simultaneously in the same field during a growing season. There are four main types of intercropping:

1. *mixed:* growing component crops simultaneously with no distinct row arrangement; commonly practiced in labor-intensive subsistence farming.
2. *row:* growing component crops simultaneously in different rows; used in mechanized agriculture systems permitting crop-specific operations.
3. *strip:* growing component crops simultaneously in different strips to allow independent cultivation of each crop, and
4. *relay:* growing component crops in relay, so that their growth cycles overlap.

Crop combinations differ with geographical location, and are primarily determined by the length of the growing season and the adaptation of crops to particular environments (Ofori and Stern 1987). In areas with annual rainfall of <60 cm and a short growing season (e.g., Africa), early-maturing and drought-tolerant crops such as millet and sorghum dominate (Baker 1979). In areas with annual rainfall >60 cm, cereals and legumes of varying maturities are used. In the tropics and subtropics, the cereal component is usually corn, sorghum, millet, or, to a lesser extent, rice; the legume is usually cowpea, peanut, soybean, chick-pea, common bean, or pigeon pea. Both early- and late-maturing crops are combined to ensure efficient utilization of the whole growing season (Baker

1979). Corn seems to dominate as the cereal component, and is combined with many different legumes.

The success of cereal–legume intercrop systems depends on minimizing the interspecific competition between the component crops for growth-limiting factors. This is regulated by basic morphophysiological differences and agronomic factors such as the proportion of crops in the mixture, fertilizer applications, and relative time of sowing. Where component crops are arranged in definite rows, the degree of competition is determined by the relative growth rates, growth durations, and the proximity of roots of the different crops. The cereal component, with relatively higher growth rate, height advantage, and a more extensive root system, is favored in the competition with the associated legume; it is therefore described as the "dominant" component, and the legume as the "dominated" one (Huxley and Maingu 1978). Competition for the growth-limiting factors could be minimized by growing component crops with contrasting maturities, so that they complement rather than compete for the same resources at the same time. This often results in substantial yield increases: For example, Willey and Osiru (1972) obtained a 55% total yield increase by growing 85-day bean and 120-day sorghum, and Reddy, Reddy, and Reddy (1980) reported a yield advantage of 31% with 82-day millet and 105-day peanut. On the other hand, in crop combinations of similar or almost overlapping growth durations, lesser or no advantages are seen. Such was the case in corn–cowpea (Wanki, Fawusi, and Nangju 1982) and sorghum–cowpea (Rees 1986) intercrop systems, where components were of similar growth durations.

The three major growth-limiting factors defining the competitive relationships between the component crops in an intercrop system include light, water, and available soil nutrients. The rate of dry-matter production in crops depends on the efficiency of the interception of photosynthetically active radiation (PAR); this, in turn, depends on the geometry of the crops and foliage architecture. Generally, the taller cereals shade the legume and, at higher plant densities, cause reduced growth and yield of the component legume. The higher productivity of intercrop systems (mainly due to their higher PAR conversion efficiencies) compared to sole crops is often attributed to the spread of light over greater leaf area and more efficient distribution of light in the intercrop canopies during the early stages of crop growth. For example, using a pearl millet–peanut system, Reddy and Willey (1981) obtained energy-conversion efficiencies at 68 days of 1.70 g/MJ in sole millet, 1.07 g/MJ in sole peanut, and 1.95 g/MJ in the mixture.

Soil moisture also plays a crucial role in intercropping systems. The differences in root systems, depth of rooting, lateral root spread, and root density are factors that affect competition for water between the component crops (Haynes 1980). The use of different parts of the soil profile by the root systems of different crop species minimizes the degree of competition for water. When component crops compete for available water, the cereal, with its higher growth rate and more extensive root system, is generally favored. Similar factors also determine the competition for available soil nutrients.

In addition to these growth-limiting factors, the productivity and efficiency of cereal–legume intercrop systems are also affected by several agronomic variables. The overall mixture densities and the relative proportions of component crops are important determinants of production efficiency. When the components are present in approximately equal numbers, productivity and efficiency appear to be determined by the more aggressive crop, usually the cereal (Ofori and Stern 1987). However, even though the density of the cereal component determines the level of combined mixture yield, the efficiency of cereal–legume intercropping systems, measured in terms of land equivalent ratio (LER), follows the trend of the legume component.

Row arrangements, in contrast to arrangements of component crops within rows, improve the amount of light transmitted to the lower legume canopy. Such arrangements can enhance legume yields and efficiency in cereal–legume intercrop systems (Mohta and De 1980). Generally, the yield of the cereal component is less affected by component densities and manipulation of spacing between the component crops (Dallal 1974, 1977; Chui and Shibles 1984; Singh 1981). Intercrop legume yield usually is reduced significantly, however, depending on the proximity of the cereal component.

The relative time of sowing of component crops is also an important management variable manipulated in cereal–legume intercrop systems, but has not been adequately studied. Andrews (1972) pointed out that differential sowing improves productivity and minimizes competition for growth-limiting factors in intercropping. Willey (1979) also suggested that sowing component crops at different times ensures full utilization of growth factors because crops occupy the land throughout the growing season. Because of the importance of cereal–legume intercropping systems in the developing countries, this factor needs to be thoroughly researched.

Another important agronomic variable affecting the efficiencies of various intercrop systems is the response of component crops to applied nitrogen fertilizers in different cereal–legume combinations. Most studies on the effects of applied nitrogen on intercropping systems are based on corn, and these indicate similar grain yield responses to applied nitrogen for sole and intercrop corn (Table 2-6). Intercrop cereal grain yields increase progressively with applied nitrogen, whereas seed yields of companion legumes decrease or are less affected. Therefore, it appears that applying nitrogen does not improve the land equivalent ratio and, thus, the efficiency of cereal–legume intercrop systems.

Perhaps the most important benefit of a cereal–legume intercrop system is the nitrogen economy of the farming system. Evidence in the literature suggests that the nitrogen fixed by the intercrop legume may be available to the associated

Table 2-6. Yields (kg/ha) and Land Equivalent Ratio (LER) of Various Cereal–Legume Intercrop Systems as Influenced by Applied Nitrogen.

Source	Treatment	N Rate (% of Maximum Applied)		
		0	50	100
Dallal (1977)	Maize			
	Sole	5,082	—	5,623
	Intercrop	4,666	—	5,099
	Soybean			
	Sole	1,478	—	1,789
	Intercrop	334	—	336
	LER	(1.15)		(1.09)
Searle et al. (1981)	Maize			
	Sole	6,680	8,604	8,941
	Intercrop	7,080	8,237	9,178
	Groundnut			
	Sole	1,741	—	—
	Intercrop	530	418	378
	LER	(1.36)	(1.20)	(1.24)
Chui and Shibles (1984)	Maize			
	Sole	6,160	—	9,160
	Intercrop	6,120	—	8,550
	Soybean			
	Sole	3,400	—	3,410
	Intercrop	570	—	420
	LER	(1.16)		(1.05)

cereal in the same growing season (Remison 1978; Pandey and Pendleton 1986) or as a residual nitrogen for the benefit of a succeeding cereal crop (Singh 1983). Both forms of nitrogen transfer are considered important and could improve the nitrogen economy of various legume-based intercrop systems. This has led to the suggestion that both current and residual nitrogen benefits be evaluated in intercrop systems in which legumes are a component (Ofori and Stern 1987). The degree to which the nitrogen from an intercrop legume may benefit a cereal crop depends on the quantity and concentration of legume nitrogen, microbial degradation (mineralization) of the legume residues, utilization of these residues, and the amount of nitrogen fixed by the legume (Ofori and Stern 1987). The nitrogen in legume residues may be tied up in the soil organic nitrogen pool and may not be readily available to the cereal crop. The rate of mineralization of organic nitrogen, determined by microbial activity, is primarily influenced by the prevailing moisture and temperature regimes. Under tropical conditions, 30% of the nitrogen in legume residues could be mineralized and taken up by the cereals after twenty-four weeks.

To summarize the available information on cereal–legume intercropping systems, it is quite apparent that light and nitrogen are the main factors influencing the production efficiency in terms of land equivalent ratio (LER), an index of intercropping efficiency. The taller cereal component suppresses the companion legume through shading, and this is accentuated by the application of nitrogen fertilizers. The cereal determines the levels of dry matter and the grain- and seed-protein yields of the intercrop mixture; the trends in the LER, however, are associated with the yields of the legume rather than of the cereal. The observation that the efficiency of cereal–legume intercropping relative to sole cropping is greatest at low levels of nitrogen fertilizers further suggests that, at low nitrogen, the intercrop legume has a greater dependence on atmospheric nitrogen. The production efficiency of cereal–legume intercropping could therefore be enhanced even more through the use of more effective strains of rhizobia and low rates of fertilizer nitrogen, so as to maximize nitrogen fixation of the intercrop legume. This will partially eliminate competition for nitrogen between cereals and legumes as intercrops. To meet the high nitrogen requirements of the intercrop cereal while at the same time promoting nitrogen fixation of the companion legume, slow-release fertilizers may be used (Ofori and Stern 1987). This will render the nitrogen available to the cereal at about the peak vegetative stage, presumably after the nitrogen-fixing system of the legume has become well established. However, in spite of the recent spurt of research interests in cereal–legume intercropping systems, there still do not seem to be any general proposals for maximizing the production efficiencies of different systems. Recently, Ofori and Stern (1987) suggested that future research in this area should be along the following lines:

1. Establish pathways of nitrogen losses from cereal–legume intercrop systems to maximize the utilization of nitrogen fertilizers, and thus to reduce wastage of an expensive input.
2. Study the application of low rates of nitrogen fertilizers early in the growth season to encourage nitrogen fixation of the intercrop legume, together with later application of nitrogen during the peak vegetative stage of the cereal to minimize competition for nitrogen.
3. Study the effects of applied nitrogen on nitrogen fixation of the intercrop legume.
4. Research the effectiveness of slow-release nitrogen fertilizers to establish whether they minimize the losses of applied nitrogen.
5. Study the amounts of fixed nitrogen in the root zones of component crops to permit accurate estimates of nitrogen balances in cereal–legume intercropping systems.
6. Establish the component density combinations that give maximum yields and efficiencies in various cereal–legume intercrop systems.

7. Find ways of improving the production efficiency of cereal–legume inter-cropping systems by giving high priority to maintaining the legume component.
8. Establish the efficiencies of specific crop combinations of cereal–legume intercropping systems in different locations.

WEED CONTROL

The association of particular weed species with legumes is much more a function of climate and location than of the crop itself. Since legumes are usually grown in a crop rotation, mainly with cereals, they suffer generally from the same species of weeds as the crops grown during the same season. The enormous number of weed species identified in association with food legume cultivation in different areas of the world makes it difficult to list them here. Hence, only the various methods available for weed control in general are described below.

Weed control is one of the most important inputs in crop production. It is one of the main reasons for most tillage operations associated with crop production. Subsistence farming, in the past, was a stable system characterized by low-population, multiple-cropping systems and prolonged fallow periods that stabilized soil fertility and kept persistent weeds in check. Early weed competition was minimized by the slash-and-burn and hand-weeding techniques practiced by these farmers. This system has been destabilized in recent times as a result of increasing human populations on limited land, decreasing fallow periods, declining soil fertility, and increasing weed problems.

There are several weed control methods applicable to tropical agriculture (Youdeowei and Adeniji 1986). These are broadly classified as cultural, biological, chemical, and integrated weed control methods.

Cultural Weed Control

This includes all aspects of good crop husbandry used to minimize weed competition with crops, excluding the manipulation of crop architecture and crop population levels and the use of chemicals or biological agents to control weeds (ICAR 1970). Some of these are briefly described below.

Burning

The primary reason for burning is to get rid of excess plant residue resulting from land-clearing operations. It also helps destroy weed seeds and other crop pests that are either on the soil surface or associated with crop residue, thus providing a weed-free environment for the establishment of crop seedlings.

Hand Weeding

Hand-pulling of weeds, slashing, or hoe weeding are efficient and practical methods of controlling weeds in most cropping systems. Hand weeding is common on smallholdings throughout the tropics and requires little or no investment in farm tools; it relies on cheap and abundant labor. The major disadvantage is that the labor requirement is high so that its effectiveness is limited to small (<2-ha) farms and to places where farm labor is cheap and readily available (Smartt 1976). Because hand weeding is generally delayed until weeds are well established, some amount of yield reduction caused by early weed competition is inevitably associated with most hand-weeding operations. In addition, there is also the risk of root damage if hoe-weeding is delayed.

Mechanical Weeding

Applicable to row crops, mechanical weeding is done with a range of interrow weeders operated by draught animals or machine. It is not labor intensive, and can be used in large-scale farming operations. A disadvantage of mechanical weeding is the inability to control weeds growing in the interrow spaces. In crops such as cowpea, where yield losses caused by weeds within and between rows are identical, interrow mechanical weeding may not reduce yield loss caused by weed competition.

Mulching

Plant residues and inorganic materials such as mulch are commonly used to conserve soil moisture and smother weeds. However, the cost of providing the mulching material makes this method unsuitable in legume cultivation.

Tillage

Agricultural land is tilled to provide a weed-free environment and to maintain soil structure. Where tillage is not carried out prior to planting, good pre- and postplanting weed control must be carried out to avoid interference with crop growth. Traditional tillage with hoe involves shallow cultivation and partial burying of weeds. The use of tractor-mounted tillage implements is an improvement over traditional tillage and animal-drawn plowing. The former also makes deep tillage possible, especially where there is a need to control stubborn weeds (Youdeowei and Adeniji 1986). Tillage controls weeds partly through burying them and partly through exposing their underground parts to desiccation.

Mowing

Mowing is aimed primarily at preventing annual weeds and simple perennials from reinfesting with a new flush of seeds, and at reducing the vigor of established perennials. Irrespective of weed type, mowing controls weeds by preventing them from either setting seed or resupplying their underground organs with assimilate. Repeated mowing, however, is necessary for this weeding practice to be effective. The main advantage of mowing over other weed control practices is that the soil is never exposed to erosion if mowing is done properly (ICAR 1970).

Cropping Systems

Each crop has its characteristic weeds, and by growing the same crop on the same piece of land year after year, these weeds tend to increase in number because they have successfully adjusted themselves to management practices used in producing the given crop (Duke 1981; Youdeowei and Adeniji 1986). Crop rotations help prevent the buildup of such weeds. Multiple-cropping systems often involve management practices that discourage weed growth, partly because of different dates in crop maturity and harvest, and partly because of a greater tendency to provide canopy cover over a longer period.

Preventive Weed Control

This method seeks to hinder the introduction and spread of weeds, and is often the most practical means of controlling weeds. Weeds are prevented from going to seed. Crop seeds intended for planting are properly cleaned to ensure that machinery and irrigation water are free of weed seeds. The spread of perennial weeds that establish vegetatively is prevented.

Biological Weed Control

In this method, weeds are controlled or suppressed by the action of one or more organisms, either naturally or by the manipulation of the weed, control organisms, or environment. Although classical biological control of weeds involving the use of insects has been demonstrated for some specific weeds, it has not been successfully demonstrated for mixed weed flora to meet the needs of the associated crops and cropping systems. Other aspects of biological control of weeds involve the use of certain plants. In this regard, specific control methods applicable in the humid and subhumid tropics are fallowing, live mulch, use of low-growing crops to smother weeds, and the manipulation of plant density and canopy (ICAR 1970; Smartt 1976; Youdeowei and Adeniji 1986). The last factor is important in cereal–legume intercropping systems, which provide different canopy structures. Weed–crop competition is also lower at higher plant populations. In order to reduce the cost of weed control, proper use should be made of optimum plant population and spatial arrangements. The major advantage of all biological weed control methods is that labor for weeding is reduced. The total energy use and the cost of energy for weed control are also reduced, since weeds are kept in check by other plants rather than by direct human effort aimed at their removal.

Chemical Weed Control

Chemical weed control refers to all weed-control practices in which toxic chemicals or herbicides are used to kill, suppress, or modify weed growth so as to prevent interference with crop establishment, growth, and production of economic yields. During the past four decades, chemical weed control became the most widely used weed control method in the developed countries of the world. It is an important method of reducing early weed competition in crops. Timely weeding through use of preemergence or early postemergence herbicides is another advantage of chemical weed control. It also makes possible cultivation of large hectarages with efficient weed control.

Based on use, herbicides can be classified as selective or nonselective. Selective herbicides will kill or impair the growth of certain plant species when applied to a mixed plant population, but cause practically no injury to other treated plants. The basis of selectivity may be marked differences between the rates of herbicide translocation in different species of weed plants, biochemical differences between plants, morphological differences, or the age and phenology of weeds. *Nonselective herbicides* will indiscriminately kill all plants with which they come in contact. The selectivity of a herbicide also depends on the chemical itself and its formulation, the amount of active ingredient applied and the quantity of the carrier, the stage of growth of the crops and weeds, and weather conditions. Generally, seedlings of most weeds are more susceptible to herbicides than are mature plants.

Based on their mode of action, the chemicals now commonly used as herbicides can be grouped as follows (Youdeowei and Adeniji 1986).

Contact Herbicides

These kill most plant tissue by contact, with little or no movement through the plant; shoots of perennials may be killed, but regrowth from the underground parts usually occurs. Some examples of this class of herbicides include dimexan, dinoseb, bentazone, ioxynil, and bromoxynil. Others such as diquat and paraquat are sometimes called contact herbicides, but they are only effective on green plant material, and involve complex chemical changes. Contact herbicides have very little or no residual action in the soil.

Translocated (Systemic) Herbicides

These chemicals act through the roots of the plant after being applied to the soil surface or worked into the soil (volatile types); some of them (e.g., linuron) are also absorbed by foliage. Most of this group act by interfering with photosynthesis. Examples include Atrazine®, simazine, ametryne, prometryne, pyrazone, lenacil, monolinuron, trifluralin, propachlor, carbetamide, and propyzamide.

Growth Regulator ("Hormone") Herbicides

These are a special group of translocated chemicals similar to substances produced naturally by plants that can regulate or control growth before dying. The important ones include MCPA®, 2,4-D, mecoprop, dichlorprop, dicamba, and benazolin.

Growth Inhibitor Herbicides

These limit or stop the growth of susceptible plants, and include chemicals such as propham, barban, TCA, and dalapon.

It should be noted here that, like pesticides, herbicides are poisonous substances that can be injurious to persons who use them carelessly. However, they are generally safe to use if the information on the label is followed, and where the operator has received proper training on herbicide handling.

Integrated Weed Management

This system suppresses weeds by combining two or more weed control methods at levels of application lower than when one control method is used alone. Environmental and socioeconomic constraints make integrated weed management one of the best options for weed control in the tropics. Light soils, high or low rainfall, a wide range of crop types and cropping systems, and abundance of persistent weeds in the tropical countries—combined with the low persistence of many herbicides—make absolute reliance on chemical weed control difficult. Cultural weed control methods, on the other hand, are often laborious, unattractive, and, in some cropping systems, ineffective. Integrated weed management has been demonstrated as effective in coping with weed problems of a wide range of cropping systems in the tropics. The progress made so far in intercropping systems, zonal tillage, no-tillage, and various mulching practices are examples of integrated weed management.

It must also be mentioned that in the developing countries, food legumes are rarely monocropped; on smallholdings, farmers normally intercrop them with cereals, root, and tuber crops (Smartt 1976). Chemical weed control looks promising in food legume cultivation, and will increase in importance as farmers increase their farm sizes in an effort to meet the demand for increased food production. Herbicides that have been identified as safe in legume cultivation are pendimethalin (to be used where itchgrass is a problem), preferably used in combination with metobromuron or metribuzin. In addition to these, trifluralin, and alachlor alone or in combination with terbutryne, are recommended for peanut. However, at least in the near future, it appears that the mainstay of weed control in legume cultivation will still be a capital- or labor-intensive system of physical weed control partly supplemented by capital-intensive chemical control.

FIELD PESTS

The variety of organisms now associated with damage or losses in cultivated crops ranges from the smallest viruses, bacteria, and insects to the higher vertebrate animals, such as birds and rodents. The science of crop protection requires a basic understanding of the nature of these organisms, whose complex interactions with cultivated crops result in symptoms of damage and disease. Effective and economical methods for the control of pests and diseases are continually under research.

Pests and diseases are among the most serious limiting factors to economically efficient crop production and utilization of natural resources in tropical agriculture. Losses from pests and diseases keep productivity low. Legumes are among the most susceptible of all crops to insect attack, and provide a nutritious and palatable substrate for a large and extremely diverse range of pests worldwide (van Emden 1981). Environmental conditions in the tropics and subtropics especially favor rapid development of dense and diverse insect communities. Problems with insect pests can therefore be expected to increase with the expansion of legume cultivation in different areas of the world, particularly where previously unnoticed native species find the new crops to their liking.

Accurate and reliable estimates of crop losses caused by pests and diseases are difficult to obtain. The average, overall losses caused by pests at different stages of production and storage in the developed and developing countries are estimated to vary from about 25% to 43% annually (Table 2-7). Sometimes crop losses may be negligible and at other times total, especially as a result of sporadic outbreaks of nonendemic pests and diseases. There is no doubt that significant increases in food production could result from efficient and effective crop protection practices.

In nature, in the absence of the influence of some external factor, insect numbers tend to fluctuate around an equilibrium position. This is commonly known as the *general equilibrium level,* and is defined as the average density of the

Table 2-7. Regional Percentage Crop Losses Caused by Pests.

Region	Insects	Diseases	Weeds	Total
Europe	5	13	7	25
North and Central America	9	11	8	28
South America	10	15	8	33
Africa	13	13	16	42
Asia	21	11	11	43

Compiled from: NAS (1978) and Youdeowei and Adeniji (1986).

population over a period in the absence of permanent environmental changes (Youdeowei and Adeniji 1986). Changes in environmental factors lead to changes in the insect population levels that affect cultivated crops. For any pest species, the damage caused to the host plant increases with increase in the population of the pest. This causes losses in yields or in the quality of the product, which in turn results in an overall loss of revenue to the farmer. An organism that causes ≥5% loss in yield in a particular crop is described as an *economic pest*. The amount of crop damage that would justify the cost of control measures is known as the *economic damage,* and the lowest pest population density that will cause economic damage is called the *economic injury level.* This level varies considerably with insect pest, crop, season, and locality. The effects of different numbers of pests on the yield of crops is very important and must be estimated in order to justify control measures.

In practice, the basis for making decisions about when to apply control measures (Youdeowei and Adeniji 1986) is the *economic threshold,* defined as the pest population density or damage level at which control measures must be applied to prevent a pest population from reaching the economic injury level. The economic thresholds of insect pest populations are very important considerations in scientific pest control. It should also be noted that several natural enemies play an important role in preventing insect pests from causing economic damage (Newsom 1978). This has been time and again demonstrated by using chemicals either to remove these natural enemies or to reduce their effectiveness. One consequence of pesticide use may be a resurgence of pest populations to densities far greater than those in untreated areas (Shepard, Carner, and Turnipseed 1977). In addition, previously minor pests may become serious when their natural enemies are killed off by chemicals. Where pesticides are necessary, their use should be restricted to selected application of chemicals that are less harmful to important beneficial species but effective in keeping pest populations under control (Turnipseed 1972).

The major field pests of food legumes are predominantly insects, but nematodes and spider mites are also troublesome pests in many areas of the world. Some pests may be quite specific to a single host plant, whereas others may attack a broad range of legume crops or be even more general feeders with hosts in other plant families. Most pests, however, are specific as to the part of the plant they attack, feeding on leaves, stems, flowers, fruits, seeds, or roots. The feeding habits of insect pests are important and often are useful in the classification of pests. The four insect orders that include most potential pest species of food legumes include the bugs (Order Hemiptera), moths and butterflies (Order Lepidoptera), beetles (Order Coleoptera), and grasshoppers and crickets (Order Orthoptera). Generally, the pest complexes that occur on food legumes in different geographical locations are rather similar; however, the presence of individual insect species and their relative abundance often varies with location and species of the legume. For example, although a pod-sucking bug complex was ubiquitous in Northern Australia, and some sucking bug species occurred in all regions and on most crops, others were observed at only one or two sites (Shepard, Lawn, and Schneider 1983). Green gram and cowpea were usually host to an abundance of sucking bugs, but adjacent areas of black gram sustained only sparse insect populations.

Table 2-8 lists the major field pests of some of the important food legume crops cultivated worldwide. These pests may be classified in the following manner.

Insects

Plant-sucking Insects

Insects that pierce the plant and feed on its juices form the most abundant complex of insect pests of food legumes. Many of them are pod suckers and cause substantial yield losses by piercing the pod wall and feeding directly from the developing seeds. However, assessment of losses caused by pod-sucking insects can be more difficult than with pod-chewing insects because the damage of the former may not be readily visible. The degree of damage depends on the stage of development of the pod and seed. When flowers and young pods are attacked, they may fall from the plant. The damaged ovules usually shrivel and die. Older seeds, however, may only show puncture marks, and the damage may not be detected until after harvest (Turner 1977). Feeding by pod-sucking insects thus may cause a reduction in seed quality and germinability, and may lower the oil content in oilseeds. Piercing and sucking insects also cause mechanical damage to the tissues they pierce and, with the accompanying loss of plant sap, seriously affect growth and development of the host. Some sucking insects also inject toxic saliva into plant tissues, and this may cause the death of such tissues. Pod-sucking bugs may also transmit other disease causal agents (especially viruses) to the seeds, or the seed may be made vulnerable to attack by diseases during subsequent germination (Daugherty et al 1964; Lawn and Russell 1978).

Table 2-8. Major Field Pests of Some Important Food Legumes.

Legume	Field Pests
Arachis hypogaea (peanut, groundnut)	*Elasmopalpus lignosellus* (lesser cornstalk borer), *Diabrotica undecimpunctata howardi* (corn rootworm), *Graphognathus* spp. (white-fringed beetles), *Pangeaus bilineatus, P. congruus* (burrowing bugs), *Heliothis zea* (corn earworm), *H. virescens* (tobacco budworm), *Spodoptera frugiperda, S. exigua* (fall armyworm), *Feltia subterranea* (granulate cutworm), *Anticarsia gemmatalis* (velvet-bean caterpillar), *Stegasta bosqueella* (red-necked peanutworm), *Frankliniella fusca* (thrips), *Tetranychus urticae, T. cinnabarinus, T. desertorum* (spider mites), *Empoasca fabae* (leafhopper)
Cajanus cajan (pigeon pea, red gram)	*Heliothis armigera* (podborer), *Melanagromyza obtusa* (podfly), *Exelastis atomosa* (plume moth), *Euchrysops chejus* (blue butterfly), *Eucosma critica* (leaf tier), *Ceuthorrhynchus aspurulus* (bud weevil), *Etiella zinckiella* (spotted podborer), *Clavigralla* spp. (pod bugs), *Frankliniella sulphurea, Taeniothrips nigricernis* (thrips), *Mylabris pustulata* (blister beetle), *Empoasca fabilis* (leafhopper), *Aphis craccivora* (aphids)
Cicer arietinum (chick-pea)	*Heliothis armigera, H. obsoleta* (gram podborer or caterpillar), *Plusia orichalcea, Autographa nigrisigna* (semilooper), *Exelastis atomosa* (plume moth), *Agrotis ipsilon, Ochropleura flammatra* (cutworms), *Spodoptera exigua* (lesser armyworm), *Lyriomyza cicerini* (miner flies), *Aphis craccivora* (aphids)
Cyamopsis tetragonoloba (guar, cluster bean)	*Stictocephla festuca* (alfalfa leafhopper), *Aspondylia cyamopsii* (pod gall midge), *Eutettix tenella* (beet leafhopper)
Dolichos biflorus (horse gram)	*Heliothis armigera* (gram caterpillar), *Exelastis atomosa* (plume moth), *Maruca testulalis* (spotted podborer), *Mylabris* spp. (flower beetles), *Cerotoma ruficormis* (bean leaf beetle), *Coptasoma eribraria* (stinkbugs), *Schizonycha* spp. (cock-shaver larvae)
Glycine max (soybean)	*Melanagromyza sojae, Ophiomyia centrosematis* (beanflies or stem miners), *Maruca testulalis, Etiella zinckiella* (podborers), *Nezara viridula, Piezodorus hybneri* (stinkbugs), *Anticarsia gemmatalis* (velvet-bean caterpillar), *Epilachna varivestis* (Mexican bean beetle), *Heliothis virescens* (tobacco budworm), *Heliothis zea* (corn earworm), *Plathypena scabra* (green clover-worm), *Pseudoplusia includens* (soybean looper), *Cydia ptychora* (seed moth)
Lathyrus sativus (kesari dhal)	*Aphis* spp. (aphids), *Halotydens destructor* (red-legged mite)
Lens esculenta (*L. culinaris*) (lentil)	*Etiella zinckenella* (podborer), *Aphis* spp. (aphids), *Sitona lineatus* (weevils), *Bruchus lentis, B. ervi* (bruchids), *Agrotis ipsilon* (cutworms), *Apion* spp. (bud weevils), *Delia platura* (seed corn maggots), *Limonius* spp., *Ctenicera* spp. (wireworms), *Macrosiphum pisi* (pea aphids), *Megalurothrips* spp. (thrips), *Heliothis obsoleta* (gram caterpillar), *Ochropleura flammatra* (gram cutworm)
Lupinus spp. (lupine)	*Sminthurus viridis* (lucerne fleas), *Hylemya lupini* (lupine maggot), *Graphognathus* spp. (white-fringed beetles), *Sitona*

Table 2-8. (*Continued*)

Legume	Field Pests
	explicata (root weevil), *Heliothis* spp. (budworms), *Halotydens destructor* (red-legged mites)
Phaseolus aureus (*Vigna radiata*) (green gram, mung bean)	*Melanagromyza phaseoli* (bean fly), *Heliothis* spp., *Etiella* spp. (podboring caterpillars), *Amsacta moorei, A. albistriga* (leaf-eating caterpillar), *Maruca testulalis* (bean podborer), *Nezara viridula* (pod-sucking bug), *Diacrisia obliqua* (hairy caterpillar), *Chrysodeixis* spp., *Mocis* spp., *Spodoptera* spp. (cutworms), *Tetranychus cinnabarinus* (red spider mite)
Phaseolus lunatus (*P. limensis*) (lima bean)	*Etiella zinckenella, Maruca testulalis, Cydia* spp. (podborers), *Hylemya platura* (corn seed maggot), *Epilachna varivestis* (Mexican bean beetle), *Peridroma saucia* (variegated cutworm), *Agrotis ipsilon* (gray cutworm), *Apion godmani* (bean pod weevil), *Megalurothrips sjostedi* (bud thrips), *Onychiurus* spp. (springtails), *Limonius* spp., *Melanotus* spp. (wireworms)
Phaseolus mungo (*Vigna mungo*) (black gram)	*Apion ampulum* (podborer), *Aphis craccivora* (aphids), *Diacrisia obliqua* (hairy caterpillar), *Ophiomyia phaseoli* (bean fly), *Madurasia obscurella* (pulse beetle fly), *Bemisia tabaci* (whitefly), *Heliothis armigera* (bollworm), *Amsacta albistriga* (leaf-eating caterpillar)
Phaseolus vulgaris (common bean, dry bean)	*Longitarsus belgaumensis* (flea beetle), *Melanagromyza phaseoli* (bean fly), *Epilachna varivestis* (Mexican bean beetle), *Cerotoma trifurcata* (bean leaf beetle), *Hylemya platura, H. cilicrura* (seed corn maggot), *Caliothrips fasciatus* (bean thrips), *Aphis rumicis* (bean aphid), *Empoasca* spp. (leafhoppers), *Apion godmani* (bean pod weevil), *Bemisia tabaci* (whitefly), *Tetranychus* spp. (mites), *Agrotis ipsilon, Spodoptera* spp. (cutworms)
Pisum sativum (pea)	*Sitona lineatus* (pea leaf weevil), *Cydia nigricana* (pea moth), *Acyrthosiphon pisum* (pea aphid), *Contarinia pisi* (pea midge), *Kakothrips pisivorus* (pea thrips), *Cnephasia interjectania* (Tortrix moth), *Thrips angusticeps* (field thrips), *Agrotis segetum* (cutworm), *Lygus* spp. (Lygus bugs), *Liriomyza* spp. (pea leafminers), *Autographa californica* (alfalfa looper)
Vicia faba (broad bean, fava bean, vetch)	*Aphis fabae* (bean aphid), *Bruchus rufimanus* (broad-bean weevil); other pests include corn ear worm, leafhoppers, cutworms, fall armyworms, and grasshoppers that also attack other legumes
Vigna unguiculata (cowpea, black-eyed pea)	*Empoasca dolichi, E. kerri, E. christiani* (leafhoppers), *Aphis craccivora* (aphids), *Bemisia tabaci* (whitefly), *Sericothrips occipitalis* (foliage thrips), *Ophiomyia phaseoli, O. spencerella* (stem flies), *Liriomyza trifolii* (leafminers), *Elasmopalpus lignosellus* (lesser cornstalk borer), *Ootheca mutabilis, O. bennigseni* (beetles), *Amsacta moorei* (hairy caterpillars), *Maruca testulalis* (podborer), *Cydia ptychora* (seed moth), *Heliothis armigera* (bollworms), *Megalurothrips sjostedti, Frankliniella schultzei* (flower bud thrips), *Melanagromyza chalcosoma* (pod flies), *Clavigralla tomentosicollis, C. elongata* (pod-sucking bug), *Nezara viridula* (green stinkbug), *Piezotrachelus varius* (pod weevils), *Chalcodermus aeneus* (cowpea curculio)

Compiled from: ICAR (1970), Smartt (1976), Singh, van Emden, and Taylor (1978), Duke (1981), and Shepard, Lawn, and Schneider (1983).

The major leaf-sucking insect pests of legumes include the leafhoppers (*Empoasca* spp.), aphids (*Aphis craccivora, A. fabae*), and spider mites (*Tetranychus* spp., *Penthaleus* spp.). Stem-sucker insects include the green stinkbug (*Nezara viridula*) and the three-cornered alfalfa hopper (*Spissistilus festinus*). Insects such as thrips, which pierce and suck cowpea flowers, cause flower abortion. This leads to fewer fruits being formed and thus considerable yield losses. Pests that attack the root system and suck juices from it are not usually a serious problem in legumes, although a number of such insects have been recorded for the peanut. The most important of these include the sap-sucking bug *Hilda patruelis* found in Southern Africa, mealy bugs, and scale insects.

Pod-chewing Insects

Although many of the pod-chewing insects also feed on foliage, blooms, and sometimes petioles and stems, most of the economic loss arises from their direct feeding on pods. Both seed and pod may be consumed, and the resulting damage to the pod wall may expose uneaten seed to weathering and to germination during rainy periods. There are many species that have been observed to chew into pods, but relatively few that cause serious economic loss. Among these are the cotton bollworm (*Heliothis armigera*) and other *Heliothis* species, the bean podborer (*Maruca testulalis*), and the lucerne seed web moth (*Etiella* spp.)

Heliothis spp. are generally found in all locations and crops, and in many cases constitute the most serious pest problems. In fact, species within this genus are probably the most important economic pests worldwide (Kogan et al. 1978), so it is not surprising that most legumes are favorable hosts. The larvae of *Heliothis* spp. feed on leaves, stems, flowers, and fruits of a wide range of cultivated and wild hosts as well as food legumes.

Like *Heliothis,* the bean podborer (*Maruca testulalis*) feeds on leaves, stems, flowers, and pods of many legume crops. The bean podborer is particularly destructive to mung beans, cowpeas, and pigeon peas, where the arrangement of pods allow the pest to web pods and adjacent leaves together to form a protective shelter.

The caterpillars of the lucerne seed web moth (*Etiella* spp.) and those of various lycaenid butterflies also cause serious damage in several legume crops. They generally web leaves, pods, and flowers together, and may cause heavy yield losses. Locusts are also occasionally observed in food legumes, and during heavy infestations pod damage from their feeding is often apparent. The larvae of a small fly (*Melanagromyza* spp.) also cause widespread damage. The fly develops entirely within the pod, pupation occurring within the empty locule created by the feeding larva. *M. obtusa* is a major economic pest of pigeon pea in India (ICRISAT 1977).

Foliage-feeding Insects

Most of the species that chew into the pods of food legumes also feed to some extent on foliage. Pests that attack the foliage of legume crops mostly belong to the two large insect orders, Coleoptera and Lepidoptera, or to the small order Thysanoptera (thrips). In the Order Coleoptera, both adult beetles and their larvae may feed on the foliage, whereas in the case of lepidopterans, it is always the larvae that cause damage. Regardless of the stage in their life cycles, the type of damage caused by beetles and caterpillars is the same: The lamina is consumed, photosynthetic area is reduced by an amount depending on the level of infestation, and the photosynthetic efficiency of the plant is reduced proportionately (Smartt 1976). Light infestations resulting in small reductions of total leaf area are probably of little or no consequence, whereas heavy infestations resulting in a more or less complete defoliation can cause a virtually complete crop loss.

Among the lepidopteran pests, the army worms (*Spodoptera* spp.), velvet-bean caterpillar (*Anticarsia gemmatalis*), corn earworm (*Heliothis zea*), webworm (*Agrotis* spp.), leaf miners (*Stomopteryx* spp.), loopers (*Achaea finita*), and hairy caterpillars (*Amsacta albistriga, Diacrisia obliqua*) are some of the major foliage feeder insect pests of food legume crops.

The leaf-eating beetles are quite commonly found on a variety of legume crops, but are not generally of much significance on the peanut (Smartt 1976). The more serious economic pests belonging to this class include the Mexican bean beetle (*Epilachna varivestis*), the bean leaf beetle (*Cerotoma trifurcata*), and the spotted cucumber beetle (*Diabrotica undecimpunctata howardi*). Among other foliage-feeding insects, thrips are commonly found in peanuts. The important thrips genera include *Franklinella, Heliothrips,* and *Taeniothrips.* The feeding of these insects, which are commonly found in flowers and stem apices, usually results in damage to young leaves and in stunted growth. Damage is most serious during the early stages of crop development, although frequently the crop outgrows the early adverse effects. Thrips populations are reduced by heavy rainfall and natural predators. The other minor foliage feeders include locusts, grasshoppers, crickets, and spider mites.

Stem-boring Insects

Some insect pests tunnel into the stems of crops and remain inside, consuming large quantities of the tissue and quickly killing the plants. Such insects have their mouth parts adapted for biting and chewing. Pests attacking the stem can be of two types: *stem eaters,* which actually devour the tissues of the stem, and *stem borers,* which extract juices from it. Stem eaters include termites, which are serious economic pests of legumes in the tropics. Stem borers generally include both lepidopteran and dipteran larvae. Among them are the lesser corn-stalk borer (*Elasmopalpus lignosellus*), the bean fly (*Melanagromyza* spp., *Ophiomyia phaseoli*), and the cutworms (*Agrotis ipsilon*). The adult females prepare egg-laying sites by chewing small areas of stems or petioles. The larvae and pupae develop inside the plant, and overwintering occurs in the plant stem just below ground level.

The larvae of several beetle species (*Diabrotica, Agriotes, Genocephalum, Strigoderma,* and *Euborellia*) also feed on the roots of legume plants, causing severe economic damage.

Nematodes

Nematodes are the most serious root pest of food legume crops, especially in the tropical regions of the world. The plant parasitic nematodes that attack legumes can be grouped into following five classes:

1. root-knot nematodes: genus *Meloidogyne*
2. lesion nematodes: genus *Pratylenchus*
3. cyst nematodes: genus *Heterodora*
4. sting nematodes: genus *Belonolaimus*
5. reniform nematodes: genus *Rotylenchus*

Of the four major species of root-knot nematodes, three (*M. incognita, M. javanica,* and *M. arenaria*) are cosmopolitan; the fourth (*M. hapla*) has a more northerly distribution. These nematodes, after invading the root system as larvae, induce gall formation, which distorts the roots and reduces their efficiency. Depending on conditions, the life cycle of these nematodes may require three weeks to three months for completion. The plants of several dicotyledon families serve as alternative hosts for such nematodes. However, resistance to their attack may be found in species of a family that is on the whole susceptible; in fact, even in a species that is for the most part susceptible, some resistant cultivars may be found (Smartt 1976). Among the four species of root-knot nematodes, *M. arenaria* is the most serious nematode pest of peanuts. Although in most legumes gall formation is confined to the root system or portions of the stem (in prostrate type legumes) that happen to become buried, in peanuts the pods are also affected, thereby severely reducing the quality and yield of seeds. Peanuts, however, are quite resistant to *M. javanica* (Smartt 1976), which is a serious pest of peas, cowpeas, dry beans, pigeon peas, broad beans, and velvet beans. Peanut is therefore quite a useful crop in rotational control of this nematode species. In general, among the commonly grown food legumes, *Phaseolus* beans are the most susceptible to nematode attack, and must be interspersed with other crops resistant to root-knot nematodes if pest occurrence and population are to be kept low (Table 2-9).

Table 2-9. Some Nematode Parasites of Tropical Food Legumes.

Species (Type)	Host	References
Sedentary endoparasites		
Meloidogyne (root-knot)		
M. arenaria	Peanut, soybean, cowpea, mung bean	Schwartz & Galvez (1980) Singh & Allen (1980)
M. hapla	Peanut, soybean, common bean	Singh & Allen (1980) Sinclair & Shurtleff (1975)
M. incognita	Soybean, common bean, lima bean, cowpea, mung bean, winged bean	Price (1976), Caveness (1975), Allen (1983)
M. javanica	Soybean, common bean, cowpea, mung bean, pigeon pea, winged bean	Singh & Allen (1980), Schwartz & Galvez (1980), Allen (1983)
M. spp.	Chick-pea, hyacinth bean, Bambara groundnut	Nene, Haware, & Reddy (1979)
Heterodera (cyst)		
H. cajani	Pigeon pea	Bridge (1981)
H. glycines	Soybean	Bridge (1981)
Migratory endoparasites		
Pratylenchus (root-lesion)		
P. brachyurus	Peanut, soybean, common bean, cowpea	Schwartz & Galvez (1980), Sinclair & Shurtleff (1975)
Radopholus (burrowing)		
R. similis	Peanut	Taylor (1976)
Ditylenchus (stem and bulb)		
D. dipsaci	Many legumes	Sinclair & Shurtleff (1975)
Aphelenchoides (bud and leaf)		
A. arachidis	Peanut, common bean	Schwartz & Galvez (1980)
Sedentary semiendoparasites		
Rotylenchus (reniform)		
R. reniformis	Many legumes	Allen (1983)
Migratory semiendoparasites		
Helicotylenchus (spiral)		
H. spp.	Soybean, common bean, cowpea	Schwartz & Galvez (1980)
Hoplolaimus (lance)		
H. spp.	Cowpea, soybean	Sinclair & Shurtleff (1975)
Scutellonema (false-spiral)		
S. cavenessi	Peanut	Taylor (1976)
Sedentary ectoparasites		
Criconemoides (ring)		
C. spp.	Peanut, soybean, common bean	Allen (1983)

Table 2-9. (*Continued*)

Species (Type)	Host	References
Migratory ectoparasites		
Belonolaimus (sting)		
B. *gracilis*	Peanut, soybean, common bean	Schwartz & Galvez (1980)
B. *longicaudatus*	Peanut, soybean, common bean	Sinclair & Shurtleff (1975)
Trichodorus (stubby root)		
T. *christiei*	Many legumes	Allen (1983)
Xiphenema (dagger)		
X. spp.	Peanut, soybean, common bean	Schwartz & Galvez (1980)

The lesion nematodes (*Pratylenchus* spp.) are among the most common nematodes and cause extensive damage to a wide range of hosts throughout the world (Table 2-9). They are not resident parasites of the root system: Both adults and larvae enter and leave roots repeatedly. These nematodes feed on the parenchymal cells of roots and peanut pods, producing lesions that provide an entry point for other pests and pathogens, leading to secondary infestations that cause substantial yield losses. Severe infestation by root-lesion nematodes, whose life cycle may take up to fifty days for completion, causes extensive damage to root system, resulting in poor, yellowish, and unthrifty plants.

The cyst nematodes (*Heterodora* spp.) can cause severe damage to soybeans and locally to pigeon peas, and are generally more important in temperate climates. The infested plants frequently show chlorosis due to an inhibition of nodulation. These nematodes are more prevalent on light, sandy, or volcanic soils, which are low in organic matter content. Genetic resistance to this species has been found in soybeans, and this should prove useful in its control (Smartt 1976). Among other food legumes, peas and dry beans are fairly resistant to cyst nematodes, whereas fava beans are quite susceptible.

The sting nematodes (*Belonolaimus* spp.) have a wide host range, attacking most commonly grown food legumes as well as corn, cotton, and barley (Table 2-9), thereby making effective rotational control difficult to devise. They feed on the root system, causing stunting of the taproot system with distortion and reduction of the lateral root branches. This species is apparently restricted to very light soils.

The reniform nematode (*Rotylenchus reniformis*) is also widely distributed in warm temperate and tropical regions, where its very broad host range includes all the major food legume crops (Table 2-9). Other nematodes of economic importance to legume crops have a more restricted geographical distribution.

Virtually all plant parasitic nematodes have a soil phase, and spread by soil is the major means by which they are locally dispersed. Over short distances, nematodes may be spread on soil adhering to farm implements, in flood and irrigation water, and in wind-blown soil. However, nematode populations in soil decline rapidly in the absence of suitable hosts, and rotations with resistant crops have provided good control (Rhoades 1976). Good cultural practices also help a long way in the control of soil nematode pests. The most effective short-term control is fumigation, but its expense can be rarely justified in legume cultivation. Wherever possible, genetic resistance should be identified in various legume crops for the effective and inexpensive control of soil nematode pests.

Beneficial Organisms

The natural predator complex of legume insect pests includes a diverse range of groups such as beetles, ants, wasps, spiders, assassin bugs, stinkbugs, earwigs, flies, mantids, lacewings, dragonflies, and damselflies. However, there are usually fewer than a dozen species abundant enough to make a significant impact by themselves on pest populations. The significance of the individual predacious species thus lies in their role as part of the overall beneficial complex. For example, labeling studies with *Heliothis* spp. in soybeans indicated that predacious species collectively can reduce populations of these pest species substantially (Shepard, Lawn, and Schneider 1983). Beetles and spiders are among the most abundant and conspicuous predators in legume crop canopies.

Parasites of insect pests also are extremely valuable in maintaining certain pests below the damage threshold. In general, parasitic species are much more susceptible to chemical insecticides than are predators, and the rapid increase in pest density after an insecticide application is at least partially a result of the destruction of naturally occurring parasites. This class of beneficial organisms includes wasps and flies. Several naturally occurring microorganisms are important disease-causing agents of insect pests. There are several distinct advantages associated with the use of microbial agents in integrated pest control programs. Whether the disease organism is a fungus, a virus, or some other type, it is normally self-perpetuating and without the harmful side effects of chemical insecticides. Generally, the well-developed canopy of legume crops provides a favorable microhabitat for the development of beneficial disease organisms, especially fungi. This subject has been comprehensively reviewed by Teakle (1977). The natural control agents of some of the important field pests of food legumes are summarized in Table 2-10.

Genetics of Pest Resistance

Food legumes are a challenging crop for the entomologists and plant breeders, since both in the field and in store they attract a variety of pests due to their high level of nutrients. To minimize predation, legumes evolved characteristic de-

Table 2-10. Selected Natural Control Agents of Some Important Field Pests of Legume Crops.

Field Pest	Control Agent
Anticarsia gemmatalis (velvet-bean caterpillar)	*Patelloa* spp., *Voria ruralis, Hypsoter* spp., *Microcharops bimaculata*
Aphis spp. (aphids)	*Brumoides foudrasi, Cheilomenes* spp., *Coccinella septumpunctata*
Bemisia tabaci (whitefly)	*Chrysopa* spp.
Elasmopalpus lignosellus (lesser cornstalk borer)	*Pristomerus* spp., *Macrocentrus muesebecki*
Empoasca spp. (leafhoppers)	*Anagrus empoascae, Erythmelus* spp., *Stethynium* spp.
Epilachna spp. (Mexican bean beetle)	*Coleomegilla* spp., *Hippodamia convergens*
Etiella zinckenella (spotted podborer)	*Exeristes roborator, Phanerotoma hendecasisella*
Eucosma aporema (leaf tier)	*Eucelatoria australis*
Heliothis armigera (gram caterpillar, podborer or bollworm)	*Carcelia illota, Exorista xanthaspis, Goniophthalmus halli, Palexorista imberbis*
Maruca testulalis (bean spotted podborer)	*Theocarcelia incedens, Talenomus* spp., *Nesalynx thymus, Dinothrombium* spp.
Melanagromyza spp. (podfly)	*Euderus* spp., *Pediobius* spp.
Nezara viridula (green stinkbug)	*Trichopoda pennipes, Trissolcus* spp., *Eutrichopodopsis niteus*
Ophiomyia phaseoli (bean fly)	*Sphegigaster* spp., *Plutarchia indefensa, Eurytoma larvicola, Eucoilidea* spp., *Opius* spp., *Testrastichus* spp.

Compiled from: Singh, van Emden, and Taylor (1978) and Shepard, Lawn, and Schneider (1983).

fense strategies before being domesticated. We are increasingly forced to recognize and use these strategies lest we be outdone by the organisms that incessantly attempt to attack legume crops. Several species of cultivated legumes exhibit various degrees of varietal resistance to some important field and storage insect pests (Table 2-11). The mechanisms of resistance in legume seeds—for example, to storage bruchids—may be manifested in several ways (Horber 1978). Some of these are briefly discussed below.

Resistance of Pods

Pods may have evolved to resist attack by producing gum to obstruct larval movement. Other forms of mechanical resistance involve smooth-surfaced pods that resist insect penetration, thin-walled pods that allow parasites to oviposit through wall into the pest, and indehiscent pods that resist shattering (Horber 1978).

Some pods contain tannins or other potentially toxic substances that protect them from larval infestation allelochemically (Janzen 1969).

Table 2-11. Host Plant Resistance of Important Food Legumes to Insects and Mites.[a]

Legume	Pest	Reference
Cajanus cajan (red gram, pigeon pea)	Callosobruchus chinensis	Regupathy & Rathnaswamy (1970)
	C. maculatus	Schalk, Evans, & Kaiser (1973)
Cicer arietinum (chick-pea)	Callosobruchus spp.	Raina (1971)
Glycine max (soybean)	Callosobruchus maculatus	Applebaum, Gestetner, & Birk (1965)
	Empoasca fabae	Broersma, Bernard, & Luckmann (1972)
	Epilachna varivestis	Kogan (1972)
	Heliothis spp.	Hatchett, Beland, & Hartwig (1976)
Phaseolus aureus (Vigna radiata) (green gram)	Epilachna varivestis	Wolfenbarger & Sleesman (1961)
Phaseolus lunatus (lima bean)	Empoasca fabae	Eckenrode & Ditman (1963)
	Epilachna varivestis	Wolfenbarger & Sleesman (1961)
Phaseolus mungo (Vigna mungo) (black gram)	Epilachna varivestis	Wolfenbarger & Sleesman (1961)
Phaseolus vulgaris (common bean)	Acanthoscelides obtectus	Zacher (1952)
	Callosobruchus maculatus	Janzen, Juster, & Liener (1976)
	Empoasca fabae	Wolfenbarger & Sleesman (1963)
	Epilachna varivestis	Wilde & van Schoonhoven (1976)
	Tetranychus spp.	Hagel, Silbernagel, & Burke (1972)
	Thrips tabaci	Hagel, Silbernagel, & Burke (1972)
Pisum sativum (pea)	Cydia nigricana	Wolfenbarger & Sleesman (1963)
	Macrosiphum pisi	Markkula & Roukka (1971)
Vicia faba (fava bean)	Aphis fabae	Bond & Lowe (1975)
	Empoasca fabae	Wolfenbarger & Sleesman (1963)
	Epilachna varivestis	Wolfenbarger & Sleesman (1961)
Vigna unguiculata (cowpea)	Callosobruchus maculatus	Nwanze, Horber, & Pitts (1975)
	Bruchus spp.	Chandola, Trehan, & Bacrecha (1969)
	Epilachna varivestis	Wolfenbarger & Sleesman (1961)

[a]Some pests listed here are pests of stored grain products covered under the "Storage" section of this chapter.

Resistance of Seeds

Seeds may be mechanically protected from infestation by hard and tough layers of seed coats. Allelochemic resistance is found in seeds that contain antibiotic or hallucinogenic compounds such as alkaloids, saponins, pentose sugars, free amino acids, L-DOPA, or phytohemagglutinins (Janzen, Juster, and Liener 1976). Alternatively, seeds may contain high levels of protease inhibitors, which obstruct digestion of proteins (Borchers and Ackerson 1947).

Other Forms of Crop Resistance

Crop resistance to insect pests may also be manifested in many other ways. Plants may grow vigorously and compensate adequately for pest damage, or show differential preference through such physical characteristics as leaf hairiness, epidermal thickness or hardness, unattractiveness of color, and unpleasantness of smell or taste. Plant breeders and entomologists must continually recognize and identify resistance in various food legumes, and standardize screening, evaluation, and selection methods.

Pest Control: Strategies and Methods

Strategies

The mere appearance of a pest population in a crop does not necessarily signal that the insects are causing damage and must immediately be controlled. One must assess the pest population density and the extent of the damage caused, and consider which control method is appropriate, when to apply it, and what its financial implications are. The principal objective of all pest control operations is to reduce pest damage and increase crop yields and revenues to the farmer. The decision at farm level, therefore, must be based on knowledge of the costs of control measures and the expected revenue from the crop due to increased yields; that is, decisions made by farmers must be based on sound economic considerations. An understanding of the relationships between pest damage and crop yields and revenue is therefore basic for effective decision making in pest control.

Pests can lower the revenue obtained from a crop in two ways: reduction of yield and reduction of quality. In the first case, pest attacks on foliage and roots either reduce the photosynthetic areas of the crop or divert synthates from the final crop products such as seeds. In the second case, damage to the product may reduce yields by the consumption of the entire product. Such is the case with bruchids, which consume stored cowpea seeds. In addition, pest attack of a crop product may also favor secondary infection by other pathogens, which cause additional losses in yield and revenue.

The injury caused by a pest to a crop is related to the level of pest population: The higher the number of insect pests per unit of habitat, the greater the injury caused. This relationship is applicable to damage both to the product and to the foliage and roots (Youdeowei and Adeniji 1986), though there are some marked differences. At a low pest population, the damage caused by a pest attacking the foliage and roots of crops is compensated for by increased vegetative growth; thus there is very little overall reduction in photosynthetic area and, therefore, in yield. As the pest population increases, damage to the crop also increases, reaching a point at which the damage becomes economic and vegetative growth is unable to compensate. On the other hand, when the insect attacks the final products (e.g., when *Maruca* sp. larvae attack cowpea pods), losses in yield are very high even at low pest populations because there is very little chance for the crop to compensate through increased production; thus the pest density threshold that will cause a severe loss in yield is very low. Extending these relationships to crop revenue, there is very little reduction in revenue at low densities of pests that attack foliage and roots (i.e., the pest density threshold for high revenue losses is high). On the other hand, even a low pest density results in high revenue losses for pests that directly attack the product (i.e., the pest density threshold for severe losses in revenue is quite low).

In general, when making a decision regarding pest control, the following factors must be be considered.

Nature of pest damage: Whether damage to foliage and roots or damage to the product, the nature and extent of damage must be carefully assessed.

Pest population: Pest densities should be assessed by various sampling techniques, and economic thresholds for the pests should be established.

Crop yield: Factors other than insect pests, such as climate, agronomic practices, and soil type, can affect the yield of a crop. The role of such factors in the presence of insect pest attack needs to be considered.

Availability of pest control inputs: The decision to use chemical pest control will depend on the availability of the pesticides at the right time, in adequate quantities, and at a cost within the resources of the farmer.

Cost–potential benefit ratio: The total cost of the control measure must be lower than the expected increase in revenue from the increased yield due to the control measure; thus this ratio must be greater than 1.

Influence on ecosystem: The pest control strategy adopted must not pollute the environment or upset the natural balance in the ecosystem.

Methods of Pest Control

The primary objective of pest control is to reduce the population of the offending pest below the economic injury level (i.e., to where the damage caused is no longer economic). A pest control method will therefore be considered successful if it can maintain the pest population well below the economic threshold. Any attempt to eradicate a pest completely from an agroecosystem is neither practical nor desirable. There are two basic approaches to pest control:

1. Prevent the pest from gaining access to the host crop (preclude pest–host interaction).
2. Attack the pest when it is on the host and is causing economic damage.

The various pest control methods can be broadly divided into indirect, biological, and direct.

Indirect Control Methods

These methods aim more at the prevention of pest attack, and generally include physical, legislative, and cultural approaches.

Physical Methods. These control methods include the use of various barriers to prevent pests from physical contact with their hosts, as well as mechanical removal or destruction of the pest. Contact-preventive barriers may be mechanical, chemical, or behavioral. Mechanical barriers may include use of fences, nets, or the use of nylon or paper bags to cover young developing pods from podborers. However, the economics of these methods cannot be justified in legume cultivation. Chemical barriers include prophylactic crop treatments that leave residual poison lethal to the pest.

Behavioral barriers exploit the fact that pests locate their hosts by responding to external stimuli such as sight and odors. Some of these barriers are meant to frighten, such as scarecrows and firing devices (used especially to protect against bird pests); others are meant to entrap pests by using light or certain attractants. In the last method, the pests respond positively to the emission of particular odors. Insects may be attracted to chemical substances in their food or to *pheromones,* chemical substances produced by members of the same species. Sex and aggregating pheromones are both attractants that may be used to combat the rapid multiplication of a particular insect species. Additionally, there are behavioral repellants that make the host unacceptable to the pest. More research is needed on behavioral barriers, since these methods eliminate the environmental pollution and toxicity problems associated with pesticide use.

Sometimes large insects (e.g., grasshoppers) and their eggs and larvae can be collected by hand and crushed. Such methods, however, tend to be labor intensive and expensive.

Legislative Control. This includes the use of laws and regulations to prevent the importation of pest organisms into a country and to restrict the spread of pests in areas where they are already established. Since the main objective here is to prevent dangerous pests from colonizing new areas, legislation involves quarantine eradication regulations and certification. In order to prevent imported plant material and plant products from introducing pests into a country, quarantine laws stipulate that such imported products must be thoroughly inspected in the country of origin and certified free of pest organisms. A phytosanitary certificate by the appropriate authority must be enclosed with the product exported. The importation of some plant materials may be totally prohibited by a country. Particularly serious pests are sometimes subject to a notification order stipulating that their presence must be reported immediately to the appropriate authorities. Warehouses at seaports and ships are regularly inspected and fumigated to eliminate pests and thereby prevent their spread. Similarly, plants, seeds, and other susceptible materials must not be sold unless they have been vigorously inspected and certified free of pests. Such certification regulations are enforced by the appropriate authorities in different countries.

Cultural Control. The agronomic practices employed in crop production have a profound influence on the incidence and populations of crop pests; the manipulation of these practices for pest control is generally termed *cultural control.* The basic principle of cultural control is the disruption of the development and life cycles of pests either by denying them their food or by exposing stages in their life cycle to adverse conditions so that they are killed. Cultural pest control is relatively cheap and effective and poses minimal damage to the environment and the natural ecosystem. Various cultural methods and their effectiveness in pest control are briefly described below.

Soil Cultivation. The preparation of soil by tillage and plowing of land destroys many soil-inhabiting pests by exposing them to adverse climatic conditions or to predatory animals such as birds. Well-prepared seedbeds encourage rapid germination and growth, often enabling a crop to grow away from pest attack.

Time of Sowing and Harvesting. Pests may be controlled by planting early or late so that the egg-laying stages of pests are avoided or the plants mature before pests attack them. Harvesting early also removes products from the field well before they are attacked by pests.

Rotations. Many pests are host-specific. When such a pest population is high, it is possible to reduce the damaging populations by changing to a non-susceptible crop between harvests of the susceptible crop. Crop rotations are particularly useful for the control of nematode pests.

Planting Resistant Crop Varieties. Cultivars that show levels of tolerance or resistance characteristics to particular pests have been developed by plant breeders. Crop resistance to insect pests may be manifested in various ways. For example, plants may grow vigorously and compensate adequately for the pest damage; or they may show differential preference through such physical characteristics as hairy leaves, thick or hard epidermis, unattractive color, and unacceptable smell or taste.

Mixed Cropping. Many subsistence farmers in the tropics practice mixed cropping. The complex ecosystem of a small mixed farm provides limited food plants for specific pests and harbors a wide variety of natural enemies that help to keep pest populations down. In general, mixed farms tend to be relatively free of serious pest problems.

Biological Control

This involves the deliberate use of organisms (parasites, predators, and pathogens) to reduce populations of pests. Such natural enemies may be arthropods (insects and mites), bacteria, protozoans, fungi, viruses, nematodes, or even vertebrates (birds, toads, and fish). This method of pest control is normally used to supplement other methods of control. Successful biological control requires that the pest population be reduced to levels well below the economic threshold but be maintained sufficiently to allow the survival of the biological control agent. Biological control also requires thorough knowledge of the ecosystem and of the ecology and behavior of both the target pest and the biocontrol agent. It is safe and cost effective, continues to be effective from year to year, and is free of the environmental pollution problems associated with chemical control. Care must be exercised, however, not to upset the ecosystem of the area by the manipulation of the controlling species.

Direct (Chemical) Control Measures

The most common and easily applicable method for reducing or preventing economic pest damage is the use of toxic substances or pesticides to kill pests or repel them from their host crops. Chemical control continues to play a significant role in solving the food and health problems of tropical developing countries. In fact, crops such as cowpea cannot be grown successfully without pesticide application. There are several advantages to direct chemical control:

It is a relatively easy method of pest control.
It produces quick and easy results.
It can be repeated as often as desirable.
Because it is cheap, individual farmers can take independent action on their own farms.
The broad-spectrum action of many pesticides makes it possible to control a complex of pests by using one or only a few pesticides.

There are, however, also several disadvantages to chemical control:

It is repetitive and must be applied whenever there is a pest outbreak; thus it is wasteful.
The pesticide applied rarely kills all the pests, and the surviving population soon develops to cause economic damage.
Pesticides can be toxic to beneficial insects, especially parasites, predators, and pollinators. They are also potentially toxic to wildlife, fish, and humans.
Pesticides cause environmental pollution and ecological disturbance; toxic residues may remain in agricultural produce.
Pests may develop resistance to a pesticide, reducing the effectiveness of that pesticide against that pest.
Chemical control provides only a temporary solution to pest problems.
Pesticides are expensive to manufacture, and usually have to be imported by the developing countries.

Pesticides can be used in several forms, including sprays and dusts, granular forms, baits for controlling soil pests, and seed dressing. Gases, smokes, and fumigants are also commonly used in greenhouses and granaries. Basically, there are two ways in which pesticides kill pests.

1. *Contact:* The pest is killed when it comes in contact with the chemical, is directly hit by the spray or dust, picks up the pesticide as it moves over treated foliages, absorbs vapor, or passes through soil that has also been treated.
2. *Ingestion:* As a stomach poison, the pest eats either foliages treated with pesticide or bait that incorporates the chemical. Systemic pesticides, when applied to the foliage or to the soil around the base of the plant, get into a plant's sap stream and poison pests that subsequently suck the sap.

Many pesticides, however, kill by more than one method, which makes them very effective. The following groups are in common use in several developing countries of the tropics.

Organochlorines. Chlorinated hydrocarbons have broad-spectrum action and are persistent in soil and water. They are usually very effective against insect pests because of the ease with which they penetrate the insect integument. DDT, chlordane, endosulfan, heptachlor, tetradifon, and tetrasul are some of the pesticides belonging to this class.

Organophosphates. In these pesticides, phosphorus is chemically bound to carbon atoms of organic radicals. Most are highly toxic to humans; therefore, safety precautions must be strictly observed when they are being used. Organophosphates are of low persistence because they are rapidly broken down into nontoxic compounds in the environment. They are highly effective stomach and contact poisons, and some also act as systemics. Some examples of this class include Diazinon®, fenthion, Malathion®, phosphamidon, and thiometon.

Carbamates. These are relatively recent compounds and are generally of very low mammalian toxicity. They have a wide range of biological activity and may act as stomach and contact poison. Some are also systemic. Examples are carbaryl, carbofuran, primicarb, and promecarb.

Botanicals. Many plant pests contain substances that have a variety of negative effects on pests. These compounds are alkaloids and are generally extracted and processed into pesticides. Nicotine, pyrethrum, and rotenone are examples.

Inorganic Salts and Elements. Some of the earliest pesticides used were inorganic salts and elements. Inorganic salts usually act as stomach poisons. Those commonly used include lead arsenate, lime sulfur, aluminum phosphide, copper sulfate, sodium fluoride, and mercury chloride.

Biological Pesticides. These are preparations of bacteria, viruses, or nematodes that are known to be natural enemies of pests.

Organic Oils. These include chemical oils from crude petroleum or coal tar. These are used against scale insects and to increase the activity of other pesticides.

Integrated Pest Control and Management

The problems arising from the use of pesticides are in themselves serious; therefore, attempts must be made to ensure that wherever pesticides are used to control pests, they must be used sensibly. These problems have led to the development of integrated control as an alternative system whereby pesticides are combined with other appropriate methods of pest control.

Integrated pest control is a pest management system that, in the context of the associated environment and the population dynamics of the pest species, utilizes all suitable techniques and methods in as compatible a manner as possible, and maintains pest populations below the economic damage threshold.

Integrated pest management or control involves the use of many pest control methods in a well-organized and harmonious way to attain long-term pest control. Techniques used must be compatible in a flexible system that preserves environmental quality. Natural pest control agencies are encouraged and supplemented with cultural and artificial methods, including the supervised and judicious use of pesticides. In this way the crop is protected effectively from the ravages of pests and enabled to produce acceptable yields while the natural ecological balance of the environment is preserved. The integrated pest management system provides lasting and environmentally acceptable methods for dealing with pest problems.

FIELD DISEASES

Subsistence agriculture tends to select continuously for "fitness" (in the genetic sense): Dependability is at a higher premium than high yields, since crop failure can mean famine to the farmer. This suggests that coevolved crops in traditional farming systems have achieved an equilibrium not only with one another and with their environment, but also with their parasites. Any agent that selectively destroys a component of an ecosystem must play a role in the evolution of that system. It is not "evolutionary strategy" for a parasite to kill its host; in an endemic situation, host and parasite accommodate to each other in a dynamic balance. That this is so is borne out by genetic analysis of obligate parasites and their hosts, suggesting that such systems are the relics of an ancient balanced polymorphism that was a necessary condition for their coevolution (Mode

1958). Furthermore, supporting evidence is also obtained from the concentration of resistant genes present in centers of origin of hosts and parasites where they have coevolved (Leppik 1970). In centers of origin and genetic diversity, the host population contains a wide spectrum of protective mechanisms, matched by broad spectra of pathogenicity in the parasite population (Anikster and Wahl 1979). Plant pathogens in their most diverse and primitive forms are likely to be found where the ancestors of cultivated crops still exist as wild species, thereby making it possible to trace the evolution of plant pathogens (Watson 1970).

Genetic diversity within a species tends to increase the stability of its reproductive success as well as contribute to the control of pests and diseases. The use of multiline cultivars has long been proposed for disease control in inbreeding cereals (Browning and Frey 1969). Such cultivars consist of a mixture of lines with similar agronomic phenotypes but differing vertical resistance genes. Where some of the component lines are susceptible, disease develops more slowly on the susceptible plants than in pure stands of the susceptible lines (Leonard 1969). Reviewing the mechanisms by which disease incidence is reduced in multiline cultivars, Browning and Frey (1969) suggested that a proportion of the initial inoculum falls on the resistant lines, thus reducing the effective dose. Of the spores produced by the infected susceptible lines, again only a proportion will land on the susceptible plants, the remainder being deposited on the resistant ones; this reduces the rate of increase of the pathogen. Another approach is to use mixtures of unrelated cultivars of a crop, each possessing different genes for resistance. Although the approach to disease control is essentially similar to that in multilines, cultivar blends offer greater diversity and flexibility in that their components may be readily varied with both site and season (Barrett 1980). Mixed cropping is yet another way of reducing the incidence of certain pests and diseases. For example, in cowpea in association with corn, the severity and rate of spread of *Ascochyta phaseolorum* was greater in sole-cropped cowpea than in the intercrop, apparently because the corn foliage impeded spore dispersal (Moreno 1975). Similarly, powdery mildew (*Erysiphe polygoni*) may initially develop more rapidly in sole-crop cowpea than when intercropped with corn (Moreno 1979). Mixed cropping may also affect the development of other groups of pathogens.

In most cases, extreme susceptibility and extreme virulence are consequences of human activities, occurring when host and pathogen are introduced for the first time (Harlan 1976). Buddenhagen (1977) has examined the nature of epidemic imbalance in tropical crops, classifying epidemics according to their origin. He shows that epidemics, resulting from an intensified union of crop and pathogen following separation, may be grouped according to the type of separation and reunion (Table 2-12). Type I epidemics are those with a long-established, coevolved host–pathogen relationship that has either remained rela-

Table 2-12. The Origin of Epidemics Relative to Crop–Pathogen Evolution.

I. Long-term crop–pathogen coevolution
   A. Smooth or cyclical intensification of relationship
   B. Reunion of coevolved systems following recent spatial separation
II. New encounters after ancient (geologic) separation
   A. Host moved to new region
   B. Pathogen moved to new region
   C. New-encounter-developed pathogen moved to separate host location
III. Man-made genetic separation followed by genetic reunion

Adapted from: Buddenhagen (1977).

tively constant (IA) or has been recently interrupted and rejoined spatially (IB). Cowpea yellow mosaic in Africa is an example of a type IA disease that may become serious through intensification of the cropping system. An example of a type IB disease is peanut rust in Africa; *Puccinia arachidis* has spread across Africa only during this decade although peanuts have been cultivated in West Africa since the sixteenth century (Grigg 1974).

Type II diseases are genetically new-encounter diseases, and follow reunion of two long-separated components of isolated evolutionary systems. These may be a result of intercontinental or regional movement of a crop into a new environment (IIA) or the movement of a pathogen into a new region where it infects a related host (IIB). Examples of type IIA diseases in legumes include various viral diseases of cowpea in the New World, whereas the southern bean mosaic of common bean is an example of a type IIB disease, resulting from the movement of a pathogen into a new region, and thence to a new host (Steiner 1975).

Type III epidemic disease is a result of overcoming artificial genetic separation through plant breeding. It is this group that has caused the greatest concern, and is characterized by the sudden breakdown of the vertical resistance by emergent matching pathotypes. Cases among legumes of type III epidemics have occurred with bean rust, bean anthracnose, and the *Phytophthora* diseases of soybean and lima bean in the United States.

The importance of a plant pathogen depends on the economic loss it causes. Alternatively, the extent of crop loss depends on both the intensity of the disease and its distribution. Although it is firmly established that plant diseases constitute major constraints to crop production, there are very few reliable data quantifying these crop losses (James and Teng 1979). Fewer still have attempted to analyze the relative importance of production constraints in tropical food crops. Estimates of yield losses may be based on experimental data from the study of a single disease, from which the relationship between disease progress and crop loss is established. However, such studies have seldom been made on legume diseases, and yield loss estimates are probably rather inaccurate. Furthermore, it is difficult to extrapolate from such estimates, made under experimental conditions, to those likely to be incurred in agricultural practice, where crop yields are limited by a complex of stress factors of which diseases are only one. Until more studies are carried out, systems of field rating of legume diseases must continue to rely on largely arbitrary scales whose relationship to crop loss is uncertain.

The major legume pathogens could be broadly classified into three distinct groups: those of fungal, bacterial, and viral origin. The importance of each of these three classes is briefly described below.

Fungal Diseases

The fungi are the most important groups of pathogens, and a very wide range of species are recognized as parasites of the legume crops. Legume pathogens have representatives among most of the major groups of the fungi. Their diversity is illustrated in Table 2-13, which lists selected species of the majority of genera parasitic on the legumes. Certain fungi, including species of *Pythium, Fusarium,* and *Rhizoctonia,* are commonly responsible for seed and seedling diseases in a wide range of legumes, including cowpea (Williams 1975), chickpea (Singh and Mehrotra 1980), winged bean (Price and Monroe 1978), common bean (Gay 1969), and soybean (Sinclair 1977). Collar and root rots, characterized by a progressive rotting of the root system or basal portion of the stem leading to chlorosis and wilting, are also caused (among others) by the species of *Pythium, Fusarium,* and *Rhizoctonia* (Singh and Allen 1980). The diseases of the stem include brown stem rot of soybeans (*Cephalosporium*), charcoal rot of various legumes caused by *Macrophomina phaseolina, Diaporthe* stem blight and *Neocosmospora* stem rot of soybean, and various species of *Colletotrichum* and *Sphaceloma* (Schwartz and Galvez 1980). True wilts are those in which wilting occurs before there is extensive damage to the root system. Vascular tissues of affected plants are typically discolored. The two principal genera involved are *Fusarium* and *Verticillium,* of which the former is the more important in legumes.

The diseases characterized by sudden and serious damage to all aerial parts of the plant are often referred to as *blight.* Examples of fungal blights are the *Phytophthora* blights of cowpea and pigeon pea, the *Ascochyta* blights of chickpea, bean, and cowpea, and *Rhizoctonia* web blight and white mold of common bean (Table 2-13). In many leaf diseases, the area of necrosis is limited and the main symptom is simply a spot of varying size and shape. The most important group responsible for leaf spot diseases of various legumes is *Cercospora* and allied genera. In some diseases, the presence of a pathogen is more obvious than any damage it induces in the plant. The mildews and rusts are examples in which their visible growth are signs of the disease. Unlike in cereals, very few of the smut fungi are known to affect the legumes (Schwartz and Galvez 1980).

Table 2-13. Some Representative Species of Legume Pathogens among the Orders of Fungi.

Order and Species	Natural Hosts	Reference
Chytridiales		
Synchytrium psophocarpi	Winged bean	Drinkall (1978)
Peronosporales		
Pythium aphanidermatum	Cowpea	Onuorah (1973)
Phytophthora drechsleri	Pigeon pea	Kannaiyan et al. (1980)
Peronospora manshurica	Soybean	Sinclair & Shurtleff (1975)
Mucorales		
Choanephora cucurbitarum	Cowpea, pigeon pea	Misra & Mehra (1969)
Erysiphales		
Erysiphe polygoni	Common bean, cowpea	Schwartz & Galvez (1980)
Leveillula taurica	Pigeon pea, cluster bean	Mukerji (1968)
Myringiales		
Elsinoe phaseoli	Lima bean, common bean	Sivanesan & Holliday (1971)
Helotiales		
Sclerotinia sclerotiorum	Common bean, soybean, chick-pea	Schwartz & Galvez (1980)
Hypocreales		
Calonectaria crotolariae	Peanut, soybean	Sinclair & Shurtleff (1975)
Nectria haematococca	Common bean, cowpea, chick-pea, pigeon pea	Booth (1971)
Sphaeriales		
Diaporthe phaseolorum	Soybean, cowpea, common bean, lima bean	Punithalingam & Holliday (1972a)
Mycosphaerella cruenta	Cowpea	Deighton (1976)
Neocosmospora vasinfecta	Soybean, chick-pea, pigeon pea	Nene (1978)
Uredinales		
Puccinia arachidis	*Arachis* spp.	Laundon & Waterston (1965a)
Uromyces appendiculatus	All legume species	Laundon & Waterston (1965b)
Phakopsora pachyrhizi	All legume species	Anahosur & Waller (1978)
Ustilaginales		
Entyloma vignae	Common bean, cowpea	Allen (1983)
Aphyllophorales		
Thanatephorus cucumeris	Most legumes	Mordue (1974a)
Corticium rolfsii	Peanut, cowpea, soybean, common bean	Mordue (1974b)
Sphaeropsidales		
Ascochyta rabiei	Chick-pea	Punithalingham & Holliday (1972b)
Septoria glycines	Soybean	Punithalingham & Holliday (1972c)
Phaeoseptoria spp.	Soybean, winged bean	Allen (1979)
Melanconiales		
Colletotrichum lindemuthianum	Most legumes	Mordue (1971)

Table 2-13. (*Continued*)

Order and Species	Natural Hosts	Reference
Sphaceloma arachidis	Peanut	Allen (1979)
Pestalotiopsis versicolor	Lima bean, peanut	Allen (1979)
Moniliales		
Cercospora canescens	Most legumes	Mulder & Holliday (1975)
Fusarium udum	Pigeon pea	Booth (1978)
Verticillium dahliae	Peanut	Purss (1961)
Aspergillus flavus	Peanut, many other legumes	McDonald (1969)
Alternaria spp.	Common bean, soybean, peanut	Schwartz & Galvez (1980)

Viral Diseases

The viruses that naturally infect legumes are representatives from almost all the major groups of plant viruses. The majority have been isolated from northern temperate, herbaceous crops, and few have been obtained from tropical, wild, or woody species (Gibbs and Watson 1980). About thirty viruses have been formally described to date. These include five potyviruses, four comoviruses, and two each belonging to cucumovirus and geminivirus groups (Table 2-14). Seed-borne infection and insect vectors play major roles in the transmission of legume viruses. Seed-borne infections are of great importance to the carryover of virus between seasons, whereas vectors are of paramount importance as agents of secondary spread.

The incidence of seed transmission depends on the virus and its strain, the host plant and its cultivar, and the environment (Nene 1972; Goodman and Bird 1978). Although natural infection of a susceptible host usually leads to the systemic spread of virus throughout the plant, seeds of infected plants do not invariably become virus-infected, and viruses in some plants are not even seed-borne. Cowpea mild mottle, tobacco ringspot, and bean common mosaic are some examples of seed-transmitted viruses; bean pod mottle, peanut rosette, and cowpea chlorotic mottle viruses are examples of non–seed-transmitted viruses (Nene 1972; Phatak 1974).

The mechanisms of seed transmission of viruses were reviewed by Bos (1977). Viruses can be seed-borne in several ways. Embryo infection, by far the commonest mode of virus transmission, leads to direct infection of progeny. Although viruses can also be carried outside the embryo in or on the seed coat, very few viruses are seed-borne in this manner. Bean common mosaic and cowpea aphid-borne mosaic viruses are examples of internally seed-borne viruses. The rate of seed transmission depends on the time of infection. Plants infected after flowering do not produce infected seeds, and transmission is successful only before cytoplasmic separation of the developing embryo from maternal tissue (Bos 1977).

Table 2-14. Some Representative Viruses Naturally Infecting Tropical Legumes.

Virus	Hosts	References
Aphid-transmitted viruses		
Potyvirus		
Bean common mosaic (BCMV)	Common bean, mung bean, tepary bean	Kaiser & Mossahebi (1975)
Bean yellow mosaic (BYMV)	Common bean, soybean, chick-pea, lentil, mung bean	Sinclair & Shurtleff (1975), Iwaki & Auzay (1978)
Soybean mosaic (SMV)	Soybean	Bos (1972)
Peanut mottle (PnMV)	Peanut, soybean, lima bean, Bambara groundnut	Ghanekar (1980), Demski et al. (1981)
Cucumoviruses		
Cucumber mosaic (CMV)	Cowpea, mung bean, common bean, chick-pea, soybean, winged bean	Schwartz & Galvez (1980), Brunt & Phillips (1981)
Peanut stunt (PnSV)	Peanut, common bean, soybean	Fischer & Lockhart (1978)
Miscellaneous		
Alfalfa mosaic (AMV)	Most legumes	Jaspars & Bos (1980)
Soybean dwarf (SDV)	Soybean	Tamada & Kojima (1977)
Beetle-transmitted viruses		
Comoviruses		
Cowpea yellow mosaic (CYMV)	Cowpea, winged bean, pigeon pea	Van Kammen & de Jager (1978)
Quail pea mosaic (QpMV)	Common bean, soybean	Moore & Scott (1981)
Miscellaneous		
Cowpea chlorotic mottle (CCMV)	Cowpea, common bean, soybean	Fulton, Gomez, & Scott (1975)
Black gram mottle (BgMeV)	Black gram	Scott & Hoy (1981)
Bean mild mosaic (BMMV)	Common bean	Waterworth (1981)
Whitefly-transmitted viruses		
Geminiviruses		
Bean golden mosaic (BGMV)	Common bean, lima bean	Goodman & Bird (1978)
Carla viruses		
Cowpea mild mottle (CMMV)	Cowpea, peanut, soybean	Allen (1983)
Leafhopper-transmitted viruses		
Beet curly top (BCTV)	Many legumes	Thomas & Mink (1979)
Thrips-transmitted viruses		
Tomato spotted wilt (TSWV)	Many legumes	Ghanekar et al. (1979)
Nematode-transmitted viruses		
Tobacco ringspot (TRSV)	Soybean, mung bean, black gram, cluster bean	Vignarajah (1978)

Table 2-14. (*Continued*)

Virus	Hosts	References
Fungus-transmitted viruses		
Tobacco necrosis (TNV)	Most legumes	Kassanis (1970)
Peanut clump (PCV)	Peanut	Ghanekar (1980)
Viruses with no known vectors		
Tobamoviruses		
Sunhemp mosaic (ShMV)	Cowpea, hyacinth bean	Kassanis & Varma (1975)
Ilarviruses		
Tobacco streak (TSV)	Soybean, common bean, peanut	Fulton (1971)

Viruses spread widely by natural means are chiefly those with efficient vectors. Aphids are the most important group of virus vectors. They include more vector species and transmit more viruses than any other group. The majority of aphid-borne viruses of food legumes are transmitted in a nonpersistent manner and include soybean dwarf, peanut rosette, and pea leafroll (Tamada and Kojima 1977; Schwartz and Galvez 1980). Some viruses of the comovirus group are transmitted by beetles (Allen et al. 1981). Whiteflies are also important vectors of several viral diseases of tropical legumes. The only other group of insect vectors of legume viruses are thrips (Ghanekar et al. 1979).

Although common viruses such as cucumber mosaic virus have little effect on legume hosts, some virus diseases can devastate legume crops. An epidemic of rosette in 1975 led to almost total loss of the peanut crop in northern Nigeria, with an estimated loss of about $300 million (Rossel 1977). Peanut yields may be reduced by as much as 90% by infection with tomato spotted wilt virus in Australia (Helms, Grylls, and Purss 1961). Seed-borne viruses, often having cosmopolitan distributions, may cause extensive losses in seed yield of up to 70–90% (Hampton 1975).

Bacterial Diseases

The principal bacterial pathogens of the food legume crops belong to the genera *Pseudomonas, Xanthomonas,* and *Corynebacterium,* the first two of which are gram-negative and the third gram-positive. The principal bacterial pathogens of food legumes are listed in Table 2-15. Unlike the fungi and viruses, there are comparatively few bacterial diseases of legume plants. Bacterial infection also less often leads to outbreaks of epidemic proportions. Nevertheless, bacterial pathogens induce a range of blights, cankers, wilt, leaf spots, and pustules in susceptible legume hosts, and often lead to significant economic crop loss. The more important diseases include halo blight of bean, bacterial blight of soybean,

Table 2-15. Bacterial Pathogens of Food Legumes.

Bacteria	Natural Hosts	References
Corynebacterium		
C. flaccumfaciens	Common bean, soybean	Schwartz & Galvez (1980), Allen (1983)
Pseudomonas		
Ps. syringae		
pv. *syringae*	Common bean, soybean, cowpea, lima bean	Kaiser & Ramos (1980), Schwartz & Galvez (1980)
pv. *glycinea*	*Glycine* spp.	Sinclair & Shurtleff (1975)
pv. *phaseolicola*	Common bean, lima bean, hyacinth bean, mung bean, pigeon pea, yam bean	Birch, Alvarez, & Patil (1981), Schwartz & Galvez (1980) Allen (1983)
pv. *tabaci*	Soybean, common bean, cowpea	Allen (1983)
Ps. solanacearum	Peanut, soybean, common bean, winged bean	Sinclair & Shurtleff (1975), Abdullah (1980)
Xanthomonas		
X. campestris		
pv. *cajani*	Pigeon pea	Sabet, Ishag, & Khalil (1969)
pv. *cassiae*	Chick-pea	Nene (1978)
pv. *cyamposidis*	Cluster bean	Patel et al (1953)
pv. *glycines*	Soybean	Sinclair & Shurtleff (1975)
pv. *phaseoli*	Hyacinth bean, moth bean, common bean, mung bean	Patel & Jindal (1972)
pv. *vignaeradiatae*	Mung bean	Sabet, Ishag, & Khalil (1969)
pv. *vignicola*	Cowpea, common bean, mung bean	Allen (1983)

and bacterial wilt of peanut, each caused by a pseudomonad; xanthomonads are responsible for the common and fuscous blights of bean, bacterial pustule, blight and canker of cowpea, and bacterial pustule of soybean (Table 2-15). Crop loss estimates range from <15% in bacterial pustule of soybean (Laviolette et al. 1970), 26% in bacterial blight of cowpea (Ekpo 1979), and up to 45% from common blight of bean (Yoshii, Galvez, and Alvarez 1976). The extent of crop loss depends in each case on the host cultivar, the time and methods of infection, and locality.

Bacteria invade plants only through wounds and natural openings; once inside the susceptible hosts, they divide and multiply rapidly in intercellular spaces. Some move systemically; others cause only local infections. After multiplication in the host, bacterial pathogens are spread in various ways. Bacterial exudates from leaves may be spread in rain or by wind. Wind-blown soil may also assist the dissemination and infection of bacterial pathogens of beans under dry conditions, and insects may be important vectors of certain bacteria (Kaiser and Vakili 1978). Many of the bacterial pathogens of legumes are also seed-borne, and may retain their viability for as long as or longer than that of the host seed. Seed transmission may result from both infected (internally borne) and contaminated seed. Although this may be the primary inoculum source of the majority of bacterial pathogens of legumes, bacteria may also persist in infected crop debris. Bacteria do not produce resistant spores, and bacterial cells are susceptible to desiccation, light, and other external factors, thus emphasizing the need for their rapid and direct dispersal.

As a ready reference, a summary of the major symptoms, spread, and control measures for some commonly occurring diseases of important food legume species is presented in Table 2-16.

Disease Control

Before deciding on control measures, it is essential to know the causative agents. Having ascertained (as far as possible) the cause, the appropriate preventive or control measures can then be applied. Several methods are available for the effective control of legume diseases; in general, they represent an approach similar to that used in weed and pest control. Some of these are briefly described below.

Crop Rotations

A good crop rotation system helps in avoiding accumulation of the pathogen. In several cases, the organism cannot exist except when living on the host. It should be remembered, however, that some pathogens may take years to die, and thus may have resting spores in the soil waiting for the susceptible crop to come along; others may survive in alternative hosts.

Removal of Weed Hosts

Some pathogens use weeds as alternative hosts. By controlling the weeds, the incidence of the disease can be minimized. Both this method and the use of crop rotations in disease management require a sound knowledge of the pathogens and their life cycles and host specificity; both are primarily preventive measures.

Clean Seed

The seed used for planting must be free from disease. It should be used only from a disease-free crop or be bought from a certified seed agency.

Table 2-16. Characteristics of Some Commonly Occurring Diseases of Major Food Legumes.

Disease	Symptoms	Spread	Control
Fungal diseases			
Alternaria leaf spot	Small brown, irregular shaped lesions develop into large gray-brown oval lesions with concentric rings; leaf necrosis; premature defoliation	Wind, rain, insects, infected seeds	Chemical control; wide plant and row spacings; crop rotations
Angular leaf spot	Angular shaped spots on leaves; black feltlike appearance on undersurface of leaves; premature defoliation; reduced vigor; poor yield	Seed-borne, wind-blown spores; fungus overwinters in infected bean debris in field	2-year crop rotation; planting pathogen-free seed in well-drained soils; deep plowing to bury infected bean debris; chemical seed treatment
Anthracnose	Brick-red to dark brown lesions on aerial parts of the plant; sunken and elongate lesions on stems; circular lesions on pods; reduced vigor and yield	Infected seeds, field debris, rain and irrigation water, insects, animals, humans, farm implements	Pathogen-free seed; chemical seed treatment; 2–3-year crop rotation
Ascochyta leaf and pod spot	Large, light to dark brown leaf lesions with concentric rings; zonate appearance; dark brown, slightly sunken, zonate pod lesions; premature defoliation and plant collapse	Seed-borne, local spread by wind and rain	Crop rotations; use disease-free seed, chemical seed, and plant treatment
Powdery mildew	All aerial parts affected; small, white powdery spots enlarge to cover entire leaf, pods covered by white powdery masses of pathogen mycelium and spores	Seed-borne, rain, wind, and insects	Disease-free seed; resistant cultivars; sulfur sprays or dusts early in the season before infection
Rust	Tiny, white, raised spots on the undersurface of leaves; enlarge to form reddish-brown pustules; severely diminished plant vigor	Spores spread by wind, insects, animals, and farm implements	Resistant cultivars; crop rotations; reduce plant density; chemical control
Ashy stem blight	Black, sunken, elongate lesions on stems causing plant wilt, premature defoliation, and death; characteristic grayish-tan-ashen color	Seed-borne and soilborne; local spread by air	Disease-free seed; chemical seed treatment; resistant cultivars; deep plowing to bury infected debris; 4–5-year crop rotations with nonsusceptible plants
Fusarium root rot	Small, elongate, tan-red lesions on roots showing reddish-brown necrosis; stunted growth	Soilborne; drainage or irrigation water	Avoid spread of infected plant debris and soil; crop rotations; avoid overirrigation; resistant cultivars; chemical control for early season control

	Symptoms	Source/Transmission	Control
Pythium root rot	Elongate, water-soaked areas on roots, becoming slightly sunken tannish brown lesions; collapsed, shrunken, tan-brown appearance	Soilborne; irrigation water, wind-blown soil, farm implements	Resistant cultivars; avoid overirrigation in early stages of crop development; rotations with grain crops; plant in well-drained soils; wide spacings; chemical seed treatment
Rhizoctonia root rot	Reddish-brown elongate, cankerous lesions on roots; red coloration of the pith	Soilborne; soil spread	Prepare soil 5 or more days in advance before planting; plant in warm soil; shallow planting; irrigate conservatively; rotations with grain crops; chemical seed and soil treatment

Viral diseases

Common mosaic	Irregular-shaped light yellow and dark green areas in a mosaic-like pattern on leaves; puckering; stunting; downward curling; systemic vein necrosis in leaves, stems, roots, and pods	Virus overwinters in weed hosts and infected seeds; mechanical transmission by pollen and aphid vectors	Resistant cultivars; disease-free seed; adjust planting date to minimize exposure to aphids; control aphids
Curly top	Leaves pucker, turn downward, curl, turn yellow, and die; severely dwarfed and bunched plants	Transmitted to beans from various perennials and winter annuals by beet leafhopper	Use certified seeds of resistant cultivars
Golden mosaic	Systemic, bright yellow or golden mosaic; leaf rolling; stunted growth; pod size reduction	Whitefly insect vector; no seed transmission is known	Crop rotations; isolate bean fields from virus reservoir plants and from whitefly sources, such as soybeans, tomatoes, tobacco, and cotton; chemical control of the vector
Yellow mosaic	Malformed and distorted leaves; intense yellow and green mottling of leaves; dwarfing and bunchiness of plant; necrosis	Mechanical transmission; aphids act as vectors from bean fields and surroundings	Resistant cultivars; chemical control of aphids; eliminate alternative hosts

Bacterial diseases

Brown spot	Small, oval, necrotic lesions on leaves; puckering; necrosis	Weed hosts; wind-blown rain; overhead sprinkler irrigation	Crop rotations; spray with copper-containing chemicals; resistant cultivars
Bacterial wilt	Gradual systemic wilting of plants; stem cankers; water-soaked pods	Seed-borne; overwinters in plant debris and weeds; surface irrigation water	Disease-free seeds; crop rotations; resistant cultivars

Table 2-16. (Continued)

Disease	Symptoms	Spread	Control
Common blight	Water-soaked spots on leaves; brown, necrotic lesions with lemon yellow margins; extensive tissue damage leading to defoliation	Seed-borne; wind-driven rain, insects, humans, farm implements	Use certified seeds, 2–3-year crop rotation, deep plowing to eliminate infested bean debris in the field
Halo blight	Small, angular water-soaked spots with halo of yellow tissue on lower leaf surface; sunken, reddish brown, oval, water-soaked spots on pods; wrinkled discolored seeds	Seed-borne; infected plant debris, splattering water, or wind-blown rain	Crop rotations, deep plowing, pathogen-free seed, resistant cultivars, early harvesting, use copper-containing chemicals
Nonparasitic diseases			
Bald head	Severely stunted and malformed seedlings, growing point is killed	External/internal seed injury during harvesting; subsequent storage and handling	Extreme care in all mechanical aspects of seed harvesting, cleaning, handling and planting, maintain seed moisture level of at least 14–15%
Nutrient deficiency and toxicity	Symptoms depend upon cultivar, nutrient involved, and environmental conditions; typically, entire foliage shows yellow–tan–bronze discoloration beginning at leaf edges with veins remaining green; plants often stunted	Soil nutrient deficiency, most commonly P and Mg; toxicities include Al, B, and Mn; soil pH	Adjust soil pH, apply appropriate amounts of deficient nutrients
Ozone injury	Tiny white spots on leaf surfaces with veins remaining green; "bronzing" or brownish-purple discoloration of leaves	Air pollution by ozone (O_3)	Use tolerant cultivars; antioxidant sprays protect against ozone injury
Sunscald	Abiotic disease; water-soaked spots on sun-exposed plant parts; spots often turn reddish-brown and coalesce to form large discolored areas	Intense sunlight; high field temperatures	Not adequately researched
Wind injury	Leaves show long ragged tears, may be torn away; plant lodging; broken stems and branches	High-velocity winds	Use short, compact cultivars with small leaves, plant rows in the direction of high winds to reduce swaying

Compiled from: Smartt (1976), Allen (1983), and Hagedorn and Inglis (1986).

Resistant Varieties

For quite some time, plant breeders have concentrated on what is called "single" or "major gene" resistance. However, with few exceptions, this resistance is overcome by the development of new races of the pathogens to which the gene is no longer resistant. Breeding programs are now concentrating on "multigene" or "field resistance," which means that a variety or cultivar has the characteristics to "tolerate" infection from a wide range of races with little lowering of the yield. The major emphasis thus is now on tolerance rather than resistance. The genetic resistance of food legumes to various diseases is described at a greater length in a subsequent section.

Control of Insects

Several leaf-sucking insects, such as aphids, thrips, and whiteflies, are important carriers of many pathogens. In addition, pathogens can often enter through plant wounds made by insects. Thus, insect control indirectly also helps prevent the spread of many diseases of fungal and viral origin.

Chemical Control

The chemical control of plant diseases often involves the use of fungicides. These may be applied to the seed before planting, to the growing plant, or to the soil, and can be used as sprays, dusts, or volatile gases. To be effective, fungicides must in no way be harmful to either the crop or (after suitable precautions have been taken) to the operator or others. They must certainly repay their cost. Seed dressing or seed disinfection is a common method to prevent several soil and seed-borne diseases. In many instances, pesticides can be used at the same time to help prevent attacks by soil-borne pests. Organomercurial compounds have been widely used as seed-dressing agents; however, safety concerns over the use of mercury and its levels in food and water have caused great concern about their use. Carboxin and ethirimol are widely used for the control of smuts and mildews, and thiram is a popular dry-seed dressing used to prevent seed decay and preemergence damping-off in legumes. These fungicides can also be used as dusts or sprays on plant foliage. Fungicides containing copper, organosulfur and organotin compounds are also widely used for the control of fungal and bacterial diseases of food legumes.

Fungicide composition varies slightly according to manufacturer, but all contain a very small amount of actual poison in a suitable carrier agent. Those used for seed dressing also contain an inert dye so that the dressed seed can easily be distinguished.

Genetics of Disease Resistance

The domestication of food legumes—and particularly, the application of modern agricultural technology—may have narrowed the genetic base of cultivars, causing them to be vulnerable to disease epidemics. Wild populations of crop or closely related species and primitive, unselected cultivars or landraces have a much broader genetic base, which includes genes for disease resistance. These gene pools have been and are being exploited as the basis for genetic sources of resistance in nearly all the food legumes.

Thus, for many diseases that attack food legumes, sources of resistance have been located and resistant cultivars have been developed or are in the process of development. Although a good deal of breeding is proceeding without the benefit of information on genetic analysis, information has been published on the genetics of disease resistance of various legumes. Some representative findings in this regard are summarized in Table 2-17. These studies suggest that most resistance in food legumes is inherited in an oligogenic manner. Thus, it may appear that food legumes are in a vulnerable position in relation to variable pathogens. However, specific resistance in the crops is not always unstable. In fact, some has held up for extended periods even with some variable pathogens, such as bean common mosaic and pea fusarium wilt, for nearly half a century. With only a few diseases, such as bean rust and lima bean downy mildew, has the specific resistance been of short duration. Thus, pathologists and breeders should continue to identify and use specific resistance wherever it can be found, since experience indicates that it is adequate for a majority of diseases of food legumes.

An advantage for the use of specific resistance in breeding programs is that it requires fewer resources than multigenic or general resistance. This is important because much of the breeding of food legumes must be undertaken by developing countries with limited resources. Specific resistance should be used with caution, however, and if possible in conjunction with other means of control.

Although specific resistance may be satisfactory and even advantageous in certain situations, general resistance should be identified genetically wherever possible and used in breeding programs. Although the literature reveals few instances of general resistance in food legumes, it may be widespread. It may not have been frequently reported because it is more difficult to identify genetically. As research on the genetics of disease resistance in food legumes becomes more sophisticated and intensive, we may expect general resistance to be identified for many diseases and to be used more extensively in breeding programs. General resistance should be especially identified genetically in instances where pathogens are known to be highly variable (e.g., rust and downy and powdery mildews) and be used to breed resistant cultivars. We must also actively encourage cooperation between breeders and pathologists to determine the genetic ba-

Table 2-17. Genetics of Disease Resistance in Food Legumes.

Species	Disease	Causal Agent	Genetics of Resistance	Reference
Cajanus cajan	Wilt	*Fusarium udum*	2 dominant genes	Joshi (1957)
Cicer arietinum	Blight	*Phytophthora drechsleri*	1 dominant gene	ICRISAT (1978)
	Blight	*Ascochyta rabiei*	1 dominant gene	Hafiz & Ashraf (1953)
	Wilt	*F. oxysporum* sp. *ciceri*	1 recessive gene	Pathak, Singh, & Lal (1975)
Lablab purpureus	Bacterial leaf spot	*Xanthomonas phaseoli*	3 pairs of genes	Sulladmath et al (1977)
Lens culinaris	Pea seedborne mosaic	PSBMV	1 recessive gene	Haddad, Meuhlbauer, & Hampton (1978)
Phaseolus lunatus	Cucumber mosaic	CMV	2 dominant complementary factors	Thomas, Zaumeyer, & Jorgensen (1951)
	Downy mildew	*Phytophthora phaseoli*	1 dominant gene	Wester. Fisher, & Blount(1972)
	Stem rot	*Rhizoctonia solani*	1 dominant gene *Pd*	Steinswat, Pollaard, & Anderson (1967)
	Root knot	*Meloidogyne incognita*	Few major genes	McGuire, Allard, & Harding(1961)
Phaseolus vulgaris	Bean common mosaic	BCMV	Gene-for-gene system	Drijfhout (1978)
	Anthracnose	*Colletotrichum lindemuthianum*	*ARE* gene	Zaumeyer & Meiners (1975)
	Rust	*Uromyces phaseoli*	1 or more dominant genes	Zaumeyer & Meiners (1975)
	Root rot	*Fusarium solani*	Polygenic	Boomstra & Bliss (1977)
	Common blight	*Xanthomonas phaseoli*	Polygenic	Zaumeyer & Meiners (1975)
	Halo blight	*Pseudomonas phaseolicola*	Polygenic	Zaumeyer & Meiners (1975)
Pisum sativum	Pea mosaic	PMV	1 recessive gene	Barton et al. (1964)
	Pea leaf roll	PLRV	1 recessive gene, *lr*	Drijfhout (1968)
	Pea seedborne mosaic	PSBMV	1 recessive gene, *sbm*	Hagedorn & Kraft (1979)
	Powdery mildew	*Erysiphe polygoni*	2 recessive genes, *er₁*, *er₂*	Heringa, Van Norel, & Tazelaar (1969)
	Leaf & pod spot	*Ascochyta pisi*	3 dominant genes	Wark (1950)
	Wilt	*Fusarium oxysporum*	1 dominant gene, *Fw*	Wade (1929)
Vigna mungo, V. radiata	Bacterial leaf spot	*Xanthomonas phaseoli*	One dominant gene, *Bls*	Fery (1980)
	Mung bean yellow virus	MYMV	1 recessive gene, *v*	Thakur, Patel, & Verma (1977)
Vigna unguiculata	Cucumber mosaic	CMV	1 dominant gene, *Cmm*	Sittiyos, Poehlman, & Sehgal (1979)
	Bean yellow mosaic	BYMV-CS	1 recessive gene, *by*	Fery (1980)
	Cowpea mosaic	CPMV	1 dominant gene, *Ymr*	Bliss & Robertson (1971)
	Leaf spot	*Cercospora cruenta*	1 dominant gene, *cls-1*	Fery (1980)
			1 recessive gene, *cls-2*	
	Stem rot	*Phytophthora vignae*	1 dominant gene *Sr*	Fery (1980)
	Powdery mildew	*Erysiphe polygoni*	Multiple recessive genes	Fennell (1948)
	Root knot	*Meloidogyne incognita*	1 dominant gene	Amosu & Franckowiak (1974)

sis of disease resistance in food legumes. On a worldwide basis, we must have adequate and stable production of food legumes if the nutritional needs of the populations are to be satisfied, since legumes are major sources of dietary protein. An adequate and stable supply of food legumes depends, in turn, on the control of pests and diseases. Breeding for resistance represents the most satisfactory means of control. To be most effective, breeding programs must be based on the knowledge of the inheritance of resistance. Thus, genetic studies of disease resistance in food legumes are vital to the world's nutritional wellbeing and must be greatly strengthened worldwide.

DRYING

After harvesting and threshing, partially field-dried seeds must be further dried to an optimum moisture content to prevent germination of seeds, retain maximum grain quality, prevent bacterial and fungal growth, and retard infestation by mites and insects. Food grains such as cereals, oilseeds, and legumes differ in their biological makeup. Hot air is the preferred drying medium both to conduct heat to the produce and to remove moist vapor from the drying produce.

The moisture content in grains varies according to grain type, chemical composition, moisture at harvest, harvesting methods, relative humidity of the atmosphere, and seasonal fluctuations (Salunkhe, Chavan, and Kadam 1985). The optimum or safe storage moisture content of grains is normally defined as the amount of water at which the rate of respiration is low enough to prevent the germination of seeds and thus consequent deterioration of their quality.

Drying methods could be broadly classified as either natural or artificial, with several systems in each class. Some of these methods are briefly described below.

Natural Sun Drying

Sun drying is the preferred method of drying grains, especially in tropical countries. Typically, the grains are spread on the threshing yard for two or three days and, once dried, are transferred to storage bins. Sun drying requires frequent turning of the layers of drying grains. This method is, however, not suitable for drying large quantities, nor under humid and cloudy weather conditions.

In natural drying, it is essential to control the rate of drying. At higher rates, rapid moisture movement, especially from the surface layers, often results in swelling and bursting of seeds. The case hardening of the surface layers under such situations also results in trapping of moisture from the internal layers of seeds, causing uneven drying, wrinkled surface appearance, and enhanced susceptibility of the seeds to microbial infections during subsequent storage.

Table 2-18. Recommended Maximum Air Temperature for Drying and Moisture Contents for the Safe Storage of Some Legumes.

Legume	Maximum Air Temperature (°C)	Moisture Content (wet basis, %)
Cowpea	38	15
Dry beans (animal feed)	45	15
Dry beans (seeds)	38	15
Lentil	38	14
Peanut	37	7
Peas	38	14
Soybean	38	11

Source: Salunkhe, Kadam, and Chavan (1985) and Kadam, Salunkhe, and Kuo (1989).

Mechanical Drying

In most developed countries, drying of legume seeds is carried out in mechanical dryers (Salunkhe, Chavan, and Kadam 1985). Continuous batch dryers or in-bin dryers are commonly used for this purpose. On-the-floor drying systems or radially ventilated bins are well suited for slow drying of legumes. Moisture removal by tray or sack dryers with shallow layers is done at high temperatures, generally 9–11 °C above the ambient temperature. Other mechanical systems commonly used are low- or medium-temperature dryers, radial flow dryers, multiduct ventilated flow dryers, and solar dryers. These drying methods have been comprehensively reviewed (Foster and Peart 1976; Salunkhe, Chavan, and Kadam 1985).

The recommended maximum air temperature for drying and the optimum moisture contents for safe storage of several legumes are summarized in Table 2-18. The legume seeds should be dried immediately following threshing. If high-moisture grains are dried at high temperatures, the outer layers become hard: The grains will appear to be properly dried, but the inside will be soft and wet. Excessive heat applied to moist beans also results in splitting. For large-seeded beans, two-stage drying is thus often recommended to ensure satisfactory moisture reduction and to keep the seed unaffected. For safe storage, the beans should be dried to about 15% moisture, although peanuts and soybeans should be dried to 8% and 11% moisture, respectively (Salunkhe, Chavan, and Kadam 1985; Kadam, Salunkhe, and Kuo 1989). Seed stock that starts at a high moisture content should be agitated during drying; otherwise, the seeds will cake together. Continuous, batch, and in-bin dryers, where automatic transfer from drying to holding bin and back can be achieved, are often useful in this regard.

Beans are larger than cereals, have a thicker seed coat, and usually contain a higher moisture level at harvesting. The recommended temperatures for drying are therefore somewhat lower than those for cereals. To obtain a relatively uniform stress, unheated air and air 3–5 °C above ambient temperatures should pass through beans stored at uniform depth. On-the-floor drying systems and radially ventilated bins are well suited to this slow but sure type of moisture removal. The bag and sack dryers with shallow layers may be operated at higher temperatures (i.e., 9–11 °C above ambient temperatures). If beans containing high moisture content are held in bulk, they heat up rapidly (Salunkhe, Chavan, and Kadam 1985). Because of their size and thick skin, they must be dried only at low temperatures to avoid caking and splitting. If continuous dryers are being used, it is impossible to reduce moisture content to a safe level in one pass without causing cracking; the seeds therefore should be passed through the dryer twice, allowing 24 h to elapse between treatments. The most suitable drying system for legume seeds is one that utilizes air at ambient temperature.

The use of ambient-temperature air (or air heated only slightly above ambient temperature) is practiced in many countries to aerate grains. This is done to lower and equalize grain temperature, to remove unpleasant odors or toxic gases after fumigation, and to reduce their moisture content by a very small amount. However, care must be taken to avoid aeration with air at temperatures and relative humidities higher than those associated with the equilibrium moisture content of grain.

STORAGE

Legumes are stored at farmer, trader, and government levels in various types of storage structure until the following season's harvest is available for consumption. Under subsistence farming in the developing countries, the farmer often retains a portion of the produce for family consumption, for seed and feed, and for payment to farm laborers; the surplus is then disposed of through marketing channels. The entire marketable surplus, however, is not disposed of at once, but rather is released into the market gradually, depending upon the economic conditions and prevailing market prices. In most developing countries, legume storage is done at trader or government levels as insurance against a subsequent crop of low yield or poor quality, fluctuation in price and market demand, and shortages and famines (Salunkhe, Chavan, and Kadam 1985).

Storage Structures

In order to avoid losses during storage, it is necessary to use a storage structure designed to help avoid losses. Storage structures suitable for farm, urban, and commercial storage in tropical countries have been described (Salunkhe, Chavan, and Kadam 1985; Pingale 1976; Birewar et al. 1980). Some of these are briefly described below.

Farm Storage

Circular Steel Bin

This bin has an opening at the top for filling and a spout at the bottom for removing the grain. The bottom is made of plain sheets of mild steel. This structure can be easily assembled on site, and can be taken apart when not in use. It has a built-in arrangement for preventing the development of uneven temperatures that lead to moisture migration and deterioration of seed quality. Grains stored in the bin can be fumigated whenever required.

Plastic Bin

This low-cost structure, suitable for indoor storage of grains, has a tube-shaped metal base with a provision for placing bamboo sticks vertically around the side of the metal drum. A cylindrical rubberized fabric is hung inside, into which the grains are loaded. The grains can be taken out from the top or through a sliding door at the bottom of the metal base. This is a compact and stable storage structure and can be dismantled when not in use.

Prefabricated Steel Bin with Hopper Bottom

This is a strong and durable outdoor structure with a sloping roof, a manhole for filling, and a hopper bottom with a sliding door for discharging grains. A natural aeration arrangement is provided in the bin to prevent the buildup of a temperature gradient and the subsequent problems of translocation of moisture and deterioration of seed quality. The bin stands on a firm support, creating a clearance of 60 cm at the bottom below the hopper. Both the manhole and the hopper gates have locking arrangements, and a metallic ladder and pulley are provided to facilitate filling of the bin.

Aluminum Bin

This outdoor storage structure consists of a cylindrical body built of several corrugated aluminum curved sheets and a conical roof of flat aluminum sheets. Constructed on a 60-cm-high platform, the bin has a spout embedded in the platform and a manhole in the roof, both provided with locking arrangements.

RCC Bin

A reinforced cement concrete (RCC) bin is circular, sturdy, weatherproof, and suitable for both indoor and outdoor storage. Its construction is otherwise similar to the storage structures described above.

PUSA Bin

This is a conventional mud bin that uses a polythene sheet to make the structure air- and moisture-tight. It is simple in design, easy to construct, and inexpensive to suit the needs of average farmers. When filled to capacity and properly closed, the bin becomes an airtight, damp-proof structure that prevents thermal conductivity.

Urban Storage

In urban areas, a rectangular steel structure—rodent- and moisture-proof, with an arrangement for controlled aeration as well as fumigation—is recommended for the compact storage of cereals and legumes in one place (Pingale 1976). Made of galvanized iron sheets, the structure is often partitioned into four or five compartments of different sizes.

Commercial Large-Scale Storage

This involves storage of large quantities of grain by government agencies who have adequate economic and technical support. Hence, more sophisticated structures for both bag and bulk storage are recommended.

Bag Storage

The buildings used for bag storage in the tropics and subtropics are generally not devised for grain storage. Most have either corrugated metal or concrete roofs on mud or brick walls and are erected for general purposes. The floors are often made of earth or masonry, and have inefficient water-proofing. Ideally, a well-planned bag storage warehouse should have waterproof walls, roof, and floor, and a sealable opening for controlled ventilation and fumigation. The opening can be used for both natural and fan-controlled aeration. If a metal roof is used, it should be insulated to minimize temperature buildup. The seed bags should be placed on wood planking erected above the floor to provide insulation against floor temperature and moisture. The building should also be made rodent-, bird-, and insect-proof.

Bulk Storage

A bulk storage strucutre should meet basic requirements similar to those for a bag storage structure; however, side-wall insulation is more important in a bulk storage structure since the grains are in direct contact with the bin walls. Depending upon the temperature, the metal skins of these bins readily transfer heat inward or outward. Moreover, the metal absorbs radiation in varying degrees depending upon the reflectivity of the exterior surface and its radiation capacity for long-wavelength heat energy. Generally, white paint is as good a reflector as aluminum and bright steel, and is a much better radiator of low-temperature heat energy. Under most clear-sky climatic conditions, the surface temperature of the white-painted material is lower than most unpainted and steel surfaces.

Depending upon the requirement, the bulk storage structure may be small or large. Large elevators may be flat or upright, whereas upright storage bins are mainly large, cylindrical, silo types. A painted metal or concrete silo can be built up singly or into a row of bins.

Factors Affecting Postharvest Storage

The deterioration of legume seed quality during postharvest storage is primarily related to the inevitable process of aging. The conditions of storage, however, influence both the rate at which aging occurs and the activity of storage microorganisms and insects. The influence of seed storage on seed quality must therefore encompass the complex interactions among storage conditions, physiological changes during aging, and the activity of storage microorganisms and insects.

Storage and Physiological Aspects of Seed Quality

The two most important factors affecting the rate of aging and, therefore, the retention of seed viability in storage are seed moisture content and temperature. The moisture content of seed in storage is related to the relative humidity (rh) of the storage atmosphere, since seeds are hygroscopic and take up or lose water until their moisture content is in equilibrium with the ambient relative humidity (James 1967; Roberts 1972; Justice and Bass 1978). Food legumes show the typical response of orthodox seed species to storage at high relative humidities and therefore high seed moisture content (Roberts 1972). Seed longevity declines as the relative humidity and moisture content (mc) increase. James, Bass, and Clark (1967) found that in conditions of high relative humidity (90% rh at 70 °F), the viability of pea seeds declined to 4% in twelve months, but it was maintained at 99% for five years in less humid conditions (50% rh at 50 °F). Similarly, the viabilities of peas, *Phaseolus* beans, and broad beans all fell more rapidly when stored at high relative humidities (Sijbring 1963).

Several researchers have also studied the influence of moisture content on the loss of viability by equilibrating seeds to different moisture contents before a period of hermetic storage. The loss of viability of soybean was greater when held at 17.5% mc than at 14.5% mc (Boakye-Boateng and Hume 1975). The fall in germination of soybean was also linearly related to increasing moisture content (Burris 1980). Peas equilibrated to 18% mc lost viability rapidly, reaching 50% germination after only 15 wk (Roberts and Abdalla 1968), whereas at lower moisture contents (15.4% and 12.5%), a similar decline occurred after 35 and 100 wk, respectively. The viability of broad beans also fell more rapidly at 19.4% mc than at 14.7% mc (Sholberg and Muir 1979). Peanuts also have limited longevity at higher moisture contents (de Tella, Lago, and Zink 1976), although in this case, the moisture contents involved were much lower, with rapid loss of viability at 8.0% and 9.1% mc compared to 4.5% and 6% mc. Despite the general rule that longevity increases as seed moisture content declines, there is a suggestion that below certain moisture contents, seeds deteriorate more rapidly (Bewley and Black 1982). For example, pea seeds stored in 1% rh at 10 °C revealed evidence of deterioration as determined by reduced vital staining and increased solute leakage (Powell and Matthews 1977).

In the studies cited above wherein reduced viability has been reported after storage at high relative humidity or moisture content, the temperature of storage was also high. Early work considered the effects of temperature alone on viability (Groves 1917), and provided evidence that viability declined with increased temperature. Groves (1917), however, noted that viability decreased at any temperature if the moisture content of the seeds was increased. In subsequent investigations, the effects of both temperature and moisture content on seed viability were considered together for several grain legumes, including soybean (Toole and Toole 1953; Burris 1980; Ellis, Osei-Bonsu, and Roberts 1982), pea (James, Bass, and Clark 1967; Roberts and Abdalla 1968), *Phaseolus vulgaris* (James, Bass, and Clark 1967), *Vicia faba* (Roberts and Abdalla 1968; Sholberg and Muir 1979), peanut (Ketring 1971), and chick-pea and cowpea (Ellis, Osei-Bonsu, and Roberts 1982). These investigations showed that the effects of temperature and moisture content are constant and independent of each other. This seems to apply over temperatures ranging widely from –20 °C to 90 °C and seed moisture content between 5% and 25% (Ellis and Roberts 1980). Harrington (1960) expressed the relationship of seed moisture content and temperature to loss of viability by a general rule for seed storage: A 10 °F (5.6 °C) reduction in temperature or a 1% reduction in seed moisture content doubles the seed's storage life. This relationship has been more accurately described in viability equations for pea and broad bean (Roberts 1972) and for chick-pea, cowpea, and soybean (Ellis, Osei-Bonsu, and Roberts 1982). The information derived from the equations for pea and broad bean has also been presented as nomographs (Roberts and Roberts 1972). These equations and nomographs make it possible to estimate the time taken for viability to decrease to a given level in various conditions of temperature and relative humidity, as well as the combination of temperature and moisture content necessary to maintain viability above a given level for a certain period.

These studies on the influence of storage conditions on seed quality have mostly concentrated on the loss of viability during storage, that is, the final stage of aging. There have been few investigations into the physiological changes occurring before the loss of viability during more prolonged storage, compared to several studies relating to changes during rapid aging. In peas, increased leakage has revealed a decline in the vigor of germinable seeds of seed lots stored for up to four years in a commercial store (Powell and Matthews 1977). Similar increases in leakage from stored soybeans have been associated with other indices of reduced vigor. Thus, reduced metabolic activity (Srivastava 1975), reduced hypocotyl length, increased free fatty acids, and increased amounts of sugars and electrolytes in the leachate (Verma and Gupta 1975) were found in soybean seeds showing increased leakage. Similarly, black gram seeds that leaked readily into soak water produced seedlings with reduced root and shoot lengths (Dharmalingam, Ramakrishnan, and Ramaswamy 1976), and a decline in the vigor of peas and broad beans (Abdalla and Roberts 1969) and *Phaseolus* beans (Harrison 1966) was reflected in a reduction in the initial growth rate of the seedlings. Toole, Toole, and Borthwick (1957) also found that following the storage of *Phaseolus* bean seeds in unfavorable conditions, the plants from them developed more slowly, reaching maximum flowering several days later than did plants from seeds stored in favorable conditions. These evidences from prolonged storage experiments therefore indicate that physiological aging also occurs, leading to loss of vigor. However, the paucity of such studies, and the recent proposal that the physiological changes during rapid aging may not be those of natural aging, suggest that there should be more work done on noninduced physiological changes during seed aging.

Preharvest Deterioration and Seed Quality in Storage

The response of seeds to storage conditions is influenced by their initial condition as they enter store. This is largely determined by the degree of preharvest deterioration that has already occurred. Amable (1976) found that the decline in the germination of soybeans in storage was most rapid after delayed harvest, and the shorter longevity of the U.S. cultivars in India compared to local cultivars has been attributed to their maturation in the rainy season, which favors field deterioration (Gupta 1976). The greater susceptibility of large-seeded cultivars of soybean to field deterioration was used to explain their poor storability in comparison to small-seeded cultivars (Verma and Gupta 1975). Agrawal and Kaur (1975) also observed differences in the longevity of soybean that were more likely to be related to seed condition than to their genetic origin. The high levels of leakage and increased fat acidity observed in seeds that rapidly lost viability also indicated that the seeds with short longevity were initially of low quality. The year of production on the longevity of peas and *Phaseolus* beans also suggested that preharvest weather conditions could have influenced the response of these seeds to storage (James, Bass, and Clark 1967).

Mechanical damage to seed during harvest can also affect seed storage potential. Reduced longevity was found in damaged soybeans (Grabe 1965) and in seed batches of both peanut (Gavrielit-Gelmond 1970) and *Phaseolus* beans (Harty 1977) showing signs of threshing damage. Toole and Toole (1953) also attributed differences in storage potential of *Phaseolus* beans to mechanical injury, and Harty (1977) further emphasized that seed production should aim to produce the maximum normal germination at harvest to achieve good storage.

Among various food legumes, soybeans have a reputation as an inherently bad storer (Delouche et al. 1973). Their rapid decrease in germination in both controlled environments (Ellis, Osei-Bonsu, and Roberts 1982) and in ambient conditions in the tropics (Boakye-Boateng and Hume 1975) is partially attributable to a very small seed-to-seed variation. The viability equations have shown soybean to be particularly sensitive to storage temperature, with chick-pea and cowpea being less sensitive; on the other hand, soybeans were less sensitive to moisture content than were either of these two species (Ellis, Osei-Bonsu, and Roberts 1982). The rapid deterioration of soybean is therefore largely due to the effects of temperature. In contrast, peanut seed appears to be very sensitive to moisture content, with serious deterioration occurring within two years of storage at a moisture content as low as 5% (Gavrielit-Gelmond 1970). Similarly, de Tella, Lago, and Zink (1976) found that the reduction of seed moisture content from an initial 7% to 4.5% was necessary to maintain high germinations beyond nine months of storage.

Storage Microorganisms and Pests and Seed Quality

The viability, vigor, and seed quality of legumes held in postharvest storage is affected not only by intrinsic factors but also by such organisms as storage fungi, insects, and other pests. Some of these factors are briefly described below.

Storage Microorganisms

A large number of fungi and bacteria have been associated with food grains. All legumes are susceptible to attack by fungi, and a few of the numerous species are commonly found in large numbers on a particular sample of produce. In conditions of low oxygen and high moisture, molds are more important than fungi. The dominant species at any one time are determined by the original inoculum, chemical composition of the produce, and the temperature conditions of storage.

Legume seeds may become contaminated by storage fungi before harvest, but invasion does not usually occur until the seeds are in store. The major storage fungi reported in food legumes are *Aspergillus* spp., although *Penicillium,* the other major group of seed storage fungi, has also been found (Table 2-19).

Table 2-19. Storage Fungi Associated with Food Legumes.

Legume	Fungal Species	References
Cowpea	A. niger, Rhizoctonia bataticola, and Cladosporium herbarum	Lalithakumari, Govidaswamy, & Vidhyasekaran (1972)
	A. flavus, Absidia spp., and Rhizopus spp.	Onesirosan (1983)
Pea	Aspergillus spp.	Carlson & King (1963)
Peanut	A. flavus, A. parasiticus	Kadam, Salunkhe, & Kuo (1989)
Phaseolus spp.	A. glaucus, A. restrictus, and Penicillium	Dorworth & Christensen (1959)
Soybean	Aspergillus flavus	Milner & Geddes (1946)
	A. glaucus	Milner & Geddes (1946), Christensen (1967)
	A. restrictus	Christensen (1967)
	A. ochraeus	Tervet (1945)
	A. niger, A. fumigatus	Tervet (1945)
	A. repens	Christensen & Dorworth (1966)

The activity of these fungi during seed storage is influenced by the relative humidity of the storage (and hence the seed moisture content), and by storage temperature. For example, Tervet (1945) reported increased isolation of storage fungi, particularly *Aspergillus* spp., from soybean as the seed moisture content increased. Later, Milner and Geddes (1946) attributed this to the reduction in the latent period of spore germination that occurred as the moisture content increased. Increased storage temperature has also been associated with high levels of infection, with maximum infection reported at either 40° (Milner and Geddes 1946) or 45 °C (Tervet 1945).

The most significant effect of infection by storage fungi on seed quality is reduction of seed viability. Soybean germination was found to decrease as seed moisture content increased to levels at which fungi grew rapidly (Tervet 1945; Milner and Geddes 1946). In both soybean and cowpea, the internal invasion of seeds by storage fungi preceded a decrease in germination (Dorworth and Christensen 1959; Onesirosan 1983). The low germination of pea seeds following commercial storage has been attributed to *Aspergillus* infection (Fields and King 1962). The infection of peanut and *Phaseolus* beans by storage fungi also caused reduced germination (Lalithakumari, Govidaswamy, and Vidhyasekaran 1972).

Kadam, Salunkhe, and Kuo (1989) reported that annual losses due to microbial spoilage of stored commodities run into millions of dollars. *Aspergillus flavus* and *A. parasiticus* molds grow and produce aflatoxins in a wide range of pulses and oilseeds, especially peanuts. The major factors that lead to high contamination levels in peanuts are shell damage, kernel splitting, poor harvesting, and drought. Aflatoxin has been detected and described in pulses from Asia, Africa, and the United States (Kadam, Salunkhe, and Kuo 1989). Aflatoxin B_1 and B_2 occur in 50% of the bean samples tested in Columbia (FAO 1975). There is little information on the storage conditions at which aflatoxin contamination of food legumes most frequently occurs. At harvest, the moist seeds, unless properly and rapidly dried, represent a good substrate for mold growth. Poor storage conditions provide further opportunities for aflatoxin growth and formation.

Storage Insects

In tropical countries, several insects attack beans and cause significant losses. The factors influencing insect development and the nature of their association with different crop seeds, including food legumes, have been extensively reviewed (Howe 1972; Singh, van Emden, and Taylor 1978). Only the salient features are described below.

Unlike fungi, insect pests cannot be clearly divided into field and storage groups. A few species such as *Bruchus pisorum* are commonly found in stores but are not storage species: Unable to grow on the stored seed, they develop in the growing and ripening pea seed in the field, then emerge in store (Powell, Matthews, and Oliveira 1984). Other species can pass to another generation in store but fail to continue development, possibly because the seeds are too dry. Two types of insect seed pests can, however, be distinguished: those more or less restricted to feeding in seeds, and general scavengers able to deal with seeds along with organic debris. It is usually the scavengers that present the greatest hazard to germination since they selectively eat the embryo; in contrast, species adapted to live in seeds feed mostly on the cotyledon or endosperm, thus causing little direct loss of germination, although germination vigor may be reduced. Insect respiration can also cause an increase in temperature, and releases moisture that raises the relative humidity and, subsequently, the seed moisture content; thus, the seeds age more rapidly.

The rate of multiplication of storage insects, like that of storage fungi, is influenced by storage temperature and relative humidity (i.e., the seed moisture content). The availability of food and light may also affect development. In general, insect activity increases as temperature and relative humidity increase. This occurs over a temperature range of about 20 °C for each species, from a poorly defined minimum temperature to a sharp maximum, with the optimum temperature differing for different processes (Powell, Matthews, and Oliveira 1984); for example, the optimum temperature for the rate of oviposition is lower than that for development. Insect activity also increases as the seed moisture content is raised above 8–9%. The food availability for insect development depends on the amount of mechanical damage to seeds, the proportion of broken seeds, and the seed moisture content, which affects the softness of the seed. Finally, insect development is influenced by light, since most insects exhibit a diurnal rhythm.

Among the beetle storage pests of legumes, the bruchids provide a good example of adaptability from life in growing seeds to life in stored seeds. *Bruchus pisorum* is a storage pest of garden and field pea, and cowpea is liable to severe damage by *Callosobruchus*, particularly *C. chinensis, C. rhodesianus, C. maculatus*, and *C. analis* (Powell, Matthews, and Oliveira 1984; Kadam, Salunkhe, and Kuo 1989). The bean weevil (*Bruchus rufimanus*) is found in cool temperate climates, whereas *Zabrotes subfasciatus* is found in tropical climates and *Achanthoscelides obtectus* lives in warm temperate climates. The only bruchid genus of serious economic importance to crops other than peas and beans is *Carydon*. It is the principal pest of peanuts stored in the shell, and has become well established in Africa, India, and more recently in the West Indies and South America. Some of the more important storage pests of various food legumes are summarized in Table 2-20.

Table 2-20. Important Storage Pests of Food Legumes.

Order and Pest	Common Name
Coleoptera	
Sitophilus granarius	Granary weevil
S. oryzae	Rice weevil
S. zeamais	Corn weevil
Tribolium castaneum	Red flour beetle
T. confusum	Confused flour beetle
Gnathocerus cornutus	Broad-horned flour beetle
Trogoderma granarium	Khapra beetle
Stegobium paniceum	Drugstore beetle
Oryzaephilus surinamensis	Saw-toothed grain beetle
Achanthoscelides obtectus	Common bean weevil
Callosobruchus spp.	Cowpea weevil
Bruchus pisorum	Pea weevil
Bruchus rufimanus	Bean weevil
Lepidoptera	
Ephestia kuehniella	Mediterranean flour moth
Cadra cautella	Almond moth
Plodia interpunctella	Indian meal moth
Nemupogon granellus	Grain moth

Compiled from: Smartt (1976), Powell, Matthews, and Oliveira (1984), and Kadam, Salunkhe, and Kuo (1989).

Rodents

Several rodent species have been known to cause damage to stored legumes, including *Rattus rattus, R. norvegicus, Bandicota indica, B. bengalensis,* and *Mus musculatus.* The quantity of food they hoard is many times greater than what they actually consume: Studies have shown that rats contaminate about twenty times the amount of food grains they consume (Salunkhe, Chavan, and Kadam 1985).

Jute bags are particularly susceptible to rodent attack and are frequently damaged beyond repair. Sometimes, plastic sacking or sheeting can also be gnawed. Since rodents cannot burrow into bulk grains and therefore feed only at the surface, there is much less damage to grain in bulk than to bagged grains. Bulk storage methods also provide fewer harborages for rats, and the containers used are also frequently rat-proof.

Rodents also carry diseases that are transmissible to humans. Stored produce may become contaminated with rodent feces, urine, and ectoparasites, and thus become a potential source of danger to persons handling or eating it.

The stored pathogens and insect pests of legumes can be controlled by fumigation of the storage chambers. Often a preharvest prophylactic spray with fungicide and/or pesticide is useful. Improvements in storage structures, containers, and packages to render them insect- and rodent-proof have also been attempted, and the results have been quite promising. Periodic sun-drying, irradiation, and vegetable oil treatment of the seeds are also useful in minimizing damage from infestation with storage pests.

Storage and "Hard-to-Cook" Defect

Several studies suggest that beans stored under inadequate conditions of temperature and relative humidity require longer cooking times as related to higher water uptake in the final product (Jones and Boulter 1983a,b; Vindiola, Seib, and Hoseney 1986). Food legumes resist cooking mainly for two reasons: In "hardshell," the seed coat is impermeable to water; in the "hard-to-cook" defect, the cotyledons do not soften during cooking, even though the seeds do absorb water. Hardshell is promoted by low humidity and high temperature, and can be reversed by hydrothermal treatment, scarification, or decortication. In contrast, the hard-to-cook condition is irreversible and is accelerated by high humidity and high temperature. Plant breeders have eliminated most hardshell varieties of bean, but most legumes remain susceptible to the hard-to-cook defect.

The mechanisms responsible for the development of the hard-to-cook defect in stored beans have not been fully understood. Vindiola, Seib, and Hoseney (1986) suggested the following three reasons:

1. limited hydration of intracellular protein;
2. pectin insolubilization in the middle lamella by calcium and/or magnesium ions after the combined action of pectin methyl esterase and phytase; and
3. cross linking of phenolics (lignification) and/or proteins in the middle lamella.

However, much research is still needed to elucidate this phenomenon in stored legumes.

ANTINUTRITIONAL FACTORS

In addition to the widely studied inhibitors of proteolytic and amylolytic enzymes and lectins, legumes also contain several other antinutritional/antiphysiological factors. They have received little attention because they occur in small amounts and under normal conditions do not pose a serious health hazard. Of these, heat-stable phytic acid and polyphenols (also refered to as "condensed tannins") are of particular significance. The commonly occurring antinutrients in food legumes and methods for their removal are described below.

Lectins (Phytohemagglutinins)

The seeds of numerous leguminous species and varieties contain a group of natural products, lectins or phytohemagglutinins, which show some apparently unrelated characteristics. Their common feature is that they are all proteins or glycoproteins. Their specificity and effects are measured in agglutination tests with treated or untreated erythrocytes from which the term "lectin" (*legere* = elect, to choose) is derived (Liener 1976a). In addition to agglutinating red blood cells, lectins exhibit a number of other interesting and unusual biological and chemical properties, including interaction with specific blood groups, mitogenesis, agglutination of tumor cells, and toxicity toward animals (Liener 1983). All these effects manifest the ability of lectins to bind to specific kinds of sugar on the surface of cells. Their reaction mechanism is comparable to that of human antibodies, but lectins are not induced or the result of an immune response. Several aspects of the chemical and biological properties of the lectins were comprehensively reviewed (Liener 1976a; Lis and Sharon 1973; Pusztai and Watt 1974; Jaffe 1980).

Lectin activity has been detected in over 800 different plant species of which more than 600 belong to the Leguminosae family (Liener 1976a). In legumes, lectins constitute 2–10% or more of the total seed protein; however, relatively few of these have been purified to the point of meaningful characterization.

Based on their sugar-binding specificity, lectins are classified into several groups. Lectins binding D-mannose and D-glucose are found in the seeds of

Pisum, Vicia, Lens, and *Canavalia,* and are mitogenic toward lymphocytes (Jaffe 1980). *N*-acetyl-D-galactosamine-binding lectins isolated from *Glycine* and *Phaseolus lunatus* are specific for blood group A and, in the case of lima beans, are also mitogenic. *Arachis* lectin is a D-galactose-binding protein and agglutinates type B erythrocytes. *Phaseolus vulgaris* produces lectins with complex carbohydrate-binding sites (Pusztai and Watt 1974). Thus, there are obviously no recognizable patterns between the chemical and biological properties of the lectins and their taxonomic distribution in the Leguminosae family. Lectins with the same specificity are therefore found in different genera, and both specific and nonspecific lectins are found within one genus.

There is great variability in the biological effects of lectins, especially in the genus *Phaseolus* (Felsted et al. 1981a,b; Brown et al. 1982a,b). These biological effects are associated with different polypeptides (Brown et al. 1982b). This may explain the observed variability in agglutinating and mitogenic activities, since the polypeptide composition may vary in protein preparations from the same source. The ability to agglutinate erythrocytes requires polyvalent binding sites. Most lectins seem to have relative masses in the range 100,000–150,000 Da (daltons), and are composed of tetramers; some, such as lentil and lima bean lectins, appear to be dimers. With few exceptions (e.g., soybeans), each subunit has a sugar-binding site (Liener 1976a). The hybrid tetramer consists of erythrocyte-reactive subunits (E) and lymphocyte-reactive subunits (L) (Felsted et al. 1981b). The five possible isolectins would have the following tetrameric structures—L4, L3E1, L2E2, L1E3, and E4—which explains the differences in the observed agglutinating and mitogenic activities of bean lectins. This property is lost if the lectins are dissociated into subunits. Most, if not all, lectins also contain up to 4–10% carbohydrates.

Data regarding the biological functions of lectins still appear to be contradictory. The ability of lectins to bind to characteristic carbohydrate structures on the cell surface, and the observed variability in lectin production in different legume genotypes, have initiated a number of systematic investigations concerning the functions of lectins in host plants. Lectins appear to be important determinants of host range specificity in *Rhizobium*–legume symbiosis (Bohlool and Schmidt 1974). Thus, the lectin of *Glycine* binds only to symbiotic strains of *Rhizobium,* although it is probably not essential for initiating the symbiotic relationship. Another biological function ascribed to the lectins is that of an insecticide (Liener 1983). This function is interpreted in terms of an adaptive significance of the lectins in *Phaseolus vulgaris* for protecting seeds from attack by insect seed predators. One interesting aspect was discussed in connection with the characterization of a lectin isolated from the seeds of *Phaseolus aureus,* which possesses a strong enzymatic activity (Hankins and Shannon 1978). By comparing data concerning the synthesis, distribution, and function within plants, it was postulated that legume lectins may, in general, be plant enzymes. However, the lack of detailed information on different aspects of the biological functions of lectins raises more questions that still need to be answered.

Lectins were one of the first toxic factors implicated in the toxicity of raw legumes to laboratory animals (Liener 1951). Purified lectins, when added to the diet, markedly reduce protein digestibility and thus exert a growth-inhibitory effect by depressing appetite. Jaffe (1980) postulated that lectins combine with the cells that line the intestinal mucosa, and thus cause a nonspecific interference with the absorption of nutrients. Lectins, however, are easily destroyed by heat; thus, there would appear to be little cause for concern in properly cooked legumes (Deshpande, Sathe, and Salunkhe 1984a; Deshpande 1985).

Proteinase Inhibitors

Protein inhibitors of proteinases are ubiquitous. They are present in multiple forms in numerous tissues of animals and plants as well as in microorganisms. Their gross physiological function is the prevention of undesirable proteolysis, but detailed physiological functions have only rarely been elucidated. These inhibitors have attracted the attention of scientists in many disciplines. Nutritionists are concerned because of their possible adverse effects on the nutritive value of plant proteins. The inhibitor–enzyme reactions have provided a simple model for the study of protein–protein interactions as well as of enzyme mechanisms. Because of their unique pharmacological properties, these inhibitors hold considerable promise in clinical applications in the field of medicine.

Although the inhibition of proteolytic enzymes by extracts from animal tissues was first demonstrated in the nineteenth century (Fredericq 1878), it was only in the 1930s that their presence in plant material was recognized. Read and Hass (1938) reported that an aqueous extract of soybean flour inhibited the ability of trypsin to liquefy gelatin. This was soon followed by the first isolation of a plant proteinase inhibitor from soybeans by Kunitz (1945, 1946). A year later, the first systematic study of plant proteinase inhibitors was made by Borchers and Ackerson (1947). Because of the great and increasing importance of grain legumes as food and feed, research during the 1950s and 1960s was mainly concentrated on seeds from the legume family.

The proteinase inhibitors are nonglycosylated, water-soluble (albumin) proteins, and account for about 0.2–2% of the total soluble protein of the legume seeds (Sgarbieri and Whitaker 1982). They are mostly low-relative-mass proteins (4,000–8,000 Da). Two major families of proteinase inhibitor have been described in legumes: the Bowman–Birk and the Kunitz-type trypsin inhibitors. They are distinct families of proteins as evidenced by their relative masses, compositions, and amino acid sequences. The important properties of these two inhibitor classes are described below.

Bowman–Birk Type Trypsin Inhibitors

The Bowman–Birk inhibitor, also referred to as the acetone-insoluble inhibitor, was first recognized by Bowman (1944) and subsequently purified and characterized by Birk and coworkers (Birk 1961; Birk, Gertler, and Khalef 1963). It is found in the seeds of all common agriculturally important legume species. These trypsin inhibitors generally contain between sixty and eighty-five amino acid residues in a single polypeptide chain (Norioka and Ikenaka 1983), yielding a relative mass of approximately 8,000 Da. However, many members of this family exhibit strong self-association in solution and thus often appear considerably larger (usually dimer or trimer) in the absence of denaturing agents such as urea (Birk 1985).

The amino acid composition of the Bowman–Birk inhibitors indicates a very high content of Cys (fourteen residues), all involved in disulfide bonds (Mossor, Skupin, and Romanowska 1984). The inhibitors also have a relatively high content of Asp, Asn, and Ser. Met, Val, Tyr, and Phe are found in small quantities, whereas Trp is generally absent. Because of their low relative mass and a high content of disulfide bonds, Bowman–Birk inhibitors are generally considered heat stable (Mossor, Skupin, and Romanowska 1984).

The primary structures of Bowman–Birk trypsin inhibitors from various sources are invariably similar (Wilson 1981; Norioka and Ikenaka 1983). They are double-headed, that is, generally capable of simultaneously and independently inhibiting two molecules of proteases (Laskowski and Kato 1980). The two enzyme molecules may be the same (e.g., trypsin) or different (e.g., one trypsin and one chymotrypsin or elastase). This property is also reflected in their amino acid sequence: A high degree of homology is observed between the first half of the sequence, which contains the reactive site for one proteinase molecule, and the second half containing the second reactive site. This internal homology suggests the evolution of the present-day double-headed inhibitors from an ancestral single-headed inhibitor by a partial gene-duplication event (Wilson 1981).

Kunitz-type Trypsin Inhibitors

Kunitz-type proteinase inhibitors typically contain 170–200 amino acid residues, with a relative mass of about 20,000 Da (Liener 1983). In soybeans, the inhibitor is a single polypeptide chain. They are single-headed, inhibiting one molecule of the enzyme (generally trypsin or chymotrypsin) per molecule of the inhibitor. While the Kunitz-type inhibitors are absent from many agriculturally important members of the legumes, such as *Phaseolus, Pisum,* and *Vigna,* they are found in soybeans and winged beans.

Since all naturally occurring trypsin inhibitors have bonds Lys–X or Arg–X in the cavity of their structure due to S–S bonds (Laskowski and Kato 1980), they can also be classified according to the requirements for either Lys or Arg at their reactive sites. Thus, Kunitz inhibitors can be classified as arginine inhibitors, whereas Bowman–Birk inhibitors are of the lysine type. The trypsin inhibitors that have Arg at the reactive site lose activity upon modification of Arg but not of Lys. Conversely, Lys-type inhibitors are still active upon modification of Arg residues (Laskowski and Kato 1980). The compositional and structural aspects of proteinase inhibitors, their physiological significance, and the mechanisms of interactions with various proteinases have been discussed in several excellent reviews (Laskowski and Kato 1980; Liener and Kakade 1980; Sgarbieri and Whitaker 1982; Liener 1983; Weder 1986).

The available literature data on proteinase inhibitors from various legumes are summarized in Table 2-21. Most inhibitors show inhibiting effects against trypsin and chymotrypsin, but some also inhibit other enzymes such as elastases, papain, plasmins, and thrombins. Also, in some species, isoinhibitors are frequently found. Examination of the compilation in Table 2-22 reveals that most legume species contain <50% of the trypsin inhibitory activity (TIA) of soybeans. Particularly low activities are present in most cultivars of *Vicia, Pisum,* and *Lupinus* and a few cultivars of *Phaseolus vulgaris.* Legumes with at least 60–75% of the TIA in soybeans include *Cajanus, Phaseolus lunatus,* and *Cicer* (Soni, Singh, and Singh 1978).

The fact that proteinase inhibitors are so widely distributed among those very plants that constitute an important source of dietary protein throughout the world has stimulated a vast amount of research regarding their possible nutritional significance. Because of the important role that soybeans play in animal feeding and its potential contribution to human nutrition, inhibitors from this particular legume have received special attention. It is now well established that most raw or partially cooked legumes are of low nutritional value, an observation attributed to the presence of the inhibitors as well as lectins. Fortunately, not only are the inhibitors found in low amounts in most legumes, but also most of them are quite heat labile. Hence, proteinase inhibitors pose little, if any, serious nutritional problems in properly processed legumes. The significance of proteinase inhibitors in human and animal nutrition has been comprehensively reviewed by several authors, yielding the following consensus:

1. Inhibitors of trypsin stimulate the biosynthesis of the enzymes of the pancreas, causing increased requirements of the necessary amino acids in animals. This leads to an increase in the transformation of Met to Cys in the pancreas. The increased requirement of S-amino acids, coupled with the fact that they are deficient in legume proteins, cannot be adequately compensated by the dietary proteins. The enhanced secretion of pancreatic enzymes results in pancreatic hypertrophy in laboratory animals fed legume-based diets.

Table 2-21. Characteristics of Proteinase Inhibitors in Food Legumes.

Legume	Rel. Mass (Da)	Specificity	Comments	References
Cicer arietinum (chick-pea)	10,000	Trypsin, chymotrypsin	Independent binding sites for trypsin and chymotrypsin, 2–4 isoinhibitors present as a result of proteolysis	Belew, Porath, & Sundberg (1975), Smirnoff et al. (1979)
Glycine max (soybean)	21,700	Trypsin	Has Trp, primary sequence of 181 amino acids is known, single-headed Kunitz type	Odani & Ikenaka (1972)
	8,000	Trypsin, chymotrypsin	Double-headed Bowman–Birk type, contains 7 disulfide bonds, fairly heat stable	Odani & Ikenaka (1972)
Phaseolus lunatus (lima bean)	9,000	Trypsin, chymotrypsin	Double-headed inhibitor, has at least 4–6 isoinhibitors	Stevens, Wuerz, & Krahn (1974)
Phaseolus vulgaris (great northern bean)	8,086 I / 8,371 II / 8,844 IIIb	Trypsin, chymotrypsin	Chymotrypsin weakly inhibited by I and II, and strongly by IIIb, which has independent sites for the two enzymes	Birk (1976)
Phaseolus vulgaris (navy bean)	23,000	Trypsin, chymotrypsin	4 possible isomers present	Whitley & Bowman (1975)
Phaseolus vulgaris (pinto bean)	7,900 / 19,000	Trypsin, chymotrypsin	2 isoinhibitors present, probably different binding sites for trypsin and chymotrypsin	Wang (1975)
Phaseolus aureus (mung bean)	12,000	Trypsin, endopeptidase of mung beans	Another inhibitor of relative mass 2,000 was also reported	Beumgartner & Chrispeels (1976)
Vicia faba (broad bean)	11,000	Trypsin, chymotrypsin	Also inhibited thrombin, pronase, and papain (slightly)	Warsy, Norton, & Steim (1974)
Vigna unguiculata (cowpea)	8,000 / 8,000	Trypsin; Trypsin, chymotrypsin	Binds with 2 molecules of trypsin simultaneously; Independent binding sites for trypsin and chymotrypsin	Gennis & Cantor (1976)

Table 2-22. Trypsin Inhibitory Activity (TIA) Content of Selected Food Legumes In Relation to Soybeans.

Legume	Relative TIA (Soy = 100%)	Reference
Cajanus cajan	60	Soni, Singh, & Singh (1978)
Cicer arietinum	66	Soni, Singh, & Singh (1978)
Lens esculenta	25	Soni, Singh, & Singh (1978)
Lupinus spp.	0	Valdebouze (1977)
Phaseolus aconitifolius	27	Soni, Singh, & Singh (1978)
Phaseolus aureus	37	Soni, Singh, & Singh (1978)
Phaseolus lunatus	77	Hove & King (1979)
Phaseolus mungo	52	Soni, Singh, & Singh (1978)
Phaseolus vulgaris	13.0–44	Hove & King (1979)
Pisum sativum	1.5–13	Valdebouze (1977)
Vicia faba	0.7–36	Valdebouze (1977)
Vigna unguiculata	11.1–28	Valdebouze (1977)

2. Trypsin inhibitors decrease the proteolysis of dietary proteins by forming trypsin–inhibitor complexes. These complexes are not broken down even in the presence of adequate amounts of enzymes. This further depresses animal growth, since such undigested complexes cannot be assimilated and hence excreted. Since the proteinase inhibitors are rich in Cys, this further lowers the availability of S-amino acids.

Although there is little doubt that proteinase inhibitors can produce adverse physiological effects in animals, the question naturally arises as to whether these are of any physiological significance to humans. Trypsin inhibitor activity is invariably measured in vitro by its ability to inhibit bovine or porcine pancreatic trypsin, which is commercially available. Human trypsin exists in both a cationic form, which is the major component of human pancreatic juice, and an anionic form, which comprises about 10–20% of the total trypsin activity (Weder 1986). While the less active anionic trypsin is fully inactivated by the soybean trypsin inhibitor, the predominant cationic species is only weakly inhibited (Figarella, Negri, and Guy 1974). Thus, it seems logical to conclude that, despite the considerable body of evidence implicating proteinase inhibitors as a contributory factor in the poor nutritive value of raw legumes in animals, their relevance to human nutrition still remains uncertain.

Amylase Inhibitors

In addition to inhibition of proteinases, several legumes also contain protein inhibitors of α-amylases. Jaffe, Moreno, and Wallis (1973) reported the presence of α-amylase inhibitory activity in seventy-nine of ninety-five legume cultivars tested; the most activity was found in a kidney bean *(Phaseolus vulgaris)* culti-var. Deshpande et al. (1982) also reported substantial α-amylase inhibitor activity in several cultivars of dry bean.

The physiological role of α-amylase inhibitors in legumes is not well understood. They are not active against the endogenous α- and β-amylases of legumes, nor against those in malt, barley, or microbial amylases (Jaffe, Moreno, and Wallis 1973; Powers and Whitaker 1977a). The bean inhibitors, however, inhibit insect larva α-amylases, and therefore may have a physiological role in protecting the seeds against insect attack (Sgarbieri and Whitaker 1982).

Amylase inhibitors have been purified to homogeneity from kidney beans (Marshall and Lauda 1975; Powers and Whitaker 1977a). They constitute about 5–6% of the total water-soluble protein of kidney beans. Their relative masses range from 45,000 to 49,000 Da, and all appear to be glycoproteins, containing 8–10% carbohydrates. On SDS-PAGE, the protein gives four subunits of three size classes of relative masses 15,000–17,000, 12,000–15,000 and 11,000–12,000 Da. The inhibitors have no Pro and two Cys residues, and are relatively rich in Trp, Tyr, Val, and Gly.

The kidney bean amylase inhibitors form a 1 : 1 complex with porcine pancreatic α-amylase (Marshall and Lauda 1975). However, the specific groups involved in the complex formation and the inhibition mechanism are not known. The carbohydrate portion of the inhibitor appears to play a crucial role in this regard, since its periodate oxidation results in a complete loss of inhibitor activity (Powers and Whitaker 1977b). Although the complex has no activity, it can still bind to maltose. This observation led the researchers to speculate that a binding site of α-amylase is still available in the inhibitor–enzyme complex even though by itself it is catalytically inactive.

On a nutritional level, amylase inhibitors appear to affect the rate of mammalian starch digestion (Saunders 1975; Pace et al. 1978), but this has been a controversial point since Kneen and Sandstedt (1946) concluded that amylase inhibitors from wheat are inactivated by pepsin and thus not of much nutritional significance. However, recently some evidence has indicated that large amounts of the inhibitor may overcome gastric digestion in laboratory animals and humans (Puls and Keup 1973). This has not been confirmed in several laboratory animal and most clinical studies (Savaiano et al. 1977; Carlson et al. 1983).

Amylase inhibitors are also being clinically evaluated as to their effectiveness in the treatment of metabolic diseases such as diabetes and adiposity (Fukuhara, Murai, and Murao 1982). On the basis of in vitro and early in vivo evidence that ingested kidney bean amylase inhibitors could block the digestion of starch in meals, starch-blocker tablets containing these inhibitors were sold for weight control. However, Carlson et al. (1983) found several reasons for the apparent commercial failure of starch blockers to work. These include inactivation of inhibitor by gastric acid and pepsin or pancreatic proteinases, intraluminal conditions not being favorable for maximum inhibitions, and insufficient prein-cubation time for the inhibitor. However, the potential of new starch blockers for such therapeutic purposes as diabetes and obesity merits long-term re-search.

Flatus-causing Raffinose Oligosaccharides

A major emphasis is placed on investigations relating to the oligosaccharides of the raffinose family of sugars. These sugars occur in appreciable amounts in mature legume seeds and comprise 30–80% of the total soluble sugars (Table 2-23). The sugars (raffinose, stachyose, and verbascose) contain α-galactosi-doglucose and α-galactosidogalactose bonds (Fig. 2-5) and are nonreducing. The ingestion of large quantities of beans, and hence of those sugars, causes flatulence in humans and animals. Accumulation of flatus in the intestinal tract results in discomfort, abdominal rumblings, cramps, pain, and diarrhea, and is characterized by the production of hydrogen, carbon dioxide, and small amounts of methane gas.

Sugars of the raffinose family are not digested by humans. Two enzymes, invertase and α-galactosidase, are required for the complete hydrolysis of those sugars. The human GI tract does not possess α-galactosidase activity, where-as the mammalian invertase is an α-glucosidase (Gitzelmann and Aurricchio 1965). Also, the raffinose family sugars are unable to pass through the intestin-al wall (Rackis 1975). The microflora in the lower intestinal tract metabolizes these oligosaccharides to produce flatus.

Table 2-23. Oligosaccharides of Food Legumes.

Legume	% Raffinose	% Stachyose	% Verbascose	Reference
Cajanus cajan	1.1	2.7	4.1	Arora (1983)
Cicer arietinum	0.7 – 2.4	2.1 – 2.6	0.4 – 4.5	Reddy et al. (1984)
Dolichos biflorus	0.7	2.0	3.1	Arora (1983)
Glycine max	0.7 – 1.0	2.2 – 4.2	0.0 – 0.3	Reddy et al. (1984)
Lens esculenta	0.4 – 1.0	1.9 – 2.7	1.0 – 3.1	Reddy et al. (1984)
Lupine spp.	0.5 – 1.1	0.9 – 7.1	0.6 – 3.4	Reddy et al. (1984)
Phaseolus aureus	0.3 – 1.1	1.7 – 2.5	2.1 – 3.8	Iyengar & Kulkarni (1977)
Phaseolus lunatus	0.2	0.6	not determined	Shallenberger (1974)
Phaseolus vulgaris	0.2 – 0.9	0.2 – 4.0	0.1 – 0.5	Reddy et al. (1984)
Phaseolus mungo	0.0 – 0.9	0.9 – 2.3	3.4 – 3.5	Reddy & Salunkhe (1980)
Pisum sativum	0.3 – 1.6	2.2 – 5.5	2.2 – 4.2	Reddy et al. (1984)
Psophocarpus tetragonolobus	0.2 – 2.0	0.1 – 3.6	0.0 – 0.9	Reddy et al. (1984)
Vicia faba	0.1 – 0.5	0.5 – 2.4	1.6 – 2.1	Reddy et al. (1984)
Vigna unguiculata	0.4 – 1.2	2.0 – 3.6	0.6 – 3.1	Reddy et al. (1984)

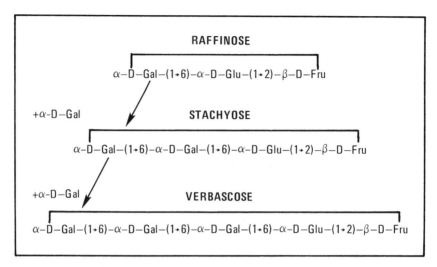

Fig. 2-5. Structural relationship of raffinose family oligosaccharides.

Sugars of the raffinose family in legumes (Table 2-23) may cause differing degrees of flatulence. However, the removal of these oligosaccharides from beans does not completely eliminate the flatus-producing capacity of legumes. The active compounds in the residue and/or extracted beans causing flatulence have not yet been identified. They seem to be quite distinct from the raffinose sugars. The protein-rich fractions in legumes do not cause flatulence in rats and human (Olson et al. 1975). Fiber, which is one of the major undigestible components in the bean residue, may be involved in the fermentation by microorganisms and subsequent flatus production (Kamat and Kulkarni 1981). Fiber is primarily composed of structural polymeric compounds including cellulose, hemicelluloses, and lignin. Tadesse and Eastwood (1978) have reported that a hemicellulose preparation increases hydrogen production in humans, whereas cellulose, lignin, and pectin do not. Further research is needed to understand the possible role of legume fiber in flatus formation and its fate in the intestinal tract.

Literature data on flatus production in humans are difficult to interpret since the results depend upon the physical state and psychological attitude of the subject. In humans, a basal diet produced an average of 13 ml of flatus per hour (Steggerda, Richards, and Rackis 1966). Soy flour diets seem to be less flatulent than those containing common beans. Compared to 30–71 ml of flatus per hour in humans on a soy diet, navy bean diets produced an average of 179 ml of flatus per hour.

Various approaches have been suggested in order to decrease the flatulence-causing factors of food legumes. Raffinose oligosaccharides are heat stable; the effects of various modes of legume consumption on these sugars are described in the "Processing" section of this chapter. Alternatively, legume varieties with low levels of the raffinose sugars can be developed by genetic manipulation. Several researchers have also demonstrated that both in vitro and in vivo flatus production can be inhibited by antibiotics (penicillin and streptomycin) and bacteriostatic agents (iodochlorhydroxyquin) when consumed along with the legume seed preparations (Steggerda 1968). Essentially, these antibiotics inhibit the intestinal microflora, and subsequently flatulence-causing compounds will be eliminated intact. The addition of these compounds to foods, however, should not be considered as an acceptable or routine practice for the prevention of flatulence in normal human subjects.

Phytates

In the plant kingdom, phosphates are stored in seeds in combination with inositol or as phytates. The term "phytic acid" implies *myo*-inositol 1,2,3,5/4,6-hexakis (dihydrogen phosphate). The Ca–Mg salts of phytic acid are designated as "phytin." The term "phytate" is applied loosely for mono- to dodeca-anions of phytate along with lower esters than hexaphosphate.

In most legume seeds, phytate phosphorus accounts for about 80% of the total phosphorus (Lolas and Markakis 1975). Most of it is present in the outer aleurone layers of the cotyledons or the endosperm (Deshpande et al. 1982). The phytic acid in legume cotyledons represents about 98.5% of the total phytate in the seed. The phytate content of various legumes is summarized in Table 2-24. It varies from 0.40 to 2.0% depending upon the species and the variety. Phytate appears to exist in most seeds as K–Mg phytate (K_2Mg_5 phytate) and not as phytin (Ca_5Mg phytate) (O'Dell and de Boland 1976).

Phytic acid has six reactive phosphates and meets the criterion of a chelating agent. In fact, a cation can complex not only within one phosphate or between two phosphate groups of the phytic acid, but also between two phytic acid mol-

Table 2-24. Phytate Content of Food Legumes.

Legume	% Phytic Acid	References
Arachis hypogaea	1.70	Dieckert et al. (1962)
Cicer arietinum	0.28	Kumar et al. (1978)
Glycine max	1.00 – 1.47	Lolas, Palamidis, & Markakis (1976)
Phaseolus aureus	0.66	Kumar et al. (1978)
Phaseolus lunatus	0.89	Chang, Schwimmer, & Burr (1977)
Phaseolus mungo	1.46 – 1.70	Reddy, Balakrishnan, & Salunkhe (1978)
Phaseolus vulgaris	0.74 – 2.10	Deshpande et al. (1982), Lolas & Markakis (1975)
Pisum sativum	1.20	Welch, House, & Allaway (1974)
Vicia faba	1.80	Bramsnaes & Olsen (1979)
Vigna unguiculata	0.44	Kumar et al. (1978)

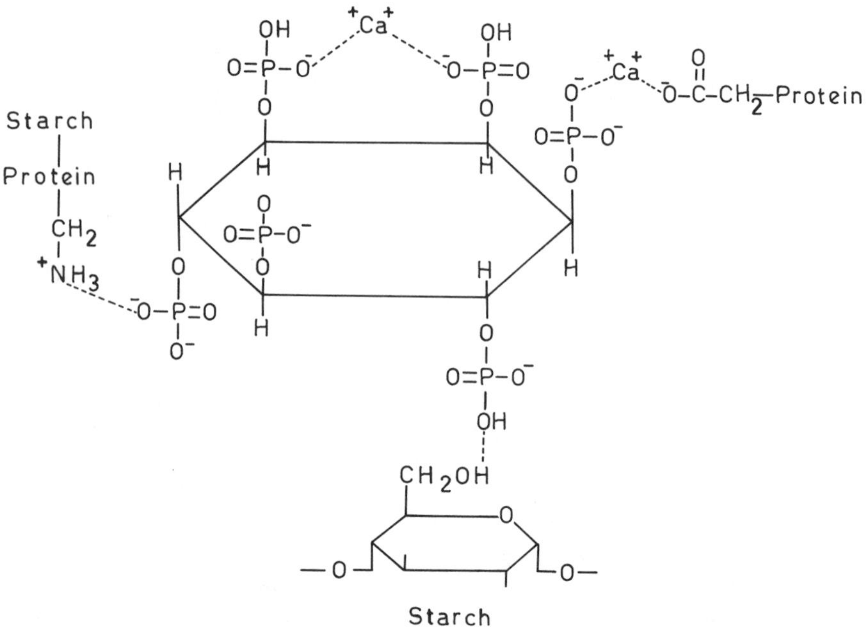

Fig. 2-6. Possible interactions of phytic acid with minerals, proteins, and starch. *Source:* Thompson (1988).

ecules (Erdman 1979). Phytate is thus largely blamed for complexing dietary essential minerals in legumes and rendering them poorly available to monogastric animals. Zinc appears to bind phytic acid in the physiological pH range more tightly than other minerals (Maddaiah, Kurnick, and Reid 1964). Phytates also interact with proteins, resulting in reduced protein solubility and availability (Sathe and Salunkhe 1984). Such a reduction in protein solubility adversely affects its functional properties. Because of the nonspecific nature of the phytate–protein interactions, phytate is also known to inhibit several enzymes such as pepsin (Camus and LaPorte 1976), α-amylase (Deshpande and Cheryan 1984a), and trypsin (Singh and Krikorian 1982). Recently, Thompson (1988) suggested that the interactions among phytate, dietary starch, and protein could be beneficially utilized in the treatment of diabetes and hyperglycemia. The possible interactions of phytic acid with minerals, proteins, and starch are shown in Fig. 2-6.

The presence of phytate in processed legumes has received considerable attention in recent years. Phytate is generally considered to be fairly heat stable. Among the processing methods, germination and fermentation appear to be quite effective in decreasing the phytate concentration, whereas soaking and cooking can remove >50–80% of the endogenous phytate in bean seeds (Sathe and Salunkhe 1984).

Table 2-25. Tannin Content of Food Legumes.

Legume	% Tannin	References
Cajanus cajan	0.03 – 1.00	Rao & Deosthale (1982), Rao & Prabhavati (1982), Price, Hagerman, & Butler (1980)
Cicer arietinum	0.03 – 0.22	Rao & Deosthale (1982), Rao & Prabhavati (1982)
Glycine max	0.045	Rao & Prabhavati (1982)
Phaseolus aureus	0.03 – 0.47	Rao & Deosthale (1982), Rao & Prabhavati (1982)
Phaseolus lunatus	0.77	Ologhobo & Fetuga (1982)
Phaseolus mungo	0.31 – 0.86	Price, Hagerman, & Butler (1980); Rao & Deosthale (1982)
Phaseolus vulgaris	0.00 – 2.00	Deshpande et al. (1982); Deshpande (1985); Elias, de Fernandez, & Bressani (1979)
Pisum sativum	0.43 – 0.47	Griffiths (1981)
Psophocarpus tetragonolobus	0.40	Tan et al. (1983)
Vicia faba	0.75 – 1.92	Griffiths (1981)
Vigna angularis	0.29 – 0.37	Price, Hagerman, & Butler (1980)
Vigna unguiculata	0.19 – 2.12	Price, Hagerman, & Butler (1980); Laurena, Van Den, & Mendoza (1984)

Condensed Tannins (Polyphenols)

The common dietary plant phenols, owing to the evolution of efficient detoxification, are not considered toxicants under normal amounts and conditions. The condensed tannins of flavonoid origin are a possible exception. They are widespread in fruits and vegetables and in certain grains. The tannin content of several legume species is summarized in Table 2-25; it varies with the type of species and variety. Generally, the pigmented varieties of beans contain greater amounts of tannins (Deshpande et al. 1982). Tannins are generally considered heat stable.

Most physiological investigations of tannins have been made with nonruminants. When fed at levels that commonly occur in legumes (about 1–2%), tannins depress the growth rate, resulting in a poor feed efficiency ratio, and increase the amount of food required per unit weight gain (Deshpande, Sathe, and Salunkhe 1984b). Other deleterious effects of tannins include damage to the mucosal lining of the GI tract, alteration in the excretion of certain cations, and increased excretion of proteins and essential amino acids. High dietary levels (about 5%) can cause death (Singleton and Kratzer 1969).

The deleterious effects of tannins in the diet seem to be related to their interactions with dietary proteins. Tannin–protein complexes are believed to be responsible for growth depression, low protein digestibility, and increased fecal nitrogen. Casein, bovine serum albumin, G1 protein from beans, and carob pod proteins resist proteolytic digestion when complexed with tannins (Deshpande

1985; Tamir and Alumot 1969). Such complexes may not be dissociated at the physiological pH and may pass out in feces. The nitrogen content of the feces generally rises in proportion to the amount of tannin fed. Tannins also inhibit important digestive enzymes (Tamir and Alumot 1969; Deshpande and Salunkhe 1982). The biochemical and nutritionally harmful effects of tannins have been discussed in several excellent reviews (Singleton 1981; Salunkhe et al. 1982; Deshpande, Sathe, and Salunkhe 1984b).

Goitrogens

The goitrogens comprise some of the most common toxicants in human food. These compounds are split in plants by the action of myrosinases and also in the intestinal tract, giving rise to isothiocyanates and oxazolidines. They act primarily by competitive inhibition of iodization of the thyroxine hormone. There is little evidence that endemic goiter in humans could be related to the consumption of goitrogenous food. This may be attributed to the fact that they are easily destroyed upon heating. Goitrogenic substances are most commonly found in *Brassica* species. Among the legumes, only soybeans and peanuts have been reported to produce goitrogenic effects in animals (Van Etten 1969). Unheated soybeans, for example, cause a marked enlargement of the thyroid gland of the rat and chick, effects easily overcome either by dietary supplementation of iodide or by heat treatment (Block et al. 1961). Konijn, Edelstein, and Guggenheim (1972) and Konijn, Gershon, and Guggenheim (1973) have purified and characterized the goitrogenic principle from soybeans. It is a low-relative-mass oligopeptide composed of two or three amino acids, or a glycopeptide consisting of one or two amino acids and a sugar. However, the goitrogenic principle in peanuts is shown to be a phenolic glycoside occurring in the seed testa. Sreenivasan, Mougdal, and Sharma (1957) suggested that the phenolic metabolites formed from this glycoside are preferentially iodinated and thereby deprive the thyroid of available iodine. Thus in this case, the goitrogenic effects could be effectively eliminated by dietary supplementation of iodide, but not by heat treatment.

Cyanogenic Glycosides

Cyanide compounds are widespread throughout the plant kingdom. The cyanide content of some legumes has been recognized as an actual or potential danger for several years (Montgomery 1964). The cyanogenic compounds in higher plants are of two types: cyanogenic glycosides and cyanogenic lipids. Both are derivatives of α-hydroxynitriles (cyanohydrins) and liberate a carbonyl compound and hydrogen cyanide (HCN) when the sugar or the respective fatty acid moiety is removed.

Among the legumes, lima beans contain the highest amounts of cyanogens (Montgomery 1964). Lima beans with colored testas are likely to have high cyanogenic glycoside contents compared to beans with white testas. Legal limits to the permissible cyanide content of lima beans have been established in the United States and some European countries. Cyanide contents in the range of 10–20 mg/100 g are considered safe (Montgomery 1964). Other legumes have been shown to contain cyanogens, but in lower than toxic quantities (Jaffe 1950; Wokes and Willimott 1951).

In lima beans, the toxic principle has been extracted and identified as a cyanogenic glycoside "linamarin" or "phaseolunatin." Upon hydrolysis by the enzyme β-glucosidase, it produces glucose, acetone, and HCN. Most of the liberated HCN is lost by volatilization. Further cooking leads to the eventual destruction of the enzyme (Liener 1983). Yet, several cases of human intoxication following the consumption of cooked lima beans led to the theory that perhaps enzymes secreted in the intestinal tract or by the microflora of the colon may be responsible for releasing HCN after ingestion of cooked beans. Large doses of cyanide cause death by inhibition of cell respiration; small doses, however, may be converted to thiocyanate, a well-known goitrogen. Although most food legumes contain only low levels of goitrogens, the conversion of cyanogens into goitrogens may explain some of the etiology of goiter in certain areas of the world.

Saponins

Saponins are glycosides that occur in a wide variety of plants. They are generally characterized by their bitter taste, foaming in aqueous solutions, and their ability to hemolyze red blood cells. Due to their surface-tension-lowering ability, saponins are highly toxic to cold-blooded animals. Saponins have been reported in soybeans, sword and jack beans, French beans, and green peas (Smartt 1976). However, in quantities normally found in legumes—and due to their heat lability—saponins are normally not considered to be a health hazard. An extensive review on various aspects of saponins has been published (Price, Johnson, and Fenwick 1987).

Allergens

Allergens are usually normal food constituents. Allergic reactions are restricted to only certain individuals. The intensity of the reaction depends on the degree of hypersensitivity of the person consuming the food rather than the quantity consumed. The response is mediated via antigen–antibody reactions due to histamine and parahistaminic compounds. Also, proteins of large relative masses are suggested to be responsible components for allergenicity (Perlman 1980).

In a survey on allergenic foods, Wraith and Young (1979) placed peanuts as eighth and soybeans as eleventh among the foods studied. Fries (1971) reported that all children showing a positive skin test to soybeans also gave a positive reaction to other legumes. Symptoms of severe allergy to soymilk in infants include diarrhea with fecal blood and vomiting. Anderson, Rackis, and Tallent (1979) have comprehensively discussed the allergenicity of soybeans.

Lathyrism

Lathyrism is a paralytic disease affecting the lower limbs in humans, and is associated with the consumption of *kesari dhal,* or chickling pea (*Lathyrus sativus*). Its outbreaks are mostly confined to some tribal regions in Central India, especially during drought periods, under which this particular legume crop does well. The danger point is apparently reached when daily consumption of *kesari dhal* exceeds about 300 g.

Two types of lathyrism are known to occur. The lathyrogen of sweet pea (*Lathyrus odoratus*), identified as β-(N-γ-glutamyl)-aminopropionitrile, causes skeletal deformities in rats; this type is known as osteolathyrism (Liener 1983). Yet rats thrive quite well on *L. sativus* and do not display the nervous disorder associated with the consumption of this species in humans. Human neurolathyrism is attributed to a neurotoxin, β-N-oxalyl-α,β-diaminopropionic acid. Because of its structural similarity to glutamic acid, this compound interferes with the action of neurotransmitters in brain tissue (Lakshaman and Padmanabhan 1974). This toxin is also known to occur in other *Lathyrus* spp. as well as in *Vicia* spp. Attempts have been made to develop varieties of *kesari dhal* lacking this toxin. It may also be removed by simple procedures such as dehulling, cooking the seeds in excess water and draining, moist heat treatment, or roasting at 150 °C for 20 min.

Favism

Favism is a disease characterized by hemolytic anemia, and is attributed to the consumption of field or broad bean (*Vicia faba*). The disease is confined largely to the inhabitants of Mediterranean countries. Individual susceptibility to this disease is believed to be of genetic origin (Liener 1983). The clinical manifestations of favism include hemolytic anemia, hemoglobinuria, and jaundice, often accompanied by high fever. It usually begins suddenly after inhalation of pollen or a few hours after eating the beans. In severe cases, death may occur in 24–48 h.

The incidence of favism is linked to a deficiency of glucose-6-phosphate dehydrogenase (G6PD) in susceptible individuals. The β-glycosides of divicine and isouramil (vicine and convicine, respectively) rapidly lower the glutathione content of red blood cells deficient in G6PD and cause hemolysis (Mager et al. 1965). Favism is not known to occur in normal individuals, and hence is not a serious problem. The only way of diminishing the risk of this disease in susceptible populations appears to be their effective removal by genetic breeding.

Alkaloids

Although widely distributed in the plant kingdom, alkaloids are not common in legumes. Only 10% of legumes grown for their seeds accumulate them (Nowacki 1980). Alkaloids are a major cause of concern in lupin seeds. These quinolizidine compounds are produced by an unusual transamination reaction, the first product being an alkaloid at the oxidation level of sparteine. This can be oxidized further to compounds with an unsaturated A (pyridone) ring. Such compounds are teratogenic to herbivores. Most large-seeded Mediterranean species of *Lupinus* contain 0.3–1.5% alkaloids, the major alkaloids therein being lupanine, angustifoline, and hydroxylupanine. Alkaloids can be removed by soaking the seeds in salt water, although in recent years, efforts to breed lupin varieties devoid of them have been quite successful (Liener 1983).

Toxic Amino Acids

The possible antinutritional properties of nonprotein amino acids in legumes have not been fully investigated. One such amino acid (canavanine) is responsible for favism. Unusual free amino acids are particularly frequent in *Lathyrus* and *Vicia* but are not distributed systematically. Dihydroxyphenylalanine (DOPA) occurs in a number of legumes. Though it is not directly toxic, plants containing it turn black as they dry, and the black compounds may make plants like *Vicia faba* and *Lathyrus niger* less nutritious. DOPA is also thought to be associated with the metabolic disorder favism. However, there are few indications that such amino acids are available in foodstuffs in amounts large enough to cause any deleterious effects.

Removal

Traditionally, several methods have been used to remove the antinutrients present in plant foods in order to improve their nutritional quality and utilization. To accomplish this goal, several approaches may be considered. Breeding plant varieties containing lower or no levels of antinutrients is one such approach; this, however, requires long-term efforts since the type and number of antinutrients present in plant foods is rather large and diverse with respect to their chemical and biochemical nature. Such efforts must also consider agronomic consequences of genetic manipulation, including crop yield, soil tolerance, light and water requirements, and resistance to pests and diseases.

Physical and chemical means of removing undesirable antinutrients include such processing methods as soaking, cooking, germination, fermentation, selective extraction, membrane filtration, irradiation, and enzymatic treatments. In many instances, the use of only one method may not effectively remove all the antinutrients present; thus, a combination of two or more methods may be required to accomplish the desired level of removal. The effectiveness of some of these methods in removing the plant antinutrients is briefly reviewed below.

Soaking usually forms an integral part of such processing methods as cooking, germination, fermentation, and roasting. Discarding soak water prior to further processing can remove several water-soluble antinutrients, such as protease inhibitors, phytates, raffinose oligosaccharides, lathyrogens, goitrogens, cyanogenic glycosides, and polyphenols. The extent of their removal depends upon soaking temperature, type of soaking medium, seed type, length of soaking, and the solubility characteristics of the soluble antinutrients. Soaking media frequently include water, salt (or combination of salts) solutions, and dilute aqueous alkali solutions. Salt and alkali help leach the solubles into the soaking medium by increasing the cell membrane permeability. However, loss of antinutrients during soaking is also associated with losses of such desirable nutrients as proteins, minerals, and vitamins.

Cooking or heat processing is probably the oldest known method of processing plant foods for human consumption. Cooking may be done at atmospheric pressure and temperature or at high pressure and temperature (autoclaving). The primary purpose of cooking is to render the food palatable and develop its aroma. The cooking water may or may not be discarded depending upon cultural and personal preferences. Cooking generally inactivates heat-sensitive factors such as enzyme inhibitors, lectins, volatile compounds such as HCN, and some off-flavor components. Heat-stable factors, such as estrogens, saponins, flatulent factors, lysinoalanine, phytate, polyphenols, and allergens, may not be affected to any significant extent by cooking. Even among the heat-labile antinutrients, complete inactivation may not always be possible. When the soaking and cooking medium (such as water) is not discarded, the heat-stable factors remain practically unchanged; on the other hand, when discarded, a significant amount of heat-stable antinutrients can be removed from plant foods. Excessive heat processing, however, should be avoided since it adversely affects the protein quality of foods.

Germination mobilizes reserve nutrients required for the growth of plant seedlings, and therefore may help in the removal of at least some of the antinutrients, such as phytates and raffinose oligosaccharides, that are thought to function as reserve nutrients. Significant reduction in phytate, lectin activity, and raffinose sugars is reported upon germination of various legumes (Deshpande, Sathe, and Salunkhe 1984a). Beneficial effects of germination in terms of reduction in enzyme inhibitory activities, however, remain controversial.

Table 2-26. A Summary of the Effects of Antinutrients of Food Legumes.

Antinutrient	Effects	Methods of Removal
Phytohemagglutinins	Growth depression, fatal	Proper thermal processing
Proteinase inhibitors	Pancreatic hypertrophy, dietary loss of S-amino acids	Proper thermal processing
Amylase inhibitors	Amylase inhibition, may hinder carbohydrate utilization	Proper thermal processing
Flatulent factors	Flatus resulting in discomfort, abdominal rumblings, cramps, pain, and diarrhea	Traditional household processes; enzyme treatment; ultrafiltration
Phytate	Reduced mineral bioavailability, altered protein solubility, enzyme inhibition	Traditional household processes remove phytate to a variable degree
Polyphenols	Reduction in protein digestibility and utilization, inhibition of several enzymes	Traditional household processes remove polyphenols to a variable degree
Cyanogens	Cyanide poisoning, act as progoitrogens	Proper processing; traditional household methods; breeding for low levels
Goitrogens	Inhibition of iodine binding to thyroid gland	Proper food processing; leaching; breeding for low levels
Saponins	Bitter taste, foaming, hemolysis	Leaching with hot water or ethanol
Allergens	Several allergic reactions	Avoid foods eliciting allergic responses
Lathyrogens	Neurotoxic, nervous paralysis of lower limbs, fatal	Breeding for low levels; leaching; roasting
Favism	Hemolytic anemia	Breeding for low levels; wet-processing methods; treatment with β-glucosidases
Off-flavors	Loss of certain amino acids, reduced product acceptability to consumers	Avoid lipid oxidation; proper thermal processing
Phytoalexins	Hemolysis, uncouple oxidative phosphorylation	Breeding for low levels
Estrogens	Growth inhibition, interference with reproduction	Breeding for low levels; reversible effects; avoid prolonged consumption of foods containing high levels
Lysinoalanine	Nephrotoxicity, reduction in available lysine, kidney cell nucleus and cytoplasm enlargement	Controlled processing; avoid use of excess alkali for prolonged periods
Amino acid racemization	Generation of D-amino acids, may act as synergist to lysinoalanine in expression of nephrocytomegaly	Controlled processing

Table 2-26. (*Continued*)

Antinutrient	Effects	Methods of Removal
Toxic amino acids	Structural analogues of protein amino acids, act as antimetabolites, potent inhibitors of several enzyme systems	Breeding for low levels
Antivitamins		
Vitamin B_{12}	Increased B_{12} requirement	
Vitamin D	Rachitogenic	Balanced nutrition; proper thermal
Vitamin E	Liver necrosis, muscular dystrophy	processing

As in germination, most of the changes occurring during the fermentation of foods are catabolic in nature, and help in the hydrolysis of such components as proteins and carbohydrates. Fermentation of foods can result in significant reduction in the quantity of certain antinutrients. The removal of raffinose oligosaccharides of legumes during fermentation, for example, is primarily due to the α-galactosidase activity present in legume seeds as well as in the microorganisms involved in the process. Depending upon the type of legume as well as fermentation, phytic acid has also been reported to be hydrolyzed during fermentation to a variable degree.

In addition to the traditional household processes for preparing plant foods for human consumption, enzymatic methods have also been used to remove certain antinutrients of plant origin including phytates and raffinose sugars. Endogenous enzymes such as linamarinase, as well as externally added β-glycosidases, are often used to remove the cyanogenic glycosides of various legumes. The HCN thus produced is water soluble and volatile, and can easily be removed by heating and/or discarding the soaking water. In addition, processes such as ultrafiltration, irradiation of foods, addition of antibiotics or bacteriostats, extrusion cooking, and protein texturization have proven useful in removing certain antinutrients present in plant foods. Table 2-26 summarizes the commonly occurring antinutrients in plant foods used for human consumption, their antinutritional effects, and methods of their removal.

Since legumes have provided a valuable source of protein, it is obvious that we have learned how to detoxify them by suitable preparative measures. We also have a capacity to handle these toxic compounds to a certain degree through the detoxifying capacity of the liver. Nonetheless, there is the ever-present possibility that the prolonged consumption of a particular legume that has been improperly processed could elicit toxic effects.

PROCESSING

Food legumes pose several problems during processing, handling, and subsequent storage and utilization. Appropriate processing is probably more important for legumes than for any other food group, primarily due to the high content of antinutrients and the indigestible nature of many raw legumes. Even though a variety of legumes are eaten in their immature state, the greatest interest from a nutritional standpoint is in the consumption of the mature, dried legumes.

Historically, the processing of food legumes in developing countries has been done in the home. Several methods are used for such home preparation (Fig. 2-7). A variety of procedures are used for the purpose of eliminating toxic substances and antinutrients, removing the seed coat, and softening the cotyledons. The initial processing steps include cooking either whole or dehulled beans. In addition, raw beans can be processed into a palatable form without cooking.

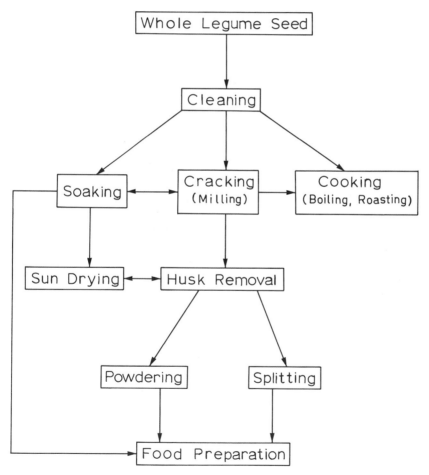

Fig. 2-7. Flowchart for the preparation of food legumes for home consumption. *Source:* Reproduced from Siegel and Fawcett (1976), with permission.

Dehulling may take place with either raw or cooked beans. Usually, the beans are mashed or pounded after cooking to facilitate removal of the husk. Fully decorticated whole or split legumes are widely used in India as flours, grits, and pastes. The techniques employed are mostly manual ones; however, in some instances, simple mechanical equipment is used.

The various traditional processing techniques for food legumes include boiling or cooking, grinding, parching, toasting, roasting, puffing, germination, and fermentation. Those processing methods apply to both raw and cooked, whole and dehulled, and whole and ground legume varieties commonly used in the semiarid tropics. The different preparatory techniques used relate to the structural and textural characteristics of the beans and the cultural habits of the people. In technologically advanced countries, industrial methods such as air classification of bean flours, canning, and preparation of protein concentrates/isolates are often used for food legume processing. In this section, the different methods of both home-scale and industrial processing of food legumes are described.

Dehulling/Decortication

Removal of the seed coat is often the first step in the processing of food legumes. Because whole beans often take a long time to cook to a soft consistency, legumes are often consumed after the removal of seed coats, with the exception of varieties with a relatively thin skin. Although not common in many parts of the world, dehulling seems to be the choice method in the Indian subcontinent.

The most common and the simplest home-scale method for decorticating legumes is pounding or grinding, or a combination of those two methods. Both dry and wet decortication methods are practiced throughout the semiarid tropics, the former having greater acceptance in Central and Northern India, Africa, and Central America (Aykroyd and Doughty 1964). A less commonly used method for preparing split, husked pulses in India consists of half-roasting the grain followed by splitting. Specific legume varieties and foods prepared from them usually dictate the choice of methods.

Because of the widespread use and importance of dehusked, split pulses in the Indian diet, most home-scale decortication methods have evolved into large-scale milling operations in India. The commercial methods use the same basic principles as in household methods (Kurien and Parpia 1968). After soaking in water for 4–12 h, the steeped grains are mixed with a paste of red earth at 2–3% level, and then kept heaped for about 16 h. After air drying for two to four days, the red earth is removed by sieving. The seeds are then passed through a power-operated stone or emery-coated vertical sheller. During this step, about 95% of the grain is dehusked and split. The husk is aspirated off and the *dhal* is separated by sieving. The wet method has the advantage of facilitating good de-husking and splitting (less breakage) of the seeds; however, it adversely affects the cooking quality (Kurien and Parpia 1968). The method is also labor inten-sive and is completely dependent upon climatic conditions. The entire process usually takes five days to a week, and only limited quantities can be processed at any given time.

In the dry method, beans are passed through an emery-coated roller for initial pitting or scratching of the husk to facilitate subsequent oil penetration. The pit-ted seeds are then thoroughly mixed with about 1% linseed oil, and the oil-coated seeds then sun-dried in thin layers for two to five days. The seeds are usually heaped at night to preserve heat. At the end of the drying period, beans are sprayed with 2–5% water, thoroughly mixed, and heaped overnight. They are subsequently passed through an abrasive roller for dehusking. In the first cycle, about 40–50% of the seeds are dehusked, and a major portion of it split simultaneously. The seed coats are removed by aspiration, and the mixture of whole and dehusked–split *dhal* is passed through a sieve to remove *dhal*. The residual unhusked and husked whole grains are passed through a second cycle. Sometimes a cone polisher with smooth rollers is used to polish the split *dhal*.

The major disadvantage of the dry method is the high milling loss due to breakage and powdering. In addition, not all seeds are decorticated. Kurien, Desikachar, and Parpia (1972) reported that the average yield of *dhal* using the traditional commercial methods is only 73% as compared to the maximum theo-retical yield of 88%. To overcome the problems of the traditional commercial milling methods, the Central Food Technological Research Institute (CFTRI) in India has developed improved methods and machinery for the efficient, uni-form, and economic milling of grain legumes. The important pretreatment (con-ditioning step) is based on the principle of removing water from the husk to facilitate its removal. Moisture is uniformly adjusted to a critical point by ex-posing the grain to hot air (approximately 300 °C) for several minutes, thereby loosening the husk and making it brittle. The second step of this process in-volves the use of pulse-dehusking machines that remove the seed coats by abra-sive (pearling) action in stone-coated rollers. Reportedly, after a single pass of properly conditioned grain through the dehusking unit, an almost complete re-moval of the husk is achieved with the least scouring of the endosperm layers. Dehusked whole pulses are subsequently split into *dhal* in a separate system. The CFTRI process gives a 10–15% increased yield over traditional commer-cial methods (Kurien, Desikachar, and Parpia 1972). This increases legume availability by about 1.0–1.2 million metric tons, equivalent to about 300,000 MT of protein.

The average yields of *dhal* from different legumes using various methods are summarized in Table 2-27.

Table 2-27. Average Yield of *Dhal* from Legumes (%).

Legume	Maximum Theoretical	Home-Scale Methods	Traditional Commercial	Improved CFTRI Process
Cajanus cajan	88	68	75	85
Cicer arietinum	88	75	75	84
Phaseolus aureus	89	62	65	83
Phaseolus mungo	87	63	71	82

Compiled from: Kurien and Parpia (1968), Kurien, Desikachar, and Parpia (1972), and Parpia (1973).

In addition to savings in fuel costs due to reduction in cooking time, the removal of seed coat may offer certain nutritional advantages. The removal of hulls has only a small effect on the total protein content and amino acid composition of legumes (Wolf 1975). The removal of seed coat also increases legume protein digestibility (Deshpande et al. 1982). Perhaps the greatest advantage is that the removal of seed coat, specially from the colored beans, eliminates tannins. In a study on the effect of dehulling on antinutrients, Deshpande (1985) reported a substantial decrease (68–95%) in the tannins of several varieties of dry bean (*Phaseolus vulgaris*).

Cooking (Boiling and Steaming)

Cooking whole or split legumes, with or without seed coats, is the common method used in most parts of the world. Cooking may be achieved at atmospheric pressure and temperature or by retorting. The primary purpose of cooking is to soften the cotyledons. Generally, soaking precedes cooking.

Several variations of the cooking method exist. In India, *dhals* are often cooked until soft, then mashed, mixed with water, and reboiled to give a consistency of a soup or gruel. Dry whole grains are similarly boiled until soft, and eaten mashed or unmashed in areas of Africa and Middle East. Cowpea paste is commonly prepared in West Africa in making a fried food product (Dolvo, Williams, and Zoaka 1975). Chick-peas are often boiled and eaten whole in parts of Afghanistan, Egypt, and Ethiopia. Whole broad beans are eaten in Lebanon in an oil sauce. In Central and South America, dry beans that have been soaked overnight are boiled to be eaten whole or mashed, or used in the preparation of other dishes. Crushed beans are commonly eaten fried.

A major factor in the underutilization of beans in developed countries is their prolonged cooking requirement prior to consumption. This has placed them at a disadvantage compared to convenience foods developed for the retail market. Similarly, the scarcity and cost of fuel in the developing countries necessitates investigations into cooking legumes by hydration. The time required for cooking of beans is a function of several factors. The thickness of the cell walls of the seed coats, and to a lesser extent those of the cotyledons, plays a major role in governing the cooking quality of legumes. Since excessive cooking leads to a lowering of protein digestibility (Kakade and Evans 1965), it is important that an optimum cooking time be used to produce an acceptable textured bean product possessing the highest nutritional value.

Several factors influence the cooking quality of legumes. Mattson (1946) reported monovalent and divalent cations and phosphates, neutral salts, environmental and varietal differences, ripeness, and storage at different humidities as factors that influenced the composition and cookability of peas. Temperature dependence of the cooking rates of legumes also has been reported (Quast and de Silva 1977). Kon and Sanshuck (1981) observed a good correlation between cooking times and phytate : Ca ratio in several legumes. More recently, Deshpande and Cheryan (1986) observed a significant correlation between cooking times of dry beans and initial water uptake during cooking ($r = -0.92$) and hardness index of beans ($r = 0.76$). They also reported that the cooking quality of beans depended on the surface area, with smaller beans (i.e., more surface area exposed per unit weight) requiring less time to cook.

The prolonged cooking requirement of legumes has generated a great deal of interest in quick-cooking bean technology. Attempts to reduce the cooking times of legumes date back to Esselen and Davis (1942), who developed dehydrated baked beans that could be reconstituted after rehydration for 1.5 h in cold water. The product was ready to eat when heated. The 1.5-h rehydration, however, was too long a preparation time to qualify the beans as "quick-cooking." Since then, several researchers have used innovative methods to lower the cooking time of beans. The different approaches used for the preparation of quick-cooking beans include pressure cooking (Subbarao, Ananthachar, and Desikachar 1964), addition of chemicals to cooking water (Mattson 1946), soaking beans in solutions of chemicals (Rockland and Metzler 1967; Kon and Sanshuck 1981), removal of testa and/or splitting into cotyledons (Subbarao, Ananthachar, and Desikachar 1964), and application of chemical coatings on legumes (Narasimha and Desikachar 1978). The technology of such processes has significant application to legume consumption in developing countries, since their preparation requires less cooking fuel; the resulting products, however, possess similar or even improved physical, chemical, and nutritional properties compared to those prepared by standard, long-time cooking processes (Rockland, Zaragosa, and Hahn 1974).

Most studies on the commercial processes for quick-cooking bean technology come from the Western Regional Research Laboratory of the USDA (Rockland and Metzler 1967). These researchers employed a combination of such chemicals as sodium chloride, sodium polyphosphates, sodium bicarbonate, and sodium carbonate in soak solutions with an intermittent vacuum treatment

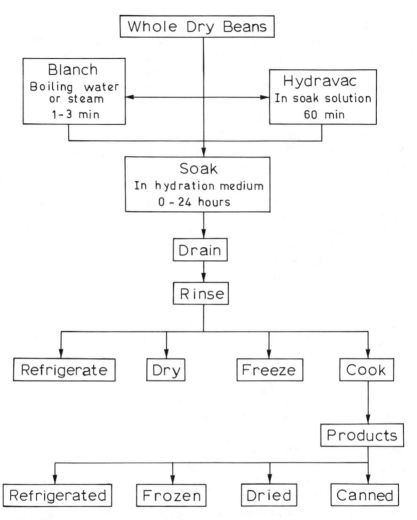

Fig. 2-8. Flowchart for the preparation of quick-cooking beans. *Source:* Rockland (1978).

(Hydravac process) to develop quick-cooking, large, dry lima beans. A flowchart for the preparation of quick-cooking beans by this process is shown in Fig. 2-8. The Hydravac process facilitates infusion of a salt solution through hilum and fissures in the hydrophobic outer layers of the seed coat. Wetted by the solution, the inner membrane hydrates rapidly, plasticizing the seed coat and causing it to expand to its maximum dimensions within a few minutes. The cotyledons, encapsulated in a uniform bath of hydration medium, imbibe the tenderizing solution rapidly and expand to fill out the seed coat. The process reduces the number of split, "fishmouth," and "butterfly" beans obtained in the dried product by minimizing the extension of seed coat fissures that would occur during normal, isobasic hydration. The Hydravac process has been successfully adapted commercially to prepare quick-cooking legumes. Thus basic research in the past two decades on the structure and composition of legume seeds and the cooking process has been successfully applied to the development and standardization of new technology for the production of more convenient and acceptable products from dry beans and other food legumes. The development of new, simple, and economical processing technology has resulted in the reduction in cooking time of legumes by over 80%.

Since cooking is the best-known method for processing food legumes, it is not surprising that much of the research on the nutritional quality of legumes has been done on beans cooked under various conditions. Several workers have studied the changes from cooking on proximate composition, minerals, and vitamin contents of legumes (Meiners et al. 1976a,b; Rockland et al. 1979; Augustin et al. 1981). With the need for accurate tables of food composition, most attention has been focused on the effects of cooking on nutrient content and nutrient retention.

If the cooking broth is not discarded, cooking in general should not influence the major food constituents (i.e., protein, starch, fat, and fiber); however, their composition may be slightly affected by the moisture content of the cooked product (Meiners et al. 1976a). Augustin et al. (1981) studied the mineral and vitamin composition of raw and cooked samples of nine classes of *P. vulgaris* species within two months after harvest. The ranges in the vitamin and mineral composition for these beans are summarized in Table 2-28. With few exceptions (thiamin, vitamin B_6, phosphorus, and potassium), variabilities of these nutrients among the bean classes exceeded those within the classes. The nutrient variabilities in the cooked samples with the above exceptions were higher than in the corresponding uncooked material. Retention values for the water-soluble vitamins during cooking averaged 70–75%. The retention of minerals during cooking ranged from a low 38.5% for sodium to a complete retention for calcium, with the majority of the minerals falling into the 80–90% level. The low sodium content of the cooked beans could be nutritionally advantageous to people who are on low-sodium diets. Ordinary cooking, thus, appears to pose few problems in retention of nutrients. Similarly, data on the proximate composition of the cooked standard and quick-cooking beans do not suggest any significant changes (Rockland and Jones 1974). However, quick-cooking beans generally contain higher levels of such minerals as sodium and phosphorus, presumably due to absorption from the original processing solution. The lower levels of calcium and magnesium in quick-cooking beans may be related to the extraction of these divalent cations as complex tripolyphosphates

Table 2-28. Ranges in the Vitamin and Mineral Composition of *Phaseolus vulgaris*.

Nutrient	Raw[a]	Cooked[a]
Thiamin (mg)	0.81 – 1.32	0.64 – 1.06
Riboflavin (mg)	0.11 – 0.41	0.09 – 0.25
Niacin (mg)	0.85 – 3.21	0.59 – 1.96
Vitamin B_6 (mg)	0.30 – 0.66	0.20 – 0.52
Folic acid (mg)	0.15 – 0.68	0.09 – 0.52
Phosphorus (g)	0.38 – 0.57	0.36 – 0.51
Sodium (mg)	4.00 – 21.0	1.50 – 6.90
Potassium (g)	1.32 – 1.78	1.10 – 1.71
Calcium (g)	0.07 – 0.21	0.07 – 0.26
Magnesium (g)	0.16 – 0.23	0.13 – 0.22
Zinc (mg)	1.90 – 6.50	1.90 – 4.00
Manganese (mg)	1.00 – 2.00	1.00 – 2.10
Copper (mg)	0.50 – 1.40	0.50 – 1.10
Iron (mg)	3.34 – 8.00	2.88 – 7.93

Source: Augustin et al (1981).
[a]Per 100 g dry weight.

in the soaking solution. The B-complex vitamin levels in the standard and quick-cooking beans vary slightly and are related to the bean type (Rockland, Hahn, and Zaragosa 1977). Quick-cooking beans thus seem to offer not only a reduction in cooking time and fuel requirements, but also appear to have nutritional qualities as good as those of the standard cooked beans.

Optimal cooking enhances the protein quality of legumes. Kakade and Evans (1966) observed a significant improvement in the in vitro protein digestibility of navy beans by a mild heat treatment. The length of cooking is an important factor governing the protein quality of cooked legumes. Cooking time beyond 30 min at 121 °C, without a previous soaking, decreases the nutritive value of legume proteins (Elias et al. 1973). The initial increase in PER is partly due to a reduction in protease inhibitory activity and lectins, as is also due to protein denaturation. The subsequent reduction in protein quality with further heating is usually due to a loss of certain essential amino acids, such as Lys, Met, and Cys. The combined effects of different periods of soaking and cooking time on protein quality are somewhat different. Literature data indicate that optimum cooking time for beans without prior soaking ranges from 20 to 30 min (Elias et al. 1973); on the other hand, soaked beans show a reduction in the nutritive value when the cooking time exceeds 10 min.

Literature data on the protein quality of cooked legumes are summarized in Table 2-29. There is considerable variation not only among the species but also within the varieties belonging to the same species. It is noteworthy that even

Table 2-29. Protein Quality of Cooked Legumes.[a]

Legume	Percent Digestibility	Net Protein Utiliz. (NPU)	References
Cajanus cajan	68	59	Geervani & Theophilus (1980)
	60		Bressani & Elias (1974)
Cicer arietinum	85–89	55–60	Khan, Jacobsen, & Eggum (1979)
	81	64	Geervani & Theophilus (1980)
Glycine max	85	59	Mitchell & Beadles (1949)
Phaseolus aureus	83–85	45–58	Khan, Jacobsen, & Eggum (1979)
Phaseolus lunatus	51		Bressani & Elias (1974)
Phaseolus mungo	78	66	Geervani & Theophilus (1980)
Phaseolus vulgaris	83	51	Khan, Jacobsen, & Eggum (1979)
	52–70		Sgarbieri, Antunes, & Almeida (1979)
Red varieties	62–74		Bressani & Elias (1974)
Black varieties	67–75		Bressani & Elias (1974)
White varieties	72–79		Bressani & Elias (1974)
Vigna unguiculata	87–92	50–51	Khan, Jacobsen, & Eggum (1979)
	72–83		Bressani & Elias (1974)

[a]Data represent observations made under in vivo conditions.

though the protein digestibility values are fairly high, the net protein utilization (NPU) appears to be quite low. The low values for NPU may be related to poor digestibility and amino acid availability of the cooked legume proteins.

Cooking generally destroys heat-sensitive antinutrients such as the protease inhibitors, lectins, such volatile compounds as HCN, and off-flavor components. The inactivation of protease inhibitors in legumes depends on the initial moisture content, particle size, temperature, and duration of the moist heat treatment (Rackis, Wolf, and Baker 1986). Heating soaked seeds of broad bean, chick-pea, cowpea, lentil, and mung bean at 121 °C for 30 min brings about a complete inactivation of trypsin inhibitors (Al-Bakir, Sachde, and Naoum 1982). Quick-cooking of beans was also reported to cause a significant reduction in proteolytic enzyme inhibitors (Iyer et al. 1980).

As a general principle, most plant protease inhibitors in purified form exhibit a much greater stability to thermal denaturation than in crude forms such as observed in aqueous extracts of soybeans, peanuts, and kidney beans (Ellenrieder, Geronazzo, and de Bojarski 1980). Similarly, in crude extracts of *kintoki* beans (*P. vulgaris*), 90% of the trypsin inhibitory activity was lost after heating at 100 °C for 60 min, whereas the purified inhibitor was heat stable (Tsukamoto, Miyoshi, and Hamaguchi 1983). The acceleration of thermal destruction of inhibitors in the crude extracts of these food legumes was attributed to the storage proteins, since the addition of several high-relative-mass proteins also inactivated the inhibitor. The residual trypsin inhibitory activity in the heated crude extracts could also be due to other food components, such as phytate or tannins (de Lumen and Salamat 1980).

The type of heating, whether moist or dry, plays an important role in the inactivation of trypsin inhibitors in legumes. Soni, Singh, and Singh (1978) found that the trypsin inhibitory activity in eleven Indian pulses exhibited varying degrees of stability to dry heating, roasting, or autoclaving. Dry heating at 75 °C for 15 min had little effect on the trypsin inhibitors of these pulses except for field peas; heating at 100 °C for 15 min destroyed considerably more activity, except for cowpeas. These studies suggested that the trypsin inhibitors were the most labile in field peas and the most stable in cowpeas. Roasting of seeds at 200 °C for 2 min was most effective in destroying the inhibitor in all pulses except lentils. The general enhancement of the nutritive value of cooked legume proteins reflects the relative ease with which the trypsin inhibitors are inactivated by appropriate methods of cooking.

Lectins seem to be completely inactivated by proper heat processing (Liener 1976a,b). Cooking inactivates certain endogenous enzymes. One such enzyme is lipoxygenase, which is responsible for lipid oxidation, which, in turn, produces several compounds of intense and undesirable off-flavors.

Cooking decreases the polyphenols in horse gram and moth beans (Satwadhar, Kadam, and Salunkhe 1981). Bressani and Elias (1980b) observed that, upon cooking, about 30–40% of polyphenols can be removed from common beans. Such reduction is most likely due to leaching out or interactions with other cell components (such as proteins) rather than to inactivation or destruction. When the soaking and cooking medium is not discarded, heat-stable factors, such as raffinose oligosaccharides and phytates, remain practically unchanged in cooked beans (Reddy, Balakrishnan, and Salunkhe 1978). On the other hand, discarding the medium could remove significant amounts of these factors from beans. As much as 57–74% phytate and 70–80% raffinose oligosaccharides were removed when beans were soaked (18 h at 22 °C) and cooked for 90 min at 100 °C (Iyer et al. 1980). Iyengar and Kulkarni (1977) have also reported 60.8%, 69.4%, 66.2%, and 72.2% removal of the raffinose oligosaccharides from red gram, chick-pea, green gram, and lentils, respectively, when the cooking water was discarded.

Roasting and Parching

Roasting as a form of preparing legumes (also referred to as toasting or parching) is practiced mainly in India and Africa. As used in the semiarid tropics, roasting refers to the method in which usually whole, husked or unhusked grains are exposed to dry heat. The traditional Indian household practice for roasting or parching pulses involves initially sprinkling the grains with a little water. The pulse is then mixed with four times its own volume of preheated sand. The pulse–sand mixture is contained in a frying pan kept on an open fire, the sand reaching a temperature of about 240 °C. The pulse is subsequently roasted (or parched) by rapid mixing. During this process, the temperature of the seeds increases from about 26 °C to 132 °C in a period of 2–3 min. The roasted material is separated from the sand by sieving. Roasted chick-peas, peanuts, and peas, prepared at home or on a commercial scale, are popular snacks in India (Deshpande, Sathe, and Salunkhe 1984a).

Puffing

Puffed grain legumes are prepared in the Indian household in a manner similar to that used for roasting. Puffing brings about a light and porous texture in split, dehusked *dhal*. Whole, unhusked grains are also commonly used for this process. For puffing, seeds are soaked in water, mixed with sand that has been heated to 250 °C, and then toasted for a short time (15–25 s). After the sand is sieved off, the grains are dehusked between a hot plate and rough roller. The more common legumes prepared in this manner are chick-peas and peas. Other dried legumes may also be suitable for this process. These products are traditionally eaten either with parched cereals or as a snack (Kurien, Desikachar, and Parpia 1972). Since the process of puffing legumes has developed in the past decade from a hand-operated home-scale system to a large-scale operation in which mechanized puffing machines are used, investigations into standardizing the optimal processing conditions for producing the best puffed products are needed.

Roasting and puffing as legume-processing methods improve the flavor and texture of the grain; however, the effects of these methods on the nutritional quality of legumes remain unexplored. Since both methods involve high-temperature treatments (160–300 °C) at low moisture contents (usually 20–25%), their effects on the nutritional characteristics of legumes likely are different than those expected during the other processing methods. Devadas, Leela, and Chandrasekaran (1964) reported that pressure cooking was much better than baking for black gram. Dry heating under low moisture conditions also destroys thiamin, pantothenic acid, and riboflavin, and reduces the availability of lysine and methionine of legumes (Rao 1974; Geervani and Theophilus 1980).

Roasting time is an important factor influencing the protein quality of legumes. About 15 min of roasting at 200 °C was optimum to enhance the protein quality of broad beans (Bressani 1983). The destruction of lysine with further increase in the roasting time lowered the PER. However, if processing conditions are well controlled, there appears to be no adverse effect on the nutritional quality of legumes.

In a more detailed study, Geervani and Theophilus (1980) investigated the effects of several home processing methods on the protein quality of black gram (*Phaseolus mungo*) and green gram (*Phaseolus aureus*). The protein quality of boiled, pressure-cooked, roasted, fermented, germinated, and parched legumes was assessed on the basis of PER, nitrogen absorption, and retention. The PER for the moist heat-treated (boiling and pressure cooking) legumes was 2.12, compared to 1.48 for unprocessed and 1.52 for dry-roasted seeds. These differences in protein quality were related to the destruction of essential amino acids during dry heat processing.

Literature data on the antinutritional factors of roasted and puffed legumes are not available. In view of the widespread use of these methods for processing legumes in Asian countries, more research is required on the protein quality and antinutrients of the roasted and puffed legumes. In particular, because of the low moisture conditions and short processing times (2–10 min), the enzyme inhibitors might not be fully inactivated. Optimization of these processes for different legumes is required to exploit the true potential of legumes as protein sources.

Germination

The development of food products from germinated legumes is another way to increase further their versatility and utility. Legume sprouts constitute a good portion of the total consumption of food legumes in the Far East. Germinated legumes are receiving increasing attention because of their improved flavor and nutritional qualities.

The preparation of germinated legumes is a method developed over the years using traditional home practices. Its importance as a processing method is recognized primarily in the Far East and to a lesser extent in India. In both regions, the process is carried out both in the home and on a village scale.

The germination process itself, as practiced in India, involves initially soaking the whole, unhusked beans for 24 h, and then spreading them on a damp cloth for up to 48 h. Under tropical conditions, sprouts up to a length of 1 cm appear. Sprouted grains are eaten raw with salt, parched, or mixed with flavorings and fried or boiled (Aykroyd and Doughty 1964).

Since germinated legume seeds and sprouts are often added to diets to increase their acceptability and nutrient content, the nutritional changes that take place during this process are of interest. However, it has received little attention and existing data tend to be contradictory. A major reason appears to be that during germination, as in soaking, there is a loss of solids that influences the overall composition of the germinated seeds.

Germination involves the breakdown of seed reserves owing to increased enzyme activity. The metabolic products are utilized by the growing shoot and root. The protein content of legumes may be slightly decreased during germination due to the action of proteases. The amino acid profile, however, does not change dramatically, and the chemical score of the seed is not decreased (Hofsten 1979). However, prolonged germination does cause a significant decrease in the nutritive value of the beans. The PER decreases after three days of germination, with an even lower value after nine days (Bressani 1983). This is generally attributed to a decrease in the total S-containing amino acids. The breakdown of proteins into free amino acids during germination results in a product that is rich in nutrients in a form readily assimilable for human nutrition.

Germinated legumes and sprouts contain significantly higher levels of vitamins than the dry seeds. They are good sources of ascorbic acid. Hofsten (1979) reported that, on a fresh-weight basis, mung bean sprouts contain more than 50 mg ascorbic acid per 100 g. He also reported an increase of about 100–300% in B-vitamins during germination, and that the sprouts are a good source of vitamin B_{12}. Germination apparently does not influence the mineral composition of beans to any significant extent. The only major changes seem to occur in phosphorus fractions of legumes (Kylen and McCready 1975; Reddy, Balakrishnan, and Salunkhe 1978). The nonphytate phosphorus increases at the expense of phytic acid. Thus, from a nutritional standpoint, germination may improve the bioavailability of certain minerals.

Phytic acid has been suggested to be a source of phosphorus, inositol, and cations for germinating seeds (Williams 1970). The breakdown of phytate during germination is attributed to an increased activity of the endogenous phytase. Data on several legumes suggest that over 20–70% of the phytic acid is hydrolyzed during germination (Reddy, Balakrishnan, and Salunkhe 1978; Tabekhia and Luh 1980; Deshpande 1985). Among the other antinutrients, conflicting data exist on the protease inhibitory and lectin activity, although over 70% of the raffinose family oligosaccharides can be removed during the germination of several legumes (Rao and Belavady 1978; Silva and Luh 1979; Gupta and Wagle 1980). Similarly, Noor, Bressani, and Elias (1980) reported a significant reduction (over 70%) in the tannin content of mung beans after four-day germination. It therefore appears that germination may be useful in removing certain unwanted and heat-stable components, such as phytates, tannins, and the flatulent factors, but has little influence on the protease inhibitory and lectin activities. However, it follows that the inactivation of these two antinutrients during the subsequent heat processing of the germinated legumes would still result in a nutritionally better food product.

Fermentation

Fermentation is probably one of the oldest methods of processing food legumes. The most notable application of this process is in the Orient, where fermented legume foods have been eaten for centuries. This technique overcomes the disadvantage of long cooking time, leads to an easily digested product, and reduces some toxic compounds. It is particularly useful for hard seeds and for those with high toxin content. In practice, fermentation breaks down starch to acid as the final end product by the action of microorganisms.

Fermented mixtures of legumes and rice are widely consumed in India. In this process, previously soaked (4–6 h) mixtures of black gram and rice (1 : 2) are mashed and left overnight to ferment. Subsequent steaming of the fermented batter produces *idli,* whereas baking or frying produces *dosai.* The preparation of a fermented paste from cooked, decorticated, dried, and crushed locust bean seeds is practiced in West Africa. The paste is subsequently cut into pieces and sun-dried, resulting in balls or sticks that are used as a condiment or relish in various dishes. An excellent description of legume-based fermented foods in various parts of the world is given by Reddy et al. (1982).

The main effect of fermentation, regardless of the fermenting organisms used, is to make more nutrients available for assimilation. Most of these changes involve the hydrolysis of protein and starch. Generally, protein digestibility improves during fermentation, since the microbial enzymes break down the legume protein. The reports on protein quality, however, are contradictory, the majority indicating a lower value than before fermentation. There is little change in the amino acid composition of the fermented products, but they are generally acknowledged as being more available (Aykroyd and Doughty 1964). Ebine (1972) has reported a biological value of 63% and an absorption rate of 83% in *natto;* this indicates an improvement in comparison with those of the raw materials. During *tempeh* production, molds break down a portion of the original protein into its constituent amino acids (Reddy et al. 1982).

The major changes during fermentation seem to occur in the vitamin content of legumes. Robinson and Kao (1974) observed an increase in the reducing sugars, soluble protein, and water-soluble vitamins during the preparation of chick-pea *tempeh.* Ramakrishnan (1979) reviewed the nutritional value of Indian fermented foods and reported an increase in thiamin, riboflavin, and niacin in fermented chick-peas, black gram, and soy products. On the other hand, Zamora and Fields (1979) found that when cowpeas and chick-peas underwent natural fermentation for four days at 25 °C, niacin decreased in both products, thiamin decreased in chick-peas, and riboflavin increased in cowpeas.

Fermentation also influences the antinutrients of legumes. The trypsin inhibitors, lectins, and saponins associated with the edible legumes are inactivated during the fermentation process (Ebine 1972). This perhaps is related to the heating process involved in the preparation of fermented foods. Reddy and Salunkhe (1980) found 28.4% hydrolysis of the raffinose oligosaccharides during a 45-h fermentation of black gram, whereas Zamora and Fields (1979) reported that 88–100% of these sugars could be hydrolyzed during a four-day fermentation of chick-peas and cowpeas. The reduction in the raffinose oligosaccharides during fermentation is primarily due to the α-galactosidase activity present in the legume seeds, as well as in the microorganisms responsible for fermentation. Phytic acid is hydrolyzed during fermentation to a variable degree, depending on the type of legume as well as fermentation (Reddy and Salunkhe 1980).

Canning

Dry beans play an important role in the canning industry in North America and, to a lesser extent, in Central and South America. In most cases, canned legumes in developing countries are consumed by the higher-income class or are exported to developed countries, since they are more expensive than traditionally processed legumes.

The most popular legumes used for canning belong to the *Phaseolus* genus. Canned kidney and pinto beans are consumed as a vegetable side dish or may be used as a basic ingredient in a salad. They are also used in preparing baked beans. Precooked canned beans are consumed in parts of Latin America. A variety of beans are available canned in water, brine, sugar solutions, tomato sauce, or mixed with other vegetables.

The following is a brief outline of a commercial procedure for canning dry beans (Deshpande, Sathe, and Salunkhe 1984a). The beans are washed and soaked in either water or salt solutions for a predetermined time and temperature depending on the variety and type of bean. After soaking, the beans are drained, washed with water, and blanched either in water or steam. The blanched beans are drained, washed, and sorted to remove broken and defective beans. They are then put into cans in water, brine, or tomato sauce, vacuum sealed, and heat processed in retorts, processing times and temperatures varying with the type of bean. The heat-processed cans are cooled in retorts and are ready for labeling, packing, and distribution.

The desired moisture content in dried beans for processing generally is in the range of 14–18%. The U.S. standards for beans permit moisture contents of up to 18% without being designated as "high-moisture" beans (USDA 1975). However, beans with a moisture content above 13% deteriorate significantly in texture and flavor after six months of storage at 25 °C (Deshpande, Sathe, and Salunkhe 1984a). Beans stored at ≤10% moisture maintain high quality and store well even after two years. On the other hand, at too low a moisture content (<6%), seed coats become brittle and crack, resulting in an inferior canned product.

Considerable losses of some of the water-soluble vitamins can occur during the presoaking (hydration) step, or if the liquid in which the beans have been cooked is not consumed. Significant amounts of riboflavin, niacin, and vitamin A have been found in the liquid medium surrounding the beans during the hydration and cooking steps (Deshpande, Sathe, and Salunkhe 1984a). Canning also results in a loss of the protein quality of legumes. Hackler (1974) reported that the PER of canned beans decreases approximately 40% as a result of canning. Elias et al. (1973) have reported that a cooking time beyond 30 min at 121 °C, without a previous soaking step, decreases the nutritive value of the protein. The lower availability of lysine is partly responsible for this effect. Moreover, soaked samples have shown a reduction in the nutritive value with processing times above 10 min. The optimum cooking time and temperature for canning beans to eliminate or minimize losses in the protein quality is an ongoing research process.

The information on antinutrients of canned legumes is at best sketchy. Changes similar to those that occur during cooking may be expected for heat-labile antinutrients. Tabekhia and Luh (1980) compared the effects of cooking and canning on inorganic phosphorus and phytic acid retention in dry beans. Canning resulted in a significant breakdown in phytic acid in four bean varieties. Retention of phytic acid was only 8.5% in canned black-eyed beans, and ranged from 25.1% to 32.4% in the other three varieties, compared to 63.7–92.3% retention of phytic acid in cooked beans. Heat processing during canning resulted in an apparent decrease in phytic acid with a concurrent increase in inorganic phosphorus. The exact mechanism of phytic acid breakdown during canning, however, is not yet known. Oberleas (1973) reported that the destruction of phytate during cooking depended on the presence of active phytase, pH, and the concentration of ionized calcium. Under the conditions of cooking and canning, phytase activity is unlikely. Soaking prior to canning and the canning media, such as brine or sucrose solution, are likely to influence phytic acid breakdown during the canning process. The work of Tabekhia and Luh (1980) on phytic acid breakdown during canning of beans suggests that the processing conditions during canning may influence other heat-stable antinutrients, such as tannins and flatulence-causing oligosaccharides.

Legume Powders

Precooked legume flours in a convenient stable form for subsequent use in convenience foods are gaining increasing attention. The initial development of instant bean powders followed three basic processing systems (Copley 1974): The first process involved soaking the whole beans, cooking them in a slurry, and drying in a drum dryer. In the second process, whole beans are ground in a mill into a fine powder, which is immediately blended with a solution of HCl to inactivate enzymes responsible for causing bitter flavor; the slurry is cooked for 5 min, neutralized by the addition of NaOH, and then further cooked to a palatable form and drum dried. A third method of legume powder preparation uses a cooked product from a quick-cooking bean process. The bean powders produced by these three methods have excellent rehydration properties.

The instant bean processes have been used commercially to prepare legume powders from dry beans, peas, and lentils. They are widely used in traditional noodle, pasta, and baked products, various snacks, and as ingredients in composite flours and instant foods.

Protein Concentrates and Isolates

The isolation of protein from aqueous solutions using a wide range of methods has been practiced for many years. In most cases, the end product is a dry powder whose protein content and quality depend on the isolation method. In addition to differences in protein content (30–90%), there are also differences in the degree of protein denaturation. Consequently, the methods will yield protein concentrates and isolates having different functional properties and potential applications in food. Generally, the undenatured form of protein is more valuable in food applications owing to its excellent functional properties, such as solubility, emulsifying capacity, and whipping and gelling properties.

Protein concentrates and isolates from oilseed meals have enjoyed great success in several food applications; they are not, however, economically viable for many food legumes. The main reason appears to be their low protein content compared to that of the oilseed meals. In addition, legume starch (50–60% yield) as a by-product cannot compete economically with cereal and tuber starches. Nevertheless, this approach to legume processing has been successful in Canada and, to a lesser extent, in some Southeast Asian countries. The two most commonly used methods for preparing legume protein concentrates and isolates are described below.

Air Classification

Much research on air classification of food legumes comes from the Prairie Regional Laboratory in Canada. Air classification to produce a protein concentrate initially involves fine grinding of the legume flour. The pin-milled flour is then separated into various fractions in a spiral air stream. Concentration of the protein by this method is possible because of the differences in size, shape, and density of the starch granules and the protein-containing particles (Sosulski 1983). In the finely ground flour, the starch fraction is present in the heavier particles, whereas the protein fraction is lighter in density. Protein separation takes place when opposing centrifugal and centripetal forces are employed; consequently, the heavier particles (starch) move in the opposite direction of the fine protein-rich particles. Since legume flours contain relatively large starch granules, preparation of protein concentrates by air classification is quite practical. The method is widely used in Canada for the preparation of crude protein concentrates (40–50% protein) from field peas and fava beans. Protein concentrates prepared by this method have a high nutritional value and are commonly used as nutritional and functional ingredients in pasta, baked goods, meat patties, and frankfurters.

Extraction and Precipitation Methods

The preparation of protein concentrates from soybeans by protein precipitation has been practiced for centuries. Hot-water extraction of protein from ground, cooked soybeans (soy milk), followed by precipitation of the protein using calcium, is a long-practiced method for preparing oriental soybean curd (tofu); soy protein concentrate is only a modern version of this age-old practice. In more recent times, research has focused on the preparation of soy protein concentrates by aqueous extraction of the protein, followed by precipitation at its isoelectric pH. This well-established technology for preparing protein concentrates and isolates from soybeans can be utilized for the preparation of similar products from food legumes. Modification of the process to establish it as a base for a small-scale industry in developing countries is receiving increasing attention.

A flowchart for the preparation of legume protein concentrates by the protein precipitation method is shown in Fig. 2-9. The bean protein can be isolated by extraction with an alkali solution at the pH of its maximum solubility, followed by precipitation at its isoelectric pH. It should be emphasized, however, that treating protein fractions with strong alkaline solutions decreases their nutritive value due to racemization of amino acids and lysinoalanine formation. Accordingly, the best and simplest method for isolating protein from dry seeds would be to extract them with salt solutions, followed by precipitation by dialysis. An alternative to the latter step could be heat denaturation of the protein. Mung bean concentrates prepared by this method are widely used in Thailand (Siegel and Fawcett 1976).

The preparation of protein concentrates from legumes using such approaches deserves attention, since they mostly stem from the conventional legume processing methods. Legume protein concentrates are nutritionally significant because they are high in protein and their physical and chemical nature make them compatible with various food applications. Both new and traditional foods can be prepared from legume protein concentrates, leading to an increased amount of protein in the diet. In addition, the use of protein concentrates may offer certain nutritional advantages. For example, Murphy, Kon, and Seifert (1964) reported preparation of protein concentrate from *P. vulgaris* void of flatulence activity. Sathe and Salunkhe (1981) observed a complete elimination of hemagglutinating activity as well as the flatulent factors during the alkali solubilization step to prepare bean protein concentrates; trypsin and chymotrypsin inhibitory activities were also significantly lower. Contrariwise, Deshpande and Cheryan (1984b) found that although trypsin inhibitory activity was lowered on a per-gram-of-protein basis, the protein concentrates prepared from three varieties of dry bean had a higher total inhibitory activity. They attributed this to a concen-

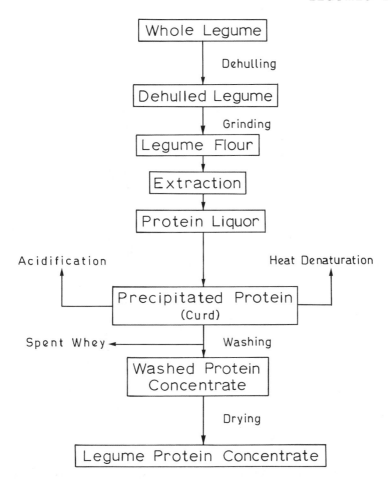

Fig. 2-9. Flowchart for the preparation of legume protein concentrates by protein precipitation method. *Source:* Reproduced from Siegel and Fawcett (1976), with permission.

tration of the inhibitors in the protein concentrates. Nutritionally, the only disadvantage of the alkali solubilization method for the preparation of protein concentrates appears to be the possibility of the formation of lysinoalanine. The prolonged exposure of food proteins to strong alkali, heat, or a combination of the two may also be accompanied by reduced protein solubility, amino acid cross linking, amino acid degradation, and amino acid–sugar complexation (Sathe and Salunkhe 1984). Protein concentrates prepared by air classification show no appreciable loss of protease inhibitory activity (Sosulski 1983). They contain higher levels of phytate, and 5–8% of the raffinose family oligosaccharides.

Oil Extraction

Soybean and peanuts are the two legumes most commonly used for oil extraction. Both are traditionally classified as "oilseeds" rather than as food legumes. Soybeans contain 20–25% oil whereas peanut kernels contain 47–50%. In recent years, winged beans are becoming a promising new source of edible oil in the developing countries of the tropics and subtropics. Unlike soybean, which is a cool-weather crop, winged beans are well adapted to the tropical climate.

Almost all of the soybeans harvested in the United States are processed into oil and meal products through a solvent extraction process. There are essentially three steps to this process: bean preparation, oil extraction, and solvent stripping and reclamation. The soybeans are dehulled and cracked to small pieces, which are then flaked using rollers to increase the surface area for oil extraction. Several types of extractor are available commercially for the extraction of oil from oilseeds. The oil is extracted using hydrocarbon solvents such as hexane. These solvents present considerable fire hazards, and precautions must be taken. Chlorinated hydrocarbons are advantageous in that they are not inflammable; they are, however, much more expensive to use. In all of the solvent recovery systems, accessory equipment for drying the meal, stripping stills, condensers, and decanters are required to effect the recovery of the solvent from the miscella and the extracted residue. Solvent extraction is the most efficient of all oil extraction methods: The oil content of the cake may be reduced to 1% or lower.

Depending on the geographical region, oil is extracted from peanuts by three methods: hydraulic pressing, expeller pressing, and solvent extraction. Both unshelled and shelled peanuts may be used for oil extraction by the first two methods, whereas solvent extraction requires pretreatments of the kernels similar to those described for soybeans. In the hydraulic pressing method, the kernels are pressed in hydraulic presses under pressures of about 2,000 lbs./sq. in. (psi). The cake is allowed to drain while under hydraulic pressure. In developing countries, peanuts are processed using traditional oil extraction methods. These include both mechanically operated and bullock-driven oil expellers. The expeller is a screw-type press in which the screw is contained in a slotted housing and operates against a restricted opening. The high pressures developed in the expeller squeezes out the oil, which escapes through the slots in the screw housing. Both hydraulic and expeller pressing methods leave a significant oil residue (up to 4–5%) in the cake, which is usually sold as high-protein animal feed. In recent years, it is also being increasingly used for the recovery of high-grade edible protein, which is used as a supplement in a variety of food products.

The crude oil thus extracted contains varying amounts of substances that may impart undesirable flavor and color, and has poor keeping quality. These substances include free fatty acids, phospholipids, carbohydrates, proteins and their degradation products, water, pigments, and fat oxidation products. Crude oils, therefore, are subjected to a number of refining processes to remove these substances. These are briefly described below.

The water phase from the crude oil is removed by settling. The oil is heated in tanks and allowed to stand until the aqueous phase separates and can be withdrawn. This allows the removal of water, proteins, some phospholipids, and carbohydrates. About 30% of the soybean oil produced in the United States is degummed to recover lecithin. Lecithin is an important food additive and is widely used as an emulsifier in the food industry. The crude or degummed oil is then treated with caustic soda to neutralize free fatty acids, hydrolyze phosphatides, and remove some color pigments and other unsaponifiable matter. This is followed by a bleaching step to remove pigments by adsorbing them on neutral or activated earth or carbon. Deodorization is the last major processing step in the refining of edible oils. This operation is designed to remove all oxidative cleavage products that impart odor or flavor to the oil. The refined oil is then used for a variety of purposes, such as a cooking or frying medium, in salad oils and dressings, or in the formulation of margarine and shortening.

Extraction

Extraction of legumes may be distinguished from normal water soaking in that it may be carried out intentionally to remove such undesirable components as flatulent factors, enzyme inhibitors, tannins, lipid-derived off-flavors, and other compounds, including the neurotoxins of *Lathyrus* species. In general, normal soaking, which forms an integral part of several legume processing operations, serves the same purpose. Although extraction processes have been successfully described for the removal of several of these compounds on a laboratory scale, their commercial viability still remains questionable. The extraction of raffinose oligosaccharides with 80% aqueous ethanol, and of tannins using dilute alkali solutions, has been reported (Deshpande and Damodaran 1990; Deshpande and Sathe, 1991). The removal of lipid-derived off-flavors by solvent extraction and a combination of solvent extraction and heat was also described (Salunkhe, Sathe, and Reddy 1982; Salunkhe, Iyer, and Deshpande 1989). Azeotropic mixtures of hexane–isopropanol, hexane–methanol, hexane–ethanol, or simple solvent systems such as ethanol have been suggested for this purpose. This is usually accompanied by an improvement in flavor scores of soya and peanut products.

Irradiation

Irradiation is generally used as a pretreatment prior to other processing operations. The γ-radiation treatment of legumes is known to reduce their cooking times, destroy several unwanted components, such as raffinose oligosaccharides, lectins, and protease inhibitors, and generally enhance their protein digestibility (Salunkhe, Iyer, and Deshpande 1989). However, due to the stigma attached to the consumption of irradiated foods, this processing method may not be commercially viable, at least in the near future.

Membrane Processing

Membrane processing of legume slurries has been shown to be a promising method for the selective removal of low-relative-mass, undesirable compounds such as phytic acid and raffinose oligosaccharides (Salunkhe, Iyer, and Deshpande 1989). However, the cost–benefit ratio, coupled with the problems associated with the commercial scaling of these processes, apparently will not make these methods economical for legume processing.

Extrusion and Texturization

Extrusion-processed foods include ready-to-eat (RTE) breakfast cereals, textured vegetable proteins (TVP), and texturized soy proteins (TSP), commonly used as meat analogues or extenders, infant food formulations, beverages, composite flours, soup bases, and precooked starches. These foods are typically blends of cereal and legume flours, the latter generally including defatted oilseed meals.

Low-cost extrusion (LCE) cooking consists of a shallow-flighted screw fitted into a stationary barrel. Flour enters the initial flight of the screw through a feed hopper and is then conveyed forward by the action of flights into constricted channels. After the addition of water, the flour is turned into dough; this is heated by a combination of heat sources, including the fluid friction dissipating the mechanical energy required to turn the screw, as well as the steam in the jackets that surround the extruder barrel. Many products are extruded at high temperatures (140–200 °C), high pressures (60–80 bars), and a moisture content <20%. The total time to accomplish this operation is typically 30–60 s. The product is finally forced out of the extruder through a variety of dies and dried on conveyer belts. This process usually destroys protease inhibitors, lipoxygenases, and urease that occur in raw flour, and thus increases the nutritive value of soy-based products.

As compared to LCE cooking, the HTST (high temperature–short time) extrusion process at 20% moisture level is greatly suited for various legumes, since their conventional cooking requires a longer time, higher moisture, and more fuel energy to inactivate the various antinutrients. Extruded products have tremendous potential in popularizing legume-based foods for the various nutritional programs in the developing countries.

The texturization of soya proteins is analogous to extrusion except that the product is extruded in the form of fibers; these are then turned into meat analogues by binding them with edible binders such as gums. These products are often used as meat extenders in a variety of convenience foods.

Freezing

Frozen foods enjoy great popularity in the developed Western world. Only those legumes used as fresh vegetables are suited for this purpose: the French beans, lima beans, and green peas. These legumes are harvested at a mature-green stage, shelled, blanched, and then quickly frozen at –20 °C. Sometimes they are individually quick-frozen (IQF) at –20 °C, then packaged and stored frozen to maintain excellent flavor, color, texture, and nutritive value (Salunkhe, Iyer, and Deshpande 1989). Overmatured and shriveled beans and peas are not suited for freezing and are often used as cattle feed. Alternatively, they can be deep-fat fried and flavored with salt and spices to produce nutritious and delicious snack foods.

UTILIZATION

Legumes are traditionally processed and consumed as human food in a variety of different forms (Deshpande, Sathe, and Salunkhe 1984a; Deshpande and Damodaran 1990). Fresh or canned mature and immature pods or seeds are used as vegetables. Split seeds or cotyledons (*dhals*) with or without seed coats, obtained after elaborate processing, can be boiled as such or made into soups or porridges. Whole and dehusked seeds are roasted, parched, or puffed. The practice of using germinated seed and young seed sprouts of pulses as fresh vegetables is widespread in the Orient. Fermented legume foods in a variety of different ways are also quite popular in Southeast Asian countries and in Africa. The practice of extracting soybean proteins in the form of soya curd (tofu) and soybean milk is common in China and Japan. Legume-based weaning foods are also common in many South and Latin American countries as well as in India. In the Western world, legumes are now promoted as a source of excellent quality dietary fiber and for their hypocholesterolemic properties. Modern legume-processing methods include using flour or isolated protein concentrates to make instant foods, simulated food products, and meat analogues, and in the fortification of cereal-based bakery products.

Several excellent reviews are available for detailed descriptions of the utilization of various traditional legume-based products (Reddy et al. 1982; Salunkhe, Kadam, and Chavan 1985; Kadam, Adsule, and Salunkhe 1989). Therefore, only a brief summary of various modes of legume utilization in the human diet is presented in Table 2-30.

Table 2-30. Utilization of Legume Products.

Mode	Country	Legumes
Whole beans		
Canned beans	USA, Europe, Canada, Mexico	Green pea, dry bean, lima bean
Precooked dehydrated	North America	Dry bean, lima bean
Puffed beans	India	Chick-pea
Boiled legumes	India	Peanuts, pigeon pea
Roasted beans	India, Middle East, N. America	Green gram, chick-pea, peanut
Milk products		
Milk	Asia, Latin America	Soybean, peanut
Curd/tofu	China, Japan	Soybean, winged bean
Fermented milk	China, Japan, India	Soybean, peanut
Cheese	Southeast Asia	Soybean
Beverages	Asia	Soybean, peanut
Yogurt	China, India	Soybean, peanut
Fermented foods		
Dawadawa	Africa	Locust bean
Ugba	West and Central Africa	African oil bean
Inyu	China	Soybean, black bean
Kecap	Indonesia	Soybean
Waries	India	Black gram
Kenima	India, Nepal	Soybean
Meitauza	China	Soybean
Taosi	Philippines	Soybean
Cotyledons		
Cooked dhal	Indian subcontinent	Most food legumes
Roasted/fried dhal	Indian subcontinent	Green gram, black gram, chick-pea
Sandage	India	Black gram
Soups	Latin America, India	Pigeon pea, chick-pea
Butter	N. America	Peanut
Edible oil	Worldwide	Soybean, peanut, winged bean
Fermented foods		
Dhokla	India	Chick-pea
Khaman	India	Chick-pea
Idli	India	Black gram
Dosai	India	Black gram
Confectionery products		
Candy, *chikki*	USA, India	Peanuts
Flours		
Composite flours	Latin America, India	Various legumes
Papad	India	Black gram
Pasta	Europe	Peas

RESEARCH NEEDS

The dietary and economic importance of food legumes is globally appreciated. Yet, besides their high protein content and certain heat-labile antinutrients, research needs on several other aspects of legume chemistry and technology seem to have been identified only recently.

In the foreseeable future, a great deal of attention will undoubtedly center on increasing legume yields using appropriate breeding techniques. There is no way of knowing with certainty what the future maximum genetic grain yield potential will be for the different legume species. A failure to achieve a green revolution in legume production technology suggests either that attaining the maximum genetic potential for these crops appears to be quite difficult, or that research efforts in this direction have been minimal or ill-directed. Seed yield per unit area is an expression of the interaction between the genetic makeup of the variety and the environment in which it is grown. Maximum yields are produced only when the variety with the highest genetic yield potential is grown in an environment that is optimum for the crop from the standpoints of sunlight, soil, moisture, plant nutrients, temperature, and insect and pest infestation. Under actual farm conditions, yields are often limited by either shortage of moisture, inadequate levels of soil fertility, or reduction in yield imposed by weeds, diseases, and insects. Obviously, it is not possible for all these considerations to be taken into account in a single cultivar; rather, breeding efforts must be targeted for specific conditions for a given locality.

Photosynthesis is the single most important process on this planet, and has considerable unutilized potential in the production of an adequate food supply. Only green plants can convert sunlight to chemical energy; however, scarcely 1% of the sunlight that falls on the plants is captured. Research on photosynthetic processes in various legumes and their influence on yield potential needs to be accelerated. Another resource that must be tapped to its full potential is the biological nitrogen fixation in legumes. Although all legumes have rhizobial associations in root nodules that provide a built-in nitrogen source, legumes often obtain as much as 75% or more of their nitrogen from that already present in soil, with only 25% being fixed in the nodules. Yet this 25% rate is limiting for growth: The production of all legumes could be substantially increased if nitrogen fixation in the nodules could be improved. Thus, a major effort should be directed toward increasing the photosynthetic energy source in legumes, and a second approach should lie in the development of super strains of *Rhizobia* for each of the several species that exhibit symbiosis with the major food legumes. The alternative is to improve the host plant, exploring the effects of variety, age, soil pH, temperature, and soil nutrient levels.

Breeding for high protein content in legume seeds, although an attractive alternative, has its drawbacks. First, seed protein content and yield are negatively correlated. Second, above a certain concentration, additional protein might be progressively lower in nutritional quality. It is therefore important to take a more critical look in concentrating our limited research sources and efforts in this direction. We need to evaluate plant breeding efforts and establish the limits of an optimum relationship between protein content and maximum yield. Breeding for high S-amino acids in legume proteins may also be a wasted effort. Legumes seldom form the sole source of nutrients in diets in most parts of the world. We are not likely to have an "ideal food source" that would take care of all our nutritional requirements. Balanced nutrition comes from a wise choice of foods belonging to the major food groups. In parts of the world where legumes serve as the "only" sources of protein, and therefore where the S-amino acid deficiency would be aggravated, research must be targeted to increase the availability of cereal-based foods.

An area beginning to receive considerable attention by molecular biologists, including those with commercial interests, is the genetic modification of plants by recombinant-DNA approaches. Although this field has lagged considerably behind bacterial, yeast, and mammalian fields in both research activity and support, advances in plant transformation indicate that plants may soon become an elegant system for studying gene expression in higher organisms. In addition, it is likely that they will be more amenable to genetic improvement than was thought possible at one time. Genetic engineering has opened several new vistas in agricultural research. The possible applications of these techniques in the area of agricultural research have been comprehensively reviewed (Beachy and Fraley 1985; Jones 1985). Those pertinent to legume research are briefly described below.

Yield

It may be possible to increase yield by improving the harvest index—that is, the ratio of harvested seed to total biomass. Since biomass production depends on photosynthesis, the various photosynthetic processes are prime candidates for the application of genetic engineering techniques.

Nitrogen Fixation

It is not clearly understood yet, at the biochemical level, what special features of leguminous plants or *Rhizobium* allow their symbiosis to take place; nevertheless, some of the possible opportunities for manipulating the system are

1. transfer of nitrogen-fixing genes from bacteria to plants,
2. expansion of the host range of symbiosis to crops other than legumes, and
3. increasing the efficiency of symbiotic bacteria to fix nitrogen.

Nitrate and Solute Uptake

In the majority of cultivated crops, the most important pathway of entry of nitrogen into the plant is nitrate uptake, followed by its reduction via nitrite to ammonia, and the assimilation of ammonia via glutamine synthetase. Higher plant nitrate and nitrite reductase have yet to be cloned. Genetic engineering techniques could be applied in this field to

1. improve NO_3 carrier uptake efficiency,
2. increase copy numbers of NO_3 reductase and NO_2 reductase, and
3. transfer NO_3 reduction to leaves (when not already present) where NO_3 reduction is energically more favorable.

Drought, Disease, Pest, and Herbicide Tolerance

Genes that directly control these traits need to be identified and cloned. Certain genetic aspects of these traits could be amenable to manipulation.

Nutritional Quality

Although breeding for overall yield is still the main objective, breeders are now almost as concerned with improving the nutritional quality of crops. The nutritional quality of the grain very much depends on the amino acid composition of its major storage proteins, which, being products directly coded by specific genes, unlike storage carbohydrates, should be easier to manipulate. In this regard, inserting extra codons for the limiting S-amino acids into cloned storage protein genomic DNA, followed by reintroduction of the gene into the legume plants, would be very useful. Similarly, several legumes contain small amounts of S-rich proteins. Thus, the expression of their genes could be modified so that these proteins are preferentially synthesized.

Recent success in gene transfer to new plants with derivatives of the Ti plasmid of *Agrobacterium tumefaciens* indicates the potential of the new genetic engineering technology. The limiting factor for proper exploitation of these techniques, however, seems to be a lack of basic knowledge of plant molecular biology, biochemistry, and plant development. In this regard, a multidisciplinary approach is clearly required, encompassing plant breeders, cell biologists, and molecular biologists. Genetic engineering technology, however, should not be looked upon as panacea for solving all the problems related to agriculture and human nutrition; it will also not replace or supplant current plant breeding practices. Nonetheless, over the next couple of decades, this technology will increasingly contribute to widening gene pools available to breeders, speed up the screening of plants, and eventually lead to the production of improved crops in the farmer's fields. This will require extensive research efforts by scientists in university, governmental, and corporate settings and a willingness to exchange information.

One of the major limiting factors in utilizing the full nutritional potential of legumes is the poor digestibility and availability of their proteins. The extent to which tannins govern legume protein quality must be elucidated. We should critically evaluate differences in the nutritional quality of various legumes. For example, why do some legumes such as chick-peas, field peas, and cowpeas perform consistently better than others? Are these differences related to their protein composition, and is it possible to obtain a similar protein profile in other legumes? The answers to these questions remain elusive.

With regard to processing, we seemed to have reached a point where the development of new technology appears to be difficult. Research in this area must be continued from the standpoint of retention of various nutrients in processed legume foods and the elimination of toxic compounds. Processing conditions also need to be standardized for different legume species. Although quick-cooking bean technology has been developed to reduce cooking times, research on the understanding of such simple basic mechanisms as the relations between water uptake and seed microstructure, the physicochemical nature and role of seed constituents, and changes that take place during storage is severely lacking. We need to establish a genetic link, if any, between cooking quality and the hardshell and hard-to-cook defects in beans, and try to eliminate this problem by suitable selection of cultivars. Reducing postharvest losses during handling and storage of legumes to a minimum should also be a high priority to increase the availability of this excellent food source.

Much attention has also been given in the past to the destruction of the well-known antiphysiological factors in legume foods, such as the enzyme inhibitors and lectins, by appropriate processing. Research over the past three decades has established the heat-labile nature of these antinutrients. Although breeding of legume cultivars for partial or complete elimination of these two antinutrients has proven successful, such a strategy still appears to be questionable. It is well known that the poor quality of legume protein is due, at least in part, to a deficiency in S-amino acids. Both lectins and enzyme inhibitors are fairly rich in these amino acids. If both compounds are easily inactivated by proper processing, an increase rather than a reduction in their concentration might be desirable. In addition, the two antinutrients may very well be involved in plant defense mechanisms and root nodulation. The biological availability of S-amino acids from the proteinase inhibitors, however, appears to be quite low. Studies are needed in the area of structure/conformation and digestibility of these inhibitors so that more of the limiting S-amino acids are made available.

The flatulence factor is another characteristic of legumes that should be genetically eliminated. Unlike the proteinase inhibitors and lectins, the flatulent sugars of the raffinose family do not seem to have any biological role. Their elimination by appropriate plant selection and breeding techniques thus does not appear to influence the seed and plant physiology adversely. Meanwhile, research for the development of appropriate processing technology to remove these sugars needs to be continued.

Problems related to the heat-stable antinutrients, such as phytates and tannins, have been identified fairly recently. Their mechanisms of destruction and interactions with other dietary components, such as proteins, carbohydrates, minerals, and vitamins, are still largely unknown and require thorough investigation. The threshold levels at which these antinutrients cause deleterious effects must be established. Other areas of research include a study of the protein-binding and enzyme-inactivation properties of phytates and tannins from different legume species, the identification of possible sites of chemical reactions, mechanisms of their detoxification, and improved experimental models and analytical methods.

Although the physiologically beneficial effects of legumes have been known for quite some time, research in this area is woefully lacking. All the three major constituents of legumes (i.e., protein, starch, and dietary fiber) have been implicated in lowering serum cholesterol and triglyceride levels in humans; however, the mechanism(s) by which such effects are induced are largely unknown. It remains to be seen whether the hypocholesterolemic effects are related to some structural and/or compositional characteristics of legume seeds. The use of low-glycemic legumes in the dietary management of diabetes and weight control also deserves further exploration.

Finally, support must also come from various public sources through national governments and international bodies to help solve some specific problems. With the exception of oilseeds such as soybeans and peanuts, none of the food legumes seems to be important cash crops. Because of low yields, they are often used as catch crops, grown on marginal land with little input of water and fertilizers, and are of little commercial interest; thus there is no economic incentive to grow more food legumes. Price increase is probably not the right solution, primarily because of their importance for the poorer part of the population in many countries around the world. Major assistance should come in terms of increasing the financial support for research in various aspects of legume production and technology. Thus, a concerted effort on parts of various agencies involved is essential if legumes are to live up to our expectations of them as an excellent nutritional source.

The world's population is now approximately 5 billion, with over 60% of these people living in developing countries. Similarly, over 70% of total food legume production is in the developing world. If human population growth continues at the present rate, the total food production will have to double by the year 2000. This will be a difficult target to achieve under the best of circumstances, and much of the success or failure will depend on our ability to increase further the yields of the major plant foods. Similarly, the production of food legumes in the developing countries needs to be doubled. Although part of the increase may come from increases in the area of cultivation under legumes, most of it will have to come from greater production per unit area. In spite of the tremendous advances made in agricultural production technology during the past three decades, extrapolations of population growth and subsistence food production among these less developed countries as studied by various international agencies (FAO, IDRC, CARE, U.S. AID, President Carter's *Global 2000 Report* [Council on Environmental Quality and U.S. Dept. of State 1980], etc.) indicate severe deficits of grain by the end of this century. These projections also anticipate little if any improvement in the present nutritional status among the world's least privileged people. These melancholy facts carry with them important economic and political considerations for the entire human race. Scientists probably bear the greatest responsibility for the worldwide failure to ensure a universally adequate food supply for all humankind. To quote Sir Francis Bacon, "If we start with certainties, we shall end with doubts; but if we begin with doubts and work patiently, we shall end with certainties." If the human concern is allowed to take precedence over restricted self-interest, patient effort can ensure the certainty of an adequate diet for all the world's people. Because legumes provide the main subsistence of peoples in the less developed countries, any effort to improve their nutritional quality and supply will certainly help alleviate the severe problem of malnutrition in many parts of the world.

REFERENCES

Abdalla, F. H., and Roberts, E. H. 1969. Effects of temperature, moisture and oxygen on the induction of chromosome damage in seeds of barley, broad beans and peas during storage. *Ann. Bot. (London) (n.s.)* 32:119–36.

Abdullah, H. 1980. A disease of winged bean (*Psophocarpus tetragonolobus*) caused by *Pseudomonas solanacearum* in Malaysia. *Pl. Dis.* 64:798–9.

Adams, M. W., and Pipoly, J. J. 1980. Biological structure, classification and distribution of economic legumes. In *Advances in Legume Science,* ed. R. J. Summerfield and A. H. Bunting, pp. 1–16. Kew: Royal Botanic Gardens.

Agrawal, P. K., and Kaur, S. 1975. Maintenance of germinability of soybean seeds from harvest to next planting under ambient conditions in Delhi. *Seed Res.* 3:81–5.

Al-Bakir, A. Y., Sachde, A. G., and Naoum, I. E. 1982. Occurrence and stability of trypsin inhibitors in Iraqi local legumes. *J. Agric. Food Chem.* 30:1184–5.

Allen, C. N. 1973. Symbiosis: Rhizobia and leguminous plants. In *Forages: The Science of Grassland Agriculture,* ed. M. E. Heath, D. S. Metcalf, and R. F. Barnes, pp. 98–104. Ames: Iowa State Univ. Press.

Allen, D. J. 1979. New disease records from grain legumes in tropical Africa. *FAO Plant Prot. Bull.* 27:134–6.

Allen, D. J. 1983. *The Pathology of Tropical Food Legumes.* New York: John Wiley and Sons.

Allen, D. J., Anno-Nyako, F. O., Ochieng, R. S., and Ratinam, M. 1981. Beetle transmission of cowpea mottle and southern bean mosaic viruses in West Africa. *Trop. Agric.* 58: 171–5.

Allen, E. K., and Allen, O. N. 1976. The nodulation profile of the genus *Cassia. Int. Biol. Progr.* 7:113–22.

Allen, O. N., and Allen, E. K. 1981. *The Leguminosae.* Madison: Univ. of Wisconsin Press.

Amable, R. 1976. The effects of harvest date and storage conditions on soybean seed quality. In *Grain Legumes,* ed. E. V. Doku, pp. 109–18. Ghana: Council of Scientific and Industrial Research.

Amosu, J. O., and Franckowiak, J. D. 1974. Inheritance of resistance to root knot nematode in cowpea. *Plant Dis. Rep.* 58:361–3.

Anahosur, K. H., and Waller, J. M. 1978. *Phakopsora packyrhizi.* CMI Descriptions of Pathogenic Fungi and Bacteria, no. 589. Kew: Commonwealth Mycological Institute.

Anderson, R. L., Rackis, J. J., and Tallent, W. H. 1979. Biologically active substances in soy products. In *Soy Protein and Human Nutrition,* ed. H. L. Wilcke, D. T. Hopkins, and D. H. Waggle, pp. 209–33. New York: Academic Press.

Andrews, D. J. 1972. Intercropping with sorghum in Nigeria. *Exp. Agric.* 8:139–50.

Anikster, Y., and Wahl, I. 1979. Co-evolution of the rust fungi on Gramineae and Liliaceae and their hosts. *Annu. Rev. Phytopathol.* 17:367–403.

Applebaum, S. W., Gestetner, B., and Birk, Y. 1965. Physiological aspects of host specificity in the Bruchidae. IV. Developmental incompatibility of soybeans for *Callosobruchus. J. Insect Physiol.* 11:611–16.

Arora, S. K. 1983. Legume carbohydrates. In *Chemistry and Biochemistry of Legumes,* ed. S. K. Arora, pp. 1–50. London: Edward Arnold.

Augustin, J., Beck, C. B., Kalbfleisch, G., Kagel, L. C., and Matthews, R. H. 1981. Variation in the vitamin and mineral content of raw and cooked commercial *Phaseolus vulgaris* classes. *J. Food Sci.* 46:1701–6.

Aykroyd, W. R., and Doughty, J. 1964. *Legumes in Human Nutrition.* Rome: Food and Agriculture Organization.

Baker, E. F. I. 1979. Mixed cropping in Northern Nigeria. III. Mixture of cereals. *Exp. Agric.* 15:41–8.

Barrett, J. A. 1980. Pathogen evolution in multilines and variety mixtures. *Pflkrankh* 87: 383–96.

Barton, D. W., Schroeder, W. T., Providenti, R., and Mishanec, W. 1964. Clones from segregating progenies of garden pea demonstrate that resistance to BV_2 and PV_2 is conditioned by the same genotype. *Plant Dis. Rep.* 48:353–5.

Beachy, R. N., and Fraley, R. T. 1985. Potentials for applications of genetic engineering technology to soybeans. In *New Protein Foods,* vol. 5, ed. A. M. Altschul, pp. 89–105. New York: Academic Press.

Beijerinck, M. W. 1888. Die bacterien der papilionaceen-knollchen. *Bot. Ztg.* 46:725–35.

Belew, M. J., Porath, J., and Sundberg, L. 1975. The trypsin and chymotrypsin inhibitors in chickpeas (*Cicer arietinum*). *Eur. J. Biochem.* 60:247–58.

Bentham, G. 1865. Leguminosae. In *Genera Plantarum,* ed. G. Bentham and J. D. Hooker, pp. 434–600. London: Bot. Soc. Edinburgh.

Beumgartner, B., and Chrispeels, M. J. 1976. Partial characterization of a protease inhibitor which inhibits the major endopeptidase present in the cotyledons of mung beans. *Plant Physiol.* 58:1–6.

Bewley, J. D., and Black, M. 1982. *Physiology and Biochemistry of Seeds,* vol. 2. Berlin: Springer–Verlag.

Bhatia, C. R. 1983. Possibilities of seed protein improvement in tropical and sub-tropical legumes. In *Seed Proteins,* ed. W. Gottschalk and H. P. Muller, pp. 451–98. The Hague: Martinus Nijhoff.

Birch, R. G., Alvarez, A. M., and Patil, S. S. 1981. A bacterial leaf spot caused in yam bean by *Pseudomonas syringae* pv. *phaseolicola. Phytopathology* 71:1289–93.

Birewar, B. R., Verma, B. K., Raman, C. P., and Kanjilal, S. C. 1980. *Traditional Storage Structures in India and Their Improvements.* Hapur (India): Indian Grain Storage Institute.

Birk, Y. 1961. Purification and some properties of a highly active inhibitor of trypsin and α–chymotrypsin from soybeans. *Biochim. Biophys. Acta* 54:378–81.

Birk, Y. 1976. Trypsin inhibitors from garden beans, *Phaseolus vulgaris. Methods Enzymol.* 45B:710–16.

Birk, Y. 1985. The Bowman–Birk inhibitor. *Int. J. Peptide Prot. Res.* 25:113–31.

Birk, Y., Gertler, A., and Khalef, S. 1963. A pure trypsin inhibitor from soya beans. *Biochem. J.* 87:281–4.

Bliss, F. A., and Robertson, D. G. 1971. Genetics of host reaction in cowpea to cowpea yellow mosaic virus and cowpea mottle virus. *Crop Sci.* 11:258–62.

Block, R. J., Mandl, R. H., Howard, H. W., Bauer, C. D., and Anderson, D. W. 1961. The curative action of iodine on soybean goiter and the changes in the distribution of iodiamino acids in the serum and in thyroid gland digests. *Arch. Biochem. Biophys.* 93:15–24.

Boakye-Boateng, K. B., and Hume, D. J. 1975. Effects of storage conditions on germination of soybean (*Glycine max* L. Merr.) seed. *Ghana J. Agric. Sci.* 8:109–14.

Bohlool, B. B., and Schmidt, E. L. 1974. Lectins: A possible basis for specificity in the *Rhizobium*–legume root nodule symbiosis. *Science* 185:269–71.

Bond, D. A., and Lowe, H. J. B. 1975. Tests for resistance to *Aphis fabae* in field beans (*Vicia faba*). *Ann. Appl. Biol.* 81:21–32.

Boomstra, A. G., and Bliss, F. A. 1977. Inheritance of resistance to *Fusarium solani* f. sp. *phaseoli* in beans (*Phaseolus vulgaris* L.) and breeding strategy to transfer resistance. *J. Am. Soc. Hort. Sci.* 102:186–8.

Booth, C. 1971. *The genus Fusarium.* Kew: Commonwealth Mycological Institute.

Booth, C. 1978. *Fusarium udum.* CMI Descriptions of Pathogenic Fungi and Bacteria, no. 575. Kew: Commonwealth Mycological Institute.

Borchers, R., and Ackerson, C. W. 1947. Trypsin inhibitor. IV. Occurrence in seeds of the Leguminosae and other seeds. *Arch. Biochem.* 13:291–3.

Bos, L. 1972. *Soybean mosaic virus.* CMI/AAB Descriptions of Plant Viruses, no. 93. Kew: Commonwealth Mycological Institute and Association of Applied Biologists.

Bos, L. 1977. Seed-borne viruses. In *Plant Health and Quarantine in International Transfer of Genetic Resources,* ed. W. B. Hewitt and L. Chiarappa, pp. 39–69. Cleveland: CRC Press.

Bowman, Y. 1944. Fractions derived from soybeans and navy beans which retard tryptic digestion of casein. *Proc. Soc. Exp. Biol. Med.* 57:139–40.

Bramsnaes, F., and Olsen, H. S. 1979. Development of field pea and faba bean proteins. *J. Am. Oil Chem. Soc.* 56:450–4.

Bressani, R. 1983. Effects of chemical changes during storage and processing on the nutritional quality of common beans. *Food Nutr. Bull.* 5:23–34.

Bressani, R., and Elias, L. G. 1974. Legume foods. In *New Protein Foods,* ed. A. M. Altschul, pp. 230–97. New York: Academic Press.

Bressani, R., and Elias, L. G. 1980a. Nutritional value of legume crops for humans and animals. In *Advances in Legume Science,* ed. R. J. Summerfield and A. H. Bunting, pp. 135–56. Kew: Royal Botanic Gardens.

Bressani, R., and Elias, L. G. 1980b. The nutritional role of polyphenols in beans. In *Polyphenols in Cereals and Legumes,* ed. J. H. Hulse, pp. 61–8, Ottawa: IDRC.

Bridge, J. 1981. Nematodes. In *Pest Control in Tropical Grain Legumes*, pp. 111–25. London: Center for Overseas Pest Research.

Broersma, D. B., Bernard, R. L., and Luckmann, W. H. 1972. Some effects of soybean pubescence on populations of the potato leafhopper. *J. Econ. Entomol.* 65:78–82.

Brown, J. W. S., Osborn, T. C., Bliss, F. A., and Hall, T. C. 1982a. Bean lectins. Part 1. Relationships between agglutinating activity and electrophoretic variation in the lectin-containing G2/albumin seed proteins of French bean (*Phaseolus vulgaris* L.). *Theor. Appl. Genet.* 62:263–71.

Brown, J. W. S., Osborn, T. C., Bliss, F. A., and Hall, T. C. 1982b. Bean lectins. Part 2. Relationship between qualitative lectin variation in *Phaseolus vulgaris* L. and previous observations on purified bean lectins. *Theor. Appl. Genet.* 62:361–7.

Browning, J. A., and Frey, K. J. 1969. Multiline cultivars as a means of disease control. *Annu. Rev. Phytopathol.* 7:355–82.

Brunt, A. A., and Phillips, S. 1981. Plant virus diseases in Fizi. *Report of the Glasshouse Crops Research Institute for 1979*, pp. 157–8. Littlehampton (England): Glasshouse Crops Res. Inst.

Buddenhagen, I. W. 1977. Resistance and vulnerability of tropical crops in relation to their evolution and breeding. *Ann. N.Y. Acad. Sci.* 287:309–26.

Burns, R. C., and Hardy, R. W. F. 1975. *Nitrogen Fixation in Bacteria and Higher Plants*. New York: Springer–Verlag.

Burris, J. 1980. Maintenance of soybean seed quality in storage as influenced by moisture, temperature and genotype. *Iowa State J. Res.* 54:377–89.

Camus, M. C., and LaPorte, J. D. 1976. Inhibition de la proteolyse pepsique in vitro par le blé; rôle de l'acide phytiquedes issues. *Ann. Biol. Anim. Biochim. Biophys.* 16:719–29.

Carlson, G. L., Li, B. U. K., Bass, P., and Olsen, W. A. 1983. A bean α–amylase inhibitor formulation (starch blocker) is ineffective in man. *Science* 219:393–4.

Carlson, L. E., and King, T. H. 1963. The effect of environmental factors on the quality of stored pea seed. *Proc. Minnesota Acad. Sci.* 30:132–5.

Caveness, F. E. 1975. Screening cowpea germplasm for resistance to root-knot nematodes at IITA. *Nematropica* 5:21.

Chandola, R. P., Trehan, K. B., and Bacrecha, L. R. 1969. Varietal resistance to *Bruchus* sp. in cowpea (*Vigna sinensis*) under storage conditions. *Curr. Sci. (Bangalore)* 38:370–1.

Chang, R., Schwimmer, S., and Burr, H. K. 1977. Phytate: Removal from whole dry beans by enzymatic hydrolysis and diffusion. *J. Food Sci.* 42:1098–101.

Christensen, C. M. 1967. Increase in invasion by storage fungi and in fat acidity values of commercial lots of soybeans stored at moisture contents of 13.0–14.0%. *Phytopathology* 57:622–4.

Christensen, C. M., and Dorworth, C. E. 1966. Influence of moisture content, temperature and time on invasion of soybeans by storage fungi. *Phytopathology* 56:412–18.

Chui, J. A. N., and Shibles, R. 1984. Influence of spatial arrangement of maize on performance of an associated soybean intercrop. *Field Crops Res.* 8:187–98.

Cobley, L. S. 1976. *Introduction to the Botany of Tropical Crops*, 2nd ed. London: Longman.

Copley, M. J. 1974. Dry bean research: Some accomplishments and unsolved problems. In *Proc. Bean Improvement Co–operative and National Dry Bean Research Association Conference*, ed. M. N. Dickson, p. 53. Geneva, N.Y.: New York Agric. Exp. Stn.

Council on Environmental Quality and U.S. Dept. of State. 1980. *The Global 2000 Report to the President: Entering the Twenty-First Century*. Washington, D.C.: USGPO, 3 vols.

Dallal, R. C. 1974. Effects of intercropping maize with pigeonpeas on grain yields and nutrient uptake. *Exp. Agric.* 10:219–24.

Dallal, R. C. 1977. Effect of intercropping of maize with soyabean on grain yield. *Trop. Agric. (Trinidad)* 54:189–91.

Daugherty, D. M., Neustadt, M. H., Gehrke, C. W., Cavanah, L. E., Williams, L. F., and Green, D. E. 1964. An evaluation of damage to soybeans by brown and green stink bugs. *J. Econ. Entomol.* 57:719–22.

de Lumen, B. O., and Salamat, L. A. 1980. Trypsin inhibitor activity in winged beans (*Psophocarpus tetragonolobus*) and the possible role of tannin. *J. Agric. Food Chem.* 28:533–6.

de Tella, R., Lago, A. A., and Zink, E. 1976. Effects of various moisture contents and fungicide treatments on the longevity of groundnut seeds. *Bragantia* 35:335–42.

Deighton, F. C. 1976. *Studies on Cercospora and allied genera. vi. Pseudocercospora Speg., Pantospora Cif. and Cercoseptoria Petr.* CMI Descriptions of Pathogenic Fungi and Bacteria, no. 140. Kew: Commonwealth Mycological Institute.

Delouche, J. C., Matthews, R. K., Dougherty, G. M., and Boyd, A. A. 1973. Storage of seed in sub-tropical and tropical regions. *Seed Sci. Technol.* 1:671–700.

Delwiche, C. C. 1978. Legumes: Past, present and future. *Bioscience* 28:565–70.

Demski, J. W., Kahn, M. A., Wells, H. D., and Miller, J. D. 1981. Peanut mottle virus in forage legumes. *Plant Dis. Rep.* 65:359–62.

Deshpande, S. S. 1985. Investigations on dry beans (*Phaseolus vulgaris* L.): Microstructure, processing, and antinutrients. Ph.D. thesis, Univ. of Illinois, Urbana–Champaign.

Deshpande, S. S., and Cheryan, M. 1984a. Effects of phytate, divalent cations, and their interactions on α-amylase activity. *J. Food Sci.* 49:516–19.

Deshpande, S. S., and Cheryan, M. 1984b. Preparation and antinutritional characteristics of dry bean protein concentrates. *Qual. Plant. Plant Foods Hum. Nutr.* 34:185–96.

Deshpande, S. S., and Cheryan, M. 1986. Water uptake during cooking of dry beans (*Phaseolus vulgaris* L.). *Qual. Plant. Plant Foods Hum. Nutr.* 36:157–65.

Deshpande, S. S., and Damodaran, S. 1990. Food legumes: Chemistry and technology. *Adv. Cereal Sci. Technol.* 10:147–241.

Deshpande, S. S., and Salunkhe, D. K. 1982. Interactions of tannic acid and catechin with legume starches. *J. Food Sci.* 47:2080–2.

Deshpande, S. S., and Sathe, S. K. 1991. Antinutrients of plant origin. In *Mycotoxins and Phytoalexins in Human Health and Animal Nutrition*, ed. R. P. Sharma and D. K. Salunkhe. Boca Raton: CRC Press.

Deshpande, S. S., Sathe, S. K., and Salunkhe, D. K. 1984a. Dry beans of *Phaseolus*. Part 3. Processing and food applications. *CRC Crit. Rev. Food Sci. Nutr.* 21:137–95.

Deshpande, S. S., Sathe, S. K., and Salunkhe, D. K. 1984b. Chemistry and safety of plant polyphenols. In *Nutritional and Toxicological Aspects of Food Safety*, ed. M. Friedman, pp. 457–96. New York: Plenum Press.

Deshpande, S. S., Sathe, S. K., Salunkhe, D. K., and Cornforth, D. P. 1982. Effects of dehulling on phytic acid, polyphenols and enzyme inhibitors of dry beans (*Phaseolus vulgaris* L.). *J. Food Sci.* 47:1846.

Devadas, R. P., Leela, R., and Chandrasekaran, K. 1964. Effect of cooking on the digestibility and nutritive value of the proteins of black gram and green gram. *Indian J. Nutr. Diet.* 1:84–7.

Dharmalingam, C., Ramakrishnan, V., and Ramaswamy, K. R. 1976. Viability and vigor of blackgram in India. *Seed Res.* 4:40–50.

Dieckert, J. W., Snowden, J. E., Moore, A. T., Heinzelman, D. C., and Altschul, A. M. 1962. Composition of some sub-cellular fractions from seeds of *Arachis hypogaea. J. Food Sci.* 27:321–5.

Doku, E. V. 1976. *Grain Legumes.* Ghana: Council of Scientific and Industrial Research.

Dolvo, F. E., Williams, C. E., and Zoaka, L. 1975. *Cowpeas: Home Preparation and Use in West Africa*. Ottawa: IDRC.

Dorworth, C. E., and Christensen, C. M. 1959. Influence of moisture content, temperature and storage time upon changes in fungus flora, germinability and fat acidity values of soybean. *Phytopathology* 58:1457–9.

Drijfhout, E. 1978. *Genetic Interaction Between Phaseolus vulgaris and Bean Common Mosaic Virus with Implications for Strain Identification and Breeding for Resistance*. Wageningen, The Netherlands: Center for Agricultural Publishing and Documentation.

Drinkall, M. J. 1978. False rust disease of the winged bean. *PANS* 24:160–6.

Duke, J. A. 1981. *Handbook of Legumes of World Economic Importance*. New York: Plenum Press.

Ebine, H. 1972. *Fermented Soybean Foods in Japan*. Tropical Agric. Res. Ser. no. 6. Tokyo: Tropical Agriculture Research Center.

Eckenrode, C. J., and Ditman, L. P. 1963. An evaluation of potato leafhopper damage to lima beans. *J. Econ. Entomol.* 56:551–3.

Ekpo, E. J. A. 1979. Effect of *Xanthomonas vignicola* on the yield of cowpea (*Vigna unguiculata*). *African J. Agric. Sci.* 5:67–9.

Elias, L. G., Conde, A., Munoz, A., and Bressani, R. 1973. Effect of germination and maturation on nutritive value of common bean (*Phaseolus vulgaris*). In *Nutritional Aspects of Common Beans and Other Legume Seeds as Animal and Human Foods*, ed. W. G. Jaffe, pp. 139–49. São Paulo, Brazil: Ribeirao Preto.

Elias, L. G., de Fernandez, D. G., and Bressani, R. 1979. Possible effect of seed coat polyphenolics on the nutritional quality of bean protein. *J. Food Sci.* 44:524–7.

Ellenrieder, G., Geronazzo, H., and de Bojarski, A. B. 1980. Thermal inactivation of trypsin inhibitors in aqueous extracts of soybeans, peanuts and kidney beans: Presence of substances that accelerate inactivation. *Cereal Chem.* 57:25–7.

Ellis, R. H., and Roberts, E. H. 1980. Improved equations for the prediction of seed longevity. *Ann. Bot. (London) (n.s.)* 45:13–30.

Ellis, R. H., Osei-Bonsu, K., and Roberts, E. H. 1982. The influence of genotype, temperature and moisture on seed longevity in chickpea, cowpea and soybean. *Ann. Bot. (London) (n.s.)* 50:69–82.

Erdman, J. W. 1979. Oilseed phytates: Nutritional implications. *J. Am. Oil Chem. Soc.* 56: 736–41.

Esselen, W. B., and Davis, S. G. 1942. Dehydrated baked beans. *Canner* 95(20):18–20.

FAO. 1975. *Production Yearbook*, vol. 29. Rome: Food and Agriculture Organization.

FAO. 1988a. *Production Yearbook*. Rome: Food and Agriculture Organization.

FAO. 1988b. *Yearbook of Fishery Statistics*. Rome: Food and Agriculture Organization.

Felsted, R. L., Leavitt, R. D., Chen, C., Bachur, N. R., and Dale, R. M. K. 1981a. Phytohemagglutinin isolectin subunit composition. *Biochim. Biophys. Acta* 668:132–40.

Felsted, R. L., Li, J., Pokrywka, G., Egorin, M. J., Spiegel, J., and Dale, R. M. K. 1981b. Comparison of *Phaseolus vulgaris* cultivars on the basis of isolectin differences. *Int. J. Biochem.* 13:549–57.

Fennell, J. L. 1948. New cowpeas resistant to mildew. *J. Hered.* 39:275–9.

Fery, R. L. 1980. Genetics of *Vigna. Hort. Rev.* 2:311–94.

Fields, R. W., and King, T. H. 1962. Influence of storage fungi on deterioration of stored pea seed. *Phytopathology* 52:336–9.

Figarella, D., Negri, G. A. and Guy, O. 1974. Studies on inhibition of the two human trypsins. In *Proteinase Inhibitors,* ed. H. Fritz, H. Tschesche, L. S. Greene, and E. Truscheit, pp. 213–22. Berlin: Springer–Verlag.

Fischer, H. U., and Lockhart, B. E. 1978. Host range and properties of peanut stunt virus from Morocco. *Phytopathology* 68:289–93.

Foster, G. H., and Peart, R. M. 1976. Solar grain drying. *U.S. Dept. Agric. Inf. Bull. no. 401*, Washington, D.C.: USDA.

Fredericq, L. 1878. Sur la digestion des albuminoides chez quelques invertebres. *Bull. Acad. R. Sci. Lett. Beaux–Arts Belg.* 46:213–28.

Fries, J. H. 1971. Studies on the allergenicity of soy bean. *Ann. Allergy* 29:1–7.

Fukuhara, K., Murai, H., and Murao, S. 1982. Amylostatins, other amylase inhibitors produced by *Streptomyces diastaticus* subsp. *Amylostaticus* No. 2476. *Agric. Biol. Chem.* 46: 2021–30.

Fulton, J. P., Gomez, R., and Scott, H. A. 1975. Cowpea chlorotic mottle and bean yellow stipple viruses. *Phytopathology* 65:741–2.

Fulton, R. W. 1971. *Tobacco streak virus*. CMI/AAB Descriptions of Plant Viruses, no. 44. Kew: Commonwealth Mycological Institute and Association of Applied Biologists.

Gavrielit-Gelmond, H. 1970. Moisture content and storage of peanut seed. *Proc. Int. Seed Test. Assoc.* 36:159–71.

Gay, J. D. 1969. Effects of temperature and moisture on snap bean damping-off caused by three isolates of *Pythium myriotylum*. *Plant Dis. Rep.* 53:707–9.

Geervani, P., and Theophilus, F. 1980. Effect of home processing on the protein quality of selected legumes. *J. Food Sci.* 45:707–10.

Gennis, L. S., and Cantor, C. R. 1976. Double-headed protease inhibitors from black-eyed peas. *J. Bio. Chem.* 251:734–40.

Ghanekar, A. M. 1980. Groundnut virus research at ICRISAT. In *Proc. Int. Workshop on Groundnuts*, pp. 211–16. Hyderabad, India: International Crops Research Institute for the Semi-Arid Tropics.

Ghanekar, A. M., Reddy, D. V. R., Iizuka, N., Amin, P. W., and Gibbons, R. W. 1979. Bud necrosis of groundnut (*Arachis hypogaea*) in India caused by tomato spotted wilt virus. *Ann. Appl. Biol.* 93:173–9.

Gibbs, A., and Watson, L. 1980. Viruses and legumes. In *Advances in Legume Science,* ed. R. J. Summerfield and A. H. Bunting, pp. 235–41. Kew: Royal Botanic Gardens.

Gitzelmann, R. and Aurricchio, S. 1965. The handling of soy α-galactosides by a normal and galactosemic child. *Pediatrics* 36:231–5.

Goodman, R. M., and Bird, J. 1978. *Bean golden mosaic virus*. CMI/AAB Descriptions of Plant Viruses, no. 192. Kew: Commonwealth Mycological Institute and Association of Applied Biologists.

Grabe, D. F. 1965. Storage of soybean for seed. *Soybean Dig.* 26:14–16.

Griffiths, D. W. 1981. The polyphenolic content and enzyme inhibitory activity of testas from bean (*Vicia faba*) and pea (*Pisum* spp.) varieties. *J. Sci. Food Agric.* 32:797–804.

Grigg, D. B. 1974. *The Agricultural Systems of the World: An Evolutionary Approach.* Cambridge: Cambridge Univ. Press.

Groves, J. F. 1917. Temperature and life duration of seeds. *Bot. Gaz. (Chicago)* 63:169–89.

Gupta, K. S., and Wagle, D. S. 1980. Changes in antinutritional factors during germination in *Phaseolus mungoreus*, a cross between *Phaseolus mungo* and *Phaseolus aureus*. *J. Food Sci.* 45:394–5, 397.

Gupta, P. C. 1976. Viability of stored soybean seeds in India. *Seed Res.* 4:32–9.

Hackler, L. R. 1974. Nutritional qualities of dry beans and the potential for improvement. In *Proc. Bean Improvement Co-operative and National Dry Bean Research Association Conference*, ed. M. N. Dickson, p. 67. Geneva, N.Y.: New York Agric. Exp. Stn.

Haddad, N. I., Meuhlbauer, F. J., and Hampton, R. O. 1978. Inheritance of resistance to pea seed-borne mosaic virus in lentils. *Crop Sci.* 18:613–15.

Hafiz, A., and Ashraf, M. 1953. Studies on the inheritance of resistance to *Mycosphaerella* blight in gram. *Phytopathology* 43:580–1.

Hagedorn, D. J., and Inglis, D. A. 1986. *Handbook of Bean Diseases.* Madison: Univ. of Wisconsin Press.

Hagel, G. T., Silbernagel, M. J., and Burke, D. W. 1972. Resistance to aphids, mites and thrips in field beans relative to infection by aphid-borne viruses. *ARS-33-139.* Washington, D.C.: USDA.

Haglund, W. A., and Kraft, J. M. 1979. *Fusarium oxysporum* f. sp. *pisi*, Race 6. Occurrence and distribution. *Phytopathology* 69:818–20.

Hampton, R. O. 1975. The nature of bean yield reduction by bean yellow and bean common mosaic virus. *Phytopathology* 65:1342–6.

Hankins, C. N., and Shannon, L. M. 1978. The physical and enzymatic properties of a phytohemagglutinin from mung beans. *J. Biol. Chem.* 253:7791–7.

Hardy, R. W. F., and Havelka, V. D. 1975. Nitrogen fixation research: A key to world food? *Science* 188:633–43.

Harlan, J. R. 1976. Disease as a factor in plant evolution. *Annu. Rev. Phytopathol.* 14:31–51.

Harrington, J. F. 1960. Seed storage and seed packages. *Seed World* 87:4–6.

Harrison, B. J. 1966. Seed deterioration in relation to storage conditions and its influence upon germination, chromosomal damage and plant performance. *J. Nat. Inst. Agric. Bot. (Great Britain)* 10:644–63.

Harty, R. L. 1977. The influence of storage conditions on bean seed quality. *Queensl. Agric. J.* 103:534–5.

Hatchett, J. H., Beland, G. L., and Hartwig, E. E. 1976. Leaf feeding resistance to bollworm and tobacco budworm in three soybean plant introductions. *Crop Sci.* 16:277–80.

Haynes, R. J. 1980. Competitive aspects of the grass–legume association. *Adv. Agron.* 33:227–61.

Heichel, G. H. 1987. Legumes as a source of nitrogen in conservation tillage. In *Role of Legumes in Conservation Tillage,* ed. J. F. Power, pp. 29–34. Ankey, Iowa: Soil Conservation Soc. Am.

Hellendoorn, E. W. 1979. Beneficial physiological activity of leguminous seeds. *Qual. Plant. Plant Foods Hum. Nutr.* 29:227–44.

Hellriegel, H., and Wilfarth, H. 1888. *Untersuchungen über die Stickstoffnahrung der Gramineen und Leguminosen.* Addendum Z. Ver Rubenzucker: Ind. Dtsch. Reichs.

Helms, K., Grylls, N. E., and Purss, G. S. 1961. Peanut plants in Queensland infected with tomato spotted wilt virus. *Aust. J. Agric. Res.* 12:239–46.

Heringa, R. J., Van Norel, A., and Tazelaar, M. F. 1969. Resistance to powdery mildew (*Erysiphe polygoni* DC) in peas (*Pisum sativum* L.). *Euphytica* 18:163–9.

Hofsten, B. V. 1979. Legume sprouts as a source of protein and other nutrients. *J. Am. Oil Chem. Soc.* 56:382.

Horber, E. 1978. Resistance to pests of grain legumes in the U.S.A. In *Pests of Grain Legumes: Ecology and Control,* ed. S. R. Singh, H. F. van Emden, and T. A. Taylor, pp. 281–95. New York: Academic Press.

Hove, E. I., and King, S. 1979. Trypsin inhibitor contents of lupin seeds and other grain legumes. *N. Z. J. Agric. Res.* 22:41–2.

Howe, R. W. 1972. Insects attacking seeds during storage. In *Seed Biology,* vol. 3, ed. T. T. Kozlowski, pp. 247–301. New York: Academic Press.

Howell, R. W. 1963. Protein in the developing soybean cotyledons. *Proc. Seed Protein Conf.*, New Orleans, La., pp. 193–5.

Hoyt, G. D., and Hargrove, W. H. 1986. Legume cover crops for improving crops and soil management in the southern United States. *Hort. Sci.* 21:97–402.

Hutchinson, J. B. 1969. The evolutionary diversity of the pulses. *Proc. Nutr. Soc.* 29:49–55.

Huxley, P. A., and Maingu, Z. 1978. Use of a systematic spacing design as an aid to the study of intercropping: Some general considerations. *Exp. Agric.* 14:49–56.

IAEA. 1980. *Nuclear Techniques in the Development of Management Practices for Multiple Cropping Systems.* Vienna: International Atomic Energy Agency.

ICAR. 1970. *Pulse Crops of India.* New Delhi: Indian Council of Agricultural Research.

ICRISAT. 1977. *Annual Report 1976/77.* Hyderabad, India: International Crops Research Institute for the Semi-Arid Tropics.

ICRISAT. 1978. *A Report for 1977–78.* Hyderabad, India: International Crops Research Institute for the Semi-Arid Tropics.

Isely, D. 1982. Leguminosae and *Homo sapiens. Econ. Bot.* 36:46–70.

Iwaki, M., and Auzay, H. 1978. Virus diseases of mungbean in Indonesia. *Proc. 1st Int. Mungbean Symp.*, pp. 169–72. Taiwan: Asian Vegetable Research and Development Center.

Iyengar, A. K., and Kulkarni, P. R. 1977. Oligosaccharide levels of processed legumes. *J. Food Sci. Technol.* 14:222–3.

Iyer, V., Salunkhe, D. K., Sathe, S. K., and Rockland, L. B. 1980. Quick-cooking beans (*Phaseolus vulgaris* L.). II. Phytates, oligosaccharides and antienzymes. *Qual. Plant. Plant Foods Hum. Nutr.* 30:45–52.

Jaffe, W. G. 1950. The comparative biological value of some legumes of importance in the Venezuelan diet. *Arch. Venez. Nutr.* 1:107–26.

Jaffe, W. G. 1980. Hemagglutinins (lectins). In: *Toxic Constituents of Plant Foodstuffs,* ed. I. E. Liener, pp. 73–102. New York: Academic Press.

Jaffe, W. G., Moreno, R., and Wallis, V. 1973. Amylase inhibitors in legume seeds. *Nutr. Rep. Int.* 7:169–74.

James, E. 1967. Preservation of seed stocks. *Adv. Agron.* 19:87–106.

James, E., Bass, L. N., and Clark, D. C. 1967. Varietal differences in longevity of vegetable seeds and their response to various storage conditions. *Proc. Am. Soc. Hort. Sci.* 91:521–8.

James, W. C., and Teng, P. S. 1979. The quantification of production constraints associated with plant diseases. *Appl. Biol.* 4:201–67.

Janzen, D. H. 1969. Seed-eaters versus seed size, number, toxicity and dispersal. *Evolution* 23:1–27.

Janzen, D. H., Juster, H. B., and Liener, I. E. 1976. Insecticidal action of the phytohemagglutinin in black beans on a Bruchid beetle. *Science* 192:795–6.

Jaspers, E. M. J., and Bos, L. 1980. *Alfalfa mosaic virus.* CMI/AAB Descriptions of Plant Viruses, no. 229. Kew: Commonwealth Mycological Institute and Association of Applied Biologists.

Jones, M. G. K. 1985. Applications of genetic engineering to agriculture. In *Plant Genetic Engineering,* ed. J. H. Dodds, pp. 269–95. Cambridge: Cambridge Univ. Press.

Jones, P. M. B., and Boulter, D. 1983a. The cause of reduced cooking rate in *Phaseolus vulgaris* following adverse storage conditions. *J. Food Sci.* 48:623–6, 649.

Jones, P. M. B., and Boulter, D. 1983b. The analysis of development of hard bean during storage of black beans (*Phaseolus vulgaris* L.). *Qual. Plant. Plant Foods Hum. Nutr.* 48:623–30.

Joshi, A. B. 1957. Genetics of resistance to diseases and pests. *Indian J. Genet. Plant Breed.* 17:305–17.

Justice, O. L., and Bass, L. N. 1978. *Principles and Practices of Seed Storage.* Washington, D.C.: USDA.

Kadam, S. S., Adsule, R. N., and Salunkhe, D. K. 1989. Utilization. In *Handbook of World Food Legumes*, ed. D. K. Salunkhe and S. S. Kadam, pp. 271–310. Boca Raton: CRC Press.

Kadam, S. S., Salunkhe, D. K., and Kuo, C. Y. 1989. Harvesting and storage of legumes. In *Legumes: Chemistry, Technology and Human Nutrition*, ed. R. H. Matthews, pp. 22–49. New York: Marcel Dekker.

Kaiser, W. J., and Mossahebi, G. H. 1975. Studies with cowpea aphid-borne mosaic virus and its effect on cowpea in Iran. *FAO Plant Prot. Bull.* 23:33–9.

Kaiser, W. J., and Ramos, A. H. 1980. Occurrence of *Pseudomonas syringae* on bean and soybean in Kenya. *Plant Dis. Rep.* 64:593–5.

Kaiser, W. J., and Vakili, N. G. 1978. Insect transmission of pathogenic *Xanthomonas phaseoli, X. Phaseoli* f. sp. *vignicola* to bean and cowpea in Puerto Rico. *Phytopathology* 68: 1057–63.

Kakade, M. L., and Evans, R. J. 1965. Nutritive value of navy bean (*Phaseolus vulgaris*). *Br. J. Nutr.* 19:269–76.

Kakade, M. L., and Evans, R. J. 1966. Growth inhibition of rats fed raw navy beans (*Phaseolus vulgaris* L.). *J. Nutr.* 90:191–8.

Kamat, A. D., and Kulkarni, P. R. 1981. Dietary effect of non-starch polysaccharides of black gram (*Phaseolus mungo* L.). *J. Food Sci. Technol.* 18:216–17.

Kannaiyan, J., Ribeiro, O. K., Erwin, D. C., and Nene, Y. L. 1980. Phytophthora blight of pigeonpea in India. *Mycologia* 72:169–81.

Kassanis, B. 1970. *Tobacco necrosis virus.* CMI/AAB Descriptions of Plant Viruses, no. 14. Kew: Commonwealth Mycological Institute and Association of Applied Biologists.

Kassanis, B., and Varma, A. 1975. *Sunhemp mosaic virus.* CMI/AAB Descriptions of Plant Viruses, no. 153. Kew: Commonwealth Mycological Institute and Association of Applied Biologists.

Ketring, D. L. 1971. Physiology of oil seeds. IV. Response of initially high and low germinating Spanish-type peanut seed to three storage environments. *Agron. J.* 63:435–8.

Khan, M. A., Jacobsen, I., and Eggum, B. O. 1979. Nutritive value of some improved varieties of legumes. *J. Sci. Food Agric.* 30:395–400.

Kneen, E., and Sandstedt, R. M. 1946. Distribution and general properties of an amylase inhibitor in cereals. *Arch. Biochem. Biophys.* 9:235–49.

Kogan, J., Sell, D. K., Stinner, R. E., Bradley, J. R., and Kogan, M. 1978. The literature of arthropods associated with soybeans. 5. A bibliography of *Heliothis zea* (Boddie) and *H. virescens* (F.) (Lepidoptera: Noctuidae). INTSOY Series no. 17. Champaign: INTSOY.

Kogan, M. 1972. Feeding and nutrition of insects associated with soybeans. 2. Soybean resistance and host preference of the Mexican bean beetle *Epilachna varivestis. Ann. Entomol. Soc. Am.* 65:675–83.

Kon, S., and Sanshuck, D. W. 1981. Phytate content and its effect on cooking quality of beans. *J. Food Proc. Pres.* 5:169–78.

Konijn, A. M., Edelstein, S., and Guggenheim, K. 1972. Separation of a thyroid-active fraction from unheated soybean flour. *J. Sci. Food Agric.* 23:549–55.

Konijn, A. M., Gershon, B., and Guggenheim, K. 1973. Further purification and mode of action of a goitrogenic material from soybean flour. *J. Nutr.* 103:378–83.

Kumar, K. G., Venkataraman, L. V., Jaya, T. V., and Krishnamurthy, K. S. 1978. Cooking characteristics of some germinated legumes: Changes in phytins, Ca^{++}, Mg^{++} and pectins. *J. Food Sci.* 43:85–8.

Kunitz, M. 1945. Crystallization of a trypsin inhibitor from soybean. *Science* 101:668–9.

Kunitz, M. 1946. Crystalline soybean trypsin inhibitor. *J. Gen. Physiol.* 29:149–54.

Kurien, P. P., Desikachar, H. S. R., and Parpia, H. A. B. 1972. Processing and utilization of grain legumes in India. In *Tropical Agric. Res. Ser. no. 6*, pp. 225–36. Tokyo: Tropical Agriculture Research Center.

Kurien, P. P., and Parpia, H. A. B. 1968. Pulse milling in India. I. Processing and milling of tur, arhar (*Cajanus cajan* Linn.). *J. Food Sci. Technol.* 5:203–7.

Kylen, A. M., and McCready, R. M. 1975. Nutrients in seeds and sprouts of alfalfa, lentils, mung beans and soybeans. *J. Food Sci.* 40:1008–9.

Lakshaman, J., and Padmanabhan, G. 1974. Effect of β-N-oxalyl-L-α,β-diaminopropionic acid on glutamate uptake by synaptosomes. *Nature* 249:469–70.

Lalithakumari, D., Govidaswamy, G. V., and Vidhyasekaran, P. 1972. Isolation of seed borne fungi from stored groundnut seeds and their role in seed spoilage. *Madras Agric. J.* 59:1–6.

LaRue, T. A., and Patterson, T. G. 1981. How much nitrogen do legumes fix? *Adv. Agron.* 34:15–38.

Laskowski, M., and Kato, I. 1980. Protein inhibitors of proteinases. *Annu. Rev. Biochem.* 49:593–626.

Laundon, G. F., and Waterson, J. M. 1965b. *Uromyces appendiculatus.* CMI Descriptions of Pathogenic Fungi and Bacteria, no. 57. Kew: Commonwealth Mycological Institute.

Laundon, G. F., and Waterson, J. M. 1965a. *Puccinia arachidis.* CMI Descriptions of Pathogenic Fungi and Bacteria, no. 53. Kew: Commonwealth Mycological Institute.

Laurena, A. C., Van Den, T., and Mendoza, E. M. T. 1984. Effects of condensed tannins on the *in vitro* protein digestibility of cowpeas (*Vigna unguiculata* L. Walp.). *J. Agric. Food Chem.* 32:1045–8.

Laviolette, F. A., Athow, K. L., Probst, A. H., and Wilcox, J. R. 1970. Effect of bacterial pustule on yield of soybeans. *Crop Sci.* 10:150–1.

Lawn, R. J., and Russell, J. S. 1978. Mungbeans: A grain legume for summer rainfall cropping areas of Australia. *J. Aust. Inst. Agric. Sci.* 44:28–41.

Leonard, K. J. 1969. Factors affecting rates of stem rust increase in mixed plantings of susceptible and resistant oat varieties. *Phytopathology* 59:1845–50.

Leppik, E. E. 1970. Gene centers of plants as sources of disease resistance. *Annu. Rev. Phytopathol.* 8:323–44.

Liener, I. E. 1951. The intraperitoneal toxicity of concentrates of soybean trypsin inhibitor. *J. Biol. Chem.* 193:183–91.

Liener, I. E. 1976a. Phytohemagglutinins (Phytolectins). *Annu. Rev. Plant Physiol.* 27:291–319.

Liener, I. E. 1976b. Legume toxins in relation to protein digestibility: A review. *J. Food Sci.* 41:1076–81.

Liener, I. E. 1983. Toxic constituents in legumes. In *Chemistry and Biochemistry of Legumes,* ed. S. K. Arora, pp. 217–57. London: Edward Arnold.

Liener, I. E., and Kakade, M. L. 1980. Protease inhibitors. In *Toxic Constituents of Plant Foodstuffs,* ed. I. E. Liener, pp. 7–71. New York: Academic Press.

Lis, H., and Sharon, N. 1973. The biochemistry of plant lectins (phytohemagglutinins). *Annu. Rev. Biochem.* 42:541–74.

Lolas, G. M., and Markakis, P. 1975. Phytic acid and other phosphorus compounds of beans (*Phaseolus vulgaris* L.). *J. Agric. Food Chem.* 23:13–15.

Lolas, G. M., Palamidis, N., and Markakis, P. 1976. The phytic acid–total phosphorus relationship in barley, oats, soybeans and wheat. *Cereal Chem.* 53:867–71.

McDonald, D. 1969. Groundnut pod diseases. *Rev. Appl. Mycol.* 48:465–74.

McGuire, D. C., Allard, R. W., and Harding, A. J. 1961. Inheritance of root-knot nematode resistance in lima beans. *Proc. Am. Soc. Hort. Sci.* 78:302–7.

Maddaiah, V. T., Kurnick, A. A., and Reid, B. L. 1964. Phytic acid studies. *Proc. Soc. Exp. Biol. Med.* 115:391–3.

Mager, L., Glaser, G., Razin, A., Izak, G., Bien, S., and Noam, M. 1965. Metabolic effects of pyrimidines derived from fava bean glycosides on human erythrocytes deficient in glucose-6-phosphate dehydrogenase. *Biochem. Biophys. Res. Commun.* 20:235–40.

Markkula, M., and Roukka, K. 1971. Resistance of plants to the pea aphid *Acyrthosiphon pisum* Harris (Hom. Aphididae). III. Fecundity on different pea varieties. *Ann. Agric. Fenn.* 10:33–7.

Marshall, J. J., and Lauda, C. M. 1975. Purification and properties of phaseolamin, an inhibitor of α–amylase from the kidney bean, *Phaseolus vulgaris*. *J. Biol. Chem.* 250:8030–7.

Matthews, R. H. 1989. *Legumes: Chemistry, Technology and Human Nutrition.* New York: Marcel Dekker.

Mattson, S. 1946. The cookability of yellow peas. *Acta Agric. Suec.* 2:185–231.

Meiners, C. R., Derise, N. L., Lau, H. C., Ritchey, S. J., and Murphy, E. W. 1976a. Proximate composition and yield of raw and cooked mature dry legumes. *J. Agric. Food Chem.* 24:1122–6.

Meiners, C. R., Derise, N. L., Lau, H. C., Ritchey, S. J., and Murphy, E. W. 1976b. The content of nine mineral elements in raw and cooked mature dry legumes. *J. Agric. Food Chem.* 24:1126–30.

Milner, M., and Geddes, W. F. 1946. Grain storage studies. II. The effect of aeration, temperature and time on the respiration of soybeans containing excessive moisture. *Cereal Chem.* 22:484–501.

Misra, D. P., and Mehra, R. C. S. 1969. *Choanephora cucurbitarum* on *Cajanus cajan* in India. *Indian Phytopathol.* 22:515–17.

Mitchell, H. H., and Beadles, J. R. 1949. Effect of storage on the nutritional qualities of the proteins of wheat, soy, and soybeans. *J. Nutr.* 39:463–84.

Mode, C. J. 1958. A mathematical model for the co-evolution of obligate parasites and their hosts. *Evolution* 12:158–65.

Mohta, N. K., and De, R. 1980. Intercropping maize and sorghum with soyabeans. *J. Agric. Sci.* 95:117–22.

Montgomery, R. D. 1964. Observations on the cyanide content and toxicity of tropical pulses. *W. Indian Med. J.* 13:1–11.

Moore, B. J., and Scott, H. A. 1981. *Quail pea mosaic virus.* CMI/AAB Descriptions of Plant Viruses, no. 238. Kew: Commonwealth Mycological Institute and Association of Applied Biologists.

Mordue, J. E. M. 1971. *Colletotrichum lindemuthianum.* CMI Descriptions of Pathogenic Fungi and Bacteria, no. 316. Kew: Commonwealth Mycological Institute.

Mordue, J. E. M. 1974a. *Thanatephorus cucumeris.* CMI Descriptions of Pathogenic Fungi and Bacteria, no. 406. Kew: Commonwealth Mycological Institute.

Mordue, J. E. M. 1974b. *Corticium rolfsii.* CMI Descriptions of Pathogenic Fungi and Bacteria, no. 410. Kew: Commonwealth Mycological Institute.

Moreno, R. 1975. Diseminacion de *Ascochyta phaseolorum* en variedades de frijol de costa bajo diferentes sistemas de cultivo. *Turrialba* 25:361–4.

Moreno, R. 1979. Crop protection implications of cassava intercropping. In *Intercropping with Cassava*, ed. E. Weber, B. Nestel, and M. Campbell, pp. 113–27. Ottawa: IDRC.

Mossor, G., Skupin, J., and Romanowska, B. 1984. Plant inhibitors of proteolytic enzymes. *Nahrung* 1:93–112.

Mukerji, K. G. 1968. *Levillula taurica*. CMI Descriptions of Pathogenic Fungi and Bacteria, no. 182. Kew: Commonwealth Mycological Institute.

Mulder, J. L., and Holliday, P. 1975. *Cercospora canescens*. CMI Descriptions of Pathogenic Fungi and Bacteria, no. 462. Kew: Commonwealth Mycological Institute.

Murphy, E. L., Kon, S., and Seifert, R. M. 1964. The preparation of bland, non-flatulent high protein concentrates from dry beans. In *Proc. 7th Annu. Res. Conf. on Dry Beans*, p. 63. Washington, D.C.: USDA.

Narasimha, H. V., and Desikachar, H. S. R. 1978. Simple procedures for reducing the cooking time of split red gram (*Cajanus cajan*). *J. Food Sci. Technol.* 15:149–51.

NAS. 1978. *Post-harvest Food Losses in Developing Countries*. Washington, D.C.: National Academy of Sciences.

NAS. 1979. *Tropical Legumes: Resources for the Future*. Washington, D.C.: National Academy of Sciences.

Nene, Y. L. 1972. *A Survey of Viral Diseases of Pulse Crops in Uttar Pradesh*. Pantnagar, India: G. B. Pant Univ. Agric. Technol.

Nene, Y. L. 1978. *Pulse Pathology Progress, Report 3*. Hyderabad, India: International Crops Research Institute for the Semi-Arid Tropics.

Nene, Y. L., Haware, M. P., and Reddy, M. V. 1979. *Diagnosis of Some Wilt-like Disorders of Chickpea (Cicer arietinum L.)*. ICRISAT Info. Bull. no. 3. Hyderabad, India: International Crops Research Institute for the Semi-Arid Tropics.

Newsom, L. D. 1978. Progress in integrated pest management of soybean pests. In *Pest Control Strategies*, ed. E. H. Smith and D. Pimentel, pp. 157–80. New York: Academic Press.

Noor, M. I., Bressani, R., and Elias, L. G. 1980. Changes in chemical and selected biochemical components, protein quality and digestibility of mung bean (*Vigna radiata*) during germination and cooking. *Qual. Plant. Plant Foods. Hum. Nutr.* 30:135–44.

Norioka, S., and Ikenaka, T. 1983. Amino acid sequences of trypsin–chymotrypsin inhibitors (A-I, A-II, B-I and B-II) from peanut (*Arachis hypogaea*): A discussion on the molecular evolution of legume Bowman–Birk type inhibitors. *J. Biochem.* 94:589–92.

Nowacki, E. 1980. Heat stable antinutritional factors in leguminous plants. In *Advances in Legume Science*, ed. R. J. Summerfield and A. H. Bunting, pp. 171–8. Kew (England): Royal Botanic Gardens.

Nwanze, K. F., Horber, E., and Pitts, C. W. 1975. Evidence for ovipositional preference of *Callosobruchus maculatus* for cowpea varieties. *Environ. Entomol.* 4:409–12.

O'Dell, B. L., and de Boland, A. 1976. Complexation of phytate with proteins and cations in corn germ and oilseed meals. *J. Agric. Food Chem.* 24:804–8.

Oberleas, D. M. 1973. Phytates. In *Toxicants Occurring Naturally in Foods*, pp. 363–71. Washington, D.C.: National Academy of Sciences.

Odani, S., and Ikenaka, T. 1972. Studies on soybean trypsin inhibitors. IV. Complete amino acid sequence and the anti-proteinase sites of Bowman–Birk soybean proteinase inhibitor. *J. Biochem.* 71:839–48.

Ofori, F., and Stern, W. R. 1987. Relative sowing time and density of component crops in a maize–cowpea intercrop system. *Exp. Agric.* 23:41–52.

Ologhobo, A. D., and Fetuga, B. L. 1982. Polyphenols, phytic acid and other phosphorus compounds of lima beans (*Phaseolus lunatus*). *Nutr. Rep. Int.* 26:605–11.

Olson, A. C., Becker, R., Miers, J. C., Gumbmann, M. R., and Wagner, J. R. 1975. Problems in the digestibility of dry beans. In *Protein Nutritional Quality of Foods and Feeds*, Part II, ed. M. Friedman, pp. 551–63. New York: Marcel Dekker.

Onesirosan, P. T. 1983. Effect of moisture content and temperature on the invasion of cowpeas by storage fungi. *Seed Sci. Technol.* 10:619–29.

Onuorah, P. E. 1973. *Pythium* seed decay and stem rot of cowpea (*Vigna sinensis* (Linn.) Savi) in southern Nigeria. *Plant Soil* 39:187–91.

Pace, W., Parlamenti, R., Urrab, A., Silano, V., and Vittozzi, L. 1978. Protein α–amylase inhibitors from wheat flour. *Cereal Chem.* 55:244–54.

Pandey, R. K., and Pendleton, J. W. 1986. Soybeans as green manure in a maize intercropping system. *Exp. Agric.* 22:179–85.

Parpia, H. A. B. 1973. Utilization problems in food legumes. In *Nutritional Improvement of Legumes by Breeding*, ed. M. Milner, pp. 281–95. New York: United Nations Organization.

Patel, M. K., Dhonde, G. W., and Kulkarni, Y. S. 1953. Bacterial leaf spot of *Cyamopsis tetragonoloba* (L.) Taub. *Curr. Sci. (Bangalore)* 22:183.

Patel, P. N., and Jindal, J. K. 1972. Occurrence of bacterial blight disease on moth bean (*Phaseolus aconitifolius*) in India. *Indian Phytopathol.* 25:464–6.

Pathak, M. M., Singh, K. P., and Lal, S. B. 1975. Inheritance of resistance to wilt (*Fusarium oxysporum* f. *ciceri*) in gram. *Indian J. Farm Sci.* 3:10–11.

Perlman, F. 1980. Allergens. In *Toxic Constituents of Plant Foodstuffs*, ed. I. E. Liener, pp. 295–327. New York: Academic Press.

Phatak, H. C. 1974. Seed-borne plant viruses—identification and diagnosis in seed health testing. *Seed Sci. Technol.* 2:22–39.

Pingale, S. V. 1976. *Storage and Handling of Food Grains*. New Delhi: Indian Council of Agriculture Research.

Poats, F. J. 1960. Guar, a summer row crop for the South West. *Econ. Bot.* 14:241–6.

Powell, A. A., and Matthews, S. 1977. The deterioration of pea seeds in humid or dry storage. *J. Exp. Bot.* 28:227–36.

Powell, A. A., Matthews, S., and Oliveira, M. de A. 1984. Seed quality in grain legumes. *Adv. Appl. Biol.* 10:217–85.

Power, J. F. 1987. *Role of Legumes in Conservation Tillage*. Ankey, Iowa: Soil Conservation Soc. Am.

Power, J. F., and Papendick, R. I. 1985. Organic sources of nutrients. In *Fertilizer Technology and Use*, ed. O. P. Engelstad, pp. 503–20. Madison: Soil Sci. Soc. Am.

Powers, J. R., and Whitaker, J. R. 1977a. Purification and some physical and chemical properties of red kidney bean (*Phaseolus vulgaris*) α-amylase inhibitor. *J. Food Biochem.* 1: 217–38.

Powers, J. R., and Whitaker, J. R. 1977b. Effect of several experimental parameters on combination of red kidney bean (*Phaseolus vulgaris*) α-amylase inhibitor with porcine pancreatic α-amylase. *J. Food Biochem.* 1:239–60.

Price, K. R., Johnson, I. T., and Fenwick, G. R. 1987. The chemistry and biological significance of saponins in foods and feeding stuffs. *CRC Crit. Rev. Food Sci. Nutr.* 26:27–135.

Price, M. L., Hagerman, A. E., and Butler, L. G. 1980. Tannin content of cowpeas, chickpeas, pigeon peas, and mung beans. *J. Agric. Food Chem.* 28:459–61.

Price, T. V. 1976. Diseases of the winged bean in Papua New Guinea. *Aust. Plant Pathol. Soc. Newsl.* 5:209 (Abstr.).

Price, T. V., and Monroe, P. E. 1978. Fungi associated with collar rot of winged bean in Papua New Guinea. *PANS* 24:53–6.

Puls, W., and Keup, N. 1973. Influence of an α-amylase inhibitor (BAY d7791) on blood glucose, serum insulin and NEFA in starch loading test in rats, dog, and man. *Diabetologia* 9:97–101.

Punithalingam, E., and Holliday, P. 1972a. *Diaporthe phaseolorum*. CMI Descriptions of Pathogenic Fungi and Bacteria, no. 336. Kew: Commonwealth Mycological Institute.

Punithalingam, E., and Holliday, P. 1972b. *Ascochyta rabiei*. CMI Descriptions of Pathogenic Fungi and Bacteria, no. 337. Kew: Commonwealth Mycological Institute.

Punithalingam, E., and Holliday, P. 1972c. *Septoria glycines*. CMI Descriptions of Pathogenic Fungi and Bacteria, no. 339. Kew: Commonwealth Mycological Institute.

Purss, G. S. 1961. Wilt of peanut (*Arachis hypogaea* L.) in Queensland, with particular reference to *Verticillium* wilt. *Queensl. J. Agric. Sci.* 18:453–62.

Pusztai, A., and Watt, W. B. 1974. Isolectins of *Phaseolus vulgaris*. A comprehensive study of fractionation. *Biochim. Biophys. Acta* 365:57–71.

Quast, D. C., and de Silva, S. D. 1977. Temperature dependence of the cooking rate of dry legumes. *J. Food Sci.* 42:1299–303.

Rackis, J. J. 1975. Oligosaccharides of food legumes: Alpha-galactosidase activity and the flatus problem. In *Physiological Effects of Food Carbohydrates,* ed. A. Jeans and J. Hodge, pp. 207–22. Washington, D.C.: Am. Chem. Soc.

Rackis, J. J., Wolf, W. J., and Baker, E. C. 1986. Protease inhibitors in plant foods: Content and inactivation. In *Nutritional and Toxicological Significance of Enzyme Inhibitors in Foods*, ed. M. Friedman, pp. 207–22. New York: Plenum Press.

Raina, A. K. 1971. Comparative resistance to three species of *Callosobruchus* in a strain of chickpea (*Cicer arietinum* L.). *J. Stored Prod. Res.* 7:213–16.

Ramakrishnan, C. V. 1979. Studies of Indian fermented foods. *Baroda J. Nutr.* 6:1–57.

Rao, B. S. N., and Prabhavati, T. 1982. Tannin content of foods commonly consumed in India and its influence on ionisable iron. *J. Sci. Food Agric.* 33:89–96.

Rao, P. G., and Deosthale, Y. G. 1982. Tannin content of pulses: Varietal differences and effects of germination and cooking. *J. Sci. Food Agric.* 33:1013–16.

Rao, P. U., and Belavady, B. 1978. Oligosaccharides in pulses: Varietal differences and effects of cooking and germination. *J. Agric. Food Chem.* 26:316–19.

Rao, R. G. 1974. Effect of heat on the proteins of groundnut and bengal gram. *Indian J. Nutr. Diet.* 11:268–75.

Read, J. W., and Haas, L. W. 1938. Studies on the baking quality of flour as affected by certain enzyme actions. II. Further studies concerning potassium bromate and enzyme activity. *Cereal Chem.* 15:59–68.

Reddy, K. A., Reddy, K. R., and Reddy, M. D. 1980. Effects of intercropping on yield and returns in corn and sorghum. *Exp. Agric.* 16:179–84.

Reddy, M. S., and Willey, R. W. 1981. Growth and resource use studies in an intercrop of pearl millet/groundnut. *Field Crops Res.* 4:13–24.

Reddy, N. R., and Salunkhe, D. K. 1980. Changes in oligosaccharides during germination and cooking of black gram and fermentation of black gram/rice blend. *Cereal Chem.* 57: 356–60.

Reddy, N. R., Balakrishnan, C. V., and Salunkhe, D. K. 1978. Phytate phosphorus and mineral changes during germination and cooking of black gram (*Phaseolus mungo*) seeds. *J. Food Sci.* 43:540–3.

Reddy, N. R., Pierson, M. D., Sathe, S. K., and Salunkhe, D. K. 1982. Legume-based fermented foods: Their preparation and nutritional quality. *CRC Crit. Rev. Food Sci. Nutr.* 17:335–70.

Reddy, N. R., Pierson, M. D., Sathe, S. K., and Salunkhe, D. K. 1984. Chemical, nutritional and physiological aspects of dry bean carbohydrates: A review. *Food Chem.* 13:25–68.

Rees, D. J. 1986. Crop growth, development and yield in semi-arid conditions in Botswana. II. The effects of intercropping *Sorghum bicolor* with *Vigna unguiculata. Exp. Agric.* 22: 169–77.

Regupathy, A., and Rathnaswamy, R. 1970. Studies on comparative susceptibility of seeds of certain redgram (*Cajanus cajan* (L.) Millsp.) varieties to the pulse beetle, *Callosobruchus chinensis* L. (Bruchidae: Coleoptera). *Madras Agric. J.* 57:106–9.

Remison, S. U. 1978. Neighbour effects between maize and cowpea at various levels of N and P. *Exp. Agric.* 14:205–12.

Renfrew, J. M. 1966. A report on recent finds of carbonized cereal grains and seeds from prehistoric Thessaly. *Thessalika* 5:21–31.

Rhoades, H. L. 1976. Effect of Indigofera hirsuta on *Belonolaimus longicaudatus, Meloidogyne incognita* and *M. javanica* and subsequent crop yields. *Plant Dis. Rep.* 60:384–6.

Roberts, E. H. 1972. Storage environment and the control of viability. In *Viability of Seeds,* ed. E. H. Roberts, pp. 14–58. London: Chapman and Hall.

Roberts, E. H., and Abdalla, F. H. 1968. The influence of temperature, moisture and oxygen on period of seed viability in barley, broad beans and peas. *Ann. Bot. (London) (n.s.)* 32: 92–117.

Roberts, E. H., and Roberts, D. L. 1972. Viability nomographs. In *Viability of Seeds,* ed. E. H. Roberts, pp. 417–23. London: Chapman and Hall.

Robinson, R. J., and Kao, C. 1974. Fermented food from chickpeas, horse beans and soybeans. *Cereal Sci. Today* 19:397.

Rockland, L. B. 1978. Relationship between fine structure and composition and development of new food products from legumes. In *Postharvest Biology and Biotechnology*, ed. H. O. Hultin and M. Milner, pp. 289–316. Westport: Food and Nutrition Press.

Rockland, L. B., and Jones, F. T. 1974. Scanning electron microscope studies: Effects of cooking on the cellular structure of cotyledons in rehydrated large lima beans. *J. Food Sci.* 39:342–6.

Rockland, L. B., and Hahn, D. M. 1977. Quick-cooking grain legumes: An alternative food processing technology. Paper presented at FAO/UN Expert Consultation of Grain Legume Processing, 14–18 November 1977, at Central Food Technol. Res. Inst., Mysore, India.

Rockland, L. B., Hahn, D. M., and Zaragosa, E. M. 1977. Frozen quick-cooking beans prepared from dry beans. *Food Prod. Dev.* 11(3):34–40.

Rockland, L. B., and Metzler, E. A. 1967. Quick-cooking lima and other dry beans. *Food Technol.* 21:344–9.

Rockland, L. B., and Nishi, S. K. 1979. Tropical grain legumes. In *Tropical Foods,* vol. II, ed. G. E. Inglett, pp. 547–74. New York: Academic Press.

Rockland, L. B., Wolf, W. R., Hahn, D. M., and Young, R. 1979. Estimated zinc and copper in raw and cooked legumes. *J. Food Sci.* 44:1711–13, 1719.

Rockland, L. B., Zaragosa, E. M., and Hahn, D. M. 1974. New information on the chemical, physical, and biological properties of dry beans. In *Proc. Bean Improvement Cooperative and National Dry Bean Res. Assoc. Conf.*, ed. M. H. Dickson, pp. 77–82. Geneva, N.Y.: New York Agric. Exp. Stn.

Rossell, H. W. 1977. Preliminary investigations on the identity and ecology of legume virus diseases in Northern Nigeria. *Trop. Grain Legume Bull.* 8:41–6.

Sabet, K. A., Ishag, F., and Khalil, O. 1969. Studies on the bacterial diseases of Sudan crops. VII. New records. *Ann. Appl. Biol.* 63:357–69.

Salunkhe, D. K. 1983. Legumes in human nutrition: Current status and future research needs. *Curr. Sci. (Bangalore)* 51:387–94.

Salunkhe, D. K., Chavan, J. K., and Kadam, S. S. 1985. *Postharvest Biotechnology of Cereals*. Boca Raton: CRC Press.

Salunkhe, D. K., Iyer, V., and Deshpande, S. S. 1989. Other methods of processing. In *Handbook of World Food Legumes*, ed. D. K. Salunkhe and S. S. Kadam, pp. 237–48. Boca Raton: CRC Press.

Salunkhe, D. K., Jadhav, S. J., Kadam, S. S., and Chavan, J. K. 1982. Chemical, biochemical, and biological significance of polyphenols in cereals and legumes. *CRC Crit. Rev. Food Sci. Nutr.* 17:277–305.

Salunkhe, D. K., Kadam, S. S., and Chavan, J. K. 1985. *Postharvest Biotechnology of Food Legumes.* Boca Raton: CRC Press.

Salunkhe, D. K., Sathe, S. K., and Reddy, N. R. 1982. Legume lipids. In *Chemistry and Biochemistry of Legumes,* ed. S. K. Arora, pp. 51–109. New Delhi: India Book House.

Sathe, S. K., and Salunkhe, D. K. 1981. Studies on trypsin and chymotrypsin inhibitory activities, hemagglutinating activity and sugars in the Great Northern bean (*Phaseolus vulgaris* L.). *J. Food Sci.* 46:626–9.

Sathe, S. K., and Salunkhe, D. K. 1984. Technology of removal of unwanted components of dry beans. *CRC Crit. Rev. Food Sci. Nutr.* 21:263–87.

Satwadhar, P. N., Kadam, S. S., and Salunkhe, D. K. 1981. Effects of germination and cooking on polyphenols and *in vitro* protein digestibility of moth bean and horse gram. *Qual. Plant. Plant Foods. Hum. Nutr.* 31:71–6.

Saunders, R. M. 1975. α–Amylase inhibitors in wheat and other cereals. *Cereal Foods World* 20:282–5.

Savaiano, D. A., Powers, J. R., Castello, M. J., Whitaker, J. R., and Clifford, A. J. 1977. The effect of an α–amylase inhibitor on the growth rate of weanling rats. *Nutr. Rep. Int.* 15:443–9.

Schalk, J. M., Evans, K. H., and Kaiser, W. J. 1973. Resistance in lines of chickpeas to attack by *Callosobruchus maculatus* in Iran. *Plant Prot. Bull. FAO* 21:126–31.

Schwartz, H. F., and Galvez, G. E. 1980. *Bean Production Problems: Disease, Insect, Soil and Climatic Constraints of Phaseolus vulgaris.* Cali, Colombia: Centro Internacional de Agricultura Tropical.

Scott, H. A., and Hoy, J. W. 1981. *Blackgram mottle virus.* CMI/AAB Descriptions of Plant Viruses, no. 237. Kew: Commonwealth Mycological Institute and Association of Applied Biologists.

Searle, P. G. E., Comudom, Y., Shedden, D. C., and Nance, R. A. 1981. Effect of maize and legume intercropping systems and fertilizer nitrogen on crop yields and residual nitrogen. *Field Crops Res.* 4:133–45.

Sgarbieri, V. C., and Whitaker, J. R. 1982. Physical, chemical and nutritional properties of common bean (*Phaseolus*) proteins. *Adv. Food Res.* 28:94–166.

Sgarbieri, V. C., Antunes, P. L., and Almeida, C. D. 1979. Nutritional evaluation of four varieties of dry beans (*Phaseolus vulgaris*). *J. Food Sci.* 44:1306–8.

Shallenberger, R. S. 1974. Occurrence of various sugars in foods. In *Sugars in Nutrition*, ed. H. L. Sipple and K. W. McNutt, pp. 67–80. New York: Academic Press.

Shepard, M., Carner, G. R., and Turnipseed, S. G. 1977. Colonization and resurgence of insect pests of soybeans in response to insecticides and field isolation. *Environ. Entomol.* 6: 501–6.

Shepard, M., Lawn, R. J., and Schneider, M. A. 1983. *Insects on Grain Legumes in Northern Australia.* Queensland: University of Queensland Press.

Sholberg, P. L., and Muir, W. E. 1979. Effect of heat treatment on the viability of faba beans. *Can. Agric. Eng.* 21:123–4.

Siegel, A., and Fawcett, B. 1976. *Food Legume Processing and Utilization.* Ottawa: IDRC.

Sijbring, P. H. 1963. Results of some storage experiments under controlled conditions (agricultural seeds). *Proc. Int. Seed Test. Assoc.* 28:845–51.

Silva, H. C., and Luh, B. S. 1979. Changes in oligosaccharides and starch granules in germinating beans. *Can. Inst. Food Sci. Technol. J.* 12:103–7.

Sinclair, J. B. 1977. Infectious soybean diseases of world importance. *PANS* 23:49–57.

Sinclair, J. B., and Shurtleff, M. C. 1975. *Compendium of Soybean Diseases.* St. Paul: American Phytopathology Society.

Singh, M., and Krikorian, A. D. 1982. Inhibition of trypsin activity *in vitro* by phytate. *J. Agric. Food Chem.* 30:799–800.

Singh, P. J., and Mehrotra, R. S. 1980. Relation between seed exudate and host-susceptibility in gram (*Cicer arietinum* L.) to *Rhizoctonia bataticola. Plant Soil* 56:265–71.

Singh, S. P. 1981. Studies on spatial arrangement in sorghum–legume intercropping systems. *J. Agric. Sci.* 97:655–61.

Singh, S. P. 1983. Summer legume intercrop effects on yield and nitrogen economy of wheat in the succeeding season. *J. Agric. Sci.* 101:401–5.

Singh, S. R., and Allen, D. J. 1980. Pests, diseases, resistance and protection in cowpeas. In *Advances in Legumes Science,* ed. R. J. Summerfield and A. H. Bunting, pp. 419–43. Kew: Royal Botanic Gardens.

Singh, S. R., van Emden, H. F., and Taylor, T. A. 1978. *Pests of Grain Legumes: Ecology and Control.* New York: Academic Press.

Singleton, V. L. 1981. Naturally occurring food toxicants: Phenolic substances of plant origin common in foods. *Adv. Food Res.* 27:149–242.

Singleton, V. L., and Kratzer, F. H. 1969. Toxicity and related physiological activity of phenolic substances of plant origin. *J. Agric. Food Chem.* 17:497–512.

Sittiyos, P., Poehlman, J. M., and Sehgal, O. P. 1979. Inheritance of resistance to cucumber mosaic virus infection in mung bean. *Crop Sci.* 19:51–3.

Sivanesan, A., and Holliday, P. 1971. *Elsinoe phaseoli.* CMI Descriptions of Pathogenic Fungi and Bacteria, no. 314. Kew: Commonwealth Mycological Institute.

Smartt, J. 1976. *Tropical Pulses.* London: Longman.

Smartt, J., and Hymowitz, T. 1985. Domestication and evolution of grain legumes. In *Grain Legume Crops,* ed. R. J. Summerfield and E. N. Roberts, pp. 37–72. London: Collins.

Smirnoff, P., Khalef, S., Birk, Y., and Applebaum, S. W. 1979. Trypsin and chymotrypsin inhibitor from chickpeas. *Int. J. Peptide Prot. Res.* 14:186–92.

Soni, G. L., Singh, T. P., and Singh, R. 1978. Comparative studies on the effects of certain treatments on the antitryptic activity of the common Indian pulses. *Indian J. Nutr. Diet.* 15:341–5.

Sosulski, F. W. 1983. Legume protein concentration by air classification. In *Developments in Food Protein,* vol. 2, ed. B. J. F. Hudson, pp. 173–213. London: Appl. Sci. Publ.

Sreenivasan, V., Mougdal, N. R., and Sharma, P. S. 1957. Goitrogenic agents in food. I. Goitrogenic action of groundnut. *J. Nutr.* 61:87–96.

Srivastava, A. K. 1975. Physiological studies on soybean seed viability during storage and its practical applicability. *Seed Res.* 4:56–61.

Steggerda, F. A. 1968. Gastrointestinal gas following food consumption. *Ann. N.Y. Acad. Sci.* 150:57–66.

Steggerda, F. R., Richards, E. R., and Rackis, J. J. 1966. Effects of various soybean products on flatulence in the adult man. *Proc. Soc. Exp. Biol. Med.* 121:1235–9.

Steiner, K. G. 1975. *Les Maladies des Plantes au Togo, Liste Commentée des Hôtes.* Rome: Service de la Protection des Vegetaux.

Steinswat, W., Pollard, L. H., and Anderson, J. L. 1967. Inheritance of resistance to a *Rhizoctonia*-induced stem rot of lima beans. *Phytopathology* 57:102 (Abstr.)

Stevens, F. C., Wuerz, S., and Krahn, J. 1974. Structure–function relationships in lima bean protease inhibitor. In *Proteinase Inhibitors*, ed. H. Fritz, H. Tschesche, L. J. Greene, and E. Truscheit, pp. 344–54. Berlin: Springer–Verlag.

Stewart, W. D. 1966. *Nitrogen Fixation in Plants*. London: Athlone.

Subbarao, P. V., Ananthachar, T. K., and Desikachar, H. S. R. 1964. Effects of certain chemicals and pressure on cookability. *Indian J. Technol.* 2:417–19.

Sulladmath, V. V., Shivshankar, G., Anilkumar, T. B., and Veerapppa, K. B. 1977. Inheritance of resistance to bacterial leaf spot in *Dolichos* crosses. *Indian J. Genet. Plant Breed.* 37:101–2.

Summerfield, R. J., and Bunting, A. H. 1980. *Advances in Legume Science*. Kew: Royal Botanic Gardens.

Tabekhia, M. M., and Luh, B. S. 1980. Effect of germination, cooking and canning on phosphorus and phytate retention in dry beans. *J. Food Sci.* 45:406–8.

Tadesse, K., and Eastwood, M. A. 1978. Metabolism of dietary fiber component in man assessed by breath hydrogen. *Brit. J. Nutr.* 40:393–6.

Tamada, T., and Kojima, M. 1977. *Soybean dwarf virus*. CMI/AAB Descriptions of Plant Viruses, no. 179. Kew: Commonwealth Mycological Institute and Association of Applied Biologists.

Tamir, M., and Alumot, E. 1969. Inhibition of digestive enzymes by condensed tannins from green and ripe carobs. *J. Sci. Food Agric.* 20:199–202.

Tan, N. H., Rahim, Z. H. A., Khor, H. T., and Wong, K. C. 1983. Winged bean (*Psophocarpus tetragonolobus*) tannin level, phytate content, and hemagglutinating activity. *J. Agric. Food Chem.* 31:916–17.

Taubert, P. 1891–4. Leguminosae. In *Die Naturlichen Pflanzenfamilien*, vol. III, ed. A. Engler and K. Prantl, pp. 70–396. Berlin: W. Engleman.

Taylor, D. P. 1976. Plant nematology problems in tropical Africa. *Helms. Abstr. B* 45:269–84.

Teakle, R. E. 1977. Disease organisms for pest control. *Queensl. Agric. J.* 103:1–4.

Tervet, I. W. 1945. The influence of fungi on storage, on seed viability and seedling vigor of soybeans. *Phytopathology* 35:3–15.

Thakur, R. P., Patel, P. N., and Verma, J. P. 1977. Independent assortment of pigmentation and resistance to cercospora leaf spot in mung bean. *Indian Phytopathol.* 30:264–5.

Thomas, H. R., Zaumeyer, W. J., and Jorgensen, H. 1951. Inheritance of resistance to lima bean mosaic virus in the lima bean. *Phytopathology* 41:231–7.

Thomas, P. E., and Mink, G. I. 1979. *Beet curly top virus*. CMI/AAB Descriptions of Plant Viruses, no. 210. Kew: Commonwealth Mycological Institute and Association of Applied Biologists.

Thompson, L. U. 1988. Antinutrients and blood glucose. *Food Technol.* 42(4):123–32.

Toole, E. H., and Toole, V. K. 1953. Relation of storage conditions to germination and to abnormal seedlings of bean. *Proc. Int. Seed Test. Assoc.* 18:123–9.

Toole, E. H., Toole, V. K., and Borthwick, H. A. 1957. Growth and production of snap beans stored under favorable and unfavorable conditions. *Proc. Int. Seed Test. Assoc.* 22:418–23.

Tsukamoto, I., Miyoshi, M., and Hamaguchi, Y. 1983. Heat inactivation of trypsin inhibitor in Kintoki bean (*Phaseolus vulgaris*). *Cereal Chem.* 60:194–7.

Turner, J. W. 1977. The nature of damage by *Nezara viridula* (L.) to soybean seed. *Queensl. J. Agric. Anim. Sci.* 24:105–7.

Turnipseed, S. G. 1972. Management of insect pests of soybean. *Proc. Tall Timbers Conf. Ecol. Anim. Control Habitat Manage.* 4:189–203.

USDA. 1975. *United States Standards for Beans.* Washington, D.C.: Agric. Mark. Serv., USDA.

Valdebouze, P. 1977. Trypsin inhibitor and hemagglutinating activities in seeds of some legume species. In *Protein Quality from Leguminous Crops*, pp. 87–98. Luxembourg: Office for Official Publications of the European Communities, Commission of the European Communities.

van Emden, H. F. 1981. Insects and mites of legume crops. In *Advances in Legume Science*, ed. R. J. Summerfield and A. H. Bunting, pp. 187–97. Kew: Royal Botanical Gardens.

Van Etten, C. H. 1969. Goitrogens. In *Toxic Constituents of Plant Foodstuffs*, ed. I. E. Liener, pp. 103–42. New York: Academic Press.

Van Kammen, A., and de Jager, C. P. 1978. *Cowpea mosaic virus.* CMI/AAB Descriptions of Plant Viruses, no. 197. Kew: Commonwealth Mycological Institute and Association of Applied Biologists.

Verma, R. S., and Gupta, P. C. 1975. Storage behavior of soybean varieties vastly differing in seed size. *Seed Res.* 3:39–44.

Vignarajah, N. 1978. Mungbean research and production in Sri Lanka. *Proc. 1st Int. Mungbean Symposium*, pp. 9–11. Taiwan: Asian Vegetable Research and Development Center.

Vindiola, O. L., Seib, P. A., and Hoseney, R. C. 1986. Accelerated development of the hardto-cook state in beans. *Cereal Foods World* 31:538–52.

Wade, B. L. 1929. The inheritance of *Fusarium* wilt resistance in canning peas. *Wisconsin Agric. Exp. Stn. Res. Bull. no. 97.*

Wang, A. 1975. A crystalline protein–proteinase inhibitor from pinto bean seeds. *Biochim. Biophys. Acta* 393:583–96.

Wanki, S. B. C., Fawusi, M. O. A., and Nangju, D. 1982. Pod and grain yields from intercropping maize and *Vigna unguiculata* (L.) Walp. in Nigeria. *J. Agric Sci.* 99:13–17.

Wark, D. C. 1950. The inheritance of resistance to *Ascochyta pisi* Lib. in *Pisum sativum* L. *Aust. J. Agric. Res.* 1:382–90.

Warsy, A. S., Norton, G., and Steim, M. 1974. Protease inhibitors from broad beans. Isolation and purification. *Phytochem.* 13:2481–6.

Waterworth, H. E. 1981. *Bean mild mosaic virus.* CMI/AAB Descriptions of Plant Viruses, no. 231. Kew: Commonwealth Mycological Institute and Association of Applied Biologists.

Watson, I. A. 1970. The utilization of wild species in the breeding of cultivated crops resistant to plant pathogens. In *Genetic Resources in Plants: Their Exploration and Conservation*, ed. O. H. Frankel and E. Bennett, pp. 441–57. Oxford: Blackwell Scientific Publ.

Weder, J. K. P. 1986. Inhibition of human proteinases by grain legumes. In *Nutritional and Toxicological Significance of Enzyme Inhibitors in Foods*, ed. M. Friedman, pp. 239–79. New York: Plenum Press.

Welch, R. M., House, W. A., and Allaway, W. H. 1974. Availability of zinc from pea seeds to rats. *J. Nutr.* 104:733–40.

Wester, R. E., Fisher, V. J., and Blount, V. L. 1972. Multiple resistance in lima beans to downy mildew (*Phytophthora phaseoli*). *Plant Dis. Rep.* 56:65–6.

Whitley, E. J., and Bowman, D. E. 1975. Isolation and properties of navy bean proteinase inhibitor component I. *Arch. Biochem. Biophys.* 169:42–50.

Wilde, G., and van Schoonhoven, A. 1976. Mechanisms of resistance to *Empoasca kraemeri* in *Phaseolus vulgaris. Environ. Entomol.* 5:251–5.

Willey, R. W. 1979. Intercropping: Its importance and research needs. *Field Crops Abstr.* 32:1–10.

Willey, R. W., and Osiru, D. S. O. 1972. Studies on mixtures of maize and beans (*Phaseolus vulgaris*) with particular reference to plant population. *J. Agric. Sci.* 79:517–29.

Williams, R. J. 1975. Diseases of cowpea (*Vigna unguiculata* (L.) Walp.) in Nigeria. *PANS* 21:253–67.

Williams, S. G. 1970. The role of phytic acid in the wheat grain. *Plant Physiol.* 45:376–81.

Wilson, K. A. 1981. The structure, function and evolution of legume proteinase inhibitors. In *Antinutrients and Natural Toxicants in Foods*, ed. R. L. Ory, pp. 187–202. Westport: Food Nutrition Press.

Wokes, F., and Willimott, S. C. 1951. Determination of cyanide in seeds. *J. Pharm. Pharmacol.* 3:905–17.

Wolf, W. J. 1975. Effects of refining operations on legumes. In *Nutritional Evaluation of Food Processing*, ed. R. S. Harris and E. Karmas, pp. 158–87. Westport: AVI Publ. Corp.

Wolfenbarger, D., and Sleesman, J. P. 1961. Resistance to the Mexican bean beetle in several bean genera and species. *J. Econ. Entomol.* 54:1018–22.

Wolfenbarger, D., and Sleesman, J. P. 1963. Variation in susceptibility of soybean pubescent types, broad bean and runner bean varieties and plant introductions to the potato leafhopper. *J. Econ. Entomol.* 56:895–7.

Wraith, D. G., and Young, G. V. W. 1979. The management of food allergy with diet and Nalcrom. In *The Mast Cell: Its Role in Health and Disease*, ed. J. Pepys and A. M. Edwards, pp. 443–6. London: Pitman.

Wydler, H. 1860. Kleinere beitrage zur kenntniss einheimischer gewachse. *Flora* 43:17–32.

Yoshii, K., Galvez, G. E., and Alvarez, G. 1976. Estimation of yield losses in beans caused by common blight. *Proc. Am. Phytopathol. Soc.* 3:298–9.

Youdeowei, A., and Adeniji, M. O. 1986. Crop protection. In *Introduction to Tropical Agriculture*, ed. A. Youdeowei, F. O. C. Ezedinma, and O. C. Onazi, pp. 132–59. New York: Longman.

Zacher, F. 1952. Die nahrpflanzen der samenkafer. *Z. Angew. Zool.* 33:460–80.

Zamora, A. F., and Fields, M. L. 1979. Nutritive quality of fermented cowpeas (*Vigna sinensis*) and chickpeas (*Cicer arietinum*). *J. Food Sci.* 44:234–6.

Zaumeyer, W. J., and Meiners, J. P. 1975. Disease resistance in beans. *Annu. Rev. Phytopathol.* 13:313–34.

Zohari, D., and Hopf, M. 1973. Domestication of pulses in the Old World. *Science* 182:887–94.

3

Fruits and Vegetables

B. B. Desai and D. K. Salunkhe

INTRODUCTION

Fruits and vegetables are soft, fleshy, edible plant products and, because of their high moisture content, are relatively perishable in the freshly harvested state. Botanically, the word "fruit" refers to the mature seed-bearing structures of flowering plants; this covers a very wide and heterogeneous group of plant products, including cereals, pulses, oilseeds, spices, and fleshy fruits. The edible fleshy fruits, however, represent a well-defined class on their own and exhibit a wide variety of plant products. They have much in common from a culinary point of view with the soft, edible structures developed from other parts of the plant body, commonly referred to as vegetables. Although botanically the line between fruits and vegetables cannot be clearly drawn, the products have been differentiated based on common verbal usage and the way in which they are consumed. Popularly, the term "fruit" has been restricted in its use to those botanical plant parts that have fragrant, aromatic flavors and are either naturally sweet or normally sweetened with sugar before eating; that is, fruits are essentially consumed as dessert items. The term "vegetable," in contrast, is applied to all the other soft, edible plant products that are usually eaten with meat, fish, or other savory dish, either fresh or cooked. Both fruits and vegetables are utilized in different ways in different parts of the world—in some instances, even within a given community. For example, banana and plantain are the fruits of two very closely related plant species but are utilized distinctively: Whereas banana is an important dessert fruit, the starchy plantain is usually consumed cooked as a vegetable.

The percentages of nutrients contributed by fruits and vegetables as a group, according to the amount consumed per year in the United States, are as follows (Salunkhe and Desai 1984a,b): vitamin C, 91%; vitamin A (β-carotene), 48%; vitamin B_6, 27%; magnesium, 26%; iron, 19%; thiamin, 17%; niacin, 15%; and calories, 9%.

Table 3-1. The Probable Original Centers of Distribution of the Ancestors of Some Presently Cultivated Fruit and Vegetable Species.

Center	Species
Central Asia	Apple, broad bean, cherry, lentil, mulberry, olive, onion, pea, pear, plum, pomegranate, quince, radish, spinach
Mediterranean	Carrot, celery, cucumber, date, eggplant, lettuce, melon, mustard, turnip
Medit. & S.E. Asia	Artichoke, asparagus, cabbage, cauliflower, fig, horseradish, parsley, parsnip
Southeast Asia	Banana, breadfruit, peach, persimmon, orange, yam
Central America	Avocado, cassava, corn, cranberry, kidney bean, lima bean, pineapple, potato, pumpkin, squash, sweet potato, tomato

Source: Duckworth (1966).

PRODUCTION HISTORY

Duckworth (1966) pointed out the probable original centers of distribution of the ancestors of some of the modern cultivated fruit and vegetable species (Table 3-1). The wild ancestors of all the important fruits and vegetables grown today were originally confined to one or another of four main centers of distribution. The ancient Greek and Roman civilizations were familiar with many edible plant species, including fruits and vegetables, that were indigenous to Central and Southwest Asia and the Mediterranean region. According to Duckworth (1966), the Greeks and Romans cultivated quite a wide range of fruits and vegetables and lived largely on a vegetarian diet. The sun drying of fruits such as grapes and prunes was already widely practiced during these times, and trade in dried fruit products flourished around the Mediterranean.

The common people realized the value of fruit and vegetable growing as a means of providing a more varied and inexpensive diet and a good source of income. The cultivation of fruits and vegetables on a commercial scale reached a high level of development in Europe during the Middle Ages. The major fruits of tropical and subtropical regions gradually spread from their original centers of distribution to other areas where the climate was suitable for their cultivation. Banana, which was grown in Malaysia since the second millennium B.C., was introduced to tropical America at the beginning of the sixteenth century; the orange, another native of Southeast Asia, also probably reached America about the same time. Greenhouse culture, introduced in the seventeenth century, enabled the small-scale cultivation of exotic species such as vines, peaches, and citrus fruits. In the following hundred years, fruit growers started to realize the problems of transporting and marketing fresh produce on a commercial scale. Eighteenth-century medical science was positively affirming that consuming

Table 3-2. World Production of Some Important Fruits and Vegetables.[a]

Produce	1983	1984	1985	1986	1987	1988
Fruits	313.9	312.9	313.0	326.7	324.7	329.3
Total nuts[b]	3.94	3.87	3.79	3.77	4.06	4.12
Root crops	560.3	594.0	578.4	582.4	584.3	583.7
Potatoes	265.4	292.3	283.1	290.2	284.1	287.2
Vegetables & melons	373.0	396.5	406.0	416.4	421.1	427.3

Adapted from: FAO Q. Bull. Stat. 1(4), 1988.
[a]In millions of metric tons.
[b]Includes both true nuts and those that are drupes or seeds.

fruits and vegetables was necessary for normal well-being. Consumption steadily increased worldwide during the nineteenth century, witnessing a marked acceleration due to an increase in the rate of population growth. During this period, foundations were laid for the subsequent exploitation of such modern methods of food preservation as cold storage, canning, and artificial drying of fruits, and commercial production of jams, jellies, and fruit juices.

Blessed with a range of climates suitable for growing a wide variety of fruit species, the newly formed United States of America quickly emerged as a leading producer of fruits and vegetables, transporting them to its southern neighbors, where the consumption of these commodities was traditionally high. The fruit processing industry rapidly expanded during the early part of this century. "Quick-freezing" was introduced in 1929, followed by the development of other branches of the processing industry. In the 1950s there was a rapid increase in the production of fruit and vegetable juices and dehydrated products, followed by the development of use of ionizing radiations to conserve perishable foods (Duckworth 1966).

A comparison of recent world production of fruit and vegetable crops is shown in Table 3-2.

FRUITS

Fruits are highly remarkable sources of wholesome food, and are valued for flavor, aroma, and texture. Fresh fruits appeal to all the senses: smell, taste, touch, sight, and even sound—as when one bites into a crunchy apple. Nutritionally, they have a vital role to play, vitamins and minerals being their major contribution to the human diet. Some fruits are considered a fairly rich source of energy and contribute notable amounts of fat (e.g., avocados and nuts), sugars (e.g., dates, figs, bananas), protein (e.g., *tucuma*) (Hall et al. 1980; Nagy and Shaw 1980), and dietary fiber (White 1979). Fruits play an especially important role in health by providing low-sodium diets to people with certain diseases, such as hypertension and kidney disorders (Goddard and Matthews 1979). One of the greatest health problems in the Western world is obesity, and fresh fruits can supply a large portion of a diet while contributing very few calories (Goddard and Matthews 1979; White 1979). Because of their higher nutrient density ratios, a normal serving of fruits will supply the recommended daily dietary allowances for most nutrients without concomitantly supplying excess calories (Hansen, Wyse, and Sorenson 1979).

Botanically, fruit is the structure that develops from the ovary wall (pericarp) as the enclosed seed or seeds mature; but although fruit is often an important feature in the diagnosis of family or genus, its classification is somewhat artificially based on gross morphology rather than on mode of origin. Thus fruits may be classified as *succulent* or *dry* depending on whether or not the middle layer (the mesocarp) of the pericarp develops into a fleshy covering. It may be further classified as *dehiscent* or *indehiscent* according to whether the fruit wall splits open to release the seed. Fruits that develop from the gynoecium of a single flower are termed *simple* or *true fruits*. If they are derived from a single ovary, they are called *monocarpellary;* those that incorporate a number of fused ovaries are termed *polycarpellary*. An aggregate fruit may develop from an apocarpous gynoecium (e.g., "pseudocarp" pomes and strawberries); others may develop from a complete inflorescence (e.g., pineapples, mulberries, and figs). Some fruits may develop even though the ovule has not been fertilized; termed *parthenocarpic* fruits, this class includes melons, figs, cucumbers, and bananas.

The various groups of fruits discussed here could be broadly defined as follows (see also Table 3-3):

Berry: A many-seeded fleshy indehiscent fruit. The epicarp usually forms a tough outer skin, especially in the pepo and hesperidium (defined below), and the mesocarp becomes massive and fleshy. The epicarp and mesocarp may be highly colored to attract animals that act as agents of dispersal. Typical examples are the tomato, grape, raspberry, blueberry, and strawberry.

Hesperidium: A type of berry that has a leathery epicarp, such as a citrus fruit. Fluid-filled trichomes fill the locule of each carpel to form the characteristic segments of the various citrus fruits.

Pepo: A type of berry with a hard exterior derived either from the epicarp or noncarpellary tissue of the plant. Examples include pumpkins, squashes, melons, and cucumbers. In members of the Cucurbitaceae (melon family), the hard exterior is formed from the receptacle of the flower.

Drupe: A fleshy, generally one-seeded, indehiscent fruit in which the seed or seeds are surrounded by a hardened schlerenchymatous endocarp, as in wild cherry. The endocarp may replace the testa in its protective role and may also play a part in the dormancy mechanism. Apricots, peaches, cherries, and plums are examples.

Table 3-3. Botanical Classification of Some Important Fruits and Nuts.

Type	Scientific Name	Family
Fruits		
Berries		
Brambles		Rosaceae
Blackberry	*Rubus* spp.	
Boysenberry	*Rubus ursinus*	
Loganberry	*Rubus ursinus* var. *loganobacus*	
Raspberry		
Black	*Rubus occidentalis*	
Red and yellow	*Rubus idaeus*	
Grapes		Vitaceae
American grape	*Vitis labrusca*	
European grape	*Vitis vinifera*	
Muscadine grape	*Vitis rotundifolia*	
Other berries		
Blueberry	*Vaccinium* spp.	Ericaceae
Cranberry		Ericaceae
American	*Vaccinium macrocarpon*	
European	*Vaccinium oxycoccus*	
Currant		Saxifragaceae
American black	*Ribes americanum*	
European black	*Ribes nigrum*	
Garden currant	*Ribes sativum*	
Northern red	*Ribes rubrum*	
Date	*Phoenix dactylifera*	Palmaceae
Gooseberry		Saxifragaceae
American	*Ribes hirtellum*	
European	*Ribes grossularia*	
Huckleberry	*Gaylussacia baccata*	Ericaceae
Strawberry	*Fragaria chiloensis* var. *ananassa*	Rosaceae
Pomegranate	*Punica granatum*	Punicaceae
Hesperidia		
Citrus		Rutaceae
Citron	*Citrus medica*	
Grapefruit		
Pomelo	*Citrus paradisi*	
Shaddock, pummelo	*Citrus grandis*	
Kumquat		
Nagami	*Fortunella margarita*	
Marumi	*Fortunella japonica*	
Lemon	*Citrus limon*	
Lime	*Citrus aurantifolia*	
Orange	*Citrus sinensis*	
Pepos		
Melons[a]		Cucurbitaceae
Melon, muskmelon	*Cucumis melo*	
Cantaloupe	*C. melo* var. *cantalupensis*	
Cassaba	*C. melo* var. *inodorus*	
Nutmeg melon	*C. melo* var. *reticulatus*	
Watermelon	*Citrullus vulgaris*	

Table 3-3. (*Continued*)

Type	Scientific Name	Family
Drupes[b]		
Apricot	*Prunus armeniaca*	Rosaceae
Avocado	*Persea americana*	Lauraceae
Cherry	*Prunus avium*	Rosaceae
Mango	*Mangifera indica*	Anacardiaceae
Olive	*Olea europaea*	Oleaceae
Peach	*Prunus persica*	Rosaceae
Plum	*Prunus domestica*	Rosaceae
Pomes		Rosaceae
Apple	*Malus sylvestric* Mill.	
Pear	*Pyrus communis*	
Quince	*Cydonia oblonga*	
Other fruits		
Banana[c]	*Musa paradisiaca* var. *sapientum*	Musaceae
Fig[d]	*Ficus carica*	Moraceae
Pineapple[d]	*Ananas comosus*	Bromeliaceae
Nuts[e]		
True nuts		
Beechnut	*Fagus grandifolia*	Fagaceae
Cashew nut*	*Anacardium occidentale*	Anacardiaceae
Chestnut	*Castanea* spp.	Fagaceae
Filberts		Corylaceae
European/common	*Corylus avellana*	
American hazelnut	*Corylus americana*	
Hickory group		
Hickory nut	*Carya* spp.	Juglandaceae
Pecan	*Carya illinoensis*	Juglandaceae
Macadamia nut*	*Macadamia ternifolia* var. *integrifolia*	Proteaceae
Pistachio nut*	*Pistacia vera*	Anacardiaceae
Drupes[b]		
Almond	*Prunus amygdalus*	Rosaceae
Coconut*	*Cocos nucifera*	Palmaceae
Walnut group		Juglandaceae
Black walnut	*Juglans nigra*	
Butternut	*Juglans cinerea*	
English/Persian walnut	*Juglans regia*	
Seeds		
Brazil nut[f]*	*Bertholletia excelsa*	Lecythidaceae
Pinenut	*Pinus* spp.	Pinaceae

[a]Although true fruits, in world trade melons are grouped with vegetables.
[b]Some so-called nuts are also drupaceous fruits.
[c]Indehiscent fleshy fruit.
[d]Multiple fruits.
[e]Asterisk = (sub)tropical; all others are from temperate or cooler climates.
[f]Borne severally in a capsule fruit.

Pome: A type of fleshy pseudocarp in which the succulent tissues are developed from a greatly enlarged urn-shaped receptacle, which encloses the real fruit at its core. The pome is typical of family Rosaceae, the apple and pear being examples.

Nut: A nut is a dry, indehiscent fruit usually shed as a one-seeded unit. Although it forms from more than one carpel, only one seed develops, the rest aborting. The pericarp is usually lignified and is often partially or completely surrounded by a cup-shaped structure or *cupule.* True nuts include the acorn, hazelnut, and beechnut. The word "nut" is often loosely applied to any woody fruit or seed, such as the walnut and almond (which are drupes) or Brazil nut (which is a seed).

Present State of Fruit Growing

Based on the size of production, Samson (1986) distinguished four groups of fruit crops in the world:

1. those having a production of more than 10 million metric tons (MT) per year—grape, citrus, banana, apple, plantain, and mango;
2. those of which 1–10 million MT were produced—pear, avocado, papaya, peach, plum, pineapple, date, fig, and strawberry;
3. those with production figures of 100,000–1 million MT, such as cashew nut; and
4. the rest, for which there are no reliable statistics, such as guava, Brazil nut, litchi, macadamia, and soursop.

The production figures for major fruit crops and their leading producers are given in Tables 3-4 and 3-5, respectively. The production of grapes, pomes, and stone fruits (drupes) has doubled since 1950, whereas that of banana and citrus has tripled, and that of pineapple has increased sixfold. Avocado, kiwi, and litchi production is developing rapidly, but that of mango and cashew nut has remained more or less stationary in recent years.

According to Samson (1986), an increase in fruit production is not always accompanied by a rise in consumption; if consumption continues to lag for many years, the resultant overproduction leads to diminishing production. However, fruit growing is a long-term process, and changes only gradually.

Pieniazek (1977) stated that the average consumption of citrus and banana in Western Europe and the United States was about 10 kg/head/year, and <1 kg for the other tropical fruits; figures are much lower in Eastern Europe, but are increasing steadily. There has been a considerable rise in consumption and export of processed fruit products, particularly fruit juices. During 1960–70, this nearly tripled for citrus fruits, occupying one-third of the Florida and Brazil markets (Samson 1986).

Table 3-4. Production of the Major Fruit Crops.[a]

Fruits	1960	1970	1980	1981	1982	1983	1984
Subtropical							
Citrus	21	38	56	55	54	57	56
Banana	15	31	39	40	41	41	41
Plantain	—[b]	—	22[c]	22	23	20	20
Mango	10	12	13	13	13.5	14	14
Pineapple	2	4.2	7.8	8.6	8.9	8.7	8.8
Date	1.4	1.3	2.7	2.7	2.6	2.8	2.4
Papaya	—	—	1.8	1.9	1.9	2.0	2.1
Avocado	—	0.9	1.6	1.5	1.5	1.6	1.6
Cashew nut	0.4	0.5	0.5	0.5	0.5	0.5	0.4
Temperate							
Grape	45	60	67	61	71	65	64
Apple	15	24	34	33	39	37	40
Pear	4.2	7.2	8.5	8.7	8.9	9.5	9.1
Peach	3.8	5.5	7.3	7.3	7.1	7.4	7.7
Plum	4.5	3.9	4.6	5.0	6.2	6.2	6.1

Source: FAO (1985).
[a]In millions of metric tons, in order of descending yield.
[b]Dashes mean data are unavailable.
[c]Formerly included in banana.

Table 3-5. Major Producers of Fruits.[a]

Country	1979–81	1983	1984	1985
Brazil	18.30	19.82	25.21	26.23
India	20.68	23.06	24.23	23.96
Italy	20.66	22.36	19.12	18.75
Spain	12.60	12.36	11.41	12.11
USA	26.55	25.41	22.89	22.46
USSR	16.04	17.99	18.54	18.20
Developed countries	130.09	137.61	129.51	126.74
Developing countries	163.09	175.28	181.37	185.61
Worldwide	293.18	312.89	310.88	312.35

Source: FAO (1985).
[a]In millions of metric tons; excludes melons, which FAO groups under vegetables.

Fruit prices vary widely between and within years, the highest generally being obtained from October to November (Fajac 1974; Naville 1975). Countries such as Brazil, South Africa, and Australia have decided price advantage, since they can deliver their fruit in the autumn of the northern hemisphere. Owing to better opportunities for travel, faster shipments with refrigeration, and better processing methods and distribution systems, there has been enormous expansion in the transport of tropical fruits to Europe and the United States (Storey 1969). Intensive research on cultivation methods, crop protection, and postharvest biotechnology, along with developments in information media, have also helped fruit industry growth worldwide (Salunkhe and Desai 1984a).

Fruits as Sources of Nutrients

Although humankind cannot live by fruit alone, fruit has been an important source of nutrients. Barring high-protein nuts and fat-rich avocado, fruits are neither good nor economic sources of protein, fat, and calories, but are indispensable as sources of vitamins and minerals.

The proximate composition of some important fruits (Table 3-6) indicates that most contain more than 80% water. This value varies considerably depending on the availability of water to the crop, especially at the time of harvest. To maintain their crisp texture and freshness after harvest, fruits are generally harvested when their moisture content is at maximum. Carbohydrates, the next most abundant group of nutrient constituents, are present as low-molecular-weight sugars (glucose, fructose, and sucrose) or their high-molecular-weight polymers (e.g., starch, hemicellulose, cellulose, and pectins). Most ripe fruits are characterized by the presence of water-soluble sugars, whereas starch is the main constituent of unripe fleshy fruits, such as bananas. Cellulose, hemicellulose, pectins, and lignin (a polymer of aromatic alcohols linked by propyl units), which together constitute the dietary fiber, are essential components of the human diet. The incidence of such diseases as constipation, diverticulosis, and colon cancer is attributed to lack of fiber in the human diet.

The protein content of most fruits varies from 0.5% to 1%. These are mostly functional proteins (e.g., globular ones, such as enzymes) rather than storage proteins. With the exception of olives and avocados, fruits generally have <1% of lipids, mostly associated with the protective cuticle layers of the fruit surface and the cell wall. Citrus fruits contain >3% of organic acids, with citric and maleic acids predominating. Tartaric and isocitric acids are predominant in grapes and blackberry, respectively (Salunkhe and Desai 1984a).

Vitamin C (ascorbic acid) is one of the most important constituents of the human diet, a deficiency of which causes scurvy. The dietary vitamin C (about 90%) is essentially obtained from fruits and vegetables. Many fruits such as citrus, cherries, berries, and guava provide the recommended dietary allowance of about 50 mg of vitamin C in <100 g of fruit tissue. Papaya and mango are rich in vitamin A (β-carotene), and nuts are excellent sources of thiamin. The human body converts β-carotene into retinol, an active vitamin A compound important to maintain visual process. Fruits are also important sources of calcium, iron, and other minerals, but generally their contribution to total dietary requirements is of less importance. Recent research on human nutrition suggests that

Table 3-6. Nutritional Values of Some Fruits (per 100 g Edible Portion).

Fruit	Water (g)	Energy (cal)	Protein (g)	Fat (g)	Carbohydrate (g)	Ca (mg)	P (mg)	Fe (mg)	Na (mg)	K (mg)	Mg (mg)	Vit. A (IU)	Thiamin (mg)	Riboflavin (mg)	Niacin (mg)	Vit. C (mg)
Apricot	85.3	51	1.0	0.2	12.8	17	23	0.5	1	281	12	2,700	0.03	0.04	0.6	10
Peach	89.1	38	0.6	0.1	9.7	9	18	0.5	1	202	10	1,330	0.02	0.05	1.0	7
Orange	86.0	49	1.0	0.2	12.2	41	20	0.4	1	200	11	200	0.10	0.04	0.4	50
Grapefruit	88.4	41	0.5	0.1	10.6	16	16	0.4	1	135	12	80	0.04	0.02	0.2	38
Plum	81.1	66	0.5	0.2[a]	17.8	18	17	0.5	2	299	9	300	0.08	0.03	0.5	5[a]
Grape	81.6	69	1.3	1.0	15.7	16	12	0.4	3	158	13	100	0.05	0.03	0.3	4
Sour cherry	83.7	58	1.2	0.3	14.3	22	19	0.4	2	191	14	1,000	0.05	0.06	0.4	10
Apple	84.4	58	0.2	0.6	14.5	7	10	0.3	1	110	8	90	0.03	0.02	0.1	4
Strawberry	89.9	37	0.7	0.5	8.4	21	21	1.0	1	164	12	60	0.03	0.07	0.6	59
Watermelon	92.6	26	0.5	0.2	6.4	7	10	0.5	1	100	8	590	0.03	0.03	0.2	7
Pear	83.2	61	0.7	0.4	15.3	8	11	0.3	2	130	7	20	0.02	0.04	0.1	4
Banana	75.7	85	1.1	0.2	22.2	8	26	0.7	1	370	33	190	0.05	0.06	0.7	10

Source: Reprinted with permission from Salunkhe, Pao, and Dull (1974), Assessment of nutritive value, quality and stability of cruciferous vegetables during storage and subsequent processing. In *Storage, Processing and Nutritional Quality of Fruits and Vegetables*, ed. D. K. Salunkhe, pp. 1–38. © CRC Press, Inc., Boca Raton, Fla.
[a]From Heinz (1959).

sodium is responsible for blood-pressure-related disorders, and that potassium acts antagonistically. Since fruits have high potassium: sodium ratios (Table 3-6), nutritionists advise a daily intake of at least 100 g of fruits and as much variety as the season permits. The total fruit production in the world is around 250 million MT per year (i.e., 50 kg/person/year or 137 g/day); however, this is spread very unevenly. In many tropical countries, such as India, there is a serious shortage of fresh fruit, at least during part of the year.

Some fruits are nutritionally harmful and even poisonous. According to Purseglove (1968), in the *akee,* the unripe aril and the pink vein that attaches it to the seed are highly poisonous. *Carambola* and *bilimbi* contain 1–6% oxalic acid, which can cause calcium deficiency and kidney stones. Plantains contain serotonin, which, when consumed in large quantities, may cause high blood pressure.

Environmental Factors

Climate

Since weather changes from day to day whereas climate has a more stable character, Samson (1986) defined climate as "average weather" or "the whole of average atmospheric phenomena for a given region, calculated for a period of thirty years." These phenomena generally include light, temperature, water, and air.

Light

Fruit trees generally require more light and must be grown in a sunny atmosphere. Some fruit crops (e.g., banana) tolerate shade, whereas others (e.g., mangosteen) need shade during their early development. A third group of fruit crops (e.g., Salak palm, *duku,* and *carambola*) requires permanent shade (Terra 1949).

Daylength, the time elapsing between dawn and dusk, may exert a profound influence on flowering. Based on the required duration of the light periods, plants can be classified as short-day, long-day, and day-neutral plants. With the exception of pineapple, most tropical fruit crops are insensitive to photoperiod (Samson 1986).

Temperature

The average temperature at sea level near the equator is about 26–27 °C, the range usually being very small (2–3 °C between months and 6–10 °C between day and night). The temperature range, however, increases farther away from the equator. The altitude lowers the temperature by 5–6 °C for every 1,000 m.

According to Samson (1986), the growth rate of plants depends on temperature; thus plants that grow optimally at sea level will grow more slowly in the mountains. For example, in Jamaica, the growth cycle of the banana cultivar "Lacatan" was shown to be thirteen months at sea level but to increase by one month for every 100 m rise in altitude.

The sum of average daily temperatures during the growth cycle of the crop is called the *heat index*. Since perennial crops stop growing under extreme climatic conditions (too cold or below the minimum temperature and too hot or above the maximum), the average temperature is not a good criterion for judging crop growth and development. It is, therefore, better to use only effective temperatures, those between the minimum and the maximum, for growth. Apples and other pome fruits require low temperatures to break their bud dormancy; thus most deciduous fruits, such as apple, pear, peach and cherry, cannot be grown in tropical climates. Some deciduous fruit crops, such as macadamia, need cooler nights and chilling temperatures to induce flowering, whereas others (apple, peach, pear), depending upon the cultivar, require 250–1,000 h of temperatures below 7 °C (Samson 1986).

Excepting citrus and dates, most tropical fruits are highly susceptible to frosts. Even a temperature several degrees above zero may be harmful. Chilling injury, in the form of coagulation of latex in the skin that turns the fruit brown, is commonly observed in such fruits as banana, soursop, and sapodilla when grown below 12 °C. In contrast, the extreme high temperatures of the arid zones cause wilting, sun-scald, necrotic spots, and even death of fruit crops. Only the date crop resists temperatures up to about 50 °C.

Samson (1986) cited Koppen, who classified the world's climates into the following five groups:

1. rainy, with coolest month above 18 °C;
2. dry, either warm or cold;
3. rainy, with a mild winter;
4. rainy, with a cold winter; and
5. polar.

The last two have winters too cold to grow any tropical or subtropical fruit crops.

Water

The importance of sufficient moisture in the production of horticultural crops like fruits cannot be overemphasized. Within a particular temperature zone, the availability of water is perhaps the most important factor determining which fruit crops can or cannot be grown. Up to 10° latitude, about 200 cm/yr of rain falls on either side of the equator. Farther away there is less rain, especially from 20 to 40 °N and from 20 to 30 °S. The amount and pattern of rainfall are influenced considerably by the mountain ranges and deserts. The distribution of rain over the year is more important than the total rainfall, the number of dry spells, in which evapotranspiration exceeds precipitation, being of greater importance. According to Terra (1949), mangosteen, *kapulasan,* banana, and papaya grow best when >100 mm of rain falls in every month, little harm resulting from one or two months having a rainfall below 60 mm. Rambutan and durian also need a great deal of water but can tolerate two or three dry months. Mango and cashew nut, on the other hand, need at least three dry months and not more than seven wet months for the normal bloom and fruit setting. Citrus occupies a position between these two extremes. Perennial fruit crops require irrigation if they are cultivated in the regions having longer dry periods. In parts of Central India, for example, there are long dry spells from November to April; fruit growing in these areas is, therefore, not possible without irrigation.

In tropical regions, rainfall of <100 mm/month is considered low because of high evapotranspiration rates of 120–150 mm. Rainfall exceeding 300 mm/mo is also not useful, since the surplus cannot be stored in the soil. Higher precipitation also causes soil erosion and losses of soil nutrients.

The potential evapotranspiration and water supply in the root zone are criteria essential to the assessment of rain's usefulness for a crop. Evapotranspiration E comprises the upward movement of water vapor from the soil (physical process), and potential evapotranspiration E_p refers to a closed leaf canopy that is well supplied with water. E_p can be estimated from E_w, the evaporation from a free water surface. It can also be calculated from Penman's formula, taking into account the increase of E_p caused by bright sunlight, high temperature, low humidity, and wind. Under average tropical conditions, E_p reaches a value of 4–5 mm/day, but may exceed 10 mm in a sunny climate. Maximum E for a fast-growing fruit crop like banana may be 50–60% higher than E_w (Samson 1986). The irrigation requirement can be calculated by adding to the E_p the water lost by runoff from the field and that lost by deep percolation. Whereas some crops are fairly drought tolerant and can sustain drier conditions for months, others (such as banana) must be irrigated more frequently.

Water is present in the atmosphere as vapor. This atmospheric humidity also influences growth and development of plants. While low humidity has a drying effect on the crop, high humidity creates favorable conditions for fungal and bacterial diseases (e.g., leaf spot of banana).

Air

The so-called trade winds blow from east-northeast in the northern and from east-southeast in the southern hemisphere, with a notable constancy for speed and direction (Lockwood 1974). In the subtropics, the wind is usually westerly. Hot desert winds, such as the notorious Harmattan of West and Central Africa, can cause a great deal of damage to fruit crops. Storms and hurricanes with wind speeds > 50–100 km/hr can ruin a banana plantation completely and heavily damage other crops like avocado, citrus, and mango. Most tropical storms originate in latitudes of 8–15° and move away from the equator.

Climate and Geographical Distribution of Fruits

Nagy and Wardowski (1988) summarized the effects of climate and geographical growing area of fruits on their nutritional composition. Any given location with its specific climate can influence the nutritional composition of fruits. Rathore (1979), for example, demonstrated that guava harvested in the winter season had a higher vitamin C content than that harvested in the spring or summer. Since the ascorbic acid content of the spring and summer fruits did not differ much, it was concluded that lower winter temperatures were responsible for the increased vitamin content of the fruits, rather than the daylength or the relative humidity (Nagy and Wardowski 1988). Similarly, bloom delay of "Bartlett" and "Bosc" pears by evaporative cooling resulted in the reduced content of soluble solids of these fruits (Collins, Lombard, and Wolfe 1978).

Climate also influences the growth and maturation of citrus fruits. Total available heat is probably the single most important factor in determining the growth rate and time of ripening of citrus fruit (Jones 1961). Scora and Newman (1967) monitored seasonal changes in the ratios of total soluble solids to titratable acidity (Brix : acid ratio) for "Valencia" oranges in six major citrus-producing regions of the United States (Weslaco, Texas; Orlando, Florida; Tempe, Arizona; and Riverside, Indigo, and Santa Paula, California). From November to March, the highest Brix : acid ratios were found in fruit from Weslaco (climate classified as warm, semiarid, subtropical, steppe) and the lowest ratios in the fruit from Santa Paula (subtropical climate; cool, dry summers; limited rainfall occurring in the late fall, winter, and early spring). Valencia oranges require about seventeen months after the mean blooming period to attain commercial maturity in the coastal areas of California (e.g., Santa Paula), but only eight months in Weslaco. Using controlled-environment techniques in Japan with fruiting satsuma trees, Kurihara (1969) showed that a programmed day/night temperature regimen of 28/23 °C applied during the three-month preharvest period produced lower total soluble solids concentration in juice than did 18/13 °C or 13/18 °C. Rygg and Getty (1955) compared the grapefruit grown in desert areas of Arizona (summer conditions of hot days and warm nights) to that grown in the coastal areas of California (cooler climate). They showed that the coastal fruit generally had higher ascorbic acid content than the desert fruit when harvested on the same date. In a controlled-atmospheric study, Reuther and Nauer (1972) demonstrated that "Frost Satsuma" fruit contained more ascorbic acid when grown under cooler temperatures (20–22 °C day, 11–13 °C night) than under hot temperatures (30–35 °C day, 20–25 °C night). Mudambi and Rajagopal (1977) concluded that tropical temperatures might have been responsible for the lower values of ascorbic acid content of Nigerian sweet oranges.

The microclimate within a tree also influences fruit quality. The shading of individual apples and entire apple-bearing trees during fruit development adversely affects the fruit's red color development, size, and storage quality (Smock 1953; Heinicke 1966; Jackson, Sharples, and Palmer 1971). According to Seeley, Micke, and Kammereck (1980), when "Delicious" apples were grown under differing radiant flux densities, red fruit color, soluble solids, starch content, and fruit size were positively correlated with high flux densities. In another study, the quality of "Concord" grapes was affected by exposure to sunlight (Wolpert, Howell, and Cress 1980). Exterior cluster grapes exposed to sunlight had a higher sugar content and weight as compared to interior cluster grapes.

The effects of light exposure on the rates of chemical changes in "Valencia" oranges were investigated (Sites and Reitz 1949, 1950). The various chemical constituents were correlated with the position of the fruit on the tree. Total soluble solids content was highest in the outside fruit, intermediate in fruit located in the canopy of the tree, and lowest in fruit located on the inside. There was an increase in soluble solids with increased height on the tree. Sites and Reitz (1951) also determined the ascorbic acid content of each orange fruit from a single "Valencia" tree. Each fruit removed from the tree was classified as to the direction of light exposure and the amount of light or shade it received. Outside fruit grown on the north and northeast side contained lower amounts of ascorbic acid than outside fruit from the south side. Canopy fruit (i.e., fruit that was partially shaded at all times) was lower in vitamin C than outside fruit from its respective sector. Canopy fruit from the north side was generally lower in ascorbic acid than that from the other sides. Inside fruit, which hung inside the main body of the leaf canopy, had the lowest amounts of vitamin C for its respective sectors (Nagy and Wardowski 1988).

Soils

One of the first requirements for the successful growing of a fruit crop is the selection of soil that allows good water drainage, aeration, and extensive root development. Russell (1973), Sanchez (1976), and Buringh (1980) have described the requirements of fruit crops for soils and fertilizers. Samson (1986) defined soil as a three-phase system in which plants grow—all three phases (viz., solid, liquid, and gas) being essential. As a growing medium for plants, soil provides not only physical support, but water and the essential plant nutrients as well. Soil is a very variable, chemically and biologically complex entity that undergoes continual change.

Soil texture depends on the size of particles: gravel, coarse and fine sand, silt, and clay. Based on the relative proportion of these particles, soils are classified texturally as clayey, silty, clay-loam, sandy-loam, sandy, and so on. (Black 1968; Russell 1973). With certain exceptions, soil texture determines whether a fruit crop can be successfully cultivated. Fruit trees differ in their requirements of rooting depth. Citrus and apple trees, for example, grow well on well-drained, sandy-loam soils, which permit deep root penetration, whereas the *annonas* are shallow-rooted and do not require deeper soils (Ochse et al. 1961).

Soil structure describes the arrangement of soil particles into bigger units. A crumb structure, ensuring the presence of sufficient pore space for the movement of soil air and water, is considered best.

Soil microorganisms break down organic matter to build up humus, a dark-colored, amorphous organic material quite resistant to further breakdown. Humus improves soil structure and fertility. Above 25 °C, organic matter is broken down faster than it is built up; under tropical conditions, it accumulates only when there is sufficient moisture in soil. When peaty soils with high organic matter are reclaimed without burning, the organic matter decays gradually. This method of reclaiming produces highly fertile soils, such as those in Surinam, where bananas are grown most successfully (Samson 1968).

Good soil must be permeable. Crusts and hard pans prevent vertical movement of water in soil and cause runoff and erosion losses. Provision of good drainage is essential for normal growth of fruit crops.

Soil air contains about 0.2% CO_2, a level six times higher than is found in the atmosphere. This air must be changed constantly by a process of diffusion to prevent CO_2 levels from rising to harmful levels. Addition of organic matter and green manuring often improves soil structure and its physical properties.

Plant Nutrition

There are sixteen elements essential for plant growth: carbon, hydrogen, oxygen, nitrogen, phosphorus, potassium, calcium, magnesium, sulfur, iron, manganese, zinc, boron, copper, molybdenum, and chlorine. Those elements required in relatively large amounts are often referred to as *macronutrients* or major nutrients (N, P, K, Ca, Mg, and S). *Micronutrients,* also called trace or minor elements, are those needed in much smaller quantities (Fe, Mn, Zn, B, Cu, Mo, and Cl). Although carbon, hydrogen, and oxygen are absolutely essential, they are not normally considered in nutritional studies, due to their ready availability from air and water.

Nitrogen, in order to be absorbed by plant roots, must be present in the form of nitrate (NO_3) or ammonia (NH_4). Some bacteria (viz., *Azotobacter* and *Rhi-*

zobium) can convert atmospheric N_2 into NH_2 provided a source of energy is available. Nitrogen-fixing bacteria either live free in the soil (*Azotobacter*) or symbiotically with leguminous plants (*Rhizobium*), forming "nodules" on the roots. The nitrogen thus fixed becomes available to the host plant either directly or after the disintegration of nodules (Cobley and Steele 1976). Leguminous crops, therefore, serve as extremely useful cover crops and green manures for fruit growing (Samson 1986).

Fruit crops remove significant amounts of nutrients from soil. Montagut and Martin-Prevel (1965) estimated that 40 metric tons of bananas removed 80 kg N, 8 kg P, 200 kg K, 10 kg Ca, and 10 kg Mg from the soil. Such nutrient losses must be replenished by the addition of manures and fertilizers. Nutrients must also be supplied for the initial growth of fruit crops.

Fruit trees show a wide tolerance to soil pH, but most thrive best under slightly acidic conditions. It may be necessary to get soil samples of the planting site analyzed for physical and chemical parameters such as texture, organic matter, water-holding capacity, nutrients, pH, and electrical conductivity. Neutral soils (pH 6–7) supply almost all plant nutrients favorably. Soils having a pH < 5 may need the addition of lime or dolomite. Iron and zinc deficiencies may be encountered in soils having pH > 7.

Nutrient deficiency or toxicity may be assessed by plant tissue tests or leaf analysis. Leaves of uniform age and position—generally from nonfruiting branches—are used for analysis. Symptoms of deficiency (hunger signs) and excesses can also be useful. Light green or yellow color of leaves, for example, indicates nitrogen deficiency, whereas dark green or purple color denotes phosphorus deficiency. Potassium deficiency is characterized by marginal scorch and lack of magnesium by the loss of chlorophyll. Leaves deficient in iron show a fine network of green veins against a lighter background. Zinc deficiency is characterized by narrow leaves with yellow bands between the veins, whereas the lack of manganese is seen by light green bands between veins of a normal-size leaf (Samson 1986).

Manures and Fertilizers

Organic manures such as compost, farmyard manure (FYM), green manures, and city wastes improve soil structure and supply fair amounts of macro- and micronutrients; being bulky in nature, however, they are not easy to handle. Concentrated inorganic fertilizers are cheaper and easy to transport. Popular nitrogenous fertilizers are urea (45% N), ammonium sulfate (21%), ammonium nitrate (33%), and calcium ammonium nitrate (21%). Important phosphatic fertilizers include superphosphate (16–20% P_2O_5), double and triple superphosphate (36–48%), basic slag (14–18%), and rock phosphate (30%). In super and double super, the phosphorus is in readily available water-soluble form; in others it dissolves slowly. These forms should not be used in soils having pH > 6. The main potassium fertilizers are muriate of potash (50–60% K_2O) and potassium sulfate (48–52%). Micronutrients are usually supplied as sulfates of zinc, iron, manganese, and copper. Boron may be added as boric acid or borax. Iron can also be applied in the form of chelates, complex organic compounds such as Fe-EDTA or Fe-EDDHA, especially on alkaline soils (Samson 1986).

The attainment of a productive level for a given fruit crop depends upon the supply of adequate levels of available plant nutrients. Although the effects of fertilization on the nutritive quality of the fruit are seldom considered (Beeson 1949; Maynard 1950, 1956), evidence shows that fertilization does influence the nutrient content of the fruits. Nagy and Wardowski (1988) reviewed the effects of the following major and minor nutrients on the chemical composition of fruits.

Nitrogen

Nitrogen is the nutrient most commonly deficient in soils (Childers 1975). Even the richest soil with high organic matter content soon becomes impoverished if it is not supplemented with nitrogen. The concentration of nitrogen in citrus fruit is usually increased by the application of nitrogenous fertilizers (Sinclair 1961). High nitrogen fertilization also increases titratable acidity (Jones and Parker 1949) and total soluble solids, mostly sugars in oranges (Koo 1979). Smith and Rasmussen (1961) and Smith (1969) reported an inverse relationship between the quantity of nitrogen applied to grapefruit trees and the amount of ascorbic acid found in fruit juices. Heavy applications of nitrogen fertilizer to fruit crops reduce levels of vitamin C in juices of oranges (Jones and Parker 1947), lemons (Jones et al. 1970), and mandarins (Marsanija 1970) as well as in cantaloupe (Finch, Jones, and Van Horn 1945) and apple (Murneek and Wittwer 1948). Harris (1975) proposed that this effect may be caused by increased acid metabolism in these fruits.

Phosphorus

Phosphorus plays an important role as an energy carrier, takes part in photosynthesis, and is a component of both storage and structural compounds, such as phytin, phospholipids, and nucleic acids. Citrus fruits show variable responses to increasing phosphorus fertilization. Although the level of phosphorus fertilization from deficient to adequate levels markedly affects fruit quality, increasing levels above those deemed optimal resulted in debatable benefits (Embleton et al. 1973). The most consistent effect in this regard was a reduction in the citric acid and vitamin C contents of orange juices (Sinclair 1961).

Potassium

Potassium deficiency in crop plants causes dysfunctions in many metabolic processes. It is essential for several enzymatically catalyzed reactions and is involved in protein synthesis and carbohydrate metabolism (Black 1968). Dalldorf (1979) studied the effects of potassium fertilization of "Smooth Cayenne" pineapples. Those from potassium-deficient soil had an average sugar content of 11.5%, whereas those from trees receiving 200 kg K_2O/ha had 14% sugar. According to Embleton, Reitz, and Jones (1973), potassium manuring influences the quality of citrus fruit more than the crop yield. High potassium fertilization was correlated with greater concentration of ascorbic acid and total acid in the juice, and with lower total soluble solids, juice percentage, and ratio of total soluble solids to acid.

Secondary Nutrients and Micronutrients

Nutritional enhancement of fruit by either soil or foliar application of secondary and trace elements is not apparent as compared to supplementation with the major elements (Nagy and Wardowski 1988). The sandy soils of Florida where citrus crop is grown are naturally deficient in Zn, Mg, Mn, and Cu. The magnesium deficiency of oranges and grapefruit grown in Florida resulted in lower total soluble solids and total acids in the juice (Stearns and Sites 1943), whereas the correction of Zn, Mg, Mn, and Cu deficiencies of Floridian soils produced citrus fruits with enhanced vitamin C levels. Sites (1947) further concluded that the addition of Zn, Mg, Mn, and Cu in amounts exceeding those needed for normal maintenance did not improve fruit quality or vitamin C levels.

Cultural Operations

Propagation and Planting

Nurseries should be located on fertile, virgin soil where the same crop or its relative has not been grown previously. Water should be made available throughout the year. Light shade may be provided to nursery plants by growing small trees of *Leucaena* or *Sesbania* or shrubs like *Cajanus*. These trees also supply mulch and serve as green manure (Samson 1986).

Fruit crops are usually planted at the beginning of the rainy season in previously dug holes. The subsoil is mixed with compost, FYM, and some phosphate; the topsoil should then be replaced on top after filling the hole. Sizaret (1983) emphasized that the soil layers should be kept separate so that they may be correctly put back in place. Extra topsoil may be added to hold the plants vertical, and planting should be done near the valley side on terraces.

Plant density and spacing vary depending on the nature of the crop—for example, mango needs more space than an orange tree, and a pineapple plant can do with far less space than a banana. If water and nutrients are in short supply, more root space per tree may be necessary. Also, trees with terminal inflorescences must not be crowded. Square planting is usually recommended. Trees with lateral inflorescences (e.g., citrus, avocado) can be set out in a rectangular planting system, which gives more room for maneuvering between the rows and for intercropping during the initial years. Trees with circular crowns, such as palms, are best planted in an equilateral triangular system, which allows cultivation in three directions and accommodates more trees per unit area.

In the subtropics, north–south orientation is preferred to take maximum advantage of the sunlight (Platt 1973), whereas in the tropics row direction makes little difference, the sun usually being directly overhead. Contour lines may be followed on slopes of 4% or more, and on steep slopes ($\geq 10\%$) the building of terraces would be advisable. Orchards must be protected by shelter belts or windbreaks, set at right angles to the prevailing wind (Samson 1986).

Rootstock Selection

Many fruit trees are propagated by budding scions to rootstocks. The selection of rootstocks depends on factors such as resistance to specific diseases, scion compatibility, drought resistance, and tolerance to soil conditions (e.g., effects of salinity on scion fruit size, quality, and other features). The chemical composition of citrus fruits is often influenced by the type of rootstock to which the scion is attached (Nagy and Wardowski 1988). Numerous reports have shown the effects of the rootstock on the scion fruit's soluble solids (Sinclair 1961; Castle and Phillips 1980), acids (Hearn and Hutchinson 1977), lipids (Nordby, Nagy, and Smoot 1979), β-carotene (Issa and Mielke 1980), and ascorbic acid (Nagy 1980).

Pruning

Fruit crops are pruned to establish a balance between vegetative growth and fruit bearing, maintaining a certain minimum leaf area for each fruit. Pruning usually depends on the natural growth habit of the tree, but may deviate from it to maintain a "profit line," above which harvest is not economic. The ideal form should be achieved with the least possible interference to the tree. Samson (1986) recommended the following when pruning a branch: Select a bud that is pointing the way one wants the new twin to grow and cut about 0.5 cm above this spot. When in doubt, pruning should not be done. Whereas the lemon tree must be pruned every year, the grapefruit may be left virtually unpruned. Trees with terminal inflorescences, such as mango and cashew, may profit from regular pruning as this allows closer spacing. Samson (1986) described three types of pruning:

1. framework (to be performed in the nursery),
2. maintenance (to preserve the status quo and to suppress "water sprouts") and
3. rejuvenation pruning (to bring trees in decline back into production).

In banana, a limited number of shoots of different ages are allowed to grow simultaneously on one stool, whereas in date palm, older leaves are cut to make the tree more accessible for harvest. In moderate climates, deciduous trees are generally pruned in winter when the leaves have fallen, but in the humid tropics, pruning may take place at almost any time of the year. Pruning also includes removal of shoots of the rootstock, dead wood, parasites, epiphytes (e.g., ferns), climbing vines, and nests of bees, wasps, ants, and termites (Samson 1986).

Preharvest Crop Protection

The term "disease" refers to any damage to crop caused by fungi, bacteria, or viruses; a "pest" is any animal or agent causing damage or injury to crops (Hill 1975; Zadoks 1975; Hill and Waller 1982). Causes of injury may be biotic (living) or abiotic (nonliving). The latter include drought and inundation, storms, deficiency and toxicity of elements, acidity and salinity of soil, chemicals, and so on. In addition to fungi and bacteria, biotic factors include mycoplasmas, insects and mites, nematodes, animals, birds, snails, weeds, and parasites. Two or more factors may contribute to crop injury—for example, a mechanical injury may provide entrance for a fungus, or an insect may be the vector (transmitter) of a virus. Wardlaw (1961) noted a synergistic effect when the burrowing nematode and a certain bacteria caused Panama disease in banana.

Fungi cause a great variety of diseases such as root rots, wilts, damping-off, leaf spots, anthracnose, fruit rots, gummosis, rusts, blights, blasts, and mildews. *Phytophthora* spp. cause root rot and damping-off of seedlings and fruit rot in many fruit crops. *Glomerella cingulata,* also known as *Colletotrichum gloeosporoides* (the imperfect form), causes anthracnose of leaves and fruits of several crops.

Bacterial diseases of economic importance are *moko* in banana and canker in citrus. Mycoplasmas, which contain both RNA and DNA, cause various types of symptom: yellowing, greening, witch's broom, and stunting. Viruses consist of either RNA or DNA, usually surrounded by a thin protein coat; they cannot reproduce themselves without the host plant. Viruses cause mosaic, flecking, vein clearing, phloem necrosis, distortion, stunting, dieback, decline, and so on. Aphids act as vectors to transmit viruses. Budding and grafting promote rapid spread of viral diseases in fruit crops. Other agents include natural grafts, budding knives, parasites, and seed.

The biting insects eat leaves (locusts, beetles) or bore in stems (cosmopolites in banana), whereas the sucking types may transmit viral diseases (aphids) or pierce holes in fruits (moths), providing an access to fruitflies and fungi. Mites feed on leaves, causing them to fade and drop. Nematodes cause widespread damage to fruit crops (e.g., root knot caused by *Meloidogyne*). The burrowing nematode, *Radopholus similis,* causes citrus decline and attacks bananas. Crop rotation and mulching help control these pests. A resistant rootstock can also be used (Samson 1986).

Ants, scales, and aphids live in symbiosis, to their mutual advantage. Scales and aphids exude a sweet sap that the ants relish; in return, the ants protect them against enemies and transport them to fresh locations. Controlling ants by spraying Diazinon® on the stem denies the entry of aphids and scales, which makes them susceptible to predators and parasites.

Pathogen population is significantly influenced by the weather and climate. Winters in temperate regions ensure a discontinuity of pathogens that is generally lacking in the tropics, where outbreaks can occur at any time of year. A population of citrus rust mite can increase a hundredfold in less than two weeks of dry weather.

Samson (1986) suggested the following general methods of controlling diseases and pests of fruit crops:

1. legislation, quarantine laws;
2. sanitation, eradication, disinfection, rotation;
3. resistance, use of resistant or tolerant cultivars;
4. mechanical means, hand-picking, flaming, banding;
5. biological means, predators, parasites;
6. chemical means, dusting, spraying; and
7. integration, a combination of methods.

Most countries have strict quarantine laws, and permit only the import of pathogen-free plants or plant parts. Sanitation prevents, destroys, or reduces sources of infection. Citrus canker was eradicated twice from Florida by destroying millions of affected nursery plants and grove trees. The spread of burrowing nematodes was also eradicated from Florida. Raccah et al. (1976) reported the eradication of tristeza virus from Israel by the destruction of every infected tree. Planting material of banana is disinfected regularly by trimming corms and dipping them in hot water (55–60 °C for 10–20 min). Various chemicals may be used to disinfect suckers and corms. Bare root citrus seedlings are dipped in warm water (45 °C) for 25 min to ward off nematodes. The planting material of pineapple is dried in the sun to prevent base rot. Several pests and diseases of citrus and papaya can be controlled by crop rotation. Resistant types of cultivar have now replaced the "Gros Michel" banana, which was susceptible to Panama disease (Samson 1986).

Use of Chemicals, Phytohormones, and Growth Regulators

Chemicals, such as fungicides, insecticides, acaricides, nematicides, and other pesticides, are relatively cheap to use and can be applied easily. They have certain disadvantages, however, such as phytotoxicity to host plants, pollution of air, soil, and water, accumulation in food chains, and increasing resistance of pathogens to chemicals; also, they are rather ineffective against viral diseases.

The action of a fungicide may be either preventive or curative. For preventive action, the crop is covered more or less permanently with a thin layer of the chemical's active ingredient; curative treatment, on the other hand, aims at killing the pathogen after infection has taken place.

Bordeaux and Burgundy mixtures are most successful as fungicides. Other copper fungicides include copper oxide, copper oxychloride, and tribasic copper. Sulfur and lime sulfur are effective against rust, mildews, and mites. Dithiocarbamates are organic compounds containing a metal, either iron (Ferbam®), zinc (Ziram®, Zineb®), or manganese (Maneb®). Ferbam® is good at controlling scab and areolate spot in citrus, Zineb® works well against greasy spot of citrus, and Maneb® controls sigatoka of banana (Samson 1986).

Contact insecticides kill by penetrating the insect body, whereas stomach poisons are taken in with food. Systemic insecticides are transported throughout a plant and act anywhere; they can be applied to either the soil or the leaves. Most chlorinated hydrocarbons are used both as stomach and contact poisons. They are very persistent and may accumulate in the body fat of vertebrates. Organophosphates are effective as contact and systemic insecticides and as acaricides. They are not persistent, and break down within a few days at high temperature. Insecticides of plant origin are nicotine, pyrethrins, and rotenone. Mineral oils, such as refined "white oil" (1–2% solution), are effective against scales and mites. DD-mixture, chloropicrin, methyl bromide, and vapam are some of the important nematicides. Cohen (1975) reported that the Mediterranean fruit fly was controlled most effectively by a combination of three methods: fly parasites on wild hosts, bait sprays on citrus, and a sex pheromone that lures males to poisoned bait.

Nagy and Wardowski (1988) reviewed the effects of chemical agents on fruit composition, citing the comprehensive works of Boysen Jenson (1936), Avery et al. (1947), Audus (1953), Evans (1963), Coggins and Hield (1968), Nitsch (1971), and Childers (1975). A variety of chemicals and growth regulators sprayed on fruit crops to improve their marketability also cause changes in their nutrient composition.

Growth regulators are extensively used in sweet cherry production. Whereas the maturity of sweet cherry is delayed by gibberellins (e.g., gibberellic acid [GA]), it is advanced by daminozide (succinic 1,1-dimethylhydrazide). GA applied four to six weeks before harvest increased ascorbic acid content, decreased anthocyanin content, and had no effect on soluble solids, maleic acid, and fruit weight (Drake et al. 1978). The application of daminozide, on the contrary, increased the anthocyanin content of "Rainer" cherries (Drake et al. 1980) and the soluble solids of "Bing" cherries (Proebsting and Mills 1976). The application of daminozide and/or Fenoprop® (2,4,5-TP) at the initiation of pit hardening enhanced ripening of nectarine fruits and decreased the content of maleic acid (Ben-Arie and Guelfat-Reich 1979). Figaron® (ethyl 5-chloro-1H-3-indazolyl acetate), initially developed as a thinning agent for satsuma mandarins (and, when sprayed at a later stage in fruit growth, to decrease acids), increases sugars and enhances peel color of the fruit (Iwahori 1978).

McGlasson (1971) reported that preharvest spraying of fruit with ethylene precursors (ethephon) or compounds like auxins, which stimulate the production of ethylene in fruit tissue, caused noticeable changes in fruit composition. In contrast, compounds that inhibit ethylene production slowed down the ripening process and, therefore, altered the fruit's nutrient content. Aminoethoxyvinylglycine (AVG) decreased ethylene production in apples (Bangerth 1978; Bramlage et al. 1980) and blueberries (Dekazos 1980). AVG-treated fruits also showed higher acid levels than the controls.

Brominated and chlorinated hydrocarbons are used as common soil fumigants. Inorganic bromine is usually found as a residue in the harvested crop. Masui et al. (1978) reported that bromine in muskmelon grown in fumigated soil was most concentrated in the pericarp, less so in the outer flesh, and least in the inner flesh. According to Kempton and Maw (1973), the bromide concentration in tomatoes grown in fumigated soil was related to the concentration of inorganic bromide present in the soil. There was no relationship between the bromide concentration found in the fruit and the state of ripeness or the position of the fruit on the plant. Working with different tomato cultivars, Wambeke, Achter, and Assche (1979) noticed proportional increases in bromide residue with the rate of methyl bromide used, but this effect was not apparent in the second crop. Potassium content was higher and pH lower in tomato fruits from plots fumigated with 25 and 50 g/m^2 methyl bromide; the titratable acid content was higher, but these changes were not seen in the second crop. Wambeke, Achter, and Assche (1979) noted that fumigation reduced the soluble sugars content of the tomato crop.

Tomato plants grown in soil treated with 75 and 150 ppm of 1,2-dibromo-3-chloropropane (DBCP) showed an increased uptake of N, P, K, S, Ca, and Mg; this uptake, however, decreased in plants treated with 300 ppm of DBCP (Elliott and Edmunds 1977). No adverse effects on any nutritional components were observed in carrots and citrus grown on EDB, DBCP, or 1,3-dichloropropane-treated soil (Thomason et al. 1971); however, these crops had higher β-carotene contents than those grown on untreated soil. The treatment of soil, two months before planting "Senga" strawberries, with Shell-DD® (a mixture of 1,3-dichloropropane, 1,2-dichloropropane, and traces of higher chlorides) increased the protein content of the fruit (Sass 1975). Nagy and Wardowski (1988) concluded that in general there are no detrimental effects from soil fumigation; indeed, some nutrients may actually increase.

Maturation

The chemical composition of the fruit varies considerably throughout its growth and maturation periods. Some fruits reach their highest nutritive value while still immature, others when mature, and some when fully mature or overmature. Even within a given species, some cultivars will differ significantly from others in their nutrient contents. The following discussion on the effects of maturation on fruits composition is mainly based on the reports of Salunkhe et al. (1975) and Nagy and Wardowski (1988).

Okuse and Ryugo (1981) observed an increase in the ascorbic acid content of kiwi fruit with maturation. Quinic acid, the main organic acid in young kiwi fruit, disappeared concurrently with the appearance of vitamin C. Papaya also showed an increase in ascorbic acid with maturation (Arriola et al. 1980), but mangoes (Askar, El-Tamini, and Raouf 1972), bananas (Thornton 1943), "Maracuya" passion fruit (Arriola, Menchu, and Rolz 1976), and acerola (Asenjo and Moscoso 1950) showed a decrease. The relationship between the stage of maturity and the vitamin C contents of oranges, grapefruit, and tangerines (Harding, Winston, and Fisher 1940; Harding and Fisher 1945; Harding and Sunday 1949) is shown in Fig. 3-1. The immature fruit had the highest concentration of vitamin C, whereas the ripe fruit contained the least. Although there was a decrease during ripening, the total vitamin C content per fruit tended to increase with increased juice volume and fruit size.

Provitamin A compounds, such as α-carotene, β-carotene, β-cryptoxanthin, and β-apo-8-carotenol, are converted into active vitamin A by the human body. John, Subbarayan, and Cama (1963) noted a significant increase in total carotenoids and β-carotenoids both in the peel and the pulp during the maturation of mangoes. At maturity, β-carotene ($=1.667$ vitamin A/μg) constituted about 50–60% of the total carotenoids in Alphonso mangoes (Jungalwala and Cama 1963). Fair quantities of carotenoid compounds have been reported in cantaloupe (Howard, McGillivray, and Yamaguchi 1962), papaya (Arriola, Madrid, and Rolz 1975), citrus (Stewart 1980), acerola (Asenjo 1980), and plantains; all these show an increase in carotenoid content with maturation.

There is an increase in thiamin content of citrus fruit with maturity (Hsu 1974). When compared at similar maturity levels, the early-season orange "Hamlin" had the lowest vitamin B_1 content, whereas "Valencia," a late-season

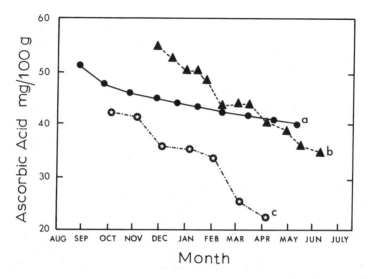

Fig. 3-1. Effect of maturation on the vitamin C contents of (a) "Duncan" grapefruit, (b) "Valencia" orange, and (c) "Dancy" tangerine. *Source:* Harding et al. (1940), Harding and Fisher (1945), and Harding and Sunday (1949).

orange, had the highest. Compared with many other fruits, grapes and black currants showed the highest level of thiamin; that of grapes also increased during ripening (Peynaud and Ribereau-Gayon 1971). Other fruits showing modest amounts of thiamin (in $\mu g/100$ g flesh) are pineapple (69–125), raspberry (20–30), mango (35–60), melon (60–80), acerola (28–30), date (80–150), fig (61–79), and tamarind (44–154) (Hulme 1971; Nagy and Shaw 1980).

Folic acid (folacin) is chemically pteroylmonoglutamic acid. Several compounds exhibiting folic acid activity may differ only in the number of glutamic acid residues they contain. With the exception of citrus, fruits generally contain low amounts of folic acid (Ting et al. 1974). Citrus fruit juice contained about 20–50 μg folacin/100 ml (Varsel 1980); its concentration increased with fruit maturation, and wide variations were observed throughout the growing season (Ting 1977). The following amounts of folic acid were found in other fruits: fig, 39 $\mu g/100$ g dried (Hall, Morgan, and Wheeler 1953); mango, 36 $\mu g/100$ g flesh (Ghosh 1960); avocado, 10–60 $\mu g/100$ g flesh (Hall, More, and Morgan 1955); and grape, 1–2 μg/liter juice (Peynaud and Ribereau-Gayon 1971).

Pantothenic acid, riboflavin, niacin, vitamin B_6 (pyridoxine, pyridoxamine, pyridoxal), vitamin B_{12}, and tocopherols are found in many fruits at levels below 10% of the U.S. RDA (Hulme 1971). Studies relating fruit maturation to changes in concentration of these minor vitamins are limited. According to Mapson (1971), apricots, gooseberries, black currants, figs, and citrus fruits contain moderate amounts of pantothenic acid. Mango, pineapple, papaya, acerola, and passion fruit are good sources of riboflavin, and tamarind, guava, and passion fruit provide niacin (Nagy and Shaw 1980). Among the twenty-six fruits tested by Polansky and Murphy (1966), bananas (5.4 μg/g) and avocados (4.5 μg/g) contained the highest amounts of vitamin B_6.

Postharvest Technology

Salunkhe and Desai (1984a) have described the effects of postharvest biotechnologies on the reduction of fruit losses.

Harvesting and Handling

Fruits picked at the appropriate stage of maturity have prolonged storage life and good quality. Most fruits overripen if left too long on trees; however, fruits like avocado, in which the climacteric sets in only after picking, may be left on the trees for a considerable length of time. Harvest may also be delayed for several weeks for some citrus fruits, even after internal maturity has been reached; however, the fruit is picked as soon as external and internal characteristics allow.

Biale (1976) grouped fruit crops into the following two classes:

1. *nonclimacteric* (e.g., citrus, grape, guava, pineapple) and
2. *climacteric* (e.g., avocado, banana, fig, mango, papaya).

There are significant differences in climacteric (characterized by a sharp rise in respiration) and nonclimacteric fruits (Table 3-7).

Leopold and Kriedemann (1975) found that ripening proceeds rapidly in banana, moderately in apple, and slowly in orange (Fig. 3-2). Fig. 3-3 shows color changes involving loss of chlorophyll and changes in the carotenoids. Fig. 3-4 shows the intensity of respiration rate in four fruit species: avocado, banana, pear, and apple (Leopold and Kriedemann 1975).

Most fruits are harvested before they reach optimum flavor, color, and nutrient content. Fruits picked before the onset of ripening tend to be firmer and less

Table 3-7. Range of Respiration[a] at 20°C

Climac-teric	Min.	Max.	Non-climacteric	Initial	Final
Avocado	35	155	Lemon	10	8
Banana	20	60	Orange	13	11
Mango	22	63	Pineapple	11	17

Source: Biale (1976).
[a]In milliliters of O_2 per kg hr^{-1}.

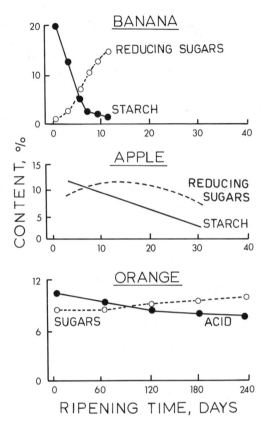

Fig. 3-2. Fruit-ripening processes in three species. *Source:* Leopold and Kriede-mann (1975).

susceptible to bruising during harvesting and subsequent handling. According to Nagy and Wardowski (1986), harvest times differ considerably and depend on the ripening pattern of the fruit. The time of harvest for climacteric fruit is critical for maximum storage and market life, as shown in Fig. 3-5 (Grierson 1973). With the exception of avocado, climacteric fruits normally ripen on the tree; however, they are usually harvested prior to the onset of the climacteric and stored under carefully controlled conditions to suppress the ripening process (Krochta and Feinberg 1975). Nonclimacteric fruits, such as citrus, are normally allowed to ripen on the parent plant prior to harvesting (Sinclair 1961; Eskin, Henderson, and Townsend 1971). In Florida, the harvesting of citrus fruits is strictly regulated; maturity tests covering color break, juice content, Brix, total titratable acidity, and ratio of Brix to total acids are conducted on citrus to ascertain whether they can be legally sold (Nagy and Wardowski 1988).

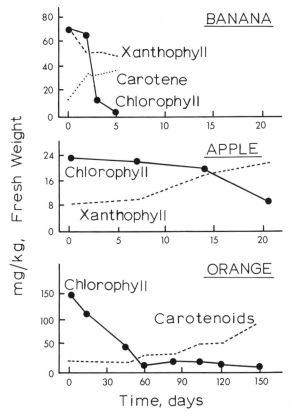

Fig. 3-3. Pigment changes in three fruit species. *Source:* Leopold and Kriede-mann (1975).

Samson (1986) pointed out the following criteria for selecting the harvest date in different fruits:

1. number of days after fruit setting (banana);
2. shape of the transversely cut fruit (banana);
3. resistance to pressure (avocado);
4. break in rind color (citrus, mango, papaya, pineapple);
5. ratio between sugars and acids (citrus, pineapple, banana); and
6. minimum juice volume (citrus).

In addition to these, other physical and chemical indexes of harvest maturi-ties, such as pulp:peel ratio, "fullness index" (weight divided by the length of an internal fruit of the first or second hand), and loss of chlorophyll in fruits like bananas have been used successfully (Desai and Deshpande 1978; Pantasti-

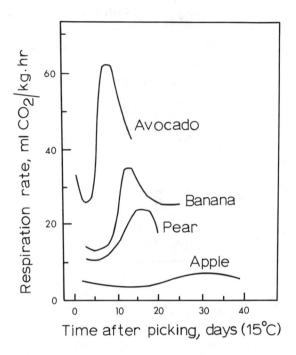

Fig. 3-4. Respiration rate during ripening of four fruits. *Source:* Leopold and Kriedemann (1975).

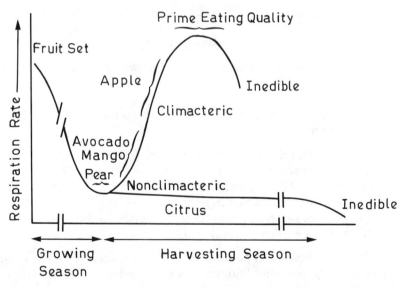

Fig. 3-5. Life cycles of typical fruits. The respiration rate of a typical "climacteric" fruit may increase tenfold after harvest, which is not true of "nonclimacteric" fruit such as citrus. *Source:* Grierson (1973).

co et al. 1975). Akamine and Goo (1971) used the relationship between the soluble solids and skin color to judge the correct harvest maturity of papaya. Pineapples are harvested at varying stages of color development depending upon the length of transport period and storage facilities available (Akamine 1977). Many fruits like tomato may be harvested at varying times depending on the market demand.

Fruit is picked by cutting, clipping, pulling, or shaking. Shaking, a labor-saving method, is usually combined with the use of abscission chemicals such as cyclohexamide, SADH, and ethephon. In the West, most citrus fruits are harvested mechanically with harvest aids (chemical pruners) and growth substances.

A trunk shaker operates with a short stroke at high frequency and has a capacity of 40–60 trees per hour. The fruit dropped on the ground is then collected with a rake-pickup; this fruit is limited to cannery use and must be processed within 36 h (Samson 1986). The fruit caught on a padded catching frame may, however, be suitable for the fresh market (Wilson and Coppock 1975). Willigen (1968) reported that the West Indian cherries in Surinam are harvested for processing by shaking into a tarpaulin.

Small fruits can best be harvested by shaking the whole tree or its branches, but in a majority of cases harvesting must be done by hand. A knife is used for larger fruits, such as papaya, pineapple, and soursop, whereas clippers are used in California for citrus. Although hand-picking is still an established practice for some fruits, there is an increasing trend toward mechanical harvesting, especially in Western countries. Woodroof (1975) listed the following advantages of hand-picking over mechanical harvesting:

1. The fruit is bruised less and can be held longer before processing.
2. The fruit may be allowed to become more mature before harvesting.
3. Picking is more complete and total yield is greater.
4. The plants themselves are bruised less and continue to produce longer.

Ever-bearing varieties are hand-picked to avoid damaging the mature and immature fruit. Fruits such as berries, which ripen over several weeks, require multiple pickings (Nagy and Wardowski 1988).

Hand methods of harvesting, picking, and catching cause less damage than do mechanical techniques, thereby extending the storage and market life of fruits (Marriott, Perkins, and Been 1979). Fresh horticultural commodities should preferably be harvested during the early part of the day to avoid a higher level of field heat. The product is collected in a suitable container, without exposing it to potentially adverse effects of sun, rain, or wind.

Ladders, bags, field boxes (to hold 30–40-kg fruit), and field containers (to hold fruit of ≤400 kg) are used. In California, a more efficient and less tiring "harness and picking bag" has been introduced (Smith 1969). According to

Johnson (1969), picking costs in California exceed all other cultural costs combined; in Israel, they represent 40% of the number of working days (Alper and Sarig 1969).

The Organization for Economic Cooperation and Development (OECD 1958), and the U.N. Industrial Development Organization (UNIDO 1972) have published alternative designs for crates and containers for handling fresh produce. These newer designs improve the storage stability of the produce resulting in substantial savings (Rawnsley 1969). Lakshminarayana et al. (1971) and Madalgatti Rao (1969) evaluated the existing and improved designs of containers used in India for transporting and handling mangoes and grapes, respectively.

O'Brien (1975) summarized different systems of mechanized handling and harvesting of fresh fruits (Table 3-8). He concluded that bin handling had the advantage of greater adaptability to a wide variety of conditions, but it required good orchard management. Harvested fruits are usually washed, disinfected, dried, waxed, and sorted for size and grade before being packed. The traditional "nailed wooden" boxes have largely been replaced by wirebound "Bruce" boxes and, more recently, by corrugated cardboard boxes for fruits like citrus and apples. Bananas are presently shipped in cardboard boxes as detached hands rather than in whole bunches.

Effect of Harvesting Methods on Nutrients

Limited studies are available on the effects of rough handling and hand-picking of fruit on its nutrient contents. Rough handling generally causes structural and

Table 3-8. Summary of Harvesting and Handling Systems.

Harvesting	Handling	Applicable Produce
Hand	Boxes	All fruits and vegetables
	Bins	Prunes, peaches, pears, citrus, apples
	Gondolas	Peaches, apples, citrus, pineapple
Picking platforms	Bins	Pears, citrus, peaches, dates, prunes
Pickup machines	Boxes	Figs, prunes
	Bins—dry	Figs, nuts, prunes
	Bins—wet	Prunes
Shake–catch	Bins—wet	Cherries
	Bins—dry	Prunes, peaches, apricots, apples, citrus
	Gondolas	Prunes, peaches, apples, citrus (short haul)
Mechanical	Boxes	Asparagus
	Bins	Tomatoes, asparagus, carrots, celery, beans, peas, potatoes
	Gondolas	Lettuce, cantaloupes, potatoes, tomatoes

Source: O'Brien (1975).

physiological disorganization of fruit tissue with a concomitant increase in the activities of degradative enzymes. As a result of cellular disorganization, oxidative destruction of vitamin C in fruits is enhanced by the action of ascorbic acid oxidase, phenolase, cytochrome oxidase, and peroxidase (Nagy and Wardowski 1988).

Vines, Grierson, and Edwards (1968) noted that dropping grapefruit from heights of up to 1.52 m onto a hard surface increased respiration and ethylene production in relation to the height of the drop. In grapefruit, ethylene evolution contributes to the overall ripening phase by causing membrane changes, increasing the activity of certain membrane-oriented enzymes and accelerating the activity of proteolytic enzymes associated with color development (Sinclair 1972). Krochta, Tillin, and Whitehead (1975) found that bruising of tomatoes had little effect on ascorbic acid content. However, dropping mangoes to the ground resulted in a significant decrease of ascorbic acid during storage (Yagi, Habish, and Agab 1978).

Mechanical harvesting of fruits may also influence the chemical composition of the fruit and/or juice product. A greater movement of tannins into the outer cortical cells during a 24-h soak was noticed in mechanically harvested "Montmorency" cherries (Arnold and Mitchell 1970). Similarly, Schumacher et al. (1974) observed that wounding of mechanically harvested "Engishofer" apples stimulated acid breakdown and increased glycerol production.

The use of abscission chemicals as aids in mechanical harvesting also causes changes in fruits. Shanmugavelu, Rao, and Srinivasan (1973) found that ethephon (2-chloroethylphosphonic acid) decreased the ascorbic acid content in papaya, but increased the total and reducing sugars and pectin content. In contrast, ethephon increased the ascorbic acid content and decreased the reducing sugars in pumpkin (Shanmugavelu, Srinivasan, and Thamburaj 1973).

The effects of ethephon on the acidity of blueberries varied with the time of application (Warren, Ballinger, and Mainland 1973). An early application of 2,000–8,000 ppm, ethephon lowered the acidity, but later application raised it. Ethephon at 50–200 ppm had no effect on the titratable acidity of four peach cultivars regardless of the date of application (Sims, Gambrell, and Stembridge 1974). Spraying ethephon (200 and 400 ppm) and GA (50 and 100 ppm) one month before the harvest of sweet oranges reduced acidity and increased the total soluble solids and total sugars (Mazumdar and Bhatt 1976). An appreciable decrease in total soluble solids (TSS) and TSS : acid ratio of the juice was observed when "Rabbab" pomegranates were treated with increasing ethephon concentration (Shaybany and Sharifi 1973).

Ethephon also influences the content of pigments. Kvale (1974) reported that ethephon at 400 ppm enhanced the anthocyanin content of "Raud Prins" apples when applied in July; the applications in June and August had no effect unless combined with daminozide. Morini, Vitagliano, and Xiloyannis (1974) also noted increased anthocyanin levels in peaches treated with ethephon. Ethephon also enhanced the synthesis of lycopene in tomatoes (Russo et al. 1975).

Mechanical harvesting in citrus is often combined with the use of abscission chemicals to reduce the force for separating the fruit from the stem. Many of these chemical pruners affect the chemical composition of cold-pressed orange oil (Moshonas, Shaw, and Sims 1976; Moshonas and Shaw 1977). These chemicals, which caused injury to the peel, also induced the formation of six phenolic ethers not reported earlier as constituents of citrus: eugenol, *cis*-methylisoeugenol, *trans*-methylisoeugenol, methyleugenol, elemicin, and iso-elemicin (Moshonas and Shaw 1978). These authors postulated that the abscission chemicals possibly enhance the aging process, thereby adversely affecting the flavor quality of the juice extracted from these fruit.

Grading, Sorting, and Packaging

Grading or sorting may be limited to removal of splits, punctures, deformed fruits, and incipient rots. Appropriate packaging, however, is necessary to assemble the produce in convenient units for handling and to protect it during the subsequent storage and marketing operations. Precooling and commodity treatments, such as waxing, disinfection (fumigation), or the use of fungicides and other growth substances, are used to prolong the shelf life of fruits (Salunkhe and Desai 1984a).

Considerable developments are taking place in the area of packaging and containerization, newer techniques and materials being added every year. The use of laminates and plastics has increased in recent years. There are many types of flexible material used singly or in combination. Fruits to be cold-stored are wrapped in flexible film; a mixture of gases is then inserted to delay post-harvest changes (gas flushing). Salunkhe and Desai (1984b) have reviewed these recent developments in packaging technology. Wills et al. (1981) also summarized the requirements of modern packaging for perishable commodities, discussing such aspects of packaging materials as mechanical strength for adequate protection; their inherent toxicity; handling and marketing requirements in terms of weight, size, and shape related to packaging; and standardization for mechanical handling. Rapid cooling of the produce in its package, permeability of plastic films to respiratory gases, and cost of the package in relation to the value of the produce are the most important factors. Hardenburg (1975) and Hall, Hardenburg, and Pantastico (1975) described the principles of packaging and use of such materials as plastics for fruits and other products.

Chemical Control of Postharvest Losses

The use of chemicals and growth substances to control postharvest losses of fruits has become an integral part of handling and successful marketing of horticultural produce in recent years. It is commercially employed for citrus, grapes, and bananas. The commodity's marketing strategy and the type of infection determine the magnitude of loss reduction enabled by the chemical.

The success of chemical treatment depends on several factors, including the initial load of microbial spores, depth of infection within the host tissue, growth rate of infection, temperature, humidity, and depth of penetration of chemical into the host tissue. The phytotoxicity of the applied chemical is very important: It should neither injure the host tissue nor leave toxic residues in the fruit (i.e., it should fall within the ambit of the local food additive laws). Eckert (1977) listed a wide range of chemicals used to control postharvest diseases of fruits (Table 3-9)—their common names, pathogens against which they are effective, and the fruits on which they are used. With the exception of chlorine and sulfur dioxide, which are true fungicides, most chemicals listed in Table 3-9 are fungistatic in action; that is, they inhibit or reduce microbial spore germination and subsequent growth. Eckert et al. (1975), Eckert (1978), and Salunkhe et al. (1975) also described the use of several chemicals, including waxes, fungicides, and growth regulators, to reduce postharvest wastage of perishable commodities. Dave, Petrie, and Kaplan (1980) reported the results of large-scale commercial field testing of a fungicide, imizalil, in a formulated product called Deccozil-EC®, for citrus; it was effective in controlling the blue-green mold rots that had developed tolerance to other commercially available fungicides, such as TBZ, 2-AB, and benomyl. Banks and Harper (1981) studied the effects of TAL-Prolong®, a coating material consisting of a mixture of sucrose esters of fatty acids and a polysaccharide, on several fruits. This compound considerably reduces the permeability of the fruit skin to oxygen while hardly affecting that to carbon dioxide. It thus creates a modified atmospheric condition without the usual technical elaboration. TAL-Prolong® was effective in extending the shelf life of bananas, apples, pears, plums, avocados, and mangoes, but had little effect on grapes, tomatoes, and strawberries. This varied response of the produce was attributed to the differential possession of stomata on the fruit surface. This coating material has enormous potential for cheaper transport of fresh fruits to distant markets.

Fruit ripening can also be delayed by treatment with certain growth hormones (e.g., gibberellic acid), growth retardants (maleic hydrazide), and metabolic inhibitors, such as vitamin K (banana), wax coating, addition of ethylene absorbents, and so on. (Salunkhe and Desai 1984a).

Fumigation of tomatoes with ethylene dibromide (EDB) reduced red color development in the outer pericarp, although the inner tissues remained unaffected at doses as high as 35 g/m^3 (Rigney, Graham, and Lee 1978). Carotene accumulation was enhanced by EDB at 4 g/m^3, but at higher doses that of the tomato pericarp was reduced. Winkler (1962) reported increased destruction of thiamin content of grapes treated with EDB.

Table 3-9. Chemicals That Have Been Used as Postharvest Fungicides.

Name and Formulation	Pathogen Controlled	Host	Remarks
Alkaline inorganic salts			
Sodium tetraborate (borax)	*Penicillium*	Citrus	Only reasonably effective; problem with boron residues
Sodium carbonate	*Penicillium*	Citrus	Only slightly effective
Sodium hydroxide	*Penicillium*	Citrus	Only slightly effective, caustic
Ammonia & aliphatic amines			
Ammonia gas	*Penicillium, Diplodia*	Citrus	Good for fumigation of degreening and storage rooms
Sec-butylamine	*Rhizopus, Penicillium,* stem-end rots	Peach	Slight control as dip or fumigant
Aromatic amines			
Dichoran	*Rhizopus, Monilia, Botrytis*	Drupes, carrots	Very effective
Benzimidazoles			
Benomyl, thiabendazole, thiophanate methyl, benzimidazole carbamate	*Penicillium, Colletotrichum,* and other fungi	Citrus, banana, apple, pear, drupes	Effective at low concentrations; resistance problem; residue tolerance 0–10 ppm
Imazalil	*Penicillium,* stem-end rots	Citrus	Effective against benomyl-resistant strains and at low concentrations
Hydrocarbons and derivatives			
Biphenyl	*Penicillium, Diplodia*	Citrus	Unpleasant smell
Methyl chloroform	*Penicillium,* stem-end rots	Citrus	Only inhibits spore germination
Oxidizers			
Hypochlorus acids	Bacteria, fungi buildup in wash water	Produce	Good sterilant, no penetration of injury sites, corrosive to metal
Iodine	Bacteria, fungi	Citrus, grapes	Staining problem, expensive
Nitrogen trichloride	*Penicillium*	Tomato, citrus	Hydrolysis to hypochlorus acid
Organic acids and aldehydes			
Dehydroacetic acid	*Botrytis* and other fungi	Strawberry	Dip not accepted by industry
Sorbic acid	*Alternaria, Cladosporium*	Fig	
Formaldehyde	Fungi		Sterilant for picking boxes, storage rooms

Table 3-9. (*Continued*)

Name and Formulation	Pathogen Controlled	Host	Remarks
Phenols			
O-Phenylphenol (HOPP)	*Penicillium*	Citrus	Causes fruit injury
Sodium-*O*-phenylphenate (SOPP)	*Penicillium*, bacteria	Produce	pH control needed to prevent injury; residue tolerance 10–12 ppm
Salicylanilide	*Penicillium, Phomopsis, Nigrospora*	Citrus, banana	Slight control
Sulfur (inorganic)			
Sulfur dust	*Monilia*	Peach	Superseded by dichloran
Lime sulfur	*Sclerotinia*		
SO$_2$ gas, bisulfite	*Botrytis*	Grapes	SO$_2$ gas needs moisture to be effective; no toxic residues
Captan®	Storage rots	Produce	
Thiram®	*Cladosporium*, crown and stem-end rots	Strawberry, banana	
Ziram®	*Alternaria*, crown and stem-end rots	Banana	
Thiourea	*Penicillium* spores	Citrus	Toxic to humans
Thioacetamide	*Diplodia*		

Compiled from: Wild (1975), Ogawa, Manji, and El-Behadli (1976), and Eckert (1977).

Holding and Storage Environment

The metabolism of harvested fruit continues until an overripe stage is reached. Although these metabolic processes cannot be stopped, they can be retarded by one or more of the following measures:

1. reduction in temperature (cold storage),
2. reduced pressure (hypobaric or subatmospheric storage),
3. controlled atmospheric (CA) storage, and
4. modified atmospheric (MA) storage.

Low-Temperature Storage

Lower holding temperatures retard the rate of respiration of fruits during storage and transport. The temperature must be maintained above the freezing point and, for most tropical fruits, should be at least 10 °C to avoid chilling injury.

Table 3-10. Recommended Holding Conditions for Various Fruits.

Fruit	Temperature (°C)	Relative Humidity (%)	Period
Orange	-1- 7	85-90	1- 6 mo
Mandarin	4- 7	85-90	3-12 wk
Grapefruit	10-15	85-90	3-13 wk
Lemon			
Green	11-14	85-90	1- 4 mo
Yellow	0-10	85-90	3- 6 wk
Lime	8-10	85-90	3- 8 wk
Banana			
Green	11-14	90-95	10-20 d
Ripe	13-16	85-90	5-10 d
Pineapple			
Green	10	90	2- 4 wk
Ripe	5-10	85-90	2- 6 wk
Avocado	5-13	85-90	2- 4 wk
Brazil nuts	0	70	8-12 mo
Cashew	0- 1	85-90	4- 5 wk
Guava	7-10	85-90	3- 4 wk
Mango	7-10	85-90	4- 7 wk
Papaya	4-10	85-90	2- 5 wk
Passion fruit	5- 7	80-85	4- 5 wk

Source: Hartoungh (1978).

The relative humidity should preferably be 85–90%. Hartoungh (1978) listed recommended temperature and relative humidity as well as probable period of storage for various fruit crops (Table 3-10). Storage requirements vary considerably depending on crop and stage of ripeness.

According to Wills et al. (1981), the storage life (in weeks) of fruits should be as follows:

at 5–9 °C—orange, 6–12; mandarin, 4–6; ripe pineapple, 4–5; avocado, 3–5; mango, 2–3; passion fruit, 3–5; and

at 10 °C—grapefruit, 6–12; lemon, 12–20; banana, 1–2; green pineapple, 4–5.

Fruits such as avocados have a longer storage life without chilling injury when packed individually in sealed polythene bags. The storage life of plantains can be extended up to 25 days at rather high temperatures by keeping ethylene absorbent (e.g., $KMnO_4$ [Purafil®]) in polythene bags; at 13 °C, it can be increased by up to 55 days. Wax coating of citrus and mango skins has an effect similar to that of the polythene bags. Coating chemicals reduce transpiration and gas exchange even at room temperatures (Samson 1986).

Low-temperature storage not only decreases the production of ethylene, but

Table 3-11. Grouping of Compatible Fruits for Transport in Mixed Loads.

Group 1 (1.0–1.1 °C, 90–95% rh)	Group 2 (12.8–18.3 °C, 85–90% rh)	Group 3 (2.2–5.0 °C, 90–95% rh)
Apple	Avocado	Cranberry
Apricot	Banana	Lemon
Berries (except cranberry)	Grapefruit	Litchi
Cherries	Guava	Orange
Fig	Lime	Tangerine
Peach	Mango	
Pear	Olive	
Persimmon	Papaya	
Plum	Pineapple	
Pomegranate		
Quince		

Source: Lipton and Harvey (1972).

also lowers the rate of response of the fruit to the applied ethylene. Fruit storage at high relative humidity may predispose the produce to microbial infection, thereby causing postharvest decays and rots. A compromise is generally effected by providing adequate air movement via ventilation and moderately high relative humidity for the freshness of the stored product. Lutz and Hardenburg (1968) determined the optimum storage temperatures and relative humidity for many tropical fruit crops. Fidler and Coursey (1969) reviewed the effects of low-temperature injury in several tropical and subtropical fruits.

Bananas and grapefruits often suffer chilling injury at low temperatures. This injury sometimes results in decay as pathogens can enter the weakened tissue. Chilling injury of grapefruit is reduced by high relative humidity (>90%) and hypobaric storage (Grierson 1976), by thiabendazole and benomyl treatments (Schiffman-Nadel et al. 1975), and even by benomyl applied several months before harvest (Wardowski et al. 1975). The green citrus fruits are most susceptible to chilling injury, the yellow ones somewhat less so, and the orange fruits most resistant (Grierson 1976).

The general compatibility of temperature and humidity requirements for fresh produce must be observed carefully during transport. Lipton and Harvey (1972) classified fruit compatibility along with the recommended temperatures and relative humidities during transport for each group (Table 3-11).

Controlled-Atmosphere (CA), Modified-Atmosphere (MA), and Subatmospheric (Hypobaric) Storage

As an adjunct to low-temperature storage or a substitute for refrigeration, the addition or removal of gases resulting in an atmosphere different from that of normal air—as in controlled atmosphere (CA), modified atmosphere (MA), or subatmospheric (hypobaric or low-pressure) storage—has been widely employed to extend the storage life of fruits. These methods aim at reducing respiration and other metabolic reactions by increasing the CO_2 and decreasing the O_2 concentrations. They also lower the rate of natural ethylene production (as in banana), as well as the sensitivity of fruits to ethylene. Controlled atmospheres with high CO_2 inhibit breakdown of pectic substances and retain fruit texture, firmness, and flavor for a longer period.

Do and Salunkhe (1975) reviewed the biochemistry and physiology of CA storage with reference to metabolic effects, accumulation of toxic substances, and other adverse effects. Ulrich (1975) also described the physiological and practical considerations of CA storage. Not all fruits respond favorably to atmospheric regulation; some are little affected by CA or MA. The use of these techniques is advantageous where the produce is harvested over a relatively short period; increasing the shelf life of such fruits can improve their marketability. CA storage, being expensive, is advocated only when there is a distinct financial gain from its use (Salunkhe and Desai 1984a).

Hypobaric storage is a form of atmospheric control in which the produce is stored in a partial vacuum. The vacuum chamber is vented continuously with water-saturated air to maintain desirable O_2 levels and minimize water loss. Reductions in the partial pressure of oxygen, as well as in ethylene levels, delays fruit ripening. The effects of subatmospheric-pressure storage on postharvest behavior, including ripening and biochemical changes of several fruits, have been comprehensively reviewed by Salunkhe and Wu (1973, 1975), Burg (1975), and Salunkhe and Desai (1984a).

Effects of Storage on Nutrients

Nagy and Wardowski (1988) have reviewed the effects of storage methods on the nutritional composition of fruit crops. Grierson and Wardowski (1978) studied the length of holding after harvest and the usual cause of the end of storage life of several fruits and vegetables. Overmaturity and the resulting decay during prolonged storage lead, in turn, to a virtually complete loss of nutrients in fruits. Most storage studies with fruits have reported changes in keeping quality, decay, weight loss, and, in the case of citrus, changes in sugar and acid content. Stahl and Camp (1936) confirmed earlier findings that for grapefruit and, even more so, for orange, citric acid decreased and sugar increased to an even greater extent during storage for several months at various temperatures. Bratley (1939) reported that, during eight weeks of storage at 0 °C, tangerines nearly maintained their vitamin C levels; but at 7–9 °C, about one-fourth was lost. Only a slight loss of vitamin C was observed for oranges held ten to 16 days under simulated marketing conditions (Harding 1954).

Anderson, Parsons, and Smith (1967) assessed the feasibility of extending the storage life of various stone fruits (viz., "Redhaven," "Sunhigh," and "Loring" peaches and "Late Le Grand" nectarines) by CA storage. Organoleptic tests favored storage of these fruits in 1% O_2 and 5% CO_2. Convey (1960) found the best CA storage for "Eldorado" plums to be 17% O_2, 7% CO_2, and 86% N_2; these conditions delayed ripening and reduced the loss of soluble solids.

Radurization

The preservation and extension of the refrigerated life of fruits by irradiation (pasteurization with ionizing radiation) has considerable potential. The attractive feature of radurization is the negligible rise in temperature even at doses that afford complete sterilization of the produce (Salunkhe, Do, and Bolin 1974). The success of this technique depends upon cultivar selection, commodity maturity, and superimposable packaging material, preirradiation chemical treatment, and storage temperatures employed. Ascorbic acid is the most radiosensitive vitamin. Salunkhe (1961) reported the results of γ-irradiation on the storage and quality of several fruits and vegetables, including its effects on nutritive values of food products.

Maxie, Sommer, and Mitchell (1971) conducted trials on irradiation of fresh fruits. The maximum tolerable dose and minimum dose required for different fruits are shown in Table 3-12. They found limited prospects for irradiation as a postharvest treatment. A joint report published by FAO/WHO (1977) on the wholesomeness of irradiated produce has largely alleviated early fears about induced radioactivity, loss of nutritive value, or the formation of harmful radiolysis products in the irradiated foods. Salunkhe (1961) also reported negligible losses of nutrients in several fruits and vegetables at pasteurization and sprout-inhibition doses of ionizing radiation.

Fruit Processing

Postharvest losses can be reduced considerably if fruits are processed into more durable food products. Fruit-processing technology must therefore be developed simultaneously with the fruit-growing business. Fruits to be processed should be ripe but firm enough to withstand the necessary heat treatment. The firmness and quality of the processed products are related to differences in pectic substances (McColloch, Nielsen, and Beavens 1950; Postlmayer, Luh, and Leonard 1956). The viscosity or consistency of such processed products as jams, jellies, juices, catsups, and preserves is also important. Rodriguez et al. (1975) reviewed the literature on the quality of raw materials for processing, factors influencing the quality of fruits used for processing, and processing qualities of individual fruit products.

Table 3-12. Comparison of Maximum Tolerable Doses and Minimum Dose Required for Desired Technical Effects on Selected Fresh Fruits and Vegetables.

Produce	Desired Technical Effect	Max. Dose Tolerable (kGy)[a]	Min. Dose Required (kGy)	Limitations for Commercial Application
Apple	Control of scald and brown core	1.0 – 1.5	1.5 – 2.5	Cheaper, more effective alternatives; tissue softening
Apricot, peach, nectarine	Inhibition of brown rot	0.5 – 1.0	2.0	Tissue softening
Avocado	Inhibition of ripening and rot	0.25	None	Cheaper, more effective alternatives; browning and softening of tissues
Banana	Inhibition of ripening	0.5	0.30 – 0.35	Cheaper, more effective alternatives
Lemon	Inhibition of Penicillium rots	0.25	1.50 – 2.0	Severe injury of fruit at doses ≥0.5 kGy
Orange	Inhibition of Penicillium rots	2	2.0	Cheaper, more effective alternatives; no technical effect under commercial conditions
Papaya	Disinfection of fruit fly	0.75 – 1.0	0.25	Not economical; inadequate acreage
Pear	Inhibition of ripening	1	2.5	Abnormal ripening; cheaper, more effective alternatives
Strawberry	Inhibition of gray mold	2	2.0	Cheaper, equally effective alternatives
Table grape	Inhibition of gray mold	0.25 – 0.50	—	Tissue softening; severe off-flavors; cheaper, more effective alternatives

Source: Maxie et al. (1971).
[a]1 kGy (kilogray) = 10^5 rad.

Losses that occur in the preparation of the material for processing can be minimized or eliminated via technological advances. Proper fruit shape and size reduce losses during mechanical trimming and handling. Varieties of fruits with improved storage characteristics and better processing properties need to be developed to reduce the cost of energy inputs and to prevent wastage and loss of quality (Rhodes 1980).

Canning, freezing, and dehydration are the major processes of food preservation. The removal of water to stop the growth and multiplication of microorganisms, heat sterilization to destroy pathogens and inactivate enzymes, lower temperature to slow down most biochemical reactions, and provision of a chemical environment to retard deterioration are the basic principles of food preservation by processing (Rasmussen, Rogers, and Michener 1966).

Salunkhe, Do, and Bolin (1974) and Salunkhe and Desai (1984a) reviewed the developments in the technology and nutritive values of dehydrated fruits and their products. They also described the modern techniques employed in the developed countries, including quick blanching, various dehydration techniques (e.g., freeze-drying, accelerated freeze-drying, liquid nitrogen, and cryogenic freezing), freeze concentration of fruit juices, foam-mat drying, and microwave drying. Dehydrofreezing and dehydrocanning are other techniques employed to reduce the weight of fruits before freezing.

The overall trend in food preservation is toward milder processing. Rather than relying on any single severe treatments to repress microbiological spoilage, combinations of less severe treatments are being developed—in particular for intermediate-moisture (IM) foods, such as raisins. Low water activity in such foods minimizes and prevents the growth of molds and bacteria. Dried fruits, jams, jellies, sausages, and pies are the traditional IM foods (Salunkhe and Desai 1984a).

VEGETABLES

As previously discussed, the term "vegetable" refers to soft edible plant parts that are eaten either fresh (salads) or cooked. All plant parts—roots, tubers, stems, leaves, flowers, and inflorescences—can be used as vegetables. Thus most cucurbits, which are actually fruits, are treated as vegetables. Some cereals and legumes may also be consumed as vegetables in their immature, unripe state. Typical examples include sweet corn of the grass family, and French beans, green beans, snap beans, and garden peas belonging to the legumes. In several parts of India, young green seeds of black gram and mung beans are also used as vegetables, whereas those of chick-pea are a popular snack. The young tender leaves of yet another legume, fenugreek, and of grain amaranth (Family Amaranthaceae) are also consumed as vegetables in several parts of the world. Winged bean is perhaps the only plant all of whose parts—including the tuberous roots, shoots, young leaves, and green pods—are consumed as vegetables.

Vegetables supply minerals, vitamins, proteins, starches, fats, and, to a certain extent, sugars for the human nutrition. They are particularly important sources of crude fiber and bulk, and provide a variety of flavors and tastes for the human palate. Typical examples of vegetables from various classes are summarized in Table 3-13.

Vegetables are highly perishable food products. Water loss and postharvest decay account for most of their losses. The postharvest losses of some vegetables are estimated to be ≥40–50% in the tropics and subtropics. Wastage is so high in some instances (e.g., onions in India) that, between the field and the consumer, bountiful amounts of highly nutritious crops are reduced to heaps of

Table 3-13. Botanical Classification of Some Important Vegetables and Mushrooms.

Type	Scientific Name	Family
Vegetables		
Bulbs		Amaryllidaceae
Garlic	*Allium sativum*	
Onion	*Allium cepa*	
Cucurbits		Cucurbitaceae
Cucumber	*Cucumis sativus*	
Pumpkin	*Cucurbita pepo*	
Winter squash	*Cucurbita maxima*	
Summer squash	*Cucurbita pepo* var. *melopepo*	
Flowers		
Artichoke	*Cynara scolymus*	Compositae
Broccoli	*Brassica oleracea* var *italica*	Cruciferae
Cauliflower	*Brassica oleracea* var. *botrytis*	Cruciferae
Fruits[a]		
Eggplant	*Solanum melongena* var. *esculentum*	Solanaceae
Garden pepper	*Capsicum frutescens* var. *grossum*	Solanaceae
Okra	*Hibiscus esculentus*	Malvaceae
Sweet corn	*Zea mays* var. *rugosa*	Gramineae
Tomato	*Lycopersicon esculentum*	Solanaceae
Leaves and stems		
Brussels sprout	*Brassica oleracea* var. *gemmifera*	Cruciferae
Cabbage	*Brassica oleracea* var. *capitata*	Cruciferae
Celery	*Apium graveolens* var. *dulce*	Umbelliferae
Chinese cabbage	*Brassica campestris* subvar. *pekinensis*	Cruciferae
Endive	*Cichorium endivia*	Compositae
Kale	*Brassica oleracea* var. *acephala*	Cruciferae
Kohlrabi	*Brassica caulorapa*	Cruciferae
Lettuce	*Lactuca sativa*	Compositae
Parsley	*Petroselinum crispum*	Umbelliferae
Rhubarb	*Rheum rhaponticum*	Polygonaceae
Spinach	*Spinacia oleracea*	Chenopodiaceae
Swiss chard	*Beta vulgaris* var. *cicla*	Chenopodiaceae
Legumes		Leguminosae
Garden pea	*Pisum sativum*	
Guar	*Cyamopsis tetragonoloba*	
Lima bean	*Phaseolus limensis*	
String bean	*Phaseolus vulgaris*	
Roots		
Beet	*Beta vulgaris*	Chenopodiaceae
Carrot	*Daucus carota* var. *sativa*	Umbelliferae
Parsnip	*Pastinaca sativa*	Umbelliferae
Radish	*Raphanus sativus*	Cruciferae
Rutabaga	*Brassica napobrassica*	Cruciferae
Sweet potato	*Ipomoea batatas*	Convolvulaceae
Turnip	*Brassica rapa*	Cruciferae

Table 3-13. (*Continued*)

Type	Scientific Name	Family
Shoots		
Asparagus	*Asparagus officinalis* var. *altilis*	Liliaceae
Tubers		
Potato	*Solanum tuberosum*	Solanaceae
Jerusalem artichoke	*Helianthus tuberosus*	Compositae
Mushrooms (nonpoisonous edible fungi)		
Common mushroom	*Agaricus campestris*	Agaricineae
Tube-bearing mushroom	*Boletus edulis*	Polyporeae

[a]Excepting cucurbits and legumes.

refuse. Lack of understanding of the pre- and postharvest etiology of vegetable crops affects both supplies and profits, even in some technologically advanced countries. Therefore, reduction of high pre- and postharvest vegetable losses entails the integration of a variety of aspects—the botany of an individual crop and its cultivars, its developmental physiology and biochemistry, types of infecting pathogens and pests, and the various feasible biotechnological measures. Preharvest biotechnology includes environmental factors such as climate (temperature, light, and water relations), soils, fertility, and crop protection during growth and development. Postharvest biotechnology deals with harvesting, handling, maturity, grading, sorting, packaging, storage, transport, use of chemicals and fungicides, irradiation, and processing of vegetables into more durable products (Salunkhe and Desai 1984b).

Present State of Vegetable Growing

Traditional "vegetable gardening" is fast becoming a commercial vegetable growing business and an important sector of the agricultural industry. A comparatively larger proportion of several important vegetables—such as potatoes, tomatoes, onions, lettuce, cabbage, cucurbits, and leafy greens—is being handled, transported, and marketed all over the world than before. Production and consumption of frozen and heat-processed vegetables are also increasing, accounting for more than 50% of the vegetables produced in the United States.

A brief history of the development of fruit and vegetable growing business was given early in this chapter. With the expansion of the fruit and vegetable processing industry, the utilization of these commodities has also improved considerably. Per capita supplies of starchy vegetables worldwide have increased about 20% since World War II; however, the levels of consumption in different countries vary over quite a wide range, from as little as 10 kg/person/ year in India and Pakistan to the exceptionally high figure of 320 kg/person/

year in West and Central Africa, an area where cassava and yam are the principal staple foods (Duckworth 1966). In China, the per capita consumption of starchy vegetables has doubled since the communist takeover of 1949.

Like fruit crops, vegetables also suffer from poor production statistics. Production data are unavailable in many countries, and available estimates refer only to crops grown in fields and market gardens for sale—excluding those cultivated in kitchen and small family gardens and meant for household consumption.

Present world production of vegetables, according to FAO estimates, is about 350 million metric tons (MT). The major vegetable-producing countries in 1985 were China, India, the USSR, the United States, Japan, and Italy (Table 3-14). China and India together produce more than one-third of the world's vegetables. As was shown in Table 3-2, the production of vegetables and melons is higher than the total production of fruits but lower than that of root crops (including potato, which are tubers). Roots and tubers (cassava, potato, sweet potato, yam, and aroid root) comprise most of the total vegetables produced in the tropical countries, providing staple food for over 500 million people. The comparison of total agricultural area covered by the vegetables and production, average yield, and import and export figures in the developing and developed countries (Table 3-15) clearly indicates that there is much to be gained in vegetable production by improvements in both preharvest and postharvest technology. Although the total vegetable growing area of the developing countries is

Table 3-14. Major Producers of Vegetables and Melons.[a]

Country	1979–81	1983	1984	1985
China	79.99	86.69	93.21	99.70
India	40.59	43.23	45.40	45.42
USSR	30.90	33.35	35.53	31.79
USA	25.46	26.02	28.02	28.10
Japan	15.23	14.89	15.26	15.41
Italy	13.40	14.85	15.35	14.68
Korea	9.05	8.43	8.56	9.46
Spain	8.55	8.71	9.27	9.10
Egypt	7.30	7.89	8.14	8.33
France	6.81	7.09	7.10	7.39
Brazil	4.35	4.58	4.85	5.00
Mexico	3.91	4.03	3.82	4.11
U.K.	3.94	3.63	3.89	3.92
Developed countries	140.84	145.38	155.60	151.51
Developing countries	212.81	228.50	239.13	250.94
Worldwide	353.65	373.88	394.72	402.45

Source: FAO (1985), courtesy Food and Agriculture Organization of the United Nations.
[a]In millions of metric tons.

Table 3-15. Vegetable Production in Developing and Developed Countries.

Agricultural Components	Developing Countries	Developed Countries
Total land area (10^6 ha)	6.6	3.3
Total agricultural area (10^6 ha)	2.0	1.3
Total vegetable area (10^3 ha)	58	10
Vegetable production (10^6 MT)	216	135
Mean yield (MT/ha)	7	14
Import (10^6 MT)	1.7	6.1
Export (10^6 MT)	2.7	5.0

Source: Pantastico and Bautista (1976).

about six times larger than that of the developed countries, the mean yield per hectare is only one-half. Export of vegetables by developing countries is also low, and there is a lack of uniformity in the vegetable quality (Pantastico and Bautista 1976). Higher production of vegetables in most developing countries is mainly due to increases of area under cultivation; yet, despite these increases, fruits and vegetables together constitute a largely neglected group of agricultural crops in these countries (Salunkhe and Desai 1984b). Apart from deficiencies in data relating to these highly perishable commodities, their production also suffers from severe handicaps, including uncertain prices received by the growers and the extreme volatility in prices at the consumer level, mitigating the interests of both the producers and consumers.

Vegetable production is lagging behind nutritional needs. India, for example, needs about 75 million MT of vegetables and fruits to meet the nutritional requirements of the existing population, as opposed to the current production of about 40 million MT. Owing to poor preharvest crop protection and improper harvesting, handling, storage, transport, processing, and marketing of these perishables, very high preharvest and postharvest losses occur in the tropical and subtropical countries, varying widely according to commodity and areas (Salunkhe and Desai 1984b).

Vegetables as Sources of Nutrients

Although vegetables generally do not show a sudden increase in metabolic activity that parallels the onset of the climacteric in fruit (unless sprouting and growth is initiated), they are notorious for losing water after harvest; this leads to rapid shriveling and wilting, which turn the vegetable tissue tough or mashy and eventually inedible. Water loss in vegetables is loss of salable weight and thus a direct loss in marketing. A loss in weight of as little as 5% will cause many perishable vegetables to appear wilty or shriveled; under warm and dry conditions, this can happen to some leafy vegetables in a few hours. Even in the absence of visible wilting, water loss can cause a loss of crispness, and undesirable changes in color and palatability may ensue in several vegetables soon after their harvest. Detention of vegetables after harvesting is thus detrimental to their quality.

In contrast to losses caused by dehydration, shriveling, and wilting, conditions that result in wetting the produce can lead to disastrous losses of both quality and nutrients in some vegetables. This is due to the encouragement of growth of decaying and rotting organisms, in some instances causing physical splitting of the commodity. Maintaining an appropriate amount of water in the marketable commodity is vital to protect its quality.

Owing to microbial spoilage, loss of water, and, in many cases, loss of the valuable nutrients (minerals, vitamins, and other soluble constituents), vegetables give up considerable amount of energy in the form of heat ($>100,000$ BTU/MT/day). Production of such heat in harvested vegetables during their storage, transportation, and marketing hastens their own deterioration, since microbial action is accelerated by higher temperatures. Both qualitative and quantitative deteriorations set in if these valuable food products are not harvested, handled, stored, transported, and marketed with due care and delicacy (Salunkhe and Desai 1984b).

In addition to a large quantity of water, the major chemical constituents of fresh vegetables are carbohydrates, proteins, fats, vitamins, minerals, and fiber. Provitamin A (β-carotene), thiamin (B_1), riboflavin (B_2), pyridoxine (B_6), niacin, pantothenic acid, folic acid (folacin), ascorbic acid (vitamin C), and vitamins E and K have been reported to be present in different vegetable products. Among the minerals present are Mg, Cu, Co, S, Zn, and F. Salunkhe and Desai (1988) reviewed the effects of various agricultural practices, handling, processing, and storage on the quality and nutritional composition of vegetables. Salunkhe, Pao, and Dull (1974) described the major functions of the nutrients in the human body. Fruits and vegetables are generally bought and consumed for their characteristic flavor and variety in taste rather than for their nutritive values. The nutritional contribution of major fruits and vegetables compared to percentage of total food supply is shown in Fig. 3-6.

Since the extent to which a food contributes nutrients to the human diet is governed by the amount of food consumed, vegetables are generally not regarded as economic sources of energy, protein, fat, calcium, or riboflavin (Vittum 1963). A vegetable may be rich in minerals and vitamins, but the consumer will need another source of food supply if only a small quantity of that vegetable is eaten. Thus, although the concentration of ascorbic acid in green peppers is about seven times higher than that in potatoes, the average consumer obtains more of this vitamin from potatoes than from peppers because of higher potato consumption. The relative concentration of ten major vitamins and minerals in

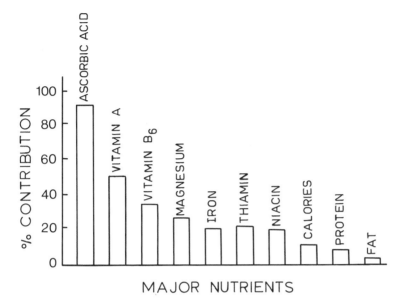

Fig. 3-6. The nutritional contribution of some important fruits and vegetables. *Source:* Reprinted with permission from Salunkhe, Pao, and Dull (1974), Assessment of nutritive value, quality and stability of cruciferous vegetables during storage and subsequent processing. In *Storage, Processing and Nutritional Quality of Fruits and Vegetables,* ed. D. K. Salunkhe, pp. 1–38. © CRC Press, Inc., Boca Raton, Fla.

some fruits and vegetables and their importance in the typical U.S. diet are shown in Table 3-16. This ranking indicates that while tomatoes and oranges are relatively low in nutrient concentration, they contribute greatly to the U.S. diet because they are consumed in large amounts (Rick 1978). Vegetables supply only negligible amounts of fat and protein (7% and 8% of the body's requirements of energy and protein, respectively); other foods, such as cereals, meat, milk, and eggs, are more efficient sources of these nutrients. Vegetables, however, contribute significantly to a well-balanced diet in that they are major sources of β-carotene and ascorbic acid, and are good sources of thiamin, niacin, and iron (Table 3-17). Tindall and Proctor (1980) summarized the nutritive values of some selected typical vegetables and concluded that vegetables contribute significantly to human dietary requirements of essential minerals, vitamins, proteins, and carbohydrates, especially in areas of low animal protein availability and where cereals comprise most of the human diet. Vegetables provide variety to an otherwise monotonous diet containing a limited number of items. They also furnish bulk (dietary fiber), which helps in the proper function of the human digestive system. Several diseases, such as appendicitis, colon cancer, constipation, deep vein thrombosis, diabetes, diverticulosis, gallstones,

Table 3-16. Nutrient Concentration and Contribution to the U.S. Diet of Fruits and Vegetables

Nutrient Concentration[a]		Contribution to U.S. Diet[b]	
Rank	Crop	Crop	Rank
1	Broccoli	Tomato	1
2	Spinach	Orange	2
3	Brussels sprout	Potato	3
4	Lima bean	Lettuce	4
5	Pea	Sweet corn	5
6	Asparagus	Banana	6
7	Artichoke	Carrot	7
8	Cauliflower	Cabbage	8
9	Sweet potato	Onion	9
10	Carrot	Sweet potato	10
12	Sweet corn	Pea	15
14	Potato	Spinach	18
15	Cabbage	Broccoli	21
16	Tomato	Lima bean	23
18	Banana	Asparagus	25
26	Lettuce	Cauliflower	30
31	Onion	Brussels sprout	34
33	Orange	Artichoke	36

Source: Rick, The Tomato. Copyright © 1978 by Scientific American, Inc. All rights reserved.
[a]Relative concentration of a group of ten vitamins and minerals in some fruits and vegetables.
[b]Relative contribution of vitamins and minerals made by these commodities to the U.S. diet.

hemorrhoids, hiatus hernia, ischemic heart disease, obesity, reactal tumors, and varicose veins, have been claimed to be due to lack of fiber in the diet (Wills et al. 1981). Most vegetables—especially such leafy greens as spinach, lettuce, celery, cabbage, and fenugreek—are characterized by a high percentage of cellulose or crude fiber. Owing to their succulence (high water content) and large bulk (roughage), leafy greens and root vegetables aid in the digestion of concentrated foods.

According to the Food and Nutrition Board of the National Academy of Sciences (NAS 1968), fats and carbohydrates provide 41% and 47% of the total calories in a typical American diet, respectively. The chemical (nutritional) composition of twelve cruciferous and eighteen other vegetables (Table 3-18) indicates that most vegetables are low in calories, fats, and carbohydrates, and rich in vitamins and minerals (Salunkhe, Pao, and Dull 1974). In general, cruciferous vegetables are the most efficient in synthesizing high concentrations of proteins, amino acids, minerals, and vitamins, and they are low in caloric content.

Table 3-17. Nutritional, Mineral, and Vitamin Content of Some Important Vegetables.[a]

Vegetable	Nutrition					Minerals					Vitamins			
	Water (g)	Energy (cal)	Protein (g)	Fat (g)	Carbohydr. (g)	Ca (mg)	P (mg)	Fe (mg)	Na (mg)	K (mg)	Thiamin (mg)	Ribofl. (mg)	Niacin (mg)	Vit. C (mg)
Roots and tubers														
Cassava	60 (ml)	153	0.7	0.2	37.0	25	—	1.0	—	—	0.07	0.03	—	30
Yam	73.0	131	2.0	0.2	32.4	10	(40)	0.3	—	(500)	0.10	0.03	0.4	10
Sweet potato	70.0	91	1.2	0.6	21.5	(22)	(47)	(0.7)	(19)	320	0.10	0.16	0.8	25
Irish potato	75.8	87	2.1	0.1	20.8	8	40	0.5	7	520	0.11	0.04	1.2	8
Other vegetables and melons														
Onion	92.8	23	0.9	trace	5.2	31	30	0.3	10	140	0.03	0.05	0.2	10
Tomato	93.4	14	0.9	trace	2.8	13	21	0.4	3	290	0.06	0.04	0.7	20
Pumpkin melon	94.7	15	0.6	trace	3.4	39	19	0.4	1	310	0.04	0.04	0.4	5
Cantaloupe	93.6	24	1.0	trace	5.3	19	30	0.8	14	320	0.05	0.03	0.5	25
Watermelon	94.0	21	0.4	trace	5.3	5	8	0.3	4	120	0.02	0.02	0.2	5
Leaves, carotene level[b]														
Low	93 (ml)	23	1.5	0.2	4.0	40	—	0.5	—	—	0.05	0.05	—	40
Medium	91 (ml)	28	2.0	0.3	4.0	80	—	2.5	—	—	0.08	0.20	—	50
High	85 (ml)	48	5.0	0.7	5.0	250	—	4.0	—	—	2.10	0.30	—	100

Source: Platt (1962), FAO (1972), Paul and Southgate (1978), Tindall and Proctor (1980).

[a]Per 100-g edible portion. Figures in parentheses are estimated from related foods or, more rarely, are tentative values based on a limited number of published sources (Paul and Southgate 1978).

[b]Low-carotene (pale green) leaves = cabbage, kohlrabi, Chinese cabbage; medium-carotene leaves = New Zealand spinach, cassava leaves, watercress, squash, pumpkin; high-carotene (dark green) leaves = spinach, sweet potato, tops of kale.

Table 3-18. Nutritional Composition of Some Cruciferous and Other Vegetables.[a]

Vegetable	Nutrition					Minerals						Vitamins				
	Water (%)	Energy (Cal)	Protein (%)	Fat (%)	Carbohydr. (%)	Ca (mg)	P (mg)	Fe (mg)	Na (mg)	K (mg)	Mg (mg)	Vit. A (IU)	Thiamin (mg)	Ribofl. (mg)	Niacin (mg)	Vit. C (mg)
Cruciferous																
Cabbage	92.2	24	1.3	0.2	5.4	49	29	0.4	20	233	13	130	0.05	0.05	0.3	47
Broccoli	89.1	32	3.6	0.3	5.9	103	78	1.1	15	382	24	2,500	0.10	0.23	0.9	113
Brussels sprout	85.2	45	4.9	0.4	8.3	36	80	1.5	14	390	29	550	0.10	0.16	0.9	102
Cauliflower	91.0	27	2.7	0.2	5.2	25	56	1.1	13	295	24	60	0.11	0.10	0.7	78
Kale	82.7	53	6.0	0.8	9.0	249	93	2.7	75	238	37	10,000	0.16	0.26	2.1	186
Watercress	93.3	19	2.2	0.3	3.0	151	54	1.7	52	282	20	4,900	0.08	0.16	0.9	79
Mustard green	89.5	31	3.0	0.5	5.6	183	50	3.0	32	377	27	7,000	0.11	0.22	0.8	97
Turnip green	90.3	28	3.0	0.3	5.0	246	58	1.8	40[b]	250[b]	58	7,600	0.21	0.39	0.8	139
Chinese cabbage	95.0	14	1.2	0.1	3.0	43	40	0.6	23	253	14	150	0.05	0.04	0.6	25
Rutabaga	87.0	46	1.1	0.1	11.0	66	39	0.4	5	239	15	580	0.07	0.07	1.1	43
Collard	85.3	45	4.8	0.8	7.5	250	82	1.5	40[b]	450	57	9,300	0.16	0.31	1.7	152
Kohlrabi	90.3	29	2.0	0.1	6.6	41	51	0.5	8	372	37	20	0.06	0.04	0.3	66
Noncruciferous																
Carrot	88.2	42	1.1	0.2	9.7	37	36	0.7	47	341	23	11,000	0.06	0.05	0.6	8
Sweet potato	70.6	114	1.7	0.4	26.3	32	47	0.7	10	243	31	8,800	0.10	0.06	0.6	21
Tomato	93.5	22	1.1	0.2	4.7	13	27	0.5	3	244	14	900	0.06	0.04	0.7	23
Sweet corn	72.7	96	3.5	1.0	22.1	3	111	0.7	10[b]	280	48	400	0.15	0.12	1.7	12
Pepper	93.4	22	1.2	0.2	4.8	9	22	0.7	13	213	18	420	0.08	0.08	0.5	128
Lettuce	95.1	14	1.2	0.2	2.5	35	26	2.0	9	264	11	900	0.06	0.06	0.3	8
Potato	79.8	76	2.1	0.1	17.1	7	53	0.6	3	407	34	20[c]	0.10	0.04	1.5	20
Squash	94.0	19	1.1	0.1	4.2	28	29	0.4	1	202	17	410	0.05	0.09	1.0	22

Vegetable															
Onion	89.1	38	1.5	0.1	8.7	27	36	0.5	10	157	12	40	0.03	0.04	0.2	10
Cucumber	95.1	15	0.9	0.1	3.4	25	27	1.1	6	160	11	250	0.03	0.04	0.2	11
Spinach	90.7	26	3.2	0.3	4.3	93	51	3.1	71	470	88	8,100	0.10	0.20	0.6	51
Lima bean	67.5	123	8.4	0.5	22.1	52	142	2.8	2	650	67	290	0.24	0.12	1.4	29
Pea	78.0	84	6.3	0.4	14.4	26	116	1.9	2	316	35	640	0.35	0.14	2.9	27
Asparagus	91.7	26	2.5	0.2	5.0	22	62	1.0	2	278	20	900	0.18	0.20	1.5	33
Cantaloupe	91.2	30	0.7	0.1	7.5	14	16	0.4	12	251	17[b]	3,400	0.04	0.03	0.6	33
Snap bean	90.1	32	1.9	0.2	7.1	56	44	0.8	7	243	32	600	0.08	0.11	0.5	19
Beet	87.3	43	1.6	0.1	9.3	16	33	0.7	60	335	25	20	0.03	0.05	0.4	10
Celery	94.1	7	0.9	0.1	3.9	39	28	0.3	126	341	22	240	0.03	0.03	0.3	9

Source: USDA (1963).
[a]Per 100-g edible portion.
[b]Nutritional composition of fresh California grown vegetables (1962), Calif. Exp. Stn. Bull. no. 788.
[c]Heinz, Handbook of Nutrition, McGraw-Hill, New York (1959).

Gopala Rao, Mallikarjuna, and Gururaja Rao (1980) analyzed β-carotene, B-vitamins (B_1, B_2, B_6, niacin), reducing and nonreducing sugars, starch, protein, soluble protein, and total nitrogen, calcium, and iron contents of several leafy greens, including amaranth (*A. tricolor* and *A. spinosus*), drumstick leaves (*Moringa oleifera*), coriander (*Coriandrum sativum*), mint (*Mentha spicata*), and garden sorrel (*Rumex acetosa*). They recommended *Trianthema portulacastrum* as a nutritionally rich, new vegetable crop.

In addition to essential nutritional attributes, flavor and taste are the most important properties of vegetables and fruits. Aroma is characterized by the presence of volatiles and by sweetness, acidity, and the astringency contributed by the phenolics. Lindstrand (1979) stressed the value of eye appeal (acceptance) of vegetables as well as the importance of the associated physiological benefits of their dietary fiber and minerals. Because of their high moisture content, vegetables help in the utilization of all other nutrients.

Vegetables also contain certain toxic factors. Cruciferous vegetables in general, and those belonging to the genus *Brassica* in particular, contain goitrogens, which cause enlargement of the thyroid glands. Natural thioglucosides (glucosinolates) are sources of goitrogens; however, these compounds, with their associated enzymes, also impart the desirable culinary flavor of cabbage, broccoli, and cauliflower. A thioglucoside, allylthioglucoside (sinigrin), is present in cabbage, kale, Brussels sprout, broccoli, cauliflower, and mustard. When these vegetables are chopped, a specific enzyme, thioglucosidase (myrosinase), hydrolyzes it into glucose, potassium bisulfate, and allylthiocyanate, a goitrogenic compound. Similarly, progoitrin or epiprogoitrin is responsible for the typical flavor of kale, rape, turnip, rutabaga, and kohlrabi. It is hydrolyzed by thioglucosidase to yield glucose, potassium bisulfate, and the highly unstable intermediate compounds thiocyanate, nitrite plus sulfur, and goitrin. Goitrin (5-vinyloxazolidine-2-thione) is a potent thyrotoxin and is formed through cyclization of an unstable isothiocyanate containing the hydroxyl group. The thyroid-inhibiting effect of goitrins is due to the irreversible inhibition of organic binding of iodine. However, thiocyanate, isothiocyanate, and nitrite ions act as goitrogens only when the iodine content of the diet is low. In such regions, benign goiter may be accentuated by eating excessive amounts of brassica vegetables (Salunkhe, Pao, and Dull 1974). Most of the goitrogen properties of vegetables, however, are lost during cooking.

Crosby (1966) reported that ethylacetate extracts from leaves of broccoli, cabbage, rutabaga, turnip, and radish inhibit human plasma choline esterase. These extracts contain chemicals that modify the functions of the nervous system. There is a need for the identification and determination of the amount of each substance. The flatulence-distress syndrome after eating cooked cruciferous vegetables is not as chronic and offensive as that produced after the consumption of beans, sweet potatoes, and onions (Murphy, pers. commun.).

Other naturally occurring toxicants of vegetables include oxalates, salicylates, arsenic, nitrite, and alkaloids such as solanine. Potatoes contain solanine, arsenic, and nitrite, and some green leafy vegetables contain toxic oxalates. The anthraquinones of rhubarb are mainly in the root, but human poisoning generally occurs from eating rhubarb leaves. The leaf poison is commonly thought to be oxalates, but other factors, possibly quinones, are also involved (Singleton and Kratzer 1973).

In terms of human lives lost due to plant phenols, the salicylate aspirin ($C_9H_8O_4$) is probably the most dangerous (four deaths per million population every year). Low-molecular-weight salicylates are associated with hyperactivity, according to Feingold (1975), who recommended omitting twenty-one fruits and vegetables containing natural salicylates for the dietary treatment of that disorder. Robertson and Kermode (1981) determined the concentration of salicylic acid in fresh vegetables. It ranged from 0.01 mg/kg in cabbage to 0.1 mg/kg in whole-kernel sweet corn. Canned sweet corn and some tomato products contained higher levels of salicylic acid than did fresh corn and tomatoes.

The distribution of oxalates in vegetables varies with species and families. Generally, leaves contain higher amounts of oxalates than stalks. The ratio of oxalates to calcium also varies widely. Based on oxalate : calcium ratio, vegetables can be divided into three classes (Fassett 1973):

1. those with a ratio > 2.0 (e.g., spinach, beet leaves, and rhubarb);
2. those with a ratio of 1–2 (e.g., potatoes); and
3. those with a ratio < 1 (e.g., lettuce, cabbage, and peas).

Several types of mushroom also contain oxalates and other toxic factors (Salunkhe and Desai 1984b, 1988).

Ingestion of large amounts of green potatoes or sprouts also causes poisoning in humans and animals. Solanine is one of the major alkaloids of potatoes. Wu and Salunkhe (1976) reported that mechanical injuries to potatoes, such as bruising, cutting, dropping, and puncturing, significantly increased glycoalkaloid synthesis in both the peel and flesh. The extent of its formation depends on the cultivar, type of injury, temperature, and the duration of storage.

Environmental Factors

Climate

Humankind has very little control over climate, but climate does indeed exert control over humankind through its effects on food production, nutritional status, and wealth. Some ecological, cultural, and physical factors significantly influence the nutritional composition and anatomical and morphological structure of vegetables. Light, daylength, mean temperature, and total heat units, as well as such extreme climates as frosts and heat waves, greatly influence plant growth and development. Air (carbon dioxide) and water relations (rainfall, water supply) influence a plant's mechanism of conversion of sucrose and hexoses into ascorbic acid and its eventual accumulation. The precursors of ascorbic acid are produced during photosynthesis, which, in turn, is significantly influenced by the environmental factors. The effects of climate on the nutritional composition of vegetables have been reviewed by Salunkhe and Desai (1988).

Light

Variations in the amount and intensity of light influence not only the growth and development of vegetable crops, but also their nutritional composition, especially the ascorbic acid content of leafy greens. Owing to the instability of ascorbic acid in the detached leaves, its loss is caused more by metabolic activity of the plant than by oxidation. Changes in light intensity greatly influence the rate of formation of precursors but do not affect the conversion of these precursors into ascorbic acid.

Winsor (1979) described various factors contributing to the overall quality of tomatoes, including appearance, firmness, and chemical composition. He reported that shading of tomato plants decreased the dry-matter content of the fruit and the sugar content of the expressed juices (Table 3-19).

Describing the influence of exogenous factors on the quality and nutritional composition of vegetables, Mengel (1979) stated that carbohydrates in vegetables are adversely influenced by the light intensity. Unlike light intensity, which promotes the production of photosynthates, warmth promotes growth processes with the consequent consumption of the photosynthates. Thus, low temperature and high light intensity favor the accumulation of carbohydrates in vegetables, whereas high temperature and low light intensity decrease the carbohydrate content (Warren-Wilson 1969). The latter type of environment often prevails under greenhouse conditions. Although carbohydrates per se are not generally regarded as nutritionally important constituents of vegetables, the

Table 3-19. Effects of Shading on Dry Matter Content of Tomato Fruit and on Sugar Content of the Expressed Juice.

Cultivar	Assessment	Unshaded	Shaded
Potentate	Dry matter (%)	6.4	5.7
	Sugars (g/100 ml)	3.8	3.0
Ailsa Craig	Dry matter (%)	7.0	5.6
	Sugars (g/100 ml)	3.7	2.7

Source: Winsor (1979).

synthesis of vitamin C is closely associated with carbohydrate metabolism. The primary precursor of ascorbic acid is glucose, which is activated by UTP and then oxidized to the activated form of glucuronic acid, the direct precursor of vitamin C. Thus, processes that promote the synthesis of UTP (or ATP) and glucose also favor the synthesis of ascorbic acid. The most important factors in this respect are light intensity and potassium supply. Light intensity is directly involved in photosynthetic ATP (or UTP) synthesis and in all plant synthetic processes.

Temperature

Temperatures optimal for the normal growth and development of vegetables are not necessarily the same for synthesizing and accumulating nutrients. Furthermore, the specific temperature promoting the greatest absorption, translocation, synthesis, and accumulation of one nutrient is often different for another. Temperature is inversely related to the synthesis of carbohydrates in vegetative plant material (Mengel 1979); high temperatures prevailing under greenhouse conditions often result in low carbohydrate content.

Rosenfeld (1979) determined the total ascorbic acid content of eight different kinds of vegetable—broad bean (*Vicia faba*), chicory (green and blanched, *Cichorium intybus*), chive (*Petroselinum crispum* Nym), cress (*Lepidium sativum*), sorrel (*Rumex acetosa*), and turnip (root and leaves, *Brassica campestris*)—grown at 3° temperature increments from 12° to 24 °C. The total vitamin C content of all vegetables was the highest at growth temperatures of 12° and 15° C, while that of turnip increased with increasing temperature. With the exception of turnip leaves, the lowest content of total ascorbic acid of all other vegetables was found at the highest growth temperatures (Fig. 3-7). Broad bean and cress showed unusually high content of total ascorbic acid at low temperatures, which was traced to the degree of development of these plants. Turnip leaves and roots showed a different pattern of total ascorbic acid content. According to Rosenfeld (1979), an increased transport of carbohydrates from the root to the leaves at higher temperatures was probably responsible for the lower ascorbic acid content of the dried turnip leaves. The total ascorbic acid and dry-matter contents were positively correlated for all kinds of vegetables. Franke (1959) reasoned that higher total ascorbic acid content at higher temperature (24 °C), especially for green chicory and turnip root, might be due to higher respiration, which probably encouraged the synthesis of total ascorbic acid.

Cantliffe (1972) reported that, under favorable light conditions, nitrate accumulation decreased from 112 kg/ha at 5 °C to 56 kg/ha at 10 °C. Nitrate accumulation did not occur where nitrogen was not applied until the temperature reached 15 °C. Mineralization and nitrification were probably impeded at the lower temperatures (Maynard et al. 1976).

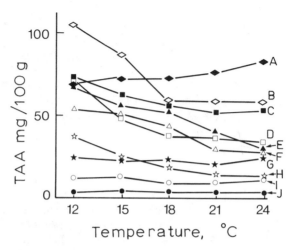

Fig. 3-7. The total ascorbic acid (TAA) content of some vegetables at different temperatures: (A) chicory (green), (B) broad bean, (C) chive, (D) cress, (E) sorrel, (F) parsley (forced), (G) turnip root, (H) spinach beet, (I) chicory (blanched), and (J) turnip leaves. *Source:* Rosenfeld (1979).

Bourne (1982) studied the effects of temperatures in the range of 0–45 °C on the firmness of several raw fruits and vegetables. For the majority of commodities tested, there was a linear relationship between decreased firmness and increased temperature.

Water

Water is a major determinant of vegetable productivity. The availability of water to plants is determined by the difference between the water evaporated from their leaves (transpiration) and its uptake from the soil through their roots. Water deficits develop within the plant tissue when the rate of transpiration exceeds that of uptake. This causes partial or complete closure of stomata, thus reducing further water loss. Since photosynthesis depends on the uptake of CO_2 through stomatal openings on leaves, the conservation of water brought about by its closure reduces photosynthesis and thus plant growth. A complex interaction among atmosphere, plant, and soil factors thus influences the development of water deficits in the plants (Fordham and Biggs 1985).

Season

The chemical composition of vegetables varies from season to season, mainly due to differences in temperature, daylength, light intensity, and light spectrum

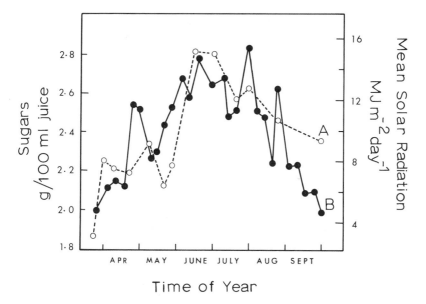

Fig. 3-8. Seasonal trends in the sugars content (A) of the fruit juices of tomato (cv. Grenadier) together with integrated data for solar radiation (B). *Source:* Winsor and Adams (1976), cited in Winsor (1979).

(Harris 1975). Winsor and Adams (1976) reported the results of a study of the composition of tomatoes (cv. Grenadier) from a commercial nursery throughout the season (late March–early October). The sugar content of the tomato juices increased from a very low value (1.9 g/100 ml) in March to about 2.8 g/100 ml in June, and then declined to 2.4 g/100 ml in early October. The data, in general, followed the same pattern as solar radiation (Fig. 3-8).

Location

Lantz, Gough, and Campbell (1958) studied the effects of cultivars and location on the protein content of dried beans (Table 3-20). Protein percentages about 1.5 times higher were found in all cultivars when they were grown at Estancia, about 2,000 ft higher from sea level than the other two locations. Lantz, Gough, and Campbell (1958) also found significant variations in nine amino acids of dried beans (Arg, His, Ile, Leu, Lys, Met, Phe, Thr, and Val) due to locality, season, and sowing time (Table 3-21).

According to Harris (1975), the effects of location or geographical area upon the nutritional status of vegetables are generally small. Salunkhe, Pao, and Dull (1974) and Salunkhe and Desai (1988) have reviewed the earlier work on this

Table 3-20. Effects of Cultivar and Location on Protein (N × 6.25) Content of Dry Beans (% Protein).

| Variety | Location (and Elevation above Sea Level) | | | |
	Deming (4,300 ft)	Estancia (6,000 ft)	State College (4,000 ft)	Mean
295	20.0	30.8	22.8	24.53
641	20.9	32.1	24.8	25.93
Michelite	23.8	34.4	25.7	27.97
Red Mexican	19.9	29.0	22.5	23.90
2574	19.9	30.9	24.4	25.07
2534	20.0	25.9	26.2	25.37
Calico	19.8	30.1	23.9	24.40
Mean	20.44	30.91	24.33	25.23

Source: Reprinted with permission from Lantz, Gough, and Campbell (1958), Nutrients in beans, effects of variety, location and years on the protein and amino acid content of dried beans. *J. Agric. Food Chem.* 6:58–60. © 1958 American Chemical Society.

subject. Klein and Perry (1982) reported reduced ascorbic acid (RAA) and provitamin A (carotenoids) activity of several vegetables grown in six different cities during two seasons of the year in the United States. The mean RAA content (in mg/100 g) of these vegetables were as follows: cabbage, 45.2; carrots, 7.8; celery, 6.0; sweet corn, 6.5; onion, 8.4; and tomato, 15.3. The vitamin C level was 22.1 mg/100 g in cooked cabbage, 6.2 in sweet corn, and 5.7 in onion. The mean vitamin A activity (in IU) was as follows: carrot, 15,228; cabbage, 114; celery, 133; corn, 219; and tomato, 217. Both RAA and vitamin A contents of vegetables varied with the location. The nutrient values of vegetables grown in different areas also varied but were not predictable. The data presented in Figs. 3-9, 3-10, and 3-11 indicate that the ascorbic acid and provitamin A activity of most vegetables are lower than the values reported in the USDA's (1963) *Agricultural Handbook no. 8* (see Table 3-18). Klein and Perry (1982) could not definitely point out whether this effect was due to different cultivars being grown or to changes in shipping and handling procedures. These authors further cautioned that if the dietary evaluation of these two important nutrients is based only on tabulated values without consideration of varietal differences, effects of season and location, or handling treatment, their consumption may be overestimated. The effects of both variety and location on the protein and amino acids contents of dried beans (see Tables 3-20 and 3-21) are of greater magnitude than that of the season.

Soils

Soil type and characteristics have a major influence on vegetable production, especially on the type of crop that can be grown. Whereas the highly intensive

Table 3-21. Effect of Locality, Year, and Planting Date on Amino Acid (and Protein) Content of Eight Varieties of Dried Bean.[a]

	Arg	His	Ile	Leu	Lys	Met	Phe	Thr	Val
Locality									
Estancia	26.0	9.4	16.5	24.7	19.8	7.2	17.1	13.3	16.1
	(8.4)	(3.0)	(5.3)	(8.0)	(6.4)	(2.3)	(5.5)	(4.3)	(5.2)
State Coll.	14.8	7.8	14.6	20.8	17.2	6.4	14.3	12.2	13.8
	(6.1)	(3.2)	(6.0)	(8.6)	(7.1)	(2.6)	(5.9)	(5.0)	(5.6)
Deming	12.1	6.8	13.6	18.4	15.4	5.5	13.0	11.3	12.5
	(5.7)	(3.2)	(6.4)	(8.6)	(7.2)	(2.6)	(6.1)	(5.3)	(5.9)
Mean	17.6[b]	8.0[b]	14.9[b]	21.3[b]	17.5[b]	6.4[b]	14.8[b]	12.3[b]	14.1[b]
	(6.7)[b]	(3.1)	(5.9)[b]	(8.4)[b]	(6.9)[b]	(2.5)[b]	(5.8)[b]	(4.9)[b]	(5.5)
LSD[c] (0.01)	3.04	1.02	0.75	1.38	0.93	0.48	9.0	0.66	2.26
	(0.66)	—	(0.48)	(0.38)	(0.21)	(0.23)	(0.30)	(0.27)	—
Season									
1948	9.5	4.8	12.2	16.6	13.9	5.9	11.2	9.2	10.9
	(4.6)	(2.4)	(6.0)	(8.2)	(6.8)	(2.9)	(3.5)	(4.5)	(5.4)
1949	12.1	6.8	13.6	18.4	15.4	5.5	13.0	11.3	12.5
	(5.7)	(3.2)	(6.4)	(8.6)	(7.2)	(22.6)	(6.1)	(5.3)	(5.9)
1950	12.7	6.6	14.4	19.8	16.5	6.6	12.8	11.2	13.0
	(5.4)	(2.8)	(6.2)	(8.5)	(7.1)	(2.8)	(5.4)	(4.8)	(5.5)
Mean	11.4[b]	6.1[b]	13.4[b]	18.3[b]	15.3[b]	6.0[b]	12.3[b]	10.6[b]	12.1[b]
	(5.2)[b]	(2.8)[b]	(6.2)	(8.4)	(7.0)	(2.8)[b]	(5.7)[d]	(4.9)[b]	(5.6)[d]
LSD (0.01)	1.26	0.45	0.60	1.23	0.66	0.33	0.75	0.63	1.17
	(0.13)	(0.30)	—	—	—	—	(0.45)	(0.48)	(0.39)
Planting date									
Early	12.3	8.0	14.4	19.0	16.5	6.0	12.8	10.6	13.2
	(5.4)	(3.6)	(6.4)	(8.4)	(7.2)	(2.7)	(5.7)	(4.7)	(5.8)
Late	12.7	6.6	14.4	19.0	16.5	6.6	12.8	11.2	13.0
	(5.4)	(2.8)	(6.4)	(8.4)	(7.1)	(2.8)	(5.4)	(4.8)	(5.5)
Mean	12.5	7.3[b]	14.4	19.4	16.5	6.3[b]	12.8	10.9[b]	13.1
	(5.4)	(3.2)[b]	(6.3)	(8.4)	(7.2)	(2.8)[b]	(5.6)	(4.8)	(5.7)
LSD (0.01)	—	1.19	—	—	—	0.38	—	0.68	—
	—	(0.45)	—	—	—	(0.12)	—	—	—

Source: Reprinted with permission from Lantz, Gough, and Campbell (1958), Nutrients in beans, effects of variety, location and years on the protein and amino acid content of dried beans. *J. Agric. Food Chem.* 6:58–60. © 1958 American Chemical Society.
[a] Amino acid content is expressed in mg/g on moisture-free basis; percent protein content is given in parentheses.
[b] Differences are significant at 1% level.
[c] Least significant difference.
[d] Differences are significant at 5% level.

production units are usually small and have considerable labor input, vegetable production on a farm scale allows the soil to be treated less intensively. In the latter case, fallowing, grass leys, or green manure crops can be introduced into the farming programs. Labor inputs per unit area or per unit output are also low-

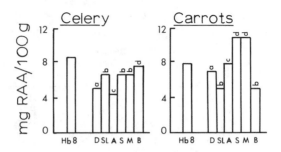

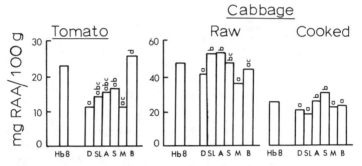

Fig. 3-9. Reduced ascorbic acid (RAA) content of celery, carrot, tomato and cabbage grown at different locations. *Abbreviations:* HB 8, USDA *Agricultural Handbook No. 8;* D, Denver, Colo.; SL, St. Louis, Mo.; A, Atlanta, Ga.; S, Seattle, Wash.; M, Minneapolis, Minn.; B, Boston, Mass. *Source:* Klein and Perry (1982).

er on large holdings; however, a high level of mechanization is required to cope with the large areas of individual crops.

The aspects of soil texture, particle size and pore space, soil textural classes, soil structure, and its maintenance and soil organic matter were discussed earlier in this chapter. Fordham and Biggs (1985) have described the soil requirements for particular vegetable crops, such as brassicas, legumes, leeks and onions, and root and salad crops.

For directly seeded crops, suitable soils are required for producing seedbeds that retain sufficient moisture to allow germination and sustain plant growth. Transplanted brassicas need fertile, moisture-retentive soils that allow rapid plant growth. Poorly drained soils are never suitable since they become wet and rutted, the passage of machines then damaging both crops and soil structure.

Whereas broad beans are tolerant vegetables and can grow on soils of only moderate fertility, French and runner beans do best in well-drained, open-textured soils to which organic manure has been added to increase fertility and capacity to retain moisture. Flower drop of runner beans can be prevented by incorporating sufficient organic matter to ensure that moisture stress conditions, which cause flower drop, do not develop.

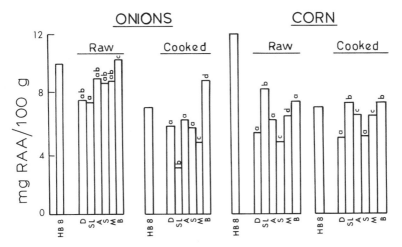

Fig. 3-10. Reduced ascorbic acid (RAA) content of onions and corn grown at different locations. Abbreviations are as described in Fig. 3-9. *Source:* Klein and Perry (1982).

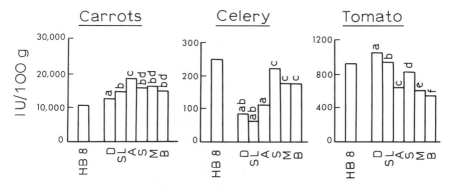

Fig. 3-11. Vitamin A activity of carrot, celery, and tomato grown at different locations. The location abbreviations are as described in Fig. 3-9. *Source:* Klein and Perry (1982).

Large quantities of green peas are produced for processing, especially for freezing and canning. Processors demand a program in which crops mature successionally, which is influenced by the soil conditions. Predetermined successional sowings can only be made in soils that are always readily cultivated into a seedbed. Although peas tolerate moderately fertile soils, they need adequate summer moisture if a contracted harvesting period is to be avoided.

Allium crops, such as leeks and onions, are sensitive to acid conditions and prefer highly fertile, moisture-retentive soils. Emergence of onion and leek seedlings is slow and can be greatly reduced on silt soils that cap badly. Stony and flinty soils should not be used for onions since the risk of mechanical damage during harvesting is greater.

Shallow soils are not suitable for root crops like carrot, beetroot, and parsnip, and stone-free soil conditions are necessary to produce good-quality roots. Bunching beetroot, whether grown for salad or processing, requires fertile, moisture-retentive soils. Carrots do not tolerate acid conditions. Generally, the harvesting of root crops is easier from loose, friable soils.

Self-blanching celery and lettuce require highly fertile soils. Because they cannot be grown efficiently and with precision without irrigation, soils must be able to withstand and retain regular applications of water. Lettuce sown using pelleted seeds requires adequate soil moisture to allow the pellets to split open, decompose, and release the seed for germination. Lettuce also does not tolerate acid conditions, especially during seedling stages (Fordham and Biggs 1985).

Plant Nutrition

Vittum (1963), Salunkhe, Pao, and Dull (1974), and Harris (1975) reviewed the early work on the effects of soil fertility on the nutrient contents of vegetables. Salunkhe and Desai (1988) also described the effects of soil fertility and fertilization on the nutritional composition of vegetables. The contradictory observations generally reported in the literature with respect to the effects of fertilization on chemical composition and the quality of vegetables are probably due to variations in soil properties, water availability, and differential environment. Adequate fertilization with N, P, K, Ca, Mg, Mn, Fe, and B is essential for normal growth and development, and for adequate yields. According to Harris (1975), the practices used for the improvement of soils are generally aimed at increasing yields rather than enhancing the nutritional quality of crop plants. Endemic goiter caused by iodine deficiency is probably the only evidence of the direct relationship between soil deficiency and malnutrition. The complex interrelationships among soil nutrient elements, the effects of one element upon the availability of others to the crop, and their antagonistic and synergistic effects upon each other have created confusion in the literature regarding the effect of mineral fertilization on the composition of the crop (Salunkhe and Desai 1988). Vittum (1963) concluded that although mineral fertilizers increase the nutritional value of vegetables, they are primarily used to rectify the nutrient status of the soil for crop growth. A well-fertilized crop is usually a high-quality crop.

Nitrogen

Crops grown on nitrogen-deficient soils show delayed growth, yellow leaves, poor yields, and, occasionally, low protein content. Nitrogen deficiency not only decreases yields but also seriously affects the quality of those vegetables in which a dark green color is desired (e.g., leafy greens). Mengel (1979) reported that nitrogen was one of the major factors influencing the protein: carbohydrate ratio. A suboptimal supply restricts protein synthesis while accentuating the accumulation of carbohydrates. A generous application of nitrogen usually lowers the ascorbic acid content of several vegetables (Table 3-22). This probably is due to the competition between the carbohydrates and the amino acid metabolism for photosynthates, the latter predominating under such conditions.

The β-carotene content of vegetables is directly linked to the supply of nitrogen to the plant. This relationship is generally associated with the increased formation of chloroplasts (Mengel 1979). Habben (1972) demonstrated that carrot roots, which normally lack chloroplasts, show a close relationship between the nitrogen supply and carotene content (Table 3-23). According to Kansal et al. (1981), leaf proteins, β-carotene, and reducing sugars were maximum when spinach was grown on sandy loam soil with the highest level of nitrogen (90 kg/ha) without FYM. However, the yield, uptake of P, Fe, Mn, Zn, and Cu, and ascorbic acid content increased with increasing rates of application of both urea and FYM.

Table 3-22. Effects of Nitrogen and Potassium Fertilizers on Vitamin C Content of Vegetables.[a]

	Vitamin C (mg/100 g fresh wt.)					
Vegetable	N_1	N_2	N_3	K_1	K_2	K_3
Beta vulgaris, type *cicla*	67.8	56.1	47.6	49.9	56.1	59.3
Brassica oleracea, type *acephala*	113.0	112.0	99.0	98.0	112.0	118.0
Brassica oleracea, type *gemmifera*	112.0	101.0	93.0	88.0	101.0	100.0
Cychorium endivia	14.0	13.8	13.1	13.1	13.8	14.2
Lactuca sativa	9.1	9.1	8.6	8.6	9.1	9.4
Spinacia oleracea	27.8	30.3	32.0	28.8	30.8	34.8

[a]*Compiled from:* Werner (1957) and Mengel (1979).

Table 3-23. Effects of Nitrogen Supply on the Degree of Maturation of Carotene Content of Carrots.[a]

Treatment (kg N/plot)	Carotene (mg/100 g dry wt.)		
	1st harvest	2nd harvest	3rd harvest
0.3	113	125	136
0.6	118	128	138
1.2	126	138	147
2.4	126	138	146

[a]*Source:* Habben (1972).

Table 3-24. Nitrate (NO₃)-N Concentrations in Edible Portions of Fresh Vegetables.[a]

Plant Part	Vegetable	NO_3–N (ppm fresh wt.)
Leaf	Cabbage	165
	Lettuce	170
	Spinach	534
Petiole	Celery	535
	Rhubarb	91
Root	Beet	600
	Carrot	32
	Sweet potato	0
	Radish	402
Fruit	Peas	26
	Snap bean	35
	Tomato	20
Stem	Asparagus	25
Bulb	Onion	14
Tuber	Potato	42

[a]*Source:* Maynard et al. (1976).

An extensive list of deficient, intermediate, and sufficient nitrate (NO₃) nitrogen concentrations at specific stages of maturity of several vegetable crops has been compiled (Geraldson, Klacan, and Lorenz 1973). Heavy nitrogen applications, however, cause accumulation of potentially hazardous concentrations of NO₃–N, thereby adversely affecting the nutritional quality of vegetables (Table 3-24) (Maynard et al. 1976).

Under normal fertilization, the nitrate content in cabbage and leek was reportedly the highest in plots receiving organic nitrogen fertilizers, whereas half the amount, regardless of the type of fertilizer applied, considerably lowered it (Nilsson 1979).This effect was more pronounced in leeks, where it decreased by about 20%. Barker, Maynard, and Lachman (1967) reported that high doses of NH₄–N induced potassium deficiency. This was evidenced by the appearance of stem lesions on tomato, the specific symptoms of NH₄ excess. Potassium deficiency can be controlled by maintaining soil pH near neutrality or by supplying equivalent potassium concentrations to enhance incorporation of NH₄–N into nontoxic nitrogen compounds (Maynard, Barker, and Lachman 1966, 1968).

Phosphorus

High rates of phosphorus fertilization increased the sugar content of tomatoes (Kattan, Stark, and Kramer 1957); however, the difference, barely significant, was detectable only in the raw tomato juice and not in the processed product.

Blackmore et al. (1942) observed that a phosphorus deficiency causes poor fill and color of sweet corn ears, similar to that caused by imperfect pollination. Although the direct effects of excess phosphorus on the composition of vegetables are not known, some secondary effects, such as phosphorus-induced deficiency of copper and zinc, may be observed (Maynard and Barker 1979).

Potassium

The differences in the vitamin C content of different vegetables are of much higher magnitude with the application of potassium fertilizers than with nitrogen (see Table 3-22). Potassium has a role in the conversion of radiant energy to chemical energy (Pfluger and Mengel 1972). Its favorable effects on the vitamin C content of vegetables are evident from the data summarized earlier in Table 3-22. Winsor (1979) also observed that increasing the levels of potassium fertilizers significantly increase the titratable (total) acidity of tomato fruits. The titratable acidity, as low as 4.3 meq/100 ml juice under conditions of severe potassium deficiency, increased to 8.3–10.9 meq/100 ml for plants grown at high potassium levels. The total acidity highly correlated ($r = .96$) with the potassium content of the tomato juice.

Pushkarnath (1976) observed no significant effects of potassium fertilization on the total solids and starch contents of several varieties of potato. At low levels (50 kg K/ha), starch content increased by only 1–2%. Nilsson (1979) also reported little changes in the vitamin C content of cabbage and leek, and the carotene content of carrots with either organic or inorganic (mineral) fertilization (Table 3-25).

Calcium and Magnesium

The levels of calcium and magnesium in the soil greatly influence its pH; adequate amounts of both are thus required to increase the availability of other nutrients (e.g., N, Fe, P, and Mn). The adverse effects of high lime concentrations are usually due to alkalinity rather than to calcium itself. High alkaline conditions of soils tend to decrease the availability of P, K, Mn, Fe, and B (Maynard 1979). Winsor (1979) reported that higher calcium influences the pectic acid content of vegetables grown in limed soil. Calcium salts are sometimes used to enhance the firmness of canned tomatoes.

The α- and β-carotene contents of carrots from plots that were not fertilized with N, P, K, or Mg (control) were markedly lower than those of carrots from fertilized plots (Vereecke et al. 1979). The ratios of β- to α-carotene decreased from 3.0 (P, K, Mg treatment) to 2.0 (N, K, Mg treatment). In general, the calcium content of carrot leaves increased while the magnesium content decreased with aging. The sum of K, Na, Mg, and Ca was almost constant, the lowest value being obtained with N, P, Mg treatment (Vereecke et al. 1979).

Table 3-25. Ascorbic Acid and Carotene Contents of Vegetables (A) at Harvest and (B) after Storage.[a]

| | Ascorbic Acid | | | | Carotene | | | |
| | Cabbage | | Leek (Stems) | | Leek (Leaves) | | Carrot | |
Fertilization	A	B	A	B	A	B	A	B
1/1 Level								
NPK	54	54	13	25	29	29	17	20
Organic N	50	50	13	23	29	18	19	19
Organic N + PK	51	52	14	23	29	17	18	19
Average	52	52	14	24	29	17	18	19
1/2 Level								
NPK	51	55	14	23	29	16	18	19
Organic N	49	50	14	23	29	16	19	20
Organic N + PK	42	55	14	23	30	15	18	18
Average	51	53	14	23	29	16	18	19
Least signif. diff. (5%)	NS[b]	1.9	NS	NS	NS	2.0	NS	NS
Fertilizers, % CV[c]	4.4	2.0	3.6	5.5	6.6	6.7	5.9	4.6
Fertilizers	—	*[d]	—	—	—	—	—	—
Levels	—	—	—	—	—	**[d]	—	—
Interaction	—	—	—	—	—	—	—	—

Source: Nilsson (1979).
[a]Mean of 1975 and 1976.
[b]NS = Not significant.
[c]Coefficient of variation.
[d]*,** Significant at 1% and 5% levels, respectively.

Micronutrients

During the growth period, the iron content of carrot leaves decreased and was not related to iron and nitrogen fertilization (Vereecke et al. 1979). Experiments carried out with onion, leek, and cauliflower indicated that manganese content of leaves was lower for treatments without nitrogen, reflecting a higher Fe : Mn ratio (Van Maercke and Vereecke 1976; Vereecke and Van Maercke 1976; Vereecke et al. 1979).

Boron-deficient radish plants show reduced growth and an increased content of the ionic toxin, thiocyanate, both in the foliage and roots. Copper is essential for normal photosynthesis. Molybdenum has an important role in nitrate reduction. NO_3 ions accumulate in molybdenum-deficient plants, leading to specific disorders such as the "whiptail" of cauliflower. Salunkhe and Desai (1988) concluded that postharvest changes in the mineral (both macro and micro) composition of vegetables are influenced by the preharvest fertilization of these mineral elements. Various physiological disorders of vegetable crops are related directly or indirectly to the deficiencies or toxicities of micronutrients, which, in turn, influence both postharvest behavior and nutritional quality of the produce.

Cultural Operations

Propagation and Plant Establishment

The world's vegetable production has not been able to keep pace with increasing nutritional demands. Vegetable growers are constantly striving to increase yields per unit area. Most vegetables are raised and established from seed, but a number are propagated vegetatively; these include potatoes, rhubarb, Jerusalem and globe artichokes, garlic, shallots, sea kale, watercress, mint, thyme, and horseradish, among others.

Vegetative propagation avoids the genetic variation associated with seed use. A uniform and adequate population of vegetable plants allows for uniform crop maturity, thereby facilitating mechanical harvesting (Fordham and Biggs 1985). Plant populations and spacings directly influence crop yield, but their effects are conditioned by other factors limiting crop growth. Plant populations can be reduced to accommodate water shortage, poor soil fertility, or limited fertilizer use. Population density also affects individual plant size and the time taken to reach maturity; market requirements thus influence the plant density at which crops are grown. Bleasdale (1973) reviewed the growing systems used for commercial vegetables grown in Britain over the past two and a half centuries. Fordham and Biggs (1985) have discussed the theoretical background and the implications of varying plant populations and spacing in vegetable production.

The genetic variation associated with seed-raised crops nonetheless has certain advantages. Because the individuals have different levels of tolerance to pests and diseases, and to environmental extremes such as cold or heat, complete crop failure is unlikely. Degenerative viral diseases are the greatest problem associated with vegetative propagation. Viral diseases do not cause plant death, but symptoms such as leaf roll, little leaf, mottling, ring spotting, and loss of vigor reduce crop yields. Macrovegetative propagation (tissue culture) is widely employed in the commercial production of Irish potatoes from tubers specially grown from mother plants that serve as "seed" for the following season. It is also used in vegetable production, both as a rapid method of multiplying plants with desirable characteristics (cauliflower, asparagus, Brussels sprout, etc.) and as a technique for eliminating viral diseases (e.g., in rhubarb).

Most other vegetables are grown from seed. Seed quality and performance are influenced by a wide range of genetic and environmental factors, such as effect of mother plant, seed dormancy, and germination. Seeds may be treated to improve emergence. They may be soaked in water, treated with nutrient solutions (e.g., potassium phosphate or potassium nitrate), wetted with water and redried, primed with polyethylene glycol, or treated with certain growth regulators (mixtures of gibberellins and other growth hormones). Although seed treatments improve performance, accurate plant spacing is equally important to ensure the most efficient use of resources, and to produce specific types of vegetables to predetermined programs. Fordham and Biggs (1985) described several techniques to enable the placement of seeds into soil in predetermined patterns and spacing (e.g., taped seed, size-graded natural seed, pelleted seed, and rubbed and graded seed).

Vegetables may also be grown by "direct seeding" on the farm or raised by transplanting young plants. Large-scale arable farms usually use direct seeding rather than transplanting as a means of crop establishment, as it often produces earlier and more uniform crop maturation. Salter and Fradgley (1969) demonstrated that increasing plant competition in the seedbed and increasing the age of transplants significantly contribute to delays in crop maturity for a number of autumn cauliflower varieties. Gray (1978) stressed the importance of uniform germination and synchronous emergence in producing evenly maturing crops of direct-seeded lettuce. The size and uniformity of transplants are particularly important in vegetables grown for vegetative characteristics (e.g., lettuce, cabbage, or leeks). Transplanting allows vegetable seedlings to be raised in isolation, where they can be given attention and protection. Damage to the root system during transplanting can be reduced by thoroughly wetting the soil before lifting, undercutting the beds of plants, and hand-forking plants out of the ground. A common horticultural practice is to harden-off (precondition) plants by withholding water and reducing temperatures before planting in order to minimize transplanting checks (Fordham and Biggs 1985). Cox et al. (1979), however, showed that successful establishment is associated with moisture stress levels in the transplant; withholding water before planting is therefore deleterious. Fordham and Biggs (1985) have described the various planting methods and postplanting cares.

Species/Varieties

The species of vegetables, as well as the varieties of cultivars within them, greatly influence their nutritional composition. Watada (1982) determined the ascorbic acid content of several species of fresh fruits and vegetables including snap bean, capsicum, kale, broccoli, cabbage, carrot, cauliflower, and tomato. Ter-Manuel'Yants (1980) estimated the vitamins of seven different brassica species; kale had the highest content (134 mg/100 g) of vitamin C, red cabbage the highest (11.2 mg/100 g) dehydroascorbic acid, broccoli the highest nicotinic acid and choline (1.44 and 90.3 mg/100 g, respectively), and Brussels sprout the highest (2.73 mg/100 g) vitamin K.

Many aspects of vegetable quality depend on the choice of variety, including uniformity of color, shape, size, and firmness. Hardh, Murmann, and Seppala (1979) reported that firmness and inner quality varied significantly in tomato fruits of different cultivars. The fruits of "Virosa" and "Sonato" had higher soluble and dry-matter content. "Virosa" also had fairly high nitrogen and potassium contents. Organoleptically, "Stella" fruits had the best flavor quality.

Irrigation

Vegetable production in the more arid regions of the world would be impossible without some form of irrigation or ensured water supply. Irrigation increases vegetable yields during prolonged droughts, improves seed germination, assists in the distribution and utilization of fertilizers, and facilitates the harvesting of root vegetable crops from dry soils.

The choice of irrigation method depends on a number of factors, including soil infiltration capacity, crop type, field shape and topography, and power and labor availability. Fordham and Biggs (1985) categorized these methods as follows:

1. *surface irrigation,* where water is run over the surface so that it infiltrates the soil;
2. *subirrigation,* where water is introduced into the soil at a depth until capillary action raises it into the root zone;
3. *overhead irrigation,* simulating the effects of rain; and
4. *trickle* or *drip irrigation.*

Although surface irrigation is one of the oldest and most widely used methods in the world, its scope is often limited when the shape, slope, and topography of the field do not allow uniform water application. Water losses from open water and wet soil surfaces can be eliminated by subirrigation, which, due to the absence of pipes or ditches, does not impede surface intercultural operations. Subirrigation, however, is largely confined to sites where the soil profile has high horizontal and low vertical permeability. Depending upon soil permeability, perforated pipes buried at definite lateral spacing to a depth of about 0.5 m can also be used.

According to Fordham and Biggs (1985), spray lines, medium–low-pressure rotary sprinklers, and high-pressure rain guns are the main types of equipment used for overhead irrigation. Each of these can be mounted on self-propelled supports, making some degree of automation possible. The use of oscillating spray-line irrigation is usually confined to high-value crops, such as salad vegetables. Overhead rotary sprinklers are widely used for irrigating vegetable crops.

Trickle systems used for greenhouse crops have been developed for use in the field production. Various types of drip nozzle and capillary tube are used to produce a trickle or series of drips from a main lateral laid polythene tubing. The tubing is either perforated or sewn along its length to permit seepage, reducing the cost of such equipment. A major advantage of trickle systems is that they reduce water loss from direct evaporation. A recent trend in irrigation is the use of automated sprinkler movement to lower rates of water application, reduce soil and crop damage, and keep labor costs to a minimum.

Use of Chemicals and Growth Regulators

Several chemicals are used to protect the quality of vegetables during their growth, development, and postharvest storage. These include insecticides, fungicides, herbicides, nematicides, growth regulators, desiccants, antioxidants, ethylene absorbents, senescence retardants, and wax emulsions. Several physiological disorders of fruits and vegetables can be controlled by the direct postharvest applications of nutrient salt solutions. Wills and Tirmazi (1979) reported that ripening of green tomatoes (cv. Daydream), as expressed by change of color, increased ethylene evolution, and respiration, was inhibited when the calcium content of the fruit was raised to >40 mg Ca/100 g fresh weight. Other divalent cations, such as manganese, cobalt, and magnesium, also inhibited tomato ripening as effectively as calcium. Monovalent metal ions, such as sodium and potassium, were less effective, but did retard the ripening.

Wu and Salunkhe (1974) described the use of several chemicals to increase the nutritional value and quality of economic plants. Growth regulators such as auxins (2,4-D, s-triazines, and other herbicides) have been successfully used to increase protein content and favorably alter the amino acid composition. Increases in carbohydrates, vitamins, minerals, and pigments of vegetables due to treatment with these chemicals have been reported. Treatment with N^6-benzyladenine (BA) at 5, 10, and 20 ppm increased the shelf life of cauliflower, endive, parsley, snap bean, lettuce, radish, bunching onion, and cabbage (Salunkhe, Dhaliwal, and Boe 1962). BA provides the necessary adenine to restore rRNA molecules, and revives protein synthesis. The maintenance of protein synthesis, in turn, enables the treated produce to stay fresh longer.

The pre- and postharvest treatment of lettuce with 6-furfurylamino purine (kinetin) or BA, followed by storage at 4.4 °C and 85% rh, resulted in higher moisture content, total chlorophyll, and total insoluble nitrogen. Inhibition of respiration (CO_2 evolution) during storage was directly related to the concentration of both BA and kinetin. The latter was more effective than BA, but both maintained higher quality ratings than the untreated (control) lettuce (El-Mansy et al. 1967).

The treatment of peas and sweet corn with s-triazine compounds (Simazine®, Igran®, or 2-methylthio-4-ethyl amino-6-isopropylamino-s-triazine, Ametryne®) at the rate of 2 lb/acre decreased the total nitrogen and soluble protein in the pea seeds. However Simazine® or Igran® at 0.5 and 0.125 lb/acre, Propazine® at 2 and 0.5 lb/acre, Prometone® at all three rates, and Ametryne® at 0.125 lb/acre significantly increased the total nitrogen and soluble protein contents, while decreasing the starch and soluble sugars of pea seeds (Tables 3-26 and 3-27). The contents of total and individual amino acids in most cases were higher when these vegetable crops were treated with s-triazine compounds. In almost every treatment, isoleucine, histidine, and cystine levels were lower than in the con-

Table 3-26. Effects of Soil Treatment of s-Triazine Compounds on the Dry Weight and Chemical Composition of Peas.

Treatment Compound	Concentration (lb/acre)	Dry Wt. (%)	Total N (%)	Soluble Protein (%)	Starch (%)	Sugar (%)
			Component (First Year, Under Field Conditions)[a]			
Control	—	35.04	4.31	14.20	51.33	5.54
Simazine®	2.0	35.11	4.06*	12.91*	49.06*	5.39
	0.5	35.03	5.28*	17.02*	47.65*	4.61*
	0.125	35.17	4.94*	16.47*	48.10*	5.43
Atrazine®	2	34.95	4.00*	13.33*	48.71*	5.04*
	0.5	34.89	4.27	14.05	51.90	5.60
	0.125	35.14	4.36	14.52	50.33	5.71
Propazine®	2	35.09	4.66*	15.89*	49.38*	5.21*
	0.5	35.04	4.70*	16.07*	49.05*	5.24*
	0.125	35.00	4.29	13.80	52.21	5.64
GS-14254	2	35.22	4.27	14.04	51.94	5.50
	0.5	35.17	4.38	14.66	50.61	5.39
	0.125	35.20	4.33	14.11	51.44	5.62
Prometone®	2	35.06	4.62*	16.35*	49.03*	4.33*
	0.5	34.93	4.98*	16.82*	46.97*	4.75*
	0.125	34.99	4.87*	16.50*	47.74*	4.38*
Prometryne®	2	35.14	4.22	14.07	52.35	5.47
	0.5	35.02	4.40	14.71	50.69	5.02
	0.125	35.15	4.36	14.43	51.18	5.60
Igran®	2	35.28	4.13*	13.58*	52.37	5.48
	0.5	35.13	4.80*	16.72*	48.15*	4.47*
	0.125	34.88	4.71*	16.64*	48.76*	4.64*
Ametryne®	2	35.06	3.94*	13.04*	51.62*	5.01*
	0.5	35.21	4.40	14.71	48.21*	4.72*
	0.125	35.19	4.71*	15.94*	47.70*	5.07*

Source: Salunkhe, Wu, and Singh (1971b).
[a]Each value represents the mean of three samples. Triplicate determinations of each of three samples were made. Dry weight is expressed as a percentage of fresh weight; other components are expressed as a percentage of the dry weight of the seeds. Asterisked data are significantly different from control at the 0.05 level; others are not.

trol pea seeds. In sweet corn, only glutamic acid was lower in both years (Salunkhe, Wu, and Singh 1971b).

Soil fumigation with Telone® (1,3-dichloropropane) and Nemagone® (1,2-dichloro-3-chloropropane) significantly increased the content of total carotenes and β-carotene of carrot and sweet corn by 10–46% and 11–48%, respectively. It also increased the total carotenes (16–45%) and β-carotene (15–48%) in car-

Table 3-27. Effects of Soil Treatment of s-Triazine Compounds on the Dry Weight and Chemical Composition of Sweet Corn.

Treatment Compound	Concen- tration (lb/acre)	Component (First Year, Under Field Conditions)[a]				
		Dry Wt. (%)	Total N (%)	Soluble Protein (%)	Starch (%)	Sugar (%)
Control	—	44.52	1.14	4.49	54.6	11.75
Simazine®	4	44.31	1.25*	4.86*	50.7*	11.55
	1	44.40	1.22*	4.73*	51.0*	11.63
	0.25	44.41	1.13	4.51	53.9	11.76
Atrazine®	4	44.37	1.20*	4.67*	52.0*	11.69
	1	44.56	1.15	4.43	54.8	11.70
	0.25	44.59	1.12	4.49	55.1	11.81
Propazine®	4	44.47	1.17	4.53	53.7	11.77
	1	44.38	1.17	4.40	54.4*	11.68
	0.25	44.51	1.13	4.49	54.9	11.73
GS-14254	4	44.40	1.15	4.51	53.8	11.70
	1	44.54	1.11	4.54	55.0	11.59
Prometone®	4	44.52	1.24*	4.79*	51.4*	11.35*
	1	44.43	1.13	4.47	54.7	11.57
	0.25	44.60	1.13	4.50	55.3	11.74
Prometryne®	4	44.53	1.11	4.48	54.1	11.80
	1	44.64	1.13	4.55	55.6	11.66
	0.25	44.57	1.17	4.53	54.0	11.71
Igran®	4	44.30	1.21*	4.69*	53.4	11.68
	1	44.37	1.14	4.40	55.2	11.76
	0.25	44.63	1.16	4.47	54.8	11.70
Ametryne®	4	44.50	1.21*	4.76*	51.6*	11.65
	1	44.60	1.12	4.39	53.8	11.71
	0.25	44.41	1.17	4.45	53.2	11.74

Source: Salunkhe, Wu, and Singh (1971b).
[a]Each value represents the mean of three samples. Triplicate determinations of each of three samples were made. Dry weight is expressed as a percentage of fresh weight; other components are expressed as a percentage of the dry weight of the seeds. Asterisked data are significantly different from control at the 0.05 level; others are not.

rots grown under field conditions (Salunkhe, Wu, and Singh 1971a). Soil fumigation with these chemicals also influenced the chemical composition of sweet corn: The total carotenoids increased by 33% in 1969 and 26% in 1970.

Processing Technology

Proctor, Goodliffe, and Coursey (1981) estimated that the postharvest losses of vegetables are particularly serious in the tropics, and may be as high as 25% for root crops and even higher for more perishable produce. Vegetables are particularly vulnerable to high evaporation rates and to high temperatures, which increase respiration rates; both cause losses in dry weight. In addition to these physiological losses, vegetables also suffer high postharvest spoilage by pests and diseases, whose incidence may be further aggravated by mechanical damage caused by harvesting and handling. *Botrytis cinerea* is the most common fungus found on stored cabbage; its incidence, however, can be reduced by pre- and postharvest treatment of the crop with fungicides such as benomyl.

Pantastico and Bautista (1976) identified general problems for several vegetable groups at each handling step, such as harvesting, packing, transporting, grading, storage, and retail marketing (Table 3-28). For each of these steps, the

Table 3-28. General Problems for Each Vegetable Group at Each Handling Step.

Produce	Harvesting	Packing	Transport	Grading	Storage	Retail
Fruits	Right stage of maturity	Overpacking, improper container	Rough handling, poor roads	Uneven ripening	Chemical changes	Overripening, shriveling, browning
Roots	Excessive moisture leading to rotting	Mechanical injury in sacks	Bruising	Malformation	Sprouting, improper curing	Sprouting
Tubers, corms	Mechanical injury	Mechanical injury in sacks	Bruising	Malformation	Improper curing, sprouting, greening	Sprouting, rotting, shriveling, weight loss
Leaves	Excessive wilting and rotting under high-moisture conditions	Unsuitable container size, mechanical injury	Rough handling, high transit temperature	Overtrimming, mixed sizes	Wilting at low rh, insufficient humidity	Overtrimming, excessive wilting, bacterial soft rot
Flowers	Flower shedding	Improper packaging	High transit temperature	Loose curds, insufficient wrapper leaves	Yellowing of curds	Loosening of curds, fading
Stems	Improper harvesting method	Breaking	High transit temperature	Malformation	Elongation of existing structure	Shriveling
Bulbs	Maturity	Bruising and other mechanical injury	Improper conditions in sacks	Misshapen	Sprouting	Shriveling and sprouting, fading

Source: Pantastico and Bautista (1976).

existing practice of produce handling must be surveyed to identify specific problems, for which solutions may then be sought.

Maturation and Harvesting

Correct harvest maturity of vegetables is directly related to consumer preference. The stage of harvest maturity depends on several considerations, including economic factors and the purpose and method of vegetable utilization. The timing and method of harvesting are determined by not only the species of vegetables in question but also the method of production and the proposed outlet. Because the consumer is becoming increasingly quality conscious, the grower must not only grow a good-quality crop, but must harvest and market it in perfect condition to command high price premiums. Delays in harvesting may result in increased yields of potatoes and carrots (which are grown for their storage organs) but in lower unit prices. Likewise, hand-harvested and trimmed Brussels sprouts may command high premiums for quality but at the expense of high labor costs (Fordham and Biggs 1985).

Vegetable harvesting techniques range from multiple, selective hand harvesting, to "once-over" harvests aided in part by machine, to completely mechanical harvesters. For "once-over" harvests, vegetable cultivars of more uniform maturity have been developed to suit the harvesting system. In addition to the use of genetic selection, growing systems have been modified to yield more uniform growth and access to machinery.

Traditionally, following harvest, produce has been transferred to a packinghouse where final trimming, grading, and packing for market takes place. The recent trend is toward carrying out as many operations in the field as possible so that the produce—especially the salad vegetables—reaches the market as quickly as possible (Fordham and Biggs 1985).

Some control over harvest date may be achieved by appropriate choice of cultivar and sowing dates. Subsequent growth and development are then determined largely by the prevailing weather and climatic conditions. Precision in forecasting harvest dates is generally poor, although empirical methods based on temperature, a major determinant of crop development, have been used successfully as a guide. For example, Ontario heat units are used with regard to harvesting crops like sweet corn and peas. The number of days, degree-days, and heat units required to grow vegetable crops depend on several factors, including species, variety, soil, climatic conditions, and plant nutrition. Salunkhe et al. (1959) reported that the number of days and degree-days required for the maturation of three varieties of lima bean (viz., "Clark's Bush," "Evergreen," and "Limagreen") were almost identical, whereas "Fordhook 242" and "Concentrated Fordhook" required longer for maturity. Total days and the length of time for maturity of each variety varied from year to year. Salunkhe et al. (1959) concluded that both total days and degree-days were too variable for the practical estimation of the harvest time of lima beans. Both riboflavin and thiamin decreased progressively with the advancing maturity of lima beans. Salunkhe, Pao, and Dull (1974) described the effects of heat units on the nutritional composition of several vegetables. Ottosson (1979) reported the changes in ascorbic acid content of vegetables during and after harvest.

The stage of maturity of a vegetable crop has an important bearing on the date of harvesting. Delays in harvesting are in many cases associated with increased yields, although with significant losses in quality and flavor. Increased maturity of garden peas is associated with a conversion of sugars to starch and a corresponding change in texture. Immature peas, like some other pulse vegetables, are smaller, sweeter, and more tender. The optimal stage of harvesting can be determined using a tenderometer to measure the shear strength of a sample. For carrots, size is particularly important for most market outlets. Although this can be controlled to some extent by the choice of variety and plant population, date of harvest has a profound influence on product quality. The lower yields resulting from earlier harvesting of many vegetable crops are usually compensated by higher price. Sweet corns should be harvested when they have a higher level of sugars, prior to their conversion to starch in the mature grain. Cabbages are usually allowed to "heart up" prior to harvest, to provide a high proportion of tender, blanched, internal leaves. Spring greens are harvested at a much earlier stage, providing a supply in a season when hearted cabbages are not readily available. Optimal harvesting dates under such circumstances depend on the prevailing market prices and the potential increases in yield from delaying the operation (Fordham and Biggs 1985).

Preharvest Treatments

All cultural operations are in effect preharvest treatments and, in some way, influence the harvesting operation. Specific treatments are carried out to facilitate harvesting or to improve some aspect of the harvested produce. These often include spraying of different chemicals and growth substances. Bulb onions intended for storage are often sprayed with maleic hydrazide (MH) two weeks in advance of harvest. The MH is translocated to the onion bulb where it acts as a sprout inhibitor. According to Fordham and Biggs (1985), practical methods for delaying senescence and aging processes should have a profound benefit in delaying harvesting dates. Preharvest applications of cytokinins show some promise in this respect, but they have not yet reached the stage of commercial application. Diquat has been used more widely to reduce foliage of root crops like potatoes effectively in order to facilitate harvesting. Defoliation is also advantageous before mechanical harvesting of Brussels sprout; but because suitable chemicals are not yet available, the leaves are either broken off or cut with specially designed knives at harvest.

Chemical sprays used for preharvest crop protection may have beneficial effects beyond the harvest date by keeping the produce free from pest damage and diseases and thus extending its shelf life. However, precautions must be taken to ensure that unacceptable residues of pesticides do not remain on the edible crops at harvest, whether it is harvested for the fresh market or for processing. Apart from any potential toxic effects, a number of crop protection chemicals can produce taints and off-flavors in the treated vegetables. According to Lyon (1981), rigorous testing is carried out on such produce to determine the likelihood of any toxic residues. Generally, recommendations on their use include information on possible tainting problems.

Methods of Harvesting

Increasing labor costs have led to a decline in the harvesting by hand of vegetable crops. Many species, however, do not lend themselves to mechanical harvesting in spite of efforts by plant breeders and agricultural engineers. Fordham and Biggs (1985) stated that the production of runner beans has dropped because they need to be hand-picked at frequent intervals if quality and yield are to be maintained. These authors also mentioned a system called "pick your own," where consumers pay for the produce they harvest themselves; thus both grower and consumer are benefited. This system, however, presents additional problems of high-level wastage and lower yields in growing the crop. Fordham and Biggs (1985) described the semiautomatic and fully mechanical harvesters used for vegetables. The latter are largely restricted to commercially grown vegetables on large farms and those meant for processing. Resistance to physical damage is the main consideration in the development of mechanical harvesters. In California, plant breeders have significantly contributed to such developments by evolving tomato cultivars with stronger skins that are more resistant to mechanical damage. Onions and root crops, which present fewer problems, are largely harvested by using appropriate machinery. Peas now marketed as frozen and canned products are also harvested mechanically. Modern harvesters run over the standing pea crop and remove the peas in a single operation.

Grading and Packing

Following harvest, vegetables are graded and packed for marketing. Depending on the crop and its intended outlet, packing and grading operations are carried out either in the field or in a specially designed and equipped packinghouse. For most vegetables, especially salads, the entire process should be executed as quickly as possible to minimize postharvest losses through deterioration, particularly under tropical conditions.

Some semiautomatic harvesters perform part of the grading and packing operation in the field. Trimming and overwrapping of lettuce are conducted on the harvest machine itself. This form of mobile packing can be adapted to many cruciferous species that require little additional treatment between harvesting and marketing.

"On-farm-machine" packing and grading operations considerably reduce delays between cutting and packing. Waste material left in the field contributes to soil nutrition and eliminates unnecessary transport costs. The problems associated with mobile packing are high investment costs for the machinery and the possible damage to soil structure.

Crops like carrots and leeks are generally transported to a central packinghouse for washing before marketing. Care must be taken to prevent damage during transport, particularly when bulk handling of the produce is involved. Careful handling of the produce at all stages is necessary, since bruises and cuts lead to increased rates of respiration and invasion by microbial spoilage.

With increasing foreign trade, international standards are being defined for the grading, packing, and quality of produce. In the European Economic Community (EEC), there are now a number of statutory grading standards for many vegetable and fruit crops, defining classes for both size and quality characteristics (Fordham and Biggs 1985).

Storage

Vegetables must be stored to ensure a continual supply through seasons when the fresh produce is not available. Market prices reflect the availability of the produce and the cost of transportation. Vegetable storage ranges from short term (one day, in the case of lettuce) to long term (onions may be stored throughout the entire winter and spring).

Only clean, healthy produce should be stored for prolonged periods. Crops should be kept free from pests and diseases. Disease infections can occur long before the crop enters the store. For example, neck rot (*Botrytis allii*) of onions, contracted in the field, may cause serious storage losses.

Prestorage Treatments

Salunkhe and Desai (1988) described various prestorage treatments, such as precooling, hydrocooling, vacuum cooling, curing, and treatment with ethylene. Leafy vegetables are difficult to cool with water or air refrigeration, but they can be field-packed and then cooled rapidly and uniformly by *vacuum cooling*— reducing the atmospheric pressure in hermetically sealed chambers until the reduced vaporizing point of water cools the produce. The speed and uniformity of cooling are the obvious advantages of this system (Ryall and Lipton 1979). Other vegetables adapted to vacuum cooling are globe artichoke, asparagus, broccoli, Brussels sprout, cabbage, celery, sweet corn, and peas.

Hydrocooling or cooling with cold water is a rapid and effective method, accomplished by flooding, spraying, or immersion. Sometimes a small amount of fungicide is dissolved in hydrocooling water to control fungal growth during the subsequent storage and transportation of vegetables.

Sweet potato, Irish potato, taro, onion, and garlic are cured under the sun to heal injured or bruised surfaces. *Curing* extends storage life of these vegetables by reducing their moisture content. It also decreases rotting by eliminating surface fungal growth and reducing internal necrosis of tissue.

An exogenous application of a low concentration of *ethylene* (1 ppm) stimulates respiration rate and hastens ripening. It also inhibits seed germination and sprouting of potatoes (Salunkhe and Wu 1974). Postharvest applications of ethephon (2-chloroethyl-phosphonic acid) to tomato had the following advantages:

1. Uniform ripening reduces sorting costs of tomatoes.
2. Fast ripening rates reduce weight loss and may prolong shelf life.
3. Ripening rooms are not necessary.
4. Yields increase from once-over harvests.
5. Maturity may be hastened early in the season to obtain marketable fruit with premium prices.

Field Storage

Vegetables such as carrots and other root crops can be left in the field for several months during the winter, either with some surface covering to prevent frost damage or in heaps or clumps. Field storage is the cheapest method of extending the supply period of such vegetables. Most hardy root crops can be stacked in heaps, which are then covered with a layer of straw or other insulating material. Celery can be stored in the field successfully for several weeks, thus benefiting from the market premium available during the early winter months. The standing crop can be protected from frost by covering it with a layer of straw or other insulating material, which is kept dry and held in place by a layer of polythene (Fordham and Biggs 1985).

Controlled-Environment Stores

Fordham and Biggs (1985) described ambient-air stores, refrigerated cold stores, and controlled-environment stores for vegetables. In temperate regions, store temperature can be lowered most economically by using the ambient air for cooling. Vegetables during winter can thus be stored by drawing external air into an insulated store during the night and early morning. At other times of the year, some form of refrigeration is required. Most vegetables are cold-stored by some form of refrigeration. Lower temperatures reduce respiration rates and water loss by lowering the vapor pressure deficit. Some humidity is necessary to prevent excessive condensation on the produce, leading to spoilage. (See also the upcoming section, "Effects of Refrigerated Storage.")

Controlled Atmosphere (CA) Storage

The store environment can also be controlled by altering the composition of the atmosphere, particularly with respect to its oxygen and carbon dioxide content. This approach is usually used in association with cooling. Respiratory rates of crop produce are reduced in gastight chambers under reduced oxygen and increased carbon dioxide concentrations; the latter has an additional benefit of slowing the growth of pathological microorganisms and reducing the loss of chlorophyll that occurs during senescence and aging of leafy vegetables. Dennis (1981) reported that high carbon dioxide levels improved tenderness of asparagus and broccoli stored in CA conditions. In practice, CA storage is largely confined to high-value fruits and has not been widely accepted to extend the shelf life of vegetables. Fordham and Biggs (1985) reasoned that this may be due to the very specific and differing conditions for different vegetable species and their cultivars. Isenberg (1979) reviewed the CA requirements for different vegetable crops. (See also the upcoming section, "Effects of Controlled Atmosphere Storage.")

Subatmospheric (Hypobaric) Storage

Subatmospheric or low-pressure (hypobaric) storage is similar to CA storage and is achieved by reducing the store pressure to one-tenth of atmosphere. Oxygen levels are correspondingly lowered, thus slowing respiration. This technique has the advantage that naturally produced gases such as ethylene do not accumulate in plant tissue. Subatmospheric storage is particularly attractive for the storage of such vegetables as tomatoes, which are susceptible to chilling injury under conventional cold storage. Lougheed, Murr, and Berard (1978) reviewed the use of low-pressure storage for horticultural commodities. (See also the upcoming section, "Effects of Subatmospheric Storage.")

Compatibility of Vegetable Storage

Although shelf life of vegetables can generally be extended by storage at low temperatures and high humidities, practical problems may arise when different types of vegetable are to be stored together. Fordham and Biggs (1985) categorized the following three sets of storage conditions to cope with the majority of vegetables:

1. *Low temperature/high humidity* (0–1°C, 90–95% rh): This range suits a wide variety of crops, including

asparagus	celery	mushrooms	radish	spinach
beet	leek	parsnip	rhubarb	sweet corn
brassicas	lettuce	peas	salad onion	turnip

2. *Low temperature/low humidity* (0–1°C, 60–65% rh): This setting is more appropriate for long-term storage of bulb onions.

3. *High temperature/high humidity* (13°C, 90–95% rh): This setting prevents chilling damage to many vegetables of tropical origin, such as

beans (runner and French)	early potatoes	tomato
cucumber	melons	

When a compromise is essential, the high-temperature and high-humidity store will cause the least damage to produce.

Fordham and Biggs (1985) stated that problems can occasionally occur from tainting of one crop by another. Ethylene production by ripe potatoes can also affect green vegetables, causing bleaching and increased incidence of rotting. Packaging techniques can reduce the extent of the problem; however, in severe cases, the vegetables must be stored separately.

Effects of Harvesting, Handling, and Storage on Nutrients

The nutritional composition of the vegetables is significantly influenced by various harvesting methods, handling procedures, and storage techniques. Salunkhe and Desai (1988) reviewed the earlier work on this subject; the following discussion is mainly based on their report.

Effects of Harvesting

Serdyukov and Emelin (1979) investigated several quality aspects of tomato, sweet potato, sweet pepper, and eggplant in relation to mechanized harvesting, storage, transport, and sale. Tomato fruits harvested by combine mechanized harvesters (SK T-2) were stored under natural conditions of storehouses for 2–3 wk before sale or transported 1,500 km with relatively small losses. Combined-harvested sweet peppers were of high market quality, and further sorting was not necessary; they were suitable for the natural conditions of storehouses or refrigerators. Hand-picking of pepper, as compared to combine-harvesting, caused yield decreases of up to 25–36% and increased the number of red and rotten fruits. The biochemical analyses of sweet peppers carried out 25–30 days after the first harvest were characterized by intensive accumulation of vitamin C in fruits (Table 3-29). Peppers of the "Mikhalev" variety also showed a 25% increase in vitamin C during this period.

Table 3-29. Effects of Mechanical Harvesting on Biochemical Composition of Sweet Peppers (1977–8).

Date of First Harvest	Days Between Harvesting	"Mikhalev" Pepper			"Padarok Moldovy"		
		Dry Matter (%)	Total Sugars (%)	Vitamin C (mg %)	Dry Matter (%)	Total Sugars (%)	Vitamin C (mg %)
August 5	20	6.2	3.4	104.4	5.0	2.6	122.2
	25	6.8	3.3	173.2	7.1	3.9	183.4
	30	7.2	3.6	220.8	6.5	3.2	200.3
August 10	20	6.1	3.2	76.8	5.5	2.6	53.9
	25	6.7	4.1	151.1	9.4	3.7	181.6
	30	7.3	3.0	198.6	6.4	9.4	190.4

Source: Serdyukov and Emelin (1979).

The combine-harvesting of tomato fruits increased the content of insoluble dry substances, decreased the acids, and approximately doubled the cellulose. The dry substances increased up to 4.6% (Serdyukov and Emelin 1979).

Effects of Handling, Transporting, and Distribution

Pantastico and Bautista (1976) described postharvest handling of tropical vegetables, the extent of their losses, handling procedures, transportation, packaging and market preparation, and problems related to preservation of quality of vegetables during storage. Distribution is an integral part of horticulture and, like production, must be managed effectively (Schoorl and Holt 1982). For fresh fruits and vegetables, the management of distribution must be based on the management of quality. This requires understanding of the nature of distribution of its components—the produce, environment, transit time, and interactions among these components. The management of quality mainly relies on the ability to predict changes in quality (or damage) of the produce. Physical deterioration leads to severe loss in nutritional quality of fresh vegetables during subsequent handling, storage, distribution, and marketing.

Effects of Refrigerated Storage

Significant changes in color, texture, flavor, and nutritional quality of vegetables occur during their storage. These are markedly influenced by temperature and storage environment (gas composition and % rh).

Nutrient loss from vegetables during storage is largely controlled by temperature and packaging medium (Salunkhe and Wu 1974). Vitamins such as thiamin are comparatively stable but are noticeably degraded during normal storage. Ascorbic acid, being heat and oxygen sensitive, is easily lost from stored vegetable products. Vitamins B_{12} and pyridoxine are stable during storage, especially in freeze-dried products (Hollingsworth 1970); riboflavin, however, is degraded somewhat during storage.

Surface color and firmness of tomato are closely related to storage temperatures (Thorne and Segurajauregui Alvarez 1982). Equations were used to predict color and firmness after storage under various irregular temperature regimes. Changes in color and firmness thus could be used to predict storage life of tomatoes held at 12–27 °C.

Smittle and Hayes (1979) stored mechanically shelled southern peas at 5°, 25°, and 45 °C for 3, 6, and 12 h. Changes in quality—decreases in percentages of green seed, total chlorophyll, sugar, starch, and protopectin, and increases in water-soluble pectin and discoloration (Table 3-30)—were minimal with 5 °C storage and increased with prolonged storage at higher temperatures. However, the total solids, hemicellulose, and cellulose contents of peas were not affected by storage treatments. Smittle and Hayes (1979) developed a response curve relating the rate of loss of green seed to storage temperature that will assist in the coordination of harvesting, transport, and processing operations for the maintenance of high-quality product during storage.

Table 3-30. Effects of Storage Treatments on Green Seed Percentage, Chlorophyll Content, and Seed Discoloration of "Purple Hull Pinkeye" Southern Pea.[a]

Storage Treatment	% Green Seed		Chlorophyll[b]		Seed Discoloration[c] (1976)
	1975	1976	1975	1976	
Initial	35a	59ab	3.0a	5.6a	1.0a
5 °C					
3 hr	33a	59ab	3.0a	5.6a	1.0a
6 hr	32a	62a	2.9ab	5.8a	1.0a
12 hr	30ab	61a	2.6ab	5.6a	1.3ab
25 °C					
3 hr	32a	57ab	2.7ab	4.6b	1.3ab
6 hr	30ab	55bc	2.4bc	4.2b	1.3ab
12 hr	27bc	53c	2.4bc	4.2b	2.0c
45 °C					
3 hr	25bc	51cd	2.5abc	4.6b	1.3ab
6 hr	24c	46d	2.3bc	4.0bc	2.0c
12 hr	12d	29c	2.1c	3.4c	3.0d

Source: Smittle and Hayes (1979).
[a]Mean separation within columns by Duncan's multiple range test at 5% level. Means followed by the same letter are not significantly different.
[b]Chlorophyll concentration in mg/kg on a fresh weight basis.
[c]Panel ratings for seed discoloration: 1 = none, 2 = marginal acceptability, 3 = unacceptable.

Salunkhe, Wu, and Jadhav (1972) reported the effects of light and temperature on the formation of solanine in potato slices. At low temperatures (0° and 8 °C) there was a slow but significant increase in solanine content during a 48-h period in the dark, whereas storage at 15° and 24 °C vigorously stimulated its formation. After 48 h at 24 °C in the dark, solanine content reached a concentration of 2.05 mg/100 g slice—seven times higher than that in the original (0-time) sample (Fig. 3-12). The rate of solanine synthesis increased at the later stages. The difference in solanine content between potato slices stored in cold (0° and 8 °C) and warm (15° and 24 °C) temperatures under light is illustrated in Fig. 3-13. In the 48-h exposure to 200-fc light at 24 °C, the solanine concentration increased up to 7.4 mg/100 g slice. In general, lighted storage increased the rate of solanine synthesis to three to four times greater than that of dark storage.

Effects of Controlled Atmosphere (CA) Storage

Chang and Kays (1981) studied the effects of lower concentration of oxygen in CA storage on the nutritional composition of sweet potatoes. These authors noted that the rate of respiration of uncured sweet potatoes was high at harvest but decreased rapidly, stabilizing at about 25 mg CO_2/kg/h after 38–40 h

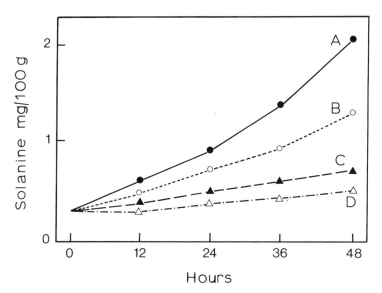

Fig. 3-12. Effects of temperature on solanine formation in potato slices stored in the dark: (A) 24 °C, (B) 15 °C, (C) 8°C, (D) 0°C. *Source:* Salunkhe, Wu, and Jadhav (1972).

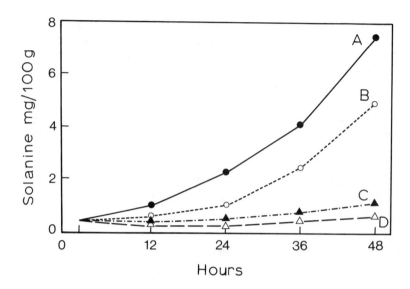

Fig. 3-13. Effects of light exposure (200 fc) on solanine formation in potato slices at different temperatures: (A) 24 °C, (B) 15 °C, (C) 8°C, (D) 0°C. *Source:* Salunkhe, Wu, and Jadhav (1972).

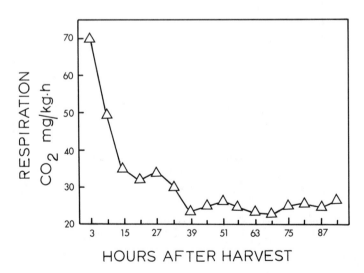

HOURS AFTER HARVEST

Fig. 3-14. Changes in respiratory rate of uncured sweet potato roots during the first 93 h after harvest when held at 21% oxygen. *Source:* Chang and Kays (1981).

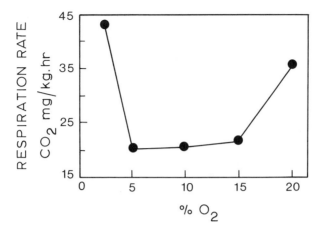

Fig. 3-15. The effect of concentration of oxygen in storage atmosphere on the respiratory rate of cured sweet potato roots at 7 days after beginning of treatment. *Source:* Chang and Kays (1981).

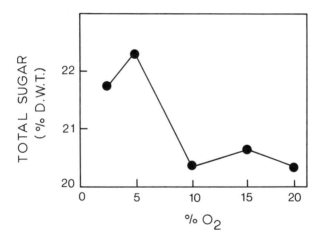

Fig. 3-16. The effect of oxygen concentration of storage gas on the sugar content (% dry weight) of stored sweet potato roots. *Source:* Chang and Kays (1981).

(Fig. 3-14). The respiratory rates of roots stored at O_2 concentrations of 5–10% were lower than those of roots held either at 2.5% or 20% O_2 (Fig. 3-15). The low oxygen concentration in the storage atmosphere also affected the carbohydrate transformations in sweet potato roots. The roots stored at <5% O_2 concentration accumulated more total sugar than roots stored at higher O_2 concentrations (Fig. 3-16). It was postulated that the reducing sugars might have been utilized via the respiratory pathway more rapidly at higher oxygen con-

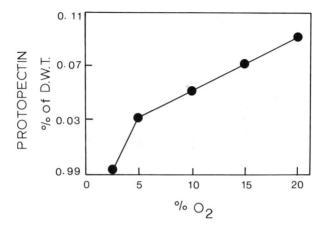

Fig. 3-17. The effect of oxygen concentration of storage gas on the content of protopectin (% dry weight) of sweet potatoes. *Source:* Chang and Kays (1981).

centration. The protopectin content of sweet potatoes also increased with increasing concentration of oxygen in the storage atmosphere (Fig. 3-17), whereas there was no significant change in water-soluble pectin.

Kurki (1979) assessed leek quality with reference to dry-matter content, vitamin C, provitamin A, reducing sugars, chlorophyll, total nitrogen, and storage loss after 3, 4, 5, and 6 mo in CA storage (1% O_2, 10% CO_2 at 0 °C and 100% rh) and in two normal-air storages (−1 °C, 75% rh and 0 °C, 100% rh). The provitamin A and chlorophyll content of vegetables stored in the optimal CA conditions were higher than in normal-air storages. The CA-stored leek had strikingly higher amounts of chlorophyll and carotene (see Table 3-31).

A prestorage treatment with Phalatan® (1,000 ppm) and polyethylene packaging inhibited chlorophyll degradation in lettuce throughout a 75-day CA storage period (Singh et al. 1972a). These authors further reported that lettuce heads could be stored for up to 75 days in CA (2.4% O_2 and 1.7 °C and 90–95% rh). Neither dry weight nor moisture content of the lettuce was affected by the CA storage. Singh et al. (1972b) reported the effects of CA storage on the biochemical composition of lettuce leaves.

Effects of Modified Atmosphere (MA) Storage

Polyethylene bags used for packaging vegetables and fruits retard respiration and transpiration, thereby increasing their shelf life (Salunkhe and Wu 1974). The use of plastic containers usually results in less spoilage of vegetables. Cellulose acetate is most promising as a wrapping material. The modified atmosphere developed (increase in CO_2 or N_2 and decrease in O_2) in the individual packages improves the quality of the produce.

Table 3-31. Effects of Controlled-Atmosphere and Cold Storages on the Nutritional Composition of Leek.

Storage Length (mo)	Dry Matter (%)	Vitamin C (mg/g, dry wt.)	Reducing Sugars (% of dry matter)	Total N (% of dry matter)	Chlorophyll (mg/g, dry wt.)	Carotene (mg/g, dry wt.)
Controlled-atmosphere (CA) storage: 0 °C , rh > 95%, O_2 = 1%, CO_2 = 10%						
0	10.1	3.68	46.5	2.82	0.860	0.150
3	8.9	2.65	37.1	3.15	0.773	0.126
4	8.1	2.50	34.4	3.07	0.625	0.100
5	8.5	2.42	32.1	3.28	0.595	0.067
6	8.3	2.04	21.5	3.18	0.510	0.046
Cold storage: –1 °C, rh = 75%, normal air						
0	10.5	3.68	46.5	2.82	0.860	0.150
3	12.0	2.24	40.9	3.01	0.467	0.044
4	12.5	1.98	36.2	3.21	0.285	0.024
5	12.9	1.12	22.0	3.28	0.165	0.012
6	13.6	1.01	14.0	3.29	0.090	0.009
Cold storage: 0 °C, rh > 95%, normal air						
0	10.1	3.68	46.5	2.82	0.860	0.150
3	9.1	2.65	41.0	3.46	0.638	0.038
4	9.3	2.59	33.1	3.30	0.190	0.004

Source: Kurki (1979).

Effects of Subatmospheric (Hypobaric) Storage

Hypobaric or subatmospheric storage increases the storage life of several perishable horticultural commodities (Burg and Burg 1966; Dilley 1977). The principal effects of hypobaric storage are retardation of ripening, lowering of respiration rate, and removal of volatiles. Salunkhe and Wu (1975) investigated the effects of hypobaric storage on biochemical composition of tomatoes, potatoes, and other vegetables. The effects of hypobaric storage on the contents of lycopene, β-carotene, starch, and sugar contents of tomatoes are depicted in Figs. 3-18, 3-19, 3-20, and 3-21, respectively. The synthesis of lycopene and β-carotene of tomato fruits was strongly inhibited by the subatmospheric pressures (Figs. 3-18 and 3-19); the lower the pressure, the longer the inhibition, especially for the lycopene content. Storage at 102 mm Hg completely inhibited lycopene formation for 100 days. After transfer to 646 mm Hg, lycopene formation was stimulated. The formation of β-carotene was less strongly inhibited by the subatmospheric storage than that of lycopene. In tomatoes, decreases in chlorophyll and starch and increases in lycopene, β-carotene, and sugars are as-

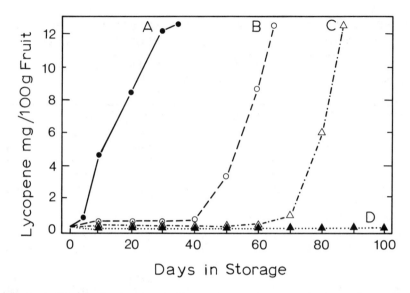

Fig. 3-18. Effects of subatmospheric pressure storage on the formation of lycopene in tomatoes at 12.8 °C and 90–95% rh. (A) 646 mm Hg (control), (B) 471 mm Hg, (C) 278 mm Hg, and (D) 102 mm Hg. *Source:* Wu, Jadhav, and Salunkhe (1972).

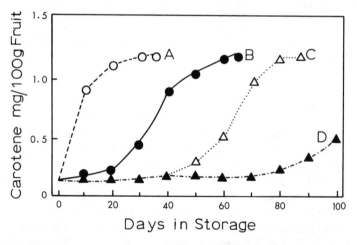

Fig. 3-19. Effects of subatmospheric pressure storage on the β-carotene content of tomatoes at 12.8 °C and 90–95% rh. (A) 646 mm Hg (control), (B) 471 mm Hg, (C) 278 mm Hg, and (D) 102 mm Hg. *Source:* Wu, Jadhav, and Salunkhe (1972).

sociated with the ripening process. The inhibition of these changes under subatmospheric pressure was attributed to the retarded ripening of tomato fruits (Salunkhe and Wu 1975).

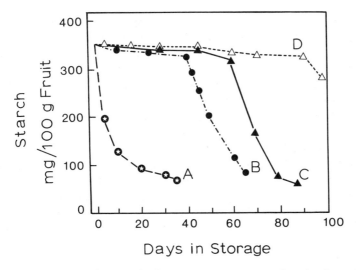

Fig. 3-20. Effects of subatmospheric pressure storage on the starch content of tomatoes at 12.8 °C and 90–95% rh. (A) 646 mm Hg (control), (B) 471 mm Hg, (C) 278 mm Hg, and (D) 102 mm Hg. *Source:* Wu, Jadhav, and Salunkhe (1972).

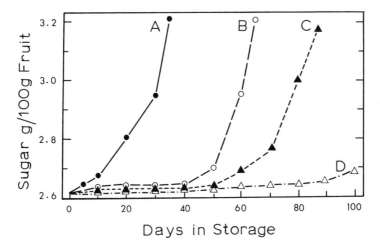

Fig. 3-21. Effects of subatmospheric pressure storage on the sugar content of tomatoes at 12.8 °C and 90–95% rh. (A) 646 mm Hg (control), (B) 471 mm Hg, (C) 278 mm Hg, and (D) 102 mm Hg. *Source:* Wu, Jadhav, and Salunkhe (1972).

Radurization

Preservation of vegetables with ionizing radiation has recently mainly been used to inhibit sprouting of potatoes and onions and to retard microbial growth and ripening in some fruits and vegetables. Salunkhe (1961) reviewed the effects of γ radiation on the storage behavior and nutritional quality of several fruits and vegetables. Ascorbic acid is the most radiosensitive vitamin. Cellulose, hemicellulose, and protopectin are degraded at higher irradiation doses ($>5 \times 10^5$ rad). These softening effects of radiation showed some promising possibilities. Slightly older sweet corns, asparagus, or peas could be irradiated to soften the pericarp of corn, the fiber of asparagus, and the cellulose of peas, to make them more edible. The storage life of mushrooms can be increased by inhibiting microbial growth.

Patil, Singh, and Salunkhe (1971) exposed "Russet Burbank" potatoes to a light intensity of 100 fc for 5 days at 21.1 °C after irradiation with γ rays in CO_2-enriched (15%) clear polyethylene packaging. The polyethylene packaging with CO_2 inhibited 33% of the chlorophyll synthesis, but neither irradiation nor the CO_2 environment, alone or in combination, affected solanine formation in potatoes.

Vegetable Processing

Processing of perishables has been a prime protector of valuable foods and a boon to vegetable growers. Processed commercial vegetable products have increased significantly in the developed countries in recent years. The vegetables are processed—by canning, freezing, dehydration, and ionizing radiation—into more stabilized products with extended storage life. Processing adds convenience by creating such products as canned soups, chutney, catsup, and instant dehydrated mashed potatoes.

Salunkhe and Desai (1984b) described many processing operations for vegetables: raw material handling, washing, trimming, blanching, salad preparations, chopping, mincing, grating and dressing, microwave cooking, preparation of frozen, canned, and fermented products, dehydration, in-package desiccants, and packaged products.

Water and Steam Blanching

Leafy vegetables are cleaned of sand and soil particles by tumbling them in a drum-type cleaner. Such mechanical cleaning operations can bruise or crush delicate tissues and increase respiration and loss of vitamin C through oxidation. The extent of nutrient losses that occur during such processing depends on the vegetable crop, cultivar, maturity, freshness, and season. When leafy vegetables are trimmed, the nutrient losses generally exceed the weight losses because nutrients tend to concentrate in the outer leaves. Moisture from leafy vegetables may be lost by evapotranspiration during holding and transportation.

Water blanching, generally employed for vegetables, can remove appreciable amounts of water-soluble nutrients from leafy vegetables, as can steam blanching, though to a lesser extent. Sulfur dioxide is generally added to the blanching water to improve the stability of the vegetables used for dehydration or freezing. Mallette et al. (1946) reported that sulfite added to the blanching water improved ascorbic acid retention in cabbage, but that the loss of thiamin could not be prevented.

Microwave Blanching

Many cruciferous vegetables are blanched with electronic energy by heating with 3,000-mCi radiation to inactivate oxidative enzymes. When broccoli was heated in plastic bags with 3,000-mCi radiation for 20–30 s, Proctor and Goldblith (1948) found that catalase and peroxidase were inactivated. There was complete retention of ascorbic acid as compared to 37–100% and 24–93% in steam and boiling water, respectively. Dielectric blanching in a closed container tended to conserve more ascorbic acid and soluble solids than did blanching in water or steam. Combination blanching by microwave energy and steam or water showed that, in Brussels sprout, peroxidase was inactivated and chlorophyll, ascorbic acid, and flavor were retained better than in conventional blanching (Dietrich, Huxsoll, and Gudagani 1970). Eheart (1967), however, found that conventional blanching was superior to microwave blanching, since it retained more chlorophyll and ascorbic acid in broccoli.

Frozen Products

After blanching, vegetables should be frozen quickly to avoid microbial changes that can impair the quality of vegetables in terms of flavor, appearance, and nutritional value (Salunkhe, Do, and Bolin 1974). Significant losses of ascorbic acid and other vitamins may occur during storage if the vegetables are frozen without blanching. The retention of vitamin C in frozen products depends upon the water vapor and permeability of the container to oxygen.

The loss of moisture from frozen vegetables during storage is associated with water-vapor transfer properties of the packaging material. The degree of carotene and ascorbic acid losses varies from vegetable to vegetable and with storage temperature. While there is no adverse effect of freezing on color and flavor of vegetable products, its major quality problem involves texture. Green beans may become rubbery and asparagus may be wilted. Melons and cantaloupes become rubbery after they are thawed. Certain types of sauce separate badly after thawing. "Quick-freezing," "rapid freezing" with liquid nitrogen at −195 °C, or "fluidized-bed freezers" offer a solution to these problems in green beans and asparagus. Rasmussen, Rogers, and Michener (1966) found a linear relationship between texture breakdown and loss of quality. The success of freezing as a method of preserving vegetables depends on product quality, variety or cultivar, size, shape, and degree of maturity, including aging or season.

Canned Products

Nonenzymatic browning reactions accompany vegetable produce during storage; their extent depends upon the concentrations of reducing sugars and amino acids. Head-space oxygen in glass jars or "tin" cans is important to stability of ascorbic acid in acid foods. With less acid foods such as vegetables, there is less effect on ascorbic acid content (Salunkhe, Do, and Bolin 1974). All vegetables sealed in cans or glass jars must be heat processed. A process known as "aseptic canning" employs new types of heat exchanger that permit extremely rapid heating and cooling of liquid foods. The sterilized food is cooled quickly and then canned under sterile conditions. The production sequence of canned vegetables is shown in Fig. 3-22 (Nickerson and Ronsivalli 1976).

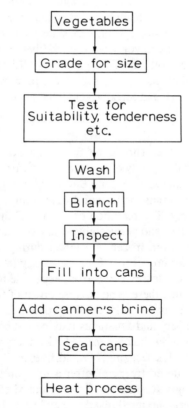

Fig. 3-22. Production sequence of canned vegetables. *Source:* Nickerson and Ronsivalli (1976).

Fermented Products

Among cruciferous vegetables, cabbage is prepared in large quantities by fermentation. Cauliflower is occasionally mixed with other vegetables for pickling. In the United States, sauerkraut is one of the most important fermented vegetable products, its quantity exceeded only by cucumber pickles. The United States produces over 200,000 MT of sauerkraut every year.

The quality and nutritive value of sauerkraut depend upon temperature, sodium chloride, and microflora during fermentation. The presence of *Leuconostoc mesenteroides* and *Lactobacillus plantarum* is particularly important for high quality of fresh and dehydrated sauerkraut (Nabors and Salunkhe 1969). Salt and vinegar (acetic acid) are the main preservatives in pickles, whereas salt is the main preservative in sauerkraut. In both pickles and sauerkraut, lactic acid produced during bacterial fermentation also acts as an additional preservative.

Sauerkraut contains as much ascorbic acid as the original cabbage; however, it is rapidly lost if the product is stored at high temperatures. According to Pederson (1956), the retention of ascorbic acid in sauerkraut depends upon the fermentation temperature and the length of time in the filling vat. Storage time and temperature also influence the retention of ascorbic acid in canned sauerkraut. Discoloration and off-flavors are usually associated with the degradation of ascorbic acid when sauerkraut is exposed to light (Sedky, Stelin, and Weckel 1953).

Dehydrated Products

Dehydration preserves foods by removing water and thus increasing the concentration of sugars and acids, thereby creating a chemical environment unfavorable for the growth of many microorganisms. Sun-dried fruits and vegetables are examples of naturally preserved foods. The weather does not always aid in the drying of the product; hence artificial drying or dehydration is generally adopted. In this process, air is heated and blown across the product. Salunkhe, Do, and Bolin (1974) and Salunkhe and Desai (1984b) described various dehydration techniques, including drum drying, spray drying, vacuum drying, forced-air dehydration, funnel drying (dry-bench-dry or DBD process), cabinet drying, continuous conveyor drying, pneumatic drying, throughflow drying (bin drying, belt-through drying, fluidized bed drying, drum drying), accelerated freeze drying (AFD), liquid nitrogen, and cryogenic freeze-drying. Other similar techniques are freeze concentration, foam-mat drying, microwave drying, dehydrofreezing, dehydrocanning, and osmotic dehydration. A flowchart for dehydration of fruit and vegetable products is shown in Fig. 3-23.

Dehydration can only slow down but not entirely stop enzyme activity; therefore, a dehydration operation must usually incorporate some method of en-

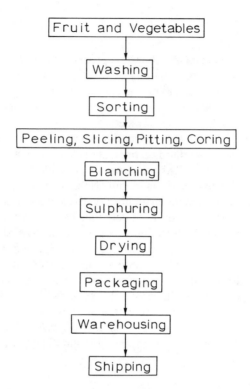

Fig. 3-23. Flowchart for dehydration of fruits and vegetables. *Source:* Salunke, Do, and Bolin (1974), Developments in technology and nutritive value of dehydrated fruits, vegetables and their products. In *Storage, Processing and Nutritional Quality of Fruits and Vegetables,* ed. D. K. Salunkhe, pp. 39–78. © CRC Press, Inc., Boca Raton, Fla.

zyme inactivation. For vegetables, heating to a boiling temperature for a few minutes (blanching) is generally employed. Sulfur dioxide treatment also effectively inactivates the enzymes, prevents discoloration, and acts as an antioxidant. Dehydrated potatoes, cabbages, carrots, and sweet potatoes may be treated with SO_2 to preserve their natural light color; this protects vegetable products during drying by minimizing oxidative changes. Carrots are often coated with starch after blanching and before dehydration to protect their color from oxidative changes (Rasmussen, Rogers, and Michener 1966).

Dehydrated products remain stable only as long as they are protected from water, air, sunlight, and contaminants; proper packaging is therefore essential to preserve them for an extended period of time. Oxidation is the primary cause of loss of vitamins, especially ascorbic acid, during drying and dehydration. Ranganna and Setty (1968) found that dehydroascorbic acid and 2,3-diketogluconic acid formed from ascorbic acid during the dehydration of cabbage react nonenzymatically with free amino acids to cause red to brown discoloration in the dried product. Harris (1945) reported a considerable loss of carotene and ascorbic acid in broccoli and Brussels sprout when dehydrated and preserved with sodium chloride.

In-Package Desiccants and Packaged Products

In-package desiccants are used to lower the moisture content of the storage environment to ≤1% to permit the storage of dehydrated vegetables for 6 mo or more at 21.1–37.8 °C without significant losses of nutrients (Salunkhe, Do, and Bolin 1974). Compression may reduce oxidative degradation of the dehydrated vegetables by the removal of air; it thus increases retention of vitamins, especially ascorbic acid and β-carotene.

Much of the losses in quality and nutritive value of the refrigerated, frozen, canned, and dehydrated products can be minimized by selecting proper packaging materials and techniques. Appropriate packaging effectively controls loss of nutrients from the adverse effects of light, oxygen, moisture, temperature, and microorganisms. Salunkhe, Do, and Bolin (1974) cautioned about probable interactions between food and packaging material, which may result in severe losses of nutrients. Light may degrade some light-sensitive vitamins, such as riboflavin, carotene, thiamin, and amino acids, in vegetable products in transparent containers. High storage temperatures accelerate microbial growth and degradation of several nutrients (e.g., ascorbic acid, thiamin, and amino ar˙ds) in packaged foods.

CONCLUSION

Pre- and postharvest biotechnologies and optimum conditions for growth, development, maturation, harvesting, handling, storage, and processing of fruits and vegetables differ greatly between crop species and even within cultivars of a given species. Recent developments in preservation and storage of fruit and vegetable products have made significant strides in extending their shelf life, enabling the producer to get a due share of profit and the consumer to obtain fresh fruits and vegetables throughout the year. However, most of the technological advances made in the more developed countries have not yet reached the developing countries. Significant losses of perishable horticultural commodities still occur in the tropical and subtropical regions, during both the preharvest phases and the postharvest handling and marketing stages. These losses may be as high as 30–40% in some instances (NRC 1978). Apart from physical losses, heavy losses also occur in the quality and nutritive values of the harvested produce, causing prices of fruits and vegetables to fluctuate considerably during the year. Improving the supply of these nutritious food products involves applying existing biotechnologies, seeking to improve them, and investigating and developing new biotechnologies, so as to minimize pre- and postharvest losses.

Existing and new preservation and processing techniques should be evaluated in terms not only of efficacy but also of producer cost–benefit ratio and producer acceptance. Depending on results, improvements can be adapted to the local situation. This process can be repeated until the best solution has been found.

Food preservation, food waste reduction and utilization, new food systems, and environmental protection—the conservation of such basic food resources as soil, water, air, and energy—may well be the greatest challenges facing humankind.

REFERENCES

Akamine, E. K. 1977. Tropical and subtropical crops in Hawaii. Commonwealth Scientific and Industrial Research Organization. *Food Res.* 37:13–18.

Akamine, E. K., and Goo, T. 1971. Relationship between surface color development and total soluble solids in papaya. *HortScience* 6(6):567–8.

Alper, Y., and Sarig, Y. 1969. Citrus harvesting mechanization in Israel. *Proc. 1st Int. Citrus Symp.* 1:623–38.

Anderson, R. E., Parsons, C. S., and Smith, W. L. 1967. For peaches, nectarines, oxygen–carbon dioxide storage. *Agric. Res. (Wash D.C.)* 15(11):7.

Arnold, C. E., and Mitchell, A. E. 1970. Histology of blemishes of cherry fruits (*Prunus cerasus* L. cv. Montmorency), resulting from mechanical harvesting. *J. Am. Hortic. Sci.* 95:723–5.

Arriola, M. C. de, Calzada, J. F. de, Menchu, J. F., Rolz, C., and Garcia, R. 1980. Papaya. In *Tropical and Subtropical Fruits,* ed. S. Nagy and P. E. Shaw, pp. 316–40. Westport: AVI Publ. Co.

Arriola, M. C. de, Madrid, M. D. de, and Rolz, C. 1975. Some physical and chemical changes in papaya during its storage. *Proc. Trop. Reg. Am. Soc. Hortic. Sci.* 19:97–109.

Arriola, M. C. de, Menchu, J. F., and Rolz, C. 1976. *Characterization, Handling and Storage of Some Tropical Fruits.* Central American Research Institute for Industry (ICAITI), Guatemala (Spanish).

Asenjo, C. F. 1980. Acerola. In *Tropical and Subtropical Fruits,* ed. S. Nagy and P. E. Shaw, pp. 341–74. Westport: AVI Publ. Co.

Asenjo, C. F., and Moscoso, C. G. 1950. Ascorbic acid content and other characteristics of the West Indian cherry. *Food Res.* 15:103–6.

Askar, A., El-Tamini, A., and Raouf, M. 1972. Constituents of mango fruits and their behavior during growth and ripening. *Mitt. Rebe Wein, Obstbau Fruchteverwert* 22:120–5.

Audus, L. J. 1953. *Plant Growth Substances.* London: Leonard Hill.

Avery, G. S., Johnson, E. B., Adams, R. M., and Thomson, B. F. 1947. *Hormones and Horticulture.* New York: McGraw–Hill.

Bangerth, F. 1978. The effect of a substituted amino acid on ethylene biosynthesis, respiration, ripening and preharvest drop of apple fruits. *J. Am. Soc. Hortic. Sci.* 103:401–4.

Banks, N. H., and Harper, G. R. 1981. Gaseous exchange, fruit surfaces and costing. In *Proc. 150th Anniv. Br. Assoc. Adv. Sci.,* Annual Meeting, Aug. 31–Sept. 4, sec. D, no. 81.

Barker, A. V., Maynard, D. N., and Lachman, W. H. 1967. Induction of tomato stem and leaf lesions and potassium deficiency by excessive ammonium nutrition. *Soil Sci.* 103:319–27.

Beeson, K. C. 1949. The soil factor in human nutrition problems. *Nutr. Rev.* 7:353–5.

Ben-Arie, R., and Guelfat-Reich, S. 1979. Advancement of nectarine fruit ripening with daminozide and fenoprop. *J. Am. Soc. Hortic. Sci.* 104:14–17.

Biale, J. B. 1976. Recent advances in postharvest physiology of tropical and subtropical fruits. In *Int. Symp. on Tropical and Subtropical Fruits,* pp. 179–87. Lima, Wageningen (The Netherlands): Int. Soc. Hortic. Sci.

Black, C. A. 1968. *Soil Plant Relationships,* 2nd ed. New York: John Wiley.

Blackmore, R., Neuman, F., Brown, H. D., and Burrell, R. C. 1942. Relation of fertility levels and temperature of the color and quality of garden beets. *Proc. Am. Soc. Hortic. Sci.* 40:545–8.

Bleasdale, J. K. A. 1973. *Plant Physiology in Relation to Horticulture.* London: Macmillan.

Bourne, M. C. 1982. Effect of temperature on firmness of raw fruits and vegetables. *J. Food Sci.* 47:440–4.

Boysen Jenson, P. 1936. *Growth Hormones in Plants.* New York: McGraw-Hill.

Bramlage, W. J., Greene, D. W., Autio, W. R., and McLaughlin, J. M. 1980. Effects of aminoethoxyvinylglycine on internal ethylene concentrations and storage of apples. *J. Am. Soc. Hortic. Sci.* 105:847–51.

Bratley, C. O. 1939. Loss of ascorbic acid (vitamin C) from tangerine during storage on the market. *Proc. Am. Soc. Hortic. Sci.* 37:526–8.

Burg, S. P. 1975. Hypobaric storage and transportation of fresh fruits and vegetables. In *Postharvest Biology and Handling of Fruits and Vegetables,* ed. N. F. Hard and D. K. Salunkhe, pp. 172–88. Westport: AVI Publ. Co.

Burg, S. P., and Burg, E. A. 1966. Fruit storage at subatmospheric pressure. *Science* 153:314–15.

Buringh, P. 1980. *Introduction to the Study of Soils in Tropical and Subtropical Regions,* 3rd ed. Wageningen (The Netherlands): Center for Agricultural Publishing and Documentation.

Cantliffe, D. J. 1972. Nitrate accumulation in spinach grown at different temperatures. *J. Am. Soc. Hortic. Sci.* 97:674–6.

Castle, W. S., and Phillips, R. L. 1980. Performance of "Marsh" grapefruit and "Valencia" orange trees on eighteen rootstocks in a closely spaced planting. *J. Am. Soc. Hortic. Sci.* 105:496–9.

Chang, L. A., and Kays, S. J. 1981. Effect of low oxygen storage on sweet potato roots. *J. Am. Soc. Hortic. Sci.* 106:481–3.

Childers, N. F. 1975. *Modern Fruit Science.* New Brunswick: Rutgers University, Horticultural Publications.

Cobley, L. S., and Steele, W. M. 1976. *An Introduction to the Botany of Tropical Crops.* London: Longman.

Coggins, C. W., and Hield, H. Z. 1968. Plant growth regulators. In *The Citrus Industry,* vol. 2, ed. W. Reuther, L. D. Batchelor, and H. J. Webber, pp. 372–89. Riverside: Univ. of California Press.

Cohen, I. 1975. From biological to internal control of citrus pests in Israel. In *Citrus,* vol. 4, pp. 38–41. Basel: CIBA–GEIGY Technical Monograph.

Collins, M. D., Lombard, P. B., and Wolfe, J. W. 1978. The effects of evaporative cooling for bloom delay in "Bartlett" and "Bosc" pear fruit maturity and quality. *J. Am. Soc. Hortic. Sci.* 103:187–9.

Convey, H. M. 1960. Effects of temperature and modified atmosphere on the storage life, ripening behavior and dessert quality of "Eldorado" plums. *Proc. Am. Soc. Hortic. Sci.* 75: 207–15.

Cox, E. F., McKee, J. M. T., Dearman, A. S., and Kratky, B. A. 1979. "Transplant Establishment," A Report of National Vegetable Research Station for 1978, pp. 97–9.

Crosby, D. G. 1966. Natural choline storage inhibitors in food. In *Toxicants Occurring Naturally in Foods,* pp. 112–29. Washington, D.C.: National Academy of Sciences and National Research Council.

Dalldorf, R. 1979. Factors influencing the sugar content of "Smooth Cayenne" pineapples. *Inf. Bull. Citr. Subtrop. Fruit Res. Inst.* 83:5–6.

Dave, B., Petrie, J., and Kaplan, H. 1980. Large scale commercial field testing of fungicides, "Deccozil-EC" to control postharvest diseases of citrus (Abstr. no. 388). *HortScience* 15: 424.

Dekazos, E. D. 1980. Effect of aminoethoxyvinylglycine, carboxymethylcellulose and growth regulators on longevity of fresh rabbiteye blueberries. *Proc. Fla. State Hortic. Soc.* 93: 145–9.

Dennis, C. 1981. The effect of storage conditions on the quality of vegetables and salad crops. In *Quality in Stored and Processed Vegetables and Fruits,* ed. P. W. Goodenough and R. K. Atkin, pp. 329–89. London: Academic Press.

Desai, B. B., and Deshpande, P. B. 1978. Effects of stage of maturity on some physical and biochemical constituents and enzyme activities of banana. *Mysore J. Agric. Sci.* 12:193–7.

Dietrich, W. C., Huxsoll, C. C., and Gudagani, D. G. 1970. Comparison of microwave, conventional and combination blanching of Brussels sprouts for frozen storage. *Food Technol.* 24:613–16.

Dilley, D. R. 1977. Hypobaric storage of perishable commodities, fruits, vegetables, flowers and seedlings. *Acta Hortic.* 62:61–70.

Do, J. Y., and Salunkhe, D. K. 1975. Controlled atmosphere storage. I. Biochemical considerations. In *Postharvest Physiology, Handling and Utilization of Tropical and Subtropical Fruits and Vegetables,* ed. E. B. Pantastico, pp. 175–86. Westport: AVI Publ. Co.

Drake, S. R., Proebsting, E. L., Carter, G. H., and Nelson, J. W. 1978. Effect of growth regulators on ascorbic acid content, drained weight and color of fresh and processed "Rainer" cherries. *J. Am. Soc. Hortic. Sci.* 105:162–4.

Drake, S. R., Proebsting, E. L., Thompson, J. B., and Nelson, J. W. 1980. Effects of daminozide, maturity and cultivar on the color grade and character of sweet cherries. *J. Am. Soc. Hortic. Sci.* 105:668–70.

Duckworth, R. B. 1966. *Fruit and Vegetables.* Oxford: Pergamon Press.

Eckert, J. W. 1977. Control of postharvest diseases. In *Antifungal Compounds,* ed. M. R. Siegel and H. D. Sisler, pp. 269–352. New York: Marcel Dekker.

Eckert, J. W. 1978. Pathological diseases of fresh fruits and vegetables. In *Postharvest Biology and Biotechnology,* ed. H. O. Hultin and M. Milner, pp. 161–209. Westport: Food and Nutrition Press.

Eckert, J. W., Rubio, P. P., Mattoo, A. K., and Thompson, A. K. 1975. Postharvest Pathology. II. Diseases of tropical crops and their control. In *Postharvest Physiology, Handling and Utilization of Tropical and Subtropical Fruits and Vegetables,* ed. E. B. Pantastico, pp. 415–466. Westport: AVI Publ. Co.

Eheart, M. S. 1967. Effect of microwave vs. water blanching on nutrients in broccoli. *J. Am. Diet. Assoc.* 50: 207–9.

El-Mansy, H. I., Salunkhe, D. K., Hurst, R. L., and Walker, D. R. 1967. Effects of pre- and postharvest applications of 6-furfuralaminopurine and N⁶-benzyladenine on physicochemical changes in lettuce (*Lactuca sativa* L.). *Int. J. Hortic. Res.* 7:81–3.

Elliott, A. P., and Edmunds, J. E. 1977. Effect of 1,2-dibromo-3-chloropropane on soil nutrients and nutrient uptake by tomatoes. *Soil Sci.* 124:343–6.

Embleton, T. W., Jones, W. W., Labanauskas, C. K., and Reuther, W. 1973. Leaf analysis as a diagnostic tool and guide to fertilization. In *The Citrus Industry*, vol. 3, ed. W. Reuther. Riverside: Univ. of California Press.

Embleton, T. W., Reitz, H. J., and Jones, W. W. 1973. Citrus fertilization. In *The Citrus Industry*, vol. 3, ed. W. Reuther. Riverside: Univ. of California Press.

Eskin, N. A. M., Henderson, H. N., and Townsend, R. J. 1971. *Biochemistry of Foods*. New York: Academic Press.

Evans, L. T. 1963. *Environmental Control of Plant Growth*. New York: Academic Press.

Fajac, I. 1974. Le marché des fruits tropicaux et subtropicaux en France en 1973. *Fruits* 29: 155–62.

FAO. 1972. *Food Composition Table for Use in East Asia*. Washington, D.C.: FAO and U.S. Dept. of Health, Education and Welfare.

FAO. 1985. *Production Yearbook*, vol. 39, Rome: Food and Agriculture Organization.

FAO. 1988. *Q. Bull. Stat.* 1(4). Rome: Food and Agriculture Organization.

FAO/WHO. 1977. *Wholesomeness of Irradiated Food*. A report of the Joint FAO/IAEA/WHO Expert Committee, Food and Nutrition Ser. no. 6, WHO Tech. Rep. Ser. no. 604, Rome, Italy.

Fassett, D. W. 1973. Oxalates. In *Toxicants Occurring Naturally in Foods*, 2nd ed, pp. 346–62. Washington, D.C.: National Academy of Sciences and National Research Council.

Feingold, B. I. 1975. *Why Your Child Is Hyperactive*. New York: Random House.

Fidler, J. C., and Coursey, D. G. 1969. Low temperature injury in tropical fruit. In *Proc. Conf. Tropical and Subtropical Fruits*. 15–19 Sept. 1969, London: Tropical Products Institute.

Finch, A. H., Jones, W. W., and Van Horn, C. W. 1945. The influence of nitrogen nutrition upon the ascorbic acid content of several vegetable crops. *Proc. Am. Soc. Hortic. Sci.* 46: 314–18.

Fordham, R., and Biggs, A. G. 1985. *Principles of Vegetable Crop Production*. London: Collins.

Franke, W. 1959. Ueber die Biosynthese des Vitamins C. 2. Mitteilung. *Planta (Berl.)* 45: 166–97.

Geraldson, C. M., Klacan, G. R., and Lorenz, O. A. 1973. Plant analysis as an aid in fertilizing vegetable crops. In *Soil Testing and Plant Analysis*, ed. L. M. Walshi and J. D. Beaton. Madison: Soil Science Society of America.

Ghosh, S. 1960. The content of folic acid and its conjugates in some common Indian fruits. *Sci. Cult.* 26:287–8.

Goddard, M. S., and Matthews, R. H. 1979. Contribution of fruits and vegetables to human nutrition. *HortScience* 14:245–7.

Gopala Rao, P. I., Mallikarjuna, K., and Gururaja Rao, G. 1980. Nutritional evaluation of some green leafy vegetables. *Indian J. Nutr. Diet.* 17:9–12.

Gray, D. 1978. Comparison of fluid drilling and conventional establishment techniques on seedling emergence and crop uniformity in lettuce. *J. Hortic. Sci.* 53:23–30.

Grierson, W. 1973. Quality of produce as affected by prestorage treatments and packaging. *Int. Inst. Refrig. Comm.* C-2, pp. 51–65.

Grierson, W. 1976. Preservation of citrus fruits. *Refrig. Serv. Eng. Soc. Sect.* 7:1–11.

Grierson, W., and Wardowski, W. F. 1978. Relative humidity effects on postharvest life of fruits and vegetables. *HortScience* 13:570–4.

Habben, J. 1972. *Einfluss von Dungung und Standort auf die Buildung Wertgebender Inhaltsstoffe in Mohren (Daucus carota L.).* Dissertation der Fakultat fur Landwirtschaft und Gartenbau der Technischen Universitat, Munchen (cited by Mengel 1979).

Hall, A. P., More, J. F., and Morgan, A. F. 1955. B-vitamin content of California grown avocados. *J. Agriċ. Food Chem.* 3:250–2.

Hall, A. P., Morgan, A. F., and Wheeler, P. 1953. The amount of six B-vitamins in fruits and dried figs. *Food Res.* 18:206–16.

Hall, C. W., Hardenburg, R. E., and Pantastico, E. B. 1975. Principles of packaging. II. Consumer packaging with plastics. In *Postharvest Physiology, Handling and Utilization of Tropical and Subtropical Fruits and Vegetables,* ed. E. B. Pantastico, pp. 303–13. Westport: AVI Publ. Co.

Hall, N. T., Smoot, J. M., Knight, R. J., and Nagy, S. 1980. Protein and amino acid compositions of ten tropical fruits by gas–liquid chromatography. *J. Agric. Food Chem.* 28: 1217–21.

Hansen, R. G., Wyse, B. W., and Sorenson, A. W. 1979. *Nutritional Quality Index of Foods.* Westport: AVI Publ. Co.

Hardenburg, R. E. 1975. Principles of packaging. I. General considerations. In *Postharvest Physiology, Handling and Utilization of Tropical and Subtropical Fruits and Vegetables,* ed. E. B. Pantastico, pp. 283–302. Westport: AVI Publ. Co.

Hardh, K., Murmann, T., and Seppala, J. 1979. Effect of chemical constituents of tomato on its keeping quality. *Acta Hortic.* 93:387–93.

Harding, P. L. 1954. Effects of simulated transit and marketing periods on quality of Florida oranges. *Food Technol.* 8:311–12.

Harding, P. L., and Fisher, D. F. 1945. Seasonal changes in Florida grapefruit. *USDA Tech. Bull. no. 886.* Washington, D.C.: USDA.

Harding, P. L., and Sunday, M. P. 1949. Seasonal changes in Florida tangerines. *USDA Tech. Bull. no. 988.* Washington, D.C.: USDA.

Harding, P. L., Winston, J. R., and Fisher, D. F. 1940. Seasonal changes in Florida oranges. *USDA Tech. Bull. no. 753.* Washington, D.C.: USDA.

Harris, S. C. 1945. Carotene and ascorbic acid in fresh and salted vegetables. *J. Am. Diet. Assoc.* 21(4):360–4.

Harris, R. S. 1975. Effects of agricultural practices on the composition of foods. In *Nutritional Evaluation of Food Processing,* 2nd ed., ed. R. S. Harris and E. Karmas, pp. 33–57. Westport: AVI Publ. Co.

Hartoungh, J. C. C. 1978. Bewaring van vruchten en groenten in de tropen. Lecture notes, Wageningen (cited by Samson 1986).

Hearn, C. J., and Hutchinson, D. J. 1977. The performance of "Robinsoni" and "Page" citrus hybrids on 10 rootstocks. *Proc. Fla. State Hortic. Soc.* 90:47–9.

Heinicke, D. R. 1966. Characteristics of "McIntosh" and "Red Delicious" apples as influenced by exposure to sunlight during the growing season. *Proc. Am. Soc. Hortic. Sci.* 89:10–13.

Heinz, M. 1959. *Handbook of Nutrition.* New York: McGraw-Hill.

Hill, D. S. 1975. *Agricultural Insect Pests of the Tropics and Their Control,* Cambridge: Cambridge University Press.

Hill, D. S., and Waller, J. M. 1982. *Pests and Diseases of Tropical Crops: Principles and Methods of Control,* vol. 7. London: Longman.

Hollingsworth, D. F. 1970. Effects of some new production and processing methods on nutritive values. *J. Am. Diet. Assoc.* 57:247–50.

Howard, F. D., McGillivray, J. H., and Yamaguchi, M. 1962. Nutrient composition of fresh California grown vegetables. *Calif. Agric. Exp. Stn. Bull. no. 778.*

Hsu, J. W. 1974. Seasonal variations of thiamin in citrus juices. Florida Dept. of Citrus (unpublished, cited by Nagy and Wardowski 1988).

Hulme, A. C. 1971. *The Biochemistry of Fruits and Their Products,* vol. 2. New York: Academic Press.

Isenberg, F. M. R. 1979. Controlled atmospheric storage of vegetables. *Hortic. Rev.* 1:337–94.

Issa, J., and Mielke, E. A. 1980. Influence of certain citrus interstocks on β-carotene and lycopene levels in 10-year-old "Redblush" grapefruit. *J. Am. Soc. Hortic. Sci.* 105:807–9.

Iwahori, S. 1978. Use of growth regulators in the control of cropping of mandarin varieties. *Proc. Int. Soc. Hort. Sci.,* Sydney, Australia, pp. 263–70 (*Hortic. Abstr.* 49:70).

Jackson, J. E., Sharples, R. O., and Palmer, J. W. 1971. The influence of shade and within-tree position on apple fruit size, color and storage quality. *J. Hortic. Sci.* 46:277–87.

John, C. J., Subbarayan, C., and Cama, H. R. 1963. Carotenoids in mango (*Mangifera indica*) fruit. *Indian J. Chem.* 1:36–40.

Johnson, M. 1969. Systems engineering for citrus production, harvest, packing and distribution. In *Proc. 1st Int. Citrus Symp.* 1:619–21.

Jones, W. W. 1961. Environmental and cultural factors influencing the chemical composition and physical characters. In *The Orange: Its Biochemistry and Physiology,* ed. W. B. Sinclair, pp. 126–68. Riverside: Univ. of California Press.

Jones, W. W., and Parker, E. R. 1947. Ascorbic acid–nitrogen relations in "Navel" orange juice as affected by fertilizer applications. *Proc. Am. Soc. Hortic. Sci.* 50:195–8.

Jones, W. W., and Parker, E. R. 1949. Effects of nitrogen, phosphorus and potassium fertilizers and of organic materials on the composition of Washington Navel orange juice. *Proc. Am. Soc. Hortic. Sci.* 53:91–102.

Jones, W. W., Embleton, T. W., Boswell, S. B., Goodall, G. E., and Barnhart, E. L. 1970. Nitrogen rate effects on lemon production, quality and leaf nitrogen. *Proc. Am. Soc. Hortic. Sci.* 95:46–9.

Jungalwala, F. B., and Cama, H. R. 1963. Carotenoids in mango (*Mangifera indica*) fruit. *Indian J. Chem.* 1:36–40.

Kansal, B. D., Singh, B., Bajaj, K. L., and Kaul, G. 1981. Effects of different levels of nitrogen and FYM on yield and quality of spinach (*Spinacia oleracea* L.). *Qual. Plant. Plant Foods Hum. Nutr.* 31:163–70.

Kattan, A. A., Stark, D. C., and Kramer, A. 1957. Effect of certain preharvest factors on yield and quality of raw and processed tomatoes. *Proc. Am. Soc. Hortic. Sci.* 69:327–42.

Kempton, R. J., and Maw, G. A. 1973. Soil fumigation with methyl bromide: The uptake and distribution of inorganic bromide in tomato plants. *Ann. Appl. Biol.* 74:91–8.

Klein, B. P., and Perry, A. K. 1982. Ascorbic acid and vitamin A activity in selected vegetables from different geographical areas of the United States. *J. Food Sci.* 47:941–5.

Koo, R. C. J. 1979. The influence of N, K and irrigation on tree size and fruit production of "Valencia" orange. *Proc. Fla. State Hortic. Soc.* 92:10–13.

Krochta, J. M., and Feinberg, B. 1975. Effects of harvesting and handling fruits and vegetables. In *Nutritional Evaluation of Food Processing,* 2nd ed., ed. R. S. Harris and E. Karmas, pp. 98–117. Westport: AVI Publ. Co.

Krochta, J. M., Tillin, S. J., and Whitehead, L. C. 1975. Ascorbic acid content of tomatoes damaged by mechanical harvesting. *Food Technol.* 29:28–30.

Kurihara, A. 1969. Fruit growth of "Satsuma" orange under controlled conditions. I. Effects of preharvest temperature on fruit growth, color development, and fruit quality in "Satsuma" orange. *Bull. Hortic. Res. Stn. (Minist. Agric. For.) Ser. A* 8:5–30.

Kurki, L. 1979. Leek quality changes in CA storage. *Acta Hortic.* 93:85–90.

Kvale, A. 1974. The effect of ethylene alone or in combination with daminozide on fruit maturation, yield and quality of "Raud Prins" apples. *Forsk. Fors. Landbruket* 25:339–46.

Lakshminarayana, S., Vijayendra Rao, A. R., Moorthy, N. V. N., Anadaswamy, B., Dalal, V. B., Narasimham, P., and Subramanyam, H. 1971. Studies on rail shipment of mango. *J. Food Sci. Technol.* 8:123–7.

Lantz, E. M., Gough, H. W., and Campbell, A. M. 1958. Nutrients in beans, effects of variety, location and years on the protein and amino acid content of dried beans. *J. Agric. Food Chem.* 6:58–60.

Leopold, A. C., and Kriedemann, P. E. 1975. *Plant Growth and Development.* London: McGraw–Hill.

Lindstrand, K. 1979. Food value of vegetables (Abstr.). *Acta Hortic.* 93:19.

Lipton, W. J., and Harvey, J. M. 1972. Compatibility of fruits and vegetables during transport of mixed loads. *Agric. Res. Stn. Bull. no. 51.* Washington, D.C.: USDA.

Lockwood, J. G. 1974. *World Climatology: An Environmental Approach.* London: Edward Arnold.

Lougheed, E. C., Murr, D. P., and Berard, L. 1978. Low pressure storage for horticultural crops. *HortScience* 13(1):21–7.

Lutz, J. M., and Hardenburg, R. E. 1968. The commercial storage of fruits, vegetables and florist and nursery stocks. *Agriculture Handbook no. 66,* Washington, D.C.: USGPO.

Lyon, D. H. 1981. Taints arising from use of crop chemicals. In *Quality in Stored and Processed Vegetables and Fruits,* ed. P. W. Goodennough and R. K. Atkin, pp. 267–72. London: Academic Press.

McColloch, R. J., Nielsen, W., and Beavens, E. A. 1950. Factors influencing the quality of tomato paste. II. Pectic changes during processing. *Food Technol.* 4:339–41.

McGlasson, W. B. 1971. The ethylene factor. In *The Biochemistry of Fruits and Their Products,* vol. 1, ed. A. C. Hulme, pp. 475–520. New York: Academic Press.

Madalgatti Rao, M. 1969. Problems and prospects of postharvest handling of grapes in India. *Punjab Hortic. J.* 9:1–11.

Mallette, M. F., Dawson, C. R., Nelson, W. L., and Gortner, W. A. 1946. Commercially dehydrated vegetables: Oxidative enzymes, vitamin contents, and other factors. *Ind. Eng. Chem.* 38:437–41.

Mapson, L. W. 1971. Vitamins in fruits. In *The Biochemistry of Fruits and Their Products,* vol. 1, ed. A. C. Hulme, pp. 369–86. New York: Academic Press.

Marriott, J., Perkins, C., and Been, B. C. 1979. Some factors affecting the storage of fresh bread fruit. *Sci. Hortic.* 10:177–80.

Marsanija, I. I. 1970. The effect of long term application of fertilizers on the vitamin C content in mandarin and lemon fruit. *Trudy suhum. opyt. Stan efirno-mas. Kul' tur* 9:49–56 (*Hortic. Abstr.* 41:9797).

Masui, M., Nukaya, A., Ogura, T., and Ishida, A. 1978. Bromine uptake of muskmelon and cucumber plants following soil fumigation with methyl bromicle. *J. Jpn. Soc. Hortic. Sci.* 47:343–50.

Maxie, E. C., Sommer, N. F., and Mitchell, F. G. 1971. Infeasibility of irradiating fresh fruits and vegetables. *HortScience* 6:202–4.

Maynard, L. A. 1950. Soils and health. Council on Food and Nutrition. *J. Am. Med. Assoc.* 143:807–9.

Maynard, L. A. 1956. Effect of fertilizers on the nutritional value of foods. *J. Amer. Med. Assoc.* 161:1478–80.

Maynard, D. N. 1979. Nutritional disorders of vegetables: A review. *J. Plant Nutr.* 1(1):1–23.

Maynard, D. N., and Barker, A. V. 1979. Regulation of nitrate accumulation in vegetables. *Acta Hortic.* 93:153–62.

Maynard, D.N., Barker, A.V., and Lachman, W.H. 1966. Ammonium-induced stem and leaf lesions of tomato plants. *Proc. Am. Soc. Hortic. Sci.* 88:516–20.

Maynard, D. N., Barker, A. V., and Lachman, W. H. 1968. Influence of potassium on the utilization of ammonium by tomato plants. *Proc. Am. Soc. Hortic. Sci.* 92:537–42.

Maynard, D. N., Barker, A. V., Minotti, P. D., and Peck, N. H. 1976. Nitrate accumulation in vegetables. *Adv. Agron.* 28:71–118.

Mazumdar, B. C., and Bhatt, D. N. V. 1976. Effect of preharvest application of GA and Etherel on sweet orange (*Citrus sinensis* Osb.) fruits. *Progr. Hortic.* 8:89–91.

Mengel, K. 1979. Influence of exogenous factors on the quality and chemical composition of vegetables. *Acta Hortic.* 93:133–51.

Montagut, G., and Martin-Prevel, P. 1965. Besoins en engrais des bananeraies antillaises. *Fruits* 20:265–73.

Morini, S., Vitagliano, C., and Xiloyannis, C. 1974. The effect of ethephon and 2,4,5-TP on fruit drop, size and ripening of peaches. *Riv. Ortoflorofruittie. Ital.* 58:235–43.

Moshonas, M. G., and Shaw, P. E. 1977. Effects of abscission agents on composition and flavor of cold-pressed orange peel oil. *J. Agric. Food Chem.* 25:1151–3.

Moshonas, M. G., and Shaw, P. E. 1978. Compounds new to essential orange oil from fruit treated with abscission chemicals. *J. Agric. Food Chem.* 26:1288–90.

Moshonas, M. G., Shaw, P. E., and Sims, D. A. 1976. Abscission agent effects on orange juice flavor. *J. Food Sci.* 41:809811.

Mudambi, S. R., and Rajagopal, M. V. 1977. Vitamin C content of some fruits grown in Nigeria. *J. Food Technol.* 12:189–91.

Murneek, A. E., and Wittwer, S. H. 1948. Some factors effecting ascorbic acid content of apples. *Proc. Am. Sco. Hortic. Sci.* 51:97–102.

Nabors, W. T., and Salunkhe, D. K. 1969. Pre-fermentation inoculations with *Leuconostoc mesenteroides* and *Lactobacillus plantarum* on physicochemical properties of fresh and dehydrated sauerkraut. *Food Technol.* 22:67–71.

Nagy, S. 1980. Vitamin C contents of citrus fruits and their products: A review. *J. Agric. Food Chem.* 28:8–18.

Nagy, S., and Shaw, P. E. 1980. *Tropical and Subtropical Fruits.* Westport: AVI Publ. Co.

Nagy, S., and Wardowski, F. 1988. Effects of agricultural practices, handling, processing and storage on fruits. In *Nutritional Evaluation of Food Processing,* 3rd ed., eds. R. S. Harris and E. Karmas, pp. 73–100. Westport: AVI Publ. Co.

NAS. 1968. *Food and Nutrition Board: Recommended Dietary Allowances.* 7th ed. Washington, D.C.: National Academy of Sciences.

Naville, R. 1975. Le marché français des fruits tropicaux et subtropicaux en 1974. *Fruits* 30: 359–66.

Nickerson, J. T. R., and Ronsivalli, L. J. 1976. *Elementary Food Science.* Westport: AVI Publ. Co.

Nilsson, T. 1979. Yield, storage ability, quality and chemical composition of carrot, cabbage and leek at conventional and organic fertilizing. *Acta Hortic.* 93:209–23.

Nitsch, J. P. 1971. Hormonal factors in growth and development. In *The Biochemistry of Fruits and Their Products,* vol. 1, ed. A. C. Hulme, pp. 428–74. New York: Academic Press.

Nordby, H. E., Nagy, S., and Smoot, J. M. 1979. Relationship of rootstock to leaf and juice lipids in citrus. *J. Am. Soc. Hortic. Sci.* 104:280–2.

NRC. 1978. *Report of the Steering Committee for Study on Postharvest Food Losses in De-*

veloping Countries. Washington, D.C.:National Research Council and National Academy of Sciences.

Nutritional composition of fresh California grown vegetables. 1962. *Calif. Exp. Stn. Bull.* no. 788, 17 pp., Davis, Calif.

O'Brien, M. 1975. Harvest and handling. II. Bulk handling methods. In *Postharvest Physiology, Handling and Utilization of Tropical and Subtropical Fruits and Vegetables,* ed. E. B. Pantastico, pp. 246–82. Westport: AVI Publ. Co.

Ochse, J. J., Soule, M. J., Dijkman, M. J., and Wehlburg, C. 1961. *Tropical and Subtropical Agriculture,* vol. 1. New York: Macmillan.

OECD. 1958. *Catalog of types and sizes of wooden packaging for fruits and vegetables used in Europe.* Report of the Organization for Economic Cooperation and Development, no. 372, Paris.

Ogawa, J. M., Manji, B. T., and El-Behadli, A. H. 1976. Chemical control of postharvest diseases. In *Proc. 3rd Int. Biodegradation Symp.,* R. I. Kingston, J. M. Sharpley, and A. M. Kaplan (ed), London: Applied Science.

Okuse, I., and Ryugo, K. 1981. Composition changes in the developing "Hayward" kiwi fruit in California. *J. Am. Soc. Hortic. Sci.* 106:73–6.

Ottosson, L. 1979. Changes in ascorbic acid of vegetables during the day and after harvest. *Acta Hortic.* 93:435–42.

Pantastico, E. B., and Bautista, O. K. 1976. Postharvest handling of tropical vegetable crops. *HortScience* 11:122–4.

Pantastico, E. B., Subramanyam, H., Bhatti, M. B., Ali, N., and Akamine, E. K. 1975. Harvesting indices. In *Postharvest Physiology, Handling and Utilization of Tropical and Subtropical Fruits and Vegetables,* ed. E. B. Pantastico, pp. 339–75. Westport: AVI Publ. Co.

Patil, B. C., Singh, B., and Salunkhe, D. K. 1971. Formation of chlorophyll and solanine in Irish potato (*Solanum tuberosum* L.) tubers and their control by gamma radiation and CO_2 enriched packaging. *Lebensm. Wiss. Technol.* 4:123–5.

Paul, A. A., and Southgate, D. A. T. 1978. Dietary fiber. In *The Composition of Foods,* 4th ed., ed. R. A. McCance and E. M. Widdowson, pp. 162–233. London: HMSO.

Pederson, C. S. 1956. The influence of temperature on sauerkraut fermentation. *Food Packer* 37:26–30.

Peynaud, E., and Ribereau-Gayon, P. 1971. The grape. In *The Biochemistry of Fruits and Their Products,* vol. 2, ed. A. C. Hulme, pp. 172–206. New York: Academic Press.

Pfluger, R., and Mengel, K. 1972. The photochemical activity of chloroplasts from various plants with different potassium nutrition. *Plant and Soil* 36:417–25.

Pieniazek, S. A. 1977. Eastern Europe—a potential market for tropical fruits. *Acta Hortic.* 53:293–6.

Platt, B. S. 1962. *Table of Representative Values of Foods Commonly Used in Tropical Countries.* Medical Research Council, Special Rep. Ser. no. 302. London: HMSO.

Platt, R. G. 1973. Planning and planting the orchard. In *The Citrus Industry,* vol. III, ed. W. Reuther, pp. 48–81. Riverside: Univ. of California Press.

Polansky, M. M., and Murphy, E. W. 1966. Vitamin B_6 components in fruits and nuts. *J. Am. Diet. Assoc.* 48:109–11.

Postlmayer, H. L., Luh, B. S., and Leonard, S. J. 1956. Characterization of pectic changes in "Freestone" and "Clingstone" peaches during ripening and processing. *Food Technol.* 10: 618–22.

Proctor, B. E., and Goldblith, S. A. 1948. Radar energy for rapid food cooking and blanching and its effect on vitamin content. *Food Technol.* 2:95–7.

Proctor, F. J., Goodliffe, J. P., and Coursey, D. G. 1981. Postharvest losses of vegetables and their control in the tropics. In *Vegetable Productivity,* ed. C. R. W. Spedding, pp. 139–72. London: Macmillan.

Proebsting, E. L., and Mills, H. H. 1976. Effect of daminozide on growth, maturity, quality and yield of sweet cherries. *J. Am. Soc. Hortic. Sci.* 101:175–9.

Purseglove, J. W. 1968. *Tropical Crops: Dicotyledons, Monocotyledons.* London: Longman.

Pushkarnath. 1976. *Potato in Subtropics and Orient.* New Delhi: Longman.

Raccah, B., Loebenstein, G., and Bar-Joseph, M. 1976. Transmission of tristeza by aphids prevalent on citrus and operation of the tristeza suppression programme in Israel. *Proc. 7th Int. Org. Citrus Virol.* 7:47–9.

Ranganna, S., and Setty, L. 1968. Nonenzymatic discoloration in dried cabbage: Ascorbic acid–amino acid interactions. *J. Agric. Food Chem.* 16:529–33.

Rasmussen, C. L., Rogers, R. O., and Michener, H. D. 1966. Processing—a prime protector. In *The Yearbook of Agriculture 1966: Protecting Our Food.* Washington, D.C.: USGPO.

Rathore, D. S. 1979. A possibility of inverse relationship between the ascorbic acid content of guava fruits and ripening temperatures. *Indian J. Hortic.* 36:128–30.

Rawnsley, J. 1969. *Crop Storage.* Tech. Rep. no. 2, Ministry of Agriculture (Accra, Ghana): Food Research and Development Unit.

Reuther, W., and Nauer, E. M. 1972. *The influence of climatic factors on the growth and fruiting of citrus and other subtropical fruits.* Univ. of California Agric. Exp. Stn. Proj. no. 2120.

Rhodes, M. J. C. 1980. The physiological basis for the conservation of food loss. *Prog. Food Nutr. Sci.* 4:11–18.

Rick, C. M. 1978. The tomato. *Sci. Am.* 239:66–76.

Rigney, C. J., Graham, D., and Lee, T. H. 1978. Changes in tomato fruit ripening caused by ethylene dibromide fumigation. *J. Am. Soc. Hortic. Sci.* 103:420–3.

Robertson, G. L., and Kermode, W. J. 1981. Salicylic acid in fresh and canned fruits and vegetables. *J. Sci. Food Agric.* 32:833–6.

Rodriguez, R., Raina, B. L., Pantastico, E. B., and Bhatt, M. B. 1975. Quality of raw materials for processing. In *Postharvest Physiology, Handling and Utilization of Tropical and Subtropical Fruits and Vegetables,* ed. E. B. Pantastico pp. 467–76. Westport: AVI Publ. Co.

Rosenfeld, H. J. 1979. Ascorbic acid in vegetables grown at different temperatures. *Acta Hortic.* 93:425–33.

Russell, E. W. 1973. *Soil Conditions and Plant Growth,* 10th ed. London: Longman.

Russo, L., Dougherty, R. H., Dostal, H. C., Wilcox, G. E., and Nelson, P. E. 1975. Quality of processed tomato products from ethephon-ripened fruit. *HortScience* 10:138–9.

Ryall, A. L., and Lipton, W. J. 1979. *Handling, Transportation and Storage of Fruits and Vegetables,* vol. 1, 2nd ed. Westport: AVI Publ. Co.

Rygg, G. L., and Getty, M. R. 1955. Seasonal changes in Arizona and California grapefruit. *USDA Tech. Bull. no. 1130.* Washington, D.C.: USDA.

Salter, P. J., and Fradgley, J. R. A. 1969. Effects on crop maturation in cauliflower: II. Effects of cultural factors on the maturity characteristics of a cauliflower crop. *J. Hortic. Sci.* 44:141–54.

Salunkhe, D. K. 1961. Gamma radiation effects on fruits and vegetables. *Econ. Bot.* 15:28–56.

Salunkhe, D. K., and Desai, B. B. 1984a. *Postharvest Biotechnology of Fruits,* vols. 1 and 2. Boca Raton: CRC Press.

Salunkhe, D. K., and Desai, B. B. 1984b. *Postharvest Biotechnology of Vegetables,* vols. 1 and 2. Boca Raton: CRC Press.

Salunkhe, D. K., and Desai, B. B. 1988. Effects of agricultural practices, handling, processing and storage on vegetables. In *Nutritional Evaluation of Food Processing*, 3rd ed., ed. E. Karmas and R. S. Harris, pp. 23–71. New York: AVI/Van Nostrand Reinhold.

Salunkhe, D. K., Dhaliwal, A. S., and Boe, A. A. 1962. N^6-benzyladenine as a senescence inhibitor for selected horticultural crops. *Nature* 195:724–5.

Salunkhe, D. K., Do, J. Y., and Bolin, H. R. 1974. Developments in technology and nutritive value of dehydrated fruits, vegetables and their products. In *Storage, Processing and Nutritional Quality of Fruits and Vegetables*, ed. D. K. Salunkhe, pp. 39–78. Boca Raton: CRC Press.

Salunkhe, D. K., Do, J. Y., Pantastico, E. B., and Chachin, K. 1975. Chemical modifications. In *Postharvest Physiology, Handling and Utilization of Tropical and Subtropical Fruits and Vegetables*, ed. E. B. Pantastico, pp. 148–85. Westport: AVI Publ. Co.

Salunkhe, D. K., Pao, S. K., and Dull, G. G. 1974. Assessment of nutritive value, quality and stability of cruciferous vegetables during storage and subsequent processing. In *Storage, Processing and Nutritional Quality of Fruits and Vegetables*, ed. D. K. Salunkhe, pp. 1–38. Boca Raton: CRC Press.

Salunkhe, D. K., Pollard, L. H., Wilcox, E. B., and Burr, H. K. 1959. Evaluation of yield and quality in relation to harvest time of lima beans grown for processing in Utah. *Utah State Agric. Exp. Stn. Bull. no. 407.*

Salunkhe, D. K., and Wu, M. T. 1973. Effect of subatmospheric pressure storage on ripening behavior and some chemical changes in certain deciduous fruits. *J. Am. Hortic. Sci.* 98: 113–17.

Salunkhe, D. K., and Wu, M. T. 1974. Development in technology of storage and handling of fresh fruits and vegetables. In *Storage, Processing and Nutritional Quality of Fruits and Vegetables*, ed. D. K. Salunkhe, pp. 121–60. Boca Raton: CRC Press.

Salunkhe, D. K., and Wu, M. T. 1975. Subatmospheric storage of fruits and vegetables. In *Postharvest Biology and Handling of Fruits and Vegetables*, ed. N. F. Haard and D. K. Salunkhe, pp. 153–71. Westport: AVI Publ. Co.

Salunkhe, D. K., Wu, M. T., and Jadhav, S. J. 1972. Effects of light and temperature on formation of solanine in potato slices. *J. Food Sci.* 37:969–70.

Salunkhe, D. K., Wu, M. T., and Singh, B. 1971a. Effects of Telone® and Nemagon® on essential nutritive components and the respiratory rates of carrot (*Daucus carota* L.) roots and sweet corn (*Zea mays* L.) seeds. *J. Am. Soc. Hortic. Sci.* 96:357–9.

Salunkhe, D. K., Wu, M. T., and Singh, B. 1971b. The nutritive composition of pea and sweet corn seeds as influenced by *s*-triazine compounds. *J. Am. Soc. Hortic. Sci.* 96:489–92.

Samson, J. A. 1968. Citrus cultivation in Surinam. *Neth. J. Agric. Sci.* 16:186–96.

Samson, J. A. 1986. *Tropical Fruits*, 2nd ed., Tropical Agriculture Series. London: Longman.

Sanchez, P. A. 1976. *Properties and Management of Soils in the Tropics.* New York: Wiley–Interscience.

Sass, B. 1975. Experiences with soil disinfection in strawberries. *Kert. Kut. Int. Kozl.* 5:73–86.

Schiffman-Nadel, M., Chalutz, E., Waks, J., and Dagan, M. 1975. Reduction of chilling injury in grapefruit by thiobendazole and benomyl during long term storage. *J. Am. Soc. Hortic. Sci.* 100:270–2.

Schoorl, D., and Holt, J. E. 1982. Fresh fruit and vegetables: Distribution, management of quality. *Scientia Hortic.* 17:1–8.

Schumacher, R., Tanner, H., Fankhauser, F., and Stadlers, W. 1974. The effect on the constituents of apple juice of harvesting method, length of storage and Ethrel treatment. *Schweiz Z. Obst. Weinbau* 110:676–81.

Scora, R. W., and Newman, J. E. 1967. A phenological study of the essential oils of the peel of "Valencia" oranges. *Agric. Meteorol.* 4:11–26.

Sedky, A., Stelin, J. A., and Weckel, K. G. 1953. Efficiency of added ascorbic acid: The control of discoloration of sauerkraut. *Food Technol.* 7:67–9.

Seeley, E. J., Micke, W. C., and Kammereck, R. 1980. "Delicious" apple fruit size and quality as influenced by radiant flux density in the immediate growing environment. *J. Am. Soc. Hortic. Sci.* 105:645–7.

Serdyukov, A. E., and Emelin, V. G. 1979. Conservation of tomato, sweet pepper, and aubergine quality under mechanical harvesting, storage and sale. *Acta Hortic.* 93:125–32.

Shanmugavelu, K. G., Rao, V. N. M., and Srinivasan, C. 1973. Studies on the effect of certain plant regulators and boron on papaya (*Carica papaya* L.). *South Indian Hortic.* 21:19–26.

Shanmugavelu, K. G., Srinivasan, C., and Thamburaj, S. 1973. Effect of Ethrel (Ethephon, 2-chloroethyl phosphoric acid) on pumpkin (*Cucurbita moschata* Poir). *South Indian Hortic.* 21:94–9.

Shaybany, B., and Sharifi, H. 1973. Effect of preharvest applications of ethephon on leaf abscission, fruit drop and constituents of fruit juice in pomegranates. *J. Hortic. Sci.* 48:293–6.

Sims, E. T., Gambrell, C. E., and Stembridge, G. E. 1974. The influence of (2-chloroethyl) phosphonic acid on peach quality and maturation. *J. Am. Soc. Hortic. Sci.* 99:152–5.

Sinclair, W. B. 1961. *The Orange: Its Biochemistry and Physiology.* Berkeley: Univ. of California Press.

Sinclair, W. B. 1972. *The Grapefruit.* Riverside: Univ. of California Press.

Singh, B., Yang, C. C., Salunkhe, D. K., and Rahman, A. R. 1972a. Controlled atmosphere storage of lettuce. II. Effects on quality and respiration rate of lettuce heads. *J. Food Sci.* 37:48–51.

Singh, B., Wang, D. J., Salunkhe, D. K., and Rahman, A. R. 1972b. Controlled atmosphere storage of lettuce. II. Effects on biochemical composition of the leaves. *J. Food Sci.* 37:52–5.

Singleton, V. L., and Kratzer, F. H. 1973. Plant phenolics. In *Toxicants Occurring Naturally in Foods,* 2nd ed., pp. 309–45. Washington, D.C.: National Academy of Sciences and National Research Council.

Sites, J. W. 1947. Internal fruit quality as related to production practices. *Proc. Fla. State Hortic. Soc.* 60:55–62.

Sites, J. W., and Reitz, H. J. 1949. The variation in individual "Valencia" oranges from different locations on the tree as a guide to sampling methods and spot-picking for quality. I. Soluble solids in the juice. *Proc. Am. Soc. Hortic. Sci.* 54:1–10.

Sites, J. W., and Reitz, H. J. 1950. The variation in individual "Valencia" oranges from different locations on the tree as a guide to sampling methods and spot-picking for quality. II. Titratable acid and soluble solids ratio of the juice. *Proc. Am. Soc. Hortic. Sci.* 55:73–80.

Sites, J. W., and Reitz, H. J. 1951. The variation in individual "Valencia" oranges from different locations on the tree as a guide to sampling methods and spot-picking for quality. III. Vitamin C and juice content of the fruit. *Proc. Am. Soc. Hortic. Sci.* 56:103–10.

Sizaret, A. 1983. Plantations fruitières sur buttes, ou le mille et une positions du collet. *Fruits* 38:397–415.

Smith, P. F. 1969. Effects of nitrogen rates and timing of application on "Marsh" grapefruit in Florida. In *Proc. 1st Int. Citrus Symp*, vol. 3, ed. H. D Chapman, pp. 1559–67. Riverside: Univ. of California Press.

Smith, P. F., and Rasmussen, G. K. 1961. Effect of nitrogen source, rate and pH on the production and quality of "Marsh" grapefruit. *Proc. Fla. State Hortic. Soc.* 74:32–8.

Smittle, D. A., and Hayes, M. J. 1979. Influence of short term storage conditions on quality of shelled southern pea. *J. Am. Soc. Hortic. Sci.* 104:783–6.

Smock, R. M. 1953. Some effects of climate during the growing season on keeping quality of apples. *Proc. Am. Soc. Hortic. Sci.* 62:272–8.

Stahl, A. L., and Camp, A. F. 1936. Cold storage studies of Florida citrus fruits. *Univ. Fla. Bull. no. 303*. Gainesville, Fla.

Stearns, C. R., and Sites, J. W. 1943. Fruit quality studies. *Fla. Agric. Exp. Stn. Annu. Rep.*, pp. 203–13. Gainesville, Fla.

Stewart, I. 1980. Color as related to quality in citrus. In *Citrus Nutrition and Quality*, ed. S. Nagy and J. A. Attaway. ACS Symp. Ser. no. 143. Washington, D.C.: Am. Chem. Soc.

Storey, W. B. 1969. Recent developments in tropical fruits crops. *Proc. Fla. State Hortic. Soc.* 82:333–9.

Ter-Manuel'Yants, E. E. 1980. Vitamin content in different Brassica species. *Tr. Prikl. Bot. Genet. Sel.* 66:99–102. (*Hortic. Abstr.* 57:783, 1982).

Terra, G. J. A. 1949. *De tuinbouw in Indonesie s' Gravenhage* (cited by Samson 1986).

Thomason, I. J., Castro, C. E., Baines, R. C., and Mankau, R. 1971. What happens to soil fumigants after nematode control. *Calif. Agric.* 25:10–12.

Thorne, S., and Segurajauregui Avarez, J. S. 1982. The effect of irregular storage temperatures on firmness and surface color in tomatoes. *J. Sci. Food Agric.* 33:671–6.

Thornton, N. C. 1943. CO_2 storage. XIV. Influence of CO_2, O_2 and ethylene on the vitamin C content of ripening bananas. *Contrib. Boyce Thompson Inst.* 13:201–20.

Tindall, H. D., and Proctor, F. J. 1980. Loss prevention of horticultural crops in the tropics. *Progr. Food Nutr. Sci.* 4:25–39.

Ting, S. V. 1977. Nutritional labelling of citrus products. In *Citrus Science and Technology*, vol. 2, ed. S. Nagy, P. E. Shaw, and M. K. Veldhuis, Westport: AVI Publ. Co.

Ting, S. V., Attaway, J. A., Deszyck, E. J., and Newhall, W. F. 1974. Nutrient assay of Florida frozen concentrated orange juice for nutrition labelling. *Proc. Fla. State Hortic. Soc.* 87:206–9.

Ulrich, R. 1975. Controlled atmosphere. II. Physiological and practical consideration. In *Postharvest Physiology, Handling and Utilization of Tropical and Subtropical Fruits and Vegetables*, ed. E. B. Pantastico, pp. 186–200. Westport: AVI Publ. Co.

UNIDO. 1972. *Wood as a Packaging Material in the Developing Countries*. ID/72, New York: United Nations Industrial Development Organization, United Nations.

USDA. 1963. *Agriculture Handbook no. 8*, Washington, D.C.: USDA.

Van Maercke, D., and Vereecke, M. 1976. Subtractive fertilization experiment on leek (*Allium porrum* L.) in relation to soil and leaf analysis, yield and quality. *Proc. 4th Int. Colloq. "Control of Plant Nutrition"* 2:217–27 (cited by Vereecke et al. 1979).

Varsel, C. 1980. Citrus juice processing as related to quality and nutrition. In *Citrus Nutrition and Quality*, pp. 225–71. Am. Chem. Soc. Symp. Ser. no. 143, Washington, D.C.: Am. Chem. Soc.

Vereecke, M., and Van Maercke, D. 1976. Influence of mineral nutrition on cauliflower in relation with leaf analysis and curd quality. *Proc. 4th Int. Colloq. "Control of Plant Nutrition"* 1:228–36 (cited by Vereecke et al. 1979).

Vereecke, M., Van Maercke, D., Bosman, G., and Cottenie, A. 1979. Subtractive fertilization experiment on carrots (*Daucus carota* L.) in relation to soil and leaf analysis, yield and quality. *Acta Hortic.* 93:197–203.

Vines, H. M., Grierson, W., and Edwards, G. J. 1968. Respiration, internal atmosphere, and ethylene evolution of citrus fruit. *Proc. Am. Soc. Hortic. Sci.* 92:227–34.

Vittum, M. T. 1963. Effect of fertilizers on the quality of vegetables. *Agron. J.* 55:425–9.

Wambeke, E. van, Achter, A. van, and Assche, C. van 1979. Influence of repeated soil disinfection with methyl bromide on bromide content in different tomato cultivars and some quality criteria of these tomato fruits. *Meded. Fac. Landbouwwet. Rijksuniv. Gent.* 44:895–900.

Wardlaw, C. W. 1961. *Banana Diseases.* London: Longman.

Wardowski, W. F., Albrigo, L. G., Grierson, W. P., Barmore, C. R., and Wheaton, T. A. 1975. Chilling injury and decay of grapefruit as affected by thiabendazole, benomyl and CO_2. *HortScience* 10:381–3.

Warren, J. M., Ballinger, W. E., and Mainland, C. M. 1973. Effects of ethephon upon fruit development and ripening of highbush blueberries in the greenhouse. *HortScience* 8:504–7.

Warren-Wilson, J. 1969. Maximum yield potential. In *Transition from Extensive to Intensive Agriculture with Fertilizers, Proc. 7th Colloq.,* pp. 34–56. Berne: Int. Potash Inst.

Watada, A. E. 1982. An HPLC method for determining ascorbic acid content of fresh fruits and vegetables. *HortScience* 17:334–5.

Werner, W. 1957. *Uber die quantitative Bestimmung and das vorkommen der Ascorbinaure (Vitamin C) inder Pflanze sowie die Abhangigkeit iher Bildung von der Ernahrung.* Diss. Landw. Fakultat der Justus Liebig Hochschule, Giessen (cited by Mengel 1979).

White, P. L. 1979. Challenge for the future: Nutritional quality of fruits and vegetables. *HortScience* 14:257–8.

Wild, B. L. 1975. Fungicides for postharvest wastage control in fruit marketing. *Food Technol. Aust.* 27:477–9.

Willigen, P. de 1968. "Kostprijsonderzoek Vruchtenproefbedrijf Boma." *Surinam Landb.* 16:99–109 (cited by Samson 1986).

Wills, R. B. H., Lee, T. H., Graham, D., McGlasson, W. B., and Hall, E. G. 1981. *Postharvest: An Introduction to the Physiology and Handling of Fruits and Vegetables.* London: Granada.

Wills, R. B. H., and Tirmazi, S. I. H. 1979. Effects of calcium and other minerals on ripening of tomatoes. *Aust. J. Plant Physiol.* 6:221–7.

Wilson, W. C., and Coppock, G. E. 1975. Citrus harvesting. In *Citrus,* vol. 4, pp. 67–71. Basel: CIBA–GEIGY Technical Monograph.

Winkler, A. J. 1962. *General Viticulture.* Berkeley: Univ. of California Press.

Winsor, G. W. 1979. Some factors affecting the quality and composition of tomatoes. *Acta Hortic.* 93:335–46.

Winsor, G. W., and Adams, P. 1976. Changes in the composition and quality of tomato fruit throughout the season. *Rep. Glasshouse Crops Res. Inst. 1975,* pp. 134–42 (cited by Winsor 1979).

Wolpert, J. A., Howell, G. S., and Cress, C. E. 1980. Sampling strategies for estimates of cluster weight, soluble solids and acidity of "Concord" grapes. *J. Am. Soc. Hortic. Sci.* 105:434–8.

Woodroof, J. G. 1975. Fruit harvesting, handling and storing. In *Commercial Fruit Processing,* ed. J. G. Woodroof and B. S. Luh, pp. 32–77. Westport: AVI Publ. Co.

Wu, M. T., Jadhav, S. J., and Salunkhe, D. K. 1972. Effects of subatmospheric pressure storage on ripening of tomato fruits. *J. Food Sci.* 37:952–6.

Wu, M. T., and Salunkhe, D. K. 1974. The use of certain chemicals to increase nutritional value and to extend quality in economic plants. In *Storage, Processing and Nutritional Quality of Fruits and Vegetables,* ed. D. K. Salunkhe, pp. 79–120. Boca Raton: CRC Press.

Wu, M. T., and Salunkhe, D. K. 1976. Changes in glycoalkaloid content following mechanical injuries to potato tubers. *J. Am. Soc. Hortic. Sci.* 101:329–31.

Yagi, M. I., Habish, H. A., and Agab, M. A. 1978. Effect of the method of harvest on the development of microorganisms and quality of mango fruit. *Sudan J. Food Sci. Technol.* 10:83–9.

Zadoks, K. C. 1975. Gewasbescherming (Lecture Notes), Agric. Univ. Wageningen, Netherlands (cited by Samson 1986).

4

Sugar Crops

B. B. Desai and D. K. Salunkhe

INTRODUCTION

Although chemists have recognized over a hundred sweet substances that have
been described as "sugars," only one of these is commonly used: the natural
sweetener sucrose, usually obtained commercially in crystalline form from
sugarcane (cane sugar) or sugar beet (beet sugar). Sucrose is a disaccharide belonging to the carbohydrate group of organic compounds. It is naturally synthesized by plants, and is composed of two monosaccharide units: glucose (dextrose) and fructose (levulose).

Sugar or sucrose is a commercially important substance owing to its versatile
use in food and a variety of industrial products (Salunkhe and Desai 1988). It
plays a unique role in varied aspects of human chemistry, biology, nutrition,
physiology, and clinical medicine. Sugar is thus of interest to a wide range of
specialists including the chemist, the biochemist, the physiologist, the nutrition-
ist, the clinician, the sociologist, and the food scientist. The research activities
of chemistry, biology, and medicine are fundamentally related to the chemical
properties of the sucrose molecule.

HISTORY OF SUGAR DEVELOPMENT

The earliest Western reference to sugar was written in 325 B.C. by an officer of
Alexander's invading army in India, where sugarcane may already have been
cultivated for several centuries. New data seem to place the origin of sugarcane
in the South Pacific about 8,000 years ago. Probably a native of New Guinea,
the plant moved northward to Southeast Asia and India. Sugarcane cultivation
and refining spread east to China about 100 B.C., but reached Mediterranean
Europe relatively late, probably as a result of Arab conquests after A.D. 636 (A
Facto Sheet 1975).

Sugar was probably introduced to the Western world in the thirteenth century, with Venetian merchants acting as intermediary traders. By the year 1300, Venice was the sugar capital of the world. The colonization of Madeira Island by the Portuguese early in the fifteenth century led to the successful introduction of sugarcane. Portuguese enterprise subsequently brought sugar to the west coast of Africa and then to Brazil. By 1583, there were over a hundred sugar factories in Brazil. The Spaniards introduced sugar cultivation in the Canary Islands, from which Columbus brought cane to the Caribbean on his second voyage, in 1493. By 1550, sugar had become one of the most valuable products on the Island of Hispaniola (now known as Haiti and the Dominican Republic) and a pirate's prize. England and France established their own refineries by 1600 to handle sugar from the West Indies (Salunkhe and Desai 1988).

SOURCES, PRODUCTION, AND CONSUMPTION

The total world sugar (sucrose) production is now well over 95 million metric tonnes (MT) per year. About 55% of this comes from cane and roughly 45% from beet. Sucrose from all other sources (sugar palm, sweet sorghum, and the maple tree) amounts to about 1% of the total. The contributions from various sources of sucrose to total annual production in 1987 are shown in Table 4-1.

World production of raw sugar has grown enormously, increasing seven- or eightfold since the year 1900. During this period, per capita sugar consumption increased about threefold despite a substantial increase in population. This increase has been greatest (about 200–300%) in the poorest countries (i.e., those in Latin America, the Near East, and Africa). The average consumption of sugar is about 15 kg/person/yr but varies widely from country to country. Affluent countries, such as the United Kingdom, Australia, Sweden, the United States, and Canada, consume on average roughly 50 kg sucrose/person/yr; the poorer countries, such as India, Pakistan, and China, consume ≤5 kg/person/yr. The major sugar-producing countries are the USSR, Cuba, Brazil, the United States, and India (Table 4-2).

Although India is the largest producer of sugarcane in the world, the third largest producer of sugar, and the fourth largest exporter of cane sugar in the free market, the cost of sugar production in India is higher than the world price. Hence, India cannot compete with other sugar-producing countries, and all exports have been heavily subsidized (Thuljaram Rao, Natarajan, and Bhagyalakshmi 1983). The Indian sugar industry—the second largest in the country—has made rapid strides during the last half-century, mainly due to the introduction of improved varieties developed at the Sugarcane Breeding Institute, Coimbtore. The current record production of cane sugar (about 9 million MT) is due to improvements in sugar technology at both the field and factory levels, variety being the most important low-cost technology. Other important technologies are

Table 4-1. Botanical Sources of Sucrose.

Source	Scientific Name	Family	Percentage of Production[a]
Sugarcane	*Saccharum officinarum*	Gramineae	55
Sugar beet	*Beta vulgaris*	Chenopodiaceae	44
Sugar palm	*Phoenix dactylifera*	Palmaceae	1
Sorghum	*Sorghum vulgare* var. *durra*	Gramineae	0.1
Maple	*Acer saccharum*	Aceraceae	0.05

[a]Production figures are from FAO (1988). Approximate total annual production in 1987 was 73 million metric tons.

Table 4-2. Major Sugar-producing Countries.[a]

Country	1979–81	1983	1984	1985
Centrifugal (raw) sugar				
USSR	7,017	8,760	8,685	8,350
Cuba	7,510	7,460	8,331	8,097
Brazil	7,991	9,576	9,332	8,300
USA	5,345	5,107	5,363	5,412
India	5,380	8,948	6,430	6,650
France	4,720	3,875	4,305	4,335
China	3,809	4,910	4,986	5,314
Australia	3,243	3,171	3,550	3,380
West Germany	3,261	2,725	3,151	3,427
Mexico	2,796	3,108	3,297	3,436
Philippines	2,360	2,540	2,400	1,780
South Africa	1,969	1,495	2,560	2,300
World	88,585	97,929	100,043	97,867
Noncentrifugal sugar				
India	8,107	8,782	9,800	9,660
Pakistan	1,766	1,295	1,570	1,400
Colombia	925	780	825	850
Thailand	733	900	900	950
Bangladesh	427	409	416	495
China	351	463	517	443
Brazil	200	200	200	200
World	13,419	13,707	15,109	14,889

Source: FAO (1986), courtesy Food and Agriculture Organization of the United Nations.
[a]In decreasing order of output (in thousands of metric tons).

the use of biofertilizers; prevention of leaching losses of nitrogen fertilizers and nitrate toxicity (coating of urea with *neem* cake); and improved water management practices (drip and sprinkler irrigation systems to save water) (Thuljaram Rao, Natarajan, and Bhagyalakshmi 1983).

Table 4-3. Effects of Average National Income on Intake of Calories, Protein, Fat, Total Carbohydrates, and Sugar.

Annual Income (£)		No. of Countries	Calories (kcal)	Fat (g)	Protein (g)	Carbohydr. (g)	Sugar	
Range	Avg.						(g)	(% of Carbohydr.)
≥50	38	6	2,060	34	52	394	35	8.9
51–100	82	6	2,500	61	68	437	59	13.5
101–200	148	7	2,700	73	78	456	86	18.9
201–350	292	7	2,970	118	86	419	102	24.3
>350	460	8	3,200	140	92	422	139	33.0

Source: Yudkin (1971).

Yudkin (1971) pointed out the relationship between sucrose consumption and a country's affluence. Poorer countries have a much slower increase in the sugar consumption rate over a much longer time as compared to wealthy countries. In the United Kingdom, for example, the average annual consumption in the early nineteenth century was 2–3 kg; by the middle of the nineteenth century it had reached 10–12 kg; and in 1971, it was 50 kg. The diets of people in affluent countries are characterized by a small rise in protein, a considerable rise in fat, and a fall in starch that is about the same as the rise in sugar. The total intake of carbohydrates in countries of very different degrees of affluence does not vary significantly (Table 4-3). Yudkin (1971) stated that the amount of sugar consumed was a function of wealth in relation to sugar prices. However, there appears to be a limit to the consumption of sugar in wealthy countries of about 50 kg/person/yr—a level that most of the less affluent countries are fast approaching. This high level of sugar intake in the wealthy countries is attributed to a greater consumption of sophisticated confectionery foods, bakery products, and soft drinks as well as to sugar itself used in the household. There appears to be a concomitant fall in the consumption of starch-containing foods, with the result that the total consumption of carbohydrates is little affected. The approximate distribution of different carbohydrates in the daily human diet globally is 175 g starch, 140 g sucrose, 20 g galactose, and 15 g other sugars—almost entirely fructose and glucose (Yudkin 1971).

UTILIZATION

Sugar as Food

Sucrose is one of the important constituents of the human diet. Much of the sucrose in the diets of the high-consumption countries is found in manufactured foods (i.e., confectionery, soft drinks, cakes, ice creams, and bakery products). In the United Kingdom, about half the sugar consumed is in the form of manufactured foods; the other half is bought as sugar and used in tea and coffee, on cereals and pudding, and in cooking and baking. According to Watson (1971), dietary sucrose is a mixed blessing. On the one hand, it is credited with making food more attractive and appetizing; on the other hand, it is claimed to leave in its trail (especially on excessive consumption) various pathological conditions, including dental caries, coronary thrombosis, diabetes, obesity, and certain diseases of the skin, the digestive tract, and the joints. Excessive consumption of sucrose has been most certainly implicated in such health disorders as ischemic heart disease and diabetes—although, as these are multifactorial ailments, its abandonment may not be justified without further evidence.

Sucrose is one of the purest raw food materials available in large quantities to the homemaker, caterer, and food manufacturer. It is also one of the most consistent in composition. To the homemaker, sugar is available in a variety of types or forms: granulated, cubed, confectioner's, and so on. The sugar refiner, therefore, supplies the food manufacturer with a variety of sucrose products tailored for specific uses (Table 4-4). Sugar for canned food, for example, is selected for its low count of bacteria that may cause spoilage. Mineral water sugar is a granulated sugar specially refined to have an extremely low ash content, a good color, and a low tendency to foam or to discolor when heated. It is also suitable for high-quality confectionery (i.e., clear mints, fruit preserves, and pharmaceuticals). Brook (1971) stated that about 65% of the sugar used by manufacturers is supplied in bulk in granulated form, but the basic grades of dry sugar are also supplied in liquid form. Mixtures of sucrose and glucose syrup or sucrose and invert sugar are also available and extensively used by food manufacturers.

The sweetness of 1 lb of sugar can be matched with that of 1 g of saccharin or 10 g of cyclamate. Sucrose thus provides bulk to the human diet in addition to sweetness. Other valuable characteristics of sucrose besides sweetness are

Table 4-4. Some Basic Grades of Industrial Sugars.

Sugar Grade	Characteristics	Some Uses
Mineral water	Pure white, low ash	Preserves, drinks, high-quality foods, medicines
Standard, granulated	High purity, consistent quality	Manufacturing
Canners	Low bacterial count	Canning
Manufacturing	White, off-white, yellow, brown, various crystal sizes	Baking, confectionery
Liquid sugars	Equivalent grades to above	As above

Source: Brook (1971).

Table 4-5. Some Characteristics of Sucrose in Foods.

Increases sweetness, osmotic pressure, viscosity, boiling point, moisture retention
Enhances flavor, appearance (improved by clarity, luster, and gloss)
Imparts plasticity
Assists emulsification and color development
Provides calories, bulk (or body) to the diet
Affects solubility of other ingredients
Penetrates other ingredients (e.g., fruits and vegetables)
Depresses freezing point (hence its use in ice cream)
Can be fermented, crystallized, and the crystal size controlled

Adapted from: Brook (1971).

summarized in Table 4-5. The relative importance of these characteristics varies by industry. It is the bulk provided by sucrose and its ability to exist in different amorphous or crystalline forms that, in addition to sweetness and ready solubility in water, provide the foundations for its largest manufacturing use in confectionery and bakery products. Foods and food products containing a significant quantity of sucrose include cakes, biscuits, jams, jellies, marmalades, syrups, molasses, soft drinks, beverages, canned fruit and vegetable products, soups, condensed milk, ice creams, cereal breakfast foods, and puddings.

Nonfood Uses

Hickson (1971) proposed the following sixteen possible markets as outlets for sucrose: foods, feeds, fuels, explosives, elastomers, lubricants, solvents, soil conditioners, fibers, adhesives, paper, pesticides, plasticizers, plastics, surface coatings, and surfactants. Foods constitute the greatest preponderance of the current market for sucrose. Of the total 1968 U.S. sugar usage, only about 2% was for such nonfood uses as the pharmaceutical and tobacco industries (Hickson 1971). Although sucrose has been demonstrated to yield useful materials through almost all standardized reactions of organic chemistry (viz., oxidation, hydrogenation, treatment with strong acid or strong base, and dehydration), it has achieved little chemical or industrial utilization; according to Hickson (1971), other lower-cost raw materials turn out to be more economical sources of these commodities. Thus sugar has failed to gain a market for products such as hydroxymethyl furfural and levulinic, oxalic, mucic, and lactic acids. Animal feed markets are available in special situations to produce feed energy at lower prices in temperate regions. Of the sixteen major areas of marketing of organic compounds, sucrose appears to have significant potential in the areas of plastics, plasticizers, surface coatings, and surfactants.

The conviction that sucrose could be used as a source of industrial chemical intermediates led to the establishment by U.S. sugar producers in 1943 of the

Sugar Research Foundation, Inc., to sponsor and coordinate research into the chemistry of sucrose. In 1968, the foundation—recognizing the worldwide interest in promoting nonfood markets for sucrose—was renamed the International Sugar Research Foundation (ISRF). In 1978, the ISRF was taken over by the World Sugar Research Organization (WSRO) Ltd., based in the United Kingdom. Numerous applications and nonfood uses of sugar derivatives have been explored and evaluated under the aegis of the ISRF and WSRO (Kollonitsch 1970). However, despite the ready availability and low cost of sugar in the world market, it has not gained any foothold in the chemical markets dominated by the surplus production capacity of the petrochemical industry (Parker 1984). Consequently, sucrochemicals are as yet confined to supplying specialty markets with high-value products, exploiting the unique properties of sucrose. Parker (1979), however, indicated that with an increase in crude oil prices and the cost of petrochemicals in the 1970s and 1980s, the chemical industry is increasingly looking toward regenerable carbon resources such as sugar for its raw materials.

ENVIRONMENTAL FACTORS

Climate

Season and Location

The climatic requirements of sugar crops vary widely for different crop species. Although considered to be a tropical crop, sugarcane has been successfully grown in subtropical areas between 15° and 30° latitude. This covers parts of south and central Brazil, Cuba, Mexico, South Africa, India, China, Australia, and Hawaii (Blackburn 1984). According to Blackburn (1984), the ideal climate for sugarcane during the growing season should be warm, with mean day temperature around 30 °C, adequate moisture, and high incident solar radiation. The ripening and harvesting season should be cool, with mean day temperatures of 10–20 °C, but frost-free, dry climate with high incident radiation. The vigorous growth of ratoon shoots requires adequate moisture, preferably provided by controlled irrigation during the harvest season, which also prevents excessive drying of cane prior to harvest.

Sugar beet, the second most important sugar crop, is cultivated successfully in a wide range of climates in different types of soil; however, it is mostly grown between 30° and 60° N latitudes as a summer crop in maritime, prairie, and semicontinental climates, and as a winter or summer crop in Mediterranean and semiarid conditions. It can also be grown with supplementary irrigation in regions of drier climate with low rainfall (Wu and Salunkhe 1976).

Temperature

Sugarcane requires temperatures of 24–30 °C for good growth and high yield. Practically no variety of sugarcane can grow in regions with temperatures below 5 °C. Both temperature fluctuations and daily sunshine hours remarkably influence the enrichment of sucrose. Minimum and maximum temperatures, as well as the rainfall distribution pattern, significantly influence the yield and quality of sugarcane. Under tropical conditions such as in India, the duration and intensity of sunshine do not limit sugarcane growth as much as the coefficient of variation in the mean monthly temperature. Cane quality, in terms of average recovery of sugar, bears no direct relationship with rainfall and temperature; however, sugar recovery is generally better in areas where a relatively dry and cool season prevails during cane ripening.

According to Blackburn (1984), the minimum temperature for active growth of sugarcane is approximately 20 °C, but varietal and cultural factors may modify this slightly. The critical temperatures for the sugarcane varieties grown in South Brazil were 19–20 °C (unirrigated) and 18–19 °C (irrigated). Temperature influences irrigation requirements in several ways. It affects the evaporative capacity of the atmosphere: Monthly evapotranspiration rates vary from 85 mm in midwinter to 200 mm in midsummer (Thompson 1976). In Hawaii, soil temperatures are more important than air temperatures for sugarcane (Mongelard and Mimura 1971). As growth ceases when mean day temperatures fall below 19–20 °C, sugarcane does not respond fully to irrigation in winter (Yates 1967). The growth rates of sugarcane are thus best correlated with antecedent mean day temperatures, and the effects of day and night temperatures tend to be additive. Final cane yield values are not necessarily reduced progressively by mean temperatures down to about 20 °C.

The length of season with temperatures significantly below 20 °C influences both growing season and the ripening of sugarcane. Low temperatures are the most effective means of ripening sugarcane and sugar beet, counteracting adverse effects of such factors as moisture or nitrogen. In Iran, the ripening effect lessens when temperatures fall below 10 °C; freezing conditions, however, rupture cells and cause irrevocable deterioration of sugarcane (Blackburn 1984). High temperatures above 38 °C have been known to reduce photosynthetic rate (Kortschak 1972). Chu and Kong (1971) observed that photorespiration in sugarcane increases with temperature.

The occurrence of frosts in Argentina, Egypt, Iran, Pakistan, Zimbabwe, South Africa, and the U.S. mainland (Florida and Louisiana) often damages sugarcane crop. Frosts are also common in the northern parts of India, adversely affecting both cane growth and yield. The cooler night temperatures of ≤14 °C reduce both the weight of sugarcane leaves and overnight translocation of sugar to approximately half that at 24 °C. Frosts also cause injury to

Table 4-6. Range of Maximum and Minimum Temperature of Some States of India.

State	Maximum Temperature (°C)	Minimum Temperature (°C)
South India		
Tamilnadu	28.7–36.8	20.1 – 27.3
Andhra Pradesh	27.8–33.4	14.6 – 26.6
North India		
Uttar Pradesh	21.7–33.4	7.7 – 27.2
Punjab	17.7–40.0	6.3 – 27.8

Source: *Handbook of Agriculture* (1966).

sugarcane buds. Singh et al. (1981) stated that cutting sunshine hours in Hawaii by 50% will reduce the yield of sugarcane by 50%. The ecological conditions of southern parts of India with their optimum sunshine hours are ideal for sugarcane cultivation when compared to the northern regions (Table 4-6). The effects of frost can be mitigated to some extent by planting resistant varieties or by irrigation; however, severe frosts can kill all varieties of sugarcane.

Light

Blackburn (1984) summarized the extensive work on photosynthesis and effects of light intensity on sugarcane. Sugarcane grown under field conditions can continue to increase its photosynthetic rate up to full natural light intensity, so that the greater the incident radiation, the higher the yields that may be expected. Effects of daylength are difficult to evaluate, as they are confounded with winter–summer temperature changes at high latitudes. Thus, cane yields in South Queensland, with a temperature-defined growing season of only seven months, are similar to those in North Queensland, where temperature does not limit plant growth.

Sugarcane flowering is controlled photoperiodically (night period of 11.25–11.5 h). According to Blackburn (1984), flowering has no adverse effect on sugarcane yield for some time (possibly one or two months), but has a progressively deleterious effect after that.

Water

An adequate supply of soil moisture is as essential for the growth of sugar crops as the dry season (or the withdrawing of water in irrigated areas) is essential for their ripening (e.g., the storage of sucrose in the stems of sugarcane). Because its vegetative portion is harvested, sugarcane is particularly more responsive to moisture than are other crops. Maximum cane yields are thus obtained only when there is uninterrupted vegetative growth. According to Blackburn (1984), about 1 MT yield of cane can be obtained per hectare per 10 mm of evapotranspiration. Despite its good response to soil moisture, sugarcane is remarkably resistant to drought, especially when grown in deep soils that allow profuse rooting. Blackburn (1984) cited examples of Bundaberg in Australia, Mtibwa estate in Tanzania, and Porvenir in the Dominican Republic, where commercially successful cane plantations have been established without irrigation. These areas receive about 1,200 mm rainfall/year. Although sugarcane has been grown without irrigation with an annual rainfall of as low as 850 mm (e.g., Cantarrnas in Honduras), zones with rainfall < 1,200 mm are generally not suitable.

Although most cane is grown without irrigation, vast areas of sugarcane heavily rely on irrigation in India, Egypt, and Peru; other areas use supplementary irrigation. In parts of Australia, Africa, and the Caribbean Islands, water is applied through irrigation only during the dry seasons.

In Hawaii, water requirements of sugarcane are determined by directly measuring soil moisture potentials with resistance blocks, and occasionally with ceramic tensiometers (Humbert 1968). Soil moisture status can also be determined by measuring the moisture content of selected tissues, such as certain leaf sheaths (Clements 1948), immature internodes (Blackburn 1984), or exposed, rolled spindle (Evans 1965; Singh 1976). These techniques have not been employed commercially to control irrigation, but they are of value in diagnosing certain growth limiting factors, such as poor drainage and inadequate aeration in the root zone. Abnormal tissue moisture levels also indicate certain nutritional deficiencies (e.g., insufficient nitrogen).

Virtually all known irrigation systems are used in sugarcane cultivation (Blackburn 1984): bay, furrow, portable, overhead, solid-set overhead, center pivot, rain guns, and drip. The degree of sophistication in the control of water applied varies as much as the techniques used. Perforated tubes are used rather than discrete emitters for drip irrigation in sugarcane because of the row planting of this crop. Factors that influence the economics of irrigating sugarcane include the source of water (surface, underground, requiring pumping head), quantity of water applied, system of irrigation and its overall efficiency, length of irrigation season, reliability of the rainy season, and the expected crop response.

High humidities encourage several fungal diseases of sugar crops. High humidity and high temperature accelerate the rate of deterioration of cut cane. Desai, Sangle, and Gaur (1985) reported significant losses in juice quality (Brix, CCS % cane and juice purity) and cane weight when the harvested cane was left in the field for up to 120 h at the ambient conditions. Rain and floodwaters aid in the transmission of numerous fungal, bacterial, and viral diseases of sugar crops, the most striking example of such transmission being the transatlantic movement of smut (*Ustilago scitaminea*) of sugarcane from Africa to the Caribbean.

Other Climatic Factors

Cyclones, hurricanes, hailstones, and winds occasionally damage sugarcane in many cane-growing areas, causing severe mechanical damage. Wind of more normal velocity is unimportant except where it affects irrigation systems. Rare instances of whirlwinds causing severe damage of sugarcane have been reported; damage is limited to the width of the "twister," and is in the form of broken stems at ground level. Damage by lightning has been reported from sugarcane-growing areas in South Africa, Mauritius, Jamaica, and other countries.

Effects of Climate on Ripening of Sugar Crops

Ripening in sugar crops is significantly influenced by such climatic factors as rainfall, humidity, the incidence of sunshine, nightlength, altitude, and temperature. According to Blackburn (1984), in equatorial regions, high temperatures and rainfall, with heavy cloud cover and little difference in the length of the nights, cause vigorous vegetative growth of sugarcane and thus militate against ripening. Cooler and longer nights immediately before and during harvest, prevailing in the subtropical regions, favor the accumulation of sucrose in the stems. In dry areas, irrigation is generally withdrawn about six weeks before harvest to encourage ripening. Blackburn (1984) concluded that, other factors being equal, cane quality at sea level is generally a function of latitude. A bimodal curve with its nadir at the equator and peaks at 18° N and 18° S is obtained when sucrose percent cane is plotted against latitude.

Soils

Sugar crops can be grown on soils varying in texture from light sands to heavy clays that supply adequate amounts of macronutrients (nitrogen, phosphorus, and potassium) as well as the trace elements. Sugarcane is tolerant to wide variations in soil pH, although the optimal pH = 6.5. Most of Guyana's sugarcane is grown on highly acidic clays with pH as low as 4, whereas in Barbados the crop is grown on alkaline soils (pH 8.5) derived from coral limestone. Nevertheless, damage at both extremes of the pH scale have been reported (Blackburn 1984). Evans (1960) reported aluminum toxicity in the pegasse soils of Guyana. Iron deficiency causing severe chlorosis of sugarcane has been reported under highly alkaline conditions (Stevenson 1957).

Growth of sugar crops is favored by deep soils (more than 1 m) with a well-structured loam or clay loam. Sugarcane particularly has the potential for very deep rooting (over 5 m), and cane planted on such soils markedly resists drought conditions. The soils should preferably have a bulk density of <1.4 g/ml and a pore space of at least 50%, which at field capacity would be half occupied by air and half by water. Severe suppression of rooting can result if cane is grown on soils with higher bulk densities (Trouse and Humbert 1961).

Soils have free internal drainage and rapid surface infiltration rates. Ideally, the available water-holding capacity of the soil should be ≥15 cm/m to ensure an adequate reservoir of available water to plant roots. Soil characteristics will define the irrigation techniques to be adopted. Sugar crops are well adapted to variations in soil characteristics. Blackburn (1984), however, pointed out the following main constraints that affect growth of sugarcane under extreme soil environmental situations:

1. Sandy and coarse-textured soils may mean nematode infestation and low available water capacity. Also, rapid movement of water in these soils increases the leaching loss of nutrients.
2. Fine-textured soils may have poor soil aeration, with too much of the pore space in the root zone occupied by water. Problems of soil capping and root penetration may be encouraged in soils with high salt content or high bulk density, respectively.
3. Soil salinity can cause damage to sugar crops, mainly due to accumulation of chloride rather than sodium ions in the soils.
4. Acid soils having very low pH cause aluminum and manganese toxicity to sugar crops.
5. Deficiencies of phosphate, iron, and zinc and volatilization of nitrogen fertilizers may be encountered when sugar crops are grown in highly calcareous soils.

Somawanshi and Kadu (1988) correlated different soil properties and plant characteristics using data from thirty-one diverse sugarcane fields in the Ahmednagar district of Maharashtra State. The results of this study indicated that high soil organic carbon and Mg : Ca ratio were associated with iron chlorosis of sugarcane grown in these areas (Table 4-7).

The cation exchange capacity of the soils for sugar crops should generally be >15 meq/100 g soil. Higher exchange capacities indicate greater retention of applied fertilizer nutrients against leaching losses. Higher soil organic matter content is also important for greater retention and supply of plant nutrients and soil moisture, as well as in the development and maintenance of favorable soil structure for plant growth. Blackburn (1984) advocated incorporation of organics such as filter-press cake from the factory into the soil at regular intervals to maintain organic matter content levels of 2–4%, which are usually considered adequate.

Table 4-7. Average Properties of Soils and Sugarcane Plants Collected from Nonchlorotic (Healthy Green) and Chlorotic Areas of 31 Sugarcane Fields.

Characteristic	Unit	Nonchlorotic Plant	Chlorotic Plant
Soils			
Conductance (soil : water, 1 : 2)	mho/cm	516.62	789.03
pH (soil : water, 1 : 2)	—	8.11	8.28
Calcium carbonate equivalence	%	8.06	6.62
Organic carbon	%	0.456	0.569
KCl-soluble Ca	meq/100 g	8.40	7.06
KCl-soluble Mg	meq/100 g	9.78	9.08
KCl-soluble Na	meq/100 g	0.56	0.53
DTPA–Fe	ppm	2.52	2.38
Sugarcane plants			
Leaf chlorophyll	mg/g	1.195	0.636
Weight of plant top	g/plant	227.7	143.2
Cane length	cm/plant	206.1	185.5
Number of nodes	nodes/plant	24.9	26.2
Internode length	cm/internode	8.26	7.17
Cane weight	g/cane	1,207.0	811.3
Juice extracted	%	61.5	62.7
Juice Brix	%	17.1	13.8
Juice pH	—	5.09	5.26
Na in juice	mg/100 ml	4.88	8.75
Dry matter of roots	g/plant	6.26	3.10
Length of rooted cane	cm/plant	18.67	15.05
Number of rooted nodes	nodes/plant	10.03	11.61
Dry matter of rooted cane	g/plant	38.41	22.36

Adapted from: Reprinted from Somawanshi and Kadu (1988), pp. 1545–5, by courtesy of Marcel Dekker, Inc.

CROP NUTRITION AND FERTILIZATION

Sugar crops remove significant quantities of major, secondary, and micro-nutrients from soils. If all the by-products of sugar factories are returned to the soil, there should be no reduction in its mineral content, since the sugar that is harvested is a compound of carbon, hydrogen, and oxygen. However, the by-products of sugar manufacture are often used for other purposes (fuel, food, yeast, paper, alcohol, acetic acid, acetone, furfurals, aldehydes, esters, waxes, etc.). The depletion of soil reserves of nutrients must, therefore, be made good by application of manures and fertilizers at regular intervals of time. Soils differ markedly in their nutritional composition (e.g., light soils are usually deficient in potassium) and must be dressed with appropriate fertilizer for satisfactory crop growth. In general, only nitrogen, potassium, and sometimes phosphorus and magnesium are required, but minor (trace) elements may be needed under special situations.

The nutritional requirements of sugarcane are high. A 100 MT/ha crop requires an average of 120 kg N, 75 kg P, and 150 kg K (de Gues 1967). Preliminary soil analysis can indicate the probable response of the crop to different types of fertilizer, but more accurate soil test–crop response studies are required to determine the optimum rates of fertilizer application.

Sonar et al. (1987, 1988) developed fertilizer adjustment equations for seasonal and *adsali* sugarcane at the Mahatma Phule Agricultural University, Rahuri, India, and tested their validity by conducting yield-targeting trials. The yield targets of 80, 100, and 120 MT/ha for seasonal sugarcane and 150, 175, and 200 MT/ha for *adsali* sugarcane were achieved within ±15–30% variation. The application of fertilizer based on the targeted-yield approach was found to be beneficial in increasing the yield and/or saving of expenditure on fertilizers.

Vaidya et al. (1987) reviewed research work on micronutrient requirements of sugarcane in Maharashtra, India. They concluded that Fe, Zn, Mn, and B were commonly deficient in sugarcane soils, and that the crop responded well to their application, both in terms of yield and juice quality. The wide variations observed in the response of sugarcane to micronutrient applications were attributed to the varying status of micronutrients in sugarcane soils.

Blackburn (1984) indicated the following approximate levels of soil nutrients below which a positive response of sugarcane can be expected to the application of appropriate amounts of fertilizer (whereas, on soils with equivalent or higher levels, a response is less likely):

available phosphorus, 25 ppm (Troug), 5 ppm (Olsen);
available potassium, 60–80 ppm (light soils), ≥250 ppm (heavy soils);
available magnesium, ≥70 ppm;
exchangeable calcium, 3.0–3.5 meq/100 g soil.

According to Blackburn (1984), foliar or tissue analysis technique is a good diagnostic tool for the estimation of sugarcane fertilizer requirements, once the crop is established. Foliar analysis is generally employed in the more sophisticated cane-growing areas. The correlation between the amounts of nutrient element in specific plant parts and fertilizer requirements for each main soil type and area have now been well established.

Nitrogen

Adequate soil nitrogen stimulates vigorous vegetative growth of sugar crops, its deficiency being indicated by stunted crop growth and yellow or pale green leaves. Nitrogen can be applied as urea, ammonium sulfate, or ammonium nitrate. Rates of application vary according to soil tests and local circumstances, such as rainfall received and availability of irrigation. For annual cropping of sugarcane, levels of nitrogen applied range from 100 to 140 kg/ha (90–125 lb/ acre). Ratoon crops usually respond better to nitrogen application than does plant cane. Timing and placement of nitrogenous fertilizer are also important. Since nitrogen promotes vegetative growth and inhibits the storage of sucrose in the parenchyma of the stems, all nitrogen should be applied about 5 mo before the cane is harvested. Overly heavy and unduly delayed nitrogen application can adversely affect juice quality. Nitrogen should be applied to ratoons as soon as possible after the previous crop has been reaped.

Singh et al. (1989) studied the effects of modified urea sources (*neem* and *karanj* cake–blended urea and urea super granules [USG]) on yield, nutrient uptake, and sugarcane quality. Although USG did not outperform prilled urea, the use of blended materials accentuated release of ammoniacal nitrogen and inhibited nitrification, resulting in higher uptake of nutrients, higher cane yield, and better juice quality.

Split applications of nitrogen are advocated in many countries, half the nitrogen being placed in bands at the time of planting, and the remainder shortly after the shoots have appeared. In Hawaii, sugarcane is grown for two years or more before being harvested. Profuse vegetation of sugarcane at the end of the first year makes it difficult for manual or mechanical application of fertilizers, which are therefore applied either in solution with irrigation water or in pellet form from the air (Blackburn 1984). Despite high costs of distribution, application of filter mud to sugarcane soils is advocated, especially on problem soils.

Draycott (1972) stated that the most difficult problem in sugar beet nutrition is deciding the appropriate amount of nitrogen fertilizer needed. Whereas inadequate nitrogen causes serious loss of yield, too much nitrogen depresses sugar percentage, purity of the juice, and the amount of white sugar extracted in the factory. Sugar beet on organic soils invariably needs less nitrogenous fertilizer than average. Also, sugar beet grown with organic manures will need considerably less fertilizer than that grown without it. Previous cropping also greatly influences optimum dressing. Other factors that affect the nitrogen requirement for sugar beet are irrigation, plant density, and pests and diseases. According to Draycott (1972), beet sugar yields increase linearly by increasing amounts of nitrogen fertilizer up to 100 lb/acre (113.4 kg/ha) on most fields. Field experiments conducted with several sugarcane varieties (Co 658, Co 449, Co 853, Co 6304, Co 671, and Co 6806) indicated that nitrogen fertilization at 250 kg N/ha would be optimal for sugarcane crop even in soils low in available nitrogen status (Kannappan, Pandian, and Kumar Swamy 1988).

Phosphorus

The formation of a healthy root system depends on adequate supply of phosphorus to sugarcane. Consequently, the growth of sugarcane on phosphate-deficient soils is inhibited and the number of tillers limited. Phosphorus deficiency is indicated by a deep purple discoloration of leaves. One hundred metric tons of cane remove about 50 kg of phosphorus from the soil (Blackburn 1984). Raw juice contains about 0.4% phosphorus of the total soluble solids; the clarified juice, only 0.08%. At the factory, the phosphorus is expressed in the raw juice, precipitated in the clarifiers, and removed in the filter mud. Because filter mud is usually not returned to the land evenly, phosphorus must be applied to sugar crops regularly.

Rock phosphate, the main source of phosphorus fertilizer, is insoluble in water; it is therefore treated either with sulfuric acid to make more soluble superphosphate, or with phosphoric acid to form triple superphosphate with a high phosphorus content. Other less used phosphatic fertilizers are ammonium phosphate and bone meal.

Phosphorus is generally applied at the time of planting, rates of application varying widely depending on soil-test values and types of soil (50–250 kg P/ha). Compound fertilizers containing more than one nutrient element are also used, especially for ratoons.

In some soils, soluble phosphorus combines with iron and aluminum to form insoluble phosphate. The problem of phosphorus fixation can be overcome by placing fertilizer in the furrows (root zone of the cane) at the time of planting, and by using pellets rather than the finely divided powder form of fertilizer.

Arable soils where sugar beet has been grown for a long time usually contain sufficient residual phosphorus; hence these soils generally do not respond to fertilizer application of phosphorus. Sugar beet removes about 63 kg/ha (56 lb/acre) of phosphorus from soil in tops and roots, half of which is returned if the tops are plowed in. Draycott (1972) recommended about 63 kg/ha of phosphorus for sugar beet. Fields needing larger doses can be recognized by soil testing.

Potassium

Potassium is directly involved in the formation of carbohydrates by photosynthesis, and in the translocation of sucrose to the parenchyma cells of the stems. Gross potassium deficiency is indicated by typical browning of leaf margins and tips and a pattern of necrosis that is quite different from that caused by salt damage. Serious potassium deficiency is also indicated by deep red discoloration, in blotches, on the upper surfaces of the midribs. Slight potassium deficiency can only be diagnosed by carefully designed fertilizer trials in combination with soil and plant tissue (juice and/or leaf) analysis (Blackburn 1984).

Raw sugarcane juice contains 1.31% potassium of the total solids; the molasses, a by-product of the sugar factory, contains 6.55% (Meade and Chen 1977). A crop of 75 MT cane/ha removes 92 kg K/ha from the soil. Since little of the molasses or the potassium-containing by-products (such as spent wash) are returned to the soil, there is a need for the application of potassic fertilizers to sugarcane soils.

Potassium may be applied in the form of potassium sulfate or muriate of potash (potassium chloride). The latter is the cheaper form of potassium and hence widely used for sugarcane. Potassium is applied either manually or with the aid of machine, alone or in combination with other fertilizers. Annual sugarcane crop requires about 115 kg K/ha, and proportionately larger amounts are applied in split doses to sugarcane crops of longer periods of growth.

Like phosphorus, potassium can get fixed and retained in insoluble form when applied in excess quantities. In India, sugarcane is cultivated on a wide variety of soils ranging from alluvial to mixed red and black soils, with a varying degree of both exchangeable and nonexchangeable potassium. Perumal and Sonar (1987) reported market increases in sugarcane yield with potassium application. This response has been quadratic in many red and black soils, and increased with higher levels of nitrogen. The optimum K:N ratio for sugarcane is 1:1.5. Cropping with application of potassium decreases available potassium in the soil, even in a single season. The uptake of potassium by sugarcane is high during the first 4–6 mo of crop growth. Excessive rainfall or irrigation reduces the cane yield due to leaching of potassium from the soil. Blackburn (1984) also pointed out the effect of nitrogen–potassium interaction on the growth of sugarcane. Heavy dressings of nitrogen, with consequent prolific vegetative growth, increase sugarcane yield without deteriorating juice quality, provided sufficient potassium is also present in the soil.

Sugar beet needs adequate supply of both potassium and sodium for maximum yield. The amounts of potassium fertilizer needed on soils not treated with sodium and containing <50 ppm of sodium are much greater than when sodium is applied or where soils contain enough sodium. Organic soils also need less potassium than most mineral soils. Draycott (1972) summarized the K and Na dressings needed by sugar beet on five different types of soil (Table 4-8). Clay

Table 4-8. Summary of Optimum Potassium and Sodium Fertilizer Dressings versus Soil Texture for Sugar Beet.

Soil Texture	K Dressing without Na		K Dressing with Na		Na Dressing with K	
	(lb/acre K_2O)	(kg/ha K)	(lb/acre K_2O)	(kg/ha K)	(lb/acre NaCl)	(kg/ha Na)
Sand	224	210	134	125	336	150
Loam	168	160	56	55	336	150
Silt	134	125	—	—	0	0
Clay	112	105	0	0	336	150
Organic	56	55	—	—	0	0

Source: Draycott (1972).

soils need the least fertilizer potassium, and organic soils usually contain sufficient sodium for maximum yield.

Calcium and Magnesium

The effects of calcium on sugarcane nutrition have been studied in relation to soil reaction, toxicity caused by aluminum and manganese, and the availability of phosphorus and molybdenum. Based on research work carried out in Hawaii and Guyana, Evans (1960) concluded that, where only calcium nutrition is concerned, the critical level in soil is 100 ppm of exchangeable calcium; however, when the calcium is to be added to increase phosphorus availability, lower toxic levels of iron or aluminum, or reduce acidity, dressings of limestone should be increased to obtain exchangeable calcium levels in soil as high as 500 ppm.

Calcium deficiency in sugar beet soils is not usually due to an actual shortage of calcium in the soil, but to unbalanced nutrient supply: An excess of sodium and magnesium ions decrease the uptake of calcium by sugar beet. Under these circumstances, neutral or alkaline soils may respond to calcium or lime applications. Since sugar beet is very sensitive to acid soil, calcium application in the form of oxide, carbonate, hydroxide, or sulfate neutralizes soil acidity. Growth of sugar beet is favored in soils having $5.3 < pH < 9.0$.

Magnesium is mobile within the plant, hence its deficiency symptoms appear on older leaves. The chlorotic spots turn brown as the tissue dies, giving a rusty appearance to leaves. There are very few reports of increases in yield of sugar crops due to the application of magnesium. In Hawaii, sugarcane crop did not respond to magnesium application despite soil exchangeable-magnesium levels of as low as 30 and 50 ppm (Blackburn 1984).

Although yields of some sugar beets have been reported to increase economically due to the application of magnesium, most sugar beet crops do not so respond. Fields with >50 ppm exchangeable magnesium have an ample supply from the soil; when the exchangeable magnesium is <25 ppm, a large increase in yield is likely (Draycott 1972).

Micronutrients (Trace Nutrients)

Iron deficiency in sugarcane is commonly encountered in several sugarcane-growing areas. Iron being relatively immobile within the plant, older leaves remain deep green in color, while young ones appear chlorotic. Iron deficiency also restricts the development of an adequate root system. In calcareous soils containing limestone, soluble iron (ferrous) is converted into insoluble ferric state. Iron deficiency also occurs if the Fe : Mn ratio in the leaf tissue is lower than 1 : 1; thus iron deficiency may be due to lack of the nutrient in the soil, lack of its mobility within the tissue, or a low Fe:Mn ratio (or possibly other elements).

Iron deficiency has become a serious problem in many parts of India and is one of the major factors in limiting yields of many important crops, including sugarcane (Kannan 1988). Due to intensive cropping with heavy irrigation, the groundwater has become salty. In Ahmednagar district of Maharashtra, sugarcane has been particularly badly affected in recent years because both the land and irrigation water have become saline. The same groundwater is exploited and practically recycled, the situation being aggravated due to poor rainfall. The typical effects on sugarcane are stunting of the plant and reduced internodal length.

The critical limits of micronutrients in soils and plants are complex functions of several interacting soil and plant factors. The concentration of iron in plant is often not related to growth: Iron chlorotic sugarcane has been reported to have as much or more iron than the comparable normal plant growing on calcareous soil (Somawanshi and Kadu 1988). Yadav and Yaduvanshi (1989) reported that it may not be possible to obtain the maximum benefit of applied NPK fertilizers without the application of the micronutrients that are commonly deficient in Indian soils—Mn, Zn, Cu, and B.

Sugarcane is also affected by iron toxicity; the symptoms are similar to those of potassium deficiency, and in Java they disappear if potassium is applied (Van Dillewijn 1952). Potassium deficiency is known to interfere with the mobility of iron within the plant. Evans (1960), however, reported iron toxicity in the presence of adequate or even high levels of available potassium.

Manganese deficiency in sugarcane areas has frequently been reported. In association with copper and zinc deficiencies, it is responsible for the poor growth of sugarcane on the organic soils of Florida, and it was the cause of Pahala blight in Hawaii (Blackburn 1984). Manganese deficiency can be controlled by adding manganese sulfate to soil (34–36 kg/ha). In Florida, in addition to manganese fertilization, it is necessary to correct soil alkalinity. Cases of manganese toxicity to sugarcane are rare and usually associated with highly acid conditions.

Total failures of sugarcane crops due to deficiency of copper have been reported. Allison, Bryan, and Hunter (1927) found that, on the raw peat soils of the Everglades in Florida, sugarcane failed to grow in the absence of copper. Sandy soils of Mossman and Innisfail in Queensland and granitic soils of South Natal also have been reported to be deficient in copper. Poor growth with few tillers and chlorotic spindles from which the leaves are reluctant to unroll are the typical symptoms of copper deficiency in sugarcane. In more mature cane, the leaves hang downward; this, together with the unrolled spindles, gives a characteristic appearance to the cane, called "droppy top" in Queensland. Significant yield increases in sugarcane were obtained in Queensland by the application of

Table 4-9. Concentration and Quantity of Micronutrients in Sugar Beet.

Micronutrient	Concentration in Dry Matter		Quantity in Crop (Tops + Roots)	
	Tops	Roots	(lb/acre)	(g/ha)
Boron	40	15	0.30	335
Chlorine	2,000	1,000	17.00	19,000
Copper	7	1	0.04	44
Iron	200	100	1.70	1,900
Manganese	50	30	0.46	520
Molybdenum	7	5	0.07	80
Zinc	20	10	0.17	190

Source: Draycott (1972).

Table 4-10. Micronutrients in Farmyard Manure.

Micronutrient	Average Concentration in Dry Matter (ppm)	Amounts in 10 MT/Acre (26 MT/ha) Dressing	
		(lb/acre)	(g/ha)
Boron	41	0.37	426
Cobalt	3	0.03	24
Copper	33	0.30	312
Manganese	264	2.40	2,500
Molybdenum	2	0.02	19
Nickel	10	0.09	94
Zinc	120	1.10	1123

Source: Draycott (1972).

60 kg/ha copper sulfate. The generally recommended dose of copper sulfate, however, is 23–57 kg/ha (20–50 lb/acre). Copper chelates can also be used successfully (Blackburn 1984).

Zinc deficiency in sugarcane soils has been reported from several sugarcane-growing areas, including the Florida Everglades, lighter soils of Queensland, and parts of India. Zinc deficiency is indicated by chlorosis of veins (in contrast to Fe- and Mn-deficiency conditions). In Florida, zinc deficiency has been overcome by applying 84 kg/ha of manganese sulfate at the time of planting, along with 34 kg/ha of both copper sulfate and zinc sulfate. Such dressings obviously also correct manganese and copper deficiencies of these soils.

The quantities of micronutrients removed by sugar beet crop at harvest, and their concentration in tops and roots, are shown in Table 4-9. According to Draycott (1972), most soils supply the needs of sugar beet crop from reserves, weathering minerals, limes, fertilizers, and organic manures. One dressing of farmyard manure (FYM) supplies more of most micronutrients than sugar beet removes (Table 4-10).

CULTURAL OPERATIONS

Cultivation of sugar crops includes preparatory tillage, propagation and plant establishment, control of weeds, pests, and diseases, and maintenance of soil fertility.

Sugarcane

Systems of Cultivation

Several different agricultural systems of cultivating sugarcane were developed in different countries based on local climatic conditions and abundance of cheap labor. In drier regions where irrigation was not available, conservation of both soil and soil moisture were of supreme importance. Blackburn (1984) described various systems of sugarcane cultivation: cane holes (Barbados, Mauritius, Reunion, parts of Jamaica, and slopes of Antigua); cambered beds (low-lying flatlands of high-rainfall areas of many countries); flood fallowing (Guyana, Florida, and Mozambique); and ridge and furrow (low-lying flatlands of Louisiana banks and India).

In India, both the flat and the trench systems of cultivation are followed. The flat system is required because of inadequate irrigation facilities. Preparatory operations include 4–8 disk or iron plowings, spreading of organic manure, compaction of soil by a wooden roller (or *pata*), opening of shallow furrows, dropping sets in furrows, and soil compaction by the *pata*. In this case, no irrigation is given.

The trench system is followed wherever irrigation is available. The land is plowed to a fine tilth with an iron plow or a tractor. Organic matter is spread before the last plowing, and trenches are dug by the ridge plow. Seed rate, planting time, and spacing between rows adopted in different states of India vary considerably (Thuljaram Rao, Natarajan, and Bhagyalakshmi 1983). In Punjab and Haryana, closer spacing of 60 cm and two-budded cuttings are recommended.

Tops are usually used as the seed material where harvesting and planting times coincide. The cuttings are treated before planting with organomercurial compounds (0.25% Aretan®, 0.5% Agallol®) to minimize the attack of soil microorganisms on the cuttings. Soil application of aldrin, dialdrin, chlordane, benzene hexachloride (BHC) dust, and heptachlor gives adequate protection against white ants. Gamma-BHC effectively controls termites and shoot-borer.

Planting and Crop Establishment

The sets of sugarcane are placed by hand or machine, end to end or slightly overlapping, with the buds on the sides and covered with soil (2–3 cm). In trench planting, the cuttings are placed at the bottom of the trenches, covered with minimum soil, and immediately irrigated. Weeds are controlled by two or three hoeings, the spreading of trash, and the use of "weedicides" (2,4-D or Simazine®).

Considerable success has been achieved in several countries by a new method of planting, called "pineapple planting," in which two rows 0.9 m apart are made simultaneously and spaced at intervals of 1.8 m. This layout facilitates other operations, especially drip irrigation.

In the flat system, lodging of cane needs to be prevented by heavy earthing-up before the start of monsoon rains. In the trench system, beside planting in deep trenches, lodging may be prevented by earthing-up or tying single cane rows by trash twisting.

Species and Varieties

Choice of variety depends on its resistance to major diseases and pests prevailing in the area where it is planted: Suitable precautions must be taken to prevent damage by disease and pests if the varieties released by cane-breeding stations for general cultivation do not have an inbuilt resistance. Yield of sugar, ability to ratoon, and growth habit in relation to use of mechanical harvesters are other criteria for selecting a variety of sugarcane. Early-ripening varieties are preferred to ensure that, when harvested at the beginning of the crop season, the juice is of high quality. Harvesting of such varieties must proceed in an orderly manner to avoid postharvest losses. Early-ripening variety B 4362, for example, quickly dries out, its stems becoming pithy and corklike, if harvesting is delayed (Blackburn 1984). Blackburn (1984) recommended that a new variety be introduced gradually, and be widely planted only after successful performance over many years.

All varieties of sugarcane are species or hybrids of the genus *Saccharum* and include *S. robustum* and *S. edule* (Stevenson 1965). For centuries, *S. sinense* has been grown in China and *S. barberi* in India, but it was the increased planting of the noble cane *S. officinarum* that resulted in the spread of the sugar industry in the tropics and subtropics. Clones of *S. officinarum* have now been replaced in commercial production by hybrid varieties. Production of new varieties, called nobilized seedlings—such as the legendary "wonder cane," POJ 2878 in Java—has revolutionized the commercial sugarcane cultivation.

Pests and Diseases

The major pests of sugarcane are moth borers, froghoppers, white grubs, and rodents. Others of minor importance are leafhoppers and aphids, which are the vectors of virus diseases.

The diseases of sugarcane can be grouped according to their causal agents as fungal, bacterial, and viral. Important fungal diseases of sugarcane are red rot, root rot, culmicolous smut eyespot, *Fusarium* set or stem rot, and pineapple disease. Bacterial diseases include gumming disease, leaf scald, and ratoon stunting disease. The viral diseases of importance are mosaic and Fiji disease. Blackburn (1984) and Salunkhe and Desai (1988) have described the nature of damage caused, symptoms, and control measures for the pests and diseases of sugarcane and other sugar crops.

Sugar Beet

Systems of Cultivation

Sugar beet is a herbaceous, long-day biennial that requires two seasons to produce seed. The crop is adapted to cooler regions of the world. Generally, areas with high humidity are favorable for seed production, but drier periods are preferable before and during seed harvest. During flowering in the second year, warm, dry weather greatly helps seed set. Early-sown beets flower at cooler temperatures than those planted late. Bolting, seedstack development, and seed yield are generally best in cooler weather (<20.5 °C) under wet and cloudy conditions (with <4–5 h sunshine per day) for roughly six weeks, followed by two weeks of cool dry weather to stimulate seed production. Bolting is probably best stimulated by a temperature range of 4–10 °C depending on the age of the plants and duration of light.

Successful sugar beet production is found only on fertile soils. A good supply of soil organic matter supplied naturally, by manuring or by legume residues, favors beet yields. Loam or sandy loam soils predominate the sugar beet cultivation areas on the North American continent; however, heavy clay soils are also used to some extent. Because of the difficulty of lifting the beets and freeing them from adhering soil, stickier soils are not favored for beet cultivation. The sugar content of beets is highest on soils that also produce the best tonnage, although excess nitrogen lowers the sugar content. Once established, sugar beet crops can endure large quantities (up to 1–1.5%) of saline salts.

Sugar beet seed germinates well when the soil temperature is about 14–16 °C. The roots usually contain the highest sugar content in regions where the summer temperatures average about 19–22 °C. The plant is not injured by cool night temperatures. Cool autumn weather favors sugar storage in roots, whereas temperatures >30 °C retard sugar accumulation. Sugar beets planted in the winter in California and harvested during the very hot July weather have a high sugar content. Newly emerged seedlings are usually susceptible to frost.

Species and Varieties

Sugar beets grown in the United States and Canada are improved hybrids or varieties developed by crossing or selection for disease resistance, monogerm seed, slow bolting, regional adaptation, high production, and other desired characteristics. Selection for disease resistance in sugar beets is essential since heavy losses are caused by curly top, leaf spot, and black root diseases.

Planting and Crop Establishment

Two methods are used for producing sugar beet seed: The crop may be over-wintered in the field, or selected roots may be lifted at the end of the first season and replanted to produce seed the following season. The first method is suitable only in areas with mild winters. In the colder climates of the Northern Hemisphere, the seed roots must be stored to prevent freezing damage.

The time of sowing varies depending on geographical location: during June–July in Canada, August–September in the United States, and October–January in South Africa. Deep plowing to a depth of 20–30 cm is usually recommended. A fine and firm seedbed is essential for prompt germination and early growth of the crop. Seed rates vary from 7–10 kg/ha in Canada and parts of the United States to 15–30 kg/ha in the Pacific Northwest and in Europe. Since little roguing is possible, only good stock seed must be sown wherever the seed crop is overwintered. In several European countries, undersowing in cereal crop for overwintering seed crop is quite a common practice. Planting is usually done with a special four- or six-row beet planter with rows 20–40 cm apart.

Sugar beets often require thinning. When the first pair of true leaves develops, the crop is thinned 20–25 cm apart by cross-row cultivation with a flexible-toothed or knife weeder. Rotary implements that uproot the plants at fixed intervals may also be used. Thinning should be completed by the time the plants have eight to ten leaves. Later on, thorough hoeing and cultivation are important to control shallow weeds.

Pests and Diseases

Cercospora leaf spot, caused by *Cercospora beticola,* is one of the most prevalent sugar beet diseases. Circular sunken spots scattered over the leaf are about 1–2 mm in diameter. When the spots are numerous, they coalesce, causing the leaf blades to become brown and dry. Under severe attack, sugar beet fields may look brown or scorched. The principal control measure for leaf spot is the use of resistant varieties and hybrids. In Germany, hot-water treatment of seeds is often used to kill the seed-borne infection.

Curly top, a viral disease, used to cause heavy losses to sugar beet growers in the Pacific Northwest and California. The upward curling of leaf is usually accompanied by a roughening and distortion of the leaf veins. These symptoms are accompanied by a shortening of the petiole as well as a general retardation in the growth of the entire plant. The stunted beets commonly develop large numbers of tiny rootlets. The disease is transmitted by the beet leafhopper, *Circulifer tenellus*. The use of resistant varieties and hybrids has brought the disease well under control.

Sugar beets are also susceptible to seedling and black root rot diseases, caused by several fungi. To control the occurrence of these diseases, long rotations, proper drainage and fertilization, seed treatment with fungicides, and use of resistant hybrids are often recommended.

Among the insects, beet leafhopper, beet webworm (*Loxostege sticticalis*), beet armyworm (*Laphrygme exigua*), sugar beet maggot (*Eurycephalomyia myopaeformis*), and sugar beet root aphids (*Pemphigus betae*) are serious pests causing huge economic losses. Use of insecticides is often recommended to control these pests in sugar beet fields.

POSTHARVEST LOSSES OF SUGAR CROPS

Magnitude of Loss

Salunkhe and Desai (1988) reviewed the research on the magnitude of losses of sugars in sugar crops. Significant losses of sugar crops occur both during pre- and postharvest phases. Cramer (1967) evaluated the extent and type of crop losses due to plant diseases and insect pests. Table 4-11 shows the annual losses of the two major sugar crops, sugarcane and sugar beet, as compared to

Table 4-11. Annual World Sugar Crop Losses.

Commodity	Tonnage (Value)[a]		Crop Loss Cause			
	Actual	Potential	Insects	Disease	Weeds	All
Sugar beet/cane	694.6	1,330.4	228.4	232.3	175.1	635.8
	(7.6)	(13.9)	(2.3)	(2.3)	(1.7)	(6.3)
All crops	2,393.1	3,854.7	510.1	539.6	412.1	1,461.6
	(139.7)	(210.5)	(25.8)	(24.8)	(20.2)	(70.8)

Adapted from: Cramer (1967).
[a]Tonnage in millions of metric tons, value in U.S.$10^9 (in parentheses).

those of other agricultural crops. Annual world losses of sugarcane and sugar beet in 1967 amounted to 636 million metric tons (U.S.$6,300 million). In terms of crop tonnage, the losses of sugar crops were the highest.

Rush (1968) estimated that about $30 million was lost annually in the United States and Canada because of sucrose losses and spoilage during storage of sugar beets after harvest. According to Stout (1957), the average total loss came to about 42 lb of sugar per MT of sugar beets per day. Barr, Guinn, and Rice (1940) determined loss of sugar by respiration at various temperatures over a 47-day storage period. The amount of CO_2 evolved accounted for about 60% of the total apparent sucrose losses in sugar beet, the loss varying with temperature. Stout and Spikes (1957) estimated that the loss of sucrose associated with sugar beet respiration was between 0.3 and 0.5 lb/MT/day at 21°C. The losses varied from 0.1 lb/MT at 3°C to 1.8 lb/MT at 35°C (Barr, Guinn, and Rice 1940).

Hughes (1956) described sugar losses from sugarcane recorded at the Hawaiian Commercial and Sugar Factory Ltd., Puunene, Maui, during the period 1929–53. He observed a vivid discrepancy between the sugar produced by the cane plant and that actually recorded in the factory. The yield increases on a U.S. ton/acre basis accompanied by processing losses increased by over 35% in 25 yr (Fig. 4-1). The burning and field inversion losses were assumed to be

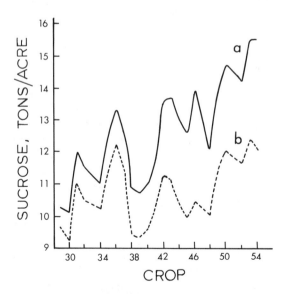

Fig. 4-1. Discrepancy between sucrose production in the field and sucrose recovery in the factory during a 24-yr period at Puunene, Maui (Hawaii): sucrose (a) produced and (b) recovered per acre (U.S. tons). *Source:* Hughes (1956).

constant during this period. The enormous quantities of sugar lost during postharvest operations point out the futility of increasing sugar production at the field level if the sugar is not proportionately recovered in the factory. Similar views were expressed by Turner and Rojas (1963) in Mexico.

Guilbeau, Coll, and Martin (1955, 1956), discussing delayed grinding of sugarcane in Louisiana, reported quality losses that exceeded those occurring in the factory. Sugar losses varied from a minimum of about 12% to as high as 50% of the recoverable sugar from fresh cane after it was held for 14 days. A maximum loss of about 37% was recorded when the stalks were held only for 9 days. Mean values from six experiments indicated that, of the recoverable sugar present in cane cut for 1 day, 11% was lost by day 9 and 23% after 13 days. This attrition stemmed from combined losses in weight, sucrose, and purity, with purity decline being the largest contributing factor. On the basis of a 25-MT yield/acre 1 day after cutting, it was estimated that >2 MT of this weight would have vanished by day 9. Guilbeau, Coll, and Martin (1955, 1956) concluded that processing 1-day-old cane would be highly unprofitable. Since most of the loss in recoverable sugar occurred before the cane was purchased, losses to sugarcane growers were substantially larger than those in the factory.

Boneta-Garcia and Lugo-Lopez (1962) measured postharvest losses of sucrose in whole stalks of six varieties of sugarcane stored in shade or sun for a 15-day period. A daily sucrose decline of statistically significant magnitude was obtained for each variety, although the rate and extent of deterioration in each variety differed considerably. A variety M 336 was least affected, whereas P.R. 1000 was more sensitive to quality decline. A slightly higher level of sucrose was generally retained in shaded areas.

Foster and Ivin (1981) reported that the immediate mass losses caused by fires varied from 0.3% to 2.6%, representing the sum of the physical losses and changes caused by rapid liquid movements within the plant tissue. With a severe fire, a mass loss of about 6% was recorded only 1 day after the fire. Egan (1969) reported that during storage over weekends in 1962, 1963, and 1966, the postharvest losses of cane harvested by chopper harvesters in Queensland represented at least 6%, 8.8%, and 11% of the original CCS percentage, as compared to 1–2% losses for the stored whole stalk.

Amin et al. (1972) studied the effects of burning and chopping on the rate of deterioration of two commercially important sugarcane varieties (N. Co 310 and Co 413) grown in Egypt. Burning followed by immediate harvesting reduced sucrose inversion to a minimum, although it resulted in a loss of weight amounting to about 8–10% after 96-h storage under open field conditions. Chopping of burned or unburned cane had no effect on the rate of deterioration except that moisture loss was enhanced by chopping. Delaying the harvesting of burned standing cane for >24 h resulted in a marked loss in sugar yield. Purity coefficient and glucose ratio, however, did not change significantly. Burned standing cane was better in its sugar yield from the manufacturing point of view than unburned cut cane, since its glucose ratio was lower.

Nature and Causes of Postharvest Losses of Sugar

Sugarcane

Postharvest deterioration in sugar crops has not always been viewed in terms of sucrose losses. In fact, reports indicate that harvested cane kept in the field for ≥ 1 wk had a higher sugar content than it did at the time of cutting. The magnitude of this so-called after-ripening appears to be far less pronounced when a full account is given to moisture or weight losses and purity changes relative to recoverable sucrose. It is generally agreed that by the second week after harvest the accumulated sugar experiences unfavorable changes such that the sucrose not already inverted will be exceedingly difficult to recover from the low-quality juice (Salunkhe and Desai 1988).

Tilbury (1968) reviewed work reported on microbiological deterioration of sugarcane stalks, milled juice, and raw sugar. The lactic acid bacterium *Leuconostoc mesenteroides* can attack the harvested sugarcane stalks to produce "sour" cane of deteriorated quality. The "sourness" stems from the odor of acidity arising from partial degradation of hexoses by *L. mesenteroides;* "staleness" of cane, on the other hand, describes the aging of cut stalks that have depleted their sucrose via continuing inversion and respiratory reactions (Alexander 1973b).

According to Wold (1946), postharvest deterioration in sugarcane was more nearly related to moisture and original condition of the cane than to storage methods (i.e., piles vs. open storage). The sound, clean, dry cane deteriorated much slower than cane that was damaged, dirty, and wet. Burning, freezing, and mechanical harvesting cause significant losses of sugarcane (Alexander 1973b). Fire causes major physiological changes in the sugarcane plant. Temperatures measured within the cane stalk and visual operations in laboratory and field tests indicated that significant loss of fluid took place by physical ejection and exudation from the stalk. Probably a substantial thermal degradation of the outer tissue also occurred (Foster and Ivin 1981).

In addition to microbiological losses between burning and milling, according to Salunkhe and Desai (1988), the causes of lowering commercial cane sugar values in the burned cane include the following:

1. thermal destruction of sucrose;
2. dilution by water flow into vascular bundles from the roots;
3. possible loss of sugar solution by flow into the root system immediately after the fire;
4. physical loss of sugar in boiling juice bursting from the cane tissue; and

5. loss of sugar by exudation onto the cane surfaces, much of which would be lost on the trash separated in the harvester.

Cross (1966) described two types of decomposition in frozen cane:

1. increased inversion and alcoholic fermentation by endogenous enzymes, and
2. bacterial decomposition leading to acid fermentation and production of gums.

Sugar Beet

In sugar beet, respiration, sprouting, and activity of various microorganisms are the main causes of postharvest deterioration (Karnik 1970). According to Mumford and Wyse (1976), the most significant factor determining the extent of fungus infection is root injury before storage. There is probably sufficient fungus inoculum in soil adhering to roots to initiate infection when conditions are favorable for fungus growth during root storage. Dexter, Frakes, and Wyse (1969) reported that wilting of beets resulted in a substantial loss of extractable sugar per (metric) ton (ESPT) in comparison with beets stored without wilting. The irrigation practice of "misting" the piles is highly desirable both in cooling the air and beets and in maintaining a higher humidity of the cooled ambient air (Vajna 1965). Wyse and Dexter (1971a,b) noted appreciable cell wall degradation during storage of sugar beet when desiccation, sprouting, and rot were prevalent.

Among various pests affecting sugar beet after harvest, molds and bacteria are the major group of microorganisms causing postharvest spoilage. Molds grow first and require air and moisture for their development and formation of colonies on the root surface. They then gradually decompose the firm outer tissue, thus providing an access to the inner parts of the root.

Sugar beets are infected by *Botrytis cinerea, Phoma betae,* and *Rhizopus betavora. Botrytis* commonly develops on wilted beets causing brown dry root rot. *P. betae* causes black dry rot. *Bacterium betae viscosum* and *B. betae flavum* are the most common bacteria causing slimy rot of beets; at lower temperatures, these bacteria develop slowly (Silin 1964). Karnik (1970) isolated the predominant fungi from sugar beet: *Penicillium, Fusarium, Botrytis, Rhizopus,* and *Aspergillus*.

In addition to spoilage caused by molds and bacteria, heavy losses of sugar beet also occur due to physical injuries and bruising of the roots (Wyse 1978; Wyse and Peterson 1979) as well as wilting of roots caused by freezing and moisture loss. Significant losses may occur when defective roots are mixed with sound material intended for long storage by creating centers of infection and rotting.

MATURATION AND RIPENING

Sugarcane

Maturation, ripening, and harvesting of sugar crops are closely related, and the ability to control the one and carry out the other has strongly influenced reaping strategy in the sugar industry. Physiologically, however, the terms aging, maturity, and ripening are not synonymous. Maturity pertains to the botanical completion of a stalk suitable to produce new plantlets from each node; the stalk contains stored sucrose to support reproduction, but its storage potential has not necessarily been realized. Maturity and age are not synonymous, since if water and nitrogen are continually abundant, the plant may never mature regardless of its age. Maturity is also not synonymous with ripening. Sugarcane can easily be made to ripen within a few months after germination by withholding water, nutrients, and other factors needed for growth, but such plants are by no means mature. From a cultural point of view, however, maturity is closely allied with ripening. Under the influence of cooler and longer nights prevailing in the Northern Hemisphere from April to June, sugarcane stems after the boom period of growth change from vegetative to reproductive phase, producing inflorescences, called "arrows" or "tassels." Flowered stems are ripe and have high sugar (16–18% sucrose by weight) content; the remaining unflowered stems continue to grow until low temperatures and/or inadequate water cause them also to ripen (Blackburn 1984).

Agee and Dass (1933) introduced the concept of "day degree" in Hawaii: the number of degrees Fahrenheit by which the maximum temperature each day exceeds 70 °F (21.1 °C). It showed that there was a significant negative correlation between this index and ripening of sugarcane. Le Grand and Martin (1966) reported a similar correlation in Florida.

According to Clements (1959), ripening of sugarcane is a physiological phase of senescence intermediate between that of rapid growth and the ultimate death of the plant. Agronomic concepts of ripening are usually based upon the appearance of internodes no longer subtended by green leaves and a parallel accumulation of sucrose in each successive internode toward a common high value.

Van Dillewijn (1952) described the ripened stalk as a succession of joints whose individual sucrose values can be plotted as the crest of a flat plateau (Fig. 4-2). Accordingly only the immature or green leaf internodes and the basal internodes with high fiber content do not retain appreciable sugar. In natural ripening, the older internodes assume an early lead and continue to store sucrose even while the younger ones are ripening above. The uppermost curve in Fig. 4-2 illustrates a fulfillment of storage capacity for receptive joints of a given variety under a given set of conditions.

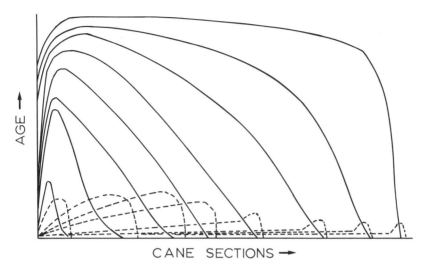

Fig. 4-2. The sucrose (solid line) and glucose (dashed line) distribution in sugarcane stalks of increasing age. The abscissa, from left to right, represents cane sections extending from the stalk base upward. Increasing age is plotted along the ordinate from bottom to top. *Source:* Van Dillewijn (1952).

Ripening of sugar crops may be induced artificially by withdrawing irrigation water prior to harvesting and by withholding nutrients. Clements (1948, 1980) in Hawaii developed the concept of crop logging, charting a log for each field. The data are derived from the measurement of temperature, sunlight, and growth as well as the analysis of young leaf sheaths for moisture, N, P, and K. These techniques have been employed successfully in several countries. According to Humbert, Zamora, and Fraser (1967) in Mexico, effective water control was largely responsible for an increase in sugar yield per metric ton of cane ground. Ripening of sugarcane is promoted by moderately cool weather and by moderate drying-off, but is interrupted by extremely cold weather and by too severe drying-off (Blackburn 1984).

Ripening is influenced not only by moisture supply and temperature but also by the age of plant, and it is modified by plant nutrition, variety, soil conditions, and other cultural practices. A majority of modern commercial canes tend to mature and ripen about 2–4 mo later than their growers desire. This has created a widespread interest in chemical "ripening agents," growth regulators, and various cultural practices (i.e., topping, water, and fertilizer regulation) to encourage the plant to ripen earlier or better.

Singh and Kanwar (1989) reported that nitrate reductase activity (NRA) could be exploited as an index to evaluate foliar vigor while selecting ideotypes in sugarcane. Late-maturing sugarcane varieties had slightly higher foliar growth and NRA than early-maturing ones. Irrespective of the varieties, NRA was significantly higher during August and September than in December–March. Foliar vigor and NRA *in vivo* showed a highly significant positive correlation between them.

Sugar Beet

Wu and Salunkhe (1976) defined ripening of sugar beet as the stage when the formation of sugar within the beet ceases. Juice purity—that is, the percentage of sucrose in the soluble solids or juice dry matter—rises during the process of sucrose synthesis, as the purifying and non-sugar-removing operation progresses during ripening. According to Dutton, Carruthers, and Oldfield (1961), both the root and the leaf of sugar beet play significant roles in the synthesis of sucrose.

Glucose and fructose are the predominating reducing sugars in the beet, with traces of galactose and arabinose (Silin 1964). The reducing sugar content of the freshly harvested beets is very low, but increases substantially during storage, particularly if mold or rotting occurs (Walker, Rorem, and McCready 1960). Increase in reducing sugar is accompanied by a concomitant decrease in recoverable sucrose.

Chemical Ripeners

Efforts to improve cane quality with chemicals have progressed along three general lines (Alexander 1973b):

1. direct ripening by treatment of standing cane shortly before harvest,
2. removal of trash, and
3. sugar retention by postharvest deterioration control.

Vlitos (1974), Nickell (1983, 1984), and Salunkhe and Desai (1988) have reviewed chemical ripeners and plant growth regulators in sugarcane cultivation. Julien (1977) stressed the importance of industrial trials before the ripeners are recommended for commercial use. Nickell (1984) concluded that, despite the fact that the use of chemical ripeners and growth regulators in sugarcane and other sugar crops is still in its infancy, there is a great potential to increase the sugar yields by use of these chemicals. As more knowledge is gained about the relationship of a given chemical to the process that it affects, and as field technology of sugar crops improves and their economy becomes more favorable, the use of chemical ripeners will undoubtedly become more widespread. Historically, agricultural research in sugar crops was primarily concerned with improvement of total crop yield by the removal of constraints to optimal production. Now that many of these limitations can also be overcome with herbicides, pesticides, fertilizers, irrigation, and improved management practices, the stage is set for further increases in yield and crop quality by the use of sophisticated techniques of physiological manipulation of the plant and its metabolism by the chemicals.

Several growth regulators have been tested to promote ripening in sugarcane, including 2,4-dichloroacetic acid (2,4-D), maleic hydrazide (MH), triiodobenzoic acid (TIBA), 2,2-dichloropropionic acid (also called dalapon or Dowpon®), 3-(p-chlorophenyl)-1,1-dimethylurea (CMU, monuron), 3-(3,4-dichlorophenyl)-1,1dimethylurea (DCMU, diuron), ethylenediaminetetraacetic acid (EDTA), Trysben® (2,3,6-trichlorobenzoic acid, dimethylamine salt), and Pesco® 1850 (a mixture of MCPA and Trysben®), as well as a number of enzyme inhibitors and metabolic inhibitors (Nickell 1983).

Preharvest Testing for Ripeness

A sugarcane field comprises stems at different stages of maturity and varying in age from young suckers a few weeks old to those that have flowered and ceased to grow. Blackburn (1984) pointed out the difficulty in obtaining a representative sample for maturity or ripeness testing from such a heterogeneous population. Other difficulties and possible errors in obtaining representative samples for analysis pertain to lodging of sugarcane. The validity of sampling methods—for example, the choice of individual stems or whole stools (Evans 1962)—is also questionable. Although Hoekstra (1978) stated that practically nothing was to be gained by carrying out maturity tests, preharvest testing for ripeness is carried out in several countries by taking samples of stools, canes, or core punches at intervals of about 2 wk. The cane is crushed in laboratory mills, the juice is analyzed, and the sugar yield is calculated.

Sugarcane can be tested for ripeness in various ways:

1. sampling of whole canes taken randomly through a field;
2. complete cutting of a selected stool;
3. punching of portions of different parts of standing cane by a simple tool; and
4. examining the juice from standing canes in the field by a hand refractometer (Barnes 1974).

The core-punch sampling method has been shown to give a close approximation of the juice character of a field cane, satisfactorily indicating whether the cane is ripe or not without destroying it. The sampling tools required are a punch, which cuts a cylindrical core transversely from the cane, and a portable hydraulic press made from a hydraulic automobile jack. Uniformly extracted juice samples are used to compare purity, sucrose, and estimated mill yields of 90° sugar.

A hand refractometer (degree Brix) may be used to examine the juice in the field. The cane is sampled by taking a small quantity of juice from the central internodes of the upper and lower thirds of the standing cane in the field. A simple tool for this purpose, usually with the refractometer, consists of a sharply pointed, rustless steel shaft. The point is pushed into the middle of an internode, groove upward with the shaft horizontal, about halfway through the stem. By moving the tool with a rotary motion and slanting the shaft downward, a small quantity of juice will run into the groove. This juice is then examined by placing a drop of it onto the prism face of the refractometer (Barnes 1974). Temperature corrections may be applied to the Brix readings, though for comparative observations in the field these are often omitted.

Modern evaluation of cane is based on its sucrose content at the time of delivery to the mill. The foundation of the price paid to the planter is the market price of the cane sugar and its proportion in the cane; thus quality and tonnage together regulate the cane price (Salunkhe and Desai 1988).

Preharvest Burning

Depending upon the variety, the older dried leaves of sugarcane either cling to the stems or gradually fall away. The resulting vegetable mass, called "trash," impedes reaping, whether manual or mechanical. Dried trash also becomes a serious fire hazard. The removal of trash (detrashing) by controlled preharvest burning, in order to facilitate reaping and lower the percentage of extraneous matter shipped to factory, has become standard practice in several regions including Hawaii, Queensland, New Guinea, Jamaica, South Africa, and the West Indies. Birkett (1953) reported that trash increases harvesting and transportation costs, contributes to fiber (thus increasing bagasse containing unextractable sugar residues), lowers juice purity, increases milling time, and adds to the wear on factory machinery. Owing to shortage of personnel and high labor costs of cutting in Hawaii and Queensland, more cane is harvested mechanically after preharvest burning.

There are obvious disadvantages of cane burning. There is a rapid deterioration in juice glucose and fructose, both of which fail to crystallize during subsequent processing and are discharged in the final molasses. This causes an imbalance between the milling plant and the boiling house. In most countries, boiling houses are equipped to handle 23–28 l of molasses/MT cane ground. When stale burnt cane is processed, the quantity of molasses increases to 55–80 l/MT. Due to the formation of dextrans and other unknown reasons, sucrose extraction becomes increasingly difficult under these conditions, congesting the boiling house. A decision must then be taken whether to abandon the burnt cane, to discharge final molasses containing more sucrose than is usual, or to delay the reaping operations. Since the purpose is to produce sugar and not cane, Blackburn (1984) suggested the following measures:

1. The time interval between burning and reaping/gleaning must be minimal.
2. Avoid burning in the daytime when the wind is high and cane might be damaged.
3. Preharvest burning should be discouraged if rigorous control cannot be exercised.

Cane fires of "unknown origin" frequently occur, constituting serious hazards; Blackburn (1984) described their causes, prevention, and control.

HARVESTING

Sugarcane

Harvesting sugar crops consists of cutting, cleaning, loading, and transport operations. It is essential to ensure proper phase of maturity and ripeness before the sugar crops are harvested. Factors influencing harvesting of sugar crops include crop age, variety, and such cultural practices as use of fertilizers, irrigation, chemical ripeners, and growth regulators. Both the growers and processors are keenly interested in achieving maximal length of the high-quality peak period in proportion to the total duration of harvesting.

For economic considerations, it is not always possible to confine the harvesting season to the peak period of cane quality. Barnes (1974) described various ways of minimizing lower returns incurred by harvesting and milling cane when it is relatively immature. Growers choose cane varieties suitable to conditions of soil, climate, and disease resistance for higher productivity throughout the harvest season. McIntyre and Hardy (1989) compared cutting methods in sugarcane grown in wet and dry areas of Mauritius and found that the yield of most varieties was depressed by stubble shaving in wet areas. In dry areas where the cutting methods and burning were tested, only one variety was adversely affected by burning and stubble shaving, but not by the cutting method in green cane. In both areas, however, neither the cutting method nor burning affected sucrose content.

Nair and Sreenivasan (1989) reported that two primary components of yield in sugarcane—number of millable stalks (NMS) and stalk weight—possessed a high level of genotypic variability in a sugarcane population of ninety-four clones. These components had negative indirect effects on stalk yield through each other. Stalk weight, however, showed very high positive correlation with stalk yield. This study indicated that selection of clones based on NMS and stalk height will be effective in improving stalk yield of sugarcane.

Manual Harvesting

The reaping of sugarcane by hand is notoriously labor intensive. It is a common practice in such countries as India and Pakistan, where labor is relatively inexpensive. The cutlass or machete is used in parts of Asia, and the cane knife or "bill" is employed in Africa. Baldwin and Fisher (1969) recommended the use of two knives, one for cutting and the other for topping, which reduced the work content by 10% and stump length by 30 mm. In South Africa, the long-handled Australian cutlass has been introduced with considerable success. It enables the cutter to work efficiently without stooping (Blackburn 1984). Output is increased considerably if the old leaves (trash) are removed by preharvest burning.

Mechanical Harvesting

Mechanical combined harvesters are being used in increasing numbers in several countries, including the United States, Australia, the Philippines, and Malaysia, as well as in new projects in Gabon, Nigeria, Swaziland, the Ivory Coast, Indonesia, and Sudan. Most of these harvesters have been designed and developed in Hawaii, the continental United States (Louisiana and Florida), Australia, or in Puerto Rico. Clayton (1969) has described these developments.

Except in Hawaii, the mechanical harvesters are of two types:

1. *whole-stick harvesters,* which deliver whole canes, and
2. *cut–chop harvesters,* which cut stems into 0.35-m-long billets.

Whole-stick harvesters readily fit into existing systems of reaping, transport, storage, and feeding into the mill, whereas cut–chop harvesters require specially built ancillary transport and sometimes need expensive transload stations. Blackburn (1984) has described different whole-stick and cut–chop harvesters in detail.

Barnes (1974) also described mechanical harvesters of two types based on design and nature of work performed:

1. Self-propelled harvesters have a second engine to provide the power for cutting the cane at the top and bottom and for stripping. Different models have been designed to work in untrashed and burned cane; the cane is left in whole lengths and dropped in bundles or loaded directly into a cart or trailer.
2. Tractor-mounted machines have a second engine to drive the harvester, which severs the cane into short lengths and loads them into a transport vehicle, leaving the tops on the ground. These work in untrashed, burned, and lodged cane. One type has also been designed to cut the young cane for seed.

In Hawaii, where there is no climatic restraint to growth, the crop may be harvested when the cane is two and even three years old; consequently, yields of 300 MT/ha are not unusual. It is rather difficult to reap such a tangled mass of vegetation. In the 1940s, the push-rake system of reaping was developed to overcome a sudden and acute shortage of labor. In this method, the cane is bulldozed into windrows by powerful crawler tractors equipped with bulldozing rakes and shearing blades. The push-rake moves along the rows, cutting the stems at their bases and rolling them into windrows. Large crawler-type mobile cranes, equipped with grabs, then load the cane from windrows into vehicles of 15–40-MT capacity for transport to the factory (Blackburn 1984).

Mechanical harvesting of sugarcane has several advantages over manual methods (Salunkhe and Desai 1988):

1. easier regulation, with fewer delays;
2. higher personnel productivity and better labor economics in terms of numbers employed (including supervisors);
3. easier maintenance of cane-processing schedules;
4. greater flexibility and speed of working, avoiding process losses caused by stale cane;
5. less field wastage of cane; and
6. fewer fire risks to standing cane.

Although it has generally been recognized that manually harvested cane delivered in clean condition to the sugar factory presents better quality raw material for processing than mechanically harvested cane, mechanical harvesting has great potential in high-production countries if all operations are conducted efficiently. Hurney, Ridge, and Dick (1984) presented the results of comprehensive studies pertaining to the efficiency of cane harvesters in removing extraneous matter and controlling postharvest losses during the cleaning process.

Chemical Desiccants to Aid Mechanical Harvesting

The use of safe and inexpensive chemicals to produce favorable burning conditions (chemical desiccation) prior to harvest has been thought an effective alternative for postharvest burning, which causes significant postharvest losses of sucrose.

In order to be suitable for use on sugarcane, a chemical desiccant should (Bates 1960):

1. be inexpensive, safe to handle, and readily disperse with low-volume aerial equipment;
2. have rapid systemic action and no undesirable residues; and
3. not affect crop quality.

Two quaternary ammonium compounds—paraquat (1,1′-dimethyl-4,4′-bipyridinium dichloride) and diquat (6,7-dihydrodipyrido-(1,2-a:2,′1′-C)-pyrazidinium dibromide)—were first discovered to have herbicidal properties in 1955 (Bates 1960). Characteristic dipyridyl effects on cane have been severe foliar drying and loss of sucrose-forming capacity, followed by a gradual recovery of the plant by producing new green leaves. Chemical desiccants have also been found to be useful in removing either meristem or green leaf spindle or both, that is, as chemical topping of sugarcane.

Several reports indicate that chemical desiccants lower the juice quality of sugarcane, but a study conducted in Mexico showed that the negative effects of diquat on juice quality were only temporary (Alexander 1973b). According to Alexander (1973b), the use of desiccants on sugarcane should be scheduled in such a way that control of tasseling results in substantial increase in cane yield. Chemical treatments, about 5–8 mo before harvest, have been known to increase yields by over 20 MT/ha. The ICI products Gramoxone®, Reglone®, and Reglox® are now being used in several countries. Humbert, Lima, and Govsas (1969) demonstrated that Reglone® (diquat) was very promising in the control of tasseling when sprayed at a rate of 0.25–1.1 l/ha in 15–70 l H_2O/ha, applied in the first week of September.

Chemical defoliation accomplished trash removal most satisfactorily. Defoliation occurs owing to formation of an abscission layer at the base of the petiole. In sugarcane leaves, leaf fall is usually prompted by mechanical disturbance after the death or partial decomposition of the leaf sheath clinging tenaciously to the stalk. Desiccation of the attached leaf and its removal by fire would be a more practical means of eliminating trash. Humbert (1974) reported effects of applying leaf desiccants prior to burning, especially at the beginning and toward the end of the harvest season, when rain might be expected. Gramoxone® applied at a rate of 1.5–3 l in 7–80 l of H_2O/ha resulted in 3–5% reduction in trash. It is important that the droplets be large enough to penetrate the lower green leaves. Of the various quaternary ammonium herbicides, paraquat has emerged as the preferred compound (Nickel 1984).

Sugar Beet

Harvesting of sugar beets in most countries begins in late September or early October and may continue until January or February, depending upon the yield and factory processing program. Delaying harvest generally increases sugar yield per unit area due to the rapid accumulation of sucrose in beet roots in the fall. However, beet raffinose content also begins to increase by the cooler temperatures during this period. The amount of raffinose accumulated is related to the average daily temperature, incidence of frost, and genetic makeup of the variety (Wood, Oldenmeyer, and Bush 1956; Finkler et al. 1959). According to

Vajna (1965), beets harvested early lose more sucrose in storage than those harvested late in the season; however, the soluble pectin content is higher in late-harvested beets (Silin 1964).

Wyse (1969) reported that sugar beets harvested in very cool, damp years had a much higher raffinose content than normal. Raffinose content increased approximately 35% between early and late harvests, and there was little difference among harvest dates in the amount accumulated after 65 days of storage at 3 °C. Early-harvested beets did not show as much increase in reducing sugar as the late-harvested beets, which tended to accumulate more reducing sugars under prolonged ideal, low-temperature storage conditions than those harvested early. The chloride content of sugar beets declined slightly with delayed harvest.

The harvest injury caused by machines may be important in determining the economic storage life of sugar beet (Wyse 1978). The respiration rates of the most severely injured, machine-harvested roots were higher than those of the hand-harvested controls. Removal of the crown reduced respiration rates slightly when compared with untopped beets, and flailing had no effect on respiration.

Sugar beet harvesting and handling equipment has been designed for maximum harvesting capacity and cleaning ability without regard for root injury. The major source of harvest injury to beets is the removal of crowns. Injury to sugar beet roots during harvesting, handling, and piling may have significant effect on their ability to be stored. The respiration rate immediately after harvest is very important, not only as a factor in sucrose loss, but also as a producer of heat (Wyse and Peterson 1979).

Although the crown contains less sucrose and has a lower purity than the root, its contribution to recoverable sugar per unit area can be considerable. Stout and Smith (1950) found that topped beets respired faster and spoiled quicker than untopped beets. The greatest spoilage was in beets topped near the center of the crown, and resulted from the exposure of the pith area to fungi (Dexter, Frakes, and Wyse 1970a; Akeson, Fox, and Stout 1974).

Sugar beets are commonly harvested by modern tractor-drawn lifters, which include one-, two-, or four-row machines directly mounted or trailed—though in some continental countries the beets are plowed out for subsequent pulling, knocking, and topping by hand. Two main types of lifter commonly used are

1. the *bow type,* with two curved arms and small shares running on each side of the row, and
2. the *sledge type,* which has converging runners on each side of the row to squeeze out the roots.

"Twin-share" and "bevel-edged lifting wheels" are the two main types of lifting mechanism employed during mechanical harvesting of beets. With the former, share setting entirely depends on soil conditions. The share heels should be about 3.1–3.8 cm apart, with the row of beets passing midway between the gap. They should be set as shallow as possible and with the minimum pitch consistent with effective lifting: Greater pitch on heavy land may bring up too much soil, causing blockages; smaller pitch breaks the tails of the beet. Bevel-edged lifting wheels are now used more commonly than twin-share lifters. They are mounted at an angle to one another to squeeze the beet out of the ground with less drag and little blockage and soil disturbance. This also reduces the amount of soil lifted onto the cleaning mechanism and increases harvesting efficiency. On heavy, sticky soils, twin-share lifters are more useful than wheels, which become blocked with mud (Salunkhe and Desai 1988).

Tractor-driven self-steering shares, in which the lifting equipment is carried on a subframe within the main chassis, are also used to harvest beets more efficiently. The subframe is free to float sideways and thus counteract any minor deviations in the steering of the tractor or the straightness of the rows. It is usually actuated through a hydraulic system from lightweight feelers on each side of the row (MAFF 1970).

Topping, cleaning of roots, and disposal of tops are the major operations involved in sugar beet harvesting. Topping involves cutting of the leaves and crown at the prescribed position. Most machines top while the roots are still in the ground. The topping unit has a feeler, with a number of serrated disks on a common axle, and a fixed knife below; the feeler holds the beet firmly while it is topped by the knife. Correct topping (not too wide or too close) is achieved by adjusting the position of the knife relative to the feeler wheel, moving it either vertically or horizontally. The horizontal distance between the center of the feeler mechanism and the knife edge can also be adjusted to suit beets of different average sizes. Incorrect topping can cause significant losses in the beet and sugar yields (Salunkhe and Desai 1988).

Tops may be disposed off either by plowing in or by collecting them for livestock feeding. They may be removed mechanically using harvesters and carting vehicles, and may be windrowed so as to make subsequent collection and grazing operations easier. In Denmark, forage harvesters are employed to remove tops by "scalping" the crowns of the roots. The more sophisticated machines collect the scalps and feed them into the discharge chute of the forage harvester, where they are mixed with the shredded leaves and carried into the silo.

The lifted roots are passed into the cleaning and conveying mechanisms. Severe cleaning and incorrect setting of "rod link conveyors," generally used for cleaning, may damage the roots, allowing subsequent ingress of rots and diseases during sugar beet storage. After passing the cleaning elevator, the beets are delivered by the same elevator to either a hopper or tank forming a part of the harvester (Fig. 4-3). Alternatively, the beets can be made to drop onto an elevator mounted at right angles to the first elevator and diverted to a trailer running alongside (MAFF 1970).

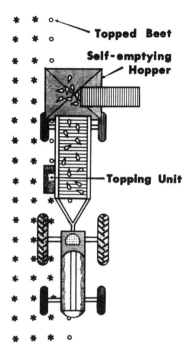

Fig. 4-3. Beet delivered to self-employing hopper on harvester. *Source:* MAFF (1970).

Two types of beet harvester are available:

1. the combined machine, which tops, lifts, cleans, and either leaves the beets in heaps or rows or elevates them into a conveyance; and
2. the two-unit machine combination, in which topping and lifting are carried out in two separate stages.

Combined machines perform harvesting in one operation and require minimum labor, although they cost more than the two unit machines initially. Machines have been developed to top beets and elevate the tops into a side or rear conveyance for carting off, thus taking the topping operation one stage further. These are known as "top savers" and are very useful when saving tops for cattle feeding purposes (Salunkhe and Desai 1988).

Other Sugar Crops

Sweet sorghum crop is harvested manually using a cane knife or mechanically by employing a suitable machine. A machine like a corn binder, though adequate, requires hand labor to load the bundles of sweet sorghum stalks (cane) onto tractor trailers or trucks. The bundles can be readily topped by hand or by a machine before milling. Chopper-harvesters are also used occasionally to cut the stalks into 15–30-cm lengths, but respiration rates and postharvest inversion losses of sugar may be very high in short, cut stalks if they are not processed in the mill immediately. Coleman (1970) reported that cutting stalks of sweet sorghum into short lengths, about the size used for ensilage, resulted in very high respiration rates and excessive breakdown of sucrose within 2–3 h on a hot day.

Harvesting machines that can cut and mill the sweet sorghum crop in the field have been used to a lesser extent. These field harvesters leave the bagasse in the field, where it is plowed under to improve the physicochemical properties of the soil; the juice is then hauled to the plant for further processing. The cost of transporting stalks can be minimized by using "mill-on-a-trailer"-type machines, which can be moved to the field.

Leaves from the stalks can be stripped by hand or via mechanical stripper. Since manual stripping is expensive and no satisfactory machines are available, some syrup processors have developed procedures of milling unstripped stalks even though processing problems are intensified.

It is well established that stripping leaves from stalks and removing seed heads and peduncles produce a better quality syrup from sweet sorghum. Coleman and Stokes (1964) reported that sweet sorghum varieties such as Wiley could be harvested for syrup anytime from flowering until the seeds were in the dough stage of maturity. The stage of maturity did not significantly influence juice extraction, but the Brix and syrup yield per metric ton of stalks increased with an advance in plant maturity up to the dough stage.

Well-manured maple trees are excellent sap producers as long as they remain vigorous. The harvesting of sap continues for 2–5 wk, between February 15 and April 15 each year. Drawing off the sap does little harm to the trees, and those that have been tapped for years can still yield good sawlogs and other wood products. Callahan (1965) observed no obvious relationship between sap yield and tree diameter, crown class, crown fullness, or the estimated apparent vigor in twenty-four maple trees studied at the Southern Indiana Forage Farm. There was, however, a relationship between temperature and sap yield: Juice Brix was apparently influenced by temperature and rate of sap flow. The maple-tapping season lasted from about mid-January to mid-March.

LOADING, TRANSPORT, AND DELIVERY

Sugarcane

By and large, road haulage of sugarcane by trucks and tractor-drawn trailers has replaced older forms of transport, such as animal-drawn carts (India) or floating canes on water (Hawaii). The vehicles may be loaded by hand or machine. Many of the machines developed solely for loading require that the cane be placed by the cutter in such a position that it can be easily grasped, that is, in heaps across the ridges on which the crop was grown (Blackburn 1984). Alternatively, the cane might be cut by machine and loaded by hand. None of these half-manual or half-mechanized systems of cutting and loading has proved to be entirely satisfactory.

The Cary Combine Harvester is a harvester-cleaner-loader designed to operate in recumbent, lodged, and tangled cane of any tonnage, and can be fitted with a device for cutting the cane into short lengths of about 38–46 cm. The cut cane is loaded into vehicles hauled alongside the machine. A selective topper and a blower remove most trash and tops. About 200–300 MT of burned or unburned cane can be cut and loaded by this combined harvester.

Deterioration in the quality of harvested cane sets in quickly with reduced recovery, leading to loss of sugar to a noticeable extent, especially if there is a serious delay in the loading and transport processes. Mechanical loading and transport are more promising in this respect (Salunkhe and Desai 1988).

Blackburn (1984) described the end-loading (e.g., Bell self-loading trailer) and side-loading (e.g., Mascane) systems of loading sugarcane. The former is used in South Africa and in the Philippines; the latter is widely used in Kenya, Malawi, South Africa, Tanzania, and Zambia. The extremely versatile Jacobyl trailer can be rear- or side-loaded, from either left or right, and thus can be operated in tandem. Loading is done by standard drum winch and cable, without requiring ramps (Blackburn 1984).

Sugar Beet

The increased output of modern sugar beet harvesters has necessitated equally efficient transport systems comprising fleets of vehicles matching the capacity of the harvesters. In addition to higher capacity, quick and efficient unloading is also required. Newer designs to build more satisfactory clamps include an entire trailer that raises itself to a height of 2.40 m before tripping and a self-unloading mechanism to throw the beet onto the heap—thereby making a clump nearly 2 m high and, at the same time, separating out some of the soil. Concrete bases are usually laid to store beets, enabling tractor-mounted front-loaders to operate without contaminating the beets with soil. The storage site should be convenient to the fields and provide access for road vehicles throughout the winter.

Root buckets on front-end loaders give good results when the beets are reasonably clean and stored on a firm base. Larger quantities of beets are usually handled using some form of cleaner-loader, especially when the soil tends to stick to the roots. Cleaner-loaders are of two kinds:

1. the cleaner-elevator with a loading hopper, and
2. the rotating drum cleaner, fed from a loading hopper and discharged into a loading elevator for further cleaning (Salunkhe and Desai 1988).

STORAGE

Sugar Beet

Low-Temperature Storage

The quality of beet roots, expressed in terms of contents of sucrose, reducing sugars, raffinose, and amino acids, can be maintained favorably when stored at 3 °C (Wyse 1969). Sucrose losses during storage can be reduced considerably at 3 °C as compared to those at 21 °C (Stout and Spikes 1957). Walker, Rorem, and McCready (1960) observed that, in beets stored at 1 °C, raffinose content increased four times after 60 days and then declined with prolonged storage. At 12 °C, raffinose content almost doubled but remained essentially constant. The effect of temperature on raffinose content of beets was reversible; they accumulated raffinose at 2 °C, but declined almost to their harvest level 25 days after being shifted to 25 °C storage. Atterson et al. (1964) noted that wilting also influenced the raffinose content of the beet root during freeze storage. Raffinose decreased markedly in beets stored under conditions permitting weight loss. Low temperature storage at 3 °C favored less accumulation of amino acids (Wyse and Dexter 1970).

Wyse (1978) found that the optimum temperature range for storing beet roots was 1.5–5 °C, and fluctuations within this range could be tolerated without increasing sucrose loss over that incurred by storage at a constant 1.5° or 5 °C. Roots stored at these temperatures could also tolerate brief exposure to warmer temperatures with only moderate damage. Beet roots were found to be damaged irreversibly, as demonstrated by loss of cellular contents and increased respiration rates, when exposed to temperatures below –2 °C.

Wyse and Holdredge (1982) compared forced ventilation and natural convection as means of cooling sugar beet storage piles at different locations. The locations having variable or mild fall harvest were found to benefit from forced-ventilation cooling of sugar beet piles. During years with mild fall temperatures, forced-air ventilation would provide a significant insurance factor for cooling the piles and thus minimizing postharvest losses. Holdredge and Wyse (1982) developed a simulation model to predict analytically the temperature variation in a sugar beet storage pile subjected to forced convection cooling. A digital computer program was designed to estimate root temperatures as a function of time and position, given the ambient air temperature, initial pile temperature, and ventilation flow rate. The predicted temperatures were in good agreement with the measured temperatures in an actual storage pile during the initial cooldown period.

Controlled Atmosphere (CA) and Modified Atmosphere (MA) Storage

Very low levels (1–2%) of CO inhibited the CO_2 output of sugar beets by 20%; increasing the concentration of CO to 10% did not increase the degree of inhibition. The rate of respiration of beet roots declined to 65% of the control when the CO concentration was 10–20%. Gassing of beets in covered piles with CO reduced sugar losses during the first few days of storage (Wyse 1969).

Vajna (1965) found that low oxygen levels (5–10%) caused accumulation of invert sugars in beet roots, owing to the onset of anaerobic respiration. Wyse (1969) noted that sugar beets stored in MA (5% CO_2 and 5% O_2) accumulated 2.5 times more raffinose than those stored at normal atmosphere. The MA did not affect the reducing sugar content of the beet roots. Wyse (1969) further reported that storage of beets in MA for 40 days increased amino acids throughout the storage period, but had no effect on raffinose and reducing sugar contents. According to Dilley, Wood, and Brimhall (1970), treatment of sugar beets with 100 ppm ethylene significantly increased sugar losses due to increased respiration. MA storage significantly decreased the loss of sugar as compared to the samples stored in air; the amount of sucrose conserved was much higher, but the accumulation of impurities caused a greater loss of juice purity (Wyse 1969).

Karnik et al. (1970a,b) extensively studied the effects of CA on storage behavior of beet roots. At 1.7 °C, control beets showed a lower rate of respiration than those stored under CA (6% CO_2 and 5% O_2); but at 10 °C, beets stored under CA had a lower respiration rate than the controls. After 200 days of stoarge at 1.7 °C, the loss of sucrose under CA averaged 54% of the loss occurring in the control beets. Similarly, at the end of 165 days of storage at 10 °C, 12.3% sucrose was retained in the CA-stored beets as compared to 11% in the control beets. Beets turned brown when stored at 10% CO_2 and 5% O_2 at both 1.7° and 10°C. They were susceptible to microbial attack, and were found to be dead at the end of 90 days of storage, as no respiration could be measured. Only 5.2% and 3.5% sucrose were retained at 1.7° and 10 °C, respectively, at the end of 165 days (Table 4-12), indicating the importance of checking the concentrations of gases in the pile routinely. The effects of CA treatments and duration on reducing sugar, raffinose, and titratable acidity showed that the percentage increase in reducing sugars was lower in CA-stored beets than in the control beets of 1.7° and 10 °C, but CA storage had little effect on raffinose accumulation of sugar beets (Table 4-12). The titratable acidity of sugar beets stored under CA, however, increased (bottom Table 4-12) and

Table 4-12. Effects of Beet Root Storage Temperatures and Duration on Various Parameters.

Days in Storage	Storage Temp. (°C)	Control (0.03% CO_2, 21% O_2)	Controlled-Atmosphere Treatments			
			0% CO_2, 5% O_2	3% CO_2, 5% O_2	6% CO_2, 5% O_2	10% CO_2, 5% O_2
Percentage sucrose retention[a]						
45	1.7	97.26	96.36	99.01	97.99	91.49
	10.0	94.66	94.65	93.39	98.10	85.56
90	1.7	93.73	93.01	95.47	96.33	85.04
	10.0	90.18	90.06	91.33	94.41	75.44
165	1.7	86.58	87.28	87.34	91.62	33.74
	10.0	72.99	76.33	80.00	81.66	21.83
200	1.7	75.10	—[b]	—	86.50	—
	10.0	61.83	66.53	—	—	—
Increase in reducing sugars[c]						
45	1.7	230.0	108.3	71.7	45.0	123.3
	10.0	421.7	381.7	323.3	260.0	343.3
90	1.7	315.2	191.7	120.0	113.3	556.7
	10.0	490.0	446.7	478.3	400.0	626.6
165	1.7	383.0	280.0	165.0	212.0	1090.0
	10.0	695.0	575.0	619.0	508.0	1354.0
200	1.7	460.0	—	—	283.0	—
	10.0	734.2	586.3	—	—	—
Increase in raffinose content[c]						
45	1.7	384.0	398.0	348.5	354.4	238.0
	10.0	156.0	134.5	147.5	148.5	118.5
90	1.7	550.0	480.0	483.0	500.0	175.0
	10.0	190.0	162.0	179.0	154.5	87.0
165	1.7	850.0	804.0	758.0	700.0	157.5
	10.0	199.5	158.0	178.5	164.0	78.0
200	1.7	888.0	—	—	776.0	—
	10.0	218.0	156.0	—	—	—
Percentage titratable acidity expressed as citric acid[d]						
45	1.7	0.28	0.35	0.31	0.45	0.26
	10.0	0.31	0.38	0.28	0.31	0.14
90	1.7	0.23	0.23	0.22	0.32	0.49
	10.0	0.25	0.35	0.24	0.24	0.24
165	1.7	0.21	0.23	0.23	0.27	1.31
	10.0	0.18	0.26	0.23	0.26	2.85
200	1.7	0.19	—	—	0.26	—
	10.0	0.14	0.19	—	—	—

Source: Karnik et al. (1970b).
[a]On the basis of 100% at the time of harvest of beet roots.
[b]Dashes mean values not determined due to shortage of samples.
[c]On the basis of 0% at the time of harvest of beet roots.
[d]Total titratable acidity = 0.332% at the time of harvest of beet roots.

was higher than that of the control beets (Karnik et al. 1970a,b). Sugar beets stored at 1.7 °C showed no sprouting during either conventional or CA storage; at 10 °C, however, beets sprouted distinctly when stored by the conventional method, and sprouting was appreciably inhibited in CA-stored beets. Sprouting significantly lowers the sugar content of beet roots (Karnik et al. 1970b).

Karnik et al. (1970a) reported the effects of CA storage on beets grown with different levels of nitrogen fertilizer. Respiration rates were significantly reduced and sucrose retention was higher in sugar beets stored under CA conditions irrespective of the level of nitrogen fertilizer (Table 4-13). CA storage

Table 4-13. Effects of Nitrogen Fertilizer, Storage Treatment, and Duration on Various Parameters of Sugar Beet at 4.4 °C.

			Days in Storage			
Parameter	Fertilizer Added[a] (lb N/acre)	Storage Treatment[b]	0	65	130	200
Respiration rate	None	CR	19.2	12.3	10.8	12.2[c]
(mg CO_2/kg/hr)		CA	19.2	11.9	8.6	9.4
	150	CR	20.4	11.4	12.2	13.4[c]
		CA	20.4	9.3	9.6	10.4
	300	CR	19.8	10.5	9.7	14.5[c]
		CA	19.8	9.9	8.6	10.4
Sucrose retention (%)[d]	None	CR	100	97.7	94.7	83.3[c]
		CA	100	98.5	97.5	86.2
	150	CR	100	96.1	88.2	78.7[c]
		CA	100	95.3	83.7	84.3
	300	CR	100	96.6	91.5	78.6
		CA	100	99.1	95.7	82.1
Reducing sugars	None	CR	95	281	347	419
(mg/100 g)		CA	95	223	282	374
	150	CR	110	260	360	445
		CA	110	186	302	413
	300	CR	123	259	410	511
		CA	123	288	330	427
Raffinose (mg/100 g)	None	CR	31	92	117[c]	124
		CA	31	86	94	114
	150	CR	34	76	97	118
		CA	34	79	95	108
	300	CR	31	88	104	123
		CA	31	78	101	117

Source: Karnik et al. (1970a).
[a]Main effects of fertilizer are nonsignificant.
[b]CR = conventional refrigeration; CA = controlled atmosphere.
[c]Storage treatments are significant at the 5% level.
[d]Initial sucrose content of 13.2%, 12.7%, and 11.0%, respectively, with 0, 150, and 300 lb N/ acre taken as 100%.

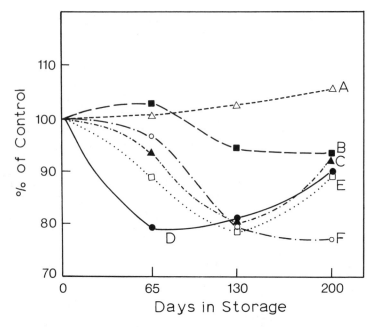

Fig. 4-4. Effects of CA storage and duration on (A) sucrose, (B) total nitrogen, (C) raffinose, (D) reducing sugars, (E) amino nitrogen, and (F) respiration at 4.4 °C in sugar beets grown without added nitrogen fertilizer, in relation to control. *Source:* Karnik et al. (1970a).

resulted in decreased accumulation of reducing sugars, raffinose, and amino nitrogen and higher accumulation of organic acids. Wu et al. (1970) confirmed the effects of MA storage (increase in CO_2 and decrease in O_2 concentration of storage environment through respiration of stored beet roots) on reduction of respiration and loss of sugar. Karnik et al. (1970a) investigated the effects of CA and duration of storage on sucrose, reducing sugars, raffinose, amino nitrogen, total nitrogen, and respiration at 4.4 °C in sugar beets grown without added nitrogen (Fig. 4-4) as well as with 150 and 300 lb N/acre (Figs. 4-5 and 4-6, respectively). Inhibition of respiration by the storage treatments appeared to be closely correlated with sucrose retention.

In general, storage of sugar beet in CA has not shown consistent effects of O_2 and CO_2 concentrations on the biochemical constituents (raffinose, reducing sugars, and amino acids) of different sugar beet varieties. CO_2 concentrations $\leq 10\%$ had no beneficial effect on sucrose conservation or impurity accumulation. Decreasing O_2 content to 3–5%, however, significantly decreased storage losses of sucrose. According to Wyse (1973), large-scale studies will be required to determine whether CA storage has any practical advantage over low-temperature storage in air.

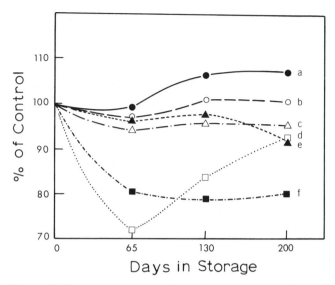

Fig. 4-5. Effects of CA storage and duration on (a) sucrose, (b) total nitrogen, (c) raffinose, (d) reducing sugars, (e) amino nitrogen, and (f) respiration at 4.4 °C in sugar beets grown with 150 lb of added nitrogen fertilizer, in relation to control. *Source:* Karnik et al. (1970a).

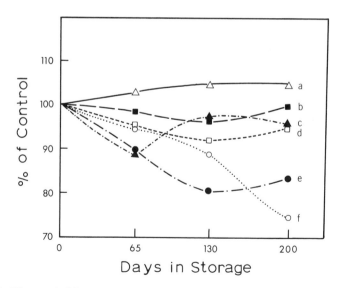

Fig. 4-6. Effects of CA storage and duration on (a) sucrose, (b) total nitrogen, (c) raffinose, (d) reducing sugars, (e) amino nitrogen, and (f) respiration at 4.4 °C in sugar beets grown with 300 lb of added nitrogen fertilizer, in relation to control. *Source:* Karnik et al. (1970a).

Sweet Sorghum

Coleman and Stokes (1964) conducted extensive studies on the storage and handling of harvested sweet sorghum. Their results indicated that the percentage of juice extracted remained constant for stalks kept wet, but decreased gradually for dry stalks during 2 wk of storage. The decrease in juice extracted from stalks was accompanied by an increase in juice Brix. Rapid inversion of sucrose into glucose and fructose in all three varieties of sweet sorghum (Iceberg, Sart, and Wiley) during storage for about a week eliminated the problem of crystallization in the syrup. The percentage of total reducing sugars (glucose and fructose) and sucrose was the same in both the juice and the syrup. The invert sugars (glucose and fructose) generally increased during the first 10 days of storage, with a concomitant decrease in sucrose content. All three sugars, however, tended to level off during the last 4 days of the 2-wk storage. Neither length of storage nor wet vs. dry conditions influenced the acidity. Storage for 6 days after harvest improved syrup quality as assessed by finishing temperature and viscosity without reducing syrup yields per metric ton of sweet sorghum stalks; the syrup, however, was slightly darker in color. Wet storage counteracted the normal benefits of storage to syrup quality. Coleman and Stokes (1964) recommended that syrup producers store enough stalks for at least 1–2 days in a dry place with good ventilation to ensure the production of high-quality syrup.

CHEMICAL CONTROL OF POSTHARVEST LOSSES

Sugarcane

Efforts to assess the extent of postharvest deterioration of sugarcane and to control its progress in the field and at the factory have met with only partial success. Juice viscosity (Brix) is a promising indicator of deterioration for routine quality control (Tilbury 1968). Other parameters of juice quality that have been found useful for cane arriving at the factory are dextran content (Vickers 1968; Tilbury 1969), titratable acidity, and gum content (Irvine and Friloux 1965). Gum content has been found to be more sensitive and accurate than titratable acidity. Both burning and freezing of cane significantly influenced the effectiveness of these parameters for quality control.

Tilbury (1969) found that the biodeterioration of cane juice quality could not be controlled by dipping stalks in formaldehyde solution. Attempts to inhibit bacterial growth inside the stalk by altering electromagnetic wave energy were also negative. Tilbury (1969) also failed to restrict bacterial growth by reducing water availability with molasses. The minimum molasses level inhibitory for *Leuconostoc* in in vitro tests was 30° Brix, but applications up to 60° Brix molasses to severed ends of the infected stalks were not effective.

Continual spraying of the chopper-harvester blade with bactericide did not prevent stalk infection (Egan 1965). Dipping stalks in bactericide solutions was also ineffective. Partial control was obtained by fumigating chopped cane in the harvester bins with formaldehyde; however, this treatment was not economically feasible (Egan 1968).

Speed of cane transport to the factory is the principal factor in controlling its biodeterioration. Cane must be delivered and crushed as quickly as possible, especially when chopper-harvesters are used. Minimum delay between cutting and grinding is the most practical means of controlling postharvest quality losses (Vickers 1968; Tilbury 1969). Amin, Sayed, and Habib (1974) recommended that the harvested cane be kept untopped, covered, and wet by daily sprinkling before it is finally transported. If covering and sprinkling are not feasible, then it should be kept untopped and unstripped until its delivery to the factory.

Tilbury (1972) developed an enzyme approach to solve the polysaccharide problem. This encouraging approach involved the hydrolysis of dextran by incorporating dextranase into bacteria-containing juice. This enzyme removed, on average, 72% of the dextrans present in the milled juice. Sugarcane juice dextrans contained both the 1,6 and 1,4 types of α-glycosidic linkages; the enzyme was apparently specific for the 1,6 type. Higher levels of dextran in the juice of cane in Jamaica were positively correlated with high rainfall and excessive maturity. In Puerto Rico, an average dextran hydrolysis of 94.6% was obtained with dextranase added to juice samples from the randomly selected mills (Tilbury 1972). Dextranase method removes massive quantities of dextran already formed and hence improves sugar recovery from juice heavily infested with *Leuconostoc* (Alexander 1973a). This, however, would not recover the sucrose already metabolized in the dextran-forming process; nor would the dextranase reaction prevent continued growth and utilization of sugar by the bacteria.

Cane and bacterial invertase in freshly milled juice may be controlled chemically to check the growth of *Leuconostoc*. The microbial growth requires sucrose inversion, either by cane or bacterial invertases, since a continued supply of carbon source in the form of glucose and fructose is needed for the growth of bacteria. Invertase inhibitors effective in vitro and absorbed by unicellular organisms might be able to control the growth of these bacteria. In vitro experiments with sodium metasilicate ($Na_2SiO_3 \cdot 9H_2O$) have shown that silica totally inhibited cane invertase within a narrow concentration range of 2–3 μmol/ml (Alexander 1973a). At slightly higher silica concentrations, cane amylase and yeast invertase were also inhibited.

Alexander, Acin-Diaz, and Montalvo-Zapata (1972) reported that sucrose inversion in sugarcane samples could be delayed for several days by adding 40–60 μmol/ml of sodium metasilicate immediately after milling; inhibitor quantity could be lowered to 2–3 μmol/ml by prior filtration and treatment of the juice with zinc sulfate and barium hydroxide. Sodium metasilicate appeared to inhibit the endogenous invertases released from stalk tissue by the grinding process.

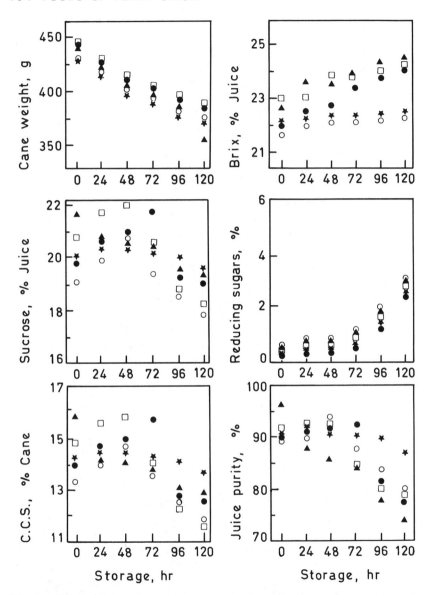

Fig. 4-7. Effects of chemical treatments on various parameters of sugarcane (cv. Co 740) biodeterioration: (○) control, (✳) H₂O, (□) benzoic acid, (▲) formaldehyde, and (●) wettable sulfur. *Source:* Desai, Sangle, and Gaur (1985).

Wong You Cheong, Heitz, and Deville (1972) reasoned that inhibition of invertase activity by silica in vitro was uniquely due to pH changes in the incubation medium brought about by the addition of sodium silicate.

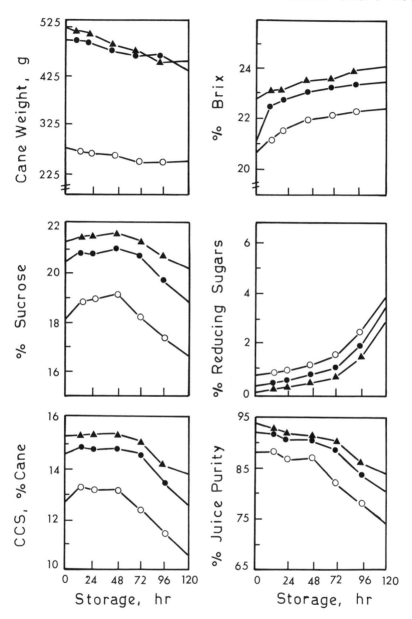

Fig. 4-8. Effects of portions of cane on various parameters of sugarcane (cv. Co 740) biodeterioration: (○) top, (•) middle, (▲) bottom. *Source:* Desai, Sangle, and Gaur (1985).

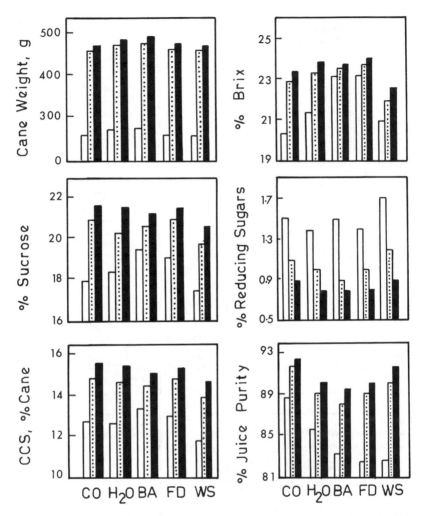

Fig. 4-9. Effects of chemical treatment on various parameters of biodeterioration in three portions (□, top; ⊡, middle; ■, bottom) of sugarcane (cv. Co 740): CO, control; H₂O, water; BA, benzoic acid; FD, formaldehyde; WS, wettable sulfur. *Source:* Desai, Sangle, and Gaur (1985).

Desai, Sangle, and Gaur (1985) investigated the effects of certain chemicals on postharvest biodeterioration of sugarcane. Benzoic acid (100 ppm) and formaldehyde (100 ppm) appeared to retard postharvest losses in juice quality as judged from changes in cane weight, Brix, contents of sucrose and reducing sugars, CCS % cane, and juice purity (Figs. 4-7, 4-8, and 4-9, and Table 4-14). The wettable sulfur had a slightly deleterious effect on juice quality. The storage period (up to 120 h) had a pronounced influence on all the parameters

Table 4-14. Statistical Constants of Chemical Treatments, Storage Time, and Portion of Cane for Different Parameters of Sugarcane Biodeterioration.

Parameters	Chemicals		Storage Time		Portion of Cane	
	SEM[a]	LSD[b] at 5%	SEM	LSD at 5%	SEM	LSD at 5%
Cane weight (g)	5.467	N.S.[c]	6.469	23.565	5.235	14.427
Brix (%)	0.016	0.059	0.019	0.070	0.013	0.046
Sucrose (%)	0.020	0.073	0.024	0.086	0.015	0.057
Reducing sugars (%)	0.009	0.036	0.012	0.042	0.008	0.028
CCS[d] (% cane)	0.015	0.055	0.018	0.065	0.012	0.042
Juice purity (%)	0.037	0.137	0.043	0.159	0.028	0.104

Source: Desai, Sangle, and Gaur (1985).
[a]Standard error of means.
[b]Least significant difference.
[c]Not significant.
[d]Commercial cane sugar equivalent.

of juice quality and significantly increased losses in quality. The highest loss of sucrose content and juice purity occurred in the top portion of sugarcane, followed by the middle and bottom portions (Fig. 4-8, Table 4-14). The top, however, responded better to the chemical treatments than either the middle or bottom portions of sugarcane (Fig. 4-9, Table 4-14).

Sugar Beet

Several chemicals have been known to control postharvest losses of sugar in beet roots effectively. Nelson (1956) found that treatment of sugar beet slices with amino triazole decreased respiration (CO_2 production); however, respiration rates were increased when whole beets were dipped in amino triazole solution. Wittwer and Patterson (1951) effectively prevented storage losses of sugar beets due to sprouting by preharvest treatment of plants with maleic hydrazide (MH). Investigating the effects of several chemicals—Randox® (α-chloro-N,N'-diallylacetamide), MH, Simazine®, N^6-benzyladenine, a mixture of N^6-benzyladenine and α-naphthalene acetic acid, Vegadex® (2-chloro-allyldiethyldithiocarbamate), chloro-IPC (isopropyl-N-(3-chlorophenyl) carbamate), Falone® (tris-2,4-dichlorophenoxy ethylphosphite), sodium hexametaphosphate, malathion, Telone®, and Captan®—Wu et al. (1970) found that the preharvest foliar application of Randox® and postharvest dips of beet roots in N^6-benzyladenine and Randox® solution reduced losses of sucrose, amounts of raffinose, and rates of respiration during storage.

Wyse and Dilley (1973) observed that wax coating of sugar beets significantly reduced desiccation and respiration, thus decreasing sucrose losses during storage. Spraying the surface of beets with wax and then covering them with straw prevented desiccation of sugar beets stored commercially in piles and reduced sucrose losses. A spray application of Benomyl® or thiabendazole (500 ppm) effectively prevented infection by *Penicillium* and *Botrytis* of injured sugar beet roots during the initial storage period (Mumford and Wyse 1976).

RADURIZATION

The growth of adventitious bacteria in stored maple sap causes deterioration that results in the production of low-grade maple syrup. Kissinger, Willits, and Bell (1969) determined the effectiveness of commercial germicidal lamps to destroy or control the bacterial populations in stored maple sap. The results of this study indicated that more effective control of bacterial population in stored maple sap could be obtained by recycling the sap under UV irradiation than by irradiation of statically stored sap. Even at the lowest recycling rate (0.1 gal/min), bacterial population decreased at 3-ft depth during the 6-h recirculation period at all storage temperatures.

Giorgi and Gontier (1980) stored sucrose solution of 65° Brix with 1% added reducing sugar for 6 mo in a stainless steel column provided with a lateral tube communicating with both the top and bottom of the column. The lateral tube housed a resistance heater, permitting circulation of the syrup to simulate the action of convection currents in the storage tank. Parallel tests were conducted with four columns in which the syrup had an initial pH of 6.5 or 8.0 and the lateral tube was either heated or unheated. A UV lamp at 400 μW cm^{-2} emitted rays of 2,537-Å wavelength onto the surface of the syrup. The results of this study indicated that in most cases the sucrose concentration increased slightly as a result of evaporation caused by lamp heat. The color of syrups having lower initial pH remained constant or even fell slightly, whereas it increased in the case of the syrup of initial pH 8. The pH fell by 1.5 units over a period of 6 mo, the fall being marked at the start of storage and attributed to the effect of UV light. In the last month of storage, there was almost complete elimination of all microorganisms determined initially in the syrup, and no subsequent development of microbes was noticed.

SUGAR PROCESSING TECHNOLOGY

Sugarcane

Sugarcane is processed into stable products like white sugar (sucrose), *Khandsari*, jaggery, cane syrup, and fancy molasses. Salunkhe and Desai (1988) have described various processing operations (e.g., extraction of juice, juice clarification and concentration by evaporation and centrifuging) involved in the production of cane sugar as well as those involved in the production of *Khandsari,* jaggery (*gur*), syrups, and molasses.

Jadhav and Londhe (1989) conducted laboratory trials to investigate effects of stale cane on the clarification process. The results indicated that mud volume increased and settling rate of juice decreased with an increase in staleness (storage time) of sugarcane, resulting in inferior sugar quality and reduced crushing rate. A significant increase in the quantity of reducing sugars suggested inversion of sucrose and greater production of molasses, making the manufacture of commercial sugar more expensive. Jadhav and Londhe (1989) stressed the industrial-economic significance of providing fresh cane.

Sugar Beet

Sugar is extracted from the beet cossettes by means of water at about 70 °C using a countercurrent flow. Traditionally, this was carried out in so-called diffusion batteries; today, these have been replaced by a modified diffusion process (an extraction drum) in a continuously operating plant. Salunkhe and Desai (1988) reviewed the developments in various beet processing operations (sugar extraction, juice filtration and purification, evaporation, and crystallization) leading to the production of sucrose and other sugar products.

Dexter, Frakes, and Wyse (1970a,b) evolved a method of evaluating the processing characteristics of sugar beet based on juice constituents. They concluded that the beet should be low in organic constituents that produce acids with soluble calcium salts, both at harvest and after storage. Soluble amino acids, a main source of acidity, did not increase in sound beets in storage, and decreased appreciably at lower temperatures. These acidic components are not removed in conventional processing and should be as low in concentration as possible to avoid exhausting the alkaline reserve. Potassium and sodium may be added, if necessary, to neutralize these acids during processing.

Other Sugar Crops

Sweet sorghum is processed into syrup, jaggery, and alcohol. Extensive research has been conducted to produce sugar (sucrose) from sweet sorghum and such crops as corn and millet. According to Brandes (1947), however, there is little prospect of developing a sorgo-sugar industry independent of the already established sugar crops, sugarcane and sugar beet. This is mainly because the harvesting and processing season for sorghum would be far too short to justify the required large investment in the elaborate and expensive processing machinery. Coleman and Stokes (1964) reported the effects of stripped and unstripped treatments on the yield and quality of juice and syrup obtained from Wiley sweet sorghum harvested at three stages of maturity (Figs. 4-10 and 4-11). The

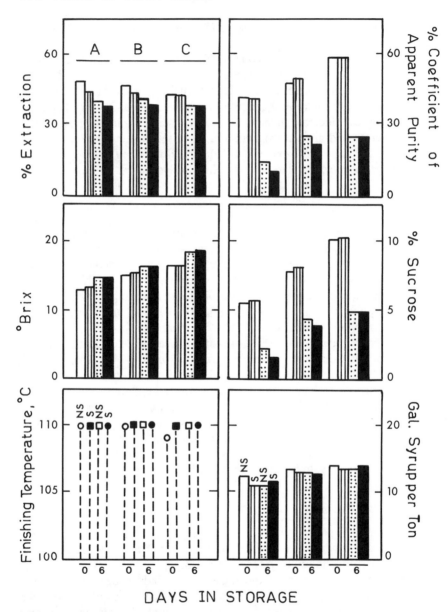

Fig. 4-10. Effects of (S) stripped and (NS) nonstripped treatments on the yield and quality of juice obtained from Wiley sweet sorghum harvested at three stages of maturity—(A) anthesis, (B) milk, and (C) dough—and stored for 0 and 6 days. *Source:* Coleman and Stokes (1964).

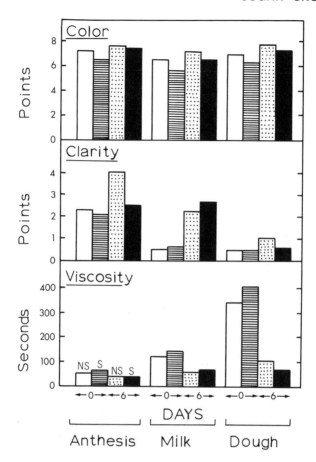

Fig. 4-11. Effects of (S) stripped and (NS) nonstripped treatments on the quality of syrup made from Wiley sweet sorghum harvested at three stages of maturity—anthesis, milk, and dough—and stored for 0 and 6 days. *Source:* Coleman and Stokes (1964).

color of syrup improved slightly (became lighter), clarity decreased, and viscosity increased with maturity (Fig. 4-11). The stripping of sweet sorghum stalks did not influence syrup yield and quality significantly. Salunkhe and Desai (1988) described milling, clarification, concentration, cooking, jellying, and crystallization operations in the production of syrup from sweet sorghum.

Bapat et al. (1986) evaluated 284 cultivars of sweet sorghum in 1984 and 1985 at the Mahatma Phule Agricultural University, Rahuri, India, for syrup and jaggery. Out of twelve promising cultivars tested for juice quality, cv SSV-108 was found to be suitable for both higher green stalk yield and juice quality

(41.0 MT/ha and 3.78 MT/ha commercial cane sugar). The cv SSV-1333 produced a high-quality juice with the highest pol percent in cane (10.41) and the lowest reducing sugar (0.73%). The cv SSV-108 produced a superior quality syrup (90.5% total soluble solids) and jaggery (63.72% nonreducing sugars and 9.32% reducing sugars). The juice characteristics of the cane of twelve sweet sorghum cultivars and the quality of syrup and jaggery prepared from the five promising cultivars are reported in Tables 4-15 and 4-16, respectively.

Maple juice is processed into maple syrup and sugar, usually in March and April. Maple sap is a dilute sugar solution containing 2–3% sugar on average

Table 4-15. Stalk Yield and Juice Characteristics of Sweet Sorghum Cultivars.

Cultivar	Green Stalk Yield (MT/ha)	CCS[a] (MT/ha)	Brix (%)	Juice Purity (%)	Pol[b] (% cane)	pH	Reducing Sugars (%)	Extraction (%)	Millable Height (cm)
SSV-74	52.2	4.07	20.0	68.2	7.8	5.1	1.42	42.6	276
SSV-84	42.2	3.24	21.6	64.8	7.7	5.1	1.68	31.8	259
SSV-108	41.2	3.78	22.0	70.8	9.2	5.0	1.24	25.6	260
SSV-111	32.9	2.36	18.3	68.2	7.2	5.2	1.99	36.9	302
SSV-119	40.0	3.41	19.1	73.6	5.8	4.9	1.39	39.0	295
SSV-685	36.6	3.07	19.1	73.0	8.4	4.9	1.33	32.1	275
SSV-956	28.5	2.37	20.0	70.7	8.3	5.2	1.28	27.3	318
SSV-1133	33.7	3.51	21.5	77.6	10.4	5.0	0.73	37.5	260
SSV-2525	57.6	4.45	19.6	68.0	7.7	5.0	1.94	29.9	344
SSV-3555	30.5	3.13	21.7	76.3	10.2	5.0	0.87	28.2	300
SSV-7073	51.7	4.85	22.2	71.4	9.4	5.1	1.28	21.8	297
SSV-2098	42.7	3.19	18.3	69.9	7.5	5.3	0.89	25.5	344

Source: Bapat et al. (1986).
[a]Commercial cane sugar equivalent.
[b]An indicator of juice quality based on sucrose content.

Table 4-16. Quality of Syrup and Jaggery Prepared from the Juice of Five Sweet Sorghum Cultivars.

Quality Parameter	Cultivar				
	SSV-74	SSV-84	SSV-108	SSV-2525	SSV-7073
Syrup, total soluble solids (%)	90.0	83.0	90.5	83.0	90.0
Jaggery					
Reducing sugars (%)	15.6	12.5	9.3	20.8	11.6
Nonreducing sugars (%)	62.0	65.4	63.7	57.5	63.2
Total sugars (%)	77.6	77.9	73.0	78.3	74.8

Source: Bapat et al. (1986).

(1–9% range). About 86 gal of maple sap containing 1% sugar produce 1 gal of syrup (65% total solids, of which sucrose is about 32%). Maple sap is concentrated in such a manner that the maple flavor is retained without the development of off-flavors.

Maple sugar is usually made in the sugar camp in a special "sugaring-off" pan, and then processed into many varieties of hard and soft sugars in molds and in cakes of about 5–10 kg.

The analysis of 481 pure samples of maple syrups from the United States and Canada showed the following range (and mean) values in percentages (Willits 1951):

moisture, 24.85–48.14 (34.22);
invert sugars, 0–11.01 (1.47);
sucrose, 47.20–70.46 (62.57); and
ash, 0.46–1.06 (0.66).

The flavor of maple syrup does not exist as such in the sap as it comes from the tree, but is developed by the postharvest treatment of the sap during heat processing. The amount of flavoring material or the amount of substances that make up the material account for <0.1% of the syrup weight (Willits 1951). The analysis of four classified and one unclassified grade of syrups produced from maple is shown in Table 4-17. The samples were produced in the same grove under identical conditions.

Maple syrups and sugars can be further processed to produce maple cream, maple butter, and candies, extending the income from maple syrups and sugars. These products are manufactured by commercial processors along with standard grades of syrups.

Willits, Porter, and Buch (1962) studied the formation of color during the evaporation of maple sap to syrup, indicating the changes in color that may occur in the sap and syrup pans of a maple syrup evaporator during commercial syrup making. Heating maple sap of different solids concentrations at the boiling point, prepared by dilution from vacuum-concentrated, colorless, and fla-

Table 4-17. Analysis of Different Grades of Syrups Produced from Maple in One Sugar Grove.

Grade	Moisture (%)	Invert Sugar (%)	Sucrose (%)	Ash (%)
Fancy	32.8	0.89	65.07	0.70
No. 1	32.6	1.52	62.90	0.68
No. 2	31.5	2.05	64.35	0.66
No. 3	32.5	1.72	65.51	0.77
Unclassified	32.7	4.86	59.83	0.68

Source: Willits (1951).

vorless maple syrup, indicated that the pH decreased with the time of heating but was not influenced by the concentration of solids. The invert sugar content remained constant irrespective of the concentration of solids and the boiling time. The rate of color development was independent of solids concentrations up to 45%; but above this limit, there was a significant increase in the rate of color development. The results of this study indicated that emphasis must be placed on the design of the evaporator so that the sap can be evaporated to syrup in the shortest possible time.

Barraclough (1952) and Salunkhe and Desai (1988) have described the preparation of maple cream, maple candies, and maple vinegar. Maple syrup skimmings, dark or slightly scorched syrup, and even maple sap or syrup that has just begun to ferment will make an excellent maple vinegar.

UTILIZATION OF SUGAR INDUSTRY BY-PRODUCTS

Sugarcane

The by-products after the extraction of sugar from sugarcane are bagasse, filter mud (press mud), and molasses. Cane trash obtained from the sugarcane field (about 25% of the cane weight) is utilized to serve as hut roofs, cattle feed (forage), and compost manure, as well as in the manufacture of paper boards and other packaging materials.

Bagasse, the residue obtained by crushing cane in one or more mills (about 32–35% of the cane weight) is used as fuel, cattle feed, organic manure, and in the manufacture of straw board and line paper, cellulose, filter aids, fiber boards, wall or insulating boards (Canec®, Celotex®, Canite®), and activated carbon (Salunkhe and Desai 1988). According to Atchison (1969), bagasse stands out as the most promising major agricultural raw material for the world pulp and paper industry. Ramos, Carlo, and Romero (1969) described simultaneous production of furfural and levulinic acid from bagasse. Keller (1963) reviewed the research carried out on the utilization of by-products of the sugarcane industry.

The press or filter mud is a residue obtained by filtration of the muds that settle out in the process of clarification of the mixed raw juice (about 2–3% of the cane weight). It is used as fuel, compost manure, and fertilizer as well as in the manufacture of cane wax, dyestuff, metal polish, and chalk.

Molasses is the heavy, dark, viscous liquid discharged by the centrifugals after no more sugar can be separated from the final low-grade massecuite by the usual factory methods (about 2.5–4.0% of the cane weight). It is used as fuel, cattle feed, manure, and tobacco curing and in the manufacture of such products as ethyl and butyl alcohols, acetone, citric acid, glycerol, and yeast. Ethanol manufactured from molasses can in turn be used to produce acetic acid, ethyl ether, and several other derivatives. The secondary fermentation products based on molasses as the raw material include ethyl acetate, butyl acetate, amyl acetate, vinegar, and CO_2 in compressed and solid forms. The best known potable spirits made from molasses are rum and gin. Special processing of molasses yields baker's and brewer's yeast and a high-protein food yeast, *Torulopsis utilis*. Fermentation also produces lactic acid, but its yields have not been commercially economical. Molasses is a valuable feed for livestock and is used as an additive in the preparation of silages. Gupta and Shukla (1969) described an industrial anaerobic fermentation process whereby cellulosic and other industrial and agricultural wastes can be rapidly converted into biogas (fuel) and biomanure (fermented mass used as a fertilizer or manure).

Porto (1984) devised a new system of achieving total utilization of crop byproducts, including sugarcane bagasse, avoiding competition both with food production and environmental pollution. In this system, alcohol is produced in mini- and microdistilleries (about 500 and 5,000 l/day) utilizing various crop residues, such as sugarcane bagasse. The findings of Kelly (1980) indicate that it would be practicable to produce alcohol from sugarcane at a cost comparable to that of petroleum-based fuels.

Paturau (1977) reviewed the main utilization of sugarcane products, indicating their present commercial value as well as the value upgrading that would result from further processing. A possibility of saving bagasse in a raw factory through better utilization of exhaust steam economy, yielding substantial fuel savings, was also stressed. Paturau (1977) considered the outlook for molasses utilization in the fermentation industry and as a cattle feed. Through utilization of by-products, sugar estates could significantly increase their revenues.

"Spent wash" is a waste by-product of alcohol distillation when molasses are used as a raw material. It is a highly colored, highly acidic by-product, toxic to normal microflora and fauna except a few fungi, which can grow only slowly. Spent wash has the following general characteristics: pH, 4.5–5.4; BOD value, 45,000 ppm; COD value, 106,000 ppm; total solids, 107,000 ppm; and volatile solids, 65,000 ppm.

Various attempts of utilizing spent wash—such as its use via irrigation water, production of cattle and poultry feed, recovery of potash by incineration, anaerobic lagooning and digestion for methane production, as well as recovery of different chemicals (e.g., glycerol, glutamic acid, and vitamin B_{12})—have not been economically viable, being highly capital intensive. Saraf (1988) proposed a combination of physicochemical anaerobic and aerobic biological methods of spent-wash disposal. The neutralized spent wash is fed to an acid phase digester, then to a gas phase digester specially designed to retain the sludge and ensure complete mixing as well as maintain the desired temperature for the maximum degradation and generation of biogas. The anaerobically treated spent wash is further treated in a modified aerobic process to further reduce the BOD value. This effluent is then disposed off for irrigation or for concentration and use as a source of potassium and other nutrients. Shaikh and Hapse (1988), however, proposed that the conversion of spent wash into organic manure would be a useful alternative in India. The process involves composting spent wash with press mud and sugarcane trash.

By and large, fresh spent wash is a harmful and corrosive product; when discharged into a natural water stream, it can affect its dissolved oxygen concentration and other temperature-dependent physical, chemical, and biological reactions. Because of its high BOD value, it gets purified rapidly, giving rise to offensive odors. It may find its way to pollute well waters, imparting its color (reddish brown and aesthetically objectionable) and odor to drinking and irrigation waters. In monsoon-zone distilleries, well waters have been reported to be colored due to seepage of spent wash (Satyanarayana, Juwarkar, and Kaul 1980). Its prolonged use as irrigation water without sufficient dilution is feared to cause soil sickness. Spent wash poses a threat to aquatic life and corrodes pumping sets.

There are about 200 distilleries in India, producing about 770 million liters of alcohol per year; the quantity of distillery waste or spent wash produced is 12–15 times that of the alcohol produced (Manohar Rao 1983)—about 10,500 million liters. Maharashtra State alone in India with its forty distilleries produces about 2,400 million liters of spent wash per year.

Various methods have been adopted by distilleries for the disposal of spent wash, the most common being lagooning. In Maharashtra State, farmers apply the sun-dried lagoon spent-wash solids to soils for crop production. The solid spent wash being concentrated, its continuous use on soils is feared to deteriorate soil health. Some distilleries burn the concentrated spent wash and apply the residual ash obtained to soils. Attempts have also been made to produce methane gas, wherein a huge quantity of spent slurry, though of lesser concentration, again poses a disposal problem. In all these methods, the secondary products need to be disposed to land, which may affect soil properties and crop production adversely.

Recently, Subba Rao (1988) proposed that spent wash could be composted with press mud, a by-product of the sugar industry that is readily available at factory sites. This method of composting spent wash may prove to be a viable technology for its most efficient utilization. Some sugar factories in Maharashtra State have already adopted this method; the compost thus prepared can be used on agricultural land on a large scale.

Arbatti (1976) described the practice of disposal of spent wash at Government Distillery at Chitali, Maharashtra. It consists of evaporating spent wash in a large number of pits under natural conditions and selling the dry residue as manures to farmers. A fivefold increase in pearl millet yield due to application of this manure was reported.

In a small-scale field trial, Subba Rao (1972) studied the accumulation of salts and organic matter in the soil due to the application of anaerobic lagoon-treated spent wash, diluted tenfold as an irrigation water, and reported the NH₄OAc-extractable potassium accumulation to the extent of about 5,000 kg/ha. The soil pH increased from 7.5 to 8.0 and electrical conductance (EC) rose from 0.1 to 0.4 mmho/cm. On the basis of one year's data, it was concluded that the addition of spent wash had no deleterious effects on either soil properties or the crop yield. Godbole (1984) suggested that spent wash from lagoons diluted with fresh water (preferably a hundredfold, so as to bring the BOD value down to 5,000 mg/l) had no adverse effect on either pH or water-holding capacity of the soil. However, he further reported that the acidity of the effluent, apart from damaging the crop, may do irreparable harm to the soil through leaching. It was also stated that the neutralization of spent wash with lime would affect the ion balance of the soil, leading to long-term deleterious effects.

Work carried out at Mahatma Phule Agricultural University, Rahuri, India, indicated that there was an adverse effect of spent wash on water retention, hydraulic conductivity, and water-stable aggregates of medium black vertic soils. However, there was a beneficial effect on available N, P, and K contents of clay soils (Jadhav 1973). Deshmane (1975) concluded from humification study that the decrease of soil organic carbon content was more rapid in spent wash–treated clay loam soil. In calcareous soils of Rahuri, Jagdale (1976) did not observe any increase in soil pH due to the application of fiftyfold diluted spent wash. It was indicated that the injudicious use of spent wash may adversely affect the growth of cane plant and soil properties. Pawar (1984) stated that the spent wash could be effectively used by diluting it with water 70–75-fold to prevent sugarcane chlorosis on saline calcareous soils of the Rahuri region.

Yadav (1989), working with a soil column, concluded that the Ca, Mg, Na, K, CO₃, Cl, SO₄, and organic carbon content of the topsoil increased but the pH decreased due to spent wash application. Initial application of diluted spent wash (1 : 50) led to substantial removal of the native cations and anions from the soil. The addition of spent wash with increasing concentrations led to increase in the soluble ion content of silty clay, gravelly loam, and silty clay loam soils of Rahuri *tehsil* (i.e., county).

According to Hanumanulu and Subramanyam (1976), high potassium concentration in soil as a result of application of spent wash is toxic and may induce magnesium deficiency and iron chlorosis in sugarcane. These authors pointed out that soils with light texture (silty, sandy, and loamy soils) and well-drained soils with sufficient rainfall (100–150 cm/yr) can tolerate as high as 4,000 mg/l of dissolved solids. Singh, Singh, and Arora (1980) applied spent wash for reclamation of saline sodic soils under sugarcane in amounts equivalent to 100%, 20%, and 10% of the gypsum requirement, and observed that the application of undiluted spent wash increased the water-intake rate of soils. Spent wash equivalent to 20% of gypsum requirement was enough to lower the pH and salt content of the soil. It was further reported that leaching with water after the application of spent wash gave results better than with the prior dilution of the spent wash. Pawar (1984), working at Rahuri, concluded that the application of spent wash followed by irrigation, rather than its dilution at the time of application, was very effective in reclaiming saline sodic soils. Dubey (1976) observed that spent-wash spraying was the best method of its disposal; however, in order to avoid the changes of undesirable levels of salt concentration, it was suggested that after every spray irrigation of the crop by spent wash, two irrigations of fresh water should be given.

Singh (1961), using neutralized spent wash because of its acidic nature, observed marginal decrease in soil pH; but the values of total nitrogen and available phosphorus and potassium content of soil were higher in spent wash–treated soil than in the control.

Agarwal and Dua (1976) applied twentyfold diluted spent wash (200 kg N/ha) to sugarcane and observed increase in cane yield by 5% over the control. At higher rates of application (300 kg N/ha), adverse effects on the yield as well as available nitrogen content of soil were noticed. Similar results were reported by Bajapai and Dua (1972).

Small distilleries supply spent wash to surrounding fields for irrigation purposes. Despite some fertilizer value, owing to its dissolved inorganic salts containing K_2O, the continuous, uncontrolled use of spent wash for irrigation can increase salinity and adversely affect soil productivity (Johari 1987).

Yang (1968) reported an increase in available potassium in sugarcane soils by use of diluted (1 : 3) spent wash. In the Philippines, Gonzales and Tianco (1982) applied spent wash to sugarcane fields in addition to regular fertilizers and found an increase in the yields of sugarcane and sugar, as well as in pH, available potassium, exchangeable calcium and magnesium content of soil, and ash content of cane juice. On the basis of field experiments conducted in Brazil, Monteiro, Pexe, and Stupeillo (1981) reported that application of spent wash at the rate of 35 MT/ha + 46 kg N/ha resulted in the highest juice purity of sugarcane grown on medium black soil, but it was lowest on the clayey soil. According to Marinho, Albuquerque, and Araujo (1982) in Brazil, the optimum dose of spent wash to sugarcane was 135 MT/ha.

In Cuba, Vieira (1982) reported significant increase in potassium content of soil, cane yield, and recoverable sugar due to the application of spent wash at the rate of 90–150 MT/ha. Several authors have reported an increase in potassium content of soil due to the application of spent wash.

According to Cantsteller (1983), an increase in crop yields due to the application of spent wash was due not only to nitrogen and mineral salts, but also to the residual sugar, which favored multiplication of microorganisms. Cooper and Prasad (1980) obtained beneficial effects of spent-wash application on the yield of sugarcane grown on sandy soil. Silva, de Castro, and Sanches (1981) and Roboina, Viera, and de Azeredo (1986) conducted experiments on soils containing <35% clay and stated that the effects of vinasse were influenced by soil texture and fertility. Marinho, Albuquerque, and Araujo (1982) stated that vinasse without mineral fertilizer did not permit maximum yield of cane in two Brazilian soils. Cesar, Delgades, and Gaban (1980), analyzing juice from four cane varieties grown on soils to which vinasse was applied as fertilizer, showed that starch and potassium contents were significantly higher than where the soil did not receive vinasse. As a consequence, processing difficulties may be expected for cane grown in treated soil.

Patil, Arbatti, and Hapse (1987) reviewed the literature on spent-wash utilization in sugarcane and concluded that the experimental data available are of a fragmentary nature and hardly applicable in practice. While utilizing the spent wash for various crops, and especially for sugarcane, due care must be taken to safeguard against the hazards of pollution of soil as well as groundwater resources. Literature survey reveals that the research on spent wash is mostly confined to its direct use in crop production, and there is no information available on the use of spent-wash solids and spent-wash press-mud cake compost in relation to their effects on soil properties and crop production.

Lipinsky (1982) presented a survey of new agricultural and processing technologies relating to liquid fuel production and transportation, and discussed the potential impacts of these developments on sugar crop growers, processors, and fuel consumers.

Sugar Beet

After the extraction of sugar from the beet roots, the residues (tops, crowns, and beet pulp) are utilized for feeding livestock, particularly cattle and sheep. Tops can also be plowed in the soil with considerable benefit to the succeeding crop (MAFF 1970). Beet roots are sliced into cossettes from which sugar is extracted with water. The beet pulp residue left after the sugar extraction is sold either as wet pulp (85–90% water), pressed pulp, or dried cake (about 10% moisture). Although generally considered a bulky feed, it is highly nutritious and rich in carbohydrates, but deficient in minerals (e.g., P).

Schwartz (1983) described a system developed by Ener Corporation, Inc., in which most of the energy consumed in fermentation and distillation of ethanol from beet molasses was in the form of solar energy. Solar energy is also used to evaporate moisture from the distillery waste in a covered pond subjected to natural ventilation.

Sweet Sorghum

Utilizing sweet sorghum for energy production, principally ethanol manufacture, Schaffert and Gourley (1982) described it as an example of an integrated food, feed, energy, and biofertilizer. The by-products of sweet sorghum can be used as animal feed, biofertilizer, fiber, and energy. The bagasse, after the extraction of sugars and other soluble solids, can be burned in the boiler to produce steam or can be used for feed, fiber, or as a cellulose feedstock for other processes. The stillage can be used as a biofertilizer and returned to the soil, or as a feedstock in biodigestor to produce methane and biofertilizer.

Wall and Blessin (1970a), citing the work of P. Lengyel and S. Annus carried out in Hungary, compared the composition of sweet sorghum stalks with respect to cellulose, pentosan, lignin, and alcohol-benzene extract (Table 4-18). Sweet sorghums have the lowest content of pentosans (20%) and lignin (10%) and highest content of alcohol-benzene-soluble compounds (25%) when compared with other sorghums and grasses. The amount and quality of cellulose in sorghum stalks have encouraged their investigation as possible sources of pulp for the paper industry. Sorgato (1949) reported that the α-cellulose in sweet sorghum stem residues from syrup manufacture accounted for 35% of the dry weight and contained about 27% pentosans and 20% lignin. A good yield of crude cellulose suitable for pulp can be obtained by treating the ground, pressed stalks of sweet sorghum with 2–5% NaOH at 120 °C for 3 h; this removes about 75% of the lignin.

Soloman, Srivastava, and Singh (1988) assessed ten sugarcane genotypes for their biomass and ethanol production capacities under subtropical conditions. Maximum bioenergy and calculated values for ethanol production were recorded in cv CoLK 8001, with a high energy produced : consumed ratio for biomass and ethanol. The high regenerative energy potential of sugarcane for biomass and ethanol makes it a potential renewable source of energy.

Sucrose can be converted into several simpler chemical intermediates by thermal degradation (Imrie and Parker 1974) and by fermentation. Numerous commercial fermentation products (Table 4-19) use sucrose as the substrate, although other hexoses such as glucose derived by the hydrolysis of starch or cellulose can also be used. Sucrose is made available for fermentation either as molasses or sugarcane juice without requiring any refining and crystallization.

Table 4-18. Composition of Sweet Sorghum Stalks and Other Related Plants Examined for Pulp Production.

Sorghum Type	Cellulose (%)	Pentosan (%)	Lignin (%)	Alcohol–Benzene Extract (%)
Sweet sorghums	26	17	10	25
Grain sorghums	29	24	16	7
Broom corns	39	24	15	8
Sudan grass	43	45	16	4
Johnson grass	42	27	17	5

Source: Lengyel and Annus, cited by Wall and Blessin (1970).

Table 4-19. Some Fermentation Products of Sugars.

Solvents	Acids	Polysaccharides	Amino Acids	Antibiotics	Gases
Ethanol	Citric acid	Alginic acid	Glutamic acid	Penicillin	Methane
Butanol	Lactic acid	Xanthan gum	Lysine	Streptomycin	Hydrogen
Acetone	Itaconic acid	Dextran	Methionine	Cephalosporin	Carbon
2 : 3 Butandiol	Gluconic acid	Pullulan		Tetracycline	dioxide
Isopropanol	Propionic acid	Poly-L-hydroxy-			
	Butyric acid	butyric acid			

Source: Blackburn (1984), *Sugar Cane,* Longman Group UK, Ltd.

CONCLUSIONS

Sugar is important in the human diet as a means of satisfying the "sweet tooth" and as an ingredient in food manufacture. Preharvest and postharvest biotechnologies and optimum conditions for growth, development, maturation, harvesting, handling, storage, and processing of sugar crops have significantly retarded the losses in the yield and quality of sugar crops. There is a need to extend the technological advances made in the more advanced countries to the developing countries—especially in the tropical and subtropical regions, where significant losses of sugar crops still occur. The newer, innovative pre- and postharvest biotechnologies being evolved to reduce losses of sugar crops will go a long way to enhance world sugar production and meet the increasing sugar demand, both for food and nonfood industrial utilization.

REFERENCES

Agarwal, M. L., and Dua, S. P. 1976. Nutritive value of distillery effluent and its effect on soil properties. Seminar on treatment and disposal of effluents from sugar and distillery industries at Bangalore, India; Distillery Section, pp. 26–9.

Agee, H. P., and Dass, U. K. 1933. The day degree. *Rep. Hawaii Sugar Technol.* 12(1):45–8.

Akeson, W. R., Fox, S. D., and Stout, E. L. 1974. Effect of topping procedure on beet quality and storage losses. *J. Am. Soc. Sugar Beet Technol.* 18(2):125–30.

Alexander, A. G. 1973a. *In vitro* effects of silicon on hydrolytic and oxidative enzymes of sugar cane. *Proc. Int. Soc. Sugar Cane Technol.* 13:532.

Alexander, A. G. 1973b. *Sugar Cane Physiology.* Amsterdam: Elsevier.

Alexander, A. G., Acin-Diaz, N., and Montalvo-Zapata, R. 1972. Inversion control in sugar cane juice by sodium metasilicate. *Proc. Int. Soc. Sugar Cane Technol.* 14:794–804.

Allison, R. V., Bryan, O. C., and Hunter, J. W. 1927. Stimulation of plant response on the raw peat soils of the Florida Everglades through the use of $CuSO_4$ and other chemicals. *Fla. Exp. Stn. Bull. no. 190.*

Amin, M. H., El-Badawi, A. A., Sayed, G., El-K., and Habib, A. T. 1972. Effect of burning and chopping on sugar cane deterioration in the UAR. *Proc. Int. Soc. Sugar Cane Technol.* 14:786–93.

Amin, M. H., Sayed, G. El-K., and Habib, A. T. 1974. Factors influencing the rate of sucrose inversion in harvested sugar cane in Egypt. *Proc. Int. Sugar Cane Technol.* 15:761–8.

Arbatti, S. V. 1976. Some considerations about spent wash disposal and its processing. Seminar on treatment and disposal of effluents from sugar and distillery industries at Bangalore, India; Distillery Section, pp. 51–8.

Atchison, J. E. 1969. Some economic factors involved in the utilization of bagasse for the manufacture of pulp and paper. *Proc. Int. Soc. Sugar Cane Technol.* 13:1858–69.

Atterson, A., Carruthers, A., Dutton, J. V., Hibbert, D., Oldfield, J. E. T., Shore, M., and Teague, H. F. 1964. Changes in beets after freezing and storage. *Z. Zuckerind Boehm.* 14: 466–70.

Bajapai, P. D., and Dua, S. P. 1972. Studies on the utility of distillery effluent (spent wash) for its manurial value and its effect on soil properties. *Indian Sugar J.* 1972:687–9.

Baldwin, A. L., and Fisher, M. V. 1969. An industrial approach to manual cane cutting. *Proc. West Indies Sugar Technol.* 1969:166–77.

Bapat, D. R., Jadhav, H. D., Gaur, S. L., and Salunkhe, C. B. 1986. Screening of sweet sorghum cultivars for production of quality syrup and jaggery. *Curr. Res. Rep.* 2(1):65–9.

Barnes, A. C. 1974. *The Sugar Cane.* London: Leonard Hill.

Barr, C., Guinn, E. M., and Rice, R. A. 1940. A preliminary report on the effect of temperature conditions on respiration and loss of sugar from beets in storage. *Proc. Am. Soc. Sugar Beet Technol.* 1(1):52–4.

Barraclough, K. E. 1952. Maple syrup and sugar production. *New Hampshire Extension Bull. no. 103,* Extension Service in Agriculture and Home Economics, Durham: Univ. of New Hampshire.

Bates, J. F. 1960. Preliminary trials with desiccants in sugar cane. *Proc. West Indies Sugar Technol.* 1960:43–8.

Birkett, L. S. 1953. The influence of tops and trash on the economics of sugar production. *Sugar Bull. Brit. Guiana Dep. Agric.* 21:1–28.

Blackburn, F. 1984. *Sugar Cane.* Tropical Agricultural Series, London: Longman.

Boneta-Garcia, E., and Lugo-Lopez, M. A. 1962. Losses of sucrose in cut cane kept under shade or sun for different periods. *J. Agric. Univ. P. R.* 46(3):189–94.

Brandes, E. W. 1947. Progress with sugar sorgo. In *Science in Farming. The Yearbook of Agriculture, 1943–1947.* Washington, D.C.: USDA, 344 p.

Brook, M. 1971. Sucrose and food manufacture. In *Sugar,* ed. J. Yudkin, J. Edelman, and L. Hough, pp. 32–48. London: Butterworths.

Callahan, J. C. 1965. Observations on the length of 1963–64 maple tapping season at the Southern Indiana forage farm. *Res. Progr. Rep. Purdue Univ. Agric. Exp. Stn. no. 175.*

Cantsteller, J. 1983. Beet vinasse as recycling for beet fields. *Zuckrindustrie* 108:1058–61.

Cesar, M. A. A., Delgades, A. A., and Gaban, L. C. 1980. *Int. Sugar J.* 1980:56; *Sugar Abstr.* 6(6):161.

Chu, C. C., and Kong, L. 1971. Photorespiration of sugar cane. *Taiwan Sugar Exp. Stn. Annu. Rep.* 1971:1–14.

Clayton, J. E. 1969. Harvester developments in Florida, Puerto Rico, Louisiana, Australia and Hawaii. *Proc. West Indies Sugar Technol.* 1969:160–5.

Clements, H. F. 1948. Crop logging of sugar cane in Hawaii. *Better Crops with Plant Food* 32(1):11–18.

Clements, H. F. 1959. Quality in sugar production—field aspects. *Rep. Hawaii Sugar Technol. Assoc., 18th Annu. Meet.* 1959:17–24.

Clements, H. F. 1980. *Sugar Cane Crop Logging and Crop Control: Principles and Practice.* London: Pitman.

Coleman, O. H. 1970. Syrup and sugar from sweet sorghum. In *Sorghum Production and Utilization of Major Feed and Food Crops in Agriculture and Food Series,* ed. J. S. Walls and W. M. Ross, pp. 416–440. Westport: AVI Publ. Co.

Coleman, O. H., and Stokes, I. E. 1964. Storage studies of sorgo. *USDA Tech. Bull. no. 1307*, Washington, D.C.: USDA.

Cooper, B. R., and Prasad, M. 1980. The use of distillery waste as a fertilizer for sugar cane in Trinidad. *Int. Sugar J.* 82:316–19.

Cramer, H. H. 1967. *Plant Protection and World Crop Production.* Leverkusen (Germany): Bayer Pflanzenschutz.

Cross, W. E. 1966. The problem of frozen cane in the Argentine. *Sugar J.* 1966(3):9–12.

de Gues, J. G. 1967. *Fertilizer Guide for Tropical and Subtropical Farming.* Zurich: Centre d'Etude de I'Azole, pp. 115–45 (cited by Blackburn 1984).

Desai, B. B., Sangle, P. B., and Gaur, S. L. 1985. Chemical control of postharvest losses in sugar cane. *Curr. Res. Rep.* 1(1):33–7.

Deshmane, A. N. 1975. Biochemical nature of spent wash (distillery waste) solids and their humification in soil. M.S. thesis, Mahatma Phule Agric. Univ., Rahuri, India.

Dexter, S. T., Frakes, M. G., and Wyse, R. E. 1969. Damage to sugar beet roots from various degrees of wilting at various temperatures. *J. Am. Soc. Sugar Beet Technol.* 15(6):480–8.

Dexter, S. T., Frakes, M. G., and Wyse, R. E. 1970a. A method of evaluating the processing characteristics of sugar beets based on juice constituents, a prescription of beet quality. *J. Am. Soc. Sugar Beet Technol.* 16(2):128–35.

Dexter, S. T., Frakes, M. G., and Wyse, R. E. 1970b. Storage and clear juice characteristics of topped and untopped sugar beets grown in 14-inch rows. *J. Am. Soc. Sugar Beet Technol.* 16(2):97–105.

Dilley, D. R., Wood, R. R., and Brimhall, P. 1970. Respiration of sugar beets following harvest in relation to temperature, mechanical injury and selected chemical treatment. *J. Am. Sugar Beet Technol.* 15(8):671–83.

Draycott, A. P. 1972. *Sugar Beet Nutrition.* United Kingdom: Applied Science Publ.

Dubey, R. S. 1976. Sugar factory and distillery effluents treatment and disposal. Seminar on treatment and disposal of effluents from sugar and distillery industries at Bangalore, India; Sugar Section, pp. 33–48.

Dutton, J. V., Carruthers, A., and Oldfield, J. F. T. 1961. The synthesis of sucrose by extracts of the root of sugar beet. *Biochem. J.* 81(3):266–9.

Egan, B.T. 1965. Investigations on the chemical control of sour storage rot. *Proc. Queensl. Soc. Sugar Cane Technol.* 32:25–30.

Egan, B. T. 1968. Investigations on the chemical control of sour storage rot. II. Formalin fumigation. *Proc. Queensl. Soc. Sugar Cane Technol.* 35:31–7.

Egan, B. T. 1969. Postharvest deterioration losses in sugar cane in Queensland. *Proc. Int. Soc. Sugar Cane Technol.* 13:1729–35.

Evans, H. 1960. Elements other than nitrogen, potassium and phosphorus in the nutrition of sugar cane. *Proc. Int. Soc. Sugar Cane Technol.* 10:473–508.

Evans, H. 1962. *Sugar in Mauritius.* New York: BWI Sugar Association, Inc.

Evans, H. 1965. In *Golden Jubilee Souvenir of the Anakapella Research Station,* A. P., India (cited by Blackburn 1984).

A Facto Sheet. A Summary of Basic Information about Sugar and Its Uses. 1975. New York: Sugar Association, Inc.

FAO. 1986. *Production Yearbook, vol. 39.* Rome: Food and Agriculture Organization.

FAO. 1988. *Production Yearbook, vol. 41.* Rome: Food and Agriculture Organization.

Finkler, R. E., Swink, J. E., Doxtator, C. W., Olson, R. F., and Hanzas, P. C. 1959. Changes in raffinose content and other characteristics of sugar beet varieties during six different harvest dates. *J. Am. Soc. Sugar Beet Technol.* 10(5):459–66.

Foster, D. H., and Ivin, P. C. 1981. Losses of sugar and water from cane in fires. *Proc. Aust. Soc. Sugar Cane Technol. Bundaberg Conf.,* Queensland, May 11–15, pp. 13–20.

Giorgi, J. C., and Gontier, R. 1980. Preservation of pure sugar syrups by UV irradiation. *Int. Sugar J.* 82(2):86–8.

Godbole, S. H. 1984. Energy generation through distillery effluent treatment. *Maharashtra Sugar* 9(7):9–12.

Gonzales, M. Y., and Tianco, A. P. 1982. Effect of volume and time of application of distillery slops on the growth and yield of sugar cane. *Proc. 29th Annu. Conv. Philippines Sugar Tech. Assoc.*, pp. 476–90.

Guilbeau, W. F., Coll, E. E., and Martin, L. F. 1955. Effects of delay in grinding on value and processing quality of sugar cane juice. *Sugar J.* 18:30–1.

Guilbeau, W. F., Coll, E. E., and Martin, L. F. 1956. Losses from delay in delivering harvested cane. *Sugar Bull.* 34:28–30.

Gupta, S. C., and Shukla, J. P. 1969. Utilization of by-products and wastes from sugar factories by cellulosic fermentation. *Proc. Int. Soc. Sugar Cane Technol.* 13:1912–21.

Handbook of Agriculture. 1966. Rev. ed., January. New Delhi: Indian Council of Agricultural Research, pp. 1–32.

Hanumanulu, V., and Subramanyam, P. V. R. 1976. Economics of treatment and disposal of distillery wastes. Seminar on treatment and disposal of effluents from sugar and distillery industries at Bangalore, India; Distillery Section, pp. 1–10.

Hickson, J. L. 1971. Utilization of sucrose by the chemist. In *Sugar,* ed. J. Yudkin, J. Edelman, and L. Hough, pp. 60–8. London: Butterworths.

Hoekstra, R. G. 1978. Investigation into the effectiveness of maturity testing for non-irrigated sugar cane fields. *Proc. Int. Soc. Sugar Cane Technol.* 16:129–33 (cited by Blackburn 1984).

Holdredge, R. M., and Wyse, R. E. 1982. Computer simulation of the forced convection cooling of sugar beets. *Trans. Am. Soc. Agric. Eng.* 25(5):1425–30.

Hughes, R. H. 1956. Sugar losses: Field and factory. *Hawaiian Planters Rec.* 55:167–75.

Humbert, R. P. 1968. *The Growing of Sugar Cane.* Amsterdam: Elsevier.

Humbert, R. P. 1974. Improving burns with desiccants as an aid to mechanical harvesting. *Proc. Int. Soc. Sugar Cane Technol.* 15:1065–73.

Humbert, R. P., Lima, G. M., Govsas, J. 1969. Tassel control progress with Reglone® in the Mexican sugar industry. *Proc. Int. Soc. Sugar Cane Technol.* 13:462–7.

Humbert, R. P., Zamora, M., and Fraser, T. B. 1967. Ripening and maturity control progress at Ingnio Las Mochis, Mexico. *Proc. Int. Soc. Sugar Cane Technol.* 12:446–52.

Hurney, A. P., Ridge, D. R., and Dick, R. G. 1984. Evaluation of the efficiency of cane harvesters in removing extraneous matter and in limiting cane losses during the cleaning process. *Proc. Aust. Soc. Sugar Cane Technol.* 1984:11–19.

Imrie, F. K. E., and Parker, K. J. 1974. Prospects for the industrial utilization of sugar. *Proc. Int. Soc. Sugar Cane Technol.* 15:1864–76.

Irvine, J. E., and Friloux, J. J. 1965. Juice acidity and gum content as measures of cane deterioration. *Sugar Azucar* 60(11):58–9.

Jadhav, H. D. 1973. Effect of spent wash (distillery waste) on the properties of non-calcareous medium black soil. M.S. thesis, Mahatma Phule Agric. Univ., Rahuri, India.

Jadhav, S. Y., and Londhe, M. B. 1989. Effect of stale cane on clarification. *Indian Sugar* 38(10):801–7.

Jagdale, H. N. 1976. Influence of spent wash (distillery waste) on the growth and chemical composition of immature sugar cane (*Saccharum officinarum* L.) cultivar CO 740. M.S. thesis, Mahatma Phule Agric. Univ., Rahuri, India.

Johari, K. K. 1987. Effluent treatment processes for distillery spent wash. *Bhartiya Sugar* 1(5):23–8.

Julien, M. H. R. 1977. Testing ripeners: Problems and prospects. *Proc. Int. Soc. Sugar Cane Technol.* 16:1791–9.

Kannan, S. 1988. Occurrence of iron deficiency in important crops in Maharashtra and Tamil Nadu States in India: A report. *J. Plant Nutr.* 11:1285–93.

Kannappan, K., Pandian, B. J., and Kumar Swamy, K. 1988. Response of sugar cane varieties to N fertilization. *Indian Sugar* 38(7):589–90.

Karnik, V. V. 1970. Selected physico-chemical, microbiological and agronomical studies on the controlled atmosphere storage of sugar beet (*Beta vulgaris*) roots. Ph.D. thesis, Utah State University, Logan, Utah.

Karnik, V. V., Olson, L. E., Salunkhe, D. K., and Singh, B. 1970a. Evaluation of effects of controlled atmosphere storage on roots of sugar beet grown at various levels of nitrogen fertilizer. *J. Am. Soc. Sugar Beet Technol.* 16(2):225–30.

Karnik, V. V., Salunkhe, D. K., Olson, L. E., and Post, F. J. 1970b. Physico-chemical and microbiological studies on controlled atmosphere storage of sugar beets. *J. Am. Soc. Sugar Beet Technol.* 16(1):156–9.

Keller, A. G. 1963. Utilization of by-products. *Proc. Int. Soc. Sugar Cane Technol.* 11: 1155–66.

Kelly, F. H. C. 1980. Cost control factors in the production of ethanol from sugar cane. *Int. Sugar J.* 82:172–7.

Kissinger, J. C., Willits, C. O., and Bell, R. A. 1969. Control of bacterial growth in stored maple sap by irradiation of the sap surface with germicidal lamps. *Dev. Ind. Microbiol.* 10: 1–140.

Kollonitsch, V. 1970. *Sucrose Chemicals.* Bethesda, Md.: The International Sugar Research Foundation, Inc.

Kortschak, H. P. 1972. Environmental studies. *HSPA Exp. Stn. Annu. Rep. 1972*, pp. 18–27.

Le Grand, F., and Martin, F. G. 1966. Maturity testing of sugar cane growing on organic soils of Florida. *Proc. West Indies Sugar Technol.* 1966:238–45.

Lipinsky, E. S. 1982. Fuels from sugar crops: Status and prospects. *Int. Sugar J.* 84:254.

McIntyre, G., and Hardy, M. 1989. The influence of cutting methods and burning on cane and sugar yield. *Sugar Cane* 1(1):2–3.

MAFF. 1970. *Sugar Beet Cultivation Bull. no. 153.* London: Ministry of Agriculture, Fisheries and Food, HMSO.

Manohar Rao. 1983. Production of methane gas from stillage on commercial scale in India. *Indian Sugar* 32(12):873–80.

Marinho, M. L., Albuquerque, G. A., and Araujo, J. T. 1982. Effects of doses of vinasse and mineral fertilizer on cane ratoon in two Lagos soils. *Brazil Acucareiro* 97(2):111–12.

Meade, G. P., and Chen, J. C. P. 1977. *Cane Sugar Handbook.* New York: Wiley.

Mongelard, J. C., and Mimura, L. 1971. Growth studies on the sguar cane plant. I. Effect of temperature. *Crop Sci.* 11:795–800.

Monteiro, H. Pexe, C. A., and Stupeillo, J. P. 1981. Use of vinasse supplemented with nitrogen and phosphorus on ratoons of sugar cane. *Brazil Acucareiro* 97(4):226–31.

Mumford, D. L., and Wyse, R. E. 1976. Effects of fungus infection on respiration and reducing sugar accumulation of sugar beet roots and use of fungicides to reduce infection. *J. Am. Soc. Sugar Beet Technol.* 19(2):157–62.

Nair, N. V., and Sreenivasan, T. V. 1989. Analysis of stalk yield components in *Saccharum officinarum* L. *Sugar Cane* 1(2):4–5.

Nelson, R. T. 1956. Effect of chemical treatment on respiration of sugar beets. *J. Am. Soc. Sugar Beet Technol.* 9(1):21–24.

Nickell, L. G. 1983. *Plant Growth Regulator Chemicals,* vol. I. Boca Raton: CRC Press.

Nickell, L. G. 1984. Review of plant growth regulators in the sugar cane industry. *Sugar Azucar* 79:17–20.

Parker, K. J. 1979. *Proc. RAPRA Diamond Jubilee Conf.,* July 1979, Rubber and Plastics Research Association, pp. 53–78.

Parker, K. J. 1984. Sucrochemistry. In *Sugar Cane,* ed. F. Blackburn, pp. 347–52. London: Longman.

Patil, J. D., Arbatti, S. V., and Hapse, D. G. 1987. A review on some aspects of distillery spent wash (vinasse) utilization in sugar cane. *Bhartiya Sugar* 1(1):9–15.

Paturau, J. M. 1977. An overview of by-products utilization in the cane industry. *Proc. Int. Sugar Cane Technol.* 16:3221–9.

Paul, H. 1954. The trace element status of peat soils in British Guiana. *Proc. Int. Soc. Sugar Cane Technol.* 8:212–17.

Pawar, R. B. 1984. Ameliorating effects of spent wash on the chlorosis of sugar cane grown on saline-calcareous soil. M.S. thesis, Mahatma Phule Agric. Univ., Rahuri, India.

Perumal, R., and Sonar, K. R. 1987. Potassium availability in soils growing sugar cane. In *Soil Testing, Plant Analysis and Fertilizer Evaluation for Potassium,* Res. Rev. Ser. no. 4., pp. 65–74. Potash Research Institute, India.

Porto, R. O. 1984. Bioenergy and animal protein production system. *Resour. Manage. Optimization* 3(2):99–112.

Ramos, E., Carlo, L. A., and Romero, R. V. 1969. The simultaneous production of furfural and levulinic acid from bagasse. *Proc. Int. Soc. Sugar Cane Technol.* 13:1900–11.

Roboina, A. A., Viera, J. R., and de Azeredo, D. F. 1986. Doses and mineral complementation of vinasse in sugar cane ratoon. *Sugarcane* 86(2):18–20.

Rush, G. 1968. *Symp. at 15th Gen. Meet. Am. Soc. Sugar Beet Technol.,* Phoenix, Ariz.

Salunkhe, D. K., and Desai, B. B. 1988. *Postharvest Biotechnology of Sugar Crops.* Boca Raton: CRC Press.

Saraf, R. V. 1988. Treatment of distillery waste. Paper presented at the National Seminar on "Sugar Factory and Allied Industries Wastes: A New Focus," June 17–18, Deccan Sugar Institute, Pune, India.

Satyanarayana, S., Juwarkar, A. S., and Kaul, S. N. 1980. Distillery waste treatment: A case study. *Natl. Seminar on Sugar Factory and Allied Industrial Wastes. Tech. Session I. P.,* pp. 37–66.

Schaffert, R. E., and Gourley, L. M. 1982. Sorghum as an energy source. In *Sorghum in the Eighties,* vol. 2, pp. 605–10. Proc. Int. Symp. on Sorghum, Nov. 1981, Patancheru (India): ICRISAT.

Schwartz, D. M. 1983. Direct application of solar energy to alcohol fuel production. *Int. Sugar J.* 85:123–5.

Shaikh, G. A., and Hapse, D. G. 1988. Future research needs for spent wash composting (Abst.). Paper presented at the National Seminar on "Sugar Factory and Allied Industries Wastes: A New Focus," June 17–18, Deccan Sugar Institute, Pune, India.

Silin, P. M. 1964. *Technology of Beet Sugar Production and Refining* (trans. from Russian, Israel Program for Scientific Translation, Ltd.), Washington, D.C.: USDA and National Science Foundation.

Silva, G. M. A., de Castro, L. J. P., and Sanches, A. C. 1981. Effects of the use of vinasse as fertilizer for sugar cane. *Int. Sugar J.* Feb. 83(1):48–9.

Singh, A. 1961. Effect of application of "spent wash" on the fertility of an alluvial soil. *Indian J. Sugarcane Res. Dev.* 5:259–60.

Singh, K. D. N., Yadav, M. D., Misra, G. K., and Sahi, B. P. 1989. Influence of modified urea sources and quality of sugar cane. *Indian Sugar* 39(3):165–72.

Singh, O., and Kanwar, R. S. 1989. Nitrate reductase activity as a factor in foliar tissue growth of sugar cane. *Indian Sugar* 39(3)159–63.

Singh, R., Singh, R. T., and Arora, Y. 1980. The use of spent wash for the reclamation of sodic soils. *J. Indian Soc. Soil Sci.* 28(1):38–41.

Singh, R., Biswas, B. C., Maheswari, S. C., and Srivastava, S. C. 1981. *Sugar Cane.* New Delhi: The Fertilizer Association of India.

Singh, Y. 1976. Preliminary studies on the effects of cold stress on sugarcane. *West Indies Sugar Technol. Conf.*, pp. 91–9 (cited by Blackburn 1984).

Soloman, S., Srivastava, K. K., and Singh, K. 1988. Evaluation of sugar cane as renewable source of energy under subtropics. *Indian Sugar* 38(7)583–7.

Somawanshi, R. N., and Kadu, P. P. 1988. Effects of soil properties on growth and chlorosis in sugar cane. *J. Plant Nutr.* 11:1545–55.

Sonar, K. R., Nazirkar, R. B., Bagul, K. M., Kanawade, C. B., and Daftardar, S. Y. 1987. A note on fertilizer requirements of seasonal sugar cane based on soil testing. *Annu. Conv., Deccan Sugar Technol. Assoc.* 37: A366–70.

Sonar, K. R., Tamboli, D. D., Kadu, P. P., Nazirkar, R. N., and Daftardar, S. Y. 1988. Fertilizer application to adsali sugar cane–summer groundnut sequence based on targeted yield approach. *Annu. Conv., Deccan Sugar Technol. Assoc.* 38:A389–94.

Sorgato, T. 1949. Cellulose and other constituents of sorghum cane. *Ind. Sac. Ital.* 42:214–18.

Stevenson, G. C. 1957. The British West Indies Sugar Cane Breeding Station: Twenty–five Years' Progress. *Proc. Bri. West Indies Sugar Technol.* 1957: 24–33.

Stevenson, G. C. 1965. *Genetics and Breeding of Sugar Cane.* London: Longman.

Stout, M. 1957. Respiratory losses from sugar beets soon after harvest. *J. Am. Soc. Sugar Beet Technol.* 9:350–3.

Stout, M., and Smith, C. H. 1950. Studies on the respiration of sugar beets as affected by bruising, by mechanical harvesting, severing into the top and bottom halves, chemical treatment, nutrition and variety. *Proc. Soc. Sugar Beet Technol.* 6(4):670–9.

Stout, M., and Spikes, J. D. 1957. Respiratory metabolism of sugar beets. *J. Am. Soc. Sugar Beet Technol.* 9(5):469–71.

Subba Rao, B. 1972. Electrical conductivity and fertility of alluvial soils supplemented with anaerobic lagoon-treated spent wash. *Madras Agric. J.* 18:49–55.

Subba Rao, B. 1988. Aerobic composting of spent wash. Paper presented at the National Seminar on "Sugar Factory and Allied Industries Wastes: A New Focus," June 17–18, Deccan Sugar Institute, Pune, India.

Thompson, G. D. 1976. Irrigation of sugar cane. *S. Afr. Sugar J.* 61:161–74.

Thuljaram Rao, J., Natarajan, B. V., and Bhagyalakshmi, K. V. 1983. *Sugar Cane.* New Delhi: Indian Council of Agriculture Research.

Tilbury, R. H. 1968. Biodeterioration of harvested sugar cane. In *Biodeterioration of Materials.* Proc. Int. Symp. on Biodeterioration, Southhampton.

Tilbury, R. H. 1969. The ecology of *Leuconostoc mesenteroides* and control of postharvest biodeterioration of sugar cane in Jamaica. In *Proc. West Indies Sugar Technol. Assoc. Annu. Meet., 1969*, pp. 126–35.

Tilbury, R. H. 1972. Dextrans and dextranase. *Proc. Int. Soc. Sugar Cane Technol.* 14:1444–58.

Trouse, A. C., and Humbert, R. P. 1961. Some aspects of soil compaction on the development of sugar cane roots. *Soil Sci.* 91(2):208–17.

Turner, A. W., and Rojas, B. A. 1963. Deterioration of sugar cane after cutting. *Proc. Int. Soc. Sugar Cane Technol.* 11:312–18.

Vaidya, B. R., Joshi, V. A., Jadhav, S. B., and Bagul, K. M. 1987. Micronutrient research pertaining to sugar cane in Maharashtra: A review. Paper presented at the Natil. Symp. on "Micronutrient Stresses in Crop Plants: Physiological and Genetical Approaches to Control Them," Dec. 16–18, Mahatma Phule Agric. Univ., Rahuri, India.

Vajna, S. 1965. Storage of sugar beets: A literature survey (trans. M. Schabit). In *Sugar Beet Storage*, Rep. no. RL 65–005, May. Longmount, Colo.: The Great Western Sugar Company Research Laboratory.

Van Dillewijn, C. 1952. *Botany of Sugar Cane*. Waltham, Mass.: Chronica Botanica.

Vickers, P. R. P. 1968. The Tully area cane deterioration investigation. *Proc. Queensl. Soc. Sugar Cane Technol.* 33:19–29.

Vieira, D. B. 1982. Methods of vinasse application in sugar cane. *Saccharum APC* (São Paulo) 5:21–6.

Vlitos, A. J. 1974. A review of plant growth regulating chemicals in sugar cane. *Proc. Int. Soc. Sugar Cane Technol.* 15:932–7.

Walker, H. G., Rorem, E. S., and McCready, R. M. 1960. Compositional changes in diffusion juices from stored sugar beets. *J. Am. Soc. Sugar Beet Technol.* 11(3):206–10.

Wall, J. S., and Blessin, C. W. 1970a. Composition of sorghum plant and grain. In *Sorghum Production and Utilization*, ed. J. S. Wall and W. M. Ross, pp. 1–118. Westport: AVI Publ. Co.

Wall, J. S., and Blessin, C. W. 1970b. Composition of sorghum plant and grain. In *Sorghum Production and Utilization*, ed. J. S. Wall and W. M. Ross, pp. 118–67. Westport: AVI Publ. Co.

Watson, R. H. J. 1971. The psychology of sweetness. In *Sweetness and Sweeteners*, ed. C. G. Birch, L. F. Green, and C. B. Coulson, pp. 1–21. London: Applied Science.

Willits, C. O. 1951. Crops from the maple trees. In *Crops in Peace and War. The Yearbook of Agriculture, 1950–51*. Washington, D.C.: USDA.

Willits, C. O., Porter, W. L., and Buch, M. L. 1962. Maple syrup. V. Formation of color during evaporation of maple sap into syrup. *Food Res.* 17(6):482–7.

Wittwer, S. H., and Patterson, D. R. 1951. Inhibition of sprouting and reduction of storage losses in onions, potato, sugar beets and vegetable root crops by spraying plants in the field with maleic hydrazide. *Mich. Agric. Exp. Stn. Q. Bull.* 34:3–6.

Wold, R. L. 1946. Cane deterioration in a storage pile. *Hawaiian Planters Rec.* 50:5–8.

Wong You Cheong Y., Heitz, A., and Deville, J. 1972. The effects of silicon on enzyme activity in vitro and sucrose production in sugar cane leaves. *Proc. Int. Soc. Sugar Cane Technol.* 14:777–85.

Wood, R. R., Oldenmeyer, R. K., and Bush, H. L. 1956. Inheritance of raffinose production in the sugar beet. *J. Am. Soc. Sugar Beet Technol.* 9:131–4.

Wu, M. T., and Salunkhe, D. K. 1976. Effects of environmental factors and agronomic and storage practices on the quality of sugar beet. *CRC Crit. Rev. Food Sci. Nutr.* 2:81–105.

Wu, M. T., Singh, B., Theurer, J. C., Olsen, L. E., and Salunkhe, D. K. 1970. Control of sucrose loss in sugar beet during storage by chemicals and modified atmosphere and certain associated changes. *J. Am. Soc. Sugar Beet Technol.* 16(2):117–27.

Wyse, R. E. 1969. Storage of sugar beets: Agronomic, physiological and quality aspects. Ph.D. thesis, Mich. State Univ., East Lansing.

Wyse, R. E. 1973. Storage of sugar beet roots in controlled atmospheres to conserve sucrose. *Crop Sci.* 13(6):701–3.

Wyse, R. E. 1978. Effect of harvest injury on respiration and sucrose loss in sugar beet roots during storage. *J. Am. Soc. Sugar Beet Technol.* 20(2):193–202.

Wyse, R. E., and Dexter, S. T. 1970. Effect of agronomic and storage practices on raffinose, reducing sugar, and amino acid content of sugar beet varieties. *J. Am. Soc. Sugar Beet Technol.* 16(5):369–80.

Wyse, R. E., and Dexter, S. T 1971a. Source of recoverable sugar losses in several sugar beet varieties during storage. *J. Am. Soc. Sugar Beet Technol.* 16(5):390–8.

Wyse, R. E., and Dexter, S. T. 1971b. A study of changes in the marc content of sugar beet during storage. *J. Am. Soc. Sugar Beet Technol.* 16(4):289–98.

Wyse, R. E., and Dilley, D. R. 1973. Evaluation of wax coatings for improving sugar beet storage. *Crop Sci.* 13(5):567–70.

Wyse, R. E., and Holdredge, R. M. 1982. A comparison of forced ventilation and natural convection as means of sugar beet storage piles in several geographical locations. *J. Am. Soc. Sugar Beet Technol.* 21(3):235–46.

Wyse, R. E., and Peterson, C. L. 1979. Effect of injury on respiration rates of sugar beet roots. *J. Am. Soc. Sugar Beet Technol.* 20(3):269–71.

Yadav, A. M. 1989. Effects of spent wash (distillery effluent) on the properties of soils and composition of leachate. M.S. thesis, Mahatma Phule Agric. Univ., Rahuri, India.

Yadav, D. V., and Yaduvanshi, N. P. S. 1989. Micronutrients for increasing sugar cane production. *Indian Sugar* 39(4):225–31.

Yang, S. C. 1968. Effects of spent wash on soil chemical and physical properties and sugar cane yield. *Soil Fertil. (Taiwan)* 7:71–4.

Yates, R. A. 1967. Studies on irrigation of sugar cane. *Aust. J. Agric. Res.* 18:903–20.

Yudkin, J. 1971. Sugar as a food: An historical survey. In *Sugar,* ed. J. Yudkin, J. Edelman, and L. Hough, pp. 11–17. London: Butterworths.

Index

Acer saccharum, see maple
Aceraceae, 415
acerola, 325–7
acid and acid–enzyme conversion, for corn syrup, 112,
 113
adzuki bean, 146
Aegilops spp., 12
African millet, see finger
 millet
Agaricineae, 345
aggregate fruit, 304
agronomic practice: cereals,
 62–71; fruits, 319–21;
 legumes, 156–78; sugar
 beet, 435–7; sugarcane,
 433–5; vegetables, 369–71
akee, 311
alkaloid, 195, 247, 355
allergen, 245–6, 249
Allium cepa, see garlic
Allium sativum, see onion
allylthioglucoside, see sinigrin
amaranth, 19, 343, 354
Amaranthaceae, 19, 343
Amaranthus spp., see
 amaranth
Amaryllidaceae, 344
amino acid: composition,
 cereal, 87, 89; deficiency,
 in legumes and cereals,
 139; location effects, in
 vegetable legumes, 359,
 361; toxic, 247, 250
amylase inhibitor, 237–9,
 249

Anacardiaceae, 306
Anacardium occidentale
 (cashew nut), see nut
Ananas comosus, see pine-
 apple
Andropogoneae, 10, 11, 17
angustifoline, 247
antinutrient: in cereals, 91–
 4; in legumes, 231–47;
 removal of, 247–50
antivitamin, 250
Apium graveolens (celery),
 see leafy green
Arachis hypogaea, see peanut
artichoke, 344, 369
Arundinaria spp., see bamboo
ascorbic acid: blanching
 effect on, 393–4; fermentation effects on, 395; and
 fertilization, 318, 365; in
 fruits, 310; in germinated
 legumes, 263; harvesting
 effect on, 314, 382–3; and
 in-package desiccant, 397;
 location effects on, 360–
 3; radiosensitivity, 392–3;
 species differences in, 370;
 storage effects on, 340,
 368; synthesis, 357; temperature effects on, 357–8;
 in vegetables, 348–4
 (canned, 394; dehydrated,
 396–7; frozen, 393)
ascorbic acid oxidase, 333
aseptic canning, of vegetables, 394

asparagus: classification,
 345; freezing, 393;
 nitrates, 366; radurization,
 392; storage conditions,
 382; vacuum cooling, 379
Asparagus officinalis, see
 asparagus
aspartic acid, 42, 44, 45
ATP synthesis, in C-3 and
 C-4 plants, 44, 45
aubergine, see eggplant
Avena spp., see oats
avocado: climate, 314; cultural operations, 320; fat,
 309; harvesting criteria,
 329; production, 307–8;
 respiration rate, 327, 330;
 storage, 338; vitamins,
 326
Azotobacter spp., 34, 317

Bacillus spp., 32, 34
bagasse, 474–5
Bambara groundnut, 147
bamboo, 11
Bambuseae, 11
banana: chemical control of
 loss of, 335–7; classification, 306; climate, 311–
 12; composition, 310;
 cultural operations, 320–
 1; definition, 301, 304;
 diseases, 321–2; harvesting criteria, 329; pests,
 321–2; production, 307–
 8; radiation tolerance, 342;
 respiration rates, 327, 330;